ASP.NET® PROGRAMMING
WITH C#® AND SQL SERVER®

ASP.NET® PROGRAMMING WITH C#® AND SQL SERVER®

DON GOSSELIN

COURSE TECHNOLOGY
CENGAGE Learning™

Australia • Brazil • Japan • Korea • Mexico • Singapore • Spain • United Kingdom • United States

COURSE TECHNOLOGY
CENGAGE Learning

**ASP.NET® Programming with C#®
and SQL Server®**
Don Gosselin

Executive Editor: Marie Lee

Acquisitions Editor: Amy Jollymore

Managing Editor: Tricia Coia

Developmental Editor: Ann Shaffer

Senior Content Project Manager:
Cathie DiMassa

Editorial Assistant: Julia Leroux-Lindsay

Marketing Manager: Bryant Chrzan

Art Director: Marissa Falco

Text Designer: Shawn Girsberger

Cover Designer: Cabbage Design Company

Cover Image: CSA Images

Print Buyer: Julio Esperas

Copy Editor: Karen Annett

Proofreader: Kim Kosmatka

Indexer: Alexandra Nickerson

Compositor: International Typesetting
and Composition

For product information and technology assistance, contact us at
Cengage Learning Customer & Sales Support, 1-800-354-9706

For permission to use material from this text or product,
submit all requests online at **www.cengage.com/permissions**
Further permissions questions can be e-mailed to
permissionrequest@cengage.com

ISBN-13: 978-1-4239-0324-6

ISBN-10: 1-4239-0324-2

Course Technology
20 Channel Center Street
Boston, MA 02210
USA

Cengage Learning is a leading provider of customized learning solutions with office locations around the globe, including Singapore, the United Kingdom, Australia, Mexico, Brazil, and Japan. Locate your local office at:
www.cengage.com/global

Cengage Learning products are represented in Canada by
Nelson Education, Ltd.

To learn more about Course Technology, visit
www.cengage.com/coursetechnology

Purchase any of our products at your local college store or at our preferred online store **www.ichapters.com**

Printed in the United States of America
1 2 3 4 5 6 7 12 11 10 09

Brief Contents

Contents

ix

CHAPTER 6   Debugging and Error Handling **308**

CHAPTER 7   Working with Databases and SQL
Server Express **365**

xi

CHAPTER 9 **Maintaining State Information 456**

CHAPTER 10 **Developing Object-Oriented C# Programs . . 525**

Preface

ASP.NET is a server-side Web development environment that you can use to build dynamic Web sites, Web applications, and XML Web services. ASP.NET is built on top of the .NET Framework, which is a platform designed for developing and running Internet applications, primarily Web-based applications and XML services. ASP.NET is not a programming language itself, but rather a development environment in which you can use one of three languages: Visual Basic, C#, or J#. Although you can use both Visual Basic and J# for developing ASP.NET applications, Microsoft developed C# specifically for use with the .NET Framework. The international standardization organization, European Computer Manufacturers Association (ECMA), first approved a standardized version of C# in 2001, based on joint recommendations from Microsoft Corporation, Hewlett-Packard, and the Intel Corporation.

This book teaches ASP.NET development with C# and SQL Server, which is a relational database management system (RDBMS) developed by Microsoft. The book covers the basics of ASP.NET, C#, and SQL Server along with advanced topics such as state preservation techniques and object-oriented programming. After completing the course, you will be able to use ASP.NET to build professional quality, database-driven Web sites.

The Approach

This book introduces a variety of techniques, focusing on what you need to know to start writing ASP.NET programs. In each chapter, you perform tasks that let you use a particular technique to build ASP.NET programs. The step-by-step tasks are guided activities that reinforce the skills you learn in the chapter and build on your learning experience by providing additional ways to apply your knowledge in new situations. In addition to step-by-step tasks, each chapter includes objectives, short quizzes, comprehension checks, and reinforcement exercises that highlight major concepts and let you practice the techniques you learn. At the end of each chapter, you will also complete Discovery Projects that let you use the skills you learned in the chapter to write ASP.NET programs on your own.

Overview of This Book

The examples and exercises in this book will help you achieve the following objectives:

- Work with ASP.NET variables and data types and learn how to use the operations that can be performed on them

- Add functions and control structures to your ASP.NET programs

- Use Web forms and controls with your Web pages

- Manipulate string data with C#

- Trace and resolve errors in ASP.NET programs

- Work with databases and SQL Server

- Manipulate SQL Server databases with ASP.NET

- Save state information across multiple Web pages

- Develop object-oriented C# programs

ASP.NET Programming with C# and SQL Server presents 10 chapters that cover specific aspects of PHP and MySQL Web development. **Chapter 1** discusses basic concepts related to the World Wide Web, the basics of Web development, how to use Microsoft Visual Studio 2008, and how to work with well-formed Web pages. In **Chapter 2,** you learn how to create basic ASP.NET Web pages and how to work with variables, data types, expressions, and operators. This early introduction of key PHP concepts gives you a framework for understanding more advanced concepts and techniques later in this book, and allows you to work on more comprehensive projects from the start. **Chapter 3** covers functions and introduces structured logic using control structures and statements. **Chapter 4** introduces the basics of ASP.NET Web Forms pages and Web server controls, including how to create dynamic forms and use complex controls, such as calendars and ad rotators. This chapter also teaches how to quickly validate user input with validation controls. **Chapter 5** discusses techniques for manipulating strings and working with regular expressions with C#. **Chapter 6** provides a thorough discussion of debugging techniques and tools that you can use to trace and resolve errors in ASP.NET programs. **Chapter 7** introduces the basics of working with SQL Server databases while **Chapter 8** goes into more detail, presenting techniques for manipulating SQL Server databases with ASP.NET. **Chapter 9** explains how to maintain state with query strings, hidden form fields, and post back/view state, and also how to work with cookies and user profiles and how to maintain session and application state. **Chapter 10** presents basic object-oriented programming techniques that you can use in your ASP.NET programs.

Features

ASP.NET Programming with C# and SQL Server is a superior textbook because it also includes the following features:

CHAPTER OBJECTIVES Each chapter begins with a list of the important concepts presented in the chapter. This list provides you with a quick reference to the contents of the chapter as well as a useful study aid.

FIGURES AND TABLES Numerous screenshots in each chapter allow you to check your screens against the desired output. Tables consolidate important material for easy reference.

CODE EXAMPLES Plentiful code examples are presented in an easy-to-read font, with key words highlighted in color.

NEW TERMS New terms are printed in boldface to draw your attention to new material.

 HELP These margin notes provide more information about the task you are currently performing.

 POINTER These useful asides, located in the margin, provide practical advice and proven strategies related to the concept being discussed.

 FACT These margin elements provide additional helpful information on specific techniques and concepts.

 CAREFUL These cautionary notes point out troublesome issues related to a particular technique or concept.

SHORT QUIZ Several short quizzes are included in each chapter. These quizzes, consisting of three to five questions each, help ensure understanding of the major points introduced in the chapter.

SUMMING UP A brief overview a the end of each chapter provides a helpful study guide.

COMPREHENSION CHECK A set of 20 to 25 end-of-chapter review questions reinforce the main ideas introduced in the chapter. These questions help you determine whether you have mastered the concepts presented in the chapter.

REINFORCEMENT EXERCISES Although it is important to understand the concepts behind every technology, no amount of theory can improve on real-world experience. To this end, each chapter includes detailed Reinforcement Exercises that provide practical experience implementing technology skills in real-world situations.

DISCOVERY PROJECTS The end-of-chapter projects are designed to help you apply what you have learned to business situations, much like those a professional Web developer would encounter. The projects give you the opportunity to independently synthesize and evaluate information, examine potential solutions, and make recommendations, similar to an actual programming situation.

Instructor Resources

The following supplemental materials are available when this book is used in a classroom setting. All of the instructor resources available with this book are provided to the instructor on a single CD-ROM.

ELECTRONIC INSTRUCTOR'S MANUAL The Instructor's Manual that accompanies this textbook includes additional instructional material to assist in class preparation, including items such as Sample Syllabi, Chapter Outlines, Technical Notes, Lecture Notes, Quick Quizzes, Teaching Tips, Discussion Topics, and Additional Case Projects.

EXAMVIEW® This textbook is accompanied by ExamView, a powerful testing software package that allows instructors to create and administer printed, computer (LAN-based), and Internet exams. ExamView includes hundreds of questions that correspond to the topics covered in this text, enabling students to generate detailed study guides that include page references for further review. The computer-based and Internet-testing components allow students to take exams at their computers, and also save the instructor's time by grading each exam automatically.

POWERPOINT® PRESENTATIONS This book comes with Microsoft PowerPoint slides for each chapter. These are included as a teaching aid for classroom presentation, to make available to students on the network for chapter review, or to be printed for classroom distribution. Instructors can add their own slides for additional topics they introduce to the class.

DATA FILES Files that contain all of the data necessary to complete the examples, Exercises, and Projects are provided through the Course Technology Web site at *www.cengage.com/coursetechnology*, and are also available on the Instructor Resources CD-ROM.

SOLUTION FILES Solutions to end-of-chapter Exercises and Projects are provided on the Instructor Resources CD and may also be found on the Course Technology Web site at *www.cengage.com/coursetechnology*. The solutions are password protected.

DISTANCE LEARNING Course Technology is proud to present online test banks in WebCT and Blackboard to provide the most complete and dynamic learning experience possible. Instructors are encouraged to make the most of the course, both online and offline. For more information on how to access your online test bank, contact your local Course Technology sales representative.

Read This Before You Begin

The following information will help you as you prepare to use this textbook.

To the User of the Data Files

To complete the steps, Exercises, and Projects in this book, you will need data files that have been created specifically for this book. These data files are available through the Course Technology Web site at *http://www.cengage.com/coursetechnology* and are also provided on the Instructor Resources CD-ROM. Note that you can use a computer in your school lab or your own computer to complete the steps, Exercises, and Projects in this book.

Using Your Own Computer

You can use a computer in your school lab or your own computer to complete the chapters. To use your own computer, you will need the following:

- **Web browser** You can use any browser you like to view the solutions to the Exercises and Projects in this text, as long as it is compatible with the standardized version of the DOM that is recommended by the World Wide Web Consortium (W3C). At the time of this writing, Internet Explorer 5.0 and higher and Netscape 6 and higher are compatible with the W3C DOM, although other browsers are also compatible.

- **Microsoft Visual Web Developer 2008 Express Edition and SQL Server 2008 Express Edition** You can download free from *www.microsoft.com/express/download/default.aspx*. Detailed installation instructions are included in Chapter 1.

To the Instructor

To complete all the steps, Projects, and Exercises in this book, your users must work with a set of user files, called data files, and download software from Web sites. The data files are located on the CD-ROM that came with this book and are also included in the Instructor's Resources. They may also be obtained electronically through the Course Technology Web site at *www.cengage.com/coursetechnology*.

Course Technology Data Files

You are granted a license to copy the data files to any computer or computer network used by individuals who have purchased this book.

Visit Our World Wide Web Site

Additional materials designed especially for this book might be available for your course. Periodically search *www.cengage.com/coursetechnology* for more information and materials to accompany this text.

Acknowledgments

A text such as this represents the hard work of many people, not just the author. I would like to thank all the people who helped make this book a reality. First and foremost, I would like to thank Ann Shaffer, Development Editor, Tricia Coia, Managing Editor, and Amy Jollymore, Acquisitions Editor, for helping me get the job done. I would also like to thank Cathie DiMassa and Anupriya Tyagi, our Project Managers, as well as Chris Scriver, Danielle Shaw, and Serge Palladino, our excellent Quality Assurance team.

Many, many thanks to the reviewers who provided plenty of comments and positive direction during the development of this book: Pat Paulson, Winona State University; Dan Hagen, Seattle Community College; and Mike Michaelson, Palomar College. A very special thanks to Ken Culp, Northern Michigan University, for helping shape the direction of this book.

On the personal side, I would like to thank my family and friends for supporting me in my career; I don't see many of you nearly as often as I'd like, but you are always in my thoughts. My most important thanks always goes to my wonderful wife Kathy for her never ending support and encouragement, and to my best (nonhuman) friend, Noah, the wonder dog.

I dedicate this book to my late mother, Pamela Rurka, who will always be fondly remembered for her love of family, devotion to friends, and obsession with karaoke.

About the Inside Front Cover

Check out our interviews with recent graduates who are now working in the IT field. One is featured on the inside front cover of this book. If someone you know recently landed a job in IT, we'd like to interview them too! Send your suggestions via e-mail to Amy Jollymore, Acquisitions Editor, at Amy.Jollymore@Cengage.com.

CHAPTER 1

Introduction to Web Development

In this chapter you will:

- ◎ Study the history of the World Wide Web
- ◎ Learn about Web development
- ◎ Learn about Microsoft Visual Web Developer 2008 Express Edition
- ◎ Work with well-formed Web pages

The original purpose of the World Wide Web (WWW) was to locate and display information. However, after the Web grew beyond a small academic and scientific community, people began to recognize that greater interactivity would make the Web more useful. As commercial applications of the Web grew, the demand for more interactive and visually appealing Web sites also grew.

But how would Web developers respond to this demand? One solution was the development of JavaScript, which is a client-side scripting language that you, as a programmer, can use to create interactive features within a Web page. However, JavaScript only works within a Web page that runs in a Web browser. Yet, a Web browser is a client in the client/server environment of the Web. Because JavaScript only works within a Web browser, it cannot take advantage of the server-side of the Web. To develop fully interactive Web sites that access databases on a server, and perform advanced e-commerce operations such as online transactions, you must use a server-side scripting tool such as ASP.NET. Combined with the C# programming language, ASP.NET is one of today's most popular technologies for Web site development. In this chapter, you learn the basics of ASP.NET and Web development.

To use this book successfully, you should already possess a strong knowledge of HTML and Web page authoring techniques. The chapter contains sections that provide a quick refresher on the history of the World Wide Web and the basic aspects of how to create Web pages with HTML and its successor, XHTML. Even if you are highly experienced with HTML, you might not be familiar with the formal terminology that is used in Web page authoring. For this reason, be certain to read through these sections to ensure that you understand the terminology used in this book.

Introduction to the World Wide Web

The Internet is a vast network that connects computers all over the world. The original plans for the Internet grew out of a series of memos written by J. C. R. Licklider of the Massachusetts Institute of Technology (MIT), in August 1962, discussing his concept of a "Galactic Network." Licklider envisioned a global computer network through which users could access data and programs from any site on the network. The Internet was actually developed in the 1960s by the Advanced Research Projects Agency (or ARPA) of the U.S. Department of Defense, which later changed its name to Defense Advanced Research Projects Agency (or DARPA). The goal of the early Internet was to connect the main computer systems of various universities and research institutions that were funded by this agency. This first implementation of the Internet was referred to as the ARPANET. More computers were connected to the ARPANET in the years following its initial development in the 1960s, although access to the ARPANET was still restricted by the U.S. government primarily to academic researchers, scientists, and the military.

The 1980s saw the widespread development of local area networks (LANs) and the personal computer. Although at one time restricted to academia and the military, computers and networks soon became common in business and everyday life. By the end of the 1980s, businesses and individual computer users began to recognize the global communications capabilities and potential of the Internet, and convinced the U.S. government to allow commercial access to the Internet.

In 1990 and 1991, Tim Berners-Lee created what would become the **World Wide Web**, or the **Web**, at the European Laboratory for Particle Physics (CERN) in Geneva, Switzerland, as a way to easily access cross-referenced documents that existed on the CERN computer network. When other academics and scientists saw the usefulness of being able to easily access cross-referenced documents using Berners-Lee's system, the Web as we know it today was born. In fact, this method of accessing cross-referenced documents, known as **hypertext linking**, is probably the most important aspect of the Web because it allows you to open other Web pages quickly. A **hypertext link**, or **hyperlink**, contains a reference to a specific Web page that you can click to open that Web page.

A document on the Web is called a **Web page** and is identified by a unique address called the **Uniform Resource Locator**, or **URL**. A URL is also commonly referred to as a **Web address**. A URL is a type of **Uniform Resource Identifier (URI)**, which is a generic term for many types of names and addresses on the World Wide Web. The term **Web site** refers to the location on the Internet of the Web pages and related files (such as graphic and video files) that belong to a company, organization, or individual. You display a Web page on your computer screen using a program called a **Web browser**. A person can retrieve and open a Web page in a Web browser either by entering a URL in the Web browser's Address box or by clicking a hypertext link. When a user wants to access a Web page, either by entering its URL in a browser's Address box or by clicking a link, the user's Web browser asks a Web server for the Web page in what is referred to as a **request**. A **Web server** is a computer that delivers Web pages. What the Web server returns to the user is called the **response**.

Understanding Web Browsers

You can choose from a number of different browsers, but at the time of this writing, Microsoft Internet Explorer is the most popular browser on the market. Although Internet Explorer is the most popular browser, it was not the first. NCSA Mosaic was created in

If you want to learn more about the history of the Internet, the Internet Society (ISOC) maintains a list of links to Internet histories at *http://www.isoc.org/internet/history/*.

A common misconception is that the words *Web* and *Internet* are synonymous. The Web is only one *part* of the Internet, and is a means of communicating on the Internet. The Internet is also composed of other communication methods such as e-mail systems that send and receive messages. However, because of its enormous influence on computing, communications, and the economy, the World Wide Web is arguably the most important part of the Internet today and is the primary focus of this book.

Prior to version 6, the Netscape Web browser was called Navigator or Netscape Navigator. With the release of version 6, however, Netscape dropped "Navigator" from the browser name, and now simply refers to its browser as "Netscape." For this reason, in this book "Navigator Web browser" refers to versions older than version 6, and "Netscape Web browser" refers to version 6 and later.

DHTML is actually a combination of HTML, Cascading Style Sheets, and JavaScript. The term Cascading Style Sheets (CSS), or style sheets, refers to a standard set by the W3C for managing Web page formatting.

The W3C does not actually release a version of a particular technology. Instead, it issues a formal recommendation for a technology, which essentially means that the technology is (or will be) a recognized industry standard.

1993 at the University of Illinois and was the first program to allow users to navigate the Web using a graphical user interface (GUI). In 1994, Netscape released Navigator, which soon controlled 75% of the market. Netscape maintained its control of the browser market until 1996, when Microsoft entered the market with the release of Internet Explorer, and the so-called browser wars began, in which Microsoft and Netscape fought for control of the browser market.

The browser wars began over DHTML, a combination of various technologies including HTML and JavaScript that allows a Web page to change after it has been loaded by a browser. Examples of DHTML include the ability to position text and elements, change document background color, and create effects such as animation.

Earlier versions of Internet Explorer and Navigator included DHTML elements that were incompatible. Furthermore, Microsoft and Netscape each wanted its version of DHTML to become the industry standard. To settle the argument, the World Wide Web Consortium set out to create a platform-independent and browser-neutral version of DHTML. The **World Wide Web Consortium**, or W3C, was established in 1994 at MIT to oversee the development of Web technology standards. While the W3C was drafting a recommendation for DHTML, versions 4 of both Internet Explorer and Navigator added a number of proprietary DHTML elements that were completely incompatible with the other browser. As a result, when working with advanced DHTML techniques such as animation, a programmer had to write a different set of HTML code for each browser type. Unfortunately for Netscape, the W3C adopted as the formal standard the version of DHTML found in version 4 of Internet Explorer, which prompted many loyal Netscape followers to defect to Microsoft.

One great benefit of the browser wars is that it has forced the Web industry to rapidly develop and adopt advanced Web page standards (including JavaScript, CSS, and DHTML) that are consistent across browser types. In 2004, Internet Explorer appeared to be winning the browser wars as it controlled 95% of the browser market. Yet, in the past few years, Internet Explorer has lost significant market share to a contentious newcomer, Mozilla Firefox. The Firefox Web browser is open source software that is developed by the Mozilla organization (*http://www.mozilla.org*). **Open source** refers to software for which the source code can be freely used and modified. At the time of this writing, Internet Explorer usage has slipped to approximately 46%, while Firefox now controls approximately 44% of the market (according to the W3 Schools browser statistics page at *http://www.w3schools.com/browsers/browsers_stats.asp*). One of the most fascinating aspects of Firefox is that it's essentially an open source version of the Netscape browser. So in a figurative sense, the original

Netscape browser has risen from the ashes to resume battle with its arch nemesis, Internet Explorer. Healthy competition is good for any market, so hopefully the renewed hostilities in the browser wars will encourage vendors to continue improving browser quality and capabilities, and to adopt and adhere to Web page standards.

Using HTML

Originally, people created Web pages using **Hypertext Markup Language**. Hypertext Markup Language, or **HTML**, is a markup language used to create the Web pages that appear on the World Wide Web. Web pages are also commonly referred to as **HTML pages** or **documents**. A **markup language** is a set of characters or symbols that define a document's logical structure—that is, it specifies how a document should be printed or displayed. HTML is based on an older language called **Standard Generalized Markup Language**, or **SGML**, which defines the data in a document independent of how the data will be displayed. In other words, SGML separates the data in a document from the way that data is formatted. Each element in an SGML document is marked according to its type, such as paragraphs, headings, and so on. Like SGML, HTML was originally designed as a way of defining the elements in a document independent of how they would appear. HTML was not intended to be used as a method of designing the actual appearance of the pages in a Web browser. However, HTML gradually evolved into a language that is capable of defining how elements should appear in a Web browser.

This textbook uses the terms *Web pages* and *HTML documents* interchangeably.

5

Basic HTML Syntax

HTML documents are text documents that contain formatting instructions, called **tags**, which determine how data is displayed on a Web page. HTML tags range from formatting commands that make text appear in boldface or italic, to controls that allow user input, such as option buttons and check boxes. Other HTML tags allow you to display graphic images and other objects in a document or Web page. Tags are enclosed in brackets (< >), and most consist of an opening tag and a closing tag that surround the text or other items they format or control. The closing tag must include a forward slash (/) immediately after the opening bracket to define it as a closing tag. For example, to make a line of text appear in boldface, you use the opening tag <b> and the closing tag </b>. Any text contained between this pair of tags appears in boldface when you open the HTML document in a Web browser.

A tag pair and any data it contains are referred to as an **element**. The information contained within an element's opening and closing tags is referred to as its **content**. Some elements do not require a closing tag. Elements that do not require a closing tag are called **empty elements**

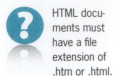

HTML documents must have a file extension of .htm or .html.

because you cannot use a tag pair to enclose text or other elements. For instance, the <hr> element, which inserts a horizontal rule on a Web page, does not include a closing tag. You simply place the <hr> element anywhere in an HTML document where you want the horizontal rule to appear.

There are literally hundreds of HTML elements. Table 1-1 lists some of the more common elements.

HTML element	Description
<b></b>	Formats enclosed text in a bold typeface
<body></body>	Encloses the body of the HTML document
 	Inserts a line break
<center>	Centers a paragraph in the middle of a Web page
<head></head>	Encloses the page header and contains information about the entire page
<h*n*></h*n*>	Indicates heading level elements, where *n* represents a number from 1 to 6
<hr>	Inserts a horizontal rule
<html></html>	Begins and ends an HTML document; these are required elements
<i></i>	Formats enclosed text in an italic typeface
<img src="..." alt="...">	Inserts an image file
<p></p>	Identifies enclosed text as a paragraph
<u></u>	Formats enclosed text as underlined

Table 1-1 Common HTML elements

All HTML documents must use the <html> element as the root element. A **root element** contains all the other elements in a document. This element tells a Web browser to assemble any instructions between the tags into a Web page. The opening and closing <html>...</html> tags are required and contain all the text and other elements that make up the HTML document.

Two other important HTML elements are the <head> element and the <body> element. The <head> element contains information that is used by the Web browser, and you place it at the beginning of an HTML document, after the opening <html> tag. You place several elements within the <head> element to help manage a document's content, including the <title> element, which contains text that appears in a browser's title bar. A <head> element must contain a <title> element. With the exception of the <title> element, elements contained in the <head> element do not affect the display of the HTML document. The <head> element and the elements it contains are referred to as the **document head**.

Following the document head is the <body> element, which contains the document body. The <body> element and the text and elements it contains are referred to as the **document body**.

When you open an HTML document in a Web browser, the document is assembled and formatted according to the instructions contained in its elements. The process by which a Web browser assembles and formats an HTML document is called **parsing** or **rendering**. The following example shows how to make a paragraph appear in boldface in an HTML document:

```
<p><b>Inventory clearance sale!</b></p>
```

HTML is not case sensitive, so you can use <B> in place of <b>. However, the next generation of HTML, a language called XHTML, is case sensitive, and you must use lowercase letters for elements. For this reason, this book uses lowercase letters for all elements. (You will learn about XHTML shortly.)

You use various parameters, called **attributes**, to configure many HTML elements. You place an attribute before the closing bracket of the opening tag, and separate it from the tag name or other attributes with a space. You assign a value to an attribute using the syntax *attribute="value"*. For example, you can configure the <img> element, which embeds an image in an HTML document, with a number of attributes, including the src attribute. The src attribute specifies the filename of an image file or video clip. To include the src attribute within the <img> element, you type <img src="mygraphic.gif">.

When a Web browser parses or renders an HTML document, it ignores nonprinting characters such as tabs and line breaks; the final document that appears in the Web browser includes only recognized HTML elements and text. You cannot use line breaks in the body of an HTML document to insert spaces before and after a paragraph; the browser recognizes only paragraph <p> and line break <br> elements for this purpose. In addition, most Web browsers ignore multiple, contiguous spaces on a Web page and replace them with a single space. The following code shows a simple HTML document, and Figure 1-1 shows how it appears in a Web browser.

```
<html>
<head>
<title>Chickasaw National Recreation Area</title>
</head>
<body>
<h1>National Parks Service</h1>
```

8

The majority of the screen captures of Web pages shown in this book were taken in Microsoft Internet Explorer 7.0, running on the Windows XP operating system. Different Web browsers might render the parts of a Web page slightly differently from other browsers. The appearance of a Web browser itself can also vary across platforms. If you are using a Web browser other than Internet Explorer and an operating system other than Windows XP, your Web pages and Web browser might not match the figures in this book.

```
<h2>Chickasaw National Recreation Area</h2>
<p><b>State</b>: Oklahoma<br>
<b>Nearest City</b>: Sulphur<br>
<b>Established</b>: July 1, 1902</p>
<img src="Arbuckle_mts.jpg" alt="Image of Travertine Creek
in the Chickasaw National Recreation Area.">
</body>
</html>
```

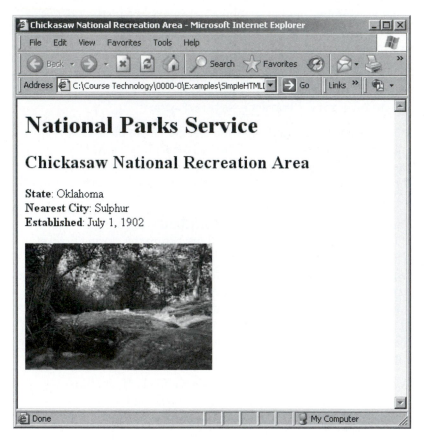

Figure 1-1   A simple HTML document in a Web browser

Creating a Web Page

Because HTML documents are text files, you can create them in any text editor, such as Notepad or WordPad, or any word-processing application capable of creating simple text files. If you use a text editor to create an HTML document, you cannot view the final result until you open the document in a Web browser. Instead of a text editor or word processor, you could choose to use an **HTML editor**, which is an application designed specifically for creating HTML documents. Some popular HTML editors, such as Macromedia Dreamweaver and Microsoft FrontPage, have graphical interfaces that allow you to create Web pages and immediately view the results, similar to the WYSIWYG (what-you-see-is-what-you-get) interface in word-processing programs. In this book, you will create Web pages with Microsoft Visual Web Developer, which is described later in this chapter. But first, you will create a simple HTML page using a simple text editor. The document you create will list specifications for the Cessna 175A Skylark airplane and will contain some of the elements you have seen in this section. You can use any text editor, such as Notepad or WordPad.

To create a simple HTML document:

1. Start your text editor and create a new document, if necessary.

2. Type the following elements to begin the HTML document. Remember that all HTML documents must begin and end with the <html> element.

```
<html>
</html>
```

3. Next add the following <head> and <title> elements between the <html>...</html> tag pair. The title appears in your Web browser's title bar. Remember that the <head> element must include the <title> element. The <title> element cannot exist outside the <head> element.

```
<head>
<title>Cessna 175A Skylark Airplane</title>
</head>
```

4. Next add the following elements above the closing </html> tag. The <body> element contains all of the elements that are rendered in a Web browser. The <basefont> element defines a base font of Arial for the Web page.

```
<body>
<basefont face="Arial">
</body>
```

5. Add the following elements and text above the closing </body> element. The code contains standard HTML elements along with the text that is displayed in the Web browser.

```
<h1>Cessna 175A Skylark Airplane</h1>
<h2>General Characteristics</h2>
<ul>
<li><b>Crew</b>: one pilot</li>
<li><b>Capacity</b>: three passengers</li>
<li><b>Length</b>: 26 ft 6 in (8.08 m)</li>
<li><b>Wingspan</b>: 36 ft 0 in (10.97 m)</li>
<li><b>Height</b>: 8 ft 11 in (2.72 m)</li>
```

10

```
<li><b>Empty weight</b>: 1,339 lb (607 kg)</li>
<li><b>Max takeoff weight</b>: 2,350 lb
   (1,066 kg)</li>
</ul>
<h2>Performance</h2>
<ul>
<li><b>Maximum speed</b>: 148 mph (236 km/h)</li>
<li><b>Range</b>: 598 miles (957 km)</li>
<li><b>Rate of climb</b>: 850 ft/min (259 m/min)</li>
```

Some Web servers do not correctly interpret spaces within the names of HTML files. For example, some Web servers might not correctly interpret the filename Dessert Shop.htm, which contains a space between Dessert and Shop. For this reason, filenames in this book do not include spaces.

6. Save the document as **CessnaSkylark.htm** in the Chapter directory for Chapter 1. Some text editors automatically add their own extensions to a document. Notepad, for instance, adds an extension of .txt. Be certain to save your document with an extension of .htm instead. Keep the document open in your text editor.

7. Open the **CessnaSkylark.htm** document in your Web browser. (You open a local document in most Web browsers by selecting Open or Open File from the File menu.) Figure 1-2 displays the CessnaSkylark.htm document as it appears in Internet Explorer.

8. Close your Web browser window.

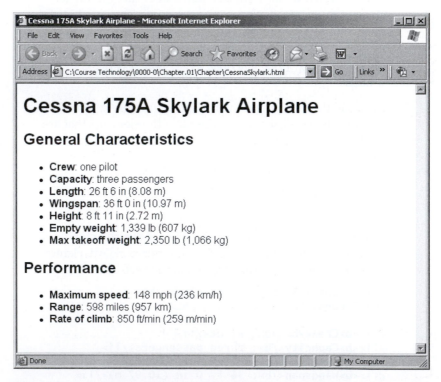

Figure 1-2   CessnaSkylark.htm in Internet Explorer

Web Communication Protocols

As you learned earlier, a Web page is identified by a unique address called the URL. A Web page's URL is similar to a telephone number. Each URL consists of two basic parts: a protocol (usually HTTP) and either the domain name for a Web server or a Web server's Internet Protocol address. **Hypertext Transfer Protocol (HTTP)** manages the hypertext links that are used to navigate the Web. HTTP ensures that Web browsers correctly process and display the various types of information contained in Web pages (text, graphics, audio, and so on). The protocol portion of a URL is followed by a colon, two forward slashes, and a host. The term **host** refers to a computer system that is being accessed by a remote computer. In the case of a URL, the host portion of a URL is usually *www* for "World Wide Web." A **domain name** is a unique address used for identifying a computer, often a Web server, on the Internet. The domain name consists of two parts separated by a period. The first part of a domain name is usually text that easily identifies a person or an organization, such as DonGosselin or Course. The last part of a domain name, known as the **domain identifier**, identifies the type of institution or organization. Common domain identifiers include .biz, .com, .edu, .info, .net, .org, .gov, .mil, or .int. Each domain identifier briefly describes the type of business or organization it represents. For instance, com (for *commercial*) represents private companies, gov (for *government*) represents government agencies, and edu (for *educational*) represents educational institutions. Therefore, the domain name consists of descriptive text for the Web site combined with the domain identifier. For example, course.com is the domain name for Course Technology. An example of an entire URL is *http://www.DonGosselin.com* or *http://www.course.com*.

 An Internet Protocol address (typically referred to as an IP address) is another way to uniquely identify computers or devices connected to the Internet. An IP address consists of a series of four groups of numbers separated by periods. Each Internet domain name is associated with a unique IP address.

In a URL, a specific filename, or a combination of directories and a filename, can follow the domain name or IP address. If the URL does not specify a filename, the requesting Web server looks for a default Web page located in the root or specified directory. Default Web pages usually have names similar to index.htm or default.htm. For instance, if you want help using Google's Web site and you enter *http://www.google.com/help/* in your browser's Address box, the Web server automatically opens a file named index.htm. Figure 1-3 identifies the parts of the URL that opens the default file in the help directory on Google's Web site.

When a URL does not specify a filename, the index.htm file or other file that opens automatically might not appear in your Address box after the document renders.

Figure 1-3   Sample URL

Although HTTP is probably the most widely used protocol on the Internet, it is not the only one. HTTP is a component of **Transmission Control Protocol/Internet Protocol (TCP/IP)**, a large collection of communication protocols used on the Internet. Another common protocol is **Hypertext Transfer Protocol Secure (HTTPS)**, which provides secure Internet connections that are used in Web-based financial transactions and other types of communication that require security and privacy. For instance, to use a Web browser to view your account information through Wells Fargo bank, you need to access the following URL:

`https://online.wellsfargo.com/`

Short Quiz 1

1. When and who developed the Internet and what was its original purpose?

2. What is the Web in relation to the Internet and how do they differ?

3. What were the browser wars, and how did they begin and end?

4. What is the process called that a Web browser uses to assemble and format an HTML document?

5. What are the basic parts of a URL and what is each part's purpose?

Introduction to Web Page Development

Web page design, or **Web design**, refers to the visual design and creation of the documents that appear on the World Wide Web. Most businesses today—both prominent and small—have Web sites. To attract and retain visitors, and to stand out from the crowd, Web sites must be exciting and visually stimulating. Quality Web design plays an important role in attracting first-time and repeat visitors. However, the visual aspect of a Web site is only one part of the story. Equally important is the content of the Web site and how that content is structured.

Web design is an extremely important topic. However, this book is not about Web design, even though you will certainly learn many

Web design concepts and techniques as you work through the chapters ahead. Instead, this book touches on both Web page authoring and Web development. **Web page authoring** (or **Web authoring**) refers to the creation and assembly of the tags, attributes, and data that make up a Web page. There is a subtle, but important distinction between Web design and Web page authoring: Web design refers to the visual and graphical design aspects of creating Web pages, whereas a book on Web page authoring refers to the physical task of assembling the Web page tags and attributes. **Web development**, or **Web programming**, refers to the design of software applications for a Web site. Generally, a Web developer works "behind the scenes" to develop software applications that access databases and file systems, communicate with other applications, and perform other advanced tasks. The programs created by a Web developer will not necessarily be seen by a visitor to a Web site, although the visitor will certainly use a Web developer's programs, particularly if the Web site writes and reads data to and from a database. Although JavaScript lives more in the realm of Web page authoring, there is certainly some overlap between Web authoring and Web development, especially when it comes to sending and receiving data to and from a Web server.

Another term that you might often see in relation to Web development is *Webmaster*. Although there is some dispute over exactly what the term means, typically Webmaster refers to a person who is responsible for the day-to-day maintenance of a Web site including the monitoring of Web site traffic and ensuring that the Web site's hardware and software are running properly. The duties of a Webmaster often require knowledge of Web page design, authoring, and development.

Understanding Client/Server Architecture

To be successful in Web development, you need to understand the basics of client/server architecture. There are many definitions of the terms *client* and *server*. In traditional client/server architecture, the **server** is usually some sort of database from which a client requests information. A server fulfills a request for information by managing the request or serving the requested information to the client—hence the term, client/server. A system consisting of a client and a server is known as a **two-tier system**.

One of the primary roles of the **client**, or **front end**, in a two-tier system is the presentation of an interface to the user. The user interface gathers information from the user, submits it to a server, or **back end**, then receives, formats, and presents the results returned from the server. The main responsibility of a server is usually data storage and management. On client/server systems, heavy processing, such as calculations, usually takes place on the server. As desktop computers become increasingly powerful, however, many client/server systems have begun placing at least some of the processing responsibilities on the client. In a typical client/server system, a client computer might contain a front end that is used for requesting information from a database on a server. The server locates records that meet the client request, performs some sort of processing, such as calculations on the data, and then returns the information to the client. The client

If you would like to study the topic of Web page design itself, refer to Joel Sklar's excellent book, *Principles of Web Design, Fourth Edition*, published by Course Technology.

computer can also perform some processing, such as building the queries that are sent to the server or formatting and presenting the returned data. Figure 1-4 illustrates the design of a two-tier client/server system.

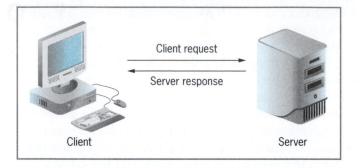

Figure 1-4   The design of a two-tier client/server system

The Web is built on a two-tier client/server system, in which a Web browser (the client) requests documents from a Web server. The Web browser is the client user interface. You can think of the Web server as a repository for Web pages. After a Web server returns the requested document, the Web browser (as the client user interface) is responsible for formatting and presenting the document to the user. The requests and responses through which a Web browser and Web server communicate happen with HTTP. For example, if a Web browser requests the URL *http://www.course.com*, the request is made with HTTP because the URL includes the HTTP protocol. The Web server then returns to the Web browser an HTTP response containing the response header and the HTML (or XHTML) for Course Technology's home page.

After you start adding databases and other types of applications to a Web server, the client/server system evolves into what is known as a three-tier client architecture. A **three-tier**, or **multitier**, **client/server system** consists of three distinct pieces: the client tier, the processing tier, and the data storage tier. The client tier, or user interface tier, is still the Web browser. However, the database portion of the two-tier client/server system is split into a processing tier and the data storage tier. The processing tier, or middle tier, handles the interaction between the Web browser client and the data storage tier. (The processing tier is also sometimes called the processing bridge.) Essentially, the client tier makes a request of a database on a Web server. The processing tier performs any necessary processing or calculations based on the request from the client tier, and then reads information from or writes information to the data storage tier. The processing tier also handles the return of any information to the client tier. Note that the processing tier is not the only place where processing can occur. The

Web browser (client tier) still renders Web page documents (which requires processing), and the database or application in the data storage tier might also perform some processing. Figure 1-5 illustrates the design of a three-tier client/server system.

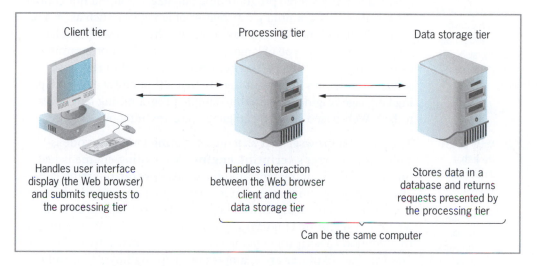

Figure 1-5   The design of a three-tier client/server system

Client-Side Scripting and JavaScript

As mentioned earlier, HTML was not originally intended to control the appearance of pages in a Web browser. When HTML was first developed, Web pages were **static**—that is, they couldn't change after the browser rendered them. However, after the Web grew beyond a small academic and scientific community, people began to recognize that greater interactivity and better visual design would make the Web more useful. As commercial applications of the Web grew, the demand for more interactive and visually appealing Web sites also grew.

HTML and XHTML could only be used to produce static documents. You can think of a static Web page written in HTML or XHTML as being approximately equivalent to a document created in a word-processing or desktop publishing program; the only thing you can do with it is view it or print it. Thus, to respond to the demand for greater interactivity, an entirely new Web programming language was needed. Netscape filled this need by developing JavaScript.

JavaScript is a client-side scripting language that allows Web page authors to develop interactive Web pages and sites. **Client-side scripting** refers to a scripting language that runs on a local browser (on the client tier) instead of on a Web server (on the processing tier).

Two-tier client/server architecture is a physical arrangement in which the client and server are two separate computers. Three-tier client/server architecture is more conceptual than physical, because the storage tier can be located on the same server.

Multitier client/server architecture is also referred to as n-tier architecture.

Originally designed for use in Navigator Web browsers, JavaScript is now also used in most other Web browsers, including Firefox and Internet Explorer.

If you want to learn more about JavaScript, refer to Don Gosselin's *JavaScript, Fourth Edition*, also published by Course Technology.

The term **scripting language** is a general term that originally referred to fairly simple programming languages that did not contain the advanced programming capabilities of languages such as Java or C++. When it comes to Web development, the term scripting language refers to any type of language that is capable of programmatically controlling a Web page or returning some sort of response to a Web browser. It's important to note that although the term scripting language originally referred to simple programming languages, today's Web-based scripting languages are anything but simple.

Many people think that JavaScript is related to or is a simplified version of the Java programming language. However, the languages are entirely different. Java is an advanced programming language that was created by Sun Microsystems and is considerably more difficult to master than JavaScript. Although Java can be used to create programs that can run from a Web page, Java programs are usually external programs that execute independently of a browser. In contrast, JavaScript programs always run within a Web page and control the browser.

The part of a browser that executes scripting language code is called the browser's **scripting engine**. A scripting engine is just one kind of interpreter, with the term **interpreter** referring generally to any program that executes scripting language code. When a scripting engine loads a Web page, it interprets any programs written in scripting languages, such as JavaScript. A Web browser that contains a scripting engine is called a **scripting host**. Firefox and Internet Explorer are examples of scripting hosts that can run JavaScript programs.

Although JavaScript is considered a programming language, it is also a critical part of Web page authoring. This is because the JavaScript language "lives" within a Web page's elements. JavaScript gives you the ability to do the following:

- Turn static Web pages into applications such as games or calculators.

- Change the contents of a Web page after a browser has rendered it.

- Create visual effects such as animation.

- Control the Web browser window itself.

For security reasons, the JavaScript programming language cannot be used outside of the Web browser. For example, to prevent mischievous scripts from stealing information, such as your e-mail address or credit card information you use for an online transaction, or from causing damage by changing or deleting files, JavaScript does not allow any file manipulation whatsoever. Similarly, JavaScript does not include any sort of mechanism for creating a network connection or accessing a database. This limitation prevents JavaScript programs from infiltrating a private network or intranet from which information might be stolen or damaged. Another helpful limitation is the fact that JavaScript cannot run system commands or execute programs on a client. The ability to read and write cookies is the only type of access to a client that JavaScript has. Web browsers, however, strictly govern cookies and do not allow access to cookies from outside the domain that created them. This security also means that you cannot use JavaScript to interact directly with Web servers that operate at the processing tier. Although the programmer can employ a few tricks (such as forms and query strings) to allow JavaScript to interact indirectly with a Web server, if you want true control over what's happening on the server, you need to use a server-side scripting language.

Server-Side Scripting and ASP.NET

Server-side scripting is a technology that processes a request for a Web page by executing a script on a server. One of the primary reasons for using server-side scripting is to develop interactive Web sites that communicate with a database. Server-side scripts work in the processing tier and have the ability to handle communication between the client tier and the data storage tier. At the processing tier, a server-side script usually prepares and processes the data in some way before submitting it to the data storage tier. Some of the more common uses of server-side scripts that you have probably already seen on the Web include the following:

- Shopping carts
- Search engines
- Mailing lists and message boards
- Web-based e-mail systems
- Authentication and security mechanisms
- Web logs (blogs)
- Games and entertainment

Figure 1-6 illustrates how a Web server processes a server-side script.

Unlike JavaScript, a server-side script can't access or manipulate a Web browser. In fact, a server-side script cannot run on a client tier at all. Instead, a server-side script exists and executes solely on a Web server, where it performs various types of processing or accesses databases. When a client requests a server-side script, the script is interpreted and executed by the scripting engine within the Web server software. After the script finishes executing, the Web server software then translates the results of the script (such as the result of a calculation or the records returned from a database) into HTML or XHTML, which it then returns to the client. In other words, a client will never see the server-side script, only the HTML or XHTML that the Web server software returns from the script.

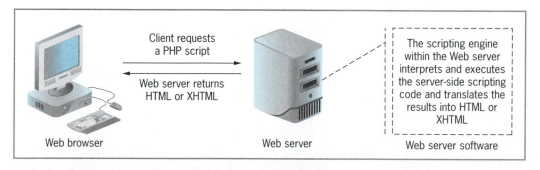

Figure 1-6 How a Web server processes a server-side script

In this book, you will use **Active Server Pages (ASP) .NET**, which is a server-side scripting technology that is part of Visual Web Developer. You can use one of two languages with ASP.NET: Visual Basic or Visual C#. In this book, the ASP.NET scripts you create use **C#** (pronounced C *sharp*), which is an object-oriented programming language based on the C++ programming language. **Object-oriented programming (OOP)** refers to the creation of reusable software objects that can be easily incorporated into another program. Popular object-oriented programming languages include C++, Java, and Visual Basic. You will learn more about C#'s object-oriented capabilities as you progress through this book.

Other popular server-side scripting tools used in Web development include PHP: Hypertext Preprocessor (PHP) and JavaServer Pages (JSP).

C# is specifically designed to create Web-based applications that run on the **.NET Framework**, which is a platform developed by Microsoft for developing and running Internet applications, primarily Web-based applications and services. The .NET Framework is automatically installed as part of Visual Web Developer.

Should You Use Client-Side or Server-Side Scripting?

An important question in the design of any client/server system is deciding how much processing to place on the client or server. In the context of Web site development, you must decide whether to use client-side JavaScript or a server-side script. This is an important consideration because the choice you make can greatly affect the performance of your program. In some cases, the decision is simple. For example, if you want to control the Web browser, you must use JavaScript. If you want to access a database on a Web server, you must use a server-side script. However, there are tasks that both languages can accomplish, such as validating forms and manipulating cookies. Further, both languages can perform the same types of calculations and data processing.

A general rule of thumb is to allow the client to handle the user interface processing and light processing, such as data validation, but have the Web server perform intensive calculations and data storage. This division of labor is especially important when dealing with clients and servers over the Web. Unlike with clients on a private network, it's not possible to know in advance the computing capabilities of each client on the Web. You cannot assume that each client (browser) that accesses your client/server application (Web site) has the necessary power to perform the processing required by the application. For this reason, intensive processing should be placed on the server.

Because servers are usually much more powerful than client computers, your first instinct might be to let the server handle all processing and only use the client to display a user interface. Although you do not want to overwhelm clients with processing they cannot handle, it is important to perform as much processing as possible on the client for several reasons:

- Distributing processing among multiple clients creates applications that are more powerful because the processing power is not limited to the capabilities of a single computer. Client computers become more powerful every day, and advanced capabilities such as JavaScript are now available in local Web browsers. Thus, it makes sense to use a **Web application** to harness some of this power and capability. A Web application is a program that executes on a server but that clients access through a Web page loaded in a browser.

- Local processing on client computers minimizes transfer times across the Internet and creates faster applications. If a client had to wait for all processing to be performed on the server, a Web application could be painfully slow over a busy Internet connection.

- Performing processing on client computers lightens the processing load on the server. If all processing in a three-tier client/server system is on the server, the server for a popular Web site could become overwhelmed trying to process requests from numerous clients.

Short Quiz 2

1. What are the differences in Web page design, Web page authoring, and Web development?

2. What are the primary roles of the client and the server in two-tier system architecture?

3. What is the purpose of the processing tier in three-tier system architecture?

4. Why are scripts written with the JavaScript programming language restricted to executing only within a Web browser?

5. How does the execution and use of client-side scripting differ from server-side scripting?

Although the express editions do not include certain types of functionality, they are ideal for educational purposes. In this book, you use Visual Web Developer 2008 Express Edition to develop ASP.NET Web sites and SQL Server 2008 Express Edition to store the information that your ASP.NET applications require. In the next section, you install the express version of Visual Web Developer.

Introduction to Microsoft Visual Studio 2008

The Microsoft Visual Studio development system is a suite of software development tools including Visual C++, Visual C#, and Visual Basic programming languages, and Visual Web Developer, which is primarily used for developing ASP.NET applications. The most recent edition is Visual Studio 2008, which is available in two commercial versions: Visual Studio 2008 Professional Edition and Visual Studio 2008 Standard Edition. The Visual Studio product line is also available in the following free but limited editions, which are known as the Visual Studio 2008 Express Editions:

- Visual Basic 2008 Express Edition
- Visual C# 2008 Express Edition
- Visual C++ 2008 Express Edition
- Visual Web Developer 2008 Express Edition
- SQL Server 2008 Express Edition

Installing Microsoft Visual Web Developer 2008 Express Edition

Microsoft Visual Web Developer 2008 Express Edition is a development environment for creating ASP.NET Web sites. Although primarily designed for creating ASP.NET Web sites, you can also use Visual Web Developer to create HTML pages, Cascading Style Sheets, XML files, JavaScript code, and various other types of files that a Web site may use. Visual Web Developer is the primary development tool that you will use with this book.

To install Microsoft Visual Web Developer and SQL Server 2008 Express Editions:

1. Start your Web browser and enter the URL for the Microsoft Visual Studio Express Editions download page: **http://www.microsoft.com/express/download/default.aspx**.

2. Scroll down to the **Web Install** section of the page and locate the Microsoft Visual Web Developer 2008 Express Edition installation section. Select **English** as your language and click the **Download** link. When prompted, save the **vwdsetup.exe** file to a temporary directory on your computer.

3. Open Windows Explorer or My Computer and navigate to the directory where you downloaded the **vwdsetup.exe** file. Double-click the file to start the installation program. The Welcome page of the installation wizard appears.

4. On the Welcome page, click **Next** to proceed with installation. The License Terms page appears.

5. On the License Terms page, click the **I have read and accept the license terms** button, and then click **Next**. The Installation Options page appears.

6. The Installation Options page allows you to choose whether to install Microsoft Silverlight Runtime and Microsoft SQL Server 2008 Express Edition along with Visual Web Developer. Silverlight is used for delivering media and interactive applications through a Web browser. If either of these products is already installed on your computer, they will not be listed on the Installation Options page. If necessary, select the **Microsoft Silverlight Runtime** box and the **Microsoft SQL Server 2008 Express Edition** box. Click **Next**. The Destination Folder page appears.

7. The Destination Folder page allows you to change the folder where Visual Web Developer will be installed. Change the destination folder if you need to, although in most cases you should accept the default value of C:\Program Files\Microsoft Visual Studio 9.0\. Click the **Install** button to begin installation. Depending on your Windows installation, you might see a dialog box prompting you to restart your computer. The dialog box contains two buttons: Restart Now and Restart Later. If you click Restart Now, your computer will restart immediately—be sure to save any open files before clicking Restart Now. If you click Restart Later, the installation wizard closes. If you do click Restart Later, be sure to restart your computer before attempting to use Visual Web Developer.

Managing Web Sites in Visual Web Developer

This section explains how to manage Web sites in Visual Web Developer. First, you learn how to create a new project.

Creating New Web Sites

To create a new Web site in Visual Web Developer, you select New Web Site from the File menu. Visual Web Developer installs the following Visual Studio templates by default:

- ASP.NET Web Site—Creates a new project with the basic files that an ASP.NET Web site requires. You will create an ASP.NET Web site in Chapter 2.

- ASP.NET Web Service—Creates a new project with the basic files that an ASP.NET Web service requires. You will create an ASP.NET Web service in Chapter 12.

- Empty Web Site—Creates an empty project that does not contain any files. You will create an empty Web site in this chapter.

- WCF Web Service—Creates a more advanced type of Web service, called a Windows Communication Foundation (WCF) Web service, which you can use to build, configure, and deploy network-distributed services. WCF Web services are a complex subject that is beyond the scope of this book. For more information on WCF Web services, refer to *Introduction to Building Windows Communication Foundation Services* at *http://msdn2.microsoft.com/en-us/library/aa480190.aspx*.

Next, you create an empty Web site.

To create an empty Web site:

1. To start Visual Web Developer, click the **Start** button, point to **All Programs**, and then click **Microsoft Visual Web Developer 2008 Express Edition**. The Visual Studio integrated development environment (IDE) opens. (You will learn more about the IDE shortly.)

2. Select the **File** menu, and then select **New Web Site**. The New Web Site dialog box opens.

3. In the Templates section, click **Empty Web Site**. Leave the Location box set to **File System**, which creates the new Web site on your local file system, and the Language box set to **Visual C#**. Click the **Browse** button. The Choose Location dialog box opens.

4. In the File System section of the Choose Location dialog box, find the Chapter folder for Chapter 1 in the location where you installed the data files. By default, the path should be C:\Course Technology\0324-2\Chapter.01\Chapter. Click the **Chapter** folder, and then click the **Create New Folder** button. For the rest of this chapter, you will work on a basic Web site that will serve the Cessna Skylark Web page, so name the new folder **Cessna**. This folder is where Visual Web Developer will store the Web site's files.

5. Click the **Open** button. The Choose Location dialog box closes and you return to the New Web Site dialog box. Click **OK** to create the new Web site.

Adding Items to a Web Site

You use the commands on the Website menu to add items, such as an HTML file, to a Web site. To add a new item, select the Website menu and then select Add New Item. To add an existing item, select the Website menu and then select Add Existing Item. The various types of items that you add to a Web site are contained in disk files and are stored in folders, just like any other files.

Next, you add an HTML file to the Cessna Web site.

To add an HTML file to the Cessna Web site:

1. Return to the Cessna project in Visual Web Developer.

2. Select the **Website** menu and then select **Add New Item**. The Add New Item dialog box opens. The Templates area of this dialog box contains various file types that you can use with a Web site. In this case, you are creating an HTML file with the HTML Page template. In the Visual Studio installed templates section of the Templates area, select **HTML Page**. Figure 1-7 shows the Add New Item dialog box with the HTML Page template selected.

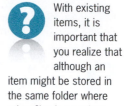

With existing items, it is important that you realize that although an item might be stored in the same folder where other files in a project are stored, the item is not actually a part of the project until you physically add it to the project within the Visual Web Developer IDE.

23

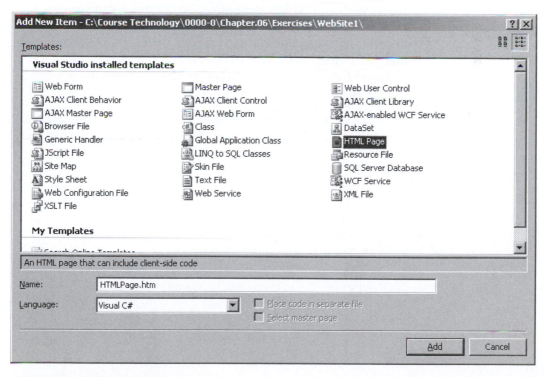

Figure 1-7 Add New Item dialog box

3. Change the suggested filename in the Name box to **CessnaSkylark.htm**, but leave the value in the Language box set to **Visual C#**.

4. Click the **Add** button to add the HTML page to the project. The new page opens in Visual Web Developer and contains an `<html>` root element, head section, and body section. The page is actually an XHTML document because it contains the following two items: a `<!DOCTYPE>` declaration and an `xmlns` attribute in the opening `<html>` tag. You will study XHTML along with the `<!DOCTYPE>` declaration and `xmlns` attribute later in this chapter. For now, you can just think of the page as an HTML document with a few extra pieces.

Opening Existing Web Sites

A Web site's project settings are stored in two files: a **Visual Studio Solution** file with an extension of .sln and a Solution User Options file with an extension of .suo. These files are referred to as solution files. The Visual Studio Solution file stores all of the settings that are required by a Web site project while the Solution User Options file stores customization options for the project. These files are assigned the name of the folder where you chose to store your Web site. For example, with the Cessna Web site that you created in the last section, the Visual Studio Solution file is named Cessna.sln and the Solution User Options file is named Cessna.suo.

The solution files are always stored in the folder that is designated as your Visual Studio projects location, although your Web site files can be stored in a separate directory. In other words, the files that make up your Web site do not need to be stored in the same folder as the project's solution files. For example, suppose you create a new project in C:\WebSites\StoreFront. This folder will contain all of your project's files, with the exception of the solution files, which will be stored in a folder named StoreFront in the designated Visual Studio projects location. The default Visual Studio projects location is usually set to C:\Documents and Settings*user name*\My Documents\Visual Studio 2008\WebSites. Because you will be saving your Web sites in the location where you installed the data files, separate folders containing solution files for each of your projects will also be created in your default Visual Studio projects location.

To open an existing Web site in Visual Web Developer, you must locate the folder where the Web site files are stored. You can actually open any Web site folder in Visual Web Developer, even Web sites that do not include solution files. However, for a folder to be recognized as a Visual Web Developer Web site, solution files for the Web site must exist. In fact, whenever you open a Web site folder in Visual Web Developer, the solution files are created automatically if they don't already exist.

To change the default Visual Studio projects location, click the Tools menu, click Options, click Show all settings, and then click Projects and Solutions.

Using the Visual Studio Integrated Development Environment (IDE)

The workspace that you use to create projects in Visual Studio is called the **integrated development environment (IDE)**. You use the same IDE no matter what type of program you are creating. However, the tools available in the IDE vary, depending on the type of project you are creating. For example, when you are working in Visual C++ 2008, the IDE displays tools related to programming in Visual C++. When you are creating a Visual Web Developer program (as you will throughout this book), the IDE provides tools related to Web site development. Within the IDE, the program you are writing is referred to as a **project** or a **solution**. The difference between projects and solutions is that a solution can contain multiple projects. In Visual Web Developer, a project is the Web site you are creating.

One reason for the popularity of ASP.NET and C# has to do with their simplicity. The C# language is relatively easy to learn, allowing nonprogrammers to quickly incorporate ASP.NET functionality into a Web site. Even though it is easier to learn than other programming languages, C# is a fast and powerful language that includes object-oriented programming capabilities found in more advanced languages such as C++ and Java. (You will study object-oriented programming in later chapters.) However, do not confuse "relatively easy to learn" with "easy to learn." Although not as involved as an advanced language such as C++ or Java, C# is nonetheless a programming language and much more complicated than simple HTML.

This chapter introduces only the basics of the Visual Studio IDE, leaving more advanced tools and windows to later chapters. Some tools and windows are only available to certain types of Web pages. Others require a solid understanding of ASP.NET and C# programming. You will learn about many of the various IDE tools and windows as necessary throughout this book.

The Start Page

The Start Page appears by default in the IDE whenever you first start Visual Web Developer. The **Start Page** contains links to recent projects, tutorials, developer information, and recent news about Visual Web Developer. When you click a link on the Start Page, a Web browser opens in a new tab and displays the URL you selected. Figure 1-8 displays how the Start Page appears the first time you open Visual Web Developer.

You can customize various aspects of the IDE by selecting the Tools menu and then by selecting Options.

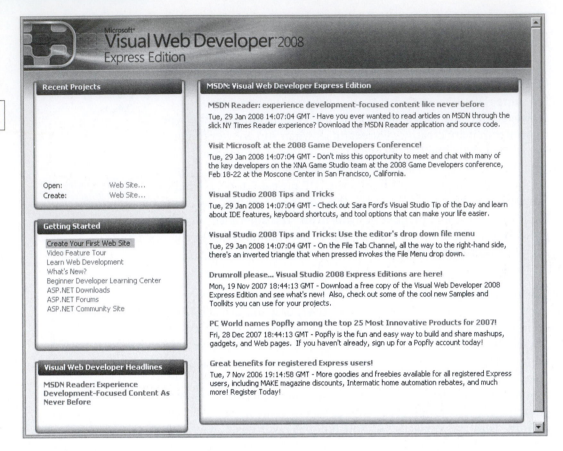

Figure 1-8 IDE Start Page

The Solution Explorer Window

Visual Web Developer projects are composed of multiple files representing a specific type of resource or object. One of the most common file types you will use when developing Web sites with Visual Web Developer are ASP.NET files, which have an extension of .aspx. Web sites can also include many other types of files, including Web pages with an extension of .htm, Cascading Style Sheets with an extension of .css, and XML files with an extension of .xml. You use the **Solution Explorer** window in the IDE to manage the various files associated with a Web site. The files in the Solution Explorer window appear in a hierarchical list that might remind you of Windows Explorer, or some other type of graphical file management system.

The Solution Explorer window should have appeared automatically when you first created the Cessna project. If it did not, click the View menu and then click Solution Explorer. The first item in the Solution Explorer window is the Solution icon. Beneath the Solution icon are the various files that make up the Web site. Figure 1-9 displays the files that the Cessna project contains.

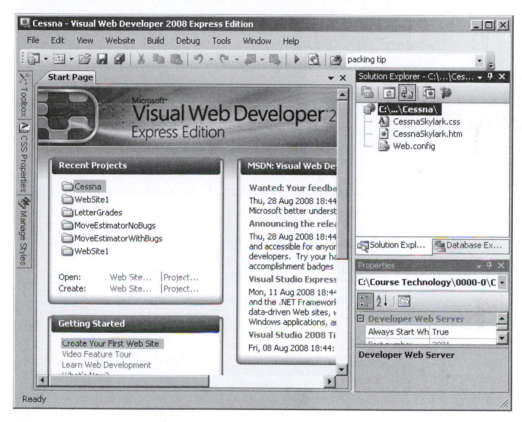

Figure 1-9 Solution Explorer window for the Cessna project

Editors and Designers

Visual Web Developer includes editors and designers (special windows for editing and designing) that streamline the process of working with the various file types that make up a Web site. The editor that you will work with the most in this book is the **Code Editor**, which you use to edit programming code. Other common editors include the **Text Editor**, which you use to edit text that is not associated with any particular programming language, and the **CSS Editor**, which you use to edit CSS files. The various editors share many of the same features and have the same text-editing capabilities as other Windows text editors: You can cut and paste, drag and drop, and

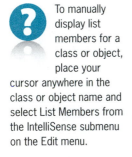

You can change editor options, including font syntax color choices, by selecting the Tools menu, selecting Options, and then by selecting Fonts and Colors.

To manually display list members for a class or object, place your cursor anywhere in the class or object name and select List Members from the IntelliSense submenu on the Edit menu.

The IntelliSense submenu on the Edit menu contains additional commands that are used with more complex types of code such as C#, Visual Basic, and JScript.

search for specific text strings. These and other text editing options are available on the Edit menu and the toolbar.

The various types of code elements in the editor windows are distinguished by special colors (known as syntax colors) that make it easier to understand the structure and code of specific types of files. For example, the default syntax coloring for HTML element names is maroon and red for attribute names. If you need to locate a statement containing an HTML <form> element, you can start by looking at just the maroon text. Of course, you can also use the Find and Replace commands on the Edit menu, but for small files, it's usually much simpler to start by looking for the correct color.

The Code Editor includes a feature called **statement completion** to aid in code creation. Statement completion is part of Microsoft's **IntelliSense** technology, which automates routine and complex tasks. As you are writing code, lists appear that you can use to quickly complete the current statement you are writing. Figure 1-10 displays an HTML file in the Code Editor. As the figure illustrates, placing your cursor before the closing bracket of the <form> tag and pressing the Spacebar displays a list of the <form> element parameters. To insert a particular parameter, you can either double-click it or move your cursor to the parameter name and press Enter.

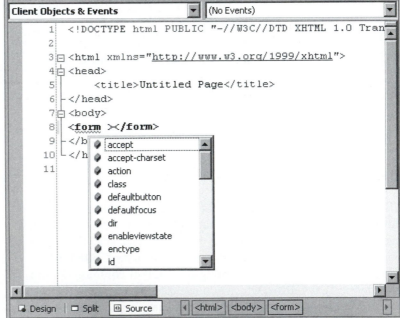

Figure 1-10   Statement completion in the Code Editor

Most editors include two views: code view, such as the Code Editor window in Figure 1-10, and design view, which displays a graphical representation of an editor that you can use to visually modify the location of controls and other elements. For example, with an HTML file that is open in the Code Editor, you can either edit the HTML statements in code view or graphically manipulate them in design view. To switch between code view and design view, click the Source or Design buttons at the bottom of the Code Editor window. You can also display both code view and design view by clicking the Split button at the bottom of the Code Editor window.

Next, you practice using the Code Editor window.

To practice using the Code Editor window:

1. Return to the Cessna project in Visual Web Developer.

2. Change the contents of the `<title>` element to **Cessna 175A Skylark Airplane**.

3. Press **Enter** and begin typing an opening **<h1>** tag. As soon as you type the opening bracket, a statement completion list appears and highlights the `<h1>` element. After you type the closing angle bracket, the closing `</h1>` tag is added automatically and your cursor is placed between the two tags. Type **Cessna 175A Skylark Airplane** as the content for the heading element.

4. Switch to the text editor window that contains the original version of the CessnaSkylark.htm file that you created earlier and copy the contents of the document body, with the exception of the opening `<h1>` element.

5. Close your text editor window.

6. Return to the Cessna project in Visual Web Developer and paste the statements that you just copied at the end of the body section. Notice that as soon as you paste the statements, the HTML element names and attributes automatically change to maroon and red, respectively.

7. Click the **Design** button at the bottom of the Code Editor window to graphically view how the page will display in a Web browser.

8. Save the CessnaSkylark.htm file by selecting the **File** menu and then by selecting **Save CessnaSkylark.htm**.

The Properties Window

An ASP.NET project contains various settings, or properties, that determine how a project and its files appear and behave. You use the **Properties window** to change the various properties, attributes, and other settings that are associated with a project. The properties listed in the Properties window change according to the programmatic element that is selected in an editor. For example, Figure 1-11 displays the properties of a `<form>` tag when it is selected in the Code Editor.

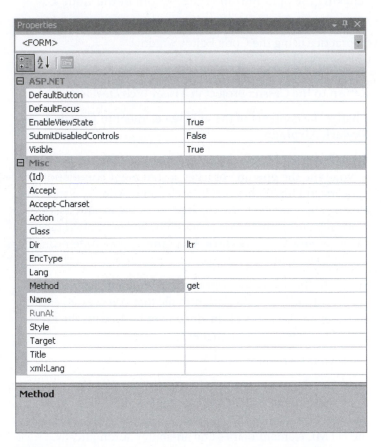

Figure 1-11 Properties of the `<form>` tag displayed in the Properties window

The Properties window contains two columns: a property column and a value column. You enter the value for a specific property into the value column. For some properties, such as the Name property of the `<form>`, you enter a text value. For other properties, such as the Method property of the `<form>` method, you select the icon to the right of the value box and select one of the available values (such as "get" or "post" for the **Method** property). Still other properties, such as the **Style** property of the **<form>** method, display a dialog box that you can use to select values for the specific property.

Managing Windows

With so many windows available in the IDE, it is easy for one window to hide another. As you work through this book, you will probably find it necessary to move and resize the windows on your screen. Certain types of windows in the IDE, such as the Solution Explorer window, can be floating or dockable. To change whether a window is floating or dockable, right-click the window's title bar and select either Floating or Dockable from the shortcut menu. Note that you can only have one of these options selected at a time. A window with its dockable property turned on "docks" or "snaps" to a position on the screen. By default, the dockable property of a tool window is turned on and the floating property is turned off. Figure 1-12 shows an example of the Solution Explorer window with its dockable property turned on and snapped to its default position.

You do not necessarily need to use the Properties window to update the properties in your file; for simple files such as an HTML file, you will often find it easier just to update the associated attribute directly in your code. However, the Properties window is useful for complex files that include numerous elements.

31

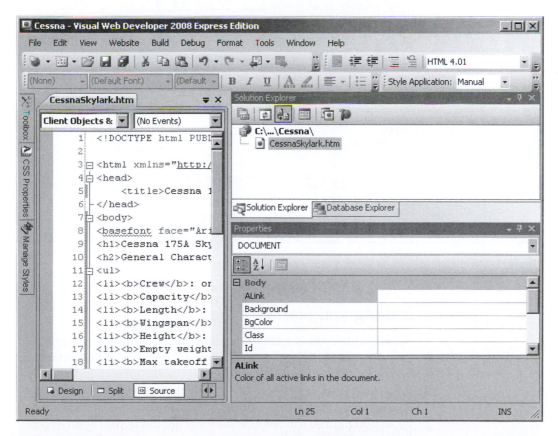

Figure 1-12 Solution Explorer window with its dockable property turned on

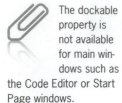

The dockable property is not available for main windows such as the Code Editor or Start Page windows.

When a window's dockable property is turned on, you can drag the window to another part of the IDE. When you are dragging the window, a guide appears on screen that identifies locations in the IDE where you can snap the window. To move a window to another part of the screen without docking it, turn the window's floating property on. Figure 1-13 shows an example of the Solution Explorer window with its floating property turned on.

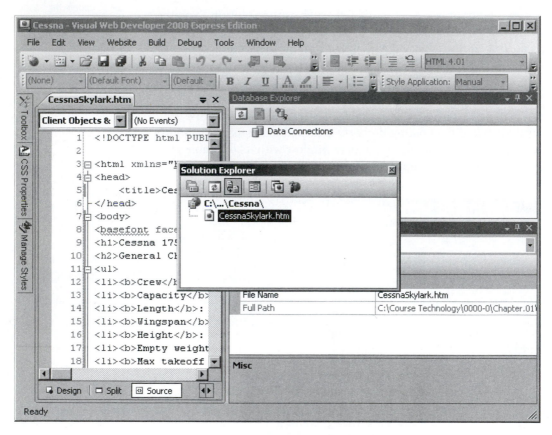

Figure 1-13   Solution Explorer window with its floating property turned on

Building and Starting a Web Site

Source code is the original programming code in which an application was written. Before you can use source code, it must be **compiled**, or processed and assembled into an executable format. In Visual Web Developer, the tools for compiling the source code that makes up a Web site are located on the Build menu. You have two options for compiling: You can compile the files containing your source code (such as ASP.NET with an extension of .aspx) individually using the

Build Page command or you can compile all the source files in the Web site simultaneously using the Build Web Site command. Both commands check code syntax and compile the source files.

When you select the Build Web Site command, Visual Web Developer compiles only the files in your Web site that have changed. However, there might be instances when you must recompile your program, even if you have made no changes to the code. For example, you would need to recompile your entire program if your compiled files become corrupt or if you want to perform some final testing before releasing a finished version of your program. You can force Visual Web Developer to recompile all files in your program, even if they have not been modified, by selecting the Rebuild Web Site command from the Build menu.

Keep in mind that even the most well-planned code can cause your computer to freeze or even crash when it runs. To protect you against this possibility, Visual Web Developer automatically saves changes to all open items during the build process. However, you must save manually if you make changes to a file and then close it without building. If your computer crashes during the build process—and it probably will on occasion—you will lose any unsaved changes to your project. Therefore, it is good practice to save your Web sites at regular intervals, especially before building and running a Web site. To save the entire Web site, select the File menu and then select Save All.

Displaying Status with the Output Window

Running any of the build commands displays the Output window at the bottom of the IDE. The **Output window** displays status messages for various IDE features. Visual Web Developer uses the Output window to display its progress when you build a program. You can display the Output window manually by selecting the View menu and then selecting Output or by pressing Ctrl+Alt+O.

Next, you practice using the Code Editor and Output windows.

To practice using the Code Editor window:

1. Return to the Cessna project in Visual Web Developer.

2. Save the CessnaSkylark.htm file by selecting the **File** menu and then by selecting **Save CessnaSkylark.htm**.

3. Click the **Source** button at the bottom of the Code Editor window.

4. Select the **Build** menu and then select **Build Web Site**. Figure 1-14 shows the Output window after successfully building the Cessna Web site.

 If at any point you become completely lost among the various floating and dockable windows that can appear in the IDE, you can start over by resetting your environment with the Reset Window Layout command on the Window menu. This command resets your environment to the default IDE settings.

 In Visual Web Developer Express Edition, the Build Page (available when you have a file selected in Solution Explorer), Build Web Site, and Rebuild Web Site commands do not actually compile the code for deployment; they just validate code syntax. To compile code that will be deployed on a production Web site, you must purchase a commercial version of Visual Studio 2008. See Appendix A, "Deploying and Configuring an ASP.NET Application," for more information on how to deploy and configure a Web site.

 You can use the Build property page to configure the options that Visual Web Developer uses to compile a page or Web site. To display the Build property page, select the Website menu, select Start Options, and then select Build.

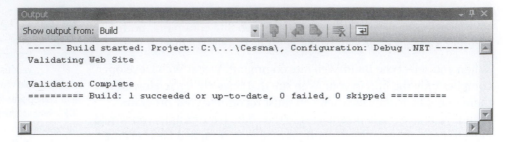

Figure 1-14   Output window after building the Cessna Web site

Finding Errors with the Error List Window

The **Error List window** lists any source file errors that Visual Web Developer finds when you run any of the build commands. Although the Error List window displays automatically if any errors are found during the build process, you can also manually display it by selecting the View menu and then by selecting Error List, or by pressing Ctrl+\ and then Ctrl+E. Figure 1-15 displays the Error List window for an ASP.NET source file that contains some errors.

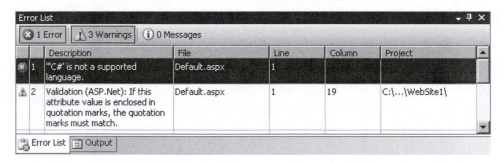

Figure 1-15   Error List window displaying errors found in an ASP.NET source file

You can quickly jump to the line that raised a build error by double-clicking the error in the Error List window.

The Error List window displays two types of messages: compiler error messages and warning messages. **Compiler error messages** occur for any syntax errors in a source file and contain a description of the error, the name of the file in which the error occurred, the line and column number in the document, and the project that contains the file. **Warning messages** occur for any potential problems that might exist in your code, but that are not serious enough to cause a compiler error message. As you progress through this book, you will learn more about the various types of ASP.NET and C# compiler error and warning messages that can occur.

Using the ASP.NET Development Server

When developing a Web site, you need to be able to open your Web sites from a Web server that is running on a local computer. Visual Web Developer includes the **ASP.NET Development Server**, which is a basic Web server that you can use to test your Web sites on your local computer. The ASP.NET Development Server is specifically designed to run under *localhost*, which is the name that a local computer uses to refer to itself. To run a Web site with the ASP.NET Development Server, select the Debug menu and then select Start Without Debugging command or press Ctrl+F5. When you run the Start Without Debugging command, Visual Web Developer runs the Build Web Site command by default, so you do not need to run it yourself. Then, Visual Web Developer launches the ASP.NET Development Server and runs the Web site in a Web browser window using *localhost* and a randomly selected port. In TCP/IP, a **port** represents the endpoint of a connection between a client and a server. Clients use a port number to identify a specific application on a Web server. Port numbers range from 0 to 65536, with ports 0 to 1024 being reserved for special purposes or well-known protocols. For example, port 80 is reserved for HTTP communications. This means that whenever you access a Web page such as *http://www.yahoo.com/*, you are really accessing it through port 80 on Yahoo's Web server.

With the exception of reserved ports such as port 80, port numbers must be specified in the URL by appending the port number with a colon to *localhost*. When the ASP.NET Development Server opens a Web page in a browser, the URL is in the format http://localhost:*port/ folder/page*. For example, the URL for a Web page named MyWebPage.htm in a Web site folder named MyWebSite that is randomly assigned port 4847 would be http://localhost:4847/MyWebSite/ MyWebPage.htm. The ASP.NET Development Server automatically shuts down when you close the browser window.

Next, you run the Cessna Web site with the ASP.NET Development Server.

To run the Cessna Web site with the ASP.NET Development Server:

1. Return to the Cessna project in Visual Web Developer.

2. Select the **Debug** menu and then select **Start Without Debugging**. The Cessna Skylark Web page opens in a Web browser window. The URL should include *localhost* and a randomly selected port.

3. Close the Web browser window.

You will learn more about the Debug menu and how to debug your code in Chapter 11.

35

Finding Help

The Microsoft Developer Network (MSDN) Library is Microsoft's official library for technical documentation. The URL for the MSDN Library is *http://msdn.microsoft.com.* You can find the Visual Studio 2008 documentation on the MSDN Library at *http://msdn2.microsoft. com/en-us/library/aa187917.aspx.* Even if you chose to install the MSDN Express Library, which contains the product documentation for Visual Studio, you should familiarize yourself with the online version of the MSDN Library. One of the benefits of the MSDN Library is that the documentation is continuously updated, so you should always refer to the online version for the most up-to-date Visual Studio documentation. The online version is available for free, but for a paid subscription, you can receive quarterly CD-ROMs or DVDs with the most recent MSDN Library. This book contains numerous references to articles and other types of documentation on the MSDN Library.

Short Quiz 3

1. What files does Visual Studio use to store a Web site's project settings and where are these files stored?

2. What is the primary difference between a Visual Web Developer project and solution?

3. What window in the IDE do you use to change the various properties, attributes, and other settings that are associated with a project?

4. What must happen before you can execute source code?

5. What is the difference between compiler error messages and warning messages?

Working with Well-Formed Web Pages

HTML first became an Internet standard in 1993 with the release of version 1.0. The next version of HTML, 2.0, was released in 1994 and included many core HTML features such as forms and the ability to bold and italicize text. However, many of the standard features that are widely used today, such as using tables to organize text and graphics on a page, were not available until the release of HTML 3.2 in 1996. The current version of HTML, 4.01, was released in 1999.

HTML 4.01, however, is the last version of the HTML language; it has been replaced with **Extensible Hypertext Markup Language**, or **XHTML**, which is the next generation markup language for creating the Web pages that appear on the World Wide Web.

HTML has been replaced because it is useful only for rendering documents in traditional Web browsers like Firefox or Internet Explorer. That worked well as long as browsers running on computers were the main source of requests for files over the Web. These days, however, many types of devices besides computers use the Web. For example, mobile phones and PDAs are commonly used to browse the Web. An application that is capable of retrieving and processing HTML and XHTML documents is called a **user agent**. A user agent can be a traditional Web browser or a device such as a mobile phone or PDA, or even an application such as a crawler for a search engine that simply collects and processes data instead of displaying it. Although user agents other than browsers can process HTML, they are not ideally suited to the task, primarily because HTML is more concerned with how data appears than with the data itself. As Web browsers have evolved over the years, they have added extensions (elements and attributes) to HTML to provide functionality for displaying and formatting Web pages. For instance, one extension to the original HTML language is the <font> element, which allows you to specify the font for data in an HTML document. The <font> element has nothing to do with the type of data in an HTML document. Instead, its sole purpose is to display data in a specific typeface within a Web browser. There is nothing wrong with continuing to author your Web pages using HTML and design elements such as the <font> element— provided your Web pages will be opened only in a Web browser. However, many user agents (such as mobile phones and PDAs) display only black-and-white or grayscale text and are incapable of processing HTML elements that handle the display and formatting of data. User agents such as these require a language that truly defines data (such as a paragraph or heading) independently of the way it is displayed.

XHTML is based on Extensible Markup Language, or XML, which is used for creating Web pages and for defining and transmitting data between applications.

The Web page examples and exercises in this book are written in XHTML. Although you need to have a solid understanding of HTML to be successful with this book, you do not necessarily need to be an expert with XHTML. Because XHTML is almost identical to HTML, you can easily adapt any of your existing HTML skills to XHTML, and vice versa.

To ensure backward compatibility with older browsers, you should save XHTML documents with an extension of .htm or .html, just like HTML documents.

XHTML Document Type Definitions (DTDs)

When a document conforms to the rules and requirements of XHTML, it is said to be **well formed**. Among other things, a well-formed document must include a <!DOCTYPE> declaration and the

<html>, <head>, and <body> elements. The **<!DOCTYPE> declaration** belongs in the first line of an XHTML document and determines the document type definition with which the document complies. A **document type definition**, or **DTD**, defines the elements and attributes that can be used in a document, along with the rules that a document must follow when it includes them. You can use three types of DTDs with XHTML documents: transitional, frameset, and strict.

To understand the differences among the three types of DTDs, you need to understand the concept of deprecated HTML elements. One of the goals of XHTML is to separate the way HTML is structured from the way the parsed Web page is displayed in the browser. To accomplish this goal, the W3C decided that several commonly used HTML elements and attributes for display and formatting would not be used in XHTML 1.0. Instead of using HTML elements and attributes for displaying and formatting Web pages, the W3C recommends you use Cascading Style Sheets (CSS), which are discussed later in this chapter.

Elements and attributes that are considered obsolete and that will eventually be eliminated are said to be **deprecated**. Table 1-2 lists the HTML elements that are deprecated in XHTML 1.0.

Element	Description
<applet>	Executes Java applets
<basefont>	Specifies the base font size
<center>	Centers text
<dir>	Defines a directory list
<font>	Specifies a font name, size, and color
<isindex>	Creates automatic document indexing forms
<menu>	Defines a menu list
<s> or <strike>	Formats strikethrough text
<u>	Formats underlined text

Table 1-2   HTML elements that are deprecated in XHTML 1.0

The three DTDs are distinguished in part by the degree to which they accept or do not accept deprecated HTML elements. This is explained in more detail in the following sections.

Transitional DTD

The **transitional DTD** allows you to use deprecated style elements in your XHTML documents. The <!DOCTYPE> declaration for the transitional DTD is as follows:

```
<!DOCTYPE html PUBLIC
"-//W3C//DTD XHTML 1.0 Transitional//EN"
"http://www.w3.org/TR/xhtml1/DTD/xhtml1-transitional.dtd">
```

Frameset DTD

The **frameset DTD** is identical to the transitional DTD, except that it includes the <frameset> and <frame> elements, which allow you to split the browser window into two or more frames. The <!DOCTYPE> declaration for the frameset DTD is as follows:

```
<!DOCTYPE html PUBLIC
"-//W3C//DTD XHTML 1.0 Frameset//EN"
"http://www.w3.org/TR/xhtml1/DTD/xhtml1-frameset.dtd">
```

Strict DTD

The **strict DTD** eliminates the elements that were deprecated in the transitional DTD and frameset DTD. The <!DOCTYPE> declaration for the strict DTD is as follows:

```
<!DOCTYPE html PUBLIC
"-//W3C//DTD XHTML 1.0 Strict//EN"
"http://www.w3.org/TR/xhtml1/DTD/xhtml1-strict.dtd">
```

If you examine the CessnaSkylark.htm file that you added to the Cessna Web site in Visual Developer Studio, you will notice that it includes the <!DOCTYPE> declaration for the transitional DTD. Next, you modify the CessnaSkylark.htm file in the Cessna project so it uses the strict DTD instead of the transitional DTD.

To add the strict DTD to the CessnaSkylark.htm file:

1. Return to the Cessna project in Visual Web Developer.

2. Replace the transitional <!DOCTYPE> declaration at the beginning of the CessnaSkylark.htm file with the following strict <!DOCTYPE> declaration:

   ```
   <!DOCTYPE html PUBLIC
   "-//W3C//DTD XHTML 1.0 Frameset//EN"
   "http://www.w3.org/TR/xhtml1/DTD/xhtml1-frameset.dtd">
   ```

3. Save the CessnaSkylark.htm file by selecting the **File** menu and then by selecting **Save CessnaSkylark.htm**.

Writing Well-Formed Documents

As you learned earlier, a well-formed document must include a <!DOCTYPE> declaration and the <html>, <head>, and <body>

You should use the transitional DTD only if you need to create Web pages that use the deprecated elements listed in Table 1-2.

You should understand that frames have been deprecated in favor of tables. However, frameset documents are still widely used, and you need to be able to recognize and work with them in the event that you need to modify an existing Web page that was created with frames.

As a rule, you should always try to use the strict DTD. This ensures that your Web pages conform to the most current Web page authoring techniques. However, because the switch to XHTML has been somewhat slow, the transitional DTD is probably the most commonly used at the time of this writing. In fact, the Visual Studio installed templates use the transitional DTD by default.

elements. The following list describes some other important components of a well-formed document:

- All XHTML documents must use `<html>` as the root element. The `xmlns` attribute is required in the `<html>` element and must be assigned the *http://www.w3.org/1999/xhtml* URI.

- XHTML is case sensitive.

- All XHTML elements must have a closing tag.

- Attribute values must appear within quotation marks.

- Empty elements must be closed.

- XHTML elements must be properly nested.

Most of the preceding rules are self-explanatory. However, the last rule requires further explanation. Nesting refers to how elements are placed inside other elements. For example, in the following code, the `<i>` element is nested within the `<b>` element, while the `<b>` element is nested within a `<p>` element.

```
<p><b><i>Think globally, act locally!</i></b></p>
```

In an HTML document, it makes no difference how the elements are nested. Examine the following modified version of the preceding statement:

```
<p><b><i>Think globally, act locally!</b></p></i>
```

In this version, the opening `<i>` element is nested within the `<b>` element, which, in turn, is nested within the `<p>` element. Notice, however, that the closing `</i>` tag is outside the closing `</p>` tag. The `<i>` is the innermost element. In XHTML, the innermost element in a statement must be closed before another element is closed. In the preceding statement, the `<b>` and `<p>` elements are closed before the `<i>` element. Although the order in which elements are closed makes no difference in HTML, the preceding code would prevent an XHTML document from being well formed.

The second-to-last rule in the list ("Empty elements must be closed.") also requires further explanation. Three of the most common empty elements in HTML are the `<hr>` element, which inserts a horizontal rule into the document, the `<br>` element, which inserts a line break, and the `<img>` element, which adds an image to the document. You close an empty element in XHTML by adding a space and a slash before the element's closing bracket. For example, the following code shows how to use the `<hr>` and `<br>` elements in an XHTML document. Figure 1-16 shows how the code appears in a Web browser.

```
<hr />
<p>Take the following steps to help curb global warming:</p>
<p>Step 1: Drive a well-tuned car with properly inflated
    tires.<br />
Step 2: Buy local and organic produce.<br />
Step 3: Support clean, renewable energy.</p>
<hr />
```

You might be wondering why XHTML documents do not use a root element of <xhtml>. The <html> element is necessary for backward compatibility with older browsers that do not recognize the <!DOCTYPE> element, which declares the DTD used by an XHTML element.

41

Figure 1-16 XHTML document with closed empty elements

Using Phrase Elements

Recall that early on, Web browser makers began to add their own extensions to HTML to provide functionality for displaying and formatting Web pages. These extensions (such as the bold and font elements) did nothing to describe the type of data being presented, but only served to instruct a Web browser how to display and format it. At the time, these extensions were considered a useful improvement. But as user agents become more complex, more nuanced elements became necessary. For example, consider the bold element. Visually, it's a great way to emphasize a word or phrase. However, it's not so useful for a user agent for the visually impaired that reads the contents of a Web page out loud. The Web developer needs some way of telling this type of user agent which text should receive extra, audible emphasis.

To address this type of issue, XHTML uses two types of inline elements for managing the formatting of text in an XHTML document: formatting

Generally, you should avoid using formatting elements, and rely on CSS instead to manage the display of elements on your Web pages. (CSS is discussed in the next section.) However, because several of the basic formatting elements are so commonly used, they are not deprecated in the strict DTD.

42

elements and phrase elements. **Formatting elements** provide specific instructions about how their contents should be displayed. Two of the most commonly used formatting elements are the <b> element (for boldface) and the <i> element (for italic). **Phrase elements**, on the other hand, primarily identify or describe their contents. For instance, the <em> element is an emphasized piece of data, similar to a quotation. How the <em> element is rendered is up to each user agent, although most current Web browsers display the contents of the <em> element using italic. However, a user agent for the vision impaired might use the <em> element to pronounce the text or phrase it contains with more emphasis, to get the meaning across to the vision-impaired visitor to the Web site. Although text-formatting elements are commonly used and work perfectly well for displaying text with a specific style of formatting, it's better to format the text on your Web pages using a phrase element that describes its content. Using phrase elements helps ensure that your Web pages are compatible with user agents that might not be capable of handling formatting elements.

Table 1-3 lists the phrase elements that are available in XHTML and explains how each element is rendered by most Web browsers.

Element	Description	Renders as
<abbr>	Specifies abbreviated text	Default text
<acronym>	Identifies an acronym	Default text
<cite>	Defines a citation	Italic
<code>	Identifies computer code	Monospace font
<dfn>	Marks a definition	Italic
<em>	Defines emphasized text	Italic
<kbd>	Indicates text that is to be entered by a visitor to a Web site	Monospace font
<q>	Defines a quotation	Italic
<samp>	Identifies sample computer code	Monospace font
<strong>	Defines strongly emphasized text	Bold
<var>	Defines a variable	Italic

Table 1-3 Phrase elements

Working with Cascading Style Sheets (CSS)

Although you should always strive to create Web pages that are compatible with all user agents, you can also design and format them so they are visually pleasing when rendered in a traditional Web browser. To design and format Web pages for traditional Web browsers, you use CSS, a standard set by the W3C for managing the design and formatting of Web pages in a Web browser. A single piece of CSS formatting information, such as text alignment or font size, is referred to as a **style**. Some of the style capabilities of CSS include the ability to change fonts, backgrounds, and colors, and to modify the layout of elements as they appear in a Web browser.

CSS information can be added directly to documents or stored in separate documents and shared among multiple Web pages. The term *cascading* refers to the ability of Web pages to use CSS information from more than one source. When a Web page has access to multiple CSS sources, the styles "cascade," or "fall together." Keep in mind that CSS design and formatting techniques are truly independent of the content of a Web page, unlike text-formatting elements, such as the <b> and <i> elements. CSS allows you to provide design and formatting specifications for well-formed documents that are compatible with all user agents.

CSS Properties

CSS styles are created with two parts separated by a colon: the **property**, which refers to a specific CSS style, and the value assigned to it, which determines the style's visual characteristics. Together, a CSS property and the value assigned to it are referred to as a **declaration** or **style declaration**. For example, `color: blue` changes the color of an element's text to blue.

Inline Styles

When you design a Web page, you often want the elements on your page to share the same formatting. For example, you might want all of the headings to be formatted in a specific font and color. Later in this section, you will learn how to use internal and external style sheets to apply the same formatting to multiple elements on a Web page. However, there might be times when you want to change the style of a single element on a Web page. The most basic method of applying styles is to use **inline styles**, which allow you to add style information to a single element in a document. You use the **style attribute** to assign inline style information to an element. You assign to the style attribute a property declaration enclosed in quotation marks.

Suppose you want to modify a single paragraph in a document so it uses the Verdana font instead of the browser's default font. You can modify the default font using the following statement, which uses an inline style declaration for the `font-family` property.

```
<p>This paragraph does not use CSS.</p>
<p style="font-family: Verdana">Paragraph formatted with
  inline styles.</p>
```

Entire books are devoted to CSS. This chapter provides only enough information to get you started. To learn more about CSS techniques, refer to Don Gosselin's *XHTML*, also published by Course Technology. For other books that cover CSS more fully, search for "css" on the Course Technology Web site at *http://www.course.com*. You can also find the latest information on CSS at the W3C's Web site: *http://www.w3.org/style/css/*.

The styles you assign to an element are automatically passed to any nested elements it contains. For example, if you use the `font-family` style to assign a font to a paragraph, that font is automatically assigned to any nested elements the paragraph contains, such as <strong> or <em> elements.

You can include multiple style declarations in an inline style by separating each declaration with a semicolon. The following statement shows the same paragraph element shown earlier, but this time with two additional style declarations: one for the `color` property, which sets an element's text color to blue, and one for the `text-align` property, which centers the paragraph in the middle of the page. Notice that the `<strong>` element, which is nested in the paragraph element, automatically takes on the paragraph element's style elements.

```
<p>This paragraph does not use CSS.</p>
<p style="font-family: Verdana; color: blue;
text-align: center">Paragraph formatted with
    <strong>inline styles</strong>.</p>
```

One of the great advantages to using CSS is that you can share styles among multiple Web pages, making it easier to create and maintain a common look and feel for an entire Web site. Inline styles, however, cannot be shared by other Web pages or even by other elements on the same page (except by elements that are nested within other elements). Plus, it is extremely time consuming to add inline styles to each and every element on a Web page. Inline styles are only useful if you need to make a one-time change to a single element on a page. If you want to apply the same formatting to multiple elements on a page or share styles with other Web pages, you need to use internal or external style sheets.

Next, you modify the Cessna Skylark page so it includes inline styles. You add some simple CSS formatting instructions that format the Web page in the Arial font, the headings in the color olive, and the body text in the color blue.

To modify the Cessna Skylark page so it includes inline styles:

1. Return to the Cessna project in Visual Web Developer.

2. Modify the opening `<body>` tag, so it includes inline styles that modify the `font-family`, `color`, and `background-color` properties, as follows:

   ```
   <body style="font-family: Arial; color: blue;
       background-color: transparent">
   ```

3. Modify the opening `<h1>` tag, so it includes inline styles that modify the `font-family` and `color` properties, as follows:

   ```
   <h1 style="font-family: Arial; color: olive">
   ```

4. Finally, modify the two opening <h2> tags, so they include the same styles as the <h1> tag. Each opening <h2> tag should appear as follows:

    ```
    <h2 style="font-family: Arial; color: olive">
    ```

5. Save the CessnaSkylark.htm file by selecting the **File** menu and then by selecting **Save CessnaSkylark.htm**. Start the Web site by selecting the **Debug** menu and then by selecting **Start Without Debugging**. The Web page should appear in Internet Explorer with the new formatting.

6. Close the Web browser window.

Internal Style Sheets

You use an **internal style sheet** to create styles that apply to an entire document. You create an internal style sheet within a <style> element placed within the document head. The <style> element must include a type attribute, which is assigned a value of "text/css", as follows:

```
<style type="text/css">
style declarations
</style>
```

Within the <style> element, you create any style instructions for a specific element that are applied to all instances of that element contained in the body of the document. The element to which specific style rules in a style sheet apply is called a **selector**. You create a style declaration for a selector in an internal style sheet by placing a list of declarations within a pair of braces { } following the name of the selector. For example, the following style declaration for the <p> element (which is the selector), changes the color property to blue:

```
p { color: blue }.
```

As with inline styles, you separate multiple properties for a selector by semicolons. The following code shows a portion of the Chickasaw National Recreation Area page you saw earlier, but this time it's valid and includes an internal style sheet for the h1, h2, and p selectors. A pair of braces containing style instructions follows each selector. All instances of the associated elements in the body of the document are formatted using these style instructions. Figure 1-17 shows how the document appears in a Web browser.

```
....
<head>
<title>Chickasaw National Recreation Area</title>
<style type="text/css">
```

You can also use an optional media attribute with the <style> element, which you use to select the destination medium for the style information. Valid values you can assign to the media attribute are screen, tty, tv, projection, handheld, print, braille, aural, and all.

```
h1 {color: navy; font-size: 2em; font-family: Arial}
h2 {color: red; font-size: 1.5em; font-family: Arial}
body {color: blue; font-family: Arial;
      font-size: .8em; font-weight: normal}
</style>
</head>
<body>
<h1>National Parks Service</h1>
<h2>Chickasaw National Recreation Area</h2>
<p><b>State</b>: Oklahoma<br />
<b>Nearest City</b>: Sulphur<br />
...
```

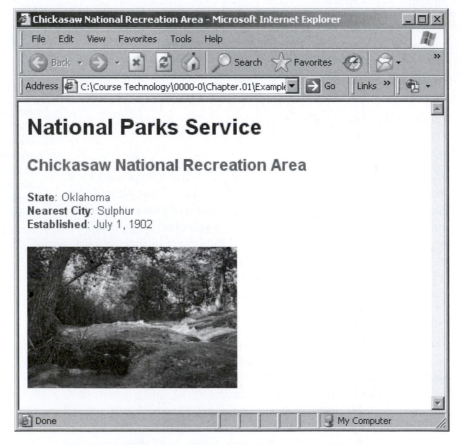

Figure 1-17   Document with an internal style sheet

You can also group selectors so they share the same style declarations by separating each selector with a comma. For example, you use the following single declaration to format all of a document's <h1>, <h2>, and <h3> elements to use the same color:

```
<style type="text/css">
h1, h2, h3 {color: navy}
</style>
```

Next, you modify the Cessna Skylark page so it uses an internal style sheet.

To modify the Cessna Skylark page so it uses an internal style sheet:

1. Return to the Cessna project in Visual Web Developer.

2. Delete the inline styles in the <body>, <h1>, and <h2> tags.

3. Add the following internal style sheet above the closing </head> tag:

```
<style type="text/css">
body { font-family: Arial; color: blue;
    background-color: transparent }
h1, h2 { font-family: Arial; color: olive }
</style>
```

4. Save the CessnaSkylark.htm file by selecting the **File** menu and then by selecting the **Save CessnaSkylark.htm** menu.

5. To start the Web site, Select the **Debug** menu and then select **Start Without Debugging**. The Web page should format the same as it did with the inline styles.

6. Close the Web browser window.

Another method of applying styles is to use class selectors, which allow you to create different groups of styles for the same element. You create a class selector within a <style> element by appending a name for the class to the selector with a period. You then assign the class name to the standard class attribute of elements in the document that you want to format with the class's style definitions.

The following code defines a class selector named danger that formats paragraph text as red and bold. The class selector is applied to two of the paragraphs in the document body.

```
...
<style type="text/css">
    p.danger
    {
        color: red;
        font-weight: bold;
    }
</style>
```

48

```
</head>
<body>
    <h1>
        Kite Flying Basics</h2>
        <h2>
            Safety Tips</h2>
        <p>
            Never fly over people.</p>
        <p>
            Never fly near trees or buildings.</p>
        <p>
            Never fly near the airport.</p>
        <p class="danger">
            Never fly in rain or thunderstorms.</p>
        <p>
            Never fly near busy streets or roadways.</p>
        <p class="danger">
            Never fly near power lines.</p>
</body>
```

When you create a class selector by appending a name for the class to a selector with a period, you can only use that class selector with the element for which it was created. For instance, you can only use the danger class selector in the preceding example with <p> elements.

You can also create a generic class selector that is not associated with any particular element. You create a generic class selector to use with any element by defining a class name preceded by a period, but without appending it to an element. The following code shows an example of the danger class selector, but this time it is not appended to the p selector. Notice that in the document body, the danger class selector is now applied to two different elements: <p> and <strong>.

```
<style type="text/css">
    .danger
    {
        color: red;
        font-weight: bold;
    }
</style>
</head>
<body>
    <h1>
        Kite Flying Basics</h2>
        <h2>
            Safety Tips</h2>
        <p>
```

```
Never fly over <strong class="danger">
   people</strong>.<p>
      <p>
         Never fly near <strong class="danger">
         trees</strong> or <strong
         class="danger">
         buildings</strong>.</p>
      <p>
         Never fly near the <strong
         class="danger">
         airport</strong>.</p>
      <p class="danger">
         Never fly in rain or thunderstorms.</p>
      <p>
         Never fly near busy <strong
         class="danger">
         streets</strong> or <strong
         class="danger">
         roadways</strong>.</p>
      <p class="danger">
         Never fly near power lines.</p>
   </body>
```

External Style Sheets

Inline styles are useful if you need to format only a single element; internal style sheets are useful for creating styles that apply to an entire document. However, most companies want all of the documents on a Web site to have the same look and feel. For this reason, it's preferable to use **external style sheets**, which are separate text documents containing style declarations that are used by multiple documents on a Web site. You should create an external style sheet whenever you need to use the same styles on multiple Web pages in the same site.

You create an external style sheet in a text editor, the same as when you create XHTML documents. However, you should save the document with an extension of .css. The style sheet document should not contain XHTML elements, only style declarations. Use the same rules for creating style declarations in an external style sheet as you use in an internal style sheet. The contents of a typical external style sheet may appear as follows. Notice that the code contains no XHTML elements.

```
h1 {color: navy; font-size: 2em; font-family: serif}
h2 {color: red; font-size: 1.5em; font-family: Arial}
body {color: blue; font-family: Arial;
     font-size: .8em; font-weight: normal}
```

The most popular way to access the styles in an external style sheet is to use the empty `<link>` element to link a document to a style sheet. You place the `<link>` element in the document head. You include three attributes in the `<link>` element: an `href` attribute that is assigned the URL of the style sheet, the `rel` attribute that is assigned a value of "stylesheet" to specify that the referenced file is a style sheet, and the `type` attribute, which is assigned the same "text/css" value as the `type` attribute used in the `<style>` element. For example, to link a document to a style sheet named company_branding.css, you include a link element in the document head, as follows:

```
<head>
...
<link rel="stylesheet" href="company_branding.css"
      type="text/css" />
</head>
```

Next, you modify the Cessna Skylark page so it uses an external style sheet.

To modify the Cessna Skylark page so it uses an external style sheet:

1. Return to the Cessna project in Visual Web Developer.

2. Copy the style declarations within the `<style>` element. Be certain not to copy the `<style>` tags.

3. Select the **Add New Item** from the **Website** menu. The Add New Item dialog box opens.

4. In the Add New Item dialog box, select **Style Sheet** from the Visual Studio installed templates section of the Templates area.

5. Change the suggested filename in the Name box to **CessnaSkylark.css**, but leave the value in the Language box set to **Visual C#**.

6. Click the **Add** button to add the external style sheet to the project. The style sheet opens in Visual Web Developer and contains an empty body selector.

7. Delete the empty body selector and paste the style declarations that you copied from the CessnaSkylark.htm file into the CessnaSkylark.css file.

8. To save and close the CessnaSkylark.css file, select the **File** menu, select **Save CessnaSkylark.css**, select the **File** menu again, and then select **Close**.

9. In the CessnaSkylark.htm file, replace the `<style>` element and the style declarations it contains with the following

<link> element that links to the CessnaSkylark.css external style sheet:

```
<link rel="stylesheet" href="CessnaSkylark.css"
type="text/css" />
```

10. Save the CessnaSkylark.htm file by selecting the **File** menu and then by selecting **Save CessnaSkylark.htm**. Start the Web site by selecting the **Debug** menu and then by selecting **Start Without Debugging**. The Web page should format the same as it did with the inline style sheet.

11. Close the Web browser window.

12. Close the Cessna project by selecting the **File** menu and then by selecting **Close Project**.

Next, you learn about content-type <meta> elements, which the W3C strongly encourages you to use to specify an XHTML document's character set.

Validating Web Pages

When you open an XHTML document that is not well formed in a Web browser, the browser simply ignores the errors, as it would with an HTML document with errors, and renders the Web page as best it can. The Web browser cannot tell whether the XHTML document is well formed. To ensure that your XHTML document is well formed and that its elements are valid, you need to use a validating parser. A **validating parser** is a program that checks whether an XHTML document is well formed and whether the document conforms to a specific DTD. The term **validation** refers to the process of verifying that your XHTML document is well formed and checking that the elements in your document are correctly written according to the element definitions in a specific DTD. If you do not validate an XHTML document and it contains errors, most Web browsers will probably treat it as an HTML document, ignore the errors, and render the page anyway. However, validation can help you spot errors in your code.

 Even the most experienced Web page authors frequently introduce typos or some other error into an XHTML document that prevents the document from being well formed.

Various Web development tools offer validation capabilities. In addition, several XHTML validating services can be found online. One of the best available is W3C Markup Validation Service, a free service that validates both HTML and XHTML. The W3C Markup Validation Service is located at *http://validator.w3.org/*. However, Visual Web Developer also automatically validates Web pages according to a specified DTD and displays any validation errors in the Error List window. To specify the DTD against which a Web

The goal of this book is to teach ASP.NET programming with C#. For this reason, the exercises in this book do not specifically instruct you to validate your Web pages. However, Web page validation is a basic skill that is expected of any Web developer. Therefore, you should always strive to ensure that your Web pages, including the ones you develop with this book, are valid. In fact, your instructor will probably require you to ensure that the Web pages you write are valid. Whenever you build a project in this book, you should always check the Error List window for any errors that Visual Web Developer generates. If there are any errors listed in the Error List window, then you've done something wrong. Go back and examine your code and ensure that it's error free before moving on to the next exercise.

page is to be validated, select the Tools menu, select the Options command, and then select Validation. Select a DTD from the Target box, and then click OK. You can also select a DTD from the Target Schema for Validation box in the HTML Source Editing toolbar. As you edit a Web page, any validation errors that it contains will be listed in the Error List window. However, the Error List window does not automatically display each time a new validation error is introduced. Instead, you must manually display the Error List window by selecting Error List from the View menu, and then periodically check the window for new validation errors.

Short Quiz 4

1. Why has XHTML replaced HTML?

2. Which HTML elements have been deprecated in XHTML?

3. What are some of the important components of a well-formed document?

4. What is the difference between formatting elements and phrase elements?

5. How will most Web browsers respond when opening an XHTML document that is not well formed?

Summing Up

- In 1990 and 1991, Tim Berners-Lee created what would become the World Wide Web, or the Web, at the European Laboratory for Particle Physics (CERN) in Geneva, Switzerland, as a way to easily access cross-referenced documents that existed on the CERN computer network.

- The World Wide Web Consortium, or W3C, was established in 1994 at the Massachusetts Institute of Technology (MIT) to oversee the development of Web technology standards.

- A system consisting of a client and a server is known as a two-tier system.

- A three-tier, or multitier, client/server system consists of three distinct pieces: the client tier, the processing tier, and the data storage tier.

- JavaScript is a client-side scripting language that allows Web page authors to develop interactive Web pages and sites.

- Active Server Pages (ASP) .NET is a server-side scripting technology that is part of Visual Web Developer.

- The Microsoft Visual Studio development system is a suite of software development tools including Visual C++, Visual C#, and Visual Basic programming languages, and Visual Web Developer, which is primarily used for developing ASP.NET applications.

- The products in the Visual Studio development system share a common workspace in Visual Studio called the integrated development environment (IDE).

- Visual Web Developer includes the ASP.NET Development Server, which is a basic Web server that you can use to test your Web sites on your local computer.

- The Microsoft Developer Network (MSDN) Library is Microsoft's official library for technical documentation. The URL for the MSDN Library is *http://msdn.microsoft.com.*

- Extensible Hypertext Markup Language, or XHTML, is the next generation markup language for creating the Web pages that appear on the World Wide Web.

- A document type definition, or DTD, defines the elements and attributes that can be used in a document, along with the rules that a document must follow when it includes them.

- To design and format the display of Web pages for traditional Web browsers, you use CSS, a standard set by the W3C for managing the design and formatting of Web pages in a Web browser.

- A validating parser is a program that checks whether an XHTML document is well formed and whether the document conforms to a specific DTD.

Comprehension Check

1. Which element is required in the `<head>` element?

   a. `<hr>`

   b. `<meta>`

   c. `<body>`

   d. `<title>`

53

2. The host portion of a URL is usually _____.

    a. web

    b. ftp

    c. http

    d. www

3. The final part of a domain name, known as the _____, identifies the type of institution or organization.

    a. domain

    b. domain identifier

    c. protocol

    d. IP address

4. If a URL does not specify a filename, the requesting Web server looks for a file with which of the following names? (Choose all that apply.)

    a. index.htm

    b. index.html

    c. default.htm

    d. default.html

5. A system consisting of a client and a server is known as a _____.

    a. mainframe topology

    b. double-system architecture

    c. two-tier system

    d. wide area network

6. What is usually the primary role of a client?

    a. locating records that match a request

    b. heavy processing, such as calculations

    c. data storage

    d. the presentation of an interface to the user

7. Which of the following functions does the processing tier not handle in a three-tier client/server system?

    a. processing and calculations

    b. reading and writing of information to the data storage tier

    c. the return of any information to the client tier

    d. data storage

8. Which function can a client safely handle?

    a. data validation

    b. data storage

    c. intensive processing

    d. heavy calculations

9. The interface shared with all members of Visual Studio is called the _____.

    a. Project Explorer

    b. application programming interface (API)

    c. Solution Developer Kit

    d. integrated development environment (IDE)

10. Visual Studio uses _____ to quickly complete the current statement you are writing.

    a. build statements

    b. statement completion

    c. online help

    d. spell checking

11. ASP.NET Development Server automatically runs on *localhost* with port 80. True or False?

12. Which of the following belongs in the first line of an XHTML document?

    a. an <html> tag

    b. an <xhtml> tag

    c. a <title> tag

    d. <!DOCTYPE> declaration

13. DTD stands for _____.

    a. data transfer display

    b. digital technology definition

    c. decimal type determinant

    d. document type definition

14. Which XHTML DTD(s) allow you to use deprecated elements? (Choose all that apply.)

    a. XML

    b. transitional

    c. strict

    d. frameset

15. Which of the following closes the empty `<hr>` element in an XHTML document?

    a. `<hr\>`

    b. `<hr \>`

    c. `<hr/>`

    d. `<hr />`

16. The information contained within an element's opening and closing tags is referred to as its _____.

    a. content

    b. data

    c. attribute

    d. meta information

17. What is the correct syntax for creating an inline style that assigns Arial to the `font-family` property?

    a. `style="font-family, Arial"`

    b. `font-family=Arial`

    c. `style="font-family: Arial"`

    d. `font-family; Arial`

18. You can include multiple style declarations in an inline style by separating each declaration with a _____.

    a. colon

    b. semicolon

    c. comma

    d. forward slash

19. Explain when you should use inline styles, internal style sheets, or external style sheets.

20. Which element do you use to create an internal style sheet?

    a. `<css>`

    b. `<link>`

    c. `<style>`

    d. `<styles>`

Reinforcement Exercises

Exercise 1-1

The HTML Page template that is part of the Visual Studio installed templates is formatted to use the transitional DTD. Although you change to the strict DTD each time you create a new file from this template, it would be easier to use a strict DTD template. In this exercise, you use the Export Template command on the File menu to create a new HTML Page template that is formatted with the strict DTD.

1. Select the **File** menu and then select **New Web Site**. The New Web Site dialog box opens.

2. Select **Empty Web Site** from the Templates section. Leave the Location box set to **File System**, which creates the new Web site on your local file system, and the Language box set to **Visual C#**. Click the **Browse** button. The Choose Location dialog box opens.

3. In the File System section of the Choose Location dialog box, find the Exercises folder for Chapter 1 in the location where you installed the data files. Click the **Exercises** folder, and then click the **Create New Folder** button. Name the new folder **StrictTemplate**.

4. Click the **Open** button to close the Choose Location dialog box and return to the New Web Site dialog box.

5. Click **OK** to create the new Web site.

6. Select the **Website** menu and then select **Add New Item**. The Add New Item dialog box opens.

7. Select **HTML Page** from the Visual Studio installed templates section of the Templates area. Change the suggested filename in the Name box to **StrictHTMLPage.htm**, but leave the value in the Language box set to **Visual C#**.

8. Click the **Add** button to add the HTML page to the project. The new page opens in Visual Web Developer.

9. Replace the transitional <!DOCTYPE> declaration at the beginning of the StrictHTMLPage.htm file file with the following strict <!DOCTYPE> declaration:

```
<!DOCTYPE html PUBLIC
"-//W3C//DTD XHTML 1.0 Strict//EN"
"http://www.w3.org/TR/xhtml1/DTD/xhtml1-strict.dtd">
```

10. Select the **File** menu and then select **Save StrictHTMLPage. htm** to save your work.

11. Select the **File** menu and then select **Export Template**. The Export Template Wizard starts, opened to the Choose Template Type page. You can use the Export Template Wizard to create either a project or an item template.

12. Select **Item template**. Also, select **StrictTemplate** from the first box and **Visual C#** from the second box, if they are not already selected, and then click **Next**. The Select Item to Export page appears.

13. Select **StrictHTMLPage.htm**, and then click **Next**. The Select Item References page appears.

14. Leave all items on the page unselected and click **Next**. The Select Template Options screen appears.

15. Change the Template name field to **StrictHTMLPage**, clear the **Display an explorer window on the output files folder** box, but leave the remaining fields set to their default settings. Click **Finish**.

16. To ensure that the template was created successfully, select the **Website** menu and then select **Add New Item**. The StrictHTMLPage template should be listed in the My Templates section of the Add New Item dialog box.

17. Click **Cancel** to close the Add New Item dialog box.

Exercise 1-2

Few of today's professional Web sites consist of a single document. Instead, most Web sites consist of numerous pages that individually contain company information, sales information, support, customer server, and countless other types of content. However, all Web sites have (or should have) a home page. In this exercise, you work with a Web site for a home furnishings company that consists of four pages: a home page, a furniture page, a bedding page, and an accessories page. Your Exercises folder for Chapter 1 contains a Web site folder named ForestvilleFurnishings that contains the files you need for this exercise. You will create a default home page using the StrictHTMLPage.htm file you created in Exercise 1-1 and configure Visual Web Developer to open the page when you start Web site with the Start Without Debugging command.

1. Select the **File** menu and then select **Open Web Site**. The Open Web Site dialog box opens.

2. Open the Exercises folder for Chapter 1 from the location where you installed the data files. Click the **ForestvilleFurnishings** folder, and then click **Open**. The Web site opens in Visual Web Developer.

3. Select the **Website** menu and then select **Add New Item**. If necessary, select **Visual C#** in the Language box, click **StrictHTMLPage** in the My Templates section, change the suggested filename to index.htm, and then click **Add**. The Web page opens in the Code Editor.

4. Change the content of the `<title>` element to "Forestville Furnishings" and add the following `<link>` element above the closing `</head>` tag to link to a style sheet named styles.css:

```
<link rel="stylesheet" href=" styles.css"
   type="text/css" />
```

5. Add the following text and elements to the document body. The code uses various styles, located in the styles.css file, to format the Web page.

```
<div id="wrapper">
  <div id="banner">
    <div id="logo">
      Forestville Furnishings</div>
  </div>
  <div id="nav-main">
    <ul title="Major Site Sections">
      <li><a href="index.htm"
        class="current">
        home</a></li>
      <li><a href="section1.htm">
        Furniture </a></li>
      <li><a href="section2.htm">
        Bath </a></li>
      <li><a href="section3.htm">
        Accessories </a></li>
    </ul>
  </div>
  <div id="homebanner">
  </div>
  <div id="col1">
    <img src="images/hmpic1.jpg"
      width="196" height="63"
      alt="Visual formatting image" />
    <h1>
      Furniture</h1>
    <p>
      We specialize in offering top quality
      home furnishings from dozens of
      manufacturers. New home furnishing
      products are added on a daily basis.
    </p>
  </div>
  <div id="col2">
    <img src="images/hmpic2.jpg" width="196"
      height="63" alt="Visual formatting image" />
    <h1>
      Bath</h1>
    <p>
      Linens and towels, in their many
      materials, colors, and textures,
      can have a dramatic effect on the
      look and feel of your bathroom.</p>
  </div>
  <div id="col3">
    <img src="images/hmpic3.jpg" width="196"
      height="63"
      alt="Visual formatting image" />
    <h1>
      Accessories</h1>
    <p>
```

```
        Beyond basic bedroom furniture like
        beds and dressers, accessories and
        accents can dress up a space and
        personalize your bedroom into a
        sanctuary designed specifically
        for your comfort.
      </p>
   </div>
   <div id="footer">
     <p>
       <a href="index.htm">Home</a>
        <span class="style1"> | </span>
        <a href="linkhere.htm">Privacy</a>
        <span class="style1"> | </span>
        <a href="linkhere.htm">About Us</a>
        <span class="style1"> | </span>
        <a href="linkhere.htm">Contact Info</a><br />
      &copy; Copyright 2009 Forestville
        Furnishings</p>
   </div>
</div>
```

6. Select the **Website** menu and then select **Start Options**.
    The Property Pages dialog box opens, with the Start Options
    property page displayed.

7. On the Start Options property page, click **Specific page** and
    then click the ellipsis button to the right of the text box. The
    Select Page to Start dialog box opens.

8. In the Contents of folder list, select **index.htm** and then click
    OK. The Select Page to Start dialog box closes and you return
    to the Property Pages dialog box. Click **OK** again to close the
    Property Pages dialog box.

9. Now you need to verify that Visual Web Developer correctly
    opens the index.htm file in the Code Editor. To do this,
    double-click the **section1.htm** filename in Solution Explorer.
    The section1.htm file opens in the Code Editor.

10. Click **Debug** menu and then click **Start Without Debugging**.
    Visual Web Developer opens the default index.htm file in
    Internet Explorer. Figure 1-18 shows the file in Internet
    Explorer.

11. Close the Web browser window.

Figure 1-18　Forestville Furnishings home page

Exercise 1-3

In this exercise, you complete the remaining pages in the Forestville Furnishings Web site.

1. Return to the Forestville Furnishings project in Visual Web Developer.

2. Search the Internet for some text and images for the Furniture, Bedding, and Accessories pages. Within each file, replace [ADD PAGE CONTENT HERE] with the appropriate text and images.

3. At the bottom of the pages in the Forestville Furnishings Web site are links to the following Web pages: Privacy, About Us, and Contact Info. Create Web pages for each of these links using the StrictHTMLPage.htm template. Use whatever information you want for each page, but be sure it's appropriate for the type of page. For example, the Contact Info page should include information such as a phone number and an e-mail address. Remember that to add a new item to a Web site, you need to select the Website menu and then select Add New Item. Don't forget to name each file so it matches the filename for each link.

4. After you finish adding the new pages, select the **Debug** menu and then select **Start Without Debugging**. Visual Web Developer opens the default index.htm file in Internet Explorer. Test all of the links on each page of the Web site, and then close the Web browser window.

5. Close the project by selecting the **File** menu and then by selecting **Close Project**.

Exercise 1-4

In this exercise, you convert a Web page's inline and internal styles into an external style sheet. Your Exercises folder for Chapter 1 contains a Web site folder named PineRidgeConstruction that contains the files you need for this exercise.

1. Select the **File** menu and then select **Open Web Site**. The Open Web Site dialog box opens.

2. Open the Exercises folder for Chapter 1 from the location where you installed the data files. Click the **PineRidgeConstruction** folder, and then click **Open**. The Web site opens in Visual Web Developer.

3. Double-click the **index.htm** file in Solution Explorer. The file opens in the Code Editor window.

4. First, highlight the style declarations in the document head and cut them to your Clipboard. Then, delete the <style> element.

5. The project contains an empty external style sheet named textstyle.css. Double-click the **textstyle.css** file in Solution Explorer. The file opens in the Code Editor window.

6. Paste the styles from the internal style sheet into the textstyle. css file.

7. Click the **index.htm** tab in the Code Editor window and locate the opening <body> tag, which contains an inline style. Highlight and cut the contents of the `style` attribute to your Clipboard, and then delete the `style` attribute from the element.

8. Click the **textstyle.css** tab in the Code Editor window and add the following style declaration to the end of the file. You can paste the properties and values from your Clipboard.

```
body { background-attachment:fixed;
        color:#333333;link:#CC0000;
        vlink=#CC6600;alink:#993300;
        margin-left:0;margin-top:0;
        margin-right:0;margin-bottom:0; }
```

9. The remaining inline styles can be replaced with class selectors. For example, the first cell in the first table contains the following inline style:

```
style="background-image:
    url(images/tablebackhome.jpg);
    background-position: left top;"
```

10. Copy the contents assigned to the style attribute to your Clipboard, and then replace the style attribute with the following class attribute: `class="tblbckhme"`.

11. Click the **textstyle.css** tab in the Code Editor window and add the following class selector declaration to the end of the file. You can paste the properties and values from your Clipboard.

```
.tblbckhme {
    background-image: url(images/tablebackhome.jpg);
    background-position: left top;
}
```

12. Work through the rest of the index.htm file and create class selectors for each of the inline styles. Keep in mind that several of the inline styles are identical, so you can apply the same class selector to multiple elements. You need to create six class selectors in addition to the `.tblbckhme` class selector. Use whatever names you like for each class selector.

13. Add the following <link> element above the closing </head> tag to link to the textstyle.css style sheet:

```
<link rel="stylesheet" href="textstyle.css"
    type="text/css" />
```

14. With the index.htm file open in the Code Editor window, select the **Debug** menu and then select **Start Without Debugging**. Visual Web Developer opens the default index. htm file in Internet Explorer. The index.htm file should appear as shown in Figure 1-19:

Figure 1-19   Pine Ridge Construction home page

15. Close your Web browser window.

Exercise 1-5

In this exercise, you fix validation errors on the Green Building page of the Pine Ridge Construction Web site.

1. Return to the PineRidgeConstruction project in Visual Web Developer.

2. Double-click the **green_building.htm** file in Solution Explorer. The file opens in the Code Editor window.

3. Select the **View** menu and then select **Error List**. You will see a list of 20 validation errors.

4. With the green_building.htm file open in the Code Editor window, select the **Debug** menu and then select **Start Without Debugging**. Visual Web Developer opens the green_building.htm file in Internet Explorer. The page should appear similar to the index.htm file that you worked with in the last project. Instead, you will see the badly formatted page shown in Figure 1-20.

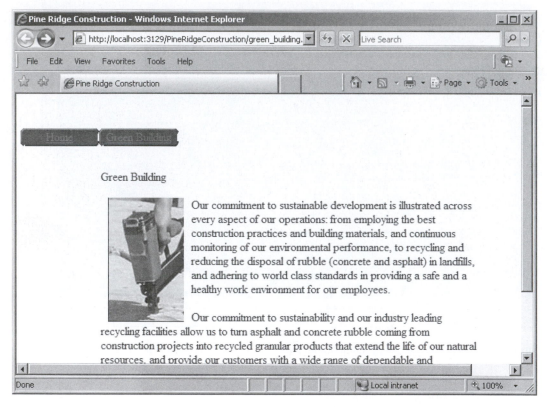

Figure 1-20   Incorrectly formatted Pine Ridge Construction Web page

5. Close your Web browser window.

6. To fix the page, work through each of the validation errors in the Error List. Many of the changes require restructuring the page and moving deprecated attributes into the style sheet. If you do not have strong HTML and CSS skills, refer to the tutorials and references that are available on the W3 Schools Web site at *http://w3schools.com/default.asp*. The fixed Web page should resemble Figure 1-21.

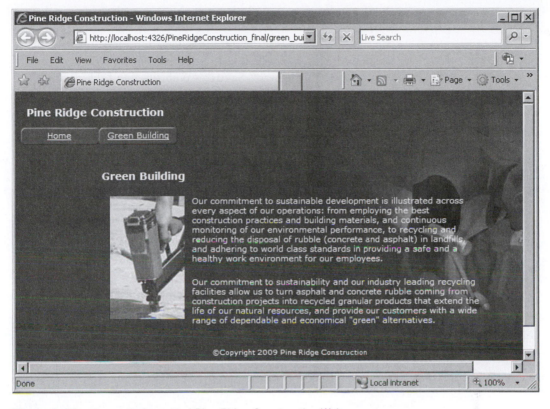

Figure 1-21 Correctly formatted Pine Ridge Construction Web page

Discovery Projects

Save your Discovery Projects in the Projects directory for Chapter 1.

Project 1-1

Create a multi-page Web site for a car dealership named Exotic Autos. Create home page that includes links to at least three other pages that contain descriptions and photos of cars such as a Ferrari and Lamborghini. Search the Internet for photos and descriptions to use on each car's page. Create the Web site so that it conforms to the transitional DTD and create an internal style sheet. Save the Web site in a folder named ExoticAutos.

Project 1-2

Create a Web site for Dubois Dentistry. Use an <h1> element to contain the dental office's name. Include an introductory paragraph that describes the care that the dental office offers. Use an <h2> element for different types of dental categories such as checkups, cleaning, cosmetic, and restoration. Beneath each category heading, include a description of the service. Write the document so that it conforms to the strict DTD (use the StrictHTMLPage template you created in the Reinforcement Exercise 1-1) and create an external style sheet that formats the document. Save the Web site in a folder named DuboisDentistry.

Project 1-3

In addition to client/server architecture, peer-to-peer architecture is also widely used. Search the Internet for information on peer-to-peer architecture. What are the differences between client/server architecture and peer-to-peer architecture? When should each type of architecture be used? Write a paper summarizing your research and conclusions.

Project 1-4

Search the Internet for information on how TCP/IP is used for communication on the Internet. How does TCP/IP work? What are the different protocols available and when should you use them? How is TCP/IP addressing used on the Internet? Write a paper summarizing your research and conclusions.

CHAPTER 2

Getting Started with ASP.NET and C#

In this chapter you will:

◎ Create basic ASP.NET Web pages

◎ Work with variables, constants, and data types

◎ Use expressions and operators

◎ Learn about operator precedence

One of the most important aspects of programming is the ability to store values in computer memory and to manipulate those values. The values stored in computer memory are called variables. The values, or data, contained in variables are classified into categories known as data types. In this chapter, you will learn about JavaScript variables, data types, and the operations that can be performed on them.

Creating Basic ASP.NET Web Pages

An ASP.NET page does not need to contain any ASP.NET code whatsoever. However, if a page you are working on contains HTML but does not contain any ASP.NET code, you should name the file with an extension of .htm.

Whenever a request is made for a document with an extension of .aspx, the Web server sends the file to the scripting engine for processing. The scripting engine then processes any ASP.NET code it encounters. Although ASP.NET pages have an extension of .aspx, they can contain the same HTML or XHTML elements you would find in a static Web page. The scripting engine ignores any non-ASP.NET code and only processes any ASP.NET code it finds within ASP.NET code blocks (which you study next). The Web server then returns the results of the ASP.NET program along with any HTML or XHTML elements found in the ASP.NET page to the client, where the client's Web browser renders it. In most cases, the results returned from an ASP.NET program, such as database records, are usually formatted with HTML or XHTML elements. This means that ASP.NET code is never sent to a client's Web browser; only the resulting Web page that is generated from the ASP.NET code and HTML or XHTML elements found within the ASP.NET page are returned to the client. Later in this chapter, you see an example of a Web page returned to a client from an ASP.NET page that contains both C# code and XHTML elements. First, you need to learn about ASP.NET code blocks.

Creating ASP.NET Code Render Blocks

Code render blocks are the most basic way of adding code to a Web page. **Code render blocks** define inline code or inline expressions that execute when a Web page renders. **Inline code** refers to one or more individual code lines, or **statements**, contained within a code render block. You use the delimiters <% and %> to designate inline code. A **delimiter** is a character or sequence of characters used to mark the beginning and end of a code segment. You include within the script delimiters any commands that are valid for the scripting language you are using. The following inline code contains two statements that writes the text "All roads lead to Rome" to a Web browser window, using the Write() method of the Response object, which you will study in the next section. For now, you only need to understand that you use the Write() method of the Response object to programmatically print text to the Web browser.

```
<%
    Response.Write("All roads ");
    Response.Write("lead to Rome.");
%>
```

Notice that the preceding statements end in a semicolon. C#, like other modern C-based programming languages including C++ and Java, requires you to end all statements with a semicolon. Note that the primary purpose of a semicolon is to identify the end of a statement, not the end of a line. Just as Web browsers ignore white space in an HTML or XHTML document, the scripting engine ignores white space within code blocks. For this reason, semicolons are critical to identifying the end of a statement. This also means that you do not need to place each statement on its own line. For example, the following code contains two `Response. Write()` statements on the same line, with each statement ending in a semicolon:

```
<%
    Response.Write("All roads "); Response.Write("lead to Rome.");
%>
```

An important requirement for code render blocks is the need to identify the language of the code segment contained within the code render block. With ASP.NET, you can use Visual Basic or C# as the language within a code render block. To declare the language that ASP.NET will use, you must use an **ASP processing directive**, which provides a Web server with information on how to process the code in an ASP.NET document. The **@ Page** processing directive defines information about the page that will be used by Visual Web Developer when it compiles the page. You use the `Language` attribute of the `@ Page` processing directive to declare a page's language. ASP.NET processing directives are created using <%@ . . .%> delimiters.

You can only declare one processing directive on a page, so it is usually declared at the top of a document.

For example, the following code contains an example of an `@ Page` processing directive that includes a `Language` attribute to define C# as the language along with a code render block:

```
<%@ Page Language="C#" %>
<%
    Response.Write("All roads ");
    Response.Write("lead to Rome.");
%>
```

To define Visual Basic as a Web page's language, you assign a value of "VB" to the `Language` attribute of the `@ Page` processing directive.

The second type of code render block is an **inline expression**, which is simply a shortcut for calling the `Write()` method of the `Response` object to print text to a Web browser. You use the delimiters <%= and %> to designate inline expressions. The following code demonstrates how to print "All roads lead to Rome." to a Web browser window by using an inline expression instead of inline code:

```
<%= "All roads lead to Rome." %>
```

Next, you will start creating a Web site that displays statistics for the 2007 NFL season. You'll begin by starting Visual Web Developer.

To create a Web site that displays statistics for the 2007 NFL season:

1. Click the **Start** button, point to **All Programs**, and then click **Microsoft Visual Web Developer 2008 Express Edition**. The Visual Studio integrated development environment (IDE) opens.

2. Return to the Visual Studio IDE, select the **File** menu, and then select **New Web Site**. The New Web Site dialog box opens. Select **ASP.NET Web Site** from the Templates section. Leave the Location box set to **File System**, which creates the new Web site on your local file system, and the Language box set to **Visual C#**. Click the **Browse** button. The Choose Location dialog box opens.

3. In the File System section of the Choose Location dialog box, find the Chapter folder for Chapter 2 in the location where you installed the data files. Click the **Chapter** folder, and then click the **Create New Folder** button. Name the new folder **NFLStats2007**.

4. Click the **Open** button to close the Choose Location dialog box, and then click **OK** in the New Web Site dialog box to create the new Web site. The Default.aspx file opens in the Code Editor.

5. Change the content of the `<title>` element to **NFL Stats 2007** and add the following `<link>` element above the closing `</head>` tag to link to the asp_styles.css style sheet in your Chapter.02 folder:

    ```
    <link rel="stylesheet" href="asp_styles.css"
    type="text/css" />
    ```

6. To add the asp_styles.css style sheet to the project, select the **Website** menu and then select **Add Existing Item**. Locate the asp_styles.css file in your Chapter.02 folder, select it, and then click the **Add** button. The file is added to the Solution Explorer window.

7. Replace the `<form>` and `<div>` elements in the document body with the following heading elements:

    ```
    <h1>NFL Stats 2007</h1>
    <h2>Interceptions</h2>
    ```

You are studying code render blocks in this chapter only to learn the basics of how to create ASP.NET pages. In practice, code render blocks are of limited use and can be difficult to maintain and debug. Further, it is considered poor programming practice to use code render blocks to create complex programs. In Chapter 3, you will learn to use code declaration blocks and code-behind forms, which are a much better solution for writing ASP.NET code.

8. Add the following code render block to the end of the document body:

```
<%
%>
```

9. To save the project, select the **File** menu and then select **Save All**.

Understanding Classes and Objects

Before you can start writing code, you need to learn some basic terminology that is commonly used in C# programming and in other kinds of programming languages. One of the most powerful aspects of C# is that it is an object-oriented programming language. **Object-oriented programming (OOP)** refers to the creation of reusable software objects that can be easily incorporated into another program. An **object** is programming code and data that can be treated as an individual unit or component. In object-oriented programming, the code that makes up an object is organized into classes. Essentially, a **class** is a template, or blueprint, that serves as the basis for new objects. When you use an object in your program, you actually create an instance of the class of the object. An **instance** is an object that has been created from an existing class. When you create an object from an existing class, you are said to be **instantiating** the object.

For example, you might create a ShoppingCart class for a Web site that calculates the total cost of a sales transaction. The ShoppingCart class might store information about the purchased items, shipping costs, and so on. To use the ShoppingCart class, you must instantiate a ShoppingCart object. Individual statements used in a computer program are often grouped into logical units called **procedures**, which are used to perform specific tasks. For example, a procedure for the ShoppingCart class might contain a group of statements that calculate the sales tax based on the sales total. The procedures associated with an object are called **methods**. A **property** is a piece of data that is associated with an object. A class's methods, properties, and other types of elements are referred to as **members**. For example, the ShoppingCart class might store the name, part number, and cost of purchased items; these data are properties, or members, of the ShoppingCart object.

To incorporate an object and an associated method in C# code, you type the object's name, followed by a period, followed by the method. For example, the following code shows the ShoppingCart object, followed by a period, followed by a method named calcShipping(), which calculates the cost of shipping the order:

```
ShoppingCart.calcShipping();
```

For many methods, you also need to provide some more specific information, called an **argument**, between the parentheses. Some methods require numerous arguments, whereas others don't require any. Providing an argument for a method is referred to as **passing arguments**. Different methods require different kinds of arguments. For example, the Write() method of the Response object requires a text string as an argument. A **text string**, or **literal string**, is text that is contained within double quotation marks. Literal strings can be also be assigned a zero-length string value called an **empty string**. The text string argument of the Write() method specifies the text that the Response object uses to create new text on a Web page. The calcShipping() method might also require a text string argument that specifies the state where the order will be shipped. In that case, the C# statement would look like this if the order were being shipped to Texas:

```
ShoppingCart.calcShipping("TX");
```

You use an object's properties in much the same way you use a method, by appending the property name to the object with a period. However, a property name is not followed by parentheses. One of the biggest differences between methods and properties is that a property does not actually do anything; you only use properties to store data. You assign a value to a property using an equal sign, as in the following example:

```
ShoppingCart.discount = .05;
```

ASP.NET includes five built-in core objects, Request, Response, Session, Application, and Server, that function at the processing tier between the client tier and the data storage tier (if there is one). You use each of these objects to access specific types of information in the processing tier and for storing information on the server. The following section focuses on the Response method as a way of helping you understand the basics of how to program with C#. You will study the other built-in core objects throughout this book.

Displaying Program Results

C# treats many things as objects. One of the most commonly used objects in C# programming is the **Response object**, which represents the information that will be sent back to the client. One of the most common uses of the Response object is to add new text to a Web page. You create new text on a Web page with the **Write() method** of the Response object. You could use the Write() method to render a Web page containing custom information such as a user's name or the result of a calculation.

You should understand that the only reason to use the `Write()` method is to add new text to a Web page while it is being rendered. For example, you might want to display a new Web page based on information a user enters into a form. A user might enter, for example, sales information into a form for an online transaction. Using the entered information, you can create a new Web page that displays their sales total, order confirmation, and so on. If you simply want to display text in a Web browser when the document is first rendered, there is no need to use anything but standard XHTML elements. The procedures for dynamically gathering information are a little too complicated for this introductory chapter. In this chapter, you will use the `Write()` method to return the results of a program to the client to learn the basics of C#.

The `Write()` method of the `Response` object requires a text string as an argument. The text string argument of the `Write()` method specifies the text that will be written to the Web browser. For example, `Response.Write("Save the whales!")` displays the text "Save the whales!" in the Web browser window (without the quotation marks). Note that you must place literal strings on a single line. If you include a line break within a literal string, you will receive an error message.

The `Write()` method performs essentially the same function that you perform when you manually add text to the body of a standard Web page document. Whether you add text to a document by using standard elements such as the <p> element or by using the `Write()` method, the text is added according to the order in which the statement appears in the document.

You can include any elements you want as part of an argument for the `Write()` method, including elements such as the <p> and <br /> elements. The following code shows several `Write()` methods containing text and various HTML elements. Figure 2-1 shows the output in a Web browser.

If you are using a version of Internet Explorer higher than 4, you need to turn on error notification. To do this, select the Tools menu, select Internet Options, and then, in the Internet Options dialog box, click the Advanced tab. In the Browsing category on the Advanced tab, make sure the "Display a notification about every script error" check box is selected, and click the OK button to close the dialog box. To view errors in Firefox, you must select the Tools menu and then select Error Console.

Programmers often talk about code that "writes to" or "prints to" a Web browser window. For example, you might say that a piece of code writes a text string to the Web browser window. This is just another way of saying that the code displays the text string in the Web browser window.

```
<%
Response.Write("<h1>String Quintet, ");
Response.Write("Op. 29 (Beethoven)</h1>");
Response.Write("<h2>Movements</h2>");
Response.Write("<ol><li>Allegro</li>");
Response.Write("<li>Adagio molto espressivo</li>");
Response.Write("<li>Scherzo. Allegro</li>");
Response.Write("<li>Presto</li></ol>");
%>
```

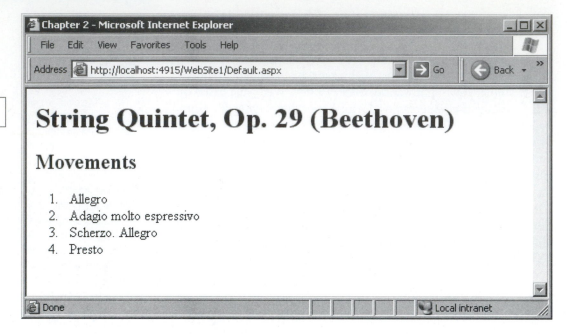

Figure 2-1 Output of a program that uses the `Write()` method of the `Response` object

Next, you will add some `Write()` methods to the NFLStats2007 project.

To add some `Write()` methods to the NFLStats2007 project:

1. Return to the **Default.aspx** file of the NFLStats2007 project in the Visual Studio IDE.

2. Add the following statements to the code render block:

```
Response.Write("<ol>");
Response.Write("<li>Antonio Cromartie (SD): 10</li>");
Response.Write("<li>Oshiomogho Atogwe (STL): 8</li>");
Response.Write("<li>Marcus Trufant (SEA): 7</li>");
Response.Write("<li>Ed Reed (BAL): 7</li>");
Response.Write("<li>Thomas Howard (OAK): 6</li>");
Response.Write("</ol>");
```

3. To save the project, select the **File** menu and then select **Save All**. To start the Web site, select the **Debug** menu and then select **Start Without Debugging**. Figure 2-2 shows how the Web page appears in a Web browser window.

4. Close your Web browser window.

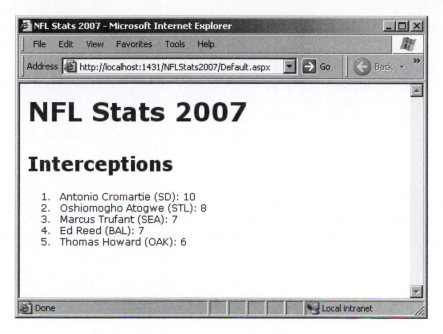

Figure 2-2   NFL Stats 2007 document in a Web browser

Case Sensitivity in ASP.NET

Like XHTML, C# is case sensitive, and within C# code, object names are usually written with initial capitalization, such as with the `Response.Write()` statement. Using lowercase letters with the `Response.Write()` statement, such as `response.write()`, will cause errors. Similarly, the following statements will also cause errors because they are not written with initial capitalization:

```
RESPONSE.Write("Save the whales!");
Response.WRITE("Save the whales!");
response.Write("Save the whales!");
```

Adding Comments to an ASP.NET Program

When you create a program, whether in C# or any other program-ming language, it is considered good programming practice to add comments to your code. In this section, you will learn how to create C# comments.

Comments are nonprinting lines that you place in your code to contain various types of remarks, including the name of the program, your name and the date you created the program, notes to yourself, or instructions to future programmers who might need to modify your work. When you are working with long programs, comments make it easier to decipher how a program is structured.

C# supports two kinds of comments: line comments and block comments. A **line comment** hides a single line of code. To create a line comment, add two slashes // before the text you want to use as a comment. The // characters instruct the ASP.NET interpreter to ignore all text immediately following the slashes to the end of the line. You can place a line comment either at the end of a line of code or on its own line. **Block comments** hide multiple lines of code. You create a block comment by adding /* to the first line that you want included in the block, and you close a comment block by typing */ after the last character in the block. Any text or lines between the opening /* characters and the closing */ characters are ignored by the ASP.NET interpreter. The following code shows a code render block containing line and block comments. If you open a document that contains the following code in a Web browser, the browser does not render the text marked with comments.

> Comments in C# use the same syntax as comments created in C++, Java, and other programming languages.

```
<%
/*
This line is part of the block comment.
This line is also part of the block comment.
*/
Response.Write("<p>Comments example</p>"); // Line comment
// This line comment takes up an entire line.
/* This is another way of creating a block comment. */
%>
```

In addition to C# comments, you can also use **server-side comments**, which allow you to leave comments anywhere within an ASP.NET file, with the exception of code render and code declaration blocks. Server-side comments are not processed on the server and do not display in the rendered page. You create server-side comments with the <%-- and --%> delimiters, as follows:

```
<%-- This program was written by Don Gosselin --%>
```

Next, you will add some comments to the NFLStats2007 project.

To add some comments to the NFLStats2007 project:

1. Return to the **Default.aspx** file of the NFLStats2007 project in the Visual Studio IDE.

2. Add the following line comments immediately after the open script delimiter, taking care to replace "your name" with your first and last name and "today's date" with the current date:

   ```
   // your name
   // today's date
   ```

3. Add the following block comment immediately after the second line comment:

```
/*
The purpose of this code is to demonstrate how
to add block comments to a C# script.
*/
```

4. To save the project, select the **File** menu and then select **Save All**. To start the Web site, select the **Debug** menu and then select **Start Without Debugging**. The comments you entered should not display.

5. Close your Web browser window.

Short Quiz 1

1. What is a processing directive and how are they used in ASP.NET?

2. What are the different types of code render blocks?

3. Should you use code render blocks in a production environment?

4. Explain the relationship between classes and objects.

5. Which processing directives are used to create server-side comments?

Using C# Variables and Constants

The values a program stores in computer memory are commonly called **variables**. Technically speaking, though, a variable is actually a specific location in the computer's memory. Data stored in a specific variable often changes. You can think of a variable as similar to a storage locker—a program can put any value into it, and then retrieve the value later for use in calculations. To use a variable in a program, you first have to write a statement that creates the variable and assigns it a name. For example, you might have a program that creates a variable named curTime and then stores the current time in that variable. Each time the program runs, the current time is different, so the value varies.

Programmers often talk about "assigning a value to a variable," which is the same as storing a value in a variable. For example, a shopping cart program might include variables that store customer names and purchase totals. Each variable will contain different values at different times, depending on the name of the customer and the items they are purchasing.

Naming Variables

The name you assign to a variable is called an **identifier**. You must observe the following rules and conventions when naming a variable in C#:

- Identifiers must begin with an uppercase or lowercase ASCII letter or underscore (_).

- You can use numbers in an identifier, but not as the first character.

- You cannot include spaces in an identifier.

- You cannot use keywords for identifiers.

Keywords (also called **reserved words**) are special words that are part of the C# language syntax. As just noted, keywords cannot be used for identifiers. Table 2-1 lists the C# keywords.

You can actually use keywords as identifiers in your C# programs if you precede them with the @ character. However, this is considered a very poor programming technique because it makes code confusing and difficult to read, so you should avoid using it in your C# programs.

abstract	event	new	struct
as	explicit	null	switch
base	extern	object	this
bool	false	operator	throw
break	finally	out	true
byte	fixed	override	try
case	float	params	typeof
catch	for	private	uint
char	foreach	protected	ulong
checked	goto	public	unchecked
class	if	readonly	unsafe
const	implicit	ref	ushort
continue	in	return	using
decimal	int	sbyte	virtual
default	interface	sealed	volatile
delegate	internal	short	void
do	is	sizeof	while
double	lock	stackalloc	
else	long	static	
enum	namespace	string	

Table 2-1   C# keywords

Contextual keywords have special meaning in the C# language, but are not actually reserved as keywords. This means that you can use them as identifiers. However, because contextual keywords might eventually become true keywords, you should avoid using them as identifiers. Table 2-2 lists the C# contextual keywords.

from	join	select	where
get	let	set	yield
group	orderby	value	
into	partial	var	

Table 2-2 C# contextual keywords

Variable names, like other C# code, are case sensitive. Therefore, the variable name `stateInterestRate` is a completely different variable than one named `stateinterestrate`, `StateInterestRate`, or `STATEINTERESTRATE`. If you receive an error when running a program, be sure that you are using the correct case when referring to any variables in your code.

Creating Variables

Before you can use a variable in your code, you have to create it. In C#, you create variables using the syntax `type variableName;`. The *type* portion of the syntax refers to the data type of the variable. The data type used to create a variable determines the type of information that can be stored in the variable. You will learn about data types shortly. For now, you will learn about a single data type, the integer data type, to understand how to work with variables. The **integer data type** stores positive or negative numbers with no decimal places or the value 0 (zero). You create an integer variable with the `int` keyword. For example, to create an integer variable named `mgSodium`, you use this statement:

```
int mgSodium;
```

When you write a statement to create a variable, you are **declaring** the variable. When you declare a variable, you can also assign a specific value to, or **initialize**, the variable using the following syntax. The equal sign in a variable declaration assigns a value to the variable.

```
type variableName = value;
```

The equal sign (=) in the preceding statement is called an **assignment operator** because it assigns the value on the right side of the expression to the variable on the left side of the expression. This is different from the standard usage of the equal sign in an algebraic formula. The value you assign to a declared variable must be appropriate for its data type or you will receive an error message when you build the project. You must assign to an integer variable a positive number with no decimal places, a negative number with no decimal places, or zero using a statement similar to the following:

```
int mgSodium = 2300;
```

It's common practice to use an underscore (_) character to separate individual words within a variable name, as in `state_interest_rate`. Another option is to use a lowercase letter for the first letter of the first word in a variable name, with subsequent words starting with an initial cap, as in `stateInterestRate`.

Although you can assign a value when a variable is declared, you are not required to do so because your program might assign the value later. However, if for some reason the program fails to assign a value to the variable and then attempts to use it, you will receive an error message when your program executes. Therefore, it is good programming practice always to initialize your variables when you declare them.

82

The values you assign to integer variables and other numeric variables are called **literal values**, or **literals**.

In addition to assigning values to a variable, you can also assign the value of one variable to another. In the following code, the first statement creates a variable named q1Headcount and assigns it an initial value of 5000. The second statement creates another variable named q2Headcount, but instead of being directly assigned a numeric value, the variable is assigned the value of the q1Headcount variable.

```
int q1Headcount = 5000;
int q2Headcount = q1Headcount;
```

Next, you will create integer variables that store the number of interceptions for each of the players in the Interceptions section of the NFLStats2007 project.

To add some integer variables to the NFLStats2007 project:

1. Return to the **Default.aspx** file of the NFLStats2007 project in the Visual Studio IDE.

2. Add the following variable declaration and initialization statements to the beginning of the code render block. Each statement creates an integer variable from the player's last name and assigns to it the number of interceptions.

    ```
    int cromartie = 10;
    int atogwe = 8;
    int trufant = 7;
    int reed = 7;
    int howard = 6;
    ```

3. To save the project, select the **File** menu and then select **Save All**.

Displaying Variables

To print a variable (that is, display its value on the screen), you pass the variable name to the `Response.Write()` method, but without enclosing it in quotation marks, as follows:

```
int mgSodium = 2300;
Response.Write(mgSodium);
```

To pass both text strings and variables to the `Response.Write()` method, you separate them with the plus sign (+), as follows:

```
int mgSodium = 2300;
Response.Write("<p>Adults should eat less than "
    + mgSodium + " milligrams of sodium a day.</p>");
```

In the preceding example, the `Response.Write()` method uses a plus sign (+) to combine a literal string with a variable containing a numeric value. You will learn more about performing similar operations as you progress through this chapter. However, you need to understand that using a plus sign to combine literal strings with variables containing numeric values does not add them together, as in an arithmetic operation. Rather, it combines the values to create a new string, which is then printed to the screen. Figure 2-3 shows how the statements appear in a Web browser.

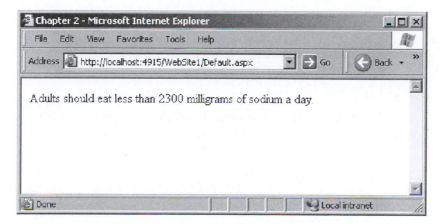

Figure 2-3 Output of a `Response.Write()` statement that combines two literal strings

Modifying Variables

Regardless of whether you assign a value to a variable when it is declared, you can change the variable's value at any point in a program by using a statement that includes the variable's name, followed by an equal sign, followed by the value you want to assign to the variable. The following code declares a variable named `salary`, assigns it an initial value of 25,000, and prints it using a `Response.Write()` method. The third statement changes the value of the `salary` variable to 28,000 and the fourth statement prints the new value. Notice that it's only necessary to declare the `salary` variable (using the `int` keyword) once. Figure 2-4 shows the output in a Web browser.

```
int salary = 25000;
Response.Write("<p>Your previous salary was $"
    + salary + ".</p>");
salary = 28000;
Response.Write("<p>Your new salary is $"
    + salary + ".</p>");
```

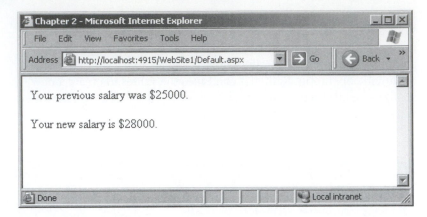

Figure 2-4   Results of program that includes a changing variable

Next, you will modify the `Response.Write()` statements in the NFL-Stats2007 project so they print each player's number of interceptions from the associated variable.

To modify the `Response.Write()` statements in the NFLStats2007 project so they print each player's number of interceptions from the associated variable:

1. Return to the **Default.aspx file** of the NFLStats2007 project in the Visual Studio IDE.

2. Modify the `Response.Write()` statements that print the number of interceptions for each player as follows:

```
Response.Write("<li>Antonio Cromartie (SD): "
    + cromartie + "</li>");
Response.Write("<li>Oshiomogho Atogwe (STL): "
    + atogwe + "</li>");
Response.Write("<li>Marcus Trufant (SEA): "
    + trufant + "</li>");
Response.Write("<li>Ed Reed (BAL): "
    + reed + "</li>");
Response.Write("<li>Thomas Howard (OAK): "
    + howard + "</li>");
```

3. To save the project, select the **File** menu and then select **Save All**. To start the Web site, select the **Debug** menu and then select **Start Without Debugging**. The results should display the same as they did before you added the variables.

4. Close your Web browser window and then, in Visual Studio, select the **File** menu and then select **Close Project**.

Creating Constants

A **constant** contains information that does not change during the course of program execution. You can think of a constant as a variable with a *constant* value. A common example of a constant is the value of pi (π), which represents the ratio of the circumference of a circle to its diameter. The value of pi never changes from the constant value 3.141592.

You use the same rules for naming constants as you do for naming variables—that is, constant names must begin with an uppercase or lowercase ASCII letter or underscore. You can use numbers in a constant name, but not as the first character, and you cannot use spaces in a constant name or use keywords for constant names. Note that it is common practice to use all uppercase letters for constant names, such as STATE_SALES_TAX.

You create a constant by placing the const keyword before the data type in a variable declaration statement. For example, the following statement declares a constant named COPYRIGHT and assigns it a value of 2009:

```
const int COPYRIGHT = 2009;
```

Unlike variables, constants must be declared and initialized in the same statement. If you attempt to declare and initialize a constant with separate statements, as shown in the following example, you will receive an error when you build your project:

```
const int COPYRIGHT;
COPYRIGHT = 2009;
```

Remember that an existing constant cannot change after it is initialized. The first statement in the following example is legal because it declares and initializes the constant on the same line, but the second statement causes an error because it attempts to assign a different value to the already existing constant:

```
const int COPYRIGHT = 2009;
COPYRIGHT = 2010;
```

Short Quiz 2

1. What rules and conventions must you observe when naming a variable in C#?

2. How can you use keywords as identifiers in C# and is this a good programming practice?

3. Why should you initialize a variable when you first declare it?

4. What convention should you follow when naming a constant?

5. Can you modify the value assigned to a constant after you first initialize it?

Working with Data Types

In addition to integers, variables can contain many different kinds of values—for example, the time of day, a dollar amount, or a person's name. A **data type** is the specific category of information that a variable contains. The concept of data types is often difficult for beginning programmers to grasp because in real life you don't often distinguish among different types of information. If someone asks you for your name, your age, or the current time, you don't usually stop to consider that your name is a text string and that your age and the current time are numbers. However, a variable's specific data type is very important in programming because the data type helps determine how much memory the computer allocates for the data stored in the variable. The data type also governs the kinds of operations that can be performed on a variable.

Data types that can be assigned only a single value are called **primitive types**. Table 2-3 lists the most commonly used C# primitive data types.

Data type	Description
`int`	A number with no decimal places between –2,147,483,648 and 2,147,483,647
`long`	A number with no decimal places between –922,337,203,685,477,508 and 922,337,203,685,477,507
`char`	Any single character contained within single quotations, such as 'A', or an escaped hexadecimal Unicode character contained within single quotations, such as '\u00A9' for the copyright symbol (©)
`float`	A floating-point number between –3.402823e38 and 3.402823e38
`double`	A floating-point number between –1.79769313486232e308 and 1.79769313486232e308; primarily used for financial calculations
`bool`	A logical value of true or false
`decimal`	Decimal numbers with 29 significant digits between $\pm1.0 \times 10e{-}28$ and $\pm7.9 \times 10e28$
`string`	Text contained within double quotations such as "Hello World"

Table 2-3 Commonly used C# primitive data types

Many programming languages require that you declare the type of data that a variable contains. Programming languages that require you to declare the data types of variables are called **strongly typed programming languages**. Strong typing is also known as **static typing** because data types do not change after they have been declared. Programming languages that do not require you to declare the data types of variables are called **loosely typed programming languages**. Loose typing is also known as **dynamic typing** because data types can change after they have been declared. C# is a strongly typed programming language.

When you declare a variable in C#, you *must* designate a data type. As with integer variables, you designate data types for other types of variables by placing the data type name and a space in front of the variable name. However, as you will learn in the following sections, there are varying requirements for initializing each of the data types.

Using Numeric Data Types

Numeric data types are an important part of any programming language, and are particularly useful for arithmetic calculations. Most programming languages support two basic numeric data types: integers and floating-point numbers. An **integer** is a positive or negative number with no decimal places. The numbers –250, –13, 0, 2, 6, 10, 100, and 10000 are examples of integers. The int and long data types listed in Table 2-3 are both integer data types.

The numbers –6.16, –4.4, 3.17, .52, 10.5, and 2.7541 are not integers; they are floating-point numbers because they contain decimal places. A **floating-point number** is a number that contains decimal places or that is written in exponential notation. **Exponential notation**, or **scientific notation**, is a shortened format for writing very large numbers or numbers with many decimal places. Numbers written in exponential notation are represented by a value between 1 and 10 multiplied by 10 raised to some power. The value of 10 is written with an uppercase or lowercase *E*. For example, the number 200,000,000,000 can be written in exponential notation as 2.0e11, which means "two times ten to the eleventh power." The float, double, and decimal data types listed in Table 2-3 store floating-point numbers.

If a right operand in an assignment operation is a literal floating-point number (such as 3.124), C# always treats it as a double data type. For this reason, if you attempt to assign a literal floating-point number to the float or decimal data types, you will receive a compiler error. To get around this problem, you need to place a letter *F* after the number for assignments to float data types or a letter *M* for assignments to decimal data types. The following two statements demonstrate how to assign floating-point literal values to float and decimal variables:

```
float mortgageRate = 6.25F;
decimal stockPrice = 21.875M;
```

Deciding which numeric data type to use is often confusing to beginning programmers. Whenever you declare a variable, C# reserves for the variable the amount of memory that the specified data type requires. How much space is reserved for the two integer data types? C# reserves 32 bits of memory for int variables and 64 bits of memory for long variables. The basic rule of thumb is to use the smallest data type possible to conserve memory. Therefore, if you need to use an integer variable in your program and you know that the values it stores will always be between –2,147,483,648 and 2,147,483,647, you should use the `int` data type because it requires less memory than the `long` data type.

Next, you will create a program that uses variables containing integers, floating-point numbers, and exponential numbers to print the 20 prefixes of the metric system. A metric prefix, or SI prefix, is a name that precedes a metric unit of measure. For example, the metric prefix for centimeter is centi, and it denotes a value of 1/100th. In other words, a centimeter is the equivalent of 1/100th of a meter.

To create a program that prints metric prefixes:

1. Return to the Visual Studio IDE, select the **File** menu and then select **New Web Site**. The New Web Site dialog box opens.

2. In the Templates section, select **ASP.NET Web Site**. Leave the Location box set to **File System**, which creates the new Web site on your local file system, and the Language box set to **Visual C#**. Click the **Browse** button. The Choose Location dialog box opens.

3. In the File System section of the Choose Location dialog box, find the Chapter folder for Chapter 2 in the location where you installed the data files. Click the **Chapter** folder, and then click the **Create New Folder** button. Name the new folder **MetricPrefixes**. Click the **Open** button, which closes the Choose Location dialog box, and then click **OK** in the New Web Site dialog box to create the new Web site. The Default. aspx file opens in the Code Editor.

4. Change the content of the `<title>` element to **Metric Prefixes** and add the following `<link>` element above the closing `</head>` tag to link to the asp_styles.css style sheet:

```
<link rel="stylesheet" href="asp_styles.css"
type="text/css" />
```

5. To add the asp_styles.css style sheet to the project, select the **Website** menu and then select **Add Existing Item**. Locate the asp_styles.css file in your Chapter.02 folder, select it, and then click the **Add** button. The file is added to the Solution Explorer window.

6. Replace the `<form>` and `<div>` elements in the document body with the following heading element:

```
<h1>Metric Prefixes</h1>
```

7. Add the following code render block to the end of the document body:

```
<%
%>
```

8. Add to the code render block the following variable declarations for the 20 metric prefixes:

```
double yotta = 1e24;
double zetta = 1e21;
double exa = 1e18;
float peta = 1e15F;
float tera = 1e12F;
float giga = 1e9F;
float mega = 1e6F;
int kilo = 1000;
int hecto = 100;
int deca = 10;
float deci = 1.1F;
float centi = .01F;
float milli = .001F;
decimal micro = 1e-6M;
decimal nano = 1e-9M;
decimal pico = 1e-12M;
decimal femto = 1e-15M;
double atto = 1e-18;
double zepto = 1e-21;
double yocto = 1e-24;
```

9. Add to the end of the code render block the following statements to print the value of each metric prefix variable as cells in a table:

```
Response.Write("<table border='1' width='100%'>
    <tr><th>Prefix</th><th>Decimal
    Equivalent</th></tr>");
Response.Write("<tr><td>Yotta</td><td>" + yotta
    + "</td></tr>");
Response.Write("<tr><td>Zetta</td><td>" + zetta
    + "</td></tr>");
Response.Write("<tr><td>Exa</td><td>" + exa
    + "</td></tr>");
Response.Write("<tr><td>Peta</td><td>" + peta
    + "</td></tr>");
Response.Write("<tr><td>Tera</td><td>" + tera
    + "</td></tr>");
Response.Write("<tr><td>Giga</td><td>" + giga
    + "</td></tr>");
Response.Write("<tr><td>Mega</td><td>" + mega
    + "</td></tr>");
Response.Write("<tr><td>Kilo</td><td>" + kilo
    + "</td></tr>");
Response.Write("<tr><td>Hecto</td><td>" + hecto
    + "</td></tr>");
Response.Write("<tr><td>Deca</td><td>" + deca
    + "</td></tr>");
Response.Write("<tr><td>Deci</td><td>" + deci
    + "</td></tr>");
Response.Write("<tr><td>Centi</td><td>" + centi
    + "</td></tr>");
```

```
Response.Write("<tr><td>Milli</td><td>" + milli
    + "</td></tr>");
Response.Write("<tr><td>Micro</td><td>" + micro
    + "</td></tr>");
Response.Write("<tr><td>Nano</td><td>" + nano
    + "</td></tr>");
Response.Write("<tr><td>Pico</td><td>" + pico
    + "</td></tr>");
Response.Write("<tr><td>Femto</td><td>" + femto
    + "</td></tr>");
Response.Write("<tr><td>Atto</td><td>" + atto
    + "</td></tr>");
Response.Write("<tr><td>Zepto</td><td>" + zepto
    + "</td></tr>");
Response.Write("<tr><td>Yocto</td><td>" + yocto
    + "</td></tr>");
Response.Write("</table>");
```

Most Web browsers automatically display very large numbers, such as the values represented by the zetta and yotta metric prefixes, in exponential format.

10. To save the project, select the **File** menu and then select **Save All**. To start the Web site, select the **Debug** menu and then select **Start Without Debugging**. Figure 2-5 shows how the Web page appears in a Web browser window.

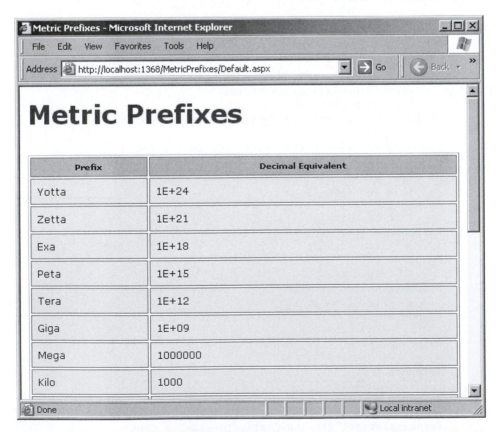

Figure 2-5   MetricPrefixes project in a Web browser

11. Close your Web browser window, and then, in Visual Studio, select the **File** menu and then select **Close Project**.

Working with Boolean Values

A **Boolean value** is a logical value of true or false. You can also think of a Boolean value as being yes or no, or on or off. Boolean values are most often used for deciding which parts of a program should execute and for comparing data. In C# programming, you can only use the words true and false to indicate Boolean values. In other programming languages, you can use the integer values of 1 and 0 to indicate Boolean values of true and false—1 indicates true and 0 indicates false. The following shows a simple example of two Boolean variables that are assigned Boolean values, one true and the other false. Figure 2-6 shows the output in a Web browser.

```
bool repeatCustomer = true;
bool corporateDiscount = false;
Response.Write("<p>Repeat customer: "
    + repeatCustomer + "</p>");
Response.Write("<p>Corporate discount: "
    + corporateDiscount + "</p>");
```

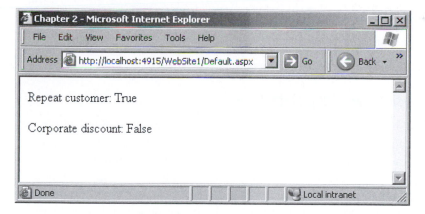

Figure 2-6   Output of a simple program with two Boolean variables

Working with Text Data Types

This section discusses how to store text with the char and string data types. First you will study the char data type.

Using the Char Data Type

The **char data type** stores any single character or escaped hexadecimal Unicode character contained within single quotations.

For example, the following statement creates a char variable named semesterGrade and assigns it a value of 'B':

```
char semesterGrade = 'B';
```

More than likely, you will not encounter many situations where you will need to use a char variable to store one of the characters that is available on your computer keyboard. Instead, the char data type is most useful in storing special characters that are not available on your keyboard, such as a copyright symbol. To assign a character that is not on your keyboard to a char variable, you need to specify an escaped hexadecimal Unicode character. **Unicode** is a standardized set of characters from many of the world's languages. A number represents each character in the Unicode character set. **Hexadecimal** is a numeral system based on a value of 16 that uses combinations of 16 characters, the numbers 0 through 9 and the letters A through F, to represent values. For example, the hexadecimal Unicode number for the copyright symbol is 00A9. To assign a hexadecimal Unicode character to a char variable, it must be preceded by the \u escape sequence and enclosed in single quotations. The following statements demonstrate how to create and print a string variable and a char variable containing the Japanese Yen character (¥), which is represented by the Unicode character 00A5.

```
string currencyText = "Japan's currency is the Yen ";
char Yen = '\u00A5';
Response.Write(currencyText + Yen);
```

You will study escape sequences later in this chapter.

Using the String Data Type

As you learned earlier, a text string is text that is contained within double quotation marks. Examples of strings you can use in a program are company names, usernames, comments, and other types of text. You can use text strings as literal values or assign them to a string variable using the string data type. You use the **string data type** to store text string variables. If you assign a literal value to a string variable, it must be contained with double quotations. For example, the first statement in the following code declares a string variable named companyName and assigns it a value of "WebAdventure". The second statement prints the companyName variable to the Web browser.

```
string companyName = "WebAdventure";
Response.Write(companyName);
```

You need to use extra care when using double quotation marks and other types of special characters within text strings. With double quotation marks, the C# interpreter always looks for the first closing double quotation mark to match an opening double quotation mark. For example, consider the following statement:

```
Response.Write("My dog's name is "Noah".");
```

This statement causes an error because the C# interpreter assumes that the literal string ends with the double quotation mark just before "Noah". To get around this problem, you include an escape character before the double quotation marks that surround "Noah". An **escape character** tells the compiler or interpreter that the character that follows it has a special purpose. In C#, the escape character is the backslash \. Placing a backslash in front of a double quotation mark tells the C# interpreter that the quotation mark is to be treated as a regular keyboard character, such as "a", "b", "1", or "2", and not as part of a double quotation mark pair that encloses a text string. The backslashes in the following statement tells the C# interpreter to print the double quotation marks surrounding "Noah" as double quotation marks:

```
Response.Write("My dog's name is \"Noah\".");
```

You can also use the escape character in combination with other characters to insert a special character into a string. When you combine the escape character with other characters, the combination is called an **escape sequence**. The backslash followed by a double quotation mark \" is an example of an escape sequence. Most escape sequences carry out special functions. For example, the escape sequence \t inserts a tab into a string. Table 2-4 lists the escape sequences that can be added to a string in C#.

Escape sequence	Character
\a	Bell (alert)
\\	Backslash
\f	Form feed
\n	New line
\r	Carriage return
\t	Horizontal tab
\v	Vertical tab
\'	Single quotation mark
\"	Double quotation mark
\b	Backspace
\?	Literal question mark
\ooo	ASCII character in octal notation
\xhh	ASCII character in hexadecimal notation
\xhhhh	Unicode character specified by the xxxx characters, which represent four hexadecimal digits

Table 2-4   C# escape sequences

 If you place a backslash before any character other than those listed in Table 2-4, the backslash is ignored.

Notice that one of the characters generated by an escape sequence is the backslash. Because the escape character itself is a backslash, you must use the escape sequence \\ to include a backslash as a character in a string. For example, to include the path "C:\My Documents\My Music\" in a string, you must include two backslashes for every single backslash you want to appear in the string, as in the following statement:

```
Response.Write("C:\\My Documents\\My Music\\");
```

The following code shows an example of a program containing strings with several escape sequences. Figure 2-7 shows the output.

```
<pre>
<%
Response.Write("<p>Printed \non two lines.</p>");
Response.Write("<p>\tIncludes a horizontal tab.</p>");
Response.Write("<p>My files are in c:\\personal.</p>");
Response.Write("<p>\x00BFQu\x00E9 pasa?</p>");
%>
</pre>
```

Several of the escape sequences, including the new line and horizontal tab escape sequences, are only recognized inside a container element such as the <pre> element.

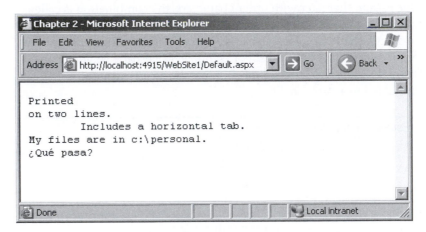

Figure 2-7 Output of program with strings containing escape sequences

Next, you will start creating a Web page that displays information about winners of the Kentucky Derby. The Web page will contain both string and numeric variables.

To create a Web page that displays information about winners of the Kentucky Derby:

1. Return to the Visual Studio IDE, select the **File** menu and then select **New Web Site**. The New Web Site dialog box opens. In the Templates section, select **ASP.NET Web Site**.

Leave the Location box set to **File System**, which creates the new Web site on your local file system, and the Language box set to **Visual C#**. Click the **Browse** button. The Choose Location dialog box opens.

2. In the File System section of the Choose Location dialog box, find the Chapter folder for Chapter 2 in the location where you installed the data files. Click the **Chapter** folder, and then click the **Create New Folder** button. Name the new folder **KentuckyDerbyWinners**. Click the **Open** button, which closes the Choose Location dialog box, and then click **OK** in the New Web Site dialog box to create the new Web site. The Default.aspx file opens in the Code Editor.

3. Change the content of the `<title>` element to **Kentucky Derby Winners** and add the following `<link>` element above the closing `</head>` tag to link to the asp_styles.css style sheet:

```
<link rel="stylesheet" href="asp_styles.css"
type="text/css" />
```

4. Add the asp_styles.css style sheet to the project by selecting the **Website** menu and then selecting **Add Existing Item**. Locate the asp_styles.css file in your Chapter.02 folder, select it, and then click the **Add** button. The file is added to the Solution Explorer window.

5. Replace the `<form>` and `<div>` elements in the document body with the following heading element:

```
<h1>Kentucky Derby Winners</h1>
```

6. Add the following code render block to the end of the document body:

```
<%
%>
```

7. Add the following variable declaration and initialization statements to the code render block. Notice that the first five variable declarations include \" escape sequences to add double quotations around each horse's name.

```
string winner2003 = "\"Funny Cide\"";
string winner2004 = "\"Smarty Jones\"";
string winner2005 = "\"Giacomo\"";
string winner2006 = "\"Barbaro\"";
string winner2007 = "\"Street Sense\"";
string jockey2003 = "J. Santos";
```

```
string jockey2004 = "S. Elliott";
string jockey2005 = "M. Smith";
string jockey2006 = "E. Prado";
string jockey2007 = "C. Borel";
float odds2003 = 12.80F;
float odds2004 = 4.10F;
float odds2005 = 50.30F;
float odds2006 = 6.10F;
float odds2007 = 4.90F;
```

8. Next, add the following statements to the end of the program section that print the values stored in each of the variables you declared and initialized in the last step:

```
Response.Write("<p>In 2003, " + jockey2003
    + " rode <strong>" + winner2003
    + "</strong> to victory with odds of "
    + odds2003 + ".<br />");
Response.Write("In 2004, " + jockey2004
    + " rode <strong>" + winner2004
    + "</strong> to victory with odds of "
    + odds2004 + ".<br />");
Response.Write("In 2005, " + jockey2005
    + " rode <strong>" + winner2005
    + "</strong> to victory with odds of "
    + odds2005 + ".<br />");
Response.Write("In 2006, " + jockey2006
    + " rode <strong>" + winner2006
    + "</strong> to victory with odds of "
    + odds2006 + ".<br />");
Response.Write("In 2007, " + jockey2007
    + " rode <strong>" + winner2007
    + "</strong> to victory with odds of "
    + odds2007 + ".</p>");
```

9. To save the project, select the **File** menu and then select **Save All**. To start the Web site, select the **Debug** menu and then select **Start Without Debugging**. Figure 2-8 shows how the Web page appears in a Web browser window.

10. Close your Web browser window.

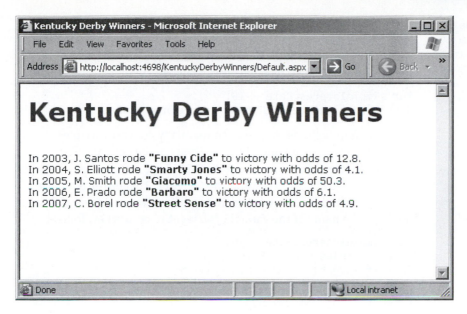

Figure 2-8   KentuckyDerbyWinners project in a Web browser

Casting Types

The data type of a variable cannot change during the course of program execution. If you attempt to assign a different data type to a variable, you will generate a compiler error or warning. If you need to use the contents of a variable as a different data type, you must cast the variable to a new data type. **Casting**, or **type casting**, copies the value contained in a variable of one data type into a variable of another data type. The C# syntax for casting types is *newVariable* = (*newType*)*oldVariable*;. The *newType* portion of the syntax is the keyword representing the type to which you want to cast the variable. Note that casting does not change the data type of the original variable. Rather, casting copies the data from the old variable, converts it to the data type of the target variable, and then assigns the value to the new variable. The following code casts an `int` variable named `simpleInterestRate` to a `float` variable named `complexInterestRate`:

```
int simpleInterestRate = 10;
double complexInterestRate = (double)simpleInterestRate;
```

If you do not explicitly cast a variable of one data type to another data type, C# attempts to automatically perform the cast for you, provided the target data type can store a larger value than the source data type. If the target data type is smaller than the source data type, you will receive an error message. The following code is identical to the preceding example, except that the `simpleInterestRate` variable is not explicitly cast to the `double`

How the C# compiler automatically converts data types is a fairly complex process. If you anticipate that your program will perform operations using multiple data types, you should always manually cast the data type of a variable before assigning its value to a variable of another data type.

data type before its value is assigned to the complexInterestRate. In this case, C# is successfully able to perform the cast because the double data type can store a larger value than the int data type, so you will not receive any errors or warnings when the project builds.

```
int simpleInterestRate = 10;
double complexInterestRate = simpleInterestRate;
```

In addition to type casting, you can manually convert variables to other types by using one of the methods of the Convert class methods. For example, the Convert.ToString() method converts a variable to string data type and the Convert.ToDouble() method converts a variable to a double data type. You pass to Convert class methods the name of the variable you want to convert, as follows:

```
int simpleInterestRate = 10;
double complexInterestRate =
Convert.ToDouble(simpleInterestRate);
```

Storing Data in Arrays

An **array** contains a set of data represented by a single variable name. You can think of an array as a collection of variables contained within a single variable. You use arrays when you want to store groups or lists of related information in a single, easily managed location. Lists of names, courses, test scores, and prices are typically stored in arrays. For example, Figure 2-9 shows that you can manage course IDs and descriptions using a single array named curriculum[]. Array names are often referred to with the array operators ([ ]) at the end of the name to clearly define them as arrays. You can use the array to refer to each department without having to retype the names and possibly introduce syntax errors through misspellings.

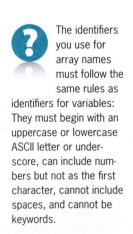

The identifiers you use for array names must follow the same rules as identifiers for variables: They must begin with an uppercase or lowercase ASCII letter or underscore, can include numbers but not as the first character, cannot include spaces, and cannot be keywords.

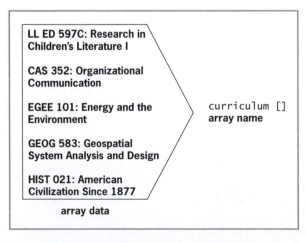

Figure 2-9 Conceptual example of an array

Declaring and Initializing Arrays

The term **element** refers to each piece of data that is stored within an array. By default, the numbering of elements within a C# array starts with an index number of zero (0). An **index** is an element's numeric position within the array. You refer to a specific element by enclosing its index in brackets at the end of the array name. For example, the first element in the curriculum[] array is curriculum[0], the second element is curriculum[1], the third element is curriculum[2], and so on. This also means that if you have an array consisting of 10 elements, the 10th element in the array is referred to using an index of 9. Because the index number of an array element is always one less than its position in the array, this numbering scheme can be confusing for beginners.

When you declare an array, you must declare the array's data type and the number of elements it will contain. The syntax for declaring an array is as follows:

```
type[] arrayName = new type[elements];
```

Notice that when declaring an array, you must declare its data type, just as you would with regular variables. Some languages, such as JavaScript and PHP, allow you to use different data types within the same array. With C#, all elements must be of the same data type.

You assign values to individual array elements in the same fashion as you assign values to a standard variable, except that you include the index for an individual element of the array. The following code demonstrates how to declare and initialize the curriculum[] array:

```
string[] curriculum = new string[5];
curriculum[0] = "LL ED 597C: Research in Children's
    Literature I";
curriculum[1] = "CAS 352: Organizational Communication";
curriculum[2] = "EGEE 101: Energy and the Environment";
curriculum[3] = "GEOG 583: Geospatial System Analysis
    and Design";
curriculum[4] = "HIST 021: American Civilization
    Since 1877";
```

Accessing Element Information

You access an element's value just as you access the value of any other variable, except you include brackets and the element index. The following code demonstrates how to print the elements in the curriculum[] array:

```
Response.Write("<p>Curriculum</p><p>");
Response.Write(curriculum[0] + "<br />");
Response.Write(curriculum[1] + "<br />");
```

```
Response.Write(curriculum[2] + "<br />");
Response.Write(curriculum[3] + "<br />");
Response.Write(curriculum[4] + "</p>");
```

Modifying Elements

You modify values in existing array elements in the same fashion as you modify values in a standard variable, except that you include brackets and the element index. The following code changes the values assigned to the first two elements in the `curriculum[]` array:

```
curriculum[0] = "HORT 101: Horticultural Science";
curriculum[1] = "IE 424: Process Quality Engineering";
```

In the following exercise, you modify the winner, jockey, and odds variables in the KentuckyDerbyWinners project so they are stored in arrays instead of as individual variables.

To add arrays to the KentuckyDerbyWinners project:

1. Return to the **Default.aspx** file of the KentuckyDerbyWinners project in the Visual Studio IDE.

2. Replace the winner variables with the following array declaration and element assignments:

    ```
    string[] winners = new string[5];
    winners[0] = "\"Funny Cide\"";
    winners[1] = "\"Smarty Jones\"";
    winners[2] = "\"Giacomo\"";
    winners[3] = "\"Barbaro\"";
    winners[4] = "\"Street Sense\"";
    ```

3. Replace the jockey variables with the following array declaration and element assignments:

    ```
    string[] jockeys = new string[5];
    jockeys[0] = "J. Santos";
    jockeys[1] = "S. Elliott";
    jockeys[2] = "M. Smith";
    jockeys[3] = "E. Prado";
    jockeys[4] = "C. Borel";
    ```

4. Replace the odds variables with the following array declaration and element assignments:

    ```
    float[] odds = new float[5];
    odds[0] = 12.80F;
    odds[1] = 4.10F;
    odds[2] = 50.30F;
    odds[3] = 6.10F;
    odds[4] = 4.90F;
    ```

5. Finally, modify the `Response.Write()` statements so they reference the new arrays and elements, as follows:

```
Response.Write("<p>In 2003, " + jockeys[0]
    + " rode <strong>" + winners[0]
    + "</strong> to victory with odds of "
    + odds[0] + ".<br />");
Response.Write("In 2004, " + jockeys[1]
    + " rode <strong>" + winners[1]
    + "</strong> to victory with odds of "
    + odds[1] + ".<br />");
Response.Write("In 2005, " + jockeys[2]
    + " rode <strong>" + winners[2]
    + "</strong> to victory with odds of "
    + odds[2] + ".<br />");
Response.Write("In 2006, " + jockeys[3]
    + " rode <strong>" + winners[3]
    + "</strong> to victory with odds of "
    + odds[3] + ".<br />");
Response.Write("In 2007, " + jockeys[4]
    + " rode <strong>" + winners[4]
    + "</strong> to victory with odds of "
    + odds[4] + ".</p>");
```

6. To save the project, select the **File** menu and then select **Save All**. To start the Web site, select the **Debug** menu and then select **Start Without Debugging**. The Web page should appear the same as it did before you replaced the variables with arrays.

7. Close your Web browser window, and then, in Visual Studio, select the **File** menu and then select **Close Project**.

Determining the Number of Elements in an Array

One useful array property that you should be aware of is the **Length property**, which returns the number of elements in an array. You append the `Length` property to the name of the array whose length you want to determine using the following syntax: *array_name.*`Length;`. Remember that property names are not followed by parentheses, as are method names. The following statements illustrate how to use the `Length` property to return the number of elements in the `curriculum[]` array:

```
Response.Write("<p>The curriculum[] array has "
    + curriculum.Length + " elements.</p>");
```

Short Quiz 3

1. What is the difference between loosely typed and strongly typed programming languages?

2. How do you decide which numeric data type to use for a variable?

3. What is the hexadecimal numeral system and how is it used with C# `char` variables?

4. What are the two techniques you can use to cast data types?

5. How do you declare and initialize an array?

Building Expressions

Variables and data become most useful when you use them in an expression. An **expression** is a literal value or variable or a combination of literal values, variables, operators, and other expressions that can be evaluated by the C# interpreter to produce a result. You use operands and operators to create expressions in C#. **Operands** are variables and literals contained in an expression. A **literal** is a value such as a literal string or a number. **Operators**, such as the addition operator (+) and multiplication operator (*), are symbols used in expressions to manipulate operands. You have worked with several simple expressions so far that combine operators and operands. Consider the following statement:

```
int simpleInterestRate = 10;
```

This statement is an expression that results in the value 10 being assigned to an integer variable named `simpleInterestRate`. The operands in the expression are the `simpleInterestRate` variable name and the integer value 10. The operator is the equal sign (=). The equal sign operator is a special kind of operator, called an assignment operator, because it assigns the value 10 on the right side of the expression to the variable (`simpleInterestRate`) on the left side of the expression. Table 2-5 lists the main types of C# operators. You'll learn more about specific operators in the following sections.

Category	Operators	Description
Arithmetic	addition (+), subtraction (–), multiplication (*), division (/), modulus (%), increment (++), decrement (--), negation (–)	Used for performing mathematical calculations
Assignment	assignment (=), compound addition assignment (+=), compound subtraction assignment (–=), compound multiplication assignment (*=), compound division assignment (/=), compound modulus assignment (%=)	Assigns values to variables
Comparison	equal (==), not equal (!=), greater than (>), less than (<), greater than or equal (>=), less than or equal (<=)	Compares operands and returns a Boolean value
Logical	and (&&), or (||), not (!)	Used for performing Boolean operations on Boolean operands
String	concatenation operator (+), compound assignment operator (+=)	Performs operations on strings
Special	property access (.), array index ([]), function calls, casts, order of precedence (()), comma (,), conditional expression (?:), delete (delete), property exists (in), object type (instanceof), new object (new), data type (typeof), void (void), pointer dereference and member access (->), variable size in bytes (sizeof)	Special operators are used for various purposes and do not fit within other operator categories

Table 2-5   C# operator categories

C# operators are binary or unary. A **binary operator** requires an operand before and after the operator. The equal sign in the statement int orderNumber = 300; is an example of a binary operator. A **unary operator** requires a single operand either before or after the operator. For example, the increment operator (++), an arithmetic operator, is used for increasing an operand by a value of one. The statement orderNumber++; changes the value of the orderNumber variable to "301".

Next, you will learn more about some of the different types of C# operators.

 Another type of C# operator, bitwise operators, operates on integer values and is a fairly complex topic. Bitwise operators and other complex operators are beyond the scope of this book.

Arithmetic Operators

Arithmetic operators are used in C# to perform mathematical calculations, such as addition, subtraction, multiplication, and division. You can also use an arithmetic operator to return the modulus of a calculation, which is the remainder left when you divide one number by another number.

Arithmetic Binary Operators

C# binary arithmetic operators and their descriptions are listed in Table 2-6.

Name	Operator	Description
Addition	+	Adds two operands
Subtraction	−	Subtracts one operand from another operand
Multiplication	*	Multiplies one operand by another operand
Division	/	Divides one operand by another operand
Modulus	%	Divides one operand by another operand and returns the remainder

Table 2-6   Arithmetic binary operators

The following code shows examples of expressions that include arithmetic binary operators. Figure 2-10 shows how the expressions appear in a Web browser.

```
// ADDITION
int x = 50;
int y = 75;
int returnValue = x + y;  // returnValue changes to 125
Response.Write("<p>Addition result: "
    + returnValue + "<br />");
// SUBTRACTION
x = 10;
y = 7;
returnValue = x - y;  // returnValue changes to 3
Response.Write("Subtraction result: "
    + returnValue + "<br />");
// MULTIPLICATION
x = 2;
y = 6;
returnValue = x * y;  // returnValue changes to 12
Response.Write("Multiplication result: "
    + returnValue + "<br />");
// DIVISION
x = 24;
y = 3;
returnValue = x / y;  // returnValue changes to 8
Response.Write("Division result: "
    + returnValue + "<br />");
// MODULUS
x = 3;
y = 2;
returnValue = x % y;  // returnValue changes to 1
Response.Write("Modulus result: "
    + returnValue + "</p>");
```

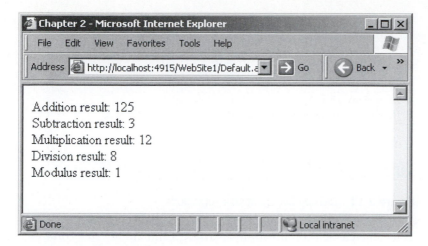

Figure 2-10 Results of arithmetic expressions

Notice in the preceding code that when C# performs an arithmetic calculation, it performs the operation on the right side of the assignment operator, and then assigns the value to a variable on the left side of the assignment operator. For example, in the statement int returnValue = x + y;, the operands x and y are added, and then the result is assigned to the returnValue variable on the left side of the assignment operator.

You might be confused by the difference between the division (/) operator and the modulus (%) operator. The division operator performs a standard mathematical division operation. For example, dividing 15 by 6 results in a value of 2.5. By contrast, the modulus operator returns the remainder that results from the division of two integers. The following code, for instance, uses the division and modulus operators to return the result of dividing 15 by 6. The division of 15 by 6 results in a value of 2.5, because 6 goes into 15 exactly 2.5 times. But if you only allow for whole numbers, 6 goes into 15 only 2 times, with a remainder of 3 left over. Therefore, the modulus of 15 divided by 6 is 3, because 3 is the remainder left over following the division. Figure 2-11 shows the output.

```
float divisionResult = 15 / 6;
float modulusResult = 15 % 6;
Response.Write("<p>15 divided by 6 is "
    + divisionResult + ".<br />"); // prints '2'
Response.Write("The whole number 6 goes into 15 twice, ");
Response.Write("with a remainder of " + modulusResult
    + ".</p>"); // prints '3'
```

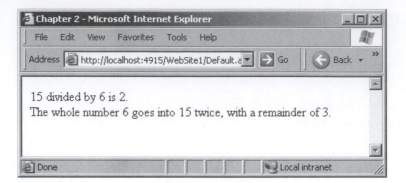

Figure 2-11   Division and modulus expressions

You can include a combination of variables and literal values on the right side of an assignment statement. For example, any of the following addition statements are correct:

```
returnValue = 100 + y;
returnValue = x + 200;
returnValue = 100 + 200;
```

However, you cannot include a literal value as the left operand because the C# interpreter must have a variable to which to assign the returned value. Therefore, the statement 100 = x + y; causes an error.

The C# interpreter does not convert strings to numbers when you use the addition operator. When you use the addition operator with strings, the strings are combined instead of being added together. In the following example, the last statement prints a value of "23" because the x and y variables contain strings instead of numbers:

```
string x = "2";
string y = "3";
Response.Write(x + y); // Prints "23"
```

Arithmetic Unary Operators

Arithmetic operations can also be performed on a single variable using unary operators. Table 2-7 lists the unary arithmetic operators available in C#.

Name	Operator	Description
Increment	++	Increases an operand by a value of one
Decrement	--	Decreases an operand by a value of one
Negation	-	Returns the opposite value (negative or positive) of an operand

Table 2-7   Arithmetic unary operators

The increment (++) and decrement (--) unary operators can be used as prefix or postfix operators. A **prefix operator** is placed before a variable. A **postfix operator** is placed after a variable. The statements ++myVariable; and myVariable++; both increase myVariable by one. However, the two statements return different values. When you use the increment operator as a prefix operator, the value of the operand is returned *after* it is increased by a value of one. When you use the increment operator as a postfix operator, the value of the operand is returned *before* it is increased by a value of one. Similarly, when you use the decrement operator as a prefix operator, the value of the operand is returned *after* it is decreased by a value of one, and when you use the decrement operator as a postfix operator, the value of the operand is returned *before* it is decreased by a value of one. If you intend to assign the incremented or decremented value to another variable, it makes a difference whether you use the prefix or postfix operator.

You use arithmetic unary operators in any situation in which you want to use a more simplified expression for increasing or decreasing a value by one. For example, the statement count = count + 1; is identical to the statement ++count;. As you can see, if your goal is only to increase a variable by one, it is easier to use the unary increment operator. But remember that with the prefix operator, the value of the operand is returned *after* it is increased or decreased by a value of one, whereas with the postfix operator, the value of the operand is returned *before* it is increased or decreased by a value of one.

For an example of when you would use the prefix operator or the postfix operator, consider an integer variable named studentID that is used for assigning student IDs in a class registration program. One way of creating a new student ID number is to store the last assigned student ID in the studentID variable. When it's time to assign a new student ID, the program could retrieve the last value stored in the studentID variable and then increase its value by one. In other words, the last value stored in the studentID variable will be the next number used for a student ID number. In this case, you would use the postfix operator to return the value of the expression *before* it is incremented by using a statement similar to currentID = studentID++;. If you are storing the last assigned student ID in the studentID variable, you would want to increment the value by one and use the result as the next student ID. In this scenario, you would use the prefix operator, which returns the value of the expression after it is incremented using a statement similar to currentID = ++studentID;.

Figure 2-12 shows a simple program that uses the prefix increment operator to assign three student IDs to a variable named curStudentID. The initial student ID is stored in the studentID variable and initialized to a starting value of "100". Figure 2-13 shows the output.

```
int studentID = 100;
int curStudentID = 0;
curStudentID = ++studentID; // assigns '101'
Response.Write("<p>The first student ID is "
    + curStudentID + ".<br />");
curStudentID = ++studentID; // assigns '102'
Response.Write("The second student ID is "
    + curStudentID + ".<br />");
curStudentID = ++studentID; // assigns '103'
Response.Write("The third student ID is "
    + curStudentID + ".<br />");
```

prefix increment operator

Figure 2-12 Program that uses the prefix increment operator

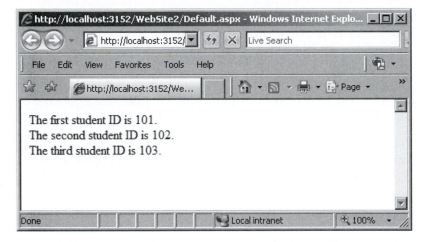

Figure 2-13 Output of the prefix version of the student ID program

The program in Figure 2-14 performs the same tasks, but using a postfix increment operator. Notice that the output in Figure 2-15 differs from the output in Figure 2-13. Because the first example of the program uses the prefix increment operator, which increments the studentID variable *before* it is assigned to curStudentID, the program does not use the starting value of "100". Rather, it first increments the studentID variable and uses "101" as the first student ID. By contrast, the second example of the program does use the initial value of "100" because the postfix increment operator increments the studentID variable *after* it is assigned to the curStudentID variable.

```
int studentID = 100;
int curStudentID = 0;
curStudentID = studentID++; // assigns '100'
Response.Write("<p>The first student ID is "
    + curStudentID + ".<br />");
curStudentID = studentID++; // assigns '101'
Response.Write("The second student ID is "
    + curStudentID + ".<br />");
curStudentID = studentID++; // assigns '102'
Response.Write("The third student ID is "
    + curStudentID + ".<br />");
```

postfix increment operator

Figure 2-14 Program that uses the postfix increment operator

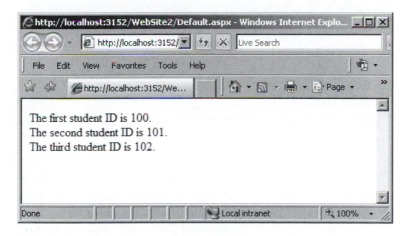

Figure 2-15 Output of the postfix version of the student ID program

Next, you will create a program that prints scoring statistics for the two highest all-time scorers in the NBA. The program uses addition, multiplication, and division to calculate total points and averages per game.

To create a program that prints the all-time NBA scoring statistics:

1. Return to the Visual Studio IDE, select the **File** menu and then select **New Web Site**. The New Web Site dialog box opens. In the Templates section, select **ASP.NET Web Site**. Leave the Location box set to **File System**, which creates the new Web site on your local file system, and the Language box set to **Visual C#**. Click the **Browse** button. The Choose Location dialog box opens.

2. In the File System section of the Choose Location dialog box, find the Chapter folder for Chapter 2 in the location where you installed the data files. Click the **Chapter** folder, and then click the **Create New Folder** button. Name the new folder

NBAScoringLeaders. Click the **Open** button, which closes the Choose Location dialog box, and then click **OK** in the New Web Site dialog box to create the new Web site. The Default.aspx file opens in the Code Editor.

3. Change the content of the `<title>` element to **NBA Scoring Leaders** and add the following `<link>` element above the closing `</head>` tag to link to the asp_styles.css style sheet:

```
<link rel="stylesheet" href="asp_styles.css"
type="text/css" />
```

4. To add the asp_styles.css style sheet to the project, select the **Website** menu and then select **Add Existing Item**. Locate the asp_styles.css file in your Chapter.02 folder, select it, and then click the **Add** button. The file is added to the Solution Explorer window.

5. Replace the `<form>` and `<div>` elements in the document body with the following heading element:

```
<h1>NBA</h1>
<h2>All-Time Scoring Leaders</h2>
```

6. Add the following code render block to the end of the document body:

```
<%
%>
```

7. Add to the script section the following statements, which create variables for the top basketball player, Michael Jordan. The first variable contains the player's name and the second variable contains the number of games played. The third variable contains the number of two-point baskets and the fourth variable contains the number of free throws. Notice that the fifth variable, which contains the total number of points, uses multiplication and addition to calculate the total number of points, whereas the sixth variable uses division to calculate the average number of points.

```
string leader1Name = "Michael Jordan";
int leader1Games = 933;
int leader1Baskets = 10989;
int leader1FreeThrows = 6814;
int leader1TotalPoints = leader1Baskets * 2
    + leader1FreeThrows;
double leader1AveragePoints = leader1TotalPoints
    / leader1Games;
```

8. Add to the end of the script section the following variable declaration and assignments for the second scoring leader, Wilt Chamberlain:

```
string leader2Name = "Wilt Chamberlain";
int leader2Games = 1045;
int leader2Baskets = 12681;
```

```
int leader2FreeThrows = 6057;
int leader2TotalPoints = leader1Baskets * 2
    + leader1FreeThrows;
double leader2AveragePoints = leader1TotalPoints
    / leader1Games;
```

9. Add the following statements to print the statistics:

```
Response.Write("<p><strong>" + leader1Name
    + "</strong> scored " + leader1Baskets
    + " two point baskets and "
    + leader1FreeThrows + " free throws in "
    + leader1Games + " games for a total of "
    + leader1TotalPoints + " points and averaging "
    + leader1AveragePoints
    + " points per game.</p>");
Response.Write("<p><strong>" + leader2Name
    + "</strong> scored " + leader2Baskets
    + " two point baskets and " + leader2FreeThrows
    + " free throws in " + leader2Games
    + " games for a total of " + leader2TotalPoints
    + " points and averaging " + leader2AveragePoints
    + " points per game.</p>");
```

10. To save the project, select the **File** menu and then select **Save All**. To start the Web site, select the **Debug** menu and then select **Start Without Debugging**. Figure 2-16 shows how the Web page appears in a Web browser window.

11. Close your Web browser window.

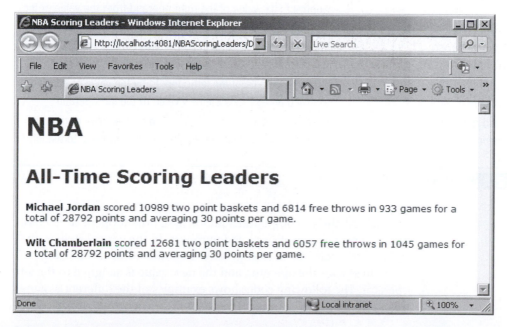

Figure 2-16 NBAScoringLeaders project in a Web browser

Assignment Operators

Assignment operators are used for assigning a value to a variable. You have already used the most common assignment operator, the equal sign (=), to initialize or assign values to variables. The equal sign assigns an initial value to a new variable or assigns a new value to an existing variable. For example, the following code creates a string variable named `language`, uses the equal sign to assign it an initial value, then uses the equal sign again to assign it a new value:

```
string language = "initial value";
language = "new value";
```

C# includes other assignment operators in addition to the equal sign. These additional assignment operators, called **compound assignment operators**, perform mathematical calculations on variables and literal values in an expression, and then assign a new value to the left operand. Table 2-8 lists the C# assignment operators.

Name	Operator	Description
Assignment	=	Assigns the value of the right operand to the left operand
Compound addition assignment	+=	Combines the value of the right operand with the value of the left operand or adds the value of the right operand to the value of the left operand and assigns the new value to the left operand
Compound subtraction assignment	-=	Subtracts the value of the right operand from the value of the left operand and assigns the new value to the left operand
Compound multiplication assignment	*=	Multiplies the value of the right operand by the value of the left operand and assigns the new value to the left operand
Compound division assignment	/=	Divides the value of the left operand by the value of the right operand and assigns the new value to the left operand
Compound modulus assignment	%=	Divides the value of the left operand by the value of the right operand and assigns the remainder (the modulus) to the left operand

Table 2-8   Assignment operators

You can use the += compound addition assignment operator to combine two strings as well as to add numbers. In the case of strings, the string on the left side of the operator is combined with the string on the right side of the operator, and the new value is assigned to the left operator. The following code shows examples of the different assignment operators.

```
float x = 100;
float y = 200;
x += y;            // x changes to 300
Response.Write(x + "<br />");
x = 10;
y = 7;
x -= y;            // x changes to 3
Response.Write(x + "<br />");
x = 2;
y = 6;
x *= y;            // x changes to 12
Response.Write(x + "<br />");
x = 24;
y = 3;
x /= y;            // x changes to 8
Response.Write(x + "<br />");
x = 3;
y = 2;
x %= y;            // x changes to 1
Response.Write(x + "</p>");
```

When used with strings, the plus sign is known as the concatenation operator. The **concatenation operator (+)** is used to combine two strings. You have already learned how to use the concatenation operator. For example, the following code combines two string variables and a literal string, and assigns the new value to another variable:

```
string city = "Llasa";
string country = "Tibet";
string destination = city
    + " is in the country of " + country;
Response.Write("<p>" + destination + ".</p>");
```

The combined value of the `city` variable, `country` variable, and string literal that is assigned to the `destination` variable is "Llasa is in the country of Tibet."

You can also use the compound assignment operator (+=) to combine two strings. The following code combines the text strings, but without using the `city` and `country` variables:

```
string destination = "Llasa";
destination += " is in the country of ";
destination += "Tibet";
Response.Write("<p>" + destination + ".</p>");
```

Comparison and Conditional Operators

Comparison operators are used to compare two operands and determine if one numeric value is greater than another. A Boolean value of true or false is returned after two operands are compared. For example, the statement 5 < 3 would return a Boolean value of false because 5 is not less than 3. Table 2-9 lists the C# comparison operators.

Name	Operator	Description
Equal	==	Returns true if the operands are equal
Not equal	!=	Returns true if the operands are not equal
Greater than	>	Returns true if the left operand is greater than the right operand
Less than	<	Returns true if the left operand is less than the right operand
Greater than or equal	>=	Returns true if the left operand is greater than or equal to the right operand
Less than or equal	<=	Returns true if the left operand is less than or equal to the right operand

Table 2-9 Comparison operators

The comparison operator (==) consists of two equal signs and performs a different function than the one performed by the assignment operator that consists of a single equal sign =. The comparison operator *compares* values, whereas the assignment operator *assigns* values.

Comparison operators are often used with two kinds of special statements: conditional statements and looping statements. You'll learn how to use comparison operators in such statements in Chapter 3.

You can use number, string, or character values as operands with comparison operators, but the values you compare must be of the same data type. When two numeric values are used as operands, the C# interpreter compares them numerically. The statement returnValue = 5 > 4; results in true because the number 5 is numerically greater than the number 4. When two nonnumeric values are used as operands, the C# interpreter compares them according to their hexadecimal Unicode number, not alphabetically. For example, the Unicode number for the uppercase letter *A* is 0041 while the Unicode number for the lowercase letter *a* is 0061. The statement returnValue = 'A' > 'a'; returns false because the lowercase letter *a* has a higher hexadecimal Unicode number than the uppercase letter *A*.

The comparison operator is often used with another kind of operator, the conditional operator. The **conditional operator** returns one of two results, based on the results of a conditional expression. The syntax for the conditional operator is *conditional_expression* ? *result1* : *result2*;. If the conditional expression evaluates to true, *result1* is assigned as the result of the operation. If the conditional expression evaluates to false, *result2* is assigned as the result of the operation. As an example, the first statement in the following code creates an integer variable named registeredStudents and assigns it a value of 25. The second statement then uses a conditional operator to determine whether the registeredStudents variable contains a value greater than or equal to 25. Because it does, the Boolean fullClass variable is assigned a value of true.

```
var registeredStudents = 25;
bool fullClass = registeredStudents >= 25
    ? true : false;
Response.Write("<p>Full class: " + fullClass + "</p>");
```

Next, you add a conditional operator to the NBAScoringLeaders project that determines which player participated in the most NBA final games.

To add a conditional operator to the NBAScoringLeaders project:

1. Return to the **Default.aspx** file of the NBAScoringLeaders project in the Visual Studio IDE.

2. Add the following conditional expression to the end of the script section. The conditional expression compares the value in the `leader1Games` and `leader2Games` variables, and then assigns an appropriate message to the `mostGames` variable, depending on which player participated in the most games.

```
string mostGames = leader1Games > leader2Games
    ? leader1Name
    + " competed in more NBA final games than "
    + leader2Name
    : leader2Name
    + " competed in more NBA final games than "
    + leader1Name;
```

3. Add the following statement to the end of the script section to print the value assigned to the `mostGames` variable:

```
Response.Write("<p>" + mostGames + ".</p>");
```

4. To save the project, select the **File** menu and then select **Save All**. To start the Web site, select the **Debug** menu and then select **Start Without Debugging**. Figure 2-17 shows how the Web page appears in a Web browser window.

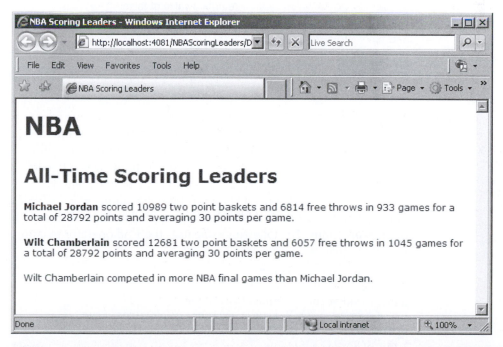

Figure 2-17 NBAScoringLeaders project in a Web browser after adding a conditional operator

5. Close your Web browser window, and then, in Visual Studio, select **File** and then click **Close Project** to close the project.

Logical Operators

Logical operators are used for comparing two Boolean operands for equality. For example, a program for an automobile insurance company might need to determine whether a customer is male *and* under 21 to determine the correct insurance quote. As with comparison operators, a Boolean value of true or false is returned after two operands are compared. Table 2-10 lists the C# logical operators.

Name	Operator	Description
And	&&	Returns true if both the left operand and right operand return a value of true; otherwise, it returns a value of false
Or	||	Returns true if either the left operand or right operand returns a value of true; if neither operand returns a value of true, the expression containing the Or || operator returns a value of false
Not	!	Returns true if an expression is false and returns false if an expression is true

Table 2-10   Logical operators

The Or (||) and the And (&&) operators are binary operators (requiring two operands), whereas the Not (!) operator is a unary operator (requiring a single operand). Logical operators are often used with comparison operators to evaluate expressions, allowing you to combine the results of several expressions into a single statement. For example, the And (&&) operator is used for determining whether two operands return an equivalent value. The operands themselves are often expressions. The following code uses the And operator to compare two separate expressions:

```
string gender = "male";
int age = 17;
bool riskFactor = gender == "male"
    && age <= 21 ? true : false; // returns true
Response.Write("<p>Insurance risk: " + riskFactor
    + "</p>");
```

In the preceding example, the conditional operator assigns the riskFactor variable a value of true because the gender value is equal to "male" and the age variable value is less than or equal to 21. Because the statement contains an And (&&) operator, it essentially says, "If variable gender is equal to "male" *and* variable age is less than or equal to 21, then assign a value of true to riskFactor. Otherwise, assign a value of false to riskFactor." In the following code, however, riskFactor is assigned a value of false because the age variable expression does not evaluate to true:

```
string gender = "male";
int age = 28;
bool riskFactor = gender == "male"
    && age <= 21 ? true : false; // returns false
Response.Write("<p>Insurance risk: " + riskFactor + "</p>");
```

The logical Or (||) operator checks to see if either expression evaluates to true. For example, the statement in the following code says, "If the variable speedingTickets is greater than 0 or variable age is less than or equal to 21, then assign a value of true to riskFactor. Otherwise, assign a value of false to riskFactor."

```
int speedingTickets = 2;
int age = 28;
bool riskFactor = speedingTickets > 0
    || age <= 21 ? true : false; // returns true
Response.Write("<p>Insurance risk: " + riskFactor + "</p>");
```

The riskFactor variable in the preceding example is assigned a value of true because the speedingTickets variable expression evaluates to true, even though the age variable expression evaluates to false. This result occurs because the Or (||) statement returns true if *either* the left *or* right operand evaluates to true.

The following code is an example of the Not (!) operator, which returns true if an operand evaluates to false and returns false if an operand evaluates to true. Notice that because the Not operator is unary, it requires only a single operand.

```
bool trafficViolations = true;
bool safeDriverDiscount = !trafficViolations
    ? true : false; // returns false
Response.Write("<p>Safe driver discount: "
    + safeDriverDiscount + "</p>");
```

Logical operators are often used within conditional and looping statements such as the if... else, for, and while statements. You will learn about conditional and looping statements in Chapter 3.

The conditional operator in the preceding example basically says, "If the trafficViolations variable is *not* false, then assign a value of true to the safeDriverDiscount variable. Otherwise, assign a value of false to the safeDriverDiscount variable." Because the trafficViolations variable is assigned a value of true, the safeDriverDiscount variable is assigned a value of false.

Short Quiz 4

1. What is the difference between operands and operators?

2. Explain the difference between binary and unary operators.

3. How do you use prefix and postfix operators?

4. Explain how the C# interpreter compares nonnumeric values.

5. How do you use the conditional operator?

Understanding Operator Precedence

When using operators to create expressions in C#, you need to be aware of the precedence of an operator. The term **operator precedence** refers to the order in which operations in an expression are evaluated. Table 2-11 shows the order of precedence for C# operators. Operators in the same grouping in Table 2-11 have the same order of precedence. When performing operations with operators in the same precedence group, the order of precedence is determined by the operator's **associativity**—that is, the order in which operators of equal precedence execute. Associativity is evaluated from left to right or from right to left depending on the operators involved, as explained shortly.

Operators	Description	Associativity
.	Objects	Left to right
()	Function calls/evaluations	
[]	Array elements	
++	Increment (postfix)	
--	Decrement (postfix)	
new	New object	
typeof	Data type	
+	Unary plus operator	Left to right
-	Unary minus operator	
!	Not	
++	Increment (prefix)	
--	Decrement (prefix)	
()	Casts	
*	Multiplication	Left to right
/	Division	
%	Modulus	
+	Addition	Left to right
-	Subtraction	
>	Greater than	Left to right
<	Less than	
>=	Greater than or equal	
<=	Less than or equal	
==	Equal to	Left to right
!=	Not equal to	
&&	Logical and	Left to right
||	Logical or	Left to right
?:	Conditional expression	Right to left
=	Assignment	Right to left
+=	Compound addition assignment	
-=	Compound subtraction assignment	
*=	Compound multiplication assignment	
/=	Compound division assignment	
%=	Compound modulus assignment	

Table 2-11 C# operator categories

Table 2-11 does not include bitwise operators and a few other advanced operators that are beyond the scope of this book.

Operators in a higher grouping have precedence over operators in a lower grouping. For example, the multiplication operator (*) has a higher precedence than the addition operator (+). Therefore, the statement 5 + 2 * 8 evaluates as follows: The numbers 2 and 8 are multiplied first for a total of 16, then the number 5 is added, resulting in a total of 21. If the addition operator had a higher precedence than the multiplication operator, the statement would evaluate to 56 because 5 would be added to 2 for a total of 7, which would then be multiplied by 8.

As an example of how associativity is evaluated, consider the multiplication and division operators. These operators have an associativity of left to right. Therefore, the statement 30 / 5 * 2 results in a value of 12. Although the multiplication and division operators have equal precedence, the division operation executes first because of the left-to-right associativity of both operators. Figure 2-18 conceptually illustrates the left-to-right associativity of the 30 / 5 * 2 statement.

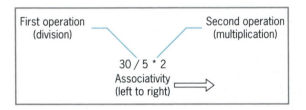

Figure 2-18   Conceptual illustration of left-to-right associativity

If the multiplication operator had higher precedence than the division operator, the statement 30 / 5 * 2 would result in a value of 3 because the multiplication operation (5 * 2) would execute first. By contrast, the assignment operator and compound assignment operators—such as the compound multiplication assignment operator (*=)—have an associativity of right to left. Therefore, in the following code, the assignment operations take place from right to left. The variable *x* is incremented by one *before* it is assigned to the *y* variable using the compound multiplication assignment operator (*=). Then, the value of variable y is assigned to variable x. The result assigned to both the *x* and *y* variables is 8. Figure 2-19 conceptually illustrates the right-to-left associativity of the x = y *= ++x statement.

```
int x = 3;
int y = 2;
x = y *= ++x;
```

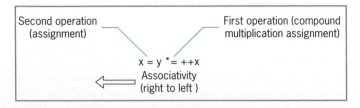

Figure 2-19   Conceptual illustration of right-to-left associativity

As you can see from Table 2-11, parentheses are in the highest order of precedence grouping. Parentheses are used with expressions to change the associativity with which individual operations in an expression are evaluated. For example, the statement 5 + 2 * 8, which evaluates to 21, can be rewritten to (5 + 2) * 8, which evaluates to 56. The parentheses tell the C# interpreter to add the numbers 5 and 2 before multiplying by the number 8. Using parentheses forces the statement to evaluate to 56 instead of 21.

Short Quiz 5

1. What is associativity and how does it affect operator precedence?

2. Which operators have the highest order of precedence?

3. Which operators have the lowest order of precedence?

Summing Up

- Code render blocks define inline code or inline expressions that execute when a Web page renders. Inline code refers to one or more individual code lines, or statements, contained within a code render block.

- To declare the language that ASP.NET will use, you must use an ASP processing directive, which provides a Web server with information on how to process the code in an ASP.NET document.

- The term object-oriented programming (OOP) refers to the creation of reusable software objects that can be easily incorporated into another program.

- Comments are nonprinting lines that you place in your code to contain various types of remarks.

- The values a program stores in computer memory are commonly called variables.

- The name you assign to a variable is called an identifier.

- Keywords (also called reserved words) are special words that are part of the C# language syntax.

- A constant contains information that does not change during the course of program execution.

- A data type is the specific category of information that a variable contains.

- C# is a strongly typed programming language.

- An integer is a positive or negative number with no decimal places.

- A floating-point number is a number that contains decimal places or that is written in exponential notation.

- A Boolean value is a logical value of true or false.

- The char data type stores any single character or escaped hexadecimal Unicode character contained within single quotation marks.

- You use the string data type to store text string variables.

- Casting, or type casting, copies the value contained in a variable of one data type into a variable of another data type.

- An array contains a set of data represented by a single variable name.

- An expression is a literal value or variable or a combination of literal values, variables, operators, and other expressions that can be evaluated by the C# interpreter to produce a result.

- Arithmetic operators are used in C# to perform mathematical calculations, such as addition, subtraction, multiplication, and division.

- Assignment operators are used for assigning a value to a variable.

- Compound assignment operators perform mathematical calculations on variables and literal values in an expression and then assign a new value to the left operand.

- Comparison operators are used to compare two operands and determine if one numeric value is greater than another.

- The conditional operator returns one of two results, based on the results of a conditional expression.

- Logical operators are used for comparing two Boolean operands for equality.

- Operator precedence refers to the order in which operations in an expression are evaluated.

- When performing operations with operators in the same precedence group, the order of precedence is determined by the operator's associativity—that is, the order in which operators of equal precedence execute.

Comprehension Check

1. Which of the following delimiters are a shortcut for calling the `Write()` method of the `Response` object?

   a. `<+ ... >`

   b. `<@ ... >`

   c. `<= ... >`

   d. `<~ ... >`

2. What is a variable and how is it used in C#?

3. Which of the following are valid identifiers? (Choose all that apply.)

   a. `int _copyrightYear = 2009;`

   b. `int 2008Copyright Year = true;`

   c. `int $CopyrightYear = 2009;`

   d. `int copyrightYear = 2009;`

4. Variable names are case sensitive. True or False?

5. Which of the following variable declaration statements is valid? (Choose all that apply.)

   a. `highwaySpeed;`

   b. `int highwaySpeed;`

   c. `int highwaySpeed = 65;`

   d. `int highwaySpeed(65);`

6. Which of the following statements correctly prints the value of a variable named `endFiscalYear`? (Choose all that apply.)

   a. `Response.Write("<p>The fiscal year ends on" + endFiscalYear + "</p>");`

   b. `Response.Write ("<p>The fiscal year ends on + endFiscalYear + </p>");`

   c. `Response.Write ("<p>endfiscalYear</p>");`

   d. `Response.Write ("endFiscalYear);`

124

7. Explain the concept of data types.

8. C# is a strongly typed programming language. True or False?

9. Which of the following values is an integer? (Choose all that apply.)

   a. 1

   b. 1.1

   c. 4e12

   d. −10

10. Which of the following letters must you append to a floating-point literal value to successfully assign it to a double variable?

    a. D

    b. F

    c. M

    d. P

11. Which of the following values can be assigned to a Boolean variable? (Choose all that apply.)

    a. 0

    b. 1

    c. true

    d. false

12. Which of the following statements contains valid syntax for casting an `int` variable named `stockPrice` to a `float` variable named `securityPrice`?

    a. `float securityPrice = stockPrice(float);`

    b. `float (float)securityPrice = stockPrice;`

    c. `float securityPrice(float) = stockPrice;`

    d. `float securityPrice = (float)stockPrice;`

13. The identifiers you use for an array name must follow the same rules as identifiers for variables. True or False?

14. What is the correct syntax for creating a double array named `taxBrackets` that contains five elements?

    a. `new double Array(taxRules) = 5;`

    b. `double Array(taxRules) + 5;`

    c. `double taxBrackets = Array(5);`

    d. `double taxBrackets = new double[5];`

15. Which of the following properties returns the number of elements in an array?

    a. `Length`

    b. `Size`

    c. `Elements`

    d. `Indexes`

16. The Or || operator returns true if _____.

    a. the left operand and right operand both return a value of true

    b. the left operand returns a value of true

    c. the left operand and right operand both return a value of false

    d. the right operand returns a value of true

17. Which of the following characters separates expressions in a conditional expression?

    a. ?

    b. :

    c. ;

    d. &&

18. The concatenation operator (+) is used for _____. (Choose all that apply.)

    a. adding numbers

    b. combining text strings

    c. combining variables

    d. incrementing numeric variables

19. Which of the following is the correct syntax for including double quotation marks within a string that is already surrounded by double quotation marks?

    a. `"Ralph Nader is a \"third party\" presidential candidate."`

    b. `"Ralph Nader is a "third party" presidential candidate."`

    c. `"Ralph Nader is a /"third party/" presidential candidate."`

    d. `"Ralph Nader is a ""third party"" presidential candidate."`

20. Which of the following expressions returns a value of 78?

    a. $6 * (9 + 4)$

    b. $(6 * 9) + 4$

    c. $(6 * 9 + 4)$

    d. $9 + 4 * 6$

Reinforcement Exercises

Exercise 1

In this project, you will create a Web page that uses variables to display information about the five largest islands in the world.

1. Open the Visual Studio IDE, select the **File** menu and then select **New Web Site**. The New Web Site dialog box opens. In the Templates section, select **ASP.NET Web Site**. Leave the Location box set to **File System**, which creates the new Web site on your local file system, and the Language box set to **Visual C#**. Click the **Browse** button. The Choose Location dialog box opens.

2. In the File System section of the Choose Location dialog box, find the Exercises folder for Chapter 2 in the location where you installed the data files. Click the **Exercises** folder, and then click the **Create New Folder** button. Name the new folder **LargestIslands**. Click the **Open** button, which closes the Choose Location dialog box, and then click **OK** in the New Web Site dialog box to create the new Web site. The Default.aspx file opens in the Code Editor.

3. Change the content of the `<title>` element to **Largest Islands** and add the following `<link>` element above the closing `</head>` tag to link to the asp_styles.css style sheet:

```
<link rel="stylesheet" href="asp_styles.css"
type="text/css" />
```

4. To add the asp_styles.css style sheet to the project, select the **Website** menu and then select **Add Existing Item**. Locate the asp_styles.css file in your Chapter.02 folder, select it, and then click the **Add** button. The file is added to the Solution Explorer window.

5. Replace the `<form>` and `<div>` elements in the document body with the following heading element:

```
<h1>Largest Islands</h1>
```

6. Add the following code render block to the end of the document body:

```
%>
<%
```

7. In the script section, type the following statements that declare variables containing the names and size of the world's five largest islands:

```
string island1Name = "Greenland";
string island2Name = "New Guinea";
string island3Name = "Borneo";
string island4Name = "Madagascar";
string island5Name = "Baffin";
int island1Size = 2175600;
int island2Size = 790000;
int island3Size = 737000;
int island4Size = 587000;
int island5Size = 507000;
```

8. Next, add the following statements to the end of the script section that print the values stored in each of the variables you declared and initialized in the preceding step:

```
Response.Write("<p>The largest island in the world is "
  + island1Name + " with " + island1Size + " miles.</p>");
Response.Write("<p>The second island in the world is "
  + island2Name + " with " + island2Size + " miles.</p>");
Response.Write("<p>The third island in the world is "
  + island3Name + " with " + island3Size + " miles.</p>");
Response.Write("<p>The fourth island in the world is "
  + island4Name + " with " + island4Size + " miles.</p>");
Response.Write("<p>The fifth island in the world is "
  + island5Name + " with " + island5Size + " miles.</p>");
```

9. To save the project, select the **File** menu and then select **Save All**. To start the Web site, select the **Debug** menu and then select **Start Without Debugging**. The island names and their size print to the browser window.

10. Close your Web browser window.

Exercise 2

In this project, you will modify the Largest Islands Web page so the island names and sizes are stored in arrays.

1. Return to the **Default.aspx** file of the LargestIslands project in the Visual Studio IDE.

2. Replace the island name variables with the following array declaration and element assignments:

```
string[] islandNames = new string[5];
islandNames[0] = "Greenland";
islandNames[1] = "New Guinea";
islandNames[2] = "Borneo";
islandNames[3] = "Madagascar";
islandNames[4] = "Baffin";
```

3. Replace the island size variables with the following array declaration and element assignments:

```
int[] islandSizes = new int[5];
islandSizes[0] = 2175600;
islandSizes[1] = 790000;
islandSizes[2] = 737000;
islandSizes[3] = 587000;
islandSizes[4] = 507000;
```

4. Finally, modify the `Response.Write()` statements so they reference the new arrays and elements. The portions of each statement that you need to modify are set in bold in the following code:

```
Response.Write("<p>The largest island in the world is "
   + islandNames[0] + " with " + islandSizes[0]
   + " miles.</p>");
Response.Write("<p>The second island in the world is "
   + islandNames[1] + " with " + islandSizes[1]
   + " miles.</p>");
Response.Write("<p>The third island in the world is "
   + islandNames[2] + " with " + islandSizes[2]
   + " miles.</p>");
Response.Write("<p>The fourth island in the world is "
   + islandNames[3] + " with " + islandSizes[3]
   + " miles.</p>");
```

```
Response.Write("<p>The fifth island in the world is "
    + islandNames[4] + " with " + islandSizes[4]
    + " miles.</p>");
```

5. To save the project, select the **File** menu and then select **Save All**. To start the Web site, select the **Debug** menu and then select **Start Without Debugging**. The output should appear the same as they did before you converted the variables to arrays.

6. Close your Web browser window, and then, in Visual Studio, select **File** and then click **Close Project** to close the project.

Exercise 3

In this project, you will create a program that uses logical operators.

1. Open the Visual Studio IDE, select the **File** menu and then select **New Web Site**. The New Web Site dialog box opens. In the Templates section, select **ASP.NET Web Site**. Leave the Location box set to **File System**, which creates the new Web site on your local file system, and the Language box set to **Visual C#**. Click the **Browse** button. The Choose Location dialog box opens.

2. In the File System section of the Choose Location dialog box, find the Exercises folder for Chapter 2 in the location where you installed the data files. Click the **Exercises** folder, and then click the **Create New Folder** button. Name the new folder **OrderFulfillment**. Click the **Open** button, which closes the Choose Location dialog box, and then click **OK** in the New Web Site dialog box to create the new Web site. The Default.aspx file opens in the Code Editor.

3. Change the content of the `<title>` element to **Order Fulfillment** and add the following `<link>` element above the closing `</head>` tag to link to the asp_styles.css style sheet:

```
<link rel="stylesheet" href="asp_styles.css"
type="text/css" />
```

4. To add the asp_styles.css style sheet to the project, select the **Website** menu and then select **Add Existing Item**. Locate the asp_styles.css file in your Chapter.02 folder, select it, and then click the **Add** button. The file is added to the Solution Explorer window.

5. Replace the `<form>` and `<div>` elements in the document body with the following heading element:

    ```
    <h1>Order Fulfillment</h1>
    ```

6. Add the following code render block to the end of the document body:

    ```
    <%
    %>
    ```

7. Add the following statements to the script section that use logical operators on two variables:

    ```
    bool orderPlaced = true;
    bool orderFilled = false;
    Response.Write("<p>Order has been placed: "
      + orderPlaced + "<br />");
    Response.Write("Order has been filled: "
      + orderFilled + "<br />");
    bool orderComplete = orderPlaced && orderFilled;
    Response.Write("Order has been placed and filled: "
      + orderComplete + "</p>");
    ```

8. To save the project, select the **File** menu and then select **Save All**. To start the Web site, select the **Debug** menu and then select **Start Without Debugging**. The output statements print to the browser window.

9. Close your Web browser window, and then, in Visual Studio, select the **File** menu and then select **Close Project** to close the project.

Exercise 4

In this project, you will create a program that contains the formula for converting Fahrenheit temperatures to Celsius. You will need to modify the formula to use the correct order of precedence to convert the temperature.

1. Open the Visual Studio IDE, select the **File** menu and then select **New Web Site**. The New Web Site dialog box opens. In the Templates section, select **ASP.NET Web Site**. Leave the Location box set to **File System**, which creates the new Web site on your local file system, and the Language box set to **Visual C#**. Click the **Browse** button. The Choose Location dialog box opens.

2. In the File System section of the Choose Location dialog box, find the Exercises folder for Chapter 2 in the location where you installed the data files. Click the **Exercises** folder, and then click the **Create New Folder** button. Name the new

folder **ConvertToCelcius**. Click the **Open** button, which closes the Choose Location dialog box, and then click **OK** in the New Web Site dialog box to create the new Web site. The Default.aspx file opens in the Code Editor.

3. Change the content of the `<title>` element to **Convert to Celcius** and add the following `<link>` element above the closing `</head>` tag to link to the asp_styles.css style sheet:

```
<link rel="stylesheet" href="asp_styles.css"
type="text/css" />
```

4. To add the asp_styles.css style sheet to the project, select the **Website** menu and then select **Add Existing Item**. Locate the asp_styles.css file in your Chapter.02 folder, select it, and then click the **Add** button. The file is added to the Solution Explorer window.

5. Replace the `<form>` and `<div>` elements in the document body with the following code render block to the end of the document body:

```
<%
%>
```

6. Add to the script section the following declaration for a variable named `fTemp` that represents a Fahrenheit temperature. The variable is assigned a value of 72 degrees.

```
int fTemp = 86;
```

7. Add the following two statements to the end of the script section. The first statement declares a variable named `cTemp` that will store the converted temperature. The right operand includes the formula for converting from Fahrenheit to Celsius. (Remember that this formula is incorrect—you still need to correct the order of precedence.) The last statement prints the value assigned to the `cTemp` variable.

```
double cTemp = fTemp - 32 * 5 / 9;
Response.Write("<p>" + fTemp
    + " Fahrenheit is equal to "
    + cTemp + " degrees Celsius.</p>");
```

8. To save the project, select the **File** menu and then select **Save All**. To start the Web site, select the **Debug** menu and then select **Start Without Debugging**. The formula is incorrectly calculating that 86 degrees Fahrenheit is equivalent to a value of 69 Celsius. Close your Web browser window and return to the **Default.aspx** document in your text editor.

9. Modify the order of precedence in the Fahrenheit-to-Celsius formula by adding parentheses as follows so it correctly calculates a value of 30 degrees Celsius for 86 degrees Fahrenheit:

```
double cTemp = (fTemp - 32) * 5 / 9;
```

10. To save the project, select the **File** menu and then select **Save All**. To start the Web site, select the **Debug** menu and then select **Start Without Debugging**. The temperature should calculate correctly as 30 degrees Celsius.

11. Close your Web browser window, and then, in Visual Studio, select the **File** menu and then click **Close Project** to close the project.

Discovery Projects

Save your Discovery Projects document in the Discovery folder for Chapter 2.

Project 2-1

The formula for calculating body mass index (BMI) is weight * 703 / height^2. For example, if you weigh 200 pounds and are 72 inches tall, you can calculate your body mass index with this expression: (200 * 703) / (72 * 72). Create a program that declares and assigns two integer variables: one for your weight in pounds and another for your height in inches. Declare another variable and assign to it the results of the body mass calculation. Use Response.Write() statements to print the value of the weight, height, and BMI variables. Include text in the Response.Write() statements that describes each measure, such as "Your weight is 200 pounds." Save the Web site in a folder named **BMI**.

Project 2-2

Table 2-12 lists the total world carbon dioxide emissions from fossil fuel consumption for various years from 1980 to 2003.

Year	Million metric tons
1980	18313.13
1985	19430.24
1990	21402.22
1995	22034.54
2000	23849.00
2002	24464.92
2003	25162.07

Table 2-12   World carbon dioxide emissions from fossil fuel

Create a program that contains two arrays: one for the emission years and one for the amount of emissions in each year. Use `Response.Write()` statements to print the amount of emissions in each year with statements similar to "In 1980, the world generated 18313.13 million metric tons of carbon dioxide emissions from fossil fuel consumption." Save the Web site in a folder named **CO2Emissions**.

Project 2-3

Write a program that calculates the cost of an event, such as a wedding. Create a string variable for the name of the event and numeric variables for the number of guests, cost per guest, and number of limousines. Also, create Boolean variables for live music, flowers, and open bar. Assign whatever value you want to the event name, number of guests, cost per guest, and number of limousines variables. Assume that each limousine costs $100 for the event. Assign the total event cost to another variable. Use a conditional expression to determine whether the value assigned to the live music variable is equal to true. If so, add $500 to the total cost of the event. Use another conditional expression to determine whether the value assigned to the flowers variable is equal to true. If so, add $300 to the total cost of the event. Use one more conditional expression to determine whether the value assigned to the open bar is equal to true. If so, add $30 for each of the expected number of guests to the total cost of the event. Use arithmetic operators to determine the cost of each item and for the entire event and `Response.Write()` statements to print a breakdown of each cost and the total estimated cost. Assume that the location of the event has a maximum capacity of 500. Use a conditional expression to determine whether the value assigned to the number of guests variable meets or exceeds the location's maximum capacity. If the number of guests exceeds the maximum capacity, print "You have invited too many guests" in parentheses at the end of the statement that prints the number of guests. Save the Web site in a folder named **Wedding Event**.

CHAPTER 3

Using Functions, Methods, and Control Structures

In this chapter you will:

◎ Learn how to use functions to organize your C# code

◎ Work with the `Request` object

◎ Use `if` statements, `if...else` statements, and `switch` statements to make decisions

◎ Use `while` statements, `do...while` statements, and `for` statements to execute code repeatedly

So far, the code you have written has consisted of simple statements placed within script sections. However, almost all programming languages, including C#, allow you to group programming statements in logical units. In C#, groups of statements that you can execute as a single unit are called functions. You'll learn how to use functions in this chapter.

The code you have written so far has also been linear in nature. In other words, your programs start at the beginning and end when the last statement in the program executes. Decision-making and flow-control statements allow you to determine the order in which statements execute in a program. Controlling the flow of code and making decisions during program execution are two of the most fundamental skills required in programming. In this chapter, you will learn about both decision-making statements and flow-control statements.

Working with Functions

In Chapter 2, you learned that procedures associated with an object are called methods. In C# programming, you can write your own procedures, called **functions**, which are used to organize a related group of C# statements as a single unit. Functions are similar to the methods associated with an object. In the following section, you'll learn more about incorporating functions in your scripts. But first, you need to learn how to create code declaration blocks.

Creating Code Declaration Blocks

In Chapter 2, you learned how to use code render blocks to define inline C# code. Although code render blocks are fine for simple ASP.NET statements, in practice, they are of limited use and can be difficult to maintain and debug. Further, it is considered poor programming practice to use code render blocks to create complex programs. A better solution is **code declaration blocks**, which use <script> elements to contain ASP.NET functions and global variables. (You will study functions and global variables later in this chapter.) With ASP.NET, you use two attributes in a code declaration block: runat="server" and language. The runat="server" attribute is required to identify the script section as an ASP.NET program. The language attribute identifies the scripting language used within the code declaration block. Recall that with ASP.NET, you can use Visual Basic or C# as the scripting language within a code render block. The following code contains an example of a code declaration block that uses C# as the scripting language:

If a Web page that contains a code declaration block includes the @ Page processing directive with a Language attribute to declare a page's scripting language, you can exclude the language attribute from the <script> element.

```
<script language="C#" runat="server">
...
</script>
```

Defining Functions

Before you can use a function in a C# program, you must first create, or define, it. The lines that make up a function are called the **function definition**. The syntax for defining a function is:

```
returnDataType nameOfFunction(parameters)
{
    statements;
}
```

In many instances, you might want your program to receive the results from a called function and then use those results in other code. In C#, you must specify the type of any data that you want to return from a function. If you do not need to return data from a function, you use the void keyword as the data type. The **void keyword** specifies that a function or method does not return a value. Later in this section, you will learn how to return data from a function.

The parentheses that follow a function name contain parameters. A **parameter** is a variable that is used within a function. Placing a parameter name within the parentheses of a function definition is the equivalent of declaring a new variable. As with regular variables, you must declare a parameter's data type.

For example, suppose you want to write a function named calcSquareRoot() that calculates the square root of a number contained in a double parameter named baseNumber. You would then write the function name as: calcSquareRoot(double baseNumber). This function declaration declares a new parameter (which is a variable) named baseNumber.

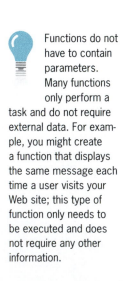

Functions do not have to contain parameters. Many functions only perform a task and do not require external data. For example, you might create a function that displays the same message each time a user visits your Web site; this type of function only needs to be executed and does not require any other information.

Functions can contain multiple parameters separated by commas. To add three separate number parameters to the calcSquareRoot() function, you would write the function name as calcSquareRoot(baseNumber1, baseNumber2, baseNumber3). Note that parameters (such as the baseNumber1, baseNumber2, and baseNumber3 parameters) receive their values when you call the function from elsewhere in your program. (You will learn how to call functions in the next section.)

Following the parentheses that contain the function parameters is a set of curly braces (called function braces) that contain the function statements. Function statements are the statements that do the actual work of the function (such as calculating the square root of the parameter, or displaying a message on the screen) and must be contained within the function braces. The following is an example of a function that prints the names of multiple companies using the Write() methods of the Response object. (Recall that functions are very similar to the methods associated with an object.)

```csharp
void printCompanyNames(string company1, string company2,
    string company3)
{
    Response.Write("<p>" + company1 + "</p>");
    Response.Write("<p>" + company2 + "</p>");
    Response.Write("<p>" + company3 + "</p>");
}
```

Notice how the preceding function is structured. Each statement between the curly braces is indented five spaces. This structure is the format preferred by many programmers. However, for simple functions it is sometimes easier to include the function name, curly braces, and statements on the same line. (Recall that C# ignores line breaks, spaces, and tabs.) The only syntax requirement for spacing in C# is that semicolons separate statements on the same line. For example, the following simplified version of the printCompanyNames() function accepts a single parameter. Notice that the function is declared with a single statement.

```csharp
void printCompanyNames(string company1)
    { Response.Write("<p>" + company1 + "</p>"); }
```

Calling Functions

A function definition does not execute the function. Creating a function definition only names the function, specifies its parameters, and organizes the statements it will execute. To execute a function, you must invoke, or **call**, it from elsewhere in your program. The code that calls a function is referred to as a **function call** and consists of the function name followed by parentheses that contain any variables or values to be assigned to the function parameters. The variables or values that you place in the parentheses of the function call statement are called **arguments** or **actual parameters**. Sending arguments to the parameters of a called function is called **passing arguments**. When you pass arguments to a function, the value of each argument is then assigned to the value of the corresponding parameter in the function definition. (Again, remember that parameters are simply variables that are declared within a function definition.) In C#, you cannot execute a function from a code declaration block. Instead, you must execute a function from a code render block or from another function. The following code demonstrates how to call the printCompanyNames() function from a code render block:

```csharp
<% printCompanyNames("Oracle", "Microsoft", "SAP"); %>
```

With some programming languages, it is necessary to put a function definition above any calling statements to ensure that the function was created before it was actually called. This convention is not necessary in C#, but other scripting languages, including JavaScript, still require you to follow this convention. Even though this convention is not required in C#, you should continue to place your function definitions above any calling statements for good programming practice and to keep your programming skills portable to other languages. The following code shows the function definition and function call for the printCompanyNames() function. Notice that the function is defined above the calling statement. Figure 3-1 shows the output in a Web browser.

```
<script runat="server">
    void printCompanyNames(string company1,
      string company2, string company3)
      {
          Response.Write("<p>" + company1 + "</p>");
          Response.Write("<p>" + company2 + "</p>");
          Response.Write("<p>" + company3 + "</p>");
      }
</script>
<% printCompanyNames("Oracle", "Microsoft", "SAP"); %>
```

The preceding program contains a statement that calls the function and passes the literal strings "Oracle", "Microsoft", and "SAP" to the function. When the printCompanyNames() function receives the literal strings, it assigns them to the company1, company2, and company3 parameters.

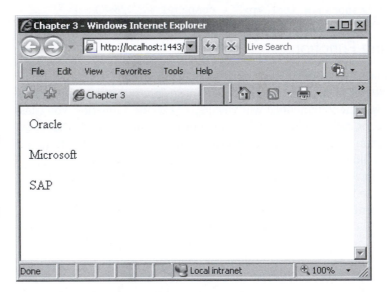

Figure 3-1   Output of a call to a custom function

Returning Values

In many instances, you might want your program to receive the results from a called function and then use those results in other code. For instance, consider a function that calculates the average of a series of numbers that are passed to it as arguments. Such a function would be useless if your program could not print or use the result elsewhere. You can return a value from a function to a calling statement by assigning the calling statement to a variable. The first statement in the following example calls a function named averageNumbers() and assigns the return value to a variable named returnValue. The statement also passes three literal values to the function. The second statement then prints the value assigned to the returnValue variable.

```
<%
    double returnValue = averageNumbers(7, 13, 25);
    Response.Write(returnValue);
%>
```

To actually return a value to a returnValue variable, the code must include a return statement within the averageNumbers() function. A **return statement** is a statement that returns a value to the statement that called the function. The following program contains the averageNumbers() function, which calculates the average of three numbers. The program also includes a return statement that returns the value (contained in the result variable) to the calling statement.

```
<script runat="server">
double averageNumbers(double paramA, double paramB,
    double paramC)
{
    double sumOfNumbers = paramA + paramB + paramC;
    double result = sumOfNumbers / 3.0;
    return result;
}
</script>
```

In scripts that include functions, where and how you declare variables is very important. In the following section, you will study variable scope, a topic that will help you understand how to use variables in scripts that include functions.

Next, you will create a program that contains two functions. The first function will print a message when it is called, and the second function will return a value that is printed after the calling statement.

To create a program that contains two functions:

1. Click the **Start** button, point to **All Programs**, and then click **Microsoft Visual Web Developer 2008 Express Edition**. The Visual Studio integrated development environment (IDE) opens.

2. Select the **File** menu and then select **New Web Site**. The New Web Site dialog box opens. Select **ASP.NET Web Site** from the Templates section. Leave the Location box set to **File System**, which creates the new Web site on your local file system, and the Language box set to **Visual C#**. Click the **Browse** button. The Choose Location dialog box opens.

3. In the File System section of the Choose Location dialog box, find the Chapter folder for Chapter 3 in the location where you installed the data files. Click the **Chapter** folder, and then click the **Create New Folder** button. Name the new folder **TwoFunctions**. Click the **Open** button, which closes the Choose Location dialog box, and then click **OK** in the New Web Site dialog box to create the new Web site. The Default.aspx file opens in the Code Editor window.

4. Change the content of the `<title>` element to **Two Functions** and add the following `<link>` element above the closing `</uhead>` tag to link to the asp_styles.css style sheet in your Chapter.03 folder:

```
<link rel="stylesheet" href="asp_styles.css"
type="text/css" />
```

5. To add the asp_styles.css style sheet to the project, select the **Website** menu and then select **Add Existing Item**. Locate the asp_styles.css file in your Chapter.03 folder, select it, and then click the **Add** button. The file is added to the Solution Explorer window.

6. Replace the `<form>` and `<div>` elements in the document body with the following heading elements:

```
<h1>Two Functions</h1>
```

7. Add the following code declaration block to the end of the document body:

```
<script runat="server">
</script>
```

8. Add the first function to the code declaration block as follows. This function writes a message to the screen using an argument that will be passed to it from the calling statement.

```
void printMessage(string firstMessage)
{
    Response.Write("<p>" + firstMessage + "</p>");
}
```

9. Add the second function, which displays a second message, to the end of the script section. In this case, the message ("This message was returned from a function.") is defined within the function itself. The only purpose of this function is to return the literal string "This message was returned from a function." to the calling statement.

```
string returnMessage()
{
    return "<p>This message was returned from
        a function.</p>";
}
```

10. Add the following code render block to the end of the document body:

```
<%
%>
```

11. Add to the code render block the following three statements, which call the functions in the document head. The first statement sends the text string "This message was printed from a function." This statement does not receive a return value. The second statement assigns the function call to a variable named return_value, but does not send any arguments to the function. The third statement writes the value of the return_value variable to the screen.

```
printMessage("This message was printed from a
    function.");
string return_value = returnMessage();
Response.Write(return_value);
```

12. Start the project by selecting the **Debug** menu and then by selecting **Start Without Debugging**. Figure 3-2 shows how the Web page opens in a Web browser window.

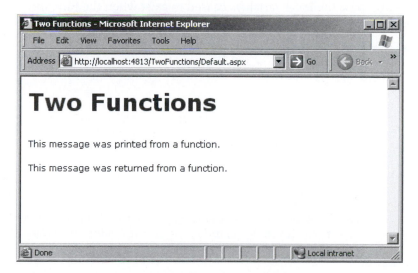

Figure 3-2   Two functions program in a Web browser

13. Close your Web browser window and then close the project by selecting the **File** menu and then selecting **Close Project**.

Understanding Variable Scope

When you use a variable in a C# program, particularly a complex ASP.NET program, you need to be aware of the **variable's scope**— that is, you need to think about where in your program a declared variable can be used. A variable's scope can be either global or local. A **global variable** is one that is declared within a code declaration block, but outside a function, and is available to all parts of your page. A **local variable** is declared inside a function or code render block and is only available within the function or code render block in which it is declared. Local variables cease to exist when the function or code render block ends. If you attempt to use a local variable outside the function in which it is declared, you will receive an error message.

The following program includes a global variable named `salesPrice` and a function containing two variable declarations. The variable declarations in the function, for the `shippingPrice` and `totalPrice` variables, are local to the function. Both the global variable and the function are contained in a code declaration block. When the function is called from the code render block, the global variable and the local variables print successfully from within the function. After the call to the function, the global variable again prints successfully from the code render block. However, when the program tries to print the local variables (`shippingPrice` and `totalPrice`) from the document body, an error message is generated because the local variables ceased to exist when the function ended.

```
<script runat="server">
    double salesPrice = 100.00;
    void applyShipping()
    {
        double shippingPrice = 8.95;
        double totalPrice = salesPrice + shippingPrice;
        Response.Write("<p>The sales price is $"
            + salesPrice + "<br />"); // prints
            successfully
        Response.Write("The shipping price is $"
          + shippingPrice + "<br />");  // prints
            successfully
        Response.Write("The sales price plus shipping is $"
          + totalPrice + "</p>"); // prints successfully
    }
</script>

<%
    applyShipping();
    Response.Write("<p>The sales price is $"
        + salesPrice + "<br />"); // prints successfully
```

```
Response.Write("The shipping price is $"
    + shippingPrice + "<br />"); // error message
Response.Write("The sales price plus shipping is $"
    + totalPrice + "</p>"); // error message
%>
```

When a program contains a global variable and a local variable with the same name, the local variable takes precedence when its function is called. The value assigned to a local variable of the same name is not assigned to a global variable of the same name. In the following code, the global variable `cityName` is assigned a value of "San Francisco" before the function that contains a local variable of the same name is called. When the function is called, the local `cityName` variable is assigned a value of "Los Angeles". After the function ends, "San Francisco" is still the value of the global `cityName` variable. Figure 3-3 shows the output in a Web browser.

```
<script runat="server">
string cityName = "San Francisco";
void printCityName()
{
    string cityName = "Los Angeles";
    Response.Write("<p>" + cityName + "</p>"); //
    prints Los Angeles
}
</script>
<%
printCityName();
Response.Write("<p>" + cityName + "</p>"); // prints
    San Francisco
%>
```

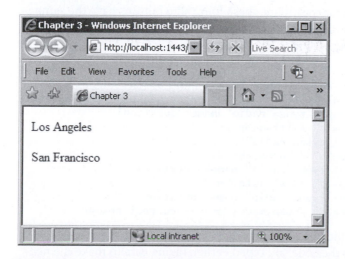

Figure 3-3 Output of a program that contains a global variable and a local variable with the same name

 Although the code that displays the output shown in Figure 3-3 is syntactically correct, it is poor programming practice to use the same name for local and global variables because it makes your scripts confusing and it is difficult to track which version of the variable is currently being used by the program.

Next, you will start creating an astronomy quiz that you will submit to an ASP.NET program for processing. The quiz will be set up in a form that allows users to select answers by means of radio buttons created with the `<input>` tag. Your Chapter folder for Chapter 3 contains a folder named AstronomyQuiz where you can find the files that you will need for this project.

To create the astronomy quiz and its form section:

1. Return to the Visual Studio IDE, select the **File** menu and then select **Open Web Site**. The Open Web Site dialog box opens. Locate and select the AstronomyQuiz folder, located in your Chapter folder for Chapter 3, and then click **Open**. The AstronomyQuiz Web site opens in the Visual Studio IDE.

2. Open the **AstronomyQuiz.htm** file from Solution Explorer.

3. Locate [ADD PAGE CONTENT HERE] and replace it with the following text and elements to the document body. The form will be submitted to an ASP.NET program named AstronomyQuiz.aspx using the post method.

   ```
   <h1>Astronomy Quiz</h1>
   <p>Answer all of the questions on the quiz, then
   select the Score button to grade the quiz. </p>
   <form action="AstronomyQuiz.aspx" method="post">
   </form>
   ```

You can build the program quickly by copying the input button code for the first question, pasting it into a new document, and then editing it to create questions two through five. If you use copy and paste to create the input buttons in the following steps, make sure you change the question number for each input button name and the function it calls.

4. Add the following lines for the first question to the `<form>` element. The four radio buttons represent the answers. Because each button within a radio button group requires the same name attribute, these four radio buttons have the same name of "question1." Each radio button is also assigned a value corresponding to its answer letter: *a*, *b*, *c*, or *d*. The correct answer is identified by the HTML comment.

   ```
   <p><strong>1. What is the name of the largest
   natural satellite in our solar system?</strong></p>
   <p><input type="radio" name="question1"
   value="a" />Titan<br />
   <input type="radio" name="question1"
   value="b" />Phobos<br />
   <input type="radio" name="question1"
   value="c" />Callisto<br />
   <input type="radio" name="question1"
   value="d" />Ganymede</p><!-- correct answer -->
   ```

5. Add the lines for the second question. If you prefer, copy and paste the code you typed earlier, taking care to make the necessary edits.

   ```
   <p><strong>2. In which constellation is the star
   Sirius located?</strong></p>
   ```

```
<p><input type="radio" name="question2"
value="a" />Ursa Major<br />
<input type="radio" name="question2"
value="b" />Orion<br />
<input type="radio" name="question2"
value="c" />Canis Major<br /><!-- correct answer -->
<input type="radio" name="question2"
value="d" />Gemini</p>
```

6. Add the lines for the third question, using copy and paste if you prefer:

```
<p><strong>3. Which meteor shower takes place every
November?</strong></p>
<p><input type="radio" name="question3"
value="a" />Quadrantids<br />
<input type="radio" name="question3"
value="b" />Perseids<br />
<input type="radio" name="question3"
value="c" />Leonids<br /><!-- correct answer -->
<input type="radio" name="question3"
value="d" />Arietids</p>
```

7. Add the lines for the fourth question:

```
<p><strong>4. What is Earth's average distance from
the Sun?</strong></p>
<p><input type="radio" name="question4"
value="a" />93 million miles<br /><!-- correct answer -->
<input type="radio" name="question4"
value="b" />93 billion miles<br />
<input type="radio" name="question4"
value="c" />93 light years<br />
<input type="radio" name="question4"
value="d" />93 trillion miles</p>
```

8. Add the lines for the fifth question:

```
<p><strong>5. An astronomical unit is the distance
between the _____.</strong></p>
<p><input type="radio" name="question5"
value="a" />Earth and the Moon<br />
<input type="radio" name="question5"
value="b" />Earth and the Sun<br /><!-- correct answer -->
<input type="radio" name="question5"
value="c" />Moon and the Sun<br />
<input type="radio" name="question5"
value="d" />Sun and the center of the Milky Way galaxy</p>
```

9. Add the following Submit button to the end of the form:

```
<p><input type="submit" value="Score" /></p>
```

10. Start the project by selecting the **Debug** menu and then by selecting **Start Without Debugging**. Figure 3-4 shows how the Web page opens in a Web browser window.

11. Close your Web browser window.

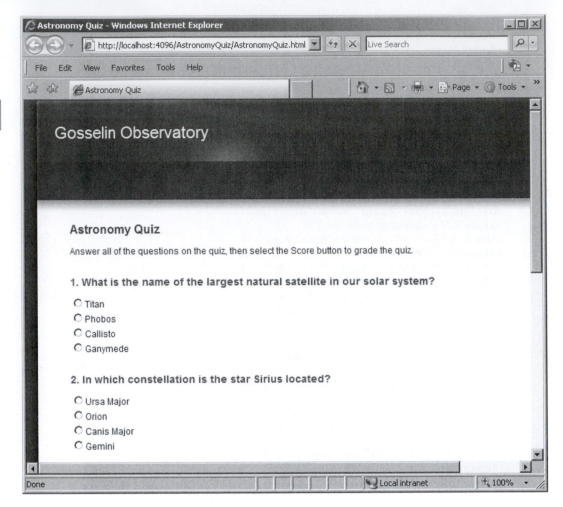

Figure 3-4   Astronomy quiz in a Web browser

Short Quiz 1

1. How do you use code declaration blocks and what types of code can they contain?

2. What is the difference between arguments and parameters?

3. How do you execute a function?

4. Why would you want to return a value from a function?

5. What is variable scope?

Working with the Request Object

As you learned in Chapter 2, ASP.NET includes various built-in core objects that you can use to access specific types of information in the processing tier and for storing information on the server. You have already used the Response object to add new text to a Web page. Another important core object is the **Request object**, which represents the current URL request from a client. For example, if users click a link or select a new URL in their browser, ASP.NET creates a Request object. The Request object and other ASP.NET core objects use **collections**, which are data structures similar to arrays that store object properties. You can access an object collection with the syntax *object.collection("property");*. Table 3-1 lists common collections of the Request object.

Collection	Contains
ClientCertificate	Field values in the client certificate sent with the request
Cookies	Cookies sent with the request
Form	The value of named form elements in the document displayed in the browser
QueryString	The name=value pairs appended to the URL in a query string
ServerVariables	Environment variables

Table 3-1   Common collections of the Request object

The Request object collection that you will use most is the Form collection, which contains variables representing form elements from a requesting Web page that is submitted with a method of "post". ASP.NET takes all of the named elements in a form on the user's browser and adds them as variables to the Form collection of the Request object. When a user clicks a form's Submit button, each field on the form is submitted to the server as a name=value pair. The name portion of the name=value pair becomes a variable name in the Form collection, and the value portion is assigned as the value of the variable. The following HTML code contains a typical form:

```
...
<body>
<h2>Customer Information</h2>
<form method="post" action="ProcessOrder.aspx">
<p>Name<br />
<input type="text" name="name" size="50" /><br />
Address<br />
```

```
<input type="text" name="address" size="50" /><br />
City, State, Zip<br />
<input type="text" name="city" size="38" />
<input type="text" name="state" size="2" maxlength="2" />
<input type="text" name="zip" size="5" maxlength="5" /><br />
E-Mail<br />
<input type="text" name="email" size="50" /></p>
<p><input type="reset" />
<input type="submit" />
</p>
</form>
</body>
</html>
```

Upon submitting the preceding form to an ASP.NET document named ProcessOrder.aspx, the field names and values are assigned as variables to the Request object Form collection. You refer to each form variable in the Request object Form collection by using the following statements:

```
Request.Form["name"]
Request.Form["address"]
Request.Form["city"]
Request.Form["state"]
Request.Form["zip"]
Request.Form["email"]
```

When you submit a form with a method of "get", name=value pairs are attached to the URL as a query string, and are assigned as variables to the Request object QueryString collection. This means that you need to refer to the form values using the QueryString collection instead of the Form collection. For example, if the sample form were submitted with a method of "get", you would refer to each form variable in the Request object QueryString collection by using the following statements:

```
Request.QueryString["name"]
Request.QueryString["address"]
Request.QueryString["city"]
Request.QueryString["state"]
Request.QueryString["zip"]
Request.QueryString["email"]
```

Similarly, if you append a query string to a URL, the name=value pairs are also assigned to the Request object QueryString collection. Consider the following code, which appends a query string to a URL:

```
<a href=" TargetPage.aspx?firstName=Don
&lastName=Gosselin&occupation=writer">Link Text</a>
```

After users click the link, TargetPage.aspx opens. Any ASP.NET code thereafter can refer to firstName, lastName, and occupation as variables in the Request object QueryString collection as follows:

148

```
Request.QueryString["firstName"]
Request.QueryString["lastName"]
Request.QueryString["occupation"]
```

ASP.NET collections support a count property, which returns the number of variables in a collection. You append the Count property to the collection name with a period. The following statements return the number of variables in the Form and QueryString collections of the Request object:

```
Request.Form.Count
Request.QueryString.Count
```

Next, you will create an ASP.NET program that displays form values submitted with the astronomy quiz.

To create an ASP.NET program that displays form values submitted with the astronomy quiz:

1. Return to the Visual Studio IDE and open the Astronomy-Quiz.aspx file from Solution Explorer.

2. Locate [ADD PAGE CONTENT HERE] and replace it with the following heading element and code render block:

   ```
   <h1>Quiz Results</h1>
   <%
   %>
   ```

3. Add to the script section the following statements, which print the values assigned to the selected radio button within each group of questions:

   ```
   Response.Write("<p>Question 1: "
     + Request.Form["question1"] + "</p>");
   Response.Write("<p>Question 2: "
     + Request.Form["question2"] + "</p>");
   Response.Write("<p>Question 3: "
     + Request.Form["question3"] + "</p>");
   Response.Write("<p>Question 4: "
     + Request.Form["question4"] + "</p>");
   Response.Write("<p>Question 5: "
     + Request.Form["question5"] + "</p>");
   ```

 Remember to use brackets ([ ]) when referring to collection variables and not parentheses as you do with functions.

4. Start the project by selecting the **Debug** menu and then by selecting **Start Without Debugging**. The AstronomyQuiz.htm file opens in a Web browser.

5. Select an answer for each question and click the **Score** button. The AstronomyQuiz.aspx file should open and display the answers you selected. Figure 3-5 shows how the AstronomyQuiz.aspx file opens in a Web browser window.

6. Close your Web browser window.

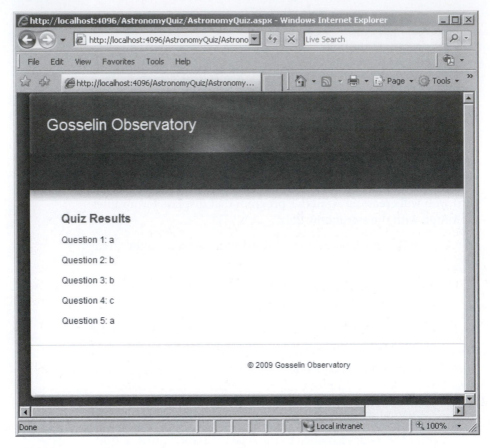

Figure 3-5   Quiz results page in a Web browser

Short Quiz 2

1. What are collections and how do you access them?

2. How do you access form data submitted with the "post" and "get" methods?

3. How do you return the number of variables in a collection?

Making Decisions

When you write a computer program, regardless of the programming language, you often need to execute different sets of statements, depending on some predetermined criteria. For example, you might create a program that needs to execute one set of code in the morning and another set of code at night. Or you might create a program that must execute one set of code when it's running in Internet Explorer and another when it runs in Firefox. Additionally, you might create a program that depends on user input to determine exactly what code to run. For instance, suppose you create a Web page through which users place online orders. If a user clicks an Add to Shopping Cart button, a set of statements that builds a list of items to be purchased must execute. However, if the user clicks a Checkout button, an entirely different set of statements, which completes the transaction, must execute. The process of determining the order in which statements execute in a program is called **decision making** or **flow control**. The special types of C# statements used for making decisions are called decision-making statements or decision-making structures. The most common type of decision-making statement is the if statement, which you will study first.

if Statements

The if statement is one of the more common ways to control program flow. The **if statement** is used to execute specific programming code if the evaluation of a conditional expression returns a value of true. The syntax for a simple if statement is as follows:

```
if (conditional expression)
    statement;
```

The if statement contains three parts: the keyword if, a conditional expression enclosed within parentheses, and executable statements. Note that the conditional expression *must* be enclosed within parentheses.

If the condition being evaluated returns a value of true, the statement immediately following the conditional expression executes. After the if statement executes, any subsequent code executes normally. Consider the following code. The if statement uses the equal (==) comparison operator to determine whether the variable exampleVar is equal to 5. (You learned about operators in Chapter 2.) Because the condition returns a value of true, two statements are printed to the Web browser. The Response.Write statement is generated by the if statement when the condition returns a value of true, and the second Response.Write statement executes after the if statement is completed.

 The statement immediately following the if statement in this code can be written on the same line as the if statement itself. However, using a line break and indentation makes the code easier for the programmer to read.

```
int exampleVar = 5;
if (exampleVar == 5)      // Condition evaluates to true
    Response.Write("<p>The variable is equal to '5'.</p>");
Response.Write("<p>Printed after the if statement.</p>");
```

In contrast, the following code displays only the second alert dialog box. The condition evaluates to false because `exampleVar` is assigned the value 4 instead of 5.

```
int exampleVar = 4;
if (exampleVar == 5)      // Condition evaluates to true
    Response.Write("<p>The variable is equal to '5'.</p>");
Response.Write("<p>Printed after the if statement.</p>");
```

You can use a command block to construct a decision-making structure containing multiple statements. A **command block** is a set of statements contained within a set of braces, similar to the way function statements are contained within a set of braces. Each command block must have an opening brace ({) and a closing brace (}). If a command block is missing either the opening or closing brace, an error occurs. The following code shows a program that runs a command block if the conditional expression within the `if` statement evaluates to true.

```
int exampleVar = 5;
if (exampleVar == 5) // Condition evaluates to true
{
    Response.Write("<p>The condition evaluates
        to true.</p>");
    Response.Write("<p><code>exampleVar</code>
        is equal to 5.</p>");
    Response.Write("<p>Each of these lines will
        be printed.</p>");
}
Response.Write("<p>Printed after the if statement.</p>");
```

When an `if` statement contains a command block, the statements in the command block execute when the `if` statement condition evaluates to true. After the command block executes, the code that follows executes normally. When the condition evaluates to false, the command block is skipped, and the statements that follow execute. If the conditional expression within the `if` statement in the preceding code evaluates to false, only the `Response.Write ()` statement following the command block executes.

Next, you will add the functions to score each of the questions in the astronomy quiz. The functions contain `if` statements that evaluate each answer.

To add functions code to score each of the questions:

1. Return to the AstronomyQuiz.aspx file in the Visual Studio IDE.

2. Add the following code declaration block above the code render block in the document body:

   ```
   <script runat="server">
   </script>
   ```

3. Add to the code declaration block the following function that scores the first question. The first statement in the function prints the question number and the selected answer. The `if` statement then prints a response of "Correct" if the user provides the correct answer and "Incorrect" if the user provides an incorrect answer.

```
void scoreQuestion1()
{
    Response.Write("<p>Question 1: "
    + Request.Form["question1"]);
    if (Request.Form["question1"] == "a")
        Response.Write(" (Incorrect)</p>");
    if (Request.Form["question1"] == "b")
        Response.Write(" (Incorrect)</p>");
    if (Request.Form["question1"] == "c")
        Response.Write(" (Incorrect)</p>");
    if (Request.Form["question1"] == "d")
        Response.Write(" (Correct!)</p>");
}
```

4. Add the `scoreQuestion2()` function after the `scoreQuestion1()` function:

```
void scoreQuestion2()
{
    Response.Write("<p>Question 2: "
    + Request.Form["question2"]);
    if (Request.Form["question2"] == "a")
        Response.Write(" (Incorrect)</p>");
    if (Request.Form["question2"] == "b")
        Response.Write(" (Incorrect)</p>");
    if (Request.Form["question2"] == "c")
        Response.Write(" (Correct!)</p>");
    if (Request.Form["question2"] == "d")
        Response.Write(" (Incorrect)</p>");
}
```

5. Add the `scoreQuestion3()` function after the `scoreQuestion2()` function:

```
void scoreQuestion3()
{
    Response.Write("<p>Question 3: "
    + Request.Form["question3"]);
    if (Request.Form["question3"] == "a")
        Response.Write(" (Incorrect)</p>");
    if (Request.Form["question3"] == "b")
        Response.Write(" (Incorrect)</p>");
    if (Request.Form["question3"] == "c")
        Response.Write(" (Correct!)</p>");
    if (Request.Form["question3"] == "d")
        Response.Write(" (Incorrect)</p>");
}
```

6. Add the scoreQuestion4() function after the scoreQuestion3() function:

```
void scoreQuestion4()
{
    Response.Write("<p>Question 4: "
    + Request.Form["question4"]);
    if (Request.Form["question4"] == "a")
        Response.Write(" (Correct!)</p>");
    if (Request.Form["question4"] == "b")
        Response.Write(" (Incorrect)</p>");
    if (Request.Form["question4"] == "c")
        Response.Write(" (Incorrect)</p>");
    if (Request.Form["question4"] == "d")
        Response.Write(" (Incorrect)</p>");
}
```

7. Add the scoreQuestion5() function after the scoreQuestion4() function:

```
void scoreQuestion5()
{
    Response.Write("<p>Question 5: "
    + Request.Form["question5"]);
    if (Request.Form["question5"] == "a")
        Response.Write(" (Incorrect)</p>");
    if (Request.Form["question5"] == "b")
        Response.Write(" (Correct!)</p>");
    if (Request.Form["question5"] == "c")
        Response.Write(" (Incorrect)</p>");
    if (Request.Form["question5"] == "d")
        Response.Write(" (Incorrect)</p>");
}
```

8. Replace the statements in the code render block with the following statements that call each function in the code declaration block:

```
scoreQuestion1();
scoreQuestion2();
scoreQuestion3();
scoreQuestion4();
scoreQuestion5();
```

9. Start the project by selecting the **Debug** menu and then by selecting **Start Without Debugging**. The AstronomyQuiz. htm file opens in a Web browser. Select an answer for each question and click the **Score** button. The AstronomyQuiz. aspx file should open and score your quiz, as shown in Figure 3-6.

10. Close your Web browser window.

154

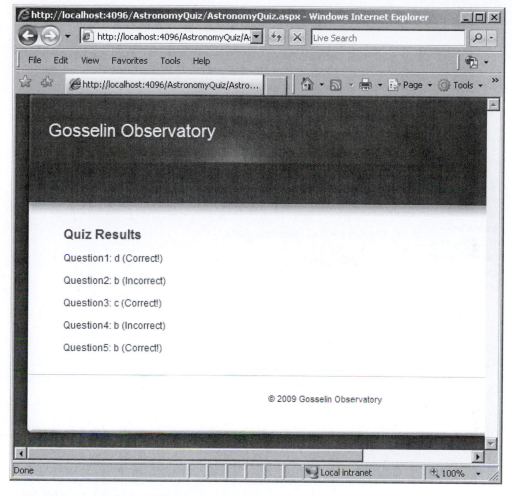

Figure 3-6 Output of astronomy quiz after adding `if` statements

if...else Statements

So far you've learned how to use an `if` statement to execute a statement (or statements) if a condition evaluates to true. In some situations, however, you might want to execute one set of statements when the condition evaluates to true, and another set of statements when the condition evaluates to false. In that case, you need to add an `else` clause to your `if` statement. For instance, suppose you create a form that includes a check box that users click to indicate whether they want to invest in the stock market. When the user submits the form to an ASP.NET program, an `if` statement in the program might contain a conditional expression that evaluates the user's input. If the condition evaluates to true (the user clicked the check box), the `if` statement displays a Web page on recommended stocks. If the condition evaluates to false (the user did not click the check box), the statements in an `else` clause display a Web page on other types of investment opportunities.

An `if` statement that includes an else clause is called an **if...else statement**. You can think of an `else` clause as being a backup plan that is implemented when the condition returns a value of false. The syntax for an `if...else` statement is as follows:

```
if (conditional expression)
      statement;
else
      statement;
```

An `if` statement can be constructed without the else clause. However, the `else` clause can only be used with an `if` statement.

You can use command blocks to construct an `if...else` statement as follows:

```
if (conditional expression)
{
      statements;
}
else
{
      statements;
}
```

The following code shows an example of an `if...else` statement:

```
string today = "Tuesday";
if (today == "Monday")
      Response.Write("<p>Today is Monday</p>");
else
      Response.Write("<p>Today is not Monday</p>");
```

In the preceding code, the `today` variable is assigned a value of "Tuesday". If the condition (`today == "Monday"`) evaluates to false, control of the program passes to the `else` clause, the statement `Response.Write("<p>Today is not Monday</p>");` executes, and the string "Today is not Monday" prints. If the `today` variable had been assigned a value of "Monday", the condition (`today == "Monday"`) would have evaluated to true, and the statement `Response.Write("<p>Today is Monday</p>");` would have executed. Only one set of statements executes: either the statements following the `if` statement or the statements following the `else` clause. When either set of statements executes, any code following the `if...else` statements executes normally.

The C# code for the astronomy quiz you created earlier uses multiple `if` statements to evaluate the results of the quiz. Although the multiple `if` statements function properly, they can be simplified using an `if...else` statement. Next, you will simplify the AstronomyQuiz. aspx program by replacing multiple `if` statements with one `if...else` statement.

1. Return to the AstronomyQuiz.aspx file in the Visual Studio IDE.

2. Because you only need the `if` statement to test for the correct answer, you can group all the incorrect answers in the `else` clause. Modify each of the functions that scores a question so that the multiple `if` statements are replaced with an `if...else` statement. The following code shows how the statements for the `scoreQuestion1()` function should look:

Keep in mind that the correct answer for Question 2 is *c*, the correct answer for Question 3 is *c*, the correct answer for Question 4 is *a*, and the correct answer for Question 5 is *b*. You need to modify the preceding code accordingly for each question. Copy and paste code and then edit it to save on typing time.

157

```
Response.Write("<p>Question 1: "
   + Request.Form["question1"]);
if (Request.Form["question1"] == "d")
    Response.Write("(Correct!)</p>");
else
    Response.Write(" (Incorrect)</p>");
```

3. Return to the AstronomyQuiz.htm file in the Visual Studio IDE, and then, start the project by selecting the **Debug** menu and then by selecting **Start Without Debugging**. The AstronomyQuiz.htm file opens in a Web browser. Select an answer for each question and click the **Score** button. The AstronomyQuiz.aspx file should open and score your quiz, the same as when it contained only `if` statements.

4. Close your Web browser window.

Nested `if` and `if...else` Statements

As you have seen, you can use a control structure such as an `if` or `if...else` statement to allow a program to make decisions about what statements to execute. In some cases, however, you might want the statements executed by the control structure to make other decisions. For instance, you might have a program that uses an `if` statement to ask users if they like sports. If users answer yes, you might want to run another `if` statement that asks users whether they like team sports or individual sports. You can include any code you want within the code block for an `if` statement or an `if...else` statement, and that includes other `if` or `if...else` statements.

When one decision-making statement is contained within another decision-making statement, they are referred to as **nested decision-making structures**. An `if` statement contained within an `if` statement or within an `if...else` statement is called a nested `if` statement. Similarly, an `if...else` statement contained within an `if` or `if...else` statement is called a nested `if...else` statement. You use nested `if` and `if...else` statements to perform conditional evaluations that must be executed after the original conditional evaluation. For example, the following code evaluates two conditional expressions before the `Write()` statement executes. The `Write()`

statement in the example only executes if the conditional expressions in both if statements evaluate to true.

```
int total = Convert.ToInt16(Request.Form["salesTotal"]);
if (total > 50)
    if (total < 100)
        Response.Write("<p>The value is between
            50 and 100.</p>");
```

The first statement in the preceding code uses the Convert class's ToInt16() method, which converts string literals to integer data types. (You first saw the Convert class in Chapter 2.) A common use of the Convert class method is to convert the value obtained from a form field text box from a string to a number. The C# interpreter does not automatically convert a text box value from a string to a number. To ensure that you can use the value from a text box in a mathematical calculation, you must use one of the methods of the Convert class to convert the string to the appropriate data type. For example, to convert a string to a long data type, you use the ToInt32() method, and to convert a string to a double data type, you use the ToDouble() method.

The C# code in the AstronomyQuiz.aspx document is somewhat inefficient because it contains multiple functions that perform essentially the same task of scoring the quiz. A more efficient method of scoring the quiz is to include the scoring statements within a single function. Another problem with the AstronomyQuiz.aspx document is that a user is not required to select answers to all of the questions. To check whether users have answered all the questions, you create an if...else statement that uses the Count property to count the number of variables in the Request.Form collection; there should be five, one for each question. If the count is equal to five, the if portion of the statement executes the code that scores the questions. However, if the count is not equal to five, the else portion of the statement prints a message instructing the user to answer all of the questions.

To modify the astronomy quiz so it contains a single function and nested if...else statements:

1. Return to the AstronomyQuiz.aspx file in the Visual Studio IDE.

2. Delete the five functions within the code declaration block, but be sure to leave the <script> element.

3. Add to the code declaration block the following function that will check all the answers:

```
void scoreQuestions()
{
}
```

4. Add the following if...else statement to the scoreQuestions() function. In the next few steps, you add code to the if

statement that scores the questions; this code only executes if the Request.Form collection contains a value of 5. If the Request.Form collection does not contain a value of 5, the else statement executes and prints a message instructing the user to answer all of the questions.

```
if (Request.Form.Count == 5) {
}
else
    Response.Write("<p>You did not answer all the
    questions! Click your browser's Back button
    to return to the quiz.</p>");
```

5. Add to the first if statement the following Response.Write() statement and nested if...else statement, which scores Question 1:

```
Response.Write("<p>Question 1: "
  + Request.Form["question1"]);
if (Request.Form["question1"] == "d")
    Response.Write(" (Correct!)</p>");
else
    Response.Write(" (Incorrect)</p>");
```

6. Add to the end of the first if statement the following Response.Write() statement and nested if...else statement, which scores Question 2:

```
Response.Write("<p>Question 2: "
  + Request.Form["question2"]);
if (Request.Form["question3"] == "c")
    Response.Write(" (Correct!)</p>");
else
    Response.Write(" (Incorrect)</p>");
```

7. Add to the end of the if statement the following Response.Write() statement and nested if...else statement, which scores Question 3:

```
Response.Write("<p>Question 3: "
  + Request.Form["question3"]);
if (Request.Form["question3"] == "c")
    Response.Write(" (Correct!)</p>");
else
    Response.Write(" (Incorrect)</p>");
```

8. Add to the end of the if statement the following Response.Write() statement and nested if...else statement, which scores Question 4:

```
Response.Write("<p>Question 4: "
  + Request.Form["question4"]);
if (Request.Form["question4"] == "a")
    Response.Write(" (Correct!)</p>");
else
    Response.Write(" (Incorrect)</p>");
```

9. Add to the end of the `if` statement the following `Response.Write()` statement and nested `if...else` statement, which scores Question 5:

```
Response.Write("<p>Question 5: "
    + Request.Form["question5"]);
if (Request.Form["question1"] == "b")
        Response.Write(" (Correct!)</p>");
else
        Response.Write(" (Incorrect)</p>");
```

10. Replace the five function calls in the code render block with a single call to the `scoreQuestions()` function:

```
scoreQuestions();
```

11. Return to the AstronomyQuiz.htm file in the Visual Studio IDE, and then, start the project by selecting the **Debug** menu and then by selecting **Start Without Debugging**. The AstronomyQuiz.htm file opens in a Web browser. Select an answer for some of the questions, but leave at least one of the questions unanswered. When you click the **Score** button, you should see the Web page shown in Figure 3-7 (assuming you did not answer all of the questions).

12. Close your Web browser window.

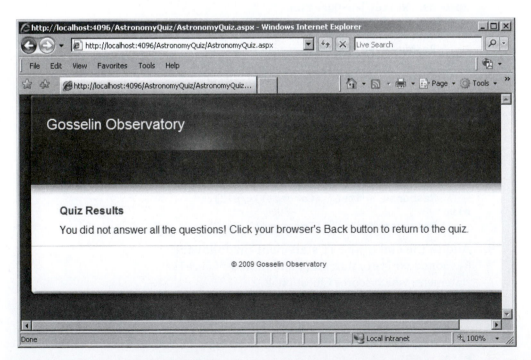

Figure 3-7 Output of astronomy quiz after adding nested `if...else` statements

switch Statements

Another statement that is used for controlling program flow is the switch statement. The **switch statement** controls program flow by executing a specific set of statements, depending on the value of an expression. The switch statement compares the value of an expression with a value contained within a special statement called a case label. A **case label** in a switch statement represents a specific value and contains one or more statements that execute if the value of the case label matches the value of the switch statement's expression. The result returned from the expression must be an integer data type, which includes the int and long types, or a string. For example, your program for an insurance company might include a variable named customerAge. A switch statement can evaluate the variable and compare it with a case label within the switch construct. The switch statement might contain several case labels for different age groups that calculate insurance rates based on a customer's age. If the customerAge variable is equal to 25, the statements that are part of the "25" case label execute and calculate insurance rates for customers who are 25 or older. Although you could accomplish the same task using if or if...else statements, a switch statement makes it easier to organize the different branches of code that can be executed.

A switch statement consists of the following components: the keyword switch, an expression, an opening brace, a case label, the executable statements, the keyword break, a default label, and a closing brace. The syntax for the switch statement is as follows:

```
switch (expression)
{
    case label:
        statement(s);
        break;
    case label:
        statement(s);
        break;
    ...
    default:
        statement(s);
}
```

A case label consists of the keyword case, followed by a literal value or variable name, followed by a colon. C# compares the value returned from the switch statement expression with the literal value or variable name following the case keyword. If a match is found, the case label statements execute. For example, case 25: represents an integer value of 25. If the value of a switch statement

A single statement or multiple statements can follow a case label. However, unlike if statements, multiple statements for a case label do not need to be enclosed within a command block.

conditional expression equals 25, the `case 25:` label statements execute. The following code shows examples of three `case` labels:

```
int customerAge = 25;
switch (customerAge)
{
    case 18:
        Response.Write("High risk");
        break;
    case 21:
        Response.Write("Medium risk");
        break;
    case 25:
        Response.Write("Low risk");
        break;
}
```

Another type of label used within `switch` statements is the `default` label. The **default label** contains statements that execute when the value returned by the `switch` statement expression does not match a `case` label. A `default` label consists of the keyword `default` followed by a colon.

When a `switch` statement executes, the value returned by the expression is compared with each `case` label in the order in which it is encountered. When a matching label is found, its statements execute. Unlike with the `if...else` statement, execution of a `switch` statement does not automatically stop after particular `case` label statements execute. Instead, the `switch` statement continues evaluating the rest of the `case` labels in the list. When a matching `case` label is found, evaluation of additional `case` labels is unnecessary. If you are working with a large `switch` statement with many `case` labels, evaluation of additional `case` labels can potentially slow down your program.

A break statement is also used to exit other types of control statements, such as the `while`, `do...while`, and `for` looping statements. You'll learn about these statements later in this chapter.

To avoid slow performance, then, you need to give some thought to how and when to end a `switch` statement. A `switch` statement ends automatically after the interpreter encounters its closing brace (`}`). You can, however, use a special kind of statement, called a **break statement**, to end a `switch` statement after it has performed its required task. To end a `switch` statement after it performs its required task, include a `break` statement within each `case` label.

The following code shows a `switch` statement contained within a function. When the function is called, it is passed an argument named `customerAge`. The `switch` statement compares the contents of the `customerAge` argument with the `case` labels. If a match is found, the risk category is returned as a string and a `break` statement ends the `switch` statement. If a match is not found, the value "Preferred customer" is returned from the default label.

```
<script runat="server">
    string checkRisk(int customerAge)
    {
        switch (customerAge)
        {
            case 18:
                return "High risk";
                break;
            case 21:
                return "Medium risk";
                break;
            case 25:
                return "Low risk";
                break;
            default:
                return "Preferred customer";
                break;
        }
    }
</script>
<%
    Response.Write(checkRisk(21));
%>
```

Next, you will add a new function to the astronomy quiz that contains a switch statement that checks each answer.

1. Return to the AstronomyQuiz.aspx file in the Visual Studio IDE.

2. Add the following new function named checkAnswer() above the scoreQuestions() function. The parameter you pass to the checkAnswer() function will contain the number of the current question (1, 2, and so on).

```
void checkAnswer(int curQuestion)
{
}
```

3. Add the following switch statement to the checkAnswer() function.

```
switch (curQuestion) {
  case 1:
  case 2:
  case 3:
  case 4:
  case 5:
  default:
  Response.Write("<p>You did not pass a valid
    question number.</p>");
  Break;
}
```

4. Move the statements that check that answer to each question from the scoreQuestions() function to the appropriate case label in the checkAnswer() function. Also, add a break

statement to the end of each `case` label. The `case` label for "question1" should appear as follows:

```
Response.Write("<p>Question 1: "
  + Request.Form["question1"]);
if (Request.Form["question1"] == "d")
    Response.Write(" (Correct!)</p>");
else
    Response.Write(" (Incorrect)</p>");
break;
```

5. Add the following call statements to the `if` statement in the `scoreQuestions()` function. Each statement calls the `checkAnswer()` function and passes to it the name of each question.

```
checkAnswer(1);
checkAnswer(2);
checkAnswer(3);
checkAnswer(4);
checkAnswer(5);
```

6. Return to the AstronomyQuiz.htm file in the Visual Studio IDE, and then start the Web site. The AstronomyQuiz.htm file opens in a Web browser. Select an answer for some of the questions, but leave at least one of the questions unanswered. When you click the **Score** button, the program should function just as it did with the single function.

7. Close your Web browser window.

Short Quiz 3

1. When will an `if` statement execute?

2. Why would you use a command block with a decision-making statement?

3. Why would you nest decision-making statements?

4. What type of label represents a specific value and contains one or more statements that execute if its value matches the value of the `switch` statement's expression?

5. Describe how the statements in a `switch` statement execute. When does a `switch` statement end?

Repeating Code

The statements you have worked with so far execute one after the other in a linear fashion. The `if`, `if...else`, and `switch` statements select only a single branch of code to execute, then continue to the statement that follows. But what if you want to repeat the same statement, function, or code section five times, 10 times, or 100 times? For example, you might want to perform the same calculation until a specific number is found. In that case, you would need to use a **loop statement**, which is a control structure that repeatedly executes a statement or a series of statements while a specific condition is true or until a specific condition becomes true. In this chapter, you'll learn about three types of loop statements: `while` statements, `do...while` statements, and `for` statements.

while Statements

One of the simplest types of loop statements is the **while statement**, which repeats a statement or series of statements as long as a given conditional expression evaluates to true. The syntax for the `while` statement is as follows:

```
while (conditional expression)
{
    statement(s);
}
```

The conditional expression in the `while` statement is enclosed within parentheses following the keyword `while`. As long as the conditional expression evaluates to true, the statement or command block that follows executes repeatedly. Each repetition of a looping statement is called an **iteration**. When the conditional expression evaluates to false, the loop ends and the next statement following the `while` statement executes.

A `while` statement keeps repeating until its conditional expression evaluates to false. To ensure that the `while` statement ends after the desired tasks have been performed, you must include code that tracks the progress of the loop and changes the value produced by the conditional expression. You track the progress of a `while` statement, or any other loop, with a counter. A **counter** is a variable that increments or decrements with each iteration of a loop statement.

The following code shows a simple program that includes a `while` statement. The program declares a variable named `count` and assigns it an initial value of 1. The `count` variable is then used in the `while` statement conditional expression (`count <= 5`). As long as the `count` variable is less than or equal to five, the `while` statement loops.

Many programmers often name counter variables `count`, `counter`, or something similar. The letters i, j, k, l, x, y, and z are also commonly used as counter names. Using a name such as `count`, or the letter i (for increment) or a higher letter, helps you remember (and lets other programmers know) that the variable is being used as a counter.

Within the body of the `while` statement, the `Response.Write()` statement prints the value of the `count` variable, then the `count` variable increments by a value of 1. The `while` statement loops until the `count` variable increments to a value of 6.

```
int count = 1;
while (count <= 5)
{
    Response.Write(count + "<br />");
    ++count;
}
Response.Write("<p>You have printed 5 numbers.</p>");
```

The preceding code uses an increment operator to print the numbers 1 to 5, with each number representing one iteration of the loop. When the counter reaches 6, the message "You have printed 5 numbers." prints, thus demonstrating that the loop has ended. Figure 3-8 shows the output of this simple program.

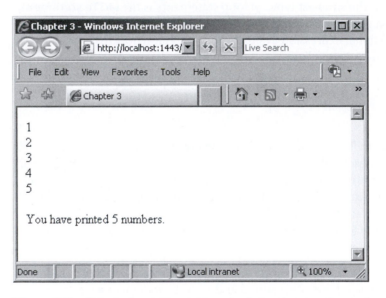

Figure 3-8   Output of a `while` statement using an increment operator

You can also control the repetitions in a `while` loop by decrementing (decreasing the value of) counter variables. Consider the following program:

```
int count = 10;
while (count > 0)
{
    Response.Write(count + "<br />");
    --count;
}
Response.Write("<p>We have liftoff.</p>");
```

In this example, the initial value of the count variable is 10, and the decrement operator (--) is used to decrease count by one. When the count variable is greater than zero, the statement within the while loop prints the value of the count variable. When the value of count is equal to zero, the while loop ends, and the statement immediately following it prints. Figure 3-9 shows the program output.

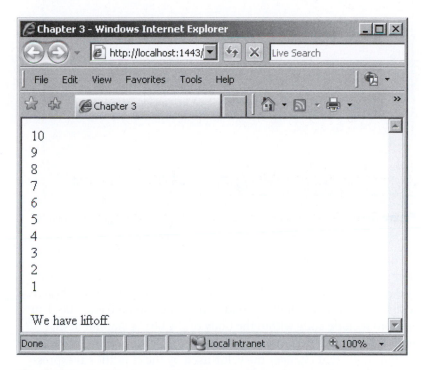

Figure 3-9 Output of a while statement using a decrement operator

There are many ways to change the value of a counter variable and to use a counter variable to control the repetitions of a while loop. The following example uses the *= assignment operator to multiply the value of the count variable by two. When the count variable reaches a value of 128, the while statement ends. Figure 3-10 shows the program output.

```
int count = 1;
while (count <= 100)
{
    Response.Write(count + "<br />");
    count *= 2;
}
```

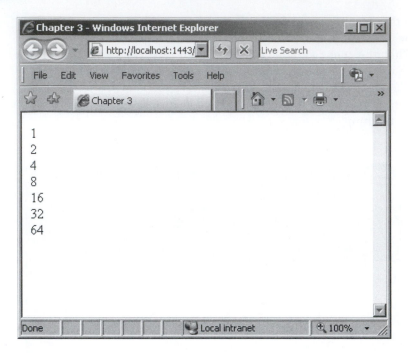

Figure 3-10 Output of a `while` statement using the `*=` assignment operator

To ensure that the `while` statement will eventually end, you must include code within the body of the `while` statement that changes the value of the conditional expression. For example, you might have a `while` statement that prints odd numbers between 0 and 100. You need to include code within the body of the `while` statement that ends the loop after the last even number (98) prints. If you do not include code that changes the value used by the conditional expression, your program will be caught in an infinite loop. In an **infinite loop**, a loop statement never ends because its conditional expression is never false. Consider the following `while` statement:

```
int count = 1;
while (count <= 10) {
    Response.Write("The number is " + count);
}
```

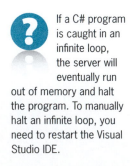

If a C# program is caught in an infinite loop, the server will eventually run out of memory and halt the program. To manually halt an infinite loop, you need to restart the Visual Studio IDE.

Although the `while` statement in the preceding example includes a conditional expression that checks the value of a `count` variable, there is no code within the `while` statement body that changes the `count` variable value. The `count` variable will continue to have a value of 1 through each iteration of the loop. That means that the text string "The number is 1" will print over and over again, until the user closes the Web browser window.

Next, you will create a new version of the astronomy quiz program that is to be scored by a single while statement containing a nested if statement. Although this while statement is somewhat more complicated than the if, if...else, and switch statements you created previously, it requires many fewer lines of code, which helps make the program run faster and more efficiently.

To create a version of the astronomy quiz that is scored by a while statement:

1. Return to the AstronomyQuiz.aspx file in the Visual Studio IDE.

2. Delete the checkAnswer() function from the program.

3. Delete the call statements in the if statement in the scoreQuestions() function, but be sure to leave the if statement's braces.

4. Add the following lines to the if statement to create an array named correctAnswers[], which holds the correct response for each of the questions.

```
char[] correctAnswers = new char[5];
correctAnswers[0] = 'd';
correctAnswers[1] = 'c';
correctAnswers[2] = 'c';
correctAnswers[3] = 'a';
correctAnswers[4] = 'b';
```

5. Add to the end of the if statement the following statement, which declares a new variable, and assign to it an initial value of 0. The totalCorrect variable holds the number of correct answers.

```
int totalCorrect = 0;
```

6. Add the following variable declaration and while statement at the end of the if statement. In this code, a counter named count is declared and initialized to a value of 0. The conditional expression within the while statement checks to see if count is less than or equal to 5, which is the number of questions in the quiz. With each iteration of the loop, the statement in the while loop increments the count variable by one.

```
int count = 1;
while (count <= 5) {
    ++count;
}
```

7. Add the following `if...else` statement to the beginning of the `while` loop, above the statement that increments the `count` variable. This `if` statement compares each element within the form values in the `Request.Form` variables with each corresponding element within the `correctAnswers[]` array. If the elements match, the `totalCorrect` variable increments by one. Notice how the statements reference the `count` variable. In the first `Response.Write()` statement and in the conditional expression, the `Request.Form` variables use the `count` variable to build the key that represents the current question. The conditional expression also uses the `count` variable to reference the correct element index by subtracting a value of 1 from the variable to account for indexed elements beginning with an index of 0.

```
Response.Write("<p>Question" + count + ": "
    + Request.Form["question" + count]);
if (Convert.ToChar(Request.Form["question"
    + count]) == correctAnswers[count-1]) {
        Response.Write(" (Correct!)</p>");
        ++totalCorrect;
}
else
        Response.Write(" (Incorrect)</p>");
```

8. Add the following statement after the `while` loop's closing brace to print the number of questions that were answered correctly.

```
Response.Write("<p><strong>You scored "
    + totalCorrect + " out of 5 answers
        correctly!</strong></p>");
```

9. Save the project, return to the AstronomyQuiz.htm file in the Visual Studio IDE, and then start the Web site. The AstronomyQuiz.htm file opens in a Web browser. Test the program by answering all five questions and clicking the **Score** button. Figure 3-11 shows how the program opens in a Web browser.

10. Close your Web browser window.

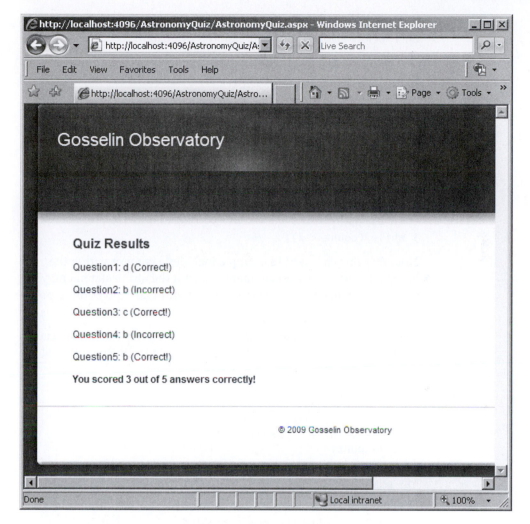

Figure 3-11 Output of astronomy quiz after adding a `while` statement

do...while Statements

Another looping statement, similar to the `while` statement, is the `do...while` statement. The **do...while statement** executes a statement or statements once, then repeats the execution as long as a given conditional expression evaluates to true. The syntax for the `do...while` statement is as follows:

```
do {
    statement(s);
} while (conditional expression);
```

As you can see in the syntax description, the statements execute before a conditional expression is evaluated. Unlike the simpler `while` statement, the statements in a do...while statement always execute once, before a conditional expression is evaluated.

The following do...while statement executes once before the conditional expression evaluates the count variable. Therefore, a single line that reads "The count is equal to 2" prints. After the conditional expression (count < 2) executes, the count variable is equal to 3. This causes the conditional expression to return a value of false, and the do...while statement ends.

```
int count = 2;
do {
    Response.Write("<p>The count is equal to "
        + count + "</p>");
    ++count;
} while (count < 2);
```

Note that this do...while example includes a counter within the body of the do...while statement. As with the while statement, you need to include code that changes the conditional expression to prevent an infinite loop.

In the following example, the while statement never executes because the count variable does not fall within the range of the conditional expression:

```
int count = 2;
while (count > 2) {
    Response.Write("<p>The count is equal to "
        + count + "</p>");
    ++count;
}
```

The following program shows an example of a do...while statement that prints the days of the week, using an array:

```
string[] daysOfWeek = new string[7];
daysOfWeek[0] = "Monday"; daysOfWeek[1] = "Tuesday";
daysOfWeek[2] = "Wednesday"; daysOfWeek[3] = "Thursday";
daysOfWeek[4] = "Friday"; daysOfWeek[5] = "Saturday";
daysOfWeek[6] = "Sunday";
int count = 0;
do
{
    Response.Write(daysOfWeek[count] + "<br />");
    ++count;
} while (count < daysOfWeek.Length);
```

In the preceding example, an array is created containing the days of the week. A variable named count is declared and initialized to zero. (Remember, the first subscript or index in an array is zero.) Therefore, in the example, the statement daysOfWeek[0]; refers to Monday. The first iteration of the do...while statement prints "Monday" and then increments the count variable by one. The conditional expression in the `while` statement then checks to determine when the last element of the array has been printed. As long as the count is less than the length of the array (which is one number higher than the largest element in the `daysOfWeek[] array`), the loop continues. Figure 3-12 shows the output of the program in a Web browser.

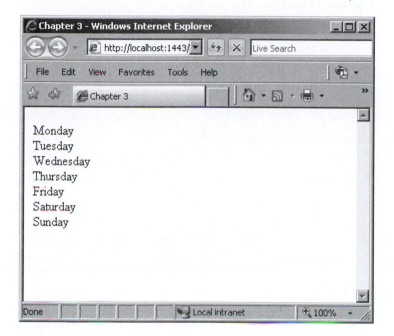

Figure 3-12 Days of week program in a Web browser

Next, you will replace the `while` statement in the astronomy quiz with a `do...while` statement. Because the `do...while` statement is very similar to the `while` statement, there is little benefit in replacing the `while` statement in the astronomy quiz. You will add a `do...while` statement to the program for practice.

To replace the `while` statement in the astronomy quiz with a `do...while` statement:

1. Return to the AstronomyQuiz.aspx file in the Visual Studio IDE.

2. Change the `while` statement within the `scoreQuestions()` function to a `do...while` statement, as follows:

```
do
{
    Response.Write("<p>Question" + count + ": "
        + Request.Form["question" + count]);
    if (Convert.ToChar(Request.Form["question"
        + count]) == correctAnswers[count - 1])
```

```
        {
            Response.Write(" (Correct!)</p>");
            ++totalCorrect;
        }
        else
            Response.Write(" (Incorrect)</p>");
        ++count;
    } while (count <= 5);
```

174

3. Save the project, return to the AstronomyQuiz.htm file
    in the Visual Studio IDE, and then start the Web site. The
    AstronomyQuiz.htm file opens in a Web browser. Test
    the program by answering all five questions and clicking
    the **Score** button. The program should function just as it
    did with the while statement.

4. Close your Web browser window.

for Statements

So far, you have learned how to use the while and the do...while statements to repeat, or loop through, code. You can also use the for statement to loop through code. The **for statement** is used for repeating a
statement or series of statements as long as a given conditional expression
evaluates to true. The for statement performs essentially the same function as the while statement: If a conditional expression within the for
statement evaluates to true, the for statement executes and will continue
to execute repeatedly until the conditional expression evaluates to false.

One of the primary differences between the while statement and the for
statement is that, in addition to a conditional expression, the for statement can also include code that initializes a counter and changes its value
with each iteration. This is useful because it provides a specific place for
you to declare and initialize a counter, and to update its value, which
helps prevent infinite loops. The syntax of the for statement is as follows:

```
for (counter declaration and initialization; condition;
    update statement)
{
    statement(s);
}
```

When the interpreter encounters a for loop, the following steps occur:

1. The counter variable is declared and initialized. For example,
    if the initialization expression in a for loop is var count = 1;,
    a variable named count is declared and assigned an initial
    value of 1. The initialization expression is only started once,
    when the for loop is first encountered.

2. The for loop condition is evaluated.

3. If the condition evaluation in Step 2 returns a value of true, the for loop statements execute, Step 4 occurs, and the process starts over again with Step 2. If the condition evaluation in Step 2 returns a value of false, the for statement ends and the next statement following the for statement executes.

4. The update statement in the for statement is executed. For example, the count variable may increment by one.

The following program shows a for statement that prints the contents of an array:

```
string[] chineseYears = new string[12];
chineseYears[0] = "Rat"; chineseYears[1] = "Ox";
chineseYears[2] = "Tiger"; chineseYears[3] = "Hare";
chineseYears[4] = "Dragon"; chineseYears[5] = "Serpent";
chineseYears[6] = "Horse"; chineseYears[7] = "Sheep";
chineseYears[8] = "Monkey"; chineseYears[9] = "Rooster";
chineseYears[10] = "Dog"; chineseYears[11] = "Boar";
for (int count = 0; count < chineseYears.Length; ++count)
{
    Response.Write(chineseYears[count] + "<br />");
}
```

As you can see in this example, the counter is initialized, evaluated, and incremented within the parentheses. You do not need to include a declaration for the count variable before the for statement, nor do you need to increment the count variable within the body of the for statement. Figure 3-13 shows the output.

> **?** You can omit any of the three parts of the for statement that are contained within the parentheses, but you must include the semicolons that separate each section. If you omit a section, be sure you include code within the body that will end the for statement or your program might get caught in an infinite loop.

175

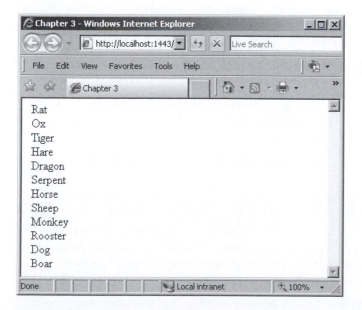

Figure 3-13 Output of the Chinese years program

The following code shows an example of the days of week program you saw earlier. This time, however, the program includes a `for` statement instead of a `do...while` statement. Notice that the declaration of the `count` variable, the conditional expression, and the statement that increments the `count` variable are now all contained within the `for` statement. Using a `for` statement instead of a `do...while` statement simplifies the program somewhat because you do not need as many lines of code.

```
string[] daysOfWeek = new string[7];
daysOfWeek[0] = "Monday"; daysOfWeek[1] = "Tuesday";
daysOfWeek[2] = "Wednesday"; daysOfWeek[3] = "Thursday";
daysOfWeek[4] = "Friday"; daysOfWeek[5] = "Saturday";
daysOfWeek[6] = "Sunday";
for (int count = 0; count < daysOfWeek.Length; ++count)
{
    Response.Write(daysOfWeek[count] + "<br />");
}
```

> You can include multiple initialization expressions in a for loop by separating them with commas.

Next, you will modify the astronomy quiz so it is scored with a `for` statement instead of a `do...while` statement.

To replace the `do...while` statement in the astronomy quiz with a `for` statement:

1. Return to the AstronomyQuiz.aspx file in the Visual Studio IDE.

2. Delete the declaration for the `count` variable within the `scoreQuestions()` function.

3. Replace the `do...while` statement within the `scoreQuestions()` function with the following `for` statement.

```
for(int count=1; count<=5; ++count)
{
    Response.Write("<p>Question" + count + ": "
        + Request.Form["question" + count]);
    if (Convert.ToChar(Request.Form["question"
        + count]) == correctAnswers[count - 1])
    {
        Response.Write(" (Correct!)</p>");
        ++totalCorrect;
    }
    else
        Response.Write(" (Incorrect)</p>");
}
```

4. Save the project, return to the AstronomyQuiz.htm file in the Visual Studio IDE, and then start the Web site. The AstronomyQuiz.htm file opens in a Web browser. Test the program by answering all five questions and clicking the **Score** button. The program should function just as it did with the `do...while` statement.

5. Close your Web browser window and then close the project by selecting the **File** menu and then selecting **Close Project**.

Using `continue` Statements to Restart Execution

When you studied `switch` statements, you learned how to use a `break` statement to exit `switch`, `while`, `do...while`, and `for` statements. A similar statement, used only with looping statements, is the `continue` statement, which halts a looping statement and restarts the loop with a new iteration. You use the **continue statement** when you want to stop the loop for the current iteration, but want the loop to continue with a new iteration. For example, suppose a company stores employee salaries in an array and wants to increase the salary by 5% for every employee who earns less than $50,000. The following program contains a `for` loop. This `for` loop contains a `continue` statement that iterates through the values in an array named `salaries[]`. The `continue` statement executes for any values in the `salaries[]` array that are higher than $50,000. The values in the `salaries[]` array that are lower than $50,000 are increased by 5% and the new value is printed.

```
double[] salaries = new double[5];
salaries[0] = 42000;
salaries[1] = 52000;
salaries[2] = 44000;
salaries[3] = 46000;
salaries[4] = 65000;
Response.Write("<p>Salary increases:</p>");
for (int count = 0; count < salaries.Length; ++count)
{
    if (salaries[count] >= 50000)
        continue;
    salaries[count] *= 1.05;
    Response.Write(salaries[count] + "<br />");
}
```

The preceding code skips the two values that are higher than $50,000 and prints the results shown in Figure 3-14.

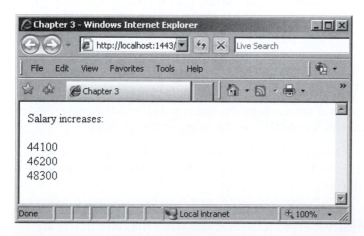

Salary increases:

44100
46200
48300

Figure 3-14   Output of a `for` loop with a `continue` statement

Short Quiz 4

1. Why is a counter critical to repetition statements?

2. How do you break out of an infinite loop?

3. Which type of repetition statement always executes its statements once, even if the conditional expression returns a value of false?

4. What are the primary differences between the `while` statement and the `for` statement?

5. How do you restart a repetition statement?

Summing Up

- Code declaration blocks use `<script>` elements to contain ASP. NET functions and global variables.

- Functions are used to organize a related group of C# statements as a single unit.

- A global variable is one that is declared within a code declaration block, but outside a function, and is available to all parts of your page.

- A local variable is declared inside a function or code render block and is only available within the function or code render block in which it is declared.

- The `Request` object represents the current URL request from a client.

- Collections are data structures similar to arrays that store object properties.

- The process of determining the order in which statements execute in a program is called decision making or flow control.

- The `if` statement is used to execute specific programming code if the evaluation of a conditional expression returns a value of true.

- An `if` statement that includes an `else` clause is called an `if...else` statement. An `else` clause executes when the condition in an `if...else` statement evaluates to false.

- When one decision-making statement is contained within another decision-making statement, they are referred to as nested decision-making structures.

- The `switch` statement controls program flow by executing a specific set of statements, depending on the value of an expression.

- A loop statement is a control structure that repeatedly executes a statement or a series of statements while a specific condition is true or until a specific condition becomes true.

- A `while` statement repeats a statement or series of statements as long as a given conditional expression evaluates to true.

- The `do...while` statement executes a statement or statements once, then repeats the execution as long as a given conditional expression evaluates to true.

- The `for` statement is used for repeating a statement or series of statements as long as a given conditional expression evaluates to true.

- You use the `continue` statement when you want to stop the loop for the current iteration, but want the loop to continue with a new iteration.

Comprehension Check

1. A(n) _____ allows you to treat a related group of C# commands as a single unit.

    a. statement

    b. variable

    c. function

    d. event

2. Functions must contain parameters. True or False?

3. Explain how to use a return statement to return a value to a statement that calls a function.

4. A variable that is declared outside a function in a code declaration block is called a _____ variable.

    a. local

    b. class

    c. program

    d. global

5. A local variable must be declared _____.

   a. before a function

   b. after a function

   c. within the braces of a function definition

   d. with the local keyword

6. If a client submits a form with the "get" method, the form's name=value pairs are stored in the _____ collection of the Request object.

   a. Form

   b. Get

   c. QueryString

   d. Cookies

7. Which of the following is the correct syntax for an if statement?

   a. `if (myVariable == 10);`
      `    Response.Write("Your variable is equal to 10.");`

   b. `if myVariable == 10`
      `    Response.Write("Your variable is equal to 10.");`

   c. `if (myVariable == 10)`
      `    Response.Write("Your variable is equal to 10.");`

   d. `if (myVariable == 10),`
      `    Response.Write("Your variable is equal to 10.");`

8. An if statement can include multiple statements provided that they _____.

   a. execute after the if statement's closing semicolon

   b. are not contained within a command block

   c. do not include other if statements

   d. are contained within a command block

9. Explain how to construct an if statement that executes multiple statements.

10. Which is the correct syntax for an `else` clause?

    a. `else (Response.Write("Printed from an else clause.");`

    b. `else Response.Write("Printed from an else clause.");`

    c. `else "Response.Write('Printed from an else clause.')";`

    d. `else; Response.Write("Printed from an else clause.");`

11. The `switch` statement controls program flow by executing a specific set of statements, depending on _____.

    a. the result of an `if...else` statement

    b. the version of C# being executed

    c. whether an `if` statement executes from within a function

    d. the value returned by a conditional expression

12. Decision-making structures cannot be nested. True or False?

13. When the value returned by a `switch` statement expression does not match a `case` label, the statements within the _____ label execute.

    a. `exception`

    b. `else`

    c. `error`

    d. `default`

14. You can exit a `switch` statement using a(n) _____ statement.

    a. `break`

    b. `end`

    c. `quit`

    d. `complete`

15. Each repetition of a looping statement is called a(n) _____.

    a. recurrence

    b. iteration

    c. duplication

    d. reexecution

16. Which of the following is the correct syntax for a `while` statement?

    a.
    ```
    while (i <= 5, ++i) {
        Response.Write("<p>i</p>");
    }
    ```

    b.
    ```
    while (i <= 5) {
        Response.Write("<p>i</p>");
        ++i;
    }
    ```

    c.
    ```
    while (i <= 5);
        Response.Write("<p>i</p>");
        ++i;
    ```

    d.
    ```
    while (i <= 5; Response.Write("<p>i</p>")) {
        ++i;
    }
    ```

17. Counter variables _____. (Choose all that apply.)

    a. can only be incremented

    b. can only be decremented

    c. can be changed using any conditional expression

    d. do not change

18. Explain how an infinite loop is caused.

19. Which of the following is the correct syntax for a `for` statement?

    a.
    ```
    for (var i = 0; i < 10; ++i)
        Response.Write("Printed from a for statement.");
    ```

    b.
    ```
    for (var i = 0, i < 10, ++i)
        Response.Write("Printed from a for statement.");
    ```

c. for {
    Response.Write("Printed from a for statement.");
    } while (var i = 0; i < 10; ++i)

d. for (var i = 0; i < 10);
    Response.Write("Printed from a for statement.");
        ++i;

20. When is a for statement initialization expression executed?

   a. when the for statement begins executing

   b. with each repetition of the for statement

   c. when the counter variable increments

   d. when the for statement ends

Reinforcement Exercises

Exercise 3-1

In this project, you will create a program for Larry's Lawn Service with a function that returns a string value.

1. Create a new ASP.NET Web site in the Visual Studio IDE and save it in a folder named LawnService in your Exercises folder for Chapter 3. Change the content of the `<title>` element in the Default.aspx file to **Larry's Lawn Service** and add a `<link>` element above the closing `</head>` tag that links to the asp_styles.css style sheet file in your Chapter.03 folder. Add the asp_styles.css style sheet to the project.

2. Replace the `<form>` and `<div>` elements in the document body with a code declaration block and function named favoriteLawnService():

```
<script runat="server">
string favoriteLawnService() {
    string companyName = "Larry's Lawn Service";
}
</script>
```

3. Modify the favoriteLawnService() function so that it returns the company name to another calling function.

4. Create a code render block at the end of the document body and add statements that call the favoriteLawnService() function and assign the return value to a variable named bestLandscaper.

5. Finally, write code that prints the contents of the bestLandscaper variable.

6. Save the project, and then test the Web site.

7. Close your Web browser window and then close the project.

Exercise 3-2

In this project, you will create a program that uses a function to print information about financing options for a company named Coast City Cars. The program will include a global variable containing the name of the company and the function will contain global variables that store financing information.

1. Create a new ASP.NET Web site in the Visual Studio IDE and save it in a folder named CoastCityCars in your Exercises folder for Chapter 3. Change the content of the <title> element in the Default.aspx file to **Coast City Cars** and add a <link> element above the closing </head> tag that links to the asp_styles.css style sheet file in your Chapter.03 folder. Add the asp_styles.css style sheet to the project.

2. Replace the <form> and <div> elements in the document body with a code declaration block.

3. Add the following global variable to the code declaration block:

```
string autoDealer = "Coast City Cars";
```

4. Add to the end of the code declaration block a function named printFinanceOptions(). Within the printFinanceOptions() function, add the following Response.Write() methods to print the available financing options:

```
Response.Write("<h2>Financing Options</h2>");
Response.Write("<ul>");
Response.Write("<li>24 months: 6.75%</li>");
Response.Write("<li>48 months: 7.15%</li>");
Response.Write("<li>72 months: 7.50%</li>");
Response.Write("</ul>");
```

5. Add a code render block to the end of the document body that prints the global variable in an <h1> element and that calls the printFinanceOptions() function.

6. Save the project, and then test the Web site.

7. Close your Web browser window and then close the project.

Exercise 3-3

In this project, you will write a `while` statement that prints all even numbers between 1 and 100 to the screen.

1. Create a new ASP.NET Web site in the Visual Studio IDE and save it in a folder named EvenNumbers in your Exercises folder for Chapter 3. Change the content of the `<title>` element of the Default.aspx file to **Even Numbers** and add a `<link>` element above the closing `</head>` tag that links to the asp_styles.css style sheet file in your Chapter.03 folder. Add the asp_styles.css style sheet to the project.

2. Replace the `<form>` and `<div>` elements in the document body with a code render block and a `while` statement that prints all even numbers between 1 and 100 to the screen.

3. Save the project, and then test the Web site.

4. Close your Web browser window and then close the project.

Exercise 3-4

In this project, you will identify and fix the logic flaws in a `while` statement.

1. Create a new ASP.NET Web Site in the Visual Studio IDE and save it in a folder named WhileLogic in your Exercises folder for Chapter 3. Change the content of the `<title>` element of the Default.aspx file to **While Logic** and add a `<link>` element above the closing `</head>` tag that links to the asp_styles.css style sheet file in your Chapter.03 folder. Add the asp_styles.css style sheet to the project.

2. Replace the `<form>` and `<div>` elements in the document body with a code render block and the following code:

```
<%
int count = 0;
int numbers = new int[100];
while (count > 100) {
    numbers[count] = count;
    ++count;
}
while (count > 100) {
    Response.Write(numbers[count] + "<br />");
    ++count;
}
%>
```

3. The code you typed in the preceding step should fill the array with the numbers 1 through 100, and then print them to the screen. However, the code contains several logic flaws that prevent it from running correctly. Identify and fix the logic flaws.

4. After fixing the errors, save the project, and then test the Web site.

5. Close your Web browser window and then close the project.

Exercise 3-5

In this project, you will modify a nested `if` statement so it uses a compound conditional expression instead. You use logical operators such as the || (OR) and && (AND) operators to execute a conditional or looping statement based on multiple criteria.

1. Create a new ASP.NET Web site in the Visual Studio IDE and save it in a folder named OilPrices in your Exercises folder for Chapter 3. Change the content of the `<title>` element of the Default.aspx file to **Oil Prices** and add a `<link>` element above the closing `</head>` tag that links to the asp_styles.css style sheet file in your Chapter.03 folder. Add the asp_styles.css style sheet to the project.

2. Replace the `<form>` and `<div>` elements in the document body with a code render block that contains the following variable declaration and nested `if` statement:

```
<%
double oilPrice = 52.85;
if (oilPrice > 50) {
    if (oilPrice < 60)
        Response.Write("<p>Oil prices are between
            $50.00 and $60.00 a barrel.</p>");
}
%>
```

3. Modify the nested `if` statement you created in the previous step so it uses a single `if` statement with a compound conditional expression to determine whether oil prices are between $50.00 and $60.00 a barrel. You will need to use the && (AND) logical operator.

4. Save the project, and then test the Web site.

5. Close your Web browser window and then close the project.

Discovery Projects

Save the following projects in the Projects folder for Chapter 3.

Project 3-1

Write a program that calculates a 15% return on an investment of
$10,000. Calculate the number of years required for a single $10,000
investment to reach $1,000,000 at an average annual return of 15%.
Use a looping statement and assume that each iteration is equivalent
to one year. Save the project as **Investments**.

Project 3-2

Use an appropriate looping statement to write a program that prints
a list of the Celsius equivalents of zero degrees Fahrenheit through
100 degrees Fahrenheit. To convert Fahrenheit to Celsius, subtract 32
from the Fahrenheit temperature, and then multiply the remainder
by .55. Save the project as **TempConversion**.

Project 3-3

Create a program that calculates an employee's weekly gross salary,
based on the number of hours worked and an hourly wage that you
choose. Use an HTML document containing a form with two text
boxes—one for the number of hours worked and the other for the
hourly wage. Submit the form to the Default.aspx file. Calculate the pay
in a function that returns a string containing the amount to the calling statement, which prints the string. Compute any hours over 40 as
time and a half. Use the appropriate decision structure to create the
program. Save the project as **Paycheck**.

Project 3-4

Create a program that calculates the square feet of carpet required
to carpet a room. Use an HTML document containing a form with
three text boxes. Create one text box for the width of the room in
linear feet and another for the length of the room in linear feet. Also,
create a text box for the cost per square foot of carpeting. When
you calculate the cost, add 25% to the total number of square feet to
account for closets and other features of the room. Save the project
as **CarpetCost**.

Project 3-5

Write a program that allows users to enter a number of cents into a
text box. Use an HTML document containing a form with a single
text box to enter the number of cents. Determine how many dollars

the cents make up and print the number of dollars and remaining cents. Save the project as **CentsToDollars**.

Project 3-6

You can determine whether a year is a leap year by testing if it is divisible by 4. However, years that are also divisible by 100 are not leap years, unless they are also divisible by 400, in which case they are leap years. Write a program that allows a user to enter a year and then determines whether the year entered is a leap year. Use an HTML document containing a form with a single text box to enter the year. Print a message to the user stating whether the year they entered is a standard year or a leap year. Save the project as **LeapYear**.

Project 3-7

The combined length of any two sides of a triangle must be greater than the length of the third side for the segments to form a triangle. For example, 8, 6, and 12 can form a triangle because the sum of any two of the three segments is greater than the third segment. However, 25, 5, and 15 cannot form a triangle because the sum of segments 5 and 15 are not greater than the length of segment 25. Using this logic, write a program that allows a user to enter three integers, one for each side of a triangle. Test whether the three sides can form a triangle. Use an HTML document containing a form with three text boxes to gather the segment lengths from the user. Print a message to the user that states whether their segments can form a triangle. Save the project as **Triangle**.

Project 3-8

Write a program that allows a user to enter a number between 1 and 999. Determine whether the number is a prime number and display your results with a `Response.Write()` statement. A prime number is a number than can only be divided by itself or by one. Examples of prime numbers include 1, 3, 5, 13, and 17. Use an HTML document containing a form with a single text box in which users can enter a number. You need to use a looping statement to test all division possibilities. Save the project as **PrimeNumbers**.

CHAPTER 4

Introduction to Web Forms and Controls

In this chapter you will:

◎ Learn about ASP.NET Web forms and server controls

◎ Work with ASP.NET Web server controls

◎ Validate user input with validation controls

Up to this point in the book, you've been coding all of the HTML elements in your projects by hand. However, one of the most important features of ASP.NET is the ability to use Web Forms pages and ASP.NET controls. With these features, you can quickly build powerful interfaces for your Web sites using special types of controls. These controls, which are similar to HTML elements such as forms and buttons, can be controlled programmatically with C#. You might be wondering: If these features are so powerful, why weren't they introduced earlier in the book? The reason is that, before you can be successful with Web Forms pages and ASP.NET controls, you need a solid understanding of the basics of ASP.NET and C#.

This chapter introduces you to the basics of ASP.NET Web Forms pages and Web server controls, including how to create dynamic forms and use complex controls, such as calendars and ad rotators, with your Web pages. You will also learn how to quickly validate user input with validation controls.

Understanding ASP.NET Web Forms and Server Controls

One of the primary uses of Web page forms is submitting user data to a server. Server-side scripting environments such as ASP.NET can then process the submitted data and return a response to the client, store the data in a database, or use the data to perform some other type of task. Typical forms that you submit to a server-side program include order forms, surveys, and applications. Another type of form frequently found on Web pages gathers search criteria from a user. After the user enters search criteria, the data is sent to a database on a Web server. The server then queries the database, using the data gathered in the search form, and returns the results to a Web browser. The data that an ASP.NET program receives from a form submission usually takes the form of a text string assigned to the `Request.QueryString` and `Request.Form` collections, which you can process with C# string functions and manipulation techniques.

JavaScript is often used with forms to validate or process form data before the data is submitted to a server-side program. For example, customers might use an online order form to order merchandise from your Web site. When a customer clicks the form's Submit button, you can use JavaScript to ensure that the customer has entered important information, such as his name, shipping address, and so on. The problem with using JavaScript to validate form data is that you cannot always ensure that the data submitted to your ASP.NET program was submitted from the Web page containing the JavaScript validation code. Every self-respecting hacker knows how to bypass JavaScript validation code in an HTML form by appending a query string directly to the URL of the ASP.NET program that processes the form. If a user does bypass the form and type the URL and a query string in the Address box of a Web browser, any JavaScript validation code in the Web page containing the form fails to execute. Because JavaScript validation code can be bypassed in this way, you should always include C# code to validate any submitted data. If your program lacks such code, you cannot be sure that all of the necessary data was submitted (such as a shipping address for an online order) nor can you tell if an unscrupulous hacker is attempting to submit malicious data that might cause problems in your script or on your Web site.

In this chapter, you will start working on a Web site for a company named Big River Kayaking that offers kayaking lessons. The Web site consists of three pages: a home page, individual reservations, and group reservations. Your Chapter folder for Chapter 4 contains a folder named BigRiverKayaking where you can find the files that you will need for this project. First, you will add a form to the Individual Reservations page that handles the submission of a form, which you will also create.

To start Visual Web Developer and add a form to the Individual Reservations page:

1. Click the **Start** button, point to **All Programs**, and then click **Microsoft Visual Web Developer 2008 Express Edition**. The Visual Studio integrated development environment (IDE) appears.

2. Click the **File** menu and then click **Open Web Site**. The Open Web Site dialog box opens. Locate the BigRiverKayaking folder in your Chapter folder for Chapter 4, highlight the folder name, and then click **Open**. After the project opens, double-click **single.aspx** in the Solution Explorer window to open it in the Code Editor.

3. Scroll down in the single.aspx file until you locate [Add form here], and replace it with the following text and elements, which create a form containing basic information for creating a reservation. Notice that the action attribute of the <form> element is assigned a value of single.aspx, which submits the form to itself. Also notice that the form contains a hidden form field; you will use this field to store a Boolean value that indicates whether the form is being opened for the first time or if it has already been submitted to itself.

```
<form action="single.aspx"
method="post">
<p>
  Last name<br />
  <input type="text" name="lastName"
  size="40" /><br />
  First name<br />
  <input type="text" name="firstName"
  size="40" /><br />
```

Recall that the POST method sends form data as a transmission separate from the URL specified by the action attribute. However, don't think that you can force users to submit form data from a Web page by specifying the POST method. Anyone who has a strong understanding of HTTP headers can construct a separate transmission containing the form data required by your program.

HTML forms are not used solely for gathering data that is submitted to users; they are also used as containers for creating interactive features such as games or calculators.

```
Telephone<br />
<input type="text" name="telephone"
size="40" /><br />
E-mail<br />
<input type="text" name="email" size="40" /><br />
Confirm e-mail<br />
<input type="text" name="confirmEmail"
size="40" /><br />
Preferred date <br />
<input type="text" name="date" size="40" />
</p>
  <p> Age (18 or older)
  <input type="text" name="age" size="10" />
  nbsp;
  <input type="submit" value="submit" />
  Text="Submit" />
  <input type="hidden" name="submitted" value="true" />
</p>
</form>
```

4. Start the Web site. Figure 4-1 shows how the Web page appears in a Web browser window.

5. Close your Web browser window.

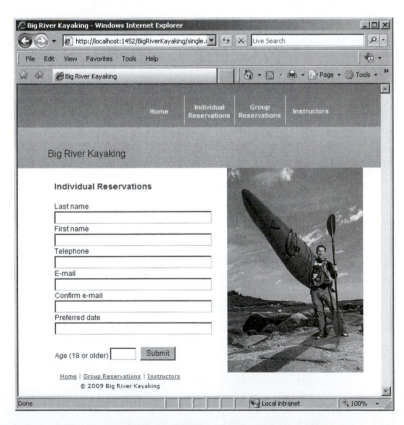

Figure 4-1 Big River Kayaking Individual Reservations page

In the next section, you will learn how to use a single page to display and process a standard HTML form. This technique helps force users to submit data from a form instead of trying to call a program directly. Then, you will learn how to perform the same technique with Web Forms pages.

Using a Single Page to Handle a Standard HTML Form

With traditional client/server architecture, a Web page form is submitted to another Web page that processes the data and returns a response to the user. However, this project requires that you develop two and sometimes more Web pages to handle the single task of gathering and processing user data. A better solution is to use a single Web page to do all of the work. To make this possible, the program must submit the form data to itself when the user clicks the Submit button. One way to do this with standard HTML is to use the `Request.QueryString` and `Request.Form` collections with validation code to ensure that the data exists when the form first opens and to ensure that the data was submitted correctly. For example, the following code contains a simple program and form that calculates body mass index with the formula `weight ÷ (height x height) x 703`.

```
<h1>Body Mass Index</h1><hr />
<%
double weight = Convert.ToDouble(Request.
QueryString["height"]);
double height = Convert.ToDouble(Request.
QueryString["weight"]);
double bodyMass = weight / (height * height) * 703;
Response.Write("<p>Your body mass index is "
   + bodyMass + "</p>");
%>
<form action="Default.aspx" method="get">
<p>Height: <input type="text" name="height" size="30"
value= <%= height %> /> (Enter a height in inches)</p>
<p>Weight: <input type="text" name="weight" size="30"
value= <%= weight %> />  (Enter a weight in pounds)</p>
<p><input type="submit" value="Calculate" />
<input type="reset" value="Reset Form" /></p>
</form><hr />
```

Notice that the ASP.NET code in the preceding example refers to the `Request.QueryString["weight"]` and `Request.QueryString["height"]` variables. However, when you first open the document, it generates errors because values have not been assigned to either variable. If your program attempts to use a nonexistent variable, you will receive an error. This problem will also occur if someone attempts to bypass the form by typing the program name and a query string in the address box of a Web browser. To prevent this problem, you can use a conditional expression to check if a submitted variable contains a null value, which means the variable does not yet exist, or if the variable contains an empty string, which means the variable exists but has not been assigned a value.

The following modified version of the body mass code uses a conditional expression that checks whether the form variables exist before the calculation is performed. Because the form was submitted with the get method, the code checks if the variables contain null values.

```csharp
double weight = 0;
double height = 0;
double bodyMass = 0;
if (Request.QueryString["height"] != null &&
        Request.QueryString["height"] != "" &&
        Request.QueryString["weight"] != null &&
        Request.QueryString["weight"] != "")
{
    weight = Convert.ToDouble(Request.QueryString["weight"]);
    height = Convert.ToDouble(Request.QueryString["height"]);
    bodyMass = weight / (height * height) * 703;
}
Response.Write("<p>Your body mass index is "
  + bodyMass + "</p>");
```

The C# interpreter does not automatically convert a text box value from a string to a number. To ensure that you can use the value from a text box in a mathematical calculation, you must use one of the methods of the Convert class to convert the string to the appropriate data type. For example, to convert a string to a long data type, you use the ToInt32() method, and to convert a string to a double data type, you use the ToDouble() method. However, you cannot be sure that a user will always enter a number into each text box. If a submitted form value must be numeric data, you should use a TryParse() method to convert a string variable to the required data type. Each of the primitive numeric data types in C# includes a **TryParse() method** that you can use to convert a string variable to that particular data type. The basic syntax for the TryParse() methods is *type*.TryParse(*string*, out *variable*). The TryParse() methods perform two tasks: They return a Boolean value indicating whether the conversion was successful and they also assign the converted value to the variable in the second argument. However, this assignment only occurs when the string value is in the proper format. If it is not in the proper format, the original value in the variable remains unaltered. Note that the TryParse() methods require the use of the out keyword as the second argument. The following statements demonstrate how to use the TryParse() method with a float value:

```csharp
string interestRateString = "6.5";
float interestRateNum = 0;
```

```
Boolean parseResult = float.TryParse(interestRateString,
    out interestRateNum);
Response.Write("<p>The parse operation returned a value of "
    + parseResult + " and the votingAgeNum variable now
    contains a value of " + interestRateNum + ".</p>");
```

The following example contains a modified version of the body mass index program. This version uses TryParse() methods to test whether the Request.QueryString["weight"] and Request.QueryString["height"] variables contain numeric values. Note that the code no longer requires the conditional expression that checks for null values or empty strings because if the variables do not exist, the TryParse() methods return a value of false.

 Later in this chapter, you will learn how to validate user data much more easily with ASP.NET validation controls.

```
double weight = 0;
double height = 0;
double bodyMass = 0;
if (double.TryParse(Request.QueryString["weight"], out weight)
    && double.TryParse(Request.QueryString["height"],
    out height))
    bodyMass = weight / (height * height) * 703;
Response.Write("<p>Your body mass index is "
    + Convert.ToInt16(bodyMass) + "</p>");
```

Next, you will add a program to the Individual Reservations page that validates the form data when it's submitted:

To add a form validation program to the Individual Reservations page:

1. Return to the **single.aspx** file in the Visual Studio IDE.

2. Add the following code render block immediately above the form:

    ```
    <%
    %>
    ```

3. Add to the code render block the following variable declaration statements. The first statement creates a Boolean variable that will be used to determine whether the form has already been submitted to itself. The remaining statements create variables to store the form values. With the exception of the last statement, which assigns a default value of 18 to the age variable, the remaining statements assign to each variable the corresponding values in the Request.Form collection.

    ```
    string lastName = Request.Form["lastName"];
    string firstName = Request.Form["firstName"];
    string telephone = Request.Form["telephone"];
    string email = Request.Form["email"];
    string confirmEmail = Request.Form["confirmEmail"];
    string date = Request.Form["date"];
    int ageCheck = 18;
    ```

4. Add the following if statement to the end of the code render block, which checks if the Request.Form["submitted"] variable exists. If the variable does not exist, it means that this is the first time the page has been loaded because the "submitted" hidden control has not been rendered. If the Request.Form["submitted"] variable does exist, the form is currently being loaded as the result of a submission.

```
if (Request.Form["submitted"] == "true")
{
}
```

5. Add the following statements to the if statement you created in the Step 4. These statements verify that each field contains a value, that the password and confirm password fields contain the same values, and that the age field contains a value of 18 or older.

```
if (Request.Form["lastName"] == null ||
    Request.Form["lastName"] == ""
    || Request.Form["firstName"] == null ||
    Request.Form["firstName"] == ""
    || Request.Form["telephone"] == null ||
    Request.Form["telephone"] == ""
    || Request.Form["email"] == null ||
    Request.Form["email"] == ""
    || Request.Form["confirmEmail"] == null ||
    Request.Form["confirmEmail"] == ""
    || Request.Form["date"] == null ||
    Request.Form["date"] == ""
    || Request.Form["age"] == null ||
    Request.Form["age"] == "") {
        Response.Write("<p><strong>You
            must enter values in each
            field.</strong></p>");
}
else if (Request.Form["email"]
  != Request.Form["confirmEmail"])
  Response.Write("<p><strong>You
    did not enter the same value in
    the e-mail and e-mail
    confirmation fields.</strong></p>");
else if (!int.TryParse(Request.Form["age"],
  out ageCheck))
  Response.Write("<p><strong>You
    must enter an integer in the
    age field.</strong></p>");
else if (ageCheck < 18)
Response.Write("<p><strong>You
  must be 18 or older.</strong></p>");
else
```

```
Response.Write("<p><strong>Your reservation
    has been submitted. A confirmation
    message has been sent to your e-mail
    address.</strong></p>");
```

6. Start the Web site. The single.aspx file opens in a Web browser. Test the validation code in the form to ensure that it requires you to enter values in each field, enter the same value in the e-mail and confirm e-mail fields, and enter a value of 18 or higher in the age field.

7. Close your Web browser window.

Using Web Forms

ASP.NET's model for handling forms represents a departure from the traditional HTML method of submitting a form. Instead of simply submitting data to a server, you can use ASP.NET's **Web forms** to quickly build dynamic interfaces containing sophisticated Web server controls that can access data sources, validate user input, handle site navigation, manage security issues such as logins and password recovery, and perform numerous other tasks. The key difference between standard HTML elements and Web forms is that Web forms (and the server controls they contain) can be controlled programmatically with ASP.NET.

When you first create a new ASP.NET Web site, the default.aspx file contains the following elements. Notice that the <form> element contains the runat="server" attribute, which identifies the form as an ASP.NET Web form that should be processed on the server instead of the client. Without the runat="server" attribute, the form would be treated as a standard HTML form.

```
<%@ Page Language="C#" AutoEventWireup="true"
CodeFile="Default.aspx.cs" Inherits="_Default" %>
<!DOCTYPE html PUBLIC "-//W3C//DTD XHTML 1.0
Transitional//EN" "http://www.w3.org/TR/xhtml1/DTD/
xhtml1-transitional.dtd">
<html xmlns="http://www.w3.org/1999/xhtml">
<head runat="server">
    <title>Untitled Page</title>
</head>
<body>
    <form ID="form1" runat="server">
    <div>
    </div>
    </form>
</body>
</html>
```

Web forms can submit data to a server, but how the server receives the data differs significantly from standard HTML forms. The most critical thing you need to understand is that a Web form only submits data to itself, in the same way that the Web page you saw in the last section submitted data to itself. In fact, you cannot submit a Web form to another URL; if you include the `action` attribute that identifies a URL to which a form should be submitted, it will be ignored. Instead, if you submit a Web form by clicking a submit button, by default its data will be posted back to the Web page itself. The process by which form data is posted back to the same page with a Web form is called **post back**. After a Web form is submitted, the post back mechanism automatically restores the form's value. Whether or not data is posted back to a Web page is determined by its **view state**. With post back and view state, you do not need to retrieve the form values that were submitted with the `Response.QueryString` or `Response.Form` collections.

You can add controls to a Web form either by dragging them from the Toolbox to the desired location in your code or by manually typing them, although it is usually easier to drag them from the Toolbox. This book simply instructs you to add controls to a Web form. If you add controls using the Toolbox, be sure they match the code lists in this book.

Consider the following Web form, which contains two Web server `TextBox` controls and a `Button` control. The `TextBox` control is equivalent to the `<input type="text">` HTML element and the `Button` control is equivalent to the HTML button element. Both the `TextBox` control and `Button` control are ASP.NET Web server controls. Later in this chapter, you will study ASP.NET Web server controls extensively. For now, you need to understand that the difference between Web server controls and HTML elements is that you can programmatically access and manipulate Web server controls on the server with an ASP.NET program. Standard HTML controls can only be accessed and manipulated programmatically on the client using JavaScript. By default, the Button control submits a form's values. Notice that all three controls include the `runat="server"` attribute. If you open the Web page containing the form in a browser, enter values in the two text fields, and then click the Submit button, the page will reload and the values you entered will appear in the reloaded page.

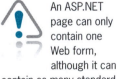

An ASP.NET page can only contain one Web form, although it can contain as many standard HTML forms as you need.

```
<form ID="form1" runat="server">
<div>
    First name <asp:TextBox ID="firstName"
    runat="server" /><br />
    Last name  <asp:TextBox ID="lastName"
    runat="server" />
    <asp:Button ID="submit" runat="server"
    Text="Submit" /></div>
</form>
```

Next, you will change the form and fields on the Individual Reservations page to a Web form and server controls.

1. Return to the **single.aspx** file in the Visual Studio IDE.

2. Replace the form with the following Web form. Note that TextBox controls support a `Width` attribute, but not the `size` attribute and that the text that appears as the label of a Button control is assigned to the `Text` attribute, not the `value` attribute that is used with standard HTML buttons. Notice that the text boxes do not include `value` attributes because they are populated automatically through post back.

```
<form ID="resForm" runat="server" >
<p>
    Last name<br />
    <asp:TextBox ID="lastName" runat="server"
        Width="265" /><br />First name<br />
    <asp:TextBox ID="firstName" runat="server"
        Width="265" /><br />Telephone<br />
    <asp:TextBox ID="telephone" runat="server"
        Width="265" /><br />E-mail<br />
    <asp:TextBox ID="email" runat="server"
        Width="265" /><br />Confirm e-mail<br />
    <asp:TextBox ID="confirmEmail" runat="server"
        Width="265" /><br />Preferred date<br />
    <asp:TextBox ID="date" runat="server"
        Width="265" />
    </p>
<p>
    Age (18 or older)
    <asp:TextBox ID="age" runat="server"
        Width="40" /> 
    <asp:Button ID="makeReservation" runat="server"
        Text="Submit" /></p>
</form>
```

3. Save the project.

View state is maintained by assigning the form values to a hidden form field named __VIEWSTATE. The form's values are assigned to the __VIEWSTATE field's `value` attribute, encoded with Base64. Because the Web form is processed on the server, you will not see the Web form or server control code if you view the source of the Web page. Instead, you will see standard HTML, and sometimes JavaScript code, that the ASP.NET program returned to the client. The following code shows how the source is rendered by a Web page for the preceding form, with the encoded values for "Don" and "Gosselin" that were assigned to the First name and Last name fields.

```
<form name="form1" method="post" action="Default.aspx"
ID="form1">
<div>
<input type="hidden" name="__VIEWSTATE" ID="__VIEWSTATE"
value="/wEPDwULLTExNTc2NTI3OTlkZGseEs16T2LhIIzZIOJ4hrz/
zDB4" />
```

 The preceding form also contains a hidden form field with an attribute named __EVENTVALIDATION. An ASP.NET security feature uses this attribute to help prevent unauthorized post back requests from hackers or other nefarious individuals.

 Base64 is a MIME content transfer encoding type that encodes data to the base-64 system, which is a numeral system based on 64. Converting form values to base-64 allows the values to contain nonalphanumeric characters that HTTP does not allow.

```
    </div>
        <div>
            First name <input name="firstName" type="text"
            value="Don" ID="firstName" /><br />
            Last name <input name="lastName" type="text"
            value="Gosselin" ID="lastName" />
            <input type="submit" name="submit" value="Submit"
              ID="submit" />
        </div>
    <div>
        <input type="hidden" name="__EVENTVALIDATION"
          ID="__EVENTVALIDATION" value="/
        wEWBALGvdGNDALniKOhBALSt4P
            gAgLcu4S2BA8quqssC6S5qn9rkT7d4aW3lB7I" />
</div></form>
```

You might be wondering why you would want to disable view state. One reason you would disable view state is to improve performance. For Web forms or individual controls that gather large amounts of data, preserving the view state for each submit request can significantly slow down the rendering of the page containing the Web form. Or, for security reasons you might want to disable view state for individual controls that contain sensitive data, such as credit card information or Social Security numbers.

By default, view state is enabled in ASP.NET Web pages, but you can disable it by assigning a value of false to the EnableViewState attribute of the @ Page processing directive, as follows:

```
<%@ Page Language="C#" EnableViewState="false" %>
```

You can also disable view state for individual controls by adding an EnableViewState attribute to the control element's opening tag and assigning it a value of false. The following example demonstrates how to disable the view state for the First name field:

```
First name <asp:TextBox ID="firstName" runat="server"
    EnableViewState="False" />
```

A Web form contains the same attributes as an HTML form, but also includes the additional ASP.NET attributes that are listed in Table 4-1.

Attribute	Description
DefaultButton	Identifies the ID of the button that should submit the form when the Enter key is pressed when the focus is on any of the form's input elements
DefaultFocus	Specifies the ID of the form element that should receive focus when the page first loads
EnableViewState	Determines whether view state is enabled for the form; accepts a value of true or false
SubmitDisabledControls	Specifies whether the values of disabled controls should be submitted with the form data; accepts a value of true or false
Visible	Determines if the form is visible; accepts a value of true or false

Table 4-1   ASP.NET Web form attributes

Like other types of attributes, you can assign values to ASP.NET attributes, such as the Web form attributes listed in Table 4-1, by assigning a value to the attribute in the `<form>` tag. For example, a form contains multiple `Button` controls. To specify which button submits the form to itself when the Enter key is pressed, you can assign the ID of the button to the `<form>` element's `DefaultButton` attribute. The following `<form>` tag demonstrates how to specify a button with an ID of `submitOrder` as the default button:

```
<form ID="form1" runat="server" DefaultButton="submitOrder">
```

ASP.NET attributes—and numerous other properties—can also be set programmatically with C# by appending the attribute or property name to the control's ID value with a period and assigning the appropriate value. The following statement demonstrates how to use C# to disable view state for a `TextBox` control with an ID of `creditCardNum`:

```
creditCardNum.EnableViewState = false;
```

To retrieve the value currently assigned to a TextBox control, you use the `Text` property of the control ID. The following statement assigns the value of a TextBox control with an ID of `address` to a string variable named `shippingAddress`.

```
string shippingAddress = address.Text;
```

You might be asking yourself an important question: If you cannot submit Web form values to another Web page, then how do you store the data in a database or process the data in some way, and then return a response to the user? If you have any experience with Web development, you are probably accustomed to using a target Web page (which is a different Web page from the requesting Web page) to process the data and return a response to the user. With ASP.NET Web forms, you use the same page to gather and process submitted data. Remember that Web forms and the server controls they contain can be manipulated programmatically on the server. After a user submits a form to the server, a server-side program within the same Web page can then process the data and return a response to the user. The trick is to use the form's `Visible` attribute to hide the form in the response that is returned after the form data is successfully processed, and then display an alternate message to the user informing him or her if the form submission was successful. For example, if a form's values validate successfully, you would call a function or method in the same form to store the data in a database or process it in some way. However, instead of displaying the form again, you would hide it and display an alternate message. The following code assumes that the data from a form with an ID attribute value of `orderForm` was processed successfully on the last form submission. Instead of displaying the form again, the code hides the form by assigning a value of false to the `Visible` property of the form, and then uses the `Response.Write()` statement to display a success message to the user.

```
orderForm.Visible = false;
Response.Write("<p>Thank you for your order!
  A confirmation message has been sent to
  your e-mail address.</p>");
```

So far, you have used a hidden form field to determine whether a page has already been submitted. With Web forms, you can use the `Page` class's **IsPostBack property** to determine whether a Web form has already been submitted. When a user opens a Web form for the first time, the `IsPostBack` property is assigned a value of false. However, after a user submits a Web form and post back occurs, the `IsPostBack` property is assigned a value of true. You can use the `IsPostBack` property to determine when to validate submitted data.

Next, you will modify the Individual Reservations page so it uses the Web form control IDs and the `IsPostBack` property to validate the submitted data.

To validate the Individual Reservations page using Web control IDs and the `IsPostBack` property:

1. Return to the **single.aspx** file in the Visual Studio IDE.

2. Delete the following variable declarations from the beginning of the code render block, but be sure to leave the `ageCheck` variable declaration.

    ```
    string lastName = Request.Form["lastName"];
    string firstName = Request.Form["firstName"];
    string telephone = Request.Form["telephone"];
    string email = Request.Form["email"];
    string confirmEmail = Request.Form["confirmEmail"];
    string date = Request.Form["date"];
    ```

3. Change the conditional expression in the first `if` statement so it checks the `IsPostBack` property instead of the value stored in the hidden form field.

    ```
    if (Page.IsPostBack)
    ```

4. Modify each of the `Request.Form` collection references in the remainder of the code render block so they reference each control's `ID` and `Text` property.

5. Finally, modify the last `else` statement as follows so it hides the Web form if the data validates:

    ```
    else
    {
        resForm.Visible = false;
    ```

```
            Response.Write("<p><strong>Your reservation
               has been submitted. A confirmation message
               has been sent to your e-mail address.
               </strong></p>");
        }
```

6. Verify that the modified code render block appears as follows:

```
<%
    int ageCheck = 18;
    if (Page.IsPostBack)
    {
        if (lastName.Text == null
            || lastName.Text == ""
            || firstName.Text == null
            || firstName.Text == ""
            || telephone.Text == null
            || telephone.Text == ""
            || email.Text == null
            || email.Text == ""
            || confirmEmail.Text == null
            || confirmEmail.Text == ""
            || date.Text == null
            || date.Text == ""
            || age.Text == null
            || age.Text == "")
        {
            Response.Write("<p><strong>You must enter
               values in each field.</strong></p>");
        }
        else if (email.Text != confirmEmail.Text)
            Response.Write("<p><strong>You did not
               enter the same value in the e-mail
               and e-mail confirmation  fields.
               </strong></p>");
        else if (!int.TryParse(age.Text,
            out ageCheck))
            Response.Write("<p><strong>You must
               enter an integer in the age field.
               </strong></p>");
        else if (ageCheck < 18)
            Response.Write("<p><strong>You must
               be 18 or older.</strong></p>");
        else
        {
            resForm.Visible = false;
            Response.Write("<p><strong>Your
               reservation has been submitted.
               A confirmation message has
               been sent to your e-mail
               address.</strong></p>");
        }
    }
%>
```

7. Start the Web site. The single.aspx file opens in a Web browser. Enter valid data into each of the fields and click Submit. The form should be hidden and you should see the confirmation message shown in Figure 4-2.

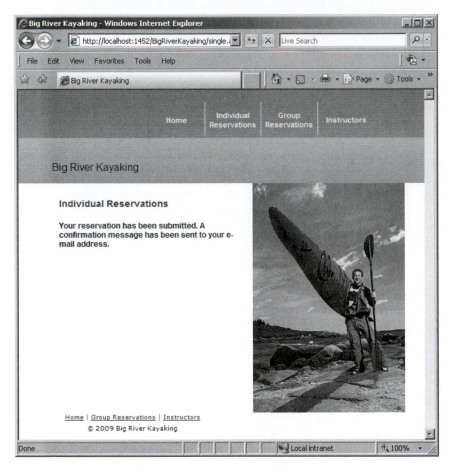

Figure 4-2 Confirmation message after successfully submitting a form

8. Close your Web browser window.

To properly use Web forms and post back, you need to understand events, which you will study next.

Understanding Events

You will study application events in Chapter 6.

The primary ways in which code is executed on a Web page is through events. An **event** is a specific circumstance (such as an action performed by a user or an action performed by the browser) that is monitored by the browser and that your program can respond to in some way. As you will see in this section, you can use events to allow users to interact with your Web pages. The most common events are actions that users perform. For example, when a user clicks a form button, a `Click` event is generated, or *raised*. You can think of an event as a trigger that fires specific code in response to a given situation. User-generated events, however, are not the only kinds of events monitored by the browser. ASP.NET supports three types of events: application events that occur automatically at different stages in an application's life cycle, page events that occur automatically at different stages in a page's life cycle, and control events that are raised by actions that are performed on individual server controls. For example, the `Load` event occurs automatically when a page finishes loading.

With standard HTML, an XHTML element can be associated with a specific event (such as a click); code written in JavaScript, VBScript, or some other client-side scripting language executes when the event occurs. For example, an HTML `<button>` element is typically associated with a `click` event; the `click` event, in turn, could contain JavaScript code that executes some sort of task, such as changing the color of the page or performing a calculation. Similarly, a text element might be associated with a `change` event that occurs when the contents of the text box or other control changes. The `change` event could, among other things, execute JavaScript code that validates the new value. Table 4-2 lists some JavaScript events and explains what triggers them.

With JavaScript, events are referred to with all lowercase letters (for example, `click` event). In ASP.NET, events are referred to with initial capitalization (for example, `Click` event).

ASP.NET supports many of the same events that JavaScript supports, and a few others that you will learn about later in this chapter. The important thing to understand about the difference between ASP.NET and JavaScript events is that ASP.NET events are processed on the server, whereas JavaScript events are processed on the client (that is, within the Web browser).

Event	Triggered when
abort	The loading of an image is interrupted
blur	An element, such as a radio button, becomes inactive
click	The user clicks an element once
change	The value of an element, such as text box, changes
error	An error occurs when a document or image is being loaded
focus	An element, such as a command button, becomes active
load	A document or image loads
mouseout	The mouse moves off an element
mouseover	The mouse moves over an element
reset	A form's fields are reset to its default values
select	A user selects a field in a form
submit	A user submits a form
unload	A document unloads

Table 4-2 JavaScript events

Writing Event Handlers

When an event occurs, your program executes the code that responds to that particular event. A function or method that executes in response to a specific event is called an **event handler**. By default, page event handlers are named Page_*event*(). For example, the event handler for the Load event, which occurs automatically when a page finishes loading, is Page_Load(). Event handler methods require two parameters: an object argument, which represents the raised event, and an EventArgs parameter, which is used for passing data with an event. These parameters are required for all event handlers although they do not contain any values for page events; they are primarily used for control events. The following code demonstrates the event handler for the Load event:

```
void Page_Load(object source, EventArgs E)
{
    statements;
}
```

So far in this book, you have embedded C# code in ASP.NET pages as inline code with code render blocks and code declaration blocks. The preferred method for working with C# code is to place it in a **code-behind page**, which is a separate class file that contains properties for an associated page. Every ASP.NET page has an associated code-behind page with an extension of .cs. For example, the code-behind page for a Default.aspx file is Default.aspx.cs. Each code-behind page is automatically created with the following code:

```
using System;
using System.Collections.Generic;
using System.Linq;
using System.Web;
using System.Web.UI;
using System.Web.UI.WebControls;
public partial class _Default : System.Web.UI.Page
{
    protected void Page_Load(object sender, EventArgs e)
    {

    }
}
```

The using statements at the beginning of the file specify namespaces to use with the program. A **namespace** is a container that manages the identifiers in a C# program. Different classes may use the same identifiers for class names, methods, and other items. With a large and complex program, then, it is only a matter of time before your program encounters two elements with identical names. Following the using statements is a class definition that contains a Page_Load() method. You will learn how classes are constructed in Chapter 10. For now, you just need to understand that methods are contained within a class, similar to the way functions are contained within a `<script>` section. A final point to mention is that the `Page_Load()` method definition is preceded by the protected access specifier. An **access specifier** determines the availability of a class's methods and properties. The **protected access specifier** only allows the class to access the method or property.

With control events, you can specify the name of the event handler by assigning the function or method name to an attribute in the format On*Event*. The following statements assign an event handler named `calcShipping_Click` to a Button Web server control. Note that you do not include the function's parentheses when you assign it to an event handler.

```
<asp:Button
ID="calcShipping"
Text="Calc Shipping Costs"
OnClick="calcShipping_Click"
Runat="server" />
```

The method definition for the `calcShipping_Click` event handler in the code-behind page would be written as follows:

```
protected void calcShipping_Click(object Source, EventArgs E)
{
    statements
}
```

 You can also quickly create an event handler for a control by double-clicking the control in Design view, which automatically creates a method in the code-behind page using the control's ID and default event type. For example, double-clicking a Button control with an ID of submitSurvey in Design view creates a method named submitSurvey_Click() in the code-behind page.

What Are the Available Page Events?

Table 4-3 lists the ASP.NET page events. Note that the events are listed in the order in which they execute.

Page event	Raised
PreInit	Before the page is initialized
Init	When the page is initialized
InitComplete	When page initialization is complete
PreLoad	Before the page is loaded
Load	When the page is loaded
Control events	After the page is loaded but before the load is complete
LoadComplete	When page loading is complete
PreRender	Before the page is rendered
SaveStateComplete	After the page finishes saving view and control state information
Render	When the page is rendered
Unload	When the page is unloaded

Table 4-3   ASP.NET page events

Page events are contained within the Page class, which, in addition to containing events, also defines numerous methods and properties for working with an ASP.NET page. You can find a complete listing of the Page class members at *http://msdn.microsoft.com/en-us/library/system. web.ui.page(VS.80).aspx.* One Page class member that you have already used is the IsPostBack property. The following Page_Load() event handler displays the confirmation text only if the IsPostBack property contains a value of true, meaning that the user has submitted the form.

```
protected void Page_Load(object Source, EventArgs E)
{
    if (Page.IsPostBack)
    {
        if (firstName.Text != "" && lastName.Text != "")
        {
            orderForm.Visible = false;
            Response.Write("<p>Thank you for your order!
                A confirmation message has been sent to
                your e-mail address.</p>");
        }
        else
            Response.Write("<p>You must enter
                values in the first and last
                name fields.</p>");
    }
}
```

The following code shows another example of the Page_Load() event handler. In this example, the Page_Load() event handler and IsPostBack property are used to calculate BMI after a user clicks the Calculate button. This version also includes code that checks if either the height or weight fields contain a value of 0, which will cause an error.

```
protected void Page_Load(object Source, EventArgs E)
{
    if (Page.IsPostBack)
    {
        double goodWeight = 0;
        double goodHeight = 0;
        double bodyMass = 0;
        if (Double.TryParse(height.Text, out goodWeight)
                && Double.TryParse(weight.Text, out goodHeight))
            if (goodHeight != 0 && goodWeight != 0)
            {
                bodyMass = goodWeight / (goodHeight
                    * goodHeight) * 703;
                Response.Write("<p>Your body mass index is "
                    + Convert.ToInt16(bodyMass) + "</p>");
            }
            else
                Response.Write("<p>You cannot enter
                    a value of 0 for your height or
                    weight!</p>");
```

```
        else
            Response.Write("<p>You did not enter
            valid values for your height and
            weight!</p>");
    }
}
```

The following code shows the Web form that uses the preceding code-behind page:

```
<form ID="form1" runat="server">
<div>
<p>Height: <asp:TextBox ID="height" runat="server"
Width="30">0</asp:TextBox>
 (Enter a height in inches)</p>
<p>Weight: <asp:TextBox ID="weight" runat="server"
Width="30">0</asp:TextBox>
 (Enter a weight in pounds)</p>
<p><asp:Button ID="submit" runat="server" Text="Calculate"
/></p>
</div>
</form>
```

Next, you will modify the Individual Reservations page so it uses the Page_Load() event handler:

To add the Page_Load() event handler to the Individual Reservations page:

1. Return to the **single.aspx** file in the Visual Studio IDE.

2. Copy the statements from the code render block, and then delete the code render block.

3. Open the single.aspx.cs file and paste the statements you copied in the previous step into the Page_Load() event handler, as follows:

   ```
   protected void Page_Load(object Source, EventArgs E)
   {
       int ageCheck = 18;
       if (Page.IsPostBack)
       {
           ...
   }
   ```

4. Start the Web site. The single.aspx file opens in a Web browser. Enter some invalid data into the form and click **Submit**. The code should function correctly, but the error messages will appear at the top of the page instead of in the page body. This occurs because the page events occur before the page finishes rendering. To fix this problem, you instead need to assign the message to a Label control that is placed above the Web form. You will learn about the Label control shortly.

5. Close your Web browser window.

Working with Control Events

Although it's easy enough to understand that page events execute automatically during the life cycle of a page (starting with `PreInit` and ending with `Unload`), it might not be so obvious to you what happens when a control event executes. If you know JavaScript, you probably understand that when an HTML event is raised, the JavaScript code that is embedded within the page executes in response. With ASP.NET server controls, post back occurs every time a server control event executes. In other words, the form is submitted each time a control event occurs. After post back occurs, the event handler for the control that raised the event executes on the server and a response is returned to the client, thus causing page events to execute.

For more information on JavaScript, refer to *JavaScript, Fourth Edition*, written by the author of this book and published by Course Technology.

This is an important concept when it comes to using Web forms, so it's worth repeating: Post back is initiated each time that a server control event is raised, which also causes each of the page events (`PreInit` through `Unload`) to execute. This means that your Web page will need to perform a round-trip to the server for every control event, which can seriously degrade the performance of your Web page. Although this book focuses on ASP.NET development, keep in mind that to improve the performance of your Web page, you might be better off using JavaScript for certain tasks. As mentioned in Chapter 1, a general rule of thumb is to allow the client to handle the user interface processing and light processing, such as data validation, but have the Web server perform intensive calculations and data storage. For example, later in this chapter you will learn how to use ASP.NET validation controls to validate user input. Although these controls are efficient and easy to use, they require a post back to the server for each validation attempt. For simple types of validation, such as verifying that a field contains a numeric value, you might be better off sticking to JavaScript validation techniques.

There are too many server control events to list here, but you can find a complete listing on the Control Events page of the Microsoft Developer Network at *http://msdn.microsoft.com/en-us/library/system.windows.forms.control_events.aspx*. Keep in mind that the events that are available to a server control vary. The `Click` event, for example, is available for the `Button` and `CheckBox` controls, but it's not available for the `MonthCalendar` and `DateTimePicker` controls. You will be introduced to the events that are available for each server control as you progress through this chapter.

What Are the Different Types of Controls?

ASP.NET supports the following types of controls:

- Server controls
- User controls
- Web parts controls

Server controls are special types of HTML controls, such as the TextBox and Button controls, that run on the server and that you can programmatically access and manipulate with an ASP.NET program. A **user control** is a customized type of control consisting of multiple server controls and HTML elements. **Web parts controls** allow users to directly control and manipulate the behavior and appearance of an ASP.NET page from within a Web browser. In this chapter, you will study the most commonly used server controls.

The ASP.NET controls you will use the most are server controls. They are broken down into the categories described in Table 4-4.

 HTML controls are the most basic types of server controls and are just some of the most commonly used HTML elements. Because you should already be familiar with HTML, this book does not cover HTML controls. However, you might find HTML controls useful for when you want to insert an HTML element without having to remember its exact syntax.

211

Category	Description
AJAX extensions	Contains controls that allow you to use AJAX programming techniques with ASP.NET pages
Data controls	Includes controls that allow you to connect ASP.NET pages to data sources, such as a SQL Server database
HTML controls	Represents standard HTML elements
Login controls	Includes security controls that you can use to create a login page
Navigation controls	Provides controls that assist users with site navigation
Standard controls	Contains common controls such as TextBox and Button controls, along with more specialized controls such as calendars and ad rotators
Validation controls	Contains controls that validate user input

Table 4-4   Server control categories

All of the ASP.NET controls are available in the Toolbox and are organized by control type, such as Standard, Data, Validation, and so on. You can quickly add a control to your form by dragging it from the Toolbox to the `<form>` element in a Web form. To display the Toolbox, select Toolbox from the View menu. The following example demonstrates the code that is added to a Web form when you drag the TextArea control (which creates an HTML `<textarea>` element) from the Toolbox to a Web form:

```
<textarea ID="TextArea1" cols="20" Rows="2"></textarea>
```

When you drag a control from the Toolbox to a Web form, the control is added as a tag pair. For example, a tag pair similar to the following is added when you drag the TextBox control from the Standard Toolbox to a Web form. The value contained within the tag pair (in this case, 6.5) becomes the control's default value:

```
<asp:TextBox ID="interestRate"
runat="server">6.5</asp:TextBox>
```

Although you need to set some ASP.NET server control properties manually, you can set many types of properties by using the Properties window.

You can also format various server controls as an empty element—that is, an element that does not require an ending tag. The following statement shows a modified version of the preceding control, but this time the control is formatted as an empty element. Notice that the control uses the Text attribute to specify the element's default text:

```
<asp:TextBox ID="interestRate" runat="server" Text="6.5" />
```

Short Quiz 1

1. Why should you use ASP.NET instead of JavaScript to validate submitted data?

2. Explain how to use the TryParse() method to convert a string variable to a particular data type.

3. How do you use a single Web form to gather and process submitted data?

4. What is a code-behind page?

5. When is a post back event initiated?

Using ASP.NET Standard Controls

In this section, you will study several of the ASP.NET standard controls, starting with the basic controls such as text boxes and hidden fields. Before beginning, you need to understand that there are many methods, properties, and events available to each server control. Methods, properties, and events that are common to more than one control are contained within the Control class. You can find a complete listing of the Control class members on the Microsoft Developer Network at *http://msdn.microsoft.com/en-us/library/system.windows.forms.control.aspx*. However, each individual control might also contain unique methods, properties, and events in a separate class that represents the control, such as the **TextBox** class that represents the TextBox control. There are too many methods, properties, and events to list in this chapter, so be sure to refer to the Microsoft Developer Network for a complete listing.

As you work through this section, keep in mind that although many of the standard server controls are very similar to their HTML counterparts, their primary purpose is to be manipulated programmatically on the server by ASP.NET code. If you do not anticipate that a particular control will need to be programmatically available to your ASP.NET program, you should use an equivalent HTML element instead. Although this section primarily focuses on describing each control's purpose and syntax, you will see many examples of how to programmatically manipulate the various controls as you progress through this book.

Text and Image Controls

This section discusses text and image controls, starting with the Label control.

Label Control

The **Label control** creates a control that is equivalent to the HTML <label> element, which associates a label with a form control, although it does not necessarily need to be associated with a label and can instead be used to programmatically set and modify text that appears on a page.

Although the Label control is equivalent to the HTML <label> element, it is rendered in a Web browser with a <span> element, not a <label> element.

In HTML, you use the **<label> element** to associate a label with a form control. You can associate a particular <label> element with only one form control. The content of the <label> element appears as the label for a control. You can include other elements, such as the <strong> and <em> elements, within the <label> element to modify the appearance of the label. In addition to allowing you to select controls by clicking a label, the <label> element allows you to select and deselect controls such as check boxes by clicking the control label. Another benefit of the <label> element is that it provides control descriptions to nonvisual browsers, helping ensure that a Web page is compatible with the widest number of user agents. You can use two attributes with the <label> element: accesskey and for. You learn about the accesskey attribute when you study form controls later in this section. You use the for attribute to associate a <label> element with a target form control. You assign to the for attribute the same value that is assigned to the target control's id attribute. When working with the ASP.NET Label control, you associate the label with a particular control by using the AssociatedControlID property instead of the for attribute.

You can use either a tag pair or an empty element to create the ASP.NET Label control. If you use a tag pair, the contents of the element are displayed as the label's text, as follows. Notice that the label is associated with a control that is assigned the ID firstName.

```
<asp:Label ID="firstNameLabel" runat="server"
AssociatedControlID="firstName">
First name: </asp:Label>
```

To create the Label control as an empty element, use the Text property to specify the label text, as follows:

```
<asp:Label ID="firstNameLabel" runat="server"
AssociatedControlID="firstName" Text="First name: " />
```

Next, you will add a Label control to the Individual Reservations page that will display the validation/submission results.

To add a validation/submission results Label control to the Individual Reservations page:

1. Return to the **single.aspx** file in the Visual Studio IDE.

2. Add the following paragraph element and Label control immediately above the Web form:

   ```
   <p><asp:Label ID="message" runat="server"
   Visible="false"></asp:Label></p>
   ```

3. Return to the **single.aspx.cs** file and replace the Response. Write() statement in the first if statement in the Page_Load() event handler with the following statements that display the Label control and assign a message to it:

   ```
   message.Visible = true;
   message.Text = "<p><strong>You must enter values in
       each field.</strong></p>";
   ```

4. Modify each of the else...if and else statement so they also display the Label control and assign a message to it, as follows:

   ```
   else if (email.Text != confirmEmail.Text) {
       message.Visible = true;
       message.Text = "<p><strong>You did not
           enter the same value in the e-mail and
           e-mail confirmation fields.</strong></p>";
   }
   else if (!int.TryParse(age.Text, out ageCheck)) {
       message.Visible = true;
       message.Text = "<p><strong>You must enter an
           integer in the age field.</strong></p>";
   }
   ```

```
else if (ageCheck < 18)
{
    message.Visible = true;
    message.Text = "<p><strong>You must be 18
      or older.</strong></p>";
}
else
{
    resForm.Visible = false;
    message.Visible = true;
    message.Text = "<p><strong>Your reservation
      has been submitted. A confirmation
      message has been sent to your e-mail
      address.</strong></p>";
}
```

5. Start the Web site. The single.aspx file opens in a Web browser. Test the validation code in the form to ensure that it works properly.

6. Close your Web browser window.

Literal Control

The **Literal control** adds literal text that is not rendered in any HTML elements, but that can be created and manipulated programmatically on the server. The difference between the Label control and the Literal control is that whereas a Label control is rendered with a `<span>` element using properties associated with the control itself, a Literal control is only rendered with the text and markup that you specify. This allows you to dynamically generate text and HTML markup with ASP.NET. You assign the text and markup that you want rendered to the Literal control's `Text` property or place it between the `<asp:Literal>` element's tag pairs. To programmatically modify the contents of a Label control, you assign a value to the `Text` property of the element ID. For example, consider a Web page that tracks checking account balances. Assume that the checking account balance is retrieved from a database. To format positive balances in blue and negative balances in red, you can use a `Page_Load()` event handler to format the text and elements that are assigned to a Literal control, as follows:

```
protected void Page_Load(object Source, EventArgs E)
{
    double checkingBalance = -1240.12;
    if (checkingBalance > 0)
        balance.Text = "<p><strong>Positive balance:
            <span style='color: blue'>"
            + String.Format("{0:C}", checkingBalance)
            + "</span></strong></p>";
```

```
else
    balance.Text = "<p><strong>Negative balance:
        <span style='color: red'>"
        + String.Format("{0:C}", checkingBalance)
        + "</span></strong></p>";
}
```

The following code shows the Web form that uses the preceding code-behind page:

```
<form ID="form1" runat="server">
<div><asp:Literal ID="balance" runat="server">
</asp:Literal></div></form>
```

Image Control

The **Image control** adds an image that is rendered with the HTML `<img>` element, and is created as an empty element, the same as with the HTML `<img>` element. To identify the image file that is associated with the Image control, you use the `ImageURL` property instead of the `src` attribute of the `<img>` element. Three additional Image control properties that you should know about are the `AlternateText`, `Height`, and `Width` properties, which are equivalent to the `alt`, `height`, and `width` attributes of the `<img>` element. For an XHTML document to be well formed, the `<img>` element must include an `src` attribute. Additionally, an `<img>` element must also include the `alt` attribute. The `alt` attribute, which specifies alternate text to display in place of the image file, is very important for user agents that do not display images (such as the text-based Lynx Web browser and Web browsers that are designed for users of Braille and speech devices). In addition, alternate text will display for the following reasons: An image has not yet downloaded, the user has turned off the display of images in her Web browser, or the image is not available.

When you create an `<img>` element that includes only the `src` and `alt` attributes, a Web browser needs to examine the image and determine the number of pixels to reserve for it. This can significantly slow down the time it takes for a Web page to render. However, if you use the `height` and `width` attributes to specify the size of an image, the Web browser will use these values to reserve enough space on the page for each image. This allows the Web browser to render all of the text on the page and then go back and render each image after it finishes downloading. Each image placeholder displays the image's alternative text until the image itself is rendered.

It is very important to assign `height` and `width` attribute values that are the exact dimensions of the original image. In other words, do not use the `height` and `width` attributes to resize an image on your Web page. If you want an image of a different size, use an image-editing program to create a new, smaller version of the image. (Most image-editing

---

The preceding code uses the `Format()` method of the `String` class to format the checking balance as currency. You will learn more about this method in Chapter 5.

The only reason to use the Image control instead of the HTML `<img>` element is if you want to programmatically manipulate the image with ASP.NET.

You can find the height and width of an image by opening the image in Internet Explorer or Firefox, right-clicking the image, and then selecting Properties from the shortcut menu. Both browsers display a Properties dialog box that shows the selected image's height and width in pixels.

programs include commands that automatically reduce the size of an image by a specified percentage or number of pixels.) Using the `height` and `width` attributes to change the size of an image on a Web page results in a poor quality image. One reason for this has to do with how you calculate the new dimensions of the image. Unless you correctly calculate the proportions of the number of pixels for both the `height` and `width` attributes that represent the image's new size, the image will appear stretched or squished and of poor quality.

The following example demonstrates an Image control that displays an image named companyLogo.jpg that is 200 pixels in height and 300 pixels in width:

```
<asp:Image ID="logo" runat="server" AlternateText="Image
of the corporate logo." ImageUrl="companyLogo.jpg"
Height="200" Width="300" />
```

Hyperlink Controls

This section discusses the controls that handle hyperlinks: HyperLink and ImageMap.

HyperLink Control

The **HyperLink control** adds a hyperlink that is rendered with the HTML <a> element, and is created as an empty element, the same as the HTML <img> element. To specify the link's target URL, you use the `NavigateURL` property. The following code shows how to use the HyperLink control to create a link to the Microsoft Developer Network:

```
<p>For comprehensive help and reference information on C#,
visit the
<asp:HyperLink ID="HyperLink1" runat="server"
NavigateUrl="http://msdn.microsoft.com/en-us/default.aspx">
Microsoft Developer Network</asp:HyperLink>.</p>
```

The HyperLink control can also be created as an empty element, as follows:

```
<p>For comprehensive help and reference information on C#,
visit the
<asp:HyperLink ID="HyperLink1" runat="server"
NavigateUrl="http://msdn.microsoft.com/en-us/default.aspx"
Text="Microsoft Developer Network" />.</p>
```

To use an image as a link anchor, assign the name of the image you want to use to the ImageURL property, as follows:

```
<p>For comprehensive help and reference information on C#,
visit the
<asp:HyperLink ID="HyperLink1" runat="server"
NavigateUrl="http://msdn.microsoft.com/en-us/default.aspx"
ImageURL="msdnLogo.jpg" />.</p>
```

The text or image used to represent a link on a Web page is called an anchor.

If a HyperLink control contains both `Text` and `ImageURL` properties, the `ImageURL` property takes precedence.

ImageMap Control

Images maps allow users to navigate to different Web pages by clicking on an area of an image. An image map consists of an image that is divided into regions. Each region is then associated with a URL; these regions are called **hot spots**. You can open the URL associated with each region by clicking the hot spot with your mouse. One of the most common uses of image maps is to create graphical menus that you can use for navigation. Using an image to create links to other Web pages gives you more flexibility than you would have by using hypertext links, allowing for a great deal more creativity. Figure 4-3 shows a typical image map that appears on the California Department of Transportation Web site at *http://www.dot.ca.gov/hq/roadinfo/ do7map.htm*. Clicking on a highlighted area displays another image map with detailed traffic information.

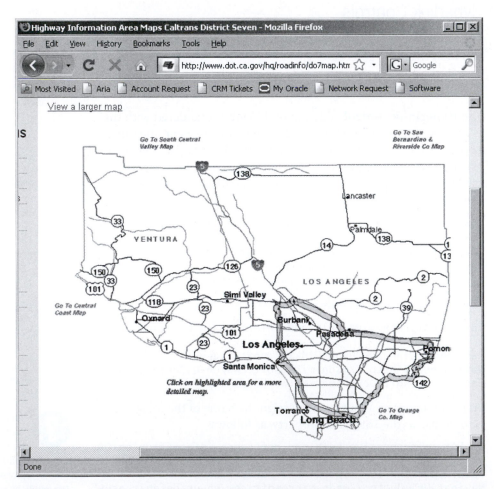

Figure 4-3 Image map on the California Department of Transportation Web site

To create an image map, you first use an **ImageMap control** to define the image. The ImageMap control accepts the same arguments as the Image control. To identify the image file that is associated with the ImageMap control, you use the `ImageURL` property instead of the `src` attribute of the `<img>` element. You can also use the `Alternate-Text` property to specify alternate text to display in place of the image file, and the `Height` and `Width` properties to declare the exact dimensions of the original image. The following ImageMap control defines an image map that uses an image file named NYCMap.jpg:

```
<asp:ImageMap ID="cityMap" ImageURL="NYCMap.jpg"
AlernateText="Map of New York City." runat="server"
Height="375" Width="282" >
</asp:ImageMap>
```

To configure each hot spot within an image map, you must nest the `<asp:circlehotspot>`, `<asp:rectanglehotspot>`, and `<asp:polygonhotspot>` controls within the ImageMap control. The **`<asp:circlehotspot>` control** defines a circular hot spot, the **`<asp:rectanglehotspot>` control** defines a rectangular hot spot, and the **`<asp:polygonhotspot>`** control defines a polygon hot spot. To identify the target alternate text for each hot spot, you assign values to the `NavigateURL` and `AlternateText` properties, the same as with the HyperLink control. The behavior of a hot spot is determined by the `HotSpotMode` property of the ImageMap control or the individual hot spot controls. You can select one of four values for the `HotSpotMode` property: Inactive, Navigate, NotSet, and Postback. The Inactive value disables the hot spot. The Navigate value causes the page to navigate to the specified URL. If the NotSet value is selected for an individual control, the control performs the behavior that is assigned to the HyperLink control's `HotSpotMode` property. However, if the HyperLink control's `HotSpotMode` property is assigned the value of NotSet, each hot spot that does not have a value assigned to its own `HotSpotMode` property navigates to its specified target URL. The Postback value causes the Web form to post back to itself.

The additional properties you must specify will depend on the type of hot spot control. You assign four properties for the rectangle hot spot, `Bottom`, `Left`, `Top`, and `Right`, which represent each corner of the rectangle. For the circle hot spot, you include the X and Y properties to identify where the center of the circle should be placed, along with the `Radius` property to determine how large the circle should be. Because a polygon can be any type of shape, you can use as many x, y pairs in the `Coordinates` property as necessary to define the shape of the object.

As an example of how to create an image map, Figure 4-4 shows an image that could be used by a medical research center to allow users to select a specific department. Following Figure 4-4, you see the code that identifies the hot spots in the image map. The code uses circle, rectangle, and polygon hot spots. Notice that the "in vitro" section of the image includes two hot spots: one for the definition of "in vitro" and another for the image of the medical researcher doing his work. Clicking each area of the image map opens a separate Web page for the selected department. Figure 4-5 shows the hot spots that are created by the code in Figure 4-5.

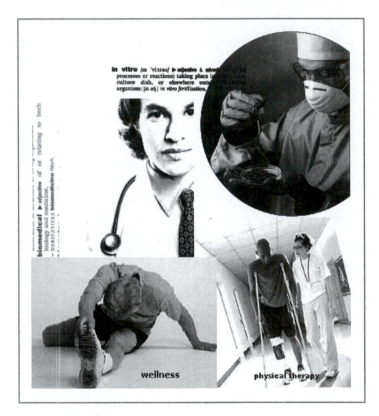

Figure 4-4   Medical research center image map

```
<asp:ImageMap ID="deptMap" ImageURL="MedicalMap.png"
HotSpotMode="Navigate"
AlernateText="Image map of additional images representing
medical departments" runat="server"
Height="446" Width="397" >
<asp:rectanglehotspot NavigateURL="invitro.htm"
AlternateText="Image containing the definition of the word
'in vitro'" Left="97" Top="39" Right="280" Bottom="81" />
<asp:circlehotspot NavigateURL="invitro.htm"
AlternateText="Image of a researcher working with a petri
dish" X="325" Y="118" Radius="115" />
<asp:rectanglehotspot NavigateURL="biomedical.htm"
```

```
AlternateText="Image of a researcher with a stethoscope
and a definition of 'biomedical'" Left="1" Top="81"
Right="207" Bottom="282" />
<asp:polygonhotspot NavigateURL="wellness.htm"
AlternateText="Image of a man stretching" Coordinates="12,
362,49,347,78,287,124,281,168,294,200,339,213,377,238,392,
231,405,199,404,166,367,137,400,92,444,55,444,50,400,12,
396" />
<asp:rectanglehotspot NavigateURL="phystherapy.htm"
AlternateText="Image of a map receiving physical therapy
from a female assistant" Left="241" Top="235" Right="397"
Bottom="445" />
</asp:ImageMap>
```

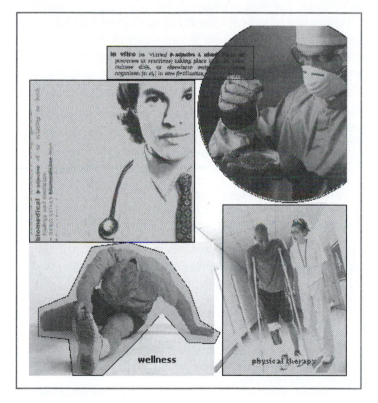

ASP.NET renders an image map with the <img>, <map>, and <area> HTML elements.

Figure 4-5 Medical research center image map hot spots

If you assign a value of "Postback" to an image map's HotSpotMode property, you need to create a click event handler to perform whatever action you would like to occur when a user clicks a hot spot. An image map's click event handler is similar to other types of event handlers, except that the second parameter must be defined with an ImageMapEventArgs parameter. With the ImageMapEventArgs parameter, you can access the PostBackValue property, which contains a value that uniquely identifies hot spots created with the <asp:circlehotspot>,

`<asp:rectanglehotspot>`, and `<asp:polygonhotspot>` controls. In the next exercise, you will create an image map with the photo on the Instructors page of the Big River Kayaking company that uses the `ImageMapEventArgs` parameter and `PostBackValue` properties to display information on the selected instructor.

To turn the instructor photo into an image map:

1. Return to the Visual Studio IDE and open the **instructors.aspx** file.

2. Locate the `<img>` element that displays the instructor photos and replace it with the following Web form and Image-Map control. The `HotSpotMode` attribute is assigned a value of "Postback" and the `OnClick` event is assigned a handler named `instructor_Clicked`. When a user clicks an instructor's image in the photo, the `instructor_Clicked()` event handler will display information about the instructor in a Label control.

```
<form runat="server">
<asp:ImageMap ID="instructorsImage"
ImageUrl="images/instructors.jpg"
    runat="server" HotSpotMode="Postback"
    AlernateText="Image of a group of kayaking
    instructors"
    Width="447" Height="266"
    OnClick="instructor_Clicked">
</asp:ImageMap></form>
```

3. Add the following hot spot controls for each instructor above the closing `</asp:ImageMap>`. Notice that each hot spot includes a `PostBackValue` property that is assigned the last name of an instructor.

```
<asp:RectangleHotSpot
    AlternateText="Image of a kayaking instructor"
    Left="20" Top="60" Right="104" Bottom="236"
    PostBackValue="Jardina" />
<asp:RectangleHotSpot
    AlternateText="Image of a kayaking instructor"
    Left="96" Top="17" Right="172" Bottom="169"
    PostBackValue="Cheung" />
<asp:RectangleHotSpot
    AlternateText="Image of a kayaking instructor"
    Left="172" Top="17" Right="235" Bottom="165"
    PostBackValue="Reimer" />
<asp:RectangleHotSpot
    AlternateText="Image of a kayaking instructor"
    Left="235" Top="26" Right="297" Bottom="155"
    PostBackValue="Miolla" />
```

```
<asp:RectangleHotSpot
    AlternateText="Image of a kayaking instructor"
    Left="297" Top="23" Right="370" Bottom="158"
    PostBackValue="Lembright" />
<asp:RectangleHotSpot
    AlternateText="Image of a kayaking instructor"
    Left="370" Top="24" Right="436" Bottom="128"
    PostBackValue="Yaron" />
```

4. Locate the paragraph that contains the text [Add label here]
    and replace the text with the following Label control, which
    will display information on the selected instructor:

    ```
    <asp:Label runat="server" ID="instructorInfo" />
    ```

5. Finally, open the **instructors.aspx.cs** file and add to the end
    of the class the following instructor_Clicked() event han-
    dler, which uses a switch statement and the PostBackValue
    property to determine which hot spot was clicked. The case
    labels then print the selected instructor's name and certifica-
    tion level.

    ```
    protected void instructor_Clicked(object sender,
    ImageMapEventArgs e)
    {
        switch (e.PostBackValue)
        {
            case "Jardina":
                instructorInfo.Text =
                    "<strong>Bob Jardina</strong><br />"
                    + "Swift-Water Rescue Instructor";
                break;
            case "Cheung":
                instructorInfo.Text =
                    "<strong>Lisa Cheung</strong><br />"
                    + "River Guide Training Instructor";
                break;
            case "Reimer":
                instructorInfo.Text =
                    "<strong>Judy Reimer</strong><br />"
                    + "Kayak Instructor II";
                break;
            case "Miolla":
                instructorInfo.Text =
                    "<strong>Wendy Miolla</strong><br />"
                    + "Kayak Instructor I";
                break;
            case "Lembright":
                instructorInfo.Text =
                    "<strong>Jody Lembright</strong><br />"
                    + "Kayak Instructor II";
                break;
    ```

```
             case "Yaron":
                 instructorInfo.Text =
                     "<strong>Dave Yaron</strong><br />"
                     + "River Guide Training Instructor";
                 break;
         }
     }
```

6.   Start the Web site. The instructors.aspx file opens in a Web browser. Click the instructor images to ensure that the image map functions properly. Figure 4-6 shows the page after selecting the first instructor on the left.

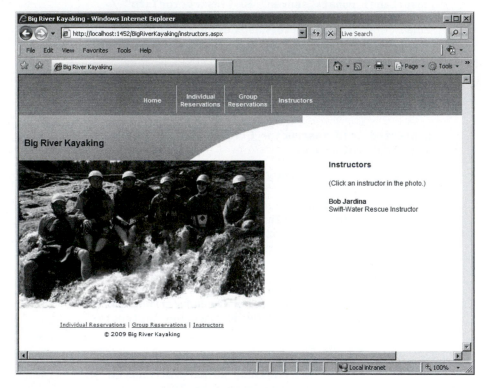

Figure 4-6   Image map on the Instructors Reservations page of the Big River Kayaking Web site

7.   Close your Web browser window.

Form Controls

With standard HTML, the `<input>` element is the most commonly used form element and allows you to create the following types of form controls:

- Text boxes
- Password boxes

- Radio buttons

- Check boxes

- Push buttons

- File boxes

- Hidden form fields

- Submit buttons

- Image submit buttons

- Reset buttons

Instead of using a single control such as the `<input>` element, ASP.
NET includes separate controls for each of the preceding items,
although each element is still rendered with the `<input>` element.
First, you will learn a little more about the TextBox control.

ASP.NET does not include a separate password box control. Instead, you create a password box with the TextBox control.

TextBox and HiddenField Controls

As you learned earlier in this chapter, the TextBox control is equivalent to the `<input type="text">` HTML element, which creates a
simple text box that accepts a single line of text. The TextBox control
can also be used to create a password text box or a multiline text
box. To specify the functionality of a TextBox control, you assign
one of the following values to the control's `TextMode` property:
SingleLine, MultiLine, or Password. The following statements demonstrate how to create a single line text box and a password text box.
Note that ASP.NET renders a password text box with the `<input
type="password">` HTML element.

For security reasons, password values are not posted back to a form unless users authorize saving them in the Web browser.

```
<p>User name: <asp:TextBox ID="firstName"
runat="server" /><br />
Password: <asp:TextBox ID="password"
runat="server" TextMode="Password" /></p>
```

Assigning the "MultiLine" value to the TextBox control's `TextMode`
property creates a control that is rendered with the HTML `<textarea>`
element, which allows users to enter multiple lines of information.
By default, 2 rows and 20 columns are displayed for a multiline text
box. To adjust the size of a multiline text box to display more lines
of text, you can assign values to the `Height` and `Width` properties or
the `Rows` and `Columns` properties. The `Height` and `Width` properties
accept values in pixels and the `Rows` and `Columns` properties accept
the number of rows and columns to display, respectively. The following statement creates a multiline text box that is 100 pixels high by
150 pixels wide:

The default TextMode value for the TextBox control is "SingleLine." For this reason, the User name control in the preceding statements does not require the TextMode property.

```
<asp:TextBox ID="shipping" runat="server"
TextMode="MultiLine" Height="100" Width="150" />
```

If you assign values to the `Height` and `Width` properties and the `Rows` and `Columns` properties, the `Height` and `Width` properties take precedence.

226

Assigning values to the `Height` and `Width` properties or the `Rows` and `Columns` properties does not limit the number of characters that a user can enter into a multiline text box.

Here is the same statement formatted to display 5 rows and 20 columns:

```
<asp:TextBox ID="shipping" runat="server" TextMode="MultiLine"
Rows="5" Columns="20" />
```

You use the HiddenField control to create a form field that you can use to hide information from users. A hidden form field is rendered in a browser with `<input type="hidden">`. The following statement demonstrates how to create a hidden field control:

```
<asp:HiddenField ID="orderNumber" runat="server" />
```

To manipulate the value in a text box or hidden field, you manipulate its `Value` property with its ID value. With a text box field, you can also manipulate the value it contains with the `Text` property.

Button, ImageButton, and LinkButton Controls

The Standard Toolbox contains three controls for creating buttons: Button, ImageButton, and LinkButton. With the Button control, you can create two types of buttons: a submit button that causes a Web form to post back to itself and a push button that is similar to the OK and Cancel buttons you see in dialog boxes. The primary purpose of push buttons is to execute code that performs some type of function, such as a calculation. The Button control's default functionality is as a submit button. However, if you have multiple Button controls in a form, you must specify which button to use as the submit button by setting the control's `UseSubmitBehavior` property to true, which is the default value. To create a push button, you set the Button control's `UseSubmitBehavior` property to false. A submit button renders with the `<input type="submit">` element and a push button renders with the `<input type="button">` element. Use the `Text` property to specify the label that appears on a button. The following statements show a submit button and a push button:

```
<asp:Button ID="calcShipping" Text="Calc Shipping Costs"
OnClick="calcShipping_Click" Runat ="server" />
<asp:Button ID="submit" runat="server" Text="Submit Query" />
```

The ImageButton control creates an image submit button that displays a graphical image and performs exactly the same function as a submit button in that it transmits a form's data to a Web server. A Web browser renders an image submit button with `<input type="image">`. As with other types of images, you specify the image to display with the `ImageURL` property and assign alternate text to display in place of the image file with the `AlternateText` property. The following code displays the image button shown in Figure 4-7.

```
<p>First name <asp:TextBox ID="firstName"
runat="server" /><br />
Last name  <asp:TextBox ID="lastName" runat="server" /><br />
E-mail <asp:TextBox ID="Email" runat="server" /></p>
<p><asp:ImageButton ID="SignGuestBook" runat="server"
ImageUrl="signbook.gif" /></p>
```

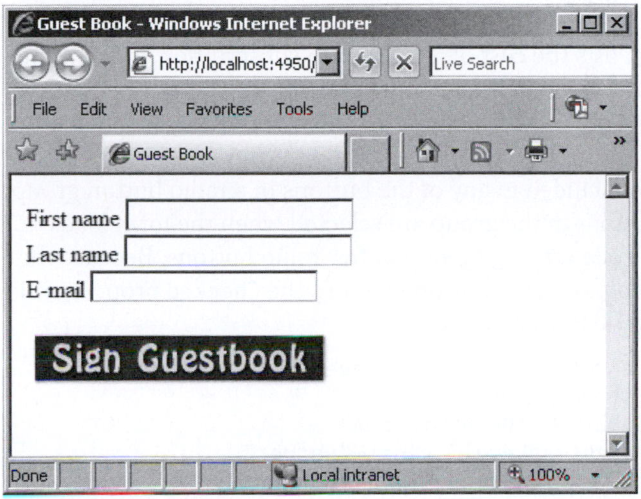

Figure 4-7   Form with an image button

The LinkButton control creates a hyperlink that posts the form to the server instead of navigating to another URL. A link button performs the same tasks as a submit button. Although a link button is rendered with the anchor element (<a>), ASP.NET adds JavaScript code on the Web page that causes post back to occur. The following statement demonstrates how to create a link button:

```
<asp:LinkButton ID="SignGuestBook" runat="server">
Sign Guest Book</asp:LinkButton>
```

RadioButton and RadioButtonList Controls

Radio buttons, or option buttons, refer to groups of controls from which the user can select only one value. Web browsers render radio buttons using an <input> element with a type of "radio" (<input type="radio" />). To create radio buttons in ASP.NET, you can use either the RadioButton or RadioButtonList controls. Note that although you can add a single radio button to a Web page, it would not be useful if it were not part of a group. If you only need a single option, a check box is a better choice. For this reason, this section focuses on creating radio button groups. (You'll learn about check boxes later in this chapter.)

To create a group of radio buttons with the RadioButton control, you must assign all radio buttons in the group the same `GroupName` property. Each radio button must also include a `Text` property that identifies the unique value associated with that button. You can also include the `Checked` property, assigned a value of true, to set an initially selected item in a group of radio buttons. For example, you might have a group of radio buttons that lists the cost of newspaper subscriptions. One button lists the cost of a one-month subscription, another button lists the cost of a six-month subscription, and another lists the cost of a yearly subscription. To encourage subscribers to purchase the yearly subscription, you could include the `Checked` property with the yearly subscription radio button. If the `Checked` property is not included in any of the buttons in a radio button group, none of the buttons in the group are selected when the form loads. The following code creates a group of five radio buttons. Because the High school diploma radio button includes the `Checked` property, it is selected when the form first loads.

```
<p><strong>Select your highest level of
education:</strong></p>
<p><asp:RadioButton ID="hsDiploma"
GroupName="educationLevel" runat="server"
Checked="True" />High school diploma<br />
<asp:RadioButton ID="associate" GroupName="educationLevel"
runat="server" />Associate degree<br />
<asp:RadioButton ID="bachelor" GroupName="educationLevel"
runat="server" />Bachelor degree<br />
<asp:RadioButton ID="master" GroupName="educationLevel"
runat="server" />Master degree<br />
<asp:RadioButton ID="doctorate" GroupName="educationLevel"
runat="server" />Doctorate<br />
<p><asp:Button ID="Button1" runat="server"
Text="Button" /></p>
```

To determine which radio button in a group is selected, you need to test the `Checked` property of each individual control using its ID value. The following `Page_Load()` function demonstrates how to determine which button in the `educationLevel` radio group is selected when the form is submitted:

```
protected void Page_Load(object Source, EventArgs E)
{
    if (Page.IsPostBack)
    {
        if (hsDiploma.Checked)
            Response.Write("<p>You have a high school
                diploma.</p>");
        else if (associate.Checked)
            Response.Write("<p>You have an Associate's
                degree.</p>");
        else if (bachelor.Checked)
```

```
            Response.Write("<p>You have a Bachelor's
              degree.</p>");
        else if (master.Checked)
            Response.Write("<p>You have a Master's
              degree.</p>");
        else if (doctorate.Checked)
            Response.Write("<p>You have a doctorate.</p>");
    }
}
```

The RadioButtonList control works the same as groups created with RadioButton controls, but it makes it easier to organize the individual radio buttons. To create a radio button list, you need to nest ListItem controls within the RadioButtonList control; each list item represents a radio button. You can then manipulate the radio buttons by using the single ID that is assigned to the RadioButtonList control. Note that to set an initially selected item in a radio button list, you must use the Selected property, not the Checked property that the RadioButton control uses. The following statements show how to use a radio button list to organize the education level radio buttons:

```
<p><strong>Select your highest level of education:
</strong></p>
<p><asp:RadioButtonList ID="educationLevel" runat="server">
        <asp:ListItem Value="hsDiploma" Selected="True">
            High school diploma</asp:ListItem>
        <asp:ListItem Value="associate">Associate
        degree</asp:ListItem>
        <asp:ListItem Value="bachelor">Bachelor
        degree</asp:ListItem>
        <asp:ListItem Value="master">Master
        degree</asp:ListItem>
        <asp:ListItem Value="doctorate">Doctorate
        </asp:ListItem>
    </asp:RadioButtonList></p>
<p><asp:Button ID="Button1" runat="server"
Text="Button" /></p>
```

To determine which radio button in a radio button list is selected, you need to check the RadioButtonList control's SelectedItem property, which returns the selected list item. You can then access the list item's Text or Value properties, as follows:

```
protected void Page_Load(object Source, EventArgs E)
{
    if (Page.IsPostBack)
    {
        Response.Write("<p>Your highest education level is: "
            + educationLevel.SelectedItem.Text + "</p>");
    }
}
```

CheckBox and CheckBoxList Controls

You use check boxes when you want users to select whether or not to include a certain item or to allow users to select multiple values from a list of items. Web browsers render check boxes using an `<input>` element with a type of "checkbox" (`<input type="checkbox" />`). To create check boxes in ASP.NET, you can use either the CheckBox or CheckBoxList controls.

You use the CheckBox control when you want to add individual check boxes to a Web form. To determine whether a check box is selected, you can use the `Checked` property. When the following simple form is submitted, the `Page_Load()` event handler prints a message if the CheckBox control's `Checked` property is selected.

```
protected void Page_Load(object Source, EventArgs E)
{
    if (Page.IsPostBack)
    {
        if (emailUpdates.Checked)
            Response.Write("<p>You have subscribed
                to environmental and energy conservation
                e-mail updates.</p>");
    }
}
```

The following code shows the Web form that uses the preceding code-behind page:

```
<form ID="form1" runat="server">
<p>E-mail address:
    <asp:TextBox ID="eMail" runat="server" /></p>
<p><asp:CheckBox ID="list9" runat="server" /><strong>
Conservation and Natural Resources</strong><br />
To receive regular updates about the President's plan
for healthy forests, programs to improve and care for our
National Park System, conservation efforts on America's
farms and protection of wildlife and environmental areas
click here.</p>
<p><asp:Button ID="Button1" runat="server"
Text="Submit" /></p>
</form>
```

One event of the CheckBox control that you should be aware of is the `CheckedChanged` event, which executes when a user clicks the check box. By default, this event does not cause the Web form to post back to the server, although you can change this behavior by assigning a value of true to the CheckBox control's `AutoPostBack` property. The following code demonstrates how you might use the `CheckedChanged` event with a check box that adds $10 to a sale total when it is selected. (For simplicity, the text box is assigned a sales total of 42.) Notice that the CheckBox control assigns a value of true to the `AutoPostBack` property and the event handler function, `calcShipping()`, to the `OnCheckedChanged` property.

```
protected void calcShipping(object Source, EventArgs E)
{
    int salesTotal = Convert.ToInt16(total.Text);
    if (shipping.Checked)
        salesTotal += 10;
    else
        salesTotal -= 10;
    total.Text = Convert.ToString(salesTotal);
}
```

The following code shows the Web form that uses the preceding code-behind page:

```
<form ID="form1" runat="server">
<p>Sales total:
    <asp:TextBox ID="total" runat="server" Value="42" /></p>
<p><asp:CheckBox ID="shipping" runat="server"
OnCheckedChanged="calcShipping" AutoPostBack="True" /> Add
$10 for express shipping</p>
</form>
```

The CheckBoxList control makes it easier to organize multiple check boxes and is very similar to the RadioButtonList control, except that you can select multiple check boxes within a check box list. To create a check box list, you use ListItem controls within the CheckBoxList control; each list item represents a check box. You can then manipulate the check boxes by using the single ID that is assigned to the CheckBoxList control. You can then access each check box programmatically through the `Items` collection of the CheckBoxList control. To determine whether a check box within a check box list is selected, you must use the `Selected` property, not the `Checked` property that the CheckBox control uses.

The following code shows a modified version of the program that allows users to select to receive environmental and energy conservation e-mail updates. This version uses a check box list that allows users to select the e-mail updates to receive. The `Page_Load()` event handler iterates through the items in the check box list to determine which check boxes are selected.

```
protected void Page_Load(object Source, EventArgs E)
{
    if (Page.IsPostBack)
    {
        Response.Write("<p>You have subscribed to the following
            e-mail updates:</p><ul>");
        for (int i = 0; i < emailUpdates.Items.Count; ++i)
        {
```

```
            if (emailUpdates.Items[i].Selected)
                Response.Write("<li>"
                    + emailUpdates.Items[i].Value
                    + "</li>");
        }
        Response.Write("</ul>");
    }
}
```

The following code shows the Web form that uses the preceding code-behind page:

```
<form id="updateReg" runat="server">
<div>
  E-mail address:
  <asp:TextBox ID="eMail" runat="server" />
  <asp:CheckBoxList ID="emailUpdates"
  runat="server">
    <asp:ListItem Value="Environmental
    and energy conservation"><strong>
    Environmental and energy conservation
    </strong><br />Learn more about
    the plans for healthy forests,
    programs to improve and care for
    our National Park System, conservation
    efforts on America's farms and
    protection of wildlife and
    environmental areas click here.
    </asp:ListItem>
    <asp:ListItem Value="Economy and jobs">
    <strong>Economy and jobs</strong>
    <br />Receive updates on efforts to
    strengthen America's economy by
    creating jobs, expanding small business
    opportunities, improving American
    competitiveness, encouraging
    entrepreneurship and promoting free and
    fair trade by clicking here.</asp:ListItem>
    <asp:ListItem Value="Education"><strong>
    Education</strong><br />Sign up for
    regular updates on the plans to improve
    our public education for all Americans.
    </asp:ListItem>
  </asp:CheckBoxList>
  <p>
    <asp:Button ID="Button1" runat="server"
    Text="Submit" /></p>
</div>
</form>
```

Three unique properties of the CheckBoxList control that are worth mentioning are the RepeatColumns, RepeatDirection, and RepeatLayout properties. These properties allow you to control the layout of the check box list. The RepeatColumns property determines how many columns will be used to format the display of the check boxes. For example, if you have 12 check boxes and you assign a value of 3 to the RepeatColumns property, the check boxes will be laid out in three columns with four rows. However, if you have 12 check boxes and you assign a value of 4 to the `RepeatColumns` property, the check boxes will be laid out in four columns with three rows. The `RepeatDirection` property determines whether the check box list is laid out horizontally or vertically. The `RepeatLayout` property determines whether the check box list is laid out in a table.

ListBox and DropDownList Controls

With HTML, you can use the `<select>` element to create a selection list that presents users with fixed lists of options from which to choose. The selection list can appear as an actual list of choices or as a drop-down menu. ASP.NET uses two separate controls to display selection lists: ListBox and DropDownList. The ListBox control creates a list of choices, whereas the DropDownList control creates a drop-down style menu. Both types of controls are rendered in a browser with the `<select>` element.

Both the ListBox and the DropDownList controls are created in the same manner as the RadioButtonList control: You nest ListItem controls within each control to represent each list item. You can then manipulate the list items by using the ID of the ListBox or DropDownList control. To set an initially selected item in a selection list, you must use the `Selected` property in a ListItem control. The ListItem control includes two additional properties that are not available to the DropDownList control: `SelectionMode` and `Rows`. The `SelectionMode` property determines whether multiple items can be selected in a selection list and the `Rows` property specifies how many list items to display. You assign to the `SelectionMode` property a value of "Single" or "Multiple" and you assign to the `Rows` property an integer representing the number of rows you want displayed.

The following code creates two selection lists. Figure 4-8 shows the output in a Web browser. Notice that because the first list's `SelectionMode` property is set to "multiple", you can select multiple options, as shown in the figure. Also notice that the "$700–$899" option is the selected value in the second list.

```
<asp:ListBox ID="brand" runat="server" SelectionMode=
"Multiple" Rows="6" Width="150">
<asp:ListItem>Apple</asp:ListItem>
<asp:ListItem>Compaq</asp:ListItem>
<asp:ListItem Selected="True">Dell</asp:ListItem>
<asp:ListItem>Gateway</asp:ListItem>
<asp:ListItem>HP</asp:ListItem>
<asp:ListItem>Lenova</asp:ListItem>
<asp:ListItem>Sony</asp:ListItem>
<asp:ListItem>Toshiba</asp:ListItem>
</asp:ListBox>
<asp:ListBox ID="priceRange" runat="server" Rows="5"
Width="150">
```

```
<asp:ListItem>Less than $700</asp:ListItem>
<asp:ListItem Selected="True">$700 - $899</asp:ListItem>
<asp:ListItem>$900 - $1199</asp:ListItem>
<asp:ListItem>$1200 - $1799</asp:ListItem>
<asp:ListItem>$1800 and Up</asp:ListItem>
</asp:ListBox>
```

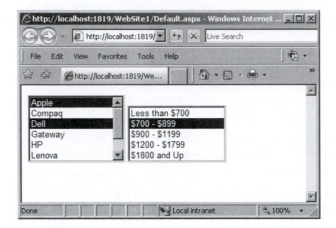

Figure 4-8   Two selection lists

The following statements demonstrate how to create the drop-down list box that is shown in Figure 4-9:

```
<asp:DropDownList ID="paymentMethod" runat="server">
<asp:ListItem>Check</asp:ListItem>
<asp:ListItem>Money Order</asp:ListItem>
<asp:ListItem>Visa</asp:ListItem>
<asp:ListItem>Mastercard</asp:ListItem>
<asp:ListItem>American Express</asp:ListItem>
<asp:ListItem>Discover</asp:ListItem>
```

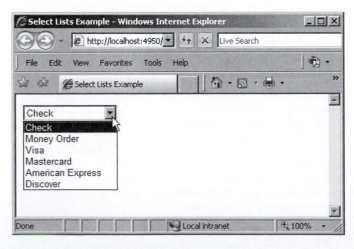

Figure 4-9   Drop-down list

You can then manipulate items in a selection list by using the ID that is assigned to the ListBox or DropDownList controls. To determine which item is selected in a single-selection list box or a drop-down list, you need to check the SelectedItem property, which returns the selected list item. You can then access the list item's Text or Value properties. For multiselection list boxes, you can access each list item programmatically through the Items collection of the ListBox control. To determine whether a list item within a multiselection list box is selected, you must use the Selected property.

Short Quiz 2

1. Explain how to use a literal control and why you would use one.

2. Why would you use an Image control instead of an `<img>` element?

3. What are the values you can assign to the HotSpotMode property and how do you use them?

4. Explain the difference between the Button, ImageButton, and LinkButton controls.

5. Explain how to use the RadioButtonList and CheckBoxList controls.

Validating User Input with Validation Controls

In this section, you will learn how to use two of the most commonly used ASP.NET validation controls: RequiredFieldValidator and CompareValidator.

RequiredFieldValidator Control

Earlier in this chapter, you learned how to perform simple validation by using a conditional expression to check if a submitted variable contained a null value, which means the variable does not yet exist, or if the variable contains an empty string, which means the variable exists but has not been assigned a value. An easier way to perform data validation is to use the **RequiredFieldValidator control**, which ensures that a value is entered into a specified field. If a user submits a form and a field that is identified with a RequiredFieldValidator control

236

does not contain a value, a message that you define prints to the Web browser. You assign the message that you want to appear to the RequiredFieldValidator control's `Text` property or place it between the `<asp:RequiredFieldValidator>` control element's tag pairs. The field that is to be validated is identified by the `ControlToValidate` property. The following code demonstrates how to use tag pairs to define a RequiredFieldValidator control that validates a field named firstName:

```
<asp:RequiredFieldValidator ID="validateFirstName"
runat="server"
ControlToValidate="height">(First name is required)
</asp:RequiredFieldValidator>
```

The preceding statements can also be written as an empty element as follows:

```
<asp:RequiredFieldValidator ID="validateFirstName"
runat="server"
ControlToValidate="height" Text="(First name is required)" />
```

By default, the validation failure message prints in red text, but you can change this with the `ForeColor` property.

The text of the validation failure message prints wherever the RequiredFieldValidator control is placed on your Web page. For example, the following is a modified version of the BMI calculator you saw earlier. This version uses RequiredFieldValidator controls to validate the height and weight fields. If either field does not contain a value when the form is submitted, the text "**Required Field**" prints next to the field.

```
protected void Page_Load(object Source, EventArgs E)
{
    if (IsPostBack)
    {
        double goodWeight = 0;
        double goodHeight = 0;
        double bodyMass = 0;
        if (Double.TryParse(height.Text, out goodWeight)
            && Double.TryParse(weight.Text, out
            goodHeight))
            if (goodHeight != 0 && goodWeight != 0)
            {
                bodyMass = goodWeight / (goodHeight
                    * goodHeight) * 703;
                Response.Write("<p>Your body mass index is "
                    + Convert.ToInt16(bodyMass) + "</p>");
            }
            else
                Response.Write("<p>You cannot enter a
                    value of 0 for your height or
                    weight!</p>");
        else
            Response.Write("<p>You did not enter valid
                values for your height and weight!</p>");
    }
}
```

The following code shows the Web form that uses the preceding code-behind page:

```
<form ID="form1" runat="server">
<div>
<p>Height: <asp:TextBox ID="height" runat="server"
Width="30" />
 (Enter a height in inches) <asp:
RequiredFieldValidator ID="validateHeight" runat="server"
ControlToValidate="height" Text="**Required field**" /></p>
<p>Weight: <asp:TextBox ID="weight" runat="server"
Width="30" />
 (Enter a weight in pounds) <asp:
RequiredFieldValidator ID="validateWeight" runat="server"
ControlToValidate="weight" Text="**Required field**" /></p>
<p><asp:Button ID="submit" runat="server"
Text="Calculate" /></p>
</div></form>
```

Figure 4-10 shows how the BMI program appears if you click the Calculate button without entering values in the height and weight fields.

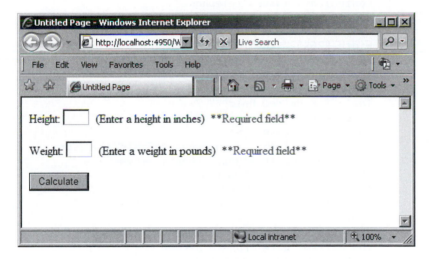

Figure 4-10 BMI program with RequiredFieldValidator controls

Notice that the `Page_Load()` event handler in the preceding example still includes the validation code that verifies the entered values are of the `Double` data type and that they are not equal to 0. To ensure that values are of a specific data type, you need to use the CompareValidator control, and to ensure that they fall within a specified value range, you need to use the RangeValidator control.

Next, you will modify the Individual Reservations page so it uses RequiredFieldValidator controls to determine whether values have been entered into each field.

When you add a validation control to a Web page, the browser automatically reserves space for it when the page renders, even if there are no validation errors. To force the browser to display a validation control only when it's needed, assign a value of "dynamic" to its `Display` property.

To add RequiredFieldValidator controls to the Individual Reservations page:

1. Return to the single.aspx file in the Visual Studio IDE.

2. Modify the form input fields so they include RequiredFieldValidator controls, as follows:

```
Last name <asp:RequiredFieldValidator
ID="lastNameValidate" runat="server"
ControlToValidate="lastName"
Text="**Required field**" /><br />
<asp:TextBox ID="lastName" runat="server"
Width="265" /><br />
First name <asp:RequiredFieldValidator
ID="firstNameValidate" runat="server"
ControlToValidate="firstName"
Text="**Required field**" /><br />
<asp:TextBox ID="firstName" runat="server"
Width="265" /><br />
Telephone <asp:RequiredFieldValidator
ID="telephoneValidate" runat="server"
ControlToValidate="telephone"
Text="**Required field**" /><br />
<asp:TextBox ID="telephone" runat="server"
Width="265" /><br />
E-mail <asp:RequiredFieldValidator
ID="emailValidate" runat="server"
ControlToValidate="email"
Text="**Required field**" /><br />
<asp:TextBox ID="email" runat="server"
Width="265" /><br />
Confirm e-mail <asp:RequiredFieldValidator
ID="confirmEmailValidate" runat="server"
ControlToValidate="confirmEmail"
Text="**Required field**" /><br />
<asp:TextBox ID="confirmEmail" runat="server"
Width="265" /><br />
Preferred date <asp:RequiredFieldValidator
ID="dateValidate" runat="server"
ControlToValidate="date"
Text="**Required field**" /><br />
<asp:TextBox ID="date" runat="server"
Width="265" /></p>
```

3. Return to the single.aspx.cs file and in the `Page_Load()` event handler, delete the first `if` statement that is nested within the `if` statement that checks the `IsPostBack` property. Also, delete "else" from the statement that compares the e-mail and e-mail address fields. The beginning of the `Page_Load()` event handler should appear as follows:

```
protected void Page_Load(object Source, EventArgs E)
{
    int ageCheck = 18;
    if (IsPostBack)
    {
        if (email.Text != confirmEmail.Text)
        {
            message.Visible = true;
...
```

4. Start the Web site. The Individual Reservations page opens in a Web browser. Test the validation functionality. Figure 4-11 shows the page if it is submitted without entering any values in the fields.

5. Close your Web browser window.

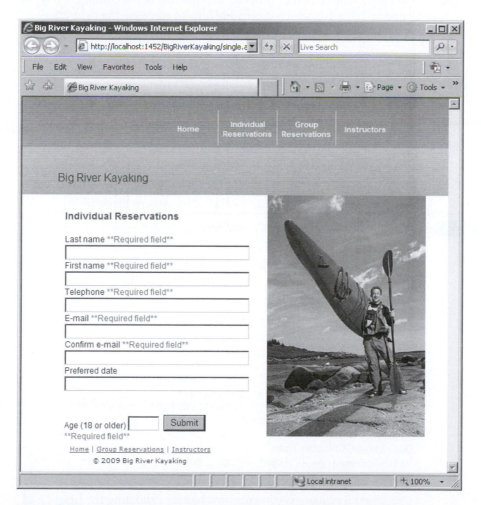

Figure 4-11   Individual Reservations page after adding validation controls

CompareValidator Control

The **CompareValidator control** verifies that a user has entered a value of a specified data type into a field. This control uses similar syntax to the RequiredFieldValidator control in that you assign the message that you want to appear to the RequiredFieldValidator control's `Text` property or place it between the `<asp:RequiredFieldValidator>` control element's tag pairs. The field that is to be validated is identified by the `ControlToValidate` property. To identify another control against which to compare the control identified with the `ControlToValidate` property, you use the `ControlToCompare` property. The CompareValidator control also includes the `Type`, `Operator`, and `ValueToCompare` properties. You assign to the Type property the data type that you want users to enter into the field: `string`, `integer`, `double`, `date`, or `currency`. The `Operator` property accepts one of the comparison types listed in Table 4-5, which determine how to compare the field value.

 Even if you select a comparison operator other than DataTypeCheck, the data type of the field will still be checked in addition to performing the selected comparison, provided that you include the Type operator in the CompareValidator control declaration.

Type	Determines whether
DataTypeCheck	The field contains the appropriate data type
Equal	The field is equal to the `ValueToCompare` property
GreaterThan	The field is greater than the `ValueToCompare` property
GreaterThanEqual	The field is greater than or equal to the `ValueToCompare` property
LessThan	The field is less than the `ValueToCompare` property
LessThanEqual	The field is less than or equal to the `ValueToCompare` property
NotEqual	The field is not equal to the `ValueToCompare` property

Table 4-5 Comparison types of the `Operator` property

The following CompareValidator controls demonstrate how to verify that the height and weight fields in the BMI calculator contain integer values greater than zero:

```
<asp:CompareValidator ID="compareHeight" runat="server"
ControlToValidate="height"
Type="Integer"
Operator="GreaterThan"
ValueToCompare="0"><p>**Height must be an integer greater
than 0**</p></asp:CompareValidator>
<asp:CompareValidator ID="compareWeight" runat="server"
ControlToValidate="weight"
Type="Integer"
Operator="GreaterThan"
ValueToCompare="0"><p>**Weight must be an integer greater
than 0**</p></asp:CompareValidator>
```

Because the validation controls now handle validating the height and width fields in the BMI calculator, you no longer need the calculation code in the `Page_Load()` event handler. The event handler is now much simpler, as follows:

```
protected void Page_Load(object Source, EventArgs E)
{
    if (Page.IsPostBack)
    {
        double goodWeight = Convert.ToDouble(weight.Text);
        double goodHeight = Convert.ToDouble(height.Text);
        double bodyMass = goodWeight / (goodHeight
            * goodHeight) * 703;
        Response.Write("<p>Your body mass index is "
            + Convert.ToInt16(bodyMass) + "</p>");
    }
}
```

Next, you will replace the remaining validation statements in the Individual Reservations page's `Page_Load()` event handler with CompareValidator controls. Recall that the last `else` statement in the `Page_Load()` event handler hides the Web form and displays a message if the fields validate successfully. To determine whether all of the validation controls on a Web form were successful, you use the `IsValid` property of the `Page` class. However, you should only check the `IsValid` property after executing the `Page.Validate()` method or you will receive an error message. The `IsValid` property contains a value of true if all the validation controls were successful or a value of false if any of them failed. You will use the `IsValid` property to determine when to display the success message after submitting the Individual Reservations page.

To add CompareValidator controls to the Individual Reservations page:

1. Return to the single.aspx file in the Visual Studio IDE.

2. Add the following CompareValidator control immediately above the Preferred date section. This control compares the values of the e-mail and confirmEmail fields.

   ```
   <asp:CompareValidator ID="compareEmail" runat="server"
   ControlToValidate="confirmEmail"
   Operator="Equal" Display="Dynamic"
   ControlToCompare="email">**You did not enter the
   same value in the e-mail and e-mail confirmation
   fields**<br /></asp:CompareValidator>
   ```

3. Replace the RequiredFieldValidator control for the date field with the following CompareValidator control, which ensures that the date field contains a valid date:

   ```
   <asp:CompareValidator ID="compareDate" runat="server"
       ControlToValidate="date" Operator="DataTypeCheck"
       Display="Dynamic" Type="Date">**You did not enter a
       valid date **</asp:CompareValidator>
   ```

4. Add the following CompareValidator control immediately before the last closing `</p>` tag in the Web form. This control ensures that the Age field contains a value of 18 or higher.

```
<p><asp:CompareValidator ID="ageCompare" runat="server"
ControlToValidate="age" Operator="GreaterThanEqual"
Display="Dynamic" ValueToCompare="18">
**You must be 18 or older**
</asp:CompareValidator><br />
```

5. Replace the contents of the `Page_Load()` event handler in the single.aspx.cs file with the following statements. After the first `if` statements determines whether the current request was caused by a post back event, it executes the `Page.Validate()` method. Then, if the `Page.IsValid` property is true, the reservation form is hidden and the success message is displayed.

```
if (Page.IsPostBack)
{
    Page.Validate();
    if (Page.IsValid)
    {
        resForm.Visible = false;
        message.Visible = true;
        message.Text = "<p><strong>Your reservation
            has been submitted. A confirmation message
            has been sent to your e-mail
            address.</strong></p>";
    }
}
```

6. Start the Web site. The single.aspx file opens in a Web browser. Test the validation functionality.

7. Close your Web browser window.

Short Quiz 3

1. Explain how to use a RequiredFieldValidator control to ensure that a user enters a value into a specified field.

2. Which validation control property identifies the control to validate?

3. How do you force the browser to display a validation control only when it's needed?

4. Explain how to use a CompareValidator control to verify that a user has entered a value of a specified data type into a field.

5. How do you configure a CompareValidator control to check a field's data type?

Summing Up

- You can use a conditional expression to check if a submitted variable contains a null value, which means the variable does not yet exist, or if the variable contains an empty string, which means the variable exists but has not been assigned a value.

- If a submitted form value must be numeric data, you should use a `TryParse()` method to convert a string variable to the required data type.

- Web Forms are an ASP.NET programming tool that you can use to quickly build dynamic interfaces containing sophisticated Web server controls that can access data sources, validate user input, handle site navigation, manage security issues such as logins and password recovery, and that can perform numerous other tasks.

- The process by which form data is posted back to the same page with a Web form is called post back. After a Web form is submitted, the post back mechanism automatically restores the form's value. Whether or not data is posted back to a Web page is determined by its view state.

- With Web forms, you can use the `Page` class's `IsPostBack` property to determine whether a Web form has already been submitted.

- An event is a specific circumstance (such as an action performed by a user or an action performed by the browser) that is monitored by the browser and that your program can respond to in some way.

- A function or method that executes in response to a specific event is called an event handler.

- A code-behind page is a separate class file that contains the C# methods and properties for an associated page.

- Post back is initiated each time that a server control event is raised, which also causes each of the page events (`PreInit` through `Unload`) to execute.

- Server controls are special types of HTML controls, such as the TextBox and Button controls, that run on the server and that you can programmatically access and manipulate with an ASP.NET program.

- A user control is a customized type of control consisting of multiple server controls and HTML elements.

- Web parts controls allow users to directly control and manipulate the behavior and appearance of an ASP.NET page from within a Web browser.

- Although many of the standard server controls are very similar to their HTML counterparts, their primary purpose is to be manipulated programmatically on the server by an ASP.NET program.

- Image maps allow users to navigate to different Web pages by clicking on an area of an image.

- The RequiredFieldValidator control ensures that a value is entered into a specified field.

- The CompareValidator control verifies that a user has entered a value of a specified data type into a field.

Comprehension Check

1. When you use JavaScript to validate form data, you can always ensure that the data submitted to your ASP.NET program was submitted from the Web page containing the JavaScript validation code. True or False?

2. Explain how to use a single page to display and process a standard HTML form.

3. If a variable contains _____, it means that the variable does not exist.

   a. empty string

   b. void

   c. a null value

   d. 0

4. Which of the following is required as the second argument of the `TryParse()` method?

   a. the out keyword

   b. the Boolean value

   c. the data type

   d. the name of the variable to parse

5. What are some of the uses of a Web form?

6. You must use the `action` attribute with a Web form. True or False?

7. Whether or not data is posted back to a Web page is determined by its _____.

    a. data type

    b. view state

    c. `request` method

    d. control type

8. Which of the following attributes identifies a form as an ASP.NET Web form that should be processed on the server instead of the client?

    a. `action`

    b. `method`

    c. `ID`

    d. `runat="server"`

9. View state is maintained by assigning the form values to a hidden form field named _____.

    a. `_VIEWSTATE`

    b. `__VIEWSTATE`

    c. `VIEW_STATE`

    d. `VIEW__STATE`

10. Explain why you would disable view state.

11. A Web browser renders ASP.NET server controls as standard HTML controls. True or False?

12. Explain how to programmatically manipulate a server control with C#.

13. Which of the following `Page` class's properties determines whether a Web form has already been submitted?

    a. `WasSubmitted`

    b. `FirstSubmit`

    c. `IsSubmit`

    d. `IsPostBack`

14. What is the correct syntax for naming a page event handler?

15. What is the difference between a Label control and a Literal control?

16. Explain how to create an image map.

17. You use the TextBox control to create a password field. True or False?

18. Which of the following properties determines whether a check box is selected?

 a. On

 b. Checked

 c. ControlSelected

 d. Active

19. Which of the following properties sets an initially selected item in a selection list?

 a. Select

 b. SelectedItem

 c. Default

 d. ItemFocus

20. Which property of the CompareValidator control identifies the data type that you want users to enter into the field?

 a. Type

 b. Data

 c. DataType

 d. Value

Reinforcement Exercises

Exercise 4-1

One of the specialty controls that ASP.NET includes is the Calendar control, which displays a graphic calendar with selectable dates. Calendars are commonly used on HTML pages to allow users to select a date that is required for different types of reservations, such as an airline reservation. In this exercise, you will add a Calendar control to the Individual Reservations page that allows users to click on the date when they would like to take kayaking lessons.

1. Return to the single.aspx file in the Visual Studio IDE.

2. Add the following `<br />` tag and Calendar control immediately after the TextBox control with an ID of "date":

    ```
    <br /><asp:Calendar ID="dateCalendar" runat="server">
        </asp:Calendar>
    ```

3. The Calendar control contains numerous properties that you can use to format the display of the calendar. However, the easiest way to format a calendar is to select a predefined auto format scheme. Select the **Design** tab at the bottom of the IDE, right-click the calendar, and then select **Auto Format** in the shortcut menu that opens. The Auto Format dialog box opens, listing several formatting schemes. Select **Colorful 2** and then click **OK**. The formatting scheme will be applied to the calendar in **Design** view. Click the **Source** tab, and you should see the various formatting properties that have been added to the Calendar control.

4. Change the `Height` and `Width` properties of the Calendar control to 120px and 185px, respectively.

5. Next, you need to add code that places the selected date into the date field. The event that executes when a user clicks a date in the calendar is the `SelectionChanged` event. Add the following `OnSelectionChanged` property to the Calendar control. The event executes a handler named `dateSelected`, which you will add next. Also, add a statement that disables post back for the control to prevent the control from submitting the form to the server each time a user clicks a date link.

    ```
    OnSelectionChanged="dateSelected"
    EnableViewState="False"
    ```

6. Return to the single.aspx.cs page and add the following bolded code to the first `if` statement. This code prevents the form from being submitted when a user clicks a date on the calendar.

    ```
    if (Page.IsPostBack && Page.Request.Params.Get(
        "__EVENTTARGET") != "dateCalendar")
            {
    ```

7. Add the following event handler to the single.aspx.cs page. The Calendar control creates a `DateTime` object that contains both date and time values. The event handler retrieves the value assigned to the `SelectedDate` property, converts it to

a string that only contains the date portion of the `DateTime` object, and then assigns the value to the `Text` property of the date control.

```
protected void dateSelected(object Source, EventArgs E)
{
    date.Text = dateCalendar
        .SelectedDate.ToString("d");
}
```

8. Finally, change the `Page_Load()` event handler to `Page_LoadComplete()`. This is necessary because the control events execute immediately after the `Page_Load()` event.

9. Start the Web site. Test the calendar to ensure that a selected date is copied to the date field.

10. Close your Web browser window.

Exercise 4-2

As you learned earlier, a user control is a customized type of control consisting of multiple server controls and HTML elements. Essentially, you create a user control to contain a logical grouping of elements and text that you want to reuse on multiple pages. For example, a banking Web site might contain a user control for calculating loan interest that is used on multiple pages on the Web site. In this exercise, you will create a user control that contains the name, telephone, and e-mail fields on the Individual Reservations page.

1. Return to the single.aspx file in the Visual Studio IDE. Select from the Last name field to the closing `</asp:CompareValidator>` tag for the `compareEmail` field. Cut the highlighted contents to the Clipboard.

2. Select the **Website** menu and then select **Add New Item**. The Add New Item dialog box opens. In the Add New Item dialog box, select **Web User Control** from the Visual Studio installed templates section of the Templates area. In the Name box, change the suggested filename to **StudentInfo.ascx**. Leave the value in the Language box set to Visual C#. Also, leave the Place code in separate file box selected. Click the **Add** button to add the user control to the project.

3. From the Clipboard, paste the text and elements you cut from the single.aspx file to the end of the user control file.

4. Return to the single.aspx file and add the following @ Register directive immediately after the @ Page directive. This directive identifies the prefix, tag name, and location of the user control.

```
<%@ Register TagPrefix="uc" TagName="StudentInfo"
    Src="StudentInfo.ascx" %>
```

5. Add the user control immediately above the preferred date field:

```
<uc:StudentInfo ID="StudentInfo" runat="server" />
```

6. Start the Web site. The Individual Reservations page should appear and function the same way as it did before you added the user control.

7. Close your Web browser window.

Exercise 4-3

In this exercise, you will build the Group Reservations page, which will include a list box to contain the names of group members.

1. Highlight and copy the form in the single.aspx file.

2. Open the groups.aspx file, locate [Add form here], and replace it with the form you copied from the single.aspx file.

3. Add the following @ Register directive immediately after the @ Page directive. This directive identifies the prefix, tag name, and location of the user control.

```
<%@ Register TagPrefix="uc" TagName="StudentInfo"
    Src="StudentInfo.ascx" %>
```

4. Add the following heading immediately after the opening <form> tag:

```
<h3>Group Leader</h3>
```

5. Add the following statements immediately after the opening <form> tag. These statements contain TextBox controls for the first and last names of additional group members, along with a ListBox control to store the names and two buttons for adding and removing group members from the list box. The Add button includes an OnClick event that calls a handler named add_Click and the Remove button includes an OnClick event that calls a handler named

remove_Click. You will create both of these event handlers next.

```
<h3>Group Members</h3>
    <p>
        Last name <br />
        <asp:TextBox ID="memberLastName"
        runat="server" Width="185px" /><br />
        First name <br />
        <asp:TextBox ID="memberFirstName"
        runat="server" Width="185px"/><br />
        <asp:Button ID="add" runat="server"
        Text="Add" OnClick="add_Click"
        CausesValidation="False"
        UseSubmitBehavior="False" />
        <asp:Button ID="remove" runat="server"
        Text="Remove" OnClick="remove_Click"
        CausesValidation="False"
        UseSubmitBehavior="False" />
        <asp:ListBox ID="groupMembers" runat="server"
        Height="120px" Width="190px"></asp:ListBox>
    </p>
```

6. Click on the single.aspx.cs tab, and then copy the Page_LoadComplete() and dateSelected() event handlers. Open the groups.aspx.cs page and replace the Page_Load() event handler with the Page_LoadComplete() and dateSelected() event handlers.

7. Add the following event handlers to the end of the groups class:

```
protected void add_Click(object Source, EventArgs E)
{
    groupMembers.Items.Add(new
    ListItem(memberLastName.Text + ", "
        + memberFirstName.Text));
}
protected void remove_Click(object Source, EventArgs E)
{
    groupMembers.Items.Remove(
      groupMembers.SelectedItem);
}
```

8. Start the Web site and test the Group Reservations page.

9. Close your Web browser window.

Discovery Projects

Project 4-1

Search the Internet for an image of a sports team photo. Use the image to create an image map that uses each player as a hot spot. Clicking on a hot spot should open a separate Web page that displays the player's statistics for the associated sport. For instance, with a photo of a baseball team, clicking on a player should open a page that displays the player's batting average, number of errors, and so on. You can make up any statistical information you want.

Project 4-2

Modify the Instructors page of the Big River Kayaking Web site so that the instructor information is listed in a table in the right column. When a user clicks a hot spot in the image map, highlight the table row for the selected instructor. For information on working with table controls, refer to the Table, TableRow, and TableCell Web Server Control Overview page on MSDN at *http://msdn.microsoft.com/ en-us/library/ty0ce8sc.aspx.*

Project 4-3

Create a user control out of the BMI calculator that you saw in this chapter, and practice using the control on at least two separate Web pages.

CHAPTER 5

Manipulating Strings with C#

In this chapter you will:

◎ Manipulate strings

◎ Parse strings

◎ Work with regular expressions

One of the most common uses of C# is for processing form data submitted by users. Because form data is submitted as strings, a good C# programmer must be adept at dealing with strings. In this chapter, you will learn how to use advanced techniques for working with strings. This chapter discusses techniques for manipulating strings and processing form data with C#. You will also learn how to employ regular expressions, which are used for matching and manipulating strings according to specified rules.

Manipulating Strings

As you learned in Chapter 2, a string is text contained within double quotation marks. You can use text strings as literal values or assign them to a variable. For example, the first statement in the following code prints a literal text string, whereas the second statement assigns a text string to a variable. The third statement then uses the `Response.Write()` statement to print the text string assigned to the variable.

```
Response.Write("<h1>2008 Highest Paid Sports Figure</h1>");
string baseballPlayer = "Alex Rodriguez";
Response.Write("<p>" + baseballPlayer + ": $ 28,000,000 </p>");
```

The preceding example demonstrates some of the basic techniques for creating and combining strings. You will often find it necessary to parse the text strings in your programs. When applied to text strings, the term **parsing** refers to the act of extracting characters or substrings from a larger string. This is essentially the same process as the parsing (rendering) that occurs in a Web browser when the Web browser extracts the necessary formatting information from a Web page before displaying it on the screen. In the case of a Web page, the document itself is one large text string from which formatting and other information needs to be extracted. However, in programming terminology, parsing usually refers to the extraction of information from string literals and variables.

To parse the text strings in your programs, you use the methods and properties of the `String` class. All literal strings and string variables in C# are represented by a **String class**, which contains methods for manipulating text strings.

In this chapter, you will create an ASP.NET program that sends e-mail messages from a Web site named Personal Web Portal, which is already created for you in your Chapter folder for Chapter 5. Figure 5-1 shows how the main page appears in a Web browser.

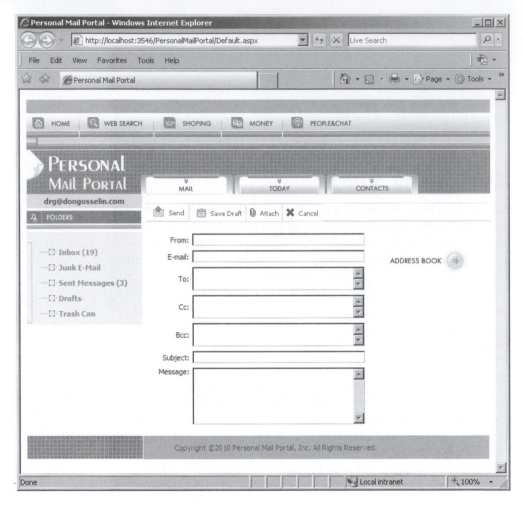

Figure 5-1 Personal Web Portal page

To send e-mail messages from an ASP.NET program, you use the **System.Net.Mail namespace**, which contains classes for sending e-mail to an SMTP server. **Simple Mail Transfer Protocol (SMTP)** is a protocol that most e-mail systems use to send messages over the Internet. A **namespace** is an abstract container that manages the identifiers in a C# program.

Different classes may use the same identifiers for class names, methods, and other items. With a large and complex program, then, it is only a matter of time before your program encounters two elements with identical names. To use a namespace in an ASP.NET Web page, you must import it with the @ import processing directive. The following @ import processing directive imports the System.Net.Mail namespace:

```
<%@ Import Namespace="System.Net.Mail" %>
```

To add a directive to a class file, you use the `using` keyword. For example, the following code demonstrates how to add the `System.Net.Mail` namespace to the default list of directives in a class file:

```
using System;
using System.Collections.Generic;
using System.Linq;
using System.Web;
using System.Net.Mail;
```

You use the **MailMessage class** to create an e-mail object that contains message information such as the sender, recipient, subject, and body. The basic syntax for creating a `MailMessage` object is as follows:

```
MailMessage emailObject = new MailMessage();
```

After initializing an object, you use properties of the `MailMessage` object to construct the message. The six basic properties of the `MailMessage` object are `From`, `To`, `CC`, `Bcc`, `Subject`, and `Body`. The values you assign to the `From`, `To`, `CC`, and `Bcc` properties can either be e-mail addresses in the format *name@domain.identifier* or an object of the **MailAddress class**, which allows you to identify the e-mail address and display name of the sender. The basic syntax for creating a `MailAddress` object is as follows:

```
MailAddress addressObject = new MailAddress(
    address[, displayName]);
```

The following example demonstrates how to construct `MailAddress` objects.

```
MailAddress from = new MailAddress(
    "refunds@centralvalleybank.com ",
    "Central Valley Bank");
MailAddress to = new MailAddress("drg@dongosselin.com",
    "Don Gosselin");
MailMessage emailMessage = new MailMessage(from, to);
```

The following statements demonstrate how to construct a new e-mail object and assign values to its `To`, `CC`, and `Bcc` properties. Note that you must use the `Add()` method to assign `MailAddress` objects the `To`, `CC`, and `Bcc` properties. You do not need to use the `Add()` method to assign a `MailAddress` object to the `From` property.

```
MailAddress from = new MailAddress(
    "refunds@centralvalleybank.com",
    "Central Valley Bank");
MailAddress to = new MailAddress("drg@dongosselin.com",
    "Don Gosselin");
MailMessage emailMessage = new MailMessage(from, to);
string subject = "Tax refund account status";
string body = "Thank you for selecting Central
    Valley Bank. You should receive your tax
    refund within seven business days.";
```

 To use the e-mail address and display name stored within a `MailAddress` object in your code, you can use the `Address` and `DisplayName` properties of the `MailAddress` class.

```
emailMessage.From = from;
emailMessage.To.Add(to);
emailMessage.Subject = subject;
emailMessage.Body = body;
```

To administer and configure your Web site, you use the **ASP.NET Web Site Administration Tool.** Before you can actually send an e-mail message, you must use the ASP.NET Web Site Administration Tool to configure your SMTP e-mail settings. Among other things, when configuring your e-mail settings, you need to specify the name of your SMTP server. (You'll need to contact your ISP for the name of your SMTP server, the server's port, and the type of authentication.) Later in this section, you learn how to use the ASP.NET Web Site Administration Tool.

After configuring your SMTP e-mail settings, you must instantiate an object of the **SmtpClient class**, which allows you to send e-mail messages with SMTP. The syntax for instantiating an SmtpClient class object is as follows:

```
SmtpClient client = new SmtpClient();
```

The main purpose of the e-mail project in this chapter is to demonstrate how to manipulate strings and validate form data with C#. Even if you do not have access to an SMTP e-mail system, you can perform the exercises in this chapter by commenting out the Send() method statement in your programs.

You need to use two members of the SmtpClient class to send an e-mail message: the UseDefaultCredentials property and the Send() method. You assign a value of true to the UseDefaultCredentials property to use the SMTP e-mail settings that you specified via the ASP.NET Web Site Administration Tool. To actually send the e-mail message, you pass the MailMessage object as an argument to the Send() method. The following statements demonstrate how to declare an SmtpClient class object, assign a value of true to the UseDefaultCredentials property, and then send the emailMessage object by passing it as an argument to the Send() method.

```
SmtpClient mailClient = new SmtpClient();
mailClient.UseDefaultCredentials = true;
mailClient.Send(emailMessage);
```

Next, you will create and work with an ASP.NET program that processes and submits e-mail messages.

To start creating the ASP.NET e-mail program:

1. Click the **Start** button, point to **All Programs**, and then click **Microsoft Visual Web Developer 2008 Express Edition**. The Visual Studio Integrated Development Environment (IDE) opens.

2. Select the **File** menu and then select **Open Web Site**. The Open Web Site dialog box opens. Locate and select the PersonalMailPortal folder, located in your Chapter folder for Chapter 5, and then click **Open**. The PersonalMailPortal Web site opens in the Visual Studio IDE.

3. Open the **Default.aspx.cs** file in the Code Editor window and add the following directive to the end of the directives section to give the class access to the `System.Net.Mail` namespace:

```
using System.Net.Mail;
```

4. Add the following statements to the `Page_Load()` event handler to determine whether the current request was caused by a post back event and if the controls on the form are valid:

```
if (Page.IsPostBack)
{
    Page.Validate();
    if (Page.IsValid)
    {
    }
}
```

5. Add the following statements to the nested `if` statement to instantiate the `MailMessage` and `MailAddress` objects:

```
MailAddress messageFrom = new
    MailAddress(senderEmail.Text, senderName.Text);
MailAddress messageTo = new MailAddress(to.Text);
MailMessage emailMessage = new MailMessage(
    messageFrom, messageTo);
string messageSubject = subject.Text;
string messageBody = message.Text;
emailMessage.Subject = messageSubject;
emailMessage.Body = messageBody;
```

6. Add the following statements to the end of nested `if` statement. These statements declare an `SmtpClient` class object, set the value of the `UseDefaultCredentials` property to true, and send the `emailMessage` object by passing it as an argument to the `Send()` method.

```
SmtpClient mailClient = new SmtpClient();
mailClient.UseDefaultCredentials = true;
mailClient.Send(emailMessage);
```

7. Add the following statement to the end of the nested `if` statements. The first statement hides the `<asp:Panel>` control that contains the e-mail form and the second statement displays a `<asp:Literal>` control that will display the sent message.

```
emailForm.Visible = false;
sentEmail.Visible = true;
```

 If you do not have access to an SMTP e-mail system, add two slashes (//) before the `Send()` statement to comment it out.

8. At the end of the nested `if` statement, add the following statements, which print the contents of the e-mail message in the `<asp:Literal>` control with an ID of `sentEmail`. Notice that the statements use properties of the `MailAddress` and `MailMessage` classes to print the contents of the e-mail message.

```
sentEmail.Text = "<p>The following message was
    sent successfully</p><hr />";
sentEmail.Text += "<p><strong>From</strong>: "
    + messageFrom.DisplayName + ", "
    + messageFrom.Address + "</p>";
sentEmail.Text += "<p><strong>To</strong>: "
    + messageTo.Address + "</p>";
sentEmail.Text += "<p><strong>Subject</strong>: "
    + emailMessage.Subject + "</p>";
sentEmail.Text += "<p><strong>Message</strong>: "
    + emailMessage.Body + "</p>";
```

Next, you will configure the SMTP e-mail settings and test the Web page.

To configure the SMTP e-mail settings and test the Web page:

1. Run the ASP.NET Web Site Administration Tool by selecting the **Website** menu and then selecting **ASP.NET Configuration**. The Welcome page of the Web Site Administration Tool displays. Click the **Application Configuration** link, and then click the **Configure SMTP e-mail settings** link to display the Configure SMTP Settings page, as shown in Figure 5-2:

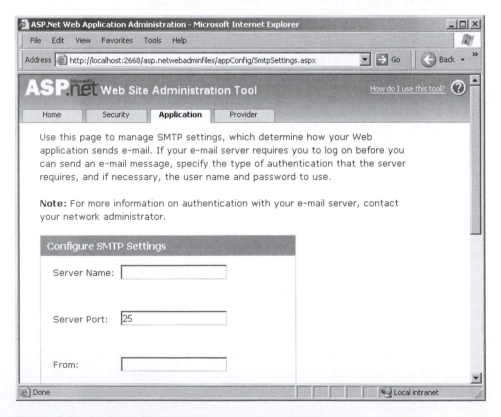

Figure 5-2 Configure SMTP Settings page of the Web Site Administration Tool

2. On the Configure SMTP Settings page, enter the name and port of your SMTP server. In the From box, you must enter a valid e-mail address. If your SMTP server requires authentication, select the **Basic** button and enter your username and password or select **NTLM (Windows authentication)**.

> You must obtain the SMTP configuration settings from your ISP or network administrator.

3. Select **Save** to save your SMTP configuration settings and then close the browser window where the Web Site Administration Tool is running.

4. Start the Web site and enter values in the From, E-mail, To, Subject, and Message fields. Be sure to enter valid e-mail addresses in the From and To fields or you will receive an error.

5. Click the **Send** button and you should see the contents of the e-mail message you sent, similar to Figure 5-3.

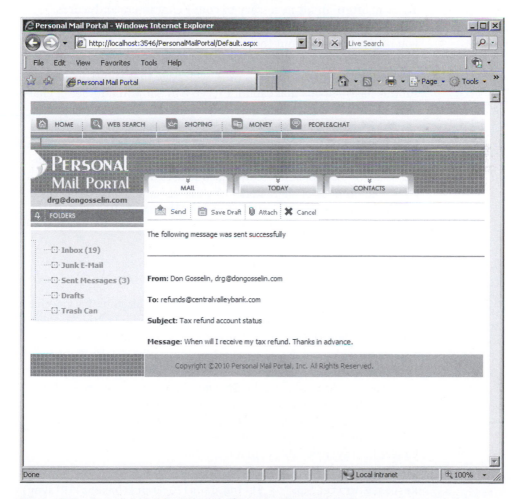

Figure 5-3 Personal Mail Portal page after submitting an e-mail

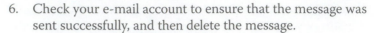

6. Check your e-mail account to ensure that the message was sent successfully, and then delete the message.

7. Close your Web browser window.

If you do receive a "relaying denied" error message, try sending and receiving your e-mail with commercial software such as Microsoft Outlook before attempting to use ASP to send e-mail messages.

Most SMTP servers can be configured to prevent relaying, or forwarding, of spam, which generally refers to unsolicited or unwanted junk e-mail. To prevent relaying, many SMTP servers require users to regularly send and receive e-mail at the same time. This allows the SMTP server to identify the user based on his IP address. Because your Web server is probably not part of your ISP's domain, you might receive a "relaying denied" error message when you attempt to send a message with the ASP e-mail program.

Counting Characters in a String

You will often find it necessary to count characters and words in strings, particularly with strings from form submissions. For example, you might need to count the number of characters in a password to ensure that a user selects a password with a minimum number of characters. Or, you might have a Web page that allows users to submit classified ads that cannot exceed a maximum number of characters. The String class contains a property, the **Length property**, which returns the number of characters in a string. To return the total number of characters in a string, you append the Length property of the String class to a literal string, variable, or object containing text. For example, the following code uses the Length property to count the number of characters in a variable named baseballPlayer. The document.write() statement prints "The baseball player's name contains 14 characters."

The Length property counts escape sequences such as \" as one character.

```
string baseballPlayer = "Alex Rodriguez";
Response.Write("<p>The baseball player's name contains "
    + baseballPlayer.Length + " characters.</p>");
```

If you only need to find out whether a string variable contains any characters at all, you can use the IsNullOrEmpty() method of the String class. The **IsNullOrEmpty() method** returns either a value of true if a string variable contains an empty string or a value of false if a string variable contains one or more characters. To use the IsNullOrEmpty() method, you append it to the String object, and then pass the name of the string variable you want to test as an argument of the IsNullOrEmpty() method. The IsNullOrEmpty() method statement in the following code returns a value of false because the baseballPlayer variable contains a value:

```
string baseballPlayer = "Alex Rodriguez";
Response.Write("<p>" + String.IsNullOrEmpty(baseballPlayer)
    + "</p>"); // prints false
```

Formatting Strings

This section describes how to use methods of the `String` class to format strings.

Using Special Characters

You learned in Chapter 2 that when you want to include basic types of special characters, such as quotation marks, within a literal string, you must use an escape sequence. The escape sequence for double quotation marks is \" and the escape sequence for single quotation marks is \'. In the following example, the text string assigned to the `baseballPlayer` variable includes escape sequences for double quotation marks. Figure 5-4 shows the output in a Web browser.

```
Response.Write("<h1>2008 Highest Paid Sports Figure</h1>");
string baseballPlayer = "Alex \"ARod\" Rodriguez";
Response.Write("<p>" + baseballPlayer + ": $ 28,000,000 </p>");
```

Figure 5-4 Output of a text string created with escape sequences and the concatenation operator

For other types of special characters, you need to use Unicode. In most cases, you can use XHTML numeric character references or character entities to represent Unicode characters in text strings. For example, the copyright symbol (©) can be represented in HTML by the numeric character reference © and the character entity is ©. To assign the text "© 2010" to a variable named `copyrightInfo` in C#, you can use either of the following statements:

```
string copyrightInfo
    = "<p>&#169; 2010</p>"; // numeric character ref
string copyrightInfo
    = "<p>&copy; 2010</p>"; // character entity
```

You can find a complete list of Unicode characters at http://www.macchiato.com/unicode/chart/.

Instead of using numeric character references or character entities within text strings, as shown in the preceding example, you can use an escape sequence, in the form \x*hhhh*. The *hhhh* characters represent the four digits of a hexadecimal Unicode symbol. The following statement use a hexadecimal Unicode symbol to print "©2010":

```
Response.Write("<p>\x00a92010</p>");
```

E-mail addresses and display names are usually displayed in the format *display name <name@domain.identifier>*, such as "Don Gosselin <drg@dongosselin.com>". By default, Web browsers always attempt to render the angle brackets (< and >) as HTML elements. To force a Web browser to display these characters instead of render them, you need to use the < character entity for the less-than character and the > character entity for the greater-than character. Next, you will add these character entities to the output statement that prints the sender's display name and e-mail address so the e-mail address is contained within less-than and greater-than characters.

To add character entities to the e-mail program:

1. Return to the **Default.aspx.cs** file in the Visual Studio IDE.

2. Modify the statement that assigns the sender's display name and e-mail address to the <asp:Literal> control so the address portion is surrounded by the character entities for the less-than and greater-than characters as follows:

```
sentEmail.Text += "<p><strong>From</strong>: "
    + messageFrom.DisplayName + " &lt;"
    + messageFrom.Address + "&gt;</p>";
```

3. Start the Web site and enter values in the From, E-mail, To, Subject, and Message fields. Click the **Send** button. The sender display name and e-mail you entered should display in the format *display name <name@domain.identifier>*.

4. Close your Web browser window.

Changing Case

To change the case of letters in a string, you use the ToLower() and ToUpper() methods of the String class. The **ToLower() method** converts a text string to lowercase, whereas the **ToUpper() method** converts a text string to uppercase. You append either method to a string or variable that contains the text for which you want to change letter case. For example, the following code uses the ToUpper() method to print the contents of the agency variable ("naacp") in uppercase letters ("NAACP"):

```
string agency = "naacp";
Response.Write("<p>" + agency.ToUpper() + "</p>");
```

Note that the `ToUpper()` method in the preceding statement does not convert the contents of the `agency` variable to uppercase letters; it only prints the text in uppercase letters. If you want to change the contents of a variable to upper- or lowercase letters, you must assign the value returned from the `ToLower()` or `ToUpper()` methods to the variable or to a different variable. The following statements demonstrate how to change the contents of the `agency` variable to uppercase letters:

```
string agency = "naacp";
agency = agency.ToUpper();
Response.Write("<p>" + agency + "</p>");
```

Next, you will add code to the e-mail program that converts the sender's e-mail address to lowercase.

To add code to the e-mail program that converts the e-mail addresses to lowercase:

1. Return to the **Default.aspx.cs** file in the Visual Studio IDE.

2. Append the `ToLower()` method to the `Request.Form["senderEmail"]` variable in the `MailAddress` object declaration, as follows:

```
MailAddress messageFrom = new
    MailAddress(senderEmail.Text.ToLower(),
    senderName.Text);
```

3. Start the Web site. The Default.aspx file opens in a Web browser.

4. Enter values in the Name, E-mail Address, To, Subject, and Message fields. Make the e-mail addresses in the E-mail Address field uppercase. Click the **Send** button and your Web browser should display "The following message was sent successfully." and the contents of the message, with the sender's e-mail address converted to lowercase.

5. Close your Web browser window.

Trimming Strings

When a form is submitted to a Web server, it's not uncommon for some of the form values to contain spaces or other characters that the user accidentally typed into a form field. For example, a user's name might be submitted with spaces before or after the text string as in "∘∘∘Don Gosselin∘∘∘" (the ∘ characters represent spaces). To remove, or trim, spaces or characters from a text string, you use the methods of the `String` class listed in Table 5-1.

E-mail addresses that are sent across the Internet are not case sensitive, although people often think that they are case sensitive.

Method	Description
Trim([char ‖ charArray])	Removes from a string all leading and trailing spaces or specified characters
TrimEnd([char ‖ charArray])	Removes from a string all trailing spaces or specified characters
TrimStart([char ‖ charArray])	Removes from a string all leading spaces or specified characters

Table 5-1   Trimming methods of the String class

If you do not include an argument with the methods listed in Table 5-1, they will automatically remove spaces from the specified string. The following example uses the Trim() method to remove the leading and trailing spaces at the beginning and end of the agency variable. In other words, the Trim() method changes the "∘NAACP∘" string to "NAACP" (without the leading and trailing spaces).

```
string agency = " NAACP ";
agency = agency.Trim(); // returns "NAACP"
```

Instead of removing spaces with one of the trim methods listed in Table 5-1, you can also specify a character to remove from the beginning or end of a string. The following statements use the TrimStart() function to remove the ^ character from the beginning of the agency variable:

```
string agency = "^NAACP";
agency = agency.TrimStart('^'); // returns "NAACP"
```

If you pass a character array argument to any of the trim methods, any character in the array argument that is found at the beginning or end of the string is removed, depending on the specific function. For example, the agency name in the following code contains various "garbage" characters at the end of the string. The TrimEnd() function uses the trimArray[] array to remove these characters from the end of the string.

```
char[] trimArray = new char[4];
trimArray[0] = '%';
trimArray[1] = '*';
trimArray[2] = '#';
trimArray[3] = '&';
string agency = "NAACP*#&%";
agency = agency.TrimEnd(trimArray); // returns "NAACP"
```

Padding Strings

In comparison to the trim methods, which remove characters from the beginning or end of a string, padding methods add characters to the beginning or end of a string. Table 5-2 lists the padding methods of the String class.

Method	Description
PadLeft(*length*[, *char*])	Adds spaces or a specified character to the beginning of a string
PadRight(*length*[, *char*])	Adds spaces or a specified character to the end of a string

Table 5-2   Padding methods of the `String` class

The value of the *length* argument of the padding methods listed in Table 5-2 determines the string's total length *after* adding spaces or specified characters; it does not represent the number of characters to add. For example, if you want to add two spaces before a string that is five characters in length, you assign a value of 7 to the argument to the `PadLeft()` method, as follows:

```
string agency = "NAACP";
agency = agency.PadLeft(7); // returns "∘∘NAACP";
```

You will rarely need to add spaces to the beginning or end of a string. (You will more likely want to remove them with the trim methods.) However, you might want to add characters to some special types of strings. For example, the written pay amount on a check is often followed by asterisks (*). The following code demonstrates how to use the `PadRight()` method to add five asterisks to the end of a variable named `payAmount`. Notice that the size of the `payAmount` variable is retrieved using the `Length` property of the `String` object.

```
string payAmount = "Sixty-five and 26/100";
payAmount = payAmount.PadRight(payAmount.Length + 5, '*');
Response.Write("<p>" + payAmount
    + "</p>"); // prints "Sixty-five and 26/100*****"
```

Short Quiz 1

1. Why do you need to manipulate data in strings? List some examples in which you would use string manipulation techniques.

2. Explain how to use the classes of the `System.Net.Mail` namespace to send e-mail to an SMTP server.

3. What Visual Studio IDE tool would you use to administer a Web site?

4. Why would you need to count the number of characters in a text string?

5. Explain the three ways in which you can include special characters within a text string.

Parsing Strings

In this section, you will study basic techniques for parsing strings, including how to find, extract, and replace characters and substrings.

Finding and Extracting Characters and Substrings

In some situations, you will need to find and extract characters and substrings from a string. For example, if your program receives an e-mail address, you might need to extract the name portion of the e-mail address or domain name. To search for and extract characters and substrings in C#, you use the methods listed in Table 5-3.

Method	Description
Contains(*string*)	Performs a case-sensitive search and returns true if the value of the *string* argument is found within the string or false if the string is not found
EndsWith(*string*)	Performs a case-sensitive search and returns true if the value of the *string* argument is found at the end of the string or false if the string is not found
IndexOf(*text*[, *index*])	Performs a case-sensitive search and returns the position number in a string of the first character in the *text* argument; if the *index* argument is included, the IndexOf() method starts searching at that position within the string; returns -1 if the character or string is not found
IndexOfAny(*charArray*[, *index*])	Returns the first position number in a string of any character in the *charArray* array argument; if the *index* argument is included, the IndexOfAny() method starts searching at that position within the string; returns -1 if the character or string is not found
LastIndexOf(*text*[, *index*])	Performs a case-sensitive search and returns the position number in a string of the last instance of the first character in the *text* argument; if the *index* argument is included, the LastIndexOf() method starts searching at that position within the string; returns -1 if the character or string is not found
LastIndexOfAny(*charArray*[, *index*])	Returns the last position number in a string of any characters in the *charArray* argument; if the *index* argument is included, the LastIndexOfAny() method starts searching at that position within the string; returns -1 if the character or string is not found

Table 5-3   Search and extraction methods of the String class *(continues)*

(continued)

Method	Description
Remove(*starting index*[, *length*])	Deletes text from a string starting with the position number in the string to the end of the string; if the *length* argument is included, the Remove() method deletes that number of characters from the string
StartsWith(*string*)	Performs a case-sensitive search and returns true if the *string* argument is found at the beginning of the string or false if the string is not found
Substring(*starting index*[, *length*])	Extracts text from a string starting with the position number in the string to the end of the string; if the *length* argument is included, the Substring() method extracts that number of characters from the string

Table 5-3   Search and extraction methods of the String class

One of the simplest methods in Table 5-3 is the Contains() method, which returns a value of true or false to indicate whether specified text is located within a string. The following statements demonstrate how to use the Contains() method to determine whether "whitehouse" is contained within the email variable containing "president@whitehouse.gov":

```
string email = "president@whitehouse.gov";
Response.Write(email.Contains("whitehouse")); // prints true
```

Two functions that are related to the Contains() method are the StartsWith() method, which determines whether the start of a string matches specified text, and the EndsWith() method, which determines whether the end of a string matches specified text. Like the Contains() method, the StartsWith() and EndsWith() methods return a value of true or false to indicate whether specified text was found. The following statements demonstrate how to use the StartsWith() and EndsWith() methods with the email variable. The StartsWith() method returns a value of true because the email variable begins with "president" and the EndsWith() method also returns a value of true because the email variable ends with "gov".

```
string email = "president@whitehouse.gov";
Response.Write(email.StartsWith("president")
  + "<br />"); // prints true
Response.Write(email.EndsWith("gov")
  + "<br />"); // prints true
```

Several of the methods listed in Table 5-3 return a numeric position in a text string. To use these methods, you need to understand that the position of characters in a text string begins with a value of 0, the same as with indexed array elements. For example, the `IndexOf()` method returns the position of the first instance of the first character of a text string that is passed as an argument. If the search string is not found, the `IndexOf()` method returns a value of -1. The following code uses the `IndexOf()` method to determine whether the `email` variable contains an @ character. Because the position of text strings begins with 0, the `Response.Write()` statement prints a value of 9, even though the @ character is the tenth character in the string.

```
string email = "president@whitehouse.gov";
Response.Write(email.IndexOf("@")); // prints 9
```

You can also pass to the `IndexOf()` method a second optional argument that specifies the position in the string where you want to start searching. If the search string is not found, the `IndexOf()` method returns a value of -1. The following code uses the `IndexOf()` method to determine whether the `email` variable contains an @ character. Because the `IndexOf()` method includes a value of 10 as the second optional argument, the `Response.Write()` statement prints a value of -1 (indicating that the search string was not found) because the method began searching in the string after the position of the @ character.

```
string email = "president@whitehouse.gov";
Response.Write(email.IndexOf("@", 10)); // prints -1
```

To extract characters from the middle or end of a string, you need to identify the position of the character in the string where you want to start the extraction. One way to do this is by using the `Substring()`, `IndexOf()`, or `LastIndexOf()` methods. The `Substring()` method extracts text from a string starting with the specified position number in the string to the end of the string or to a specific position within the string if the *ending index* argument is included. The `LastIndexOf()` method works the same as the `IndexOf()` method, except that it returns the position of the last occurrence of one string in another string instead of the first. The following code uses the `LastIndexOf()` method to return the position of the period within the e-mail address in the `email` variable. The `Substring()` method then uses the index returned from the `lastIndexOf()` method to return the domain identifier of the e-mail address.

```
string email = "president@whitehouse.gov";
int startDomainID = email.LastIndexOf('.');
Response.Write(
   "<p>The domain identifier of the e-mail address is "
   + email.Substring(startDomainID) + ".</p>");
```

The following code contains another example of the `Substring()` method. In this version, the code uses `Substring()`, `IndexOf()`, and `LastIndexOf()` methods to return the domain name of the e-mail address. Notice that the second statement increments the position returned from the `Substring()` method by one. This prevents the @ character from being included in the substring returned from the `Substring()` method. The third statement determines the number of characters to extract by subtracting the index number of the `domainBegin` variable from the index number returned from the `LastIndexOf()` method.

```
string email = "president@whitehouse.gov";
int domainBegin = email.IndexOf("@") + 1;
int domainEnd = email.LastIndexOf(".") - domainBegin;
Response.Write(
    "<p>The domain name portion of the e-mail address is '"
    + email.Substring(domainBegin, domainEnd) + "'.</p>");
```

In addition to the search and extraction methods listed in Table 5-3, the `String` class also includes a **Chars property** that you can use to retrieve a character by its specified index in a text string. The `Chars` property in C# is unlike other properties in that you do not refer to it in your code. Instead, you use the `Chars` property to retrieve a character by appending brackets and a character position to a string, similar to the way you append brackets and an element number to an array. The following statements demonstrate how to use the `Chars` property to print the character at position 9 (the @ symbol) in the `email` variable:

```
string email = "president@whitehouse.gov";
Response.Write(email[9]); // prints @
```

Later in this chapter, you will learn how to use regular expressions to validate strings, including e-mail addresses. For now, you use the `IndexOf()` method to simply check whether the e-mail addresses entered into the form contain an @ symbol and a period to separate the domain and identifier.

To use the `IndexOf()` method to check whether the e-mail addresses entered into the form contain @ symbols and periods to separate the domain and identifier:

1. Return to the **Default.aspx.cs** file in the Visual Studio IDE.

2. Add the following function to the end of the class declaration. The function uses two `IndexOf()` methods to determine whether the string passed to it contains an @ symbol and a period. If the string does contain both characters, a value of true is returned. If not, a value of false is returned.

    ```
    protected Boolean validateAddress(string address)
    {
        if (address.IndexOf("@") > 0
            && address.IndexOf(".") > 0)
            return true;
        else
            return false;
    }
    ```

3. Add the following `if` clause immediately before the statement that instantiates the `messageFrom` object. This clause prints an alternate message if the e-mail address does not contain an @ symbol. The conditional expression passes the text in the `senderName` field to the `validateAddress()` function.

```csharp
if (validateAddress(senderEmail.Text) == false)
{
    emailForm.Visible = false;
    sentEmail.Visible = true;
    sentEmail.Text = "<p>The sender's e-mail address
        does not appear to be valid. Click your browser's
        Back button to return to the message.</p>";
}
```

4. Modify the remaining statements in the nested `if` statement so they are contained within an `else if` clause, as follows:

```csharp
else
{
    MailAddress messageFrom = new
        MailAddress(senderEmail.Text.ToLower(),
        senderName.Text);
    MailAddress messageTo = new MailAddress(to.Text);
    MailMessage emailMessage = new MailMessage(
        messageFrom, messageTo);
    string messageSubject = subject.Text;
    string messageBody = message.Text;
    emailMessage.Subject = messageSubject;
    emailMessage.Body = messageBody;
    SmtpClient mailClient = new SmtpClient();
    mailClient.UseDefaultCredentials = true;
    mailClient.Send(emailMessage);
    emailForm.Visible = false;
    sentEmail.Visible = true;
    sentEmail.Text = "<p>The following
        message was sent successfully</p><hr />";
    sentEmail.Text += "<p><strong>From</strong>: "
        + messageFrom.DisplayName + " &lt;"
        + messageFrom.Address + "&gt;</p>";
    sentEmail.Text += "<p><strong>To</strong>: "
        + messageTo.Address + "</p>";
    sentEmail.Text += "<p><strong>Subject</strong>: "
        + emailMessage.Subject + "</p>";
    sentEmail.Text += "<p><strong>Message</strong>: "
        + emailMessage.Body + "</p>";
}
```

5. Start the Web site and enter values in the From, E-mail, To, Subject, and Message fields. In the E-Mail field, enter an invalid e-mail address that is missing either an @ symbol or period. Click the **Send** button and you should see the message indicating that the e-mail address is invalid.

6. Click your browser's **Back** button, enter a valid e-mail address in the E-Mail field, and then click the **Send** button. In your Web browser window, you should see "The following message was sent successfully." You should also see the contents of the message printed to your Web browser window.

7. Close your Web browser window.

Replacing Characters and Substrings

In addition to finding and extracting characters in a string, you might also need to replace them. You use the **Replace() method** of the String class to replace all instances of a specified character or text within a string. The syntax for using the Replace() method to replace all instances of text within a text string is *string*.Replace(*oldText*, *newText*).

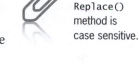

The Replace() method is case sensitive.

The following example demonstrates how to use the Replace() method to replace "president" in the email variable with "vice.president".

```
string email = "president@whitehouse.gov";
string newEmail = email.Replace("president", "vice.president");
Response.Write("<p>" + newEmail
    + "</p>"); // prints 'vice.president@whitehouse.gov'
```

The syntax for using the Replace() method to replace all instances of a specific character within a text string is *string*.Replace(*oldChar*, *newChar*). The Replace() method in the following example replaces the periods in the phoneNumber variable with dashes:

```
string phoneNumber = "212.555.1234";
string newphoneNumber = phoneNumber.Replace('.', '-');
Response.Write("<p>" + newphoneNumber
    + "</p>"); // prints '212-555-1234'
```

You can send e-mails to multiple recipients with the SmtpClient class by separating multiple e-mail addresses with commas in the strings that you assign to the To, CC, Bcc properties of the MailMessage object. However, the e-mail form instructs users to place multiple e-mail addresses in the To, Cc, and Bcc fields on separate lines results in carriage return and newline escape sequences (\r\n) between each address. Next, you will use the Replace() method to replace the carriage return and newline escape sequences with commas and spaces.

To use the Replace() method to replace the carriage return and new-line escape sequences with commas and spaces in the e-mail form:

1. Return to the **Default.aspx.cs** file in the Visual Studio IDE.

2. Add the following statements above the if statement that validates the senderEmail field. These statements use the

Replace() method to replace the carriage return and new-line escape sequences with commas and spaces in the to, cc, and bcc fields. The results are then assigned to string variables.

```
string toAddress = to.Text.Replace("\r\n", ", ");
string ccAddress = cc.Text.Replace("\r\n", ", ");
string bccAddress = bcc.Text.Replace("\r\n", ", ");
```

3. Save the project. Do not run the program yet because you still need to add some additional code to process the recipient e-mails.

Converting Between Strings and Arrays

Depending on the type of data stored in a string, you might often find it easier to manipulate the data by converting it into an array. You use the **Split() method** of the String class to split a string into an indexed array. The Split() method splits each character in a string into an array element, using the syntax *array* = *string*.Split(*separator*[, *limit*]);. The value of the *separator* argument specifies the character where the string will be separated into array elements, and the value of the *limit* argument determines the maximum length of the returned array. If the string does not contain the specified separators, the entire string is assigned to the first element of the array.

The following code demonstrates how to convert a string variable named beneluxNationsString into an array named beneluxNationsArray. A comma separates the country names in the beneluxNationsString variable. After the Split() method converts the string to an array, a for loop prints the contents of each array element. Notice that the for loop also uses the TrimEnd() method of the String class to strip the extra space at the end of each element. Figure 5-5 shows the output.

```
string beneluxNationsString
    = "Belgium, Netherlands, Luxembourg";
string[] beneluxNationsArray
    = beneluxNationsString.Split(',');
for (int i = 0; i < beneluxNationsArray.Length; ++i)
{
    beneluxNationsArray[i].TrimEnd(' ');
    Response.Write(beneluxNationsArray[i] + "<br />");
}
```

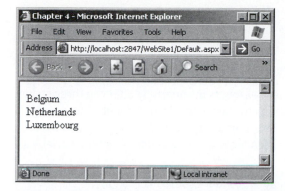

Figure 5-5 Output of an array that was converted from a string

The opposite of the Split() method is the String class's **Join() method**, which combines array elements into a string, separated by specified characters. The syntax for the Join() method is *stringVariable* = String.Join(["*separator*", *arrayName*]);. The value of the *separator* argument specifies the character or characters that will separate the contents of each array element in the returned string. If you do not include the *separator* argument, the Join() method automatically separates elements with a comma. To prevent the elements from being separated by any characters in the new string, pass an empty string ("") as the *separator* argument. The following code demonstrates how to use the Join() method to create a string from an array containing the names of the Benelux nations. Figure 5-6 shows the output.

```
string[] beneluxNationsArray = new string[3];
beneluxNationsArray[0] = "Belgium";
beneluxNationsArray[1] = "Netherlands";
beneluxNationsArray[2] = "Luxembourg";
string beneluxNationsString
    = String.Join(", ", beneluxNationsArray);
Response.Write(beneluxNationsString);
```

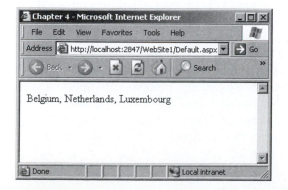

Figure 5-6 Output of a string that was converted from an array

To copy the characters in a string to a character array, use the ToCharArray() method of the String class.

To use the `Replace()` method to replace the carriage return escape sequences with commas and spaces in the to, cc, and bcc fields of the e-mail form:

1. Return to the **Default.aspx.cs** file in the Visual Studio IDE.

2. Add the following statements immediately after the three string variable declarations in the nested `if` statement. These statements use the `Split()` method to convert the e-mail addresses in the `toAddress`, `ccAddress`, and `bccAddress` string variables to arrays.

```
string[] toArray = toAddress.Split(',');
string[] ccArray = ccAddress.Split(',');
string[] bccArray = bccAddress.Split(',');
```

3. Add the following `checkAddresses()` function to the end of the class declaration. This function trims the empty spaces from the end of each e-mail address and also calls the `validateAddress()` method to validate each e-mail address.

```
protected Boolean checkAddresses(string[] address)
{
    for (int i = 0; i < address.Length; ++i)
    {
        address[i].TrimEnd(' ');
        if (!validateAddress(address[i]))
            return false;
    }
    return true;
}
```

4. Add the following `else...if` statements immediately above the `else` clause in the `Page_Load()` event handler. The `if` conditional expressions pass the arrays you created in Step 2 to a function named `checkAddresses()` that will perform further processing on the e-mail addresses. (You will create the `checkAddresses()` next.) Notice that the conditional expression for the To addresses is slightly different from the conditional expressions for the Cc and Bcc addresses; it requires that the `Length` property of the to field be greater than 0 because an e-mail message must have at least one recipient. Because the Cc and Bcc addresses are optional, their conditional expressions pass the `ccArray[]` and `bccArray[]` to the `checkAddresses()` function only if the `Length` properties for the `ccAddress` and `bccAddress` variables are greater than 0.

```
    else if (to.Text.Length == 0
        || !checkAddresses(toArray))
    {
        emailForm.Visible = false;
        sentEmail.Visible = true;
        sentEmail.Text = "One or more of the
          To e-mail address does not appear
          to be valid. Click your browser's Back
          button to return to the message.";
    }
    else if (cc.Text.Length > 0
        && !checkAddresses(ccArray))
    {
        emailForm.Visible = false;
        sentEmail.Visible = true;
        sentEmail.Text = "One or more of the
          Cc e-mail address does not appear
          to be valid. Click your browser's Back
          button to return to the message.";
    }
    else if (bcc.Text.Length > 0 && !checkAddresses(bccArray))
    {
        emailForm.Visible = false;
        sentEmail.Visible = true;
        sentEmail.Text = "One or more of the
          Bcc e-mail address does not appear
          to be valid. Click your browser's Back
          button to return to the message.";
    }
```

5. Delete the following statement from the else clause in the code render block. You will replace this statement with a for statement that assigns recipients for the To field to the MailAddress.

```
MailAddress messageTo = new MailAddress(to.Text);
```

6. Delete the arguments that are passed to the MailMessage object constructor and add a statement that assigns the messageFrom variable to the From property of the MailMessage object. The statements should appear as follows:

```
MailMessage emailMessage = new MailMessage();
emailMessage.From = messageFrom;
```

7. Add the following for statement immediately after the statement that instantiates the emailMessage object. This statement loops through the toArray[] array and assigns the e-mail addresses in each element to the To property of the MailMessage object.

```
for (int i = 0; i < toArray.Length; ++i)
{
    MailAddress messageTo
      = new MailAddress(toArray[i]);
    emailMessage.To.Add(messageTo.Address);
}
```

8. Add the following `if` and nested `for` statements immediately after the `for` statement you just created. Because the Cc and Bcc addresses are optional, the `if` statements first determine whether the `ccAddress` and `bccAddress` variables contain values by checking their `Length` properties. The `for` statement in the first `if` statement loops through the `ccArray[]` array and assigns the e-mail addresses in each element to the CC property of the `MailMessage` object and the `for` statement in the second `if` statement loops through the `bccArray[]` array and assigns the e-mail addresses in each element to the Bcc property of the `MailMessage` object.

```
if (ccAddress.Length > 0)
{
    for (int i = 0; i < ccArray.Length; ++i)
    {
        MailAddress messageTo
            = new MailAddress(ccArray[i]);
        emailMessage.CC.Add(messageTo.Address);
    }
}
if (bccAddress.Length > 0)
{
    for (int i = 0; i < bccArray.Length; ++i)
    {
        MailAddress messageTo
            = new MailAddress(bccArray[i]);
        emailMessage.Bcc.Add(messageTo.Address);
    }
}
```

9. Modify the statement that assigns the e-mail address of the To recipients to the `Text` property of the `sentEmail` field so it assigns the value of the `toAddress` variable instead of the `Address` property of the `messageTo` object (which you just deleted), as follows:

```
sentEmail.Text += "<p><strong>To</strong>: "
    + toAddress + "</p>";
```

10. Finally, add the following statements immediately after the assignment statement that assigns the e-mail address of the To recipients to the `Text` property of the `sentEmail` field. These statements print the addresses in the `ccAddress` and `bccAddress` fields.

```
sentEmail.Text += "<p><strong>To</strong>: "
    + ccAddress + "</p>";
sentEmail.Text += "<p><strong>To</strong>: "
    + bccAddress + "</p>";
```

11. Start the Web site and test the form by entering values in each field and clicking the **Send** button. Be sure to test the multiple recipient functionality of the To, CC, and Bcc fields.

12. Close your Web browser window.

Comparing Strings

In Chapter 2, you studied various operators that you can use with C#, including comparison operators. Although comparison operators are most often used with numbers, they can also be used with strings. The following statements use the comparison operator (==) to compare two variables containing text strings. Because the text strings are not the same, the `else` clause prints the text "Different locations."

```
string france = "Paris is in France.";
string england = "London is in England.";
if (france == england)
    Response.Write("<p>Same location.</p>");
else
    Response.Write("<p>Different locations.</p>");
```

You can also compare strings by using the methods of the `String` class that are listed in Table 5-4.

Method	Description
Equals(*string*)	Determines whether a string contains the same case-sensitive values as the value of the *string* argument
Compare(*string1*, *string2*)	Compares the value of the *string1* argument with the value of the *string2* argument
CompareOrdinal(*string1*, *string2*)	Compares value of the *string1* argument with the value of *string2* argument according to the numeric values of the characters within each string
CompareTo(*string*)	Compares a string with the value of the *string* argument

Table 5-4   Comparison methods of the `String` class

The `Equals()` method performs the same function as the comparison operator in that it determines whether two strings contain the same value. It returns either a value of true if the two strings are equal or false if they are not. The syntax for the `Equals()` method is *string.*`Equals(`*string*`);`. The following statements use the `Equals()` method to compare the `france` and `england` variables:

```
string france = "Paris is in France.";
string england = "London is in England.";
if (france.Equals(england))
    Response.Write("<p>Same location.</p>");
else
    Response.Write("<p>Different locations.</p>");
```

The String class includes several compare methods that compare strings according to the particular sort order of a language or country. For example, the Compare() method compares two strings that are passed as arguments. The syntax for the Compare() method is string.Compare(*string1*, *string2*). If *string1* is equivalent to *string2*, the method returns a value of 0; if *string2* sorts before *string1*, the method returns a value greater than 0, usually 1; if *string2* sorts after *string1*, the method returns a value less than 0, usually -1. For example, consider the following Compare() method, which compares the strings "Dan" and "Don". Because "Dan" sorts before "Don", the method returns a value of 1.

```
string stringA = "Don";
string stringB = "Dan";
Response.Write(string.Compare(stringA,
    stringB)); // prints 1
```

By contrast, the following statement, which switches the "Dan" and "Don" arguments in the Compare() method, returns a value of -1:

```
string stringA = "Don";
string stringB = "Dan";
Response.Write(string.Compare(stringB,
    stringA)); // prints -1
```

If both strings' values are equal, the Compare() method returns a value of 0, as in the following example:

```
string stringA = "Don";
string stringB = "Don";
Response.Write(string.Compare(stringA,
    stringB)); // prints 0
```

Keep in mind that the Compare() method performs a case-sensitive comparison of two strings. The following statements return a value of 1 because the lowercase "d" in the comparison string sorts before the uppercase "D" in the source string:

```
string stringA = "Don";
string stringB = "don";
Response.Write(string.Compare(stringA,
    stringB)); // prints 1
```

If you want to perform a case-insensitive comparison of two strings, you need to pass a value of true as a third argument to the Compare() method. Because the Compare() method in the following code includes a third argument of true, it returns a value of 0 because it ignores the case of the two strings:

```
string stringA = "Don";
string stringB = "don";
Response.Write(string.Compare(stringA,
    stringB, true)); // prints 0
```

Combining Characters and Substrings

So far, you have used the concatenation operator (+) and the compound assignment operator (+=) to combine text strings. The String class also includes the **Concat() method**, which creates a new string by combining strings that are passed as arguments. The syntax for the Concat() method is string.concat(*string1*, *string2*, ...). Note that the Concat() method does not change the original string but returns a new string. The values of the *string* arguments are combined in the order in which they are passed to the Concat() method. The following statements demonstrate how to use the Concat() method to build a string that is printed using a Write() statement. Figure 5-7 shows the output in a Web browser.

```
string name = "Samuel Clemens";
string penName = "Mark Twain";
Response.Write("<p>" + string.Concat(penName,
    " was the pen name of ", name) + ".</p>");
```

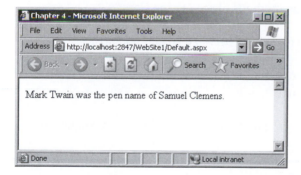

Figure 5-7 Output generated with the Concat() method of the String class

In most cases, you do not need to use the Concat() method. Instead, it is usually easier to use the concatenation operator and the compound assignment operator to combine text strings. The following code shows the same statements from the preceding example, but this time using concatenation operators:

```
string name = "Samuel Clemens";
string penName = "Mark Twain";
Response.Write("<p>" + penName +
    " was the pen name of " + name + ".</p>");
```

The Concat() method, concatenation operator, and the compound assignment operator append text strings to one another. If you want to insert text into a string, you use the **Insert() method** of the String class to insert the text after a specified index position within the string. The syntax for the Insert() method is *string. concat(index, text)*. The third statement in the following code uses the Concat() method to combine the name and penName variables into a new variable named alias. The fourth statement then uses the Insert() method to insert the text " was the pen name of " into the alias variable. Notice that the Insert() method uses the Length property to determine where to insert the text into the string.

```
string name = "Samuel Clemens";
string penName = "Mark Twain";
string alias = string.Concat(penName, name);
alias = alias.Insert(penName.Length,
    " was the pen name of ");
Response.Write("<p>" + alias + ".</p>");
```

Short Quiz 2

1. Explain why you might need to find and extract characters and substrings from a string.

2. What types of values are returned from the various search and extraction methods of the String class?

3. Explain how to convert between strings and arrays.

4. What operators and String class methods can you use to compare strings?

5. What operators and String class methods can you use to combine strings?

Working with Regular Expressions

To use regular expressions, you must add a using directive to your class file that imports the System.Text. RegularExpressions namespace.

One of the more complex methods of working with strings involves the use of **regular expressions**, which are patterns that are used for matching and manipulating strings according to specified rules. With scripting languages, regular expressions are most commonly used for validating submitted form data. For example, you can use a regular expression to ensure that a user enters a date in a specific format, such as *mm/dd/yyyy*, or a telephone number in the format (###) ###-####. Most scripting languages support some form of regular expressions.

Defining Regular Expressions in C#

To define a regular expression pattern in C#, you must use the `Regex()` constructor. The `Regex()` constructor is part of the **Regex class**, which represents regular expressions in C# and contains methods and properties for working with regular expressions. The syntax for creating a regular expression with the `Regex()` constructor is as follows:

```
Regex regularExpressionName = new Regex("pattern");
```

The following statement defines a regular expression pattern for determining whether a text string contains "https" and assigns it to a variable named `urlProtocol`.

```
Regex urlProtocol = new Regex("https");
```

To determine whether a particular string matches a regular expression pattern, you must use the **Match class**, which represents the results of a regular expression match. You instantiate an object of the `Match` class and assign to it the results from the `Match()` method of the `Regex` class. The `Match()` method returns a value of true or false, depending on whether the string matches the regular expression. The following code demonstrates how to search a variable named `url` for the `urlProtocol` regular expression. The third statement assigns the result returned from the `Match()` method of the `Regex` class to a `Match` object named `regExMatch`:

```
Regex urlProtocol = new Regex("https");
string url = "http://www.dongosselin.com";
Match regExMatch = urlProtocol.Match(url);
```

The `Match()` class contains various methods and properties, the most important of which is the **Success property**, which returns a value of true or false, depending on the result of the `Match()` method. The `Success` property in the following code contains a value of false because the regular expression pattern was not found in the `url` variable:

```
Regex urlProtocol = new Regex("https");
string url = "http://www.dongosselin.com";
Match regExMatch = urlProtocol.Match(url);
Response.Write("<p>" + regExMatch.Success
    + "</p>"); // prints false
```

Next, you modify the `validateAddress()` method so it searches for the @ symbol in the e-mail addresses using a regular expression.

To modify the `validateAddress()` method so it searches for the @ symbol in the e-mail addresses using a regular expression:

1. Return to the **Default.aspx.cs** file in the Visual Studio IDE.

2. Add the following using statement to the directives list to import the `System.Text.RegularExpressions` namespace.

    ```
    using System.Text.RegularExpressions;
    ```

3. Add the following statements to the beginning of the validateAddress() method. These statements use a regular expression to determine whether the address parameter contains an @ symbol.

```
Regex atSymbolPattern = new Regex("@");
Match atSymbolMatch = atSymbolPattern.Match(address);
```

4. Locate the if statement in the validateAddress() method and modify the conditional expression so that it checks the Success property of the atSymbolMatch variable to determine whether the address contains an @ symbol, as follows:

```
...
if (atSymbolMatch.Success && address.IndexOf(".") > 0)
    return true;
...
```

5. Start the Web site. The Default.aspx file opens in a Web browser.

6. Enter e-mail addresses in the sender and recipient e-mail fields that do not include @ symbols, and then click the **Send** button. You should see the message informing you that one or more of the e-mail addresses are invalid.

7. Close your Web browser window.

Writing Regular Expression Patterns

Notice that the argument containing the pattern string in the Regex() constructor syntax is preceded by an @ symbol. The @ symbol forces C# to ignore the escaped characters in a regular expression pattern.

You can find many types of prewritten regular expressions on the Regular Expression Library Web page at http://www. regexlib.com/.

The hardest part of working with regular expressions is writing the patterns and rules that are used for matching and manipulating strings. As an example of a common, albeit complicated, regular expression, consider the following code:

```
Regex emailPattern = new Regex(@"^[_a-z0-9\\-]
    +(\.[_a-z0-9\\-] +)*@[a-z0-9\\-]+(\.[a-z0-9\\-]+)*
    (\.[a-z]{2,3})$");
string email = "dongosselin@webadventure.com";
Match regExMatch = emailPattern.Match(email);
if (regExMatch.Success)
    Response.Write("<p>Valid e-mail address.</p>");
else
    Response.Write("<p>Invalid e-mail address.</p.");
```

The preceding code uses the Match() method to determine whether the email variable contains a valid e-mail address. If the Match() method returns a value of true, the code prints "Valid e-mail address." As you can see, the logic is straightforward: If the e-mail address doesn't match the regular expression, the code prints "Invalid e-mail address." The complex part of the code is the pattern that is defined in the first statement.

Regular expression patterns consist of literal characters and **metacharacters**, which are special characters that define the pattern matching rules in a regular expression. Table 5-5 lists the metacharacters that you can use with regular expressions.

Metacharacter	Description
.	Matches any single character
\	Identifies the next character as a literal value
^	Matches characters at the beginning of a string
$	Matches characters at the end of a string
()	Specifies required characters to include in a pattern match
[]	Specifies alternate characters allowed in a pattern match
[^]	Specifies characters to exclude in a pattern match
-	Identifies a possible range of characters to match
|	Specifies alternate sets of characters to include in a pattern match

Table 5-5   Regular expression metacharacters

Matching Any Character

You use a period (.) to match any single character in a pattern. A period in a regular expression pattern really specifies that the pattern must contain a value where the period is located. For example, the following code specifies that the zip variable must contain five characters. Because the variable only contains three characters, the Match() method returns a value of false.

```
Regex zipPattern = new Regex(".....");
string zip = "015";
Match regExMatch = zipPattern.Match(zip);
Response.Write("<p>" + regExMatch.Success
  + "</p>"); // prints false
```

In comparison, the following Match() method returns a value of true because the zip variable contains five characters:

```
Regex zipPattern = new Regex(".....");
string zip = "01562";
Match regExMatch = zipPattern.Match(zip);
Response.Write("<p>" + regExMatch.Success
  + "</p>"); // prints true
```

Because the period only specifies that a character must be included in the designated location within the pattern, you can also include additional characters within the pattern. The following Match() method returns a value of true because the zip variable contains the required five characters along with the ZIP+4 characters.

```
Regex zipPattern = new Regex(".....");
string zip = "01562-2706";
Match regExMatch = zipPattern.Match(zip);
Response.Write("<p>" + regExMatch.Success
  + "</p>"); // prints true
```

Matching Characters at the Beginning or End of a String

A pattern that matches the beginning or end of a line is called an **anchor**. To specify an anchor at the beginning of a line, the pattern must begin with the ^ metacharacter. The ^ metacharacter matches characters at the beginning of a string, and the $ metacharacter matches characters at the end of a string.

The following example specifies that the url variable begin with "http". Because the variable does begin with "http", the Match() method returns a value of true.

```
Regex urlProtocol = new Regex("^http");
string url = "http://www.dongosselin.com";
Match regExMatch = urlProtocol.Match(url);
Response.Write("<p>" + regExMatch.Success
  + "</p>"); // prints true
```

All literal characters following the ^ metacharacter in a pattern compose the anchor. This means that the following example returns false because the url variable does not begin with "https" (only "http" without the 's'), as is specified by the anchor in the pattern:

```
Regex urlProtocol = new Regex("^https");
string url = "http://www.dongosselin.com";
Match regExMatch = urlProtocol.Match(url);
Response.Write("<p>" + regExMatch.Success
  + "</p>"); // prints false
```

To specify an anchor at the end of a line, the pattern must end with the $ metacharacter. The following demonstrates how to specify that a URL ends with "com":

```
Regex urlIdentifier = new Regex("com$");
string url = "http://www.dongosselin.com";
Match regExMatch = urlIdentifier.Match(url);
Response.Write("<p>" + regExMatch.Success
  + "</p>"); // prints true
```

The preceding code returns true because the URL assigned to the urlIdentifier variable ends with "com". However, the following code returns false because the URL assigned to the urlIdentifier variable does not end with "gov".

```
Regex urlIdentifier = new Regex("gov$");
string url = "http://www.dongosselin.com";
Match regExMatch = urlIdentifier.Match(url);
Response.Write("<p>" + regExMatch.Success
  + "</p>"); // prints false
```

Matching Special Characters

To match any metacharacters as literal values in a regular expression, you must precede the character with a backslash. For example, a period (.) metacharacter matches any single character in a pattern. If you want to ensure that a string contains an actual period and not any character, you need to escape it with a backslash. The domain identifier in the following code is appended to the domain name with a comma instead of a period. However, the regular expression returns true because the period in the expression is not escaped.

```
Regex urlIdentifier = new Regex(".com");
string url = "http://www.dongosselin,com";
Match regExMatch = urlIdentifier.Match(url);
Response.Write("<p>" + regExMatch.Success
  + "</p>"); // prints true
```

To correct the problem, you must escape the period as follows:

```
Regex urlIdentifier = new Regex(@"\.com");
string url = "http://www.dongosselin,com";
Match regExMatch = urlIdentifier.Match(url);
Response.Write("<p>" + regExMatch.Success
  + "</p>"); // prints false
```

Notice that the regular expression pattern in the preceding code is preceded by an at symbol to force C# to ignore the escaped character.

Next, you modify the `validateAddress()` method so it uses a conditional expression to determine whether a domain identifier is appended to the domain name with a period.

To modify the `validateAddress()` method so it uses a conditional expression to determine whether a domain identifier is appended to the domain name with a period:

1. Return to the **Default.aspx.cs** file in the Visual Studio IDE.

2. Add the following `Regex` and `Match` declaration statements above the `if` statement. These statements use the conditional expression `"\....$"` to determine whether a domain identifier is appended to the domain name with a period.

   ```
   Regex identifierPattern = new Regex(@"\....$");
   Match identifierMatch
     = identifierPattern.Match(address);
   ```

3. Modify the conditional expression so that it also checks the `Success` property of the `identifierMatch` variable, as follows:

   ```
   ...
   if (atSymbolMatch.Success && identifierMatch.Success
       && address.IndexOf(".") > 0)
       return true;
   ...
   ```

4. Start the Web site. The Default.aspx file opens in a Web browser.

5. Enter e-mail addresses in the sender and recipient e-mail fields that do not include @ symbols or a domain identifier appended to the domain name with a period, and then click the **Send** button. You should see the message informing you that one or more of the e-mail addresses are invalid.

6. Close your Web browser window.

Specifying Quantity

Metacharacters that specify the number of matches are called **quantifiers**. Table 5-6 lists the quantifiers that you can use with regular expressions.

Quantifier	Description
?	Specifies that the preceding character is optional
+	Specifies that one or more of the preceding characters must match
*	Specifies that zero or more of the preceding characters can match
{n}	Specifies that the preceding character repeat exactly n times
{n,}	Specifies that the preceding character repeat at least n times
{n1, n2}	Specifies that the preceding character repeat at least $n1$ times but no more than $n2$ times

Table 5-6   Regular expression quantifiers

The question mark quantifier specifies that the preceding character in the pattern is optional. The following code demonstrates how to use the question mark quantifier to specify that the protocol assigned to the beginning of the url variable can be either http or https:

```
Regex urlProtocol = new Regex("^https?");
string url = "http://www.dongosselin,com";
Match regExMatch = urlProtocol.Match(url);
Response.Write("<p>" + regExMatch.Success
    + "</p>"); // prints true
```

The addition quantifier (+) specifies that one or more of the preceding characters match, while the asterisk quantifier (*) specifies that zero or more of the preceding characters match. As a simple example, the following code demonstrates how to ensure that a variable containing a string of name=value pairs contains at least one equal sign:

```
Regex stringPattern = new Regex("=+");
string queryString = "sport=football";
Match regExMatch = stringPattern.Match(queryString);
Response.Write("<p>" + regExMatch.Success
    + "</p>"); // prints true
```

Similarly, for a string that consists of multiple name=value pairs separated by ampersands (&), the following code demonstrates how to check whether the `queryString` variable contains zero or more ampersands:

```
Regex stringPattern = new Regex("=+&*");
string queryString = "sport=football&sport=baseball";
Match regExMatch = stringPattern.Match(queryString);
Response.Write("<p>" + regExMatch.Success
  + "</p>"); // prints true
```

The { } quantifiers allow you to specify more precisely the number of times that a character must repeat. The following code shows a simple example of how to use the { } quantifiers to ensure that a zip code consists of at least five characters:

```
Regex zipPattern = new Regex(".{5}");
string zip = "01562";
Match regExMatch = zipPattern.Match(zip);
Response.Write("<p>" + regExMatch.Success
  + "</p>"); // prints true
```

Specifying Subexpressions

As you learned earlier, regular expression patterns can include literal values; any strings you validate against a regular expression must contain exact matches for the literal values contained in the pattern. You can also use parentheses metacharacters ( ) to specify the required characters to include in a pattern match. Characters contained in a set of parentheses within a regular expression are referred to as a **subexpression** or **subpattern**. Subexpressions allow you to determine the format and quantities of the enclosed characters as a group. As an example, consider the following pattern, which defines a regular expression for a telephone number:

```
"^(1-)?(\(.{3}\) )?(.{3})(\-.{4})$"
```

Notice that the preceding pattern includes the ^ and $ metacharacters to anchor both the beginning and end of the pattern. This ensures that a string exactly matches the pattern in a regular expression.

The first and second groups in the preceding pattern include the ? quantifier. This allows a string to optionally include a 1 and the area code. If the string does include these groups, they must be in the exact format of 1-*nnn* (where *nnn* represents the area code), including the space following the area code. Similarly, the telephone number itself includes two groups that require the number to be in the format of "555-1212." Because the 1 and area code are optional, each of the Match() methods in the following code return a value of true:

```
Regex phonePattern = new Regex(
  @"^(1 )?(\(.{3}\) )?(.{3})(\-.{4})$");
Match regExMatch = phonePattern.Match("555-1234");
Response.Write("<p>" + regExMatch.Success
  + "</p>"); prints true
```

```
regExMatch = phonePattern.Match("(707) 555-1234");
Response.Write("<p>" + regExMatch.Success
  + "</p>"); // prints true
regExMatch = phonePattern.Match("1 (707) 555-1234");
Response.Write("<p>" + regExMatch.Success
  + "</p>"); // prints true
```

Defining Character Classes

You use **character classes** in regular expressions to treat multiple characters as a single item. You create a character class by enclosing the characters that make up the class with bracket [] metacharacters. Any characters included in a character class represent alternate characters that are allowed in a pattern match. As an example of a simple character class, consider the word *analyze*, which the British spell as *analyse*. Both of the following Match() methods return true because the character class allows either spelling of the word:

```
Regex wordPattern = new Regex("analy[sz]e");
Match regExMatch = wordPattern.Match("analyse");
Response.Write("<p>" + regExMatch.Success
  + "</p>"); // prints true
regExMatch = wordPattern.Match("analyze");
Response.Write("<p>" + regExMatch.Success
  + "</p>"); // prints true
```

In comparison, the following Match() method returns false because "analyce" is not an accepted spelling of the word:

```
regExMatch = wordPattern.Match("analyce");
Response.Write("<p>" + regExMatch.Success
  + "</p>"); // prints false
```

You use a hyphen metacharacter (-) to specify a range of values in a character class. You can include alphabetical or numerical ranges. You specify all lowercase letters as "[a-z]" and all uppercase letters as "[A-Z]". The following statements demonstrate how to ensure that only the values A, B, C, D, or F are assigned to the letterGrade variable. The character class in the regular expression specifies a range of A-D or the character "F" as valid values in the variable. Because the variable is assigned a value of "B", the Match() method returns true.

```
Regex gradeRange = new Regex("[A-DF]");
string letterGrade = "B";
Match regExMatch = gradeRange.Match(letterGrade);
Response.Write("<p>" + regExMatch.Success
  + "</p>"); // prints true
```

In comparison, the following Match() method returns false because "E" is not a valid value in the character class:

```
Regex gradeRange = new Regex("[A-DF]");
string letterGrade = "E";
```

```
Match regExMatch = gradeRange.Match(letterGrade);
Response.Write("<p>" + regExMatch.Success
    + "</p>"); // prints false
```

To specify optional characters to exclude in a pattern match, include the ^ metacharacter immediately before the characters in a character class. The following examples demonstrate how to exclude the letters E and G-Z from an acceptable pattern in the letterGrade variable. The first Match() method returns a value of true because the letter "A" is not excluded from the pattern match, while the second Match() method returns a value of false because the letter "E" is excluded from the pattern match.

```
Regex gradeRange = new Regex("[^EG-Z]");
string letterGrade = "A";
Match regExMatch = gradeRange.Match(letterGrade);
Response.Write("<p>" + regExMatch.Success
    + "</p>"); // prints true
letterGrade = "E";
regExMatch = gradeRange.Match(letterGrade);
Response.Write("<p>" + regExMatch.Success
    + "</p>"); // prints false
```

The following statements demonstrate how to include or exclude numeric characters from a pattern match. The first Match() method returns true because it allows any numeric character, while the second Match() method returns false because it excludes any numeric character.

```
Regex numberPattern = new Regex("[0-9]");
string numString = "5";
Match regExMatch = numberPattern.Match(numString);
Response.Write("<p>" + regExMatch.Success
    + "</p>"); // prints true
numberPattern = new Regex("[^0-9]");
regExMatch = numberPattern.Match(numString);
Response.Write("<p>" + regExMatch.Success
    + "</p>"); // prints false
```

Note that you can combine ranges in a character class. The first of the following statements demonstrates how to include all alphanumeric characters, and the second demonstrates how to exclude all lowercase and uppercase letters:

```
Regex alphaPattern = new Regex("[0-9a-zA-Z]");
string numString = "7";
Match regExMatch = alphaPattern.Match(numString);
Response.Write("<p>" + regExMatch.Success
    + "</p>"); // prints true
alphaPattern = new Regex("[^a-zA-Z]");
numString = "Q";
regExMatch = alphaPattern.Match(numString);
Response.Write("<p>" + regExMatch.Success
    + "</p>"); // prints false
```

The following statements demonstrate how to use character classes to create a phone number regular expression pattern:

```
Regex phonePattern = new Regex(
    @"^(1 )?(\([0-9]{3}\) )?([1-9]{3})(\-[1-9]{4})$");
string phone = "1 (212) 555-1234";
Match regExMatch = phonePattern.Match(phone);
Response.Write("<p>" + regExMatch.Success
    + "</p>"); // prints true
phone = "(212) 555-1234";
regExMatch = phonePattern.Match(phone);
Response.Write("<p>" + regExMatch.Success
    + "</p>"); // prints true
phone = "555-1234";
regExMatch = phonePattern.Match(phone);
Response.Write("<p>" + regExMatch.Success
    + "</p>"); // prints true
```

As a more complex example of a character class, examine the following e-mail validation regular expression you saw earlier in the chapter. At this point, you should recognize how the regular expression pattern is constructed. The anchor at the beginning of the pattern specifies that the first part of the e-mail address must include one or more of the characters A-Z (upper- or lowercase), 0-9, or an underscore (_) or hyphen (-). The second portion of the pattern specifies that the e-mail address can optionally include a dot separator, as in "don.gosselin". The pattern also requires the @ character. Following the literal @ character, the regular expression uses patterns that are similar to the patterns in the name portion of the e-mail address to specify the required structure of the domain name. The last portion of the pattern specifies that the domain identifier must consist of at least two, but not more than three alphabetic characters.

```
Regex emailPattern = new Regex(
    @"^[_a-z0-9\-]+(\.[_a-z0-9\-]+)*
    @[a-z0-9\-]+(\.[a-z0-9\-]+)*(\.[a-z]{2,3})$");
```

Regular expressions include special escape characters that you can use in character classes to represent different types of data. For example, the "\w" expression can be used instead of the "0-9a-zA-Z" pattern to allow any alphanumeric characters in a character class. Table 5-7 lists the character class expressions.

Expression	Description
\w	Alphanumeric characters
\D	Alphabetic characters
\d	Numeric characters
\S	All printable characters
\s	White space characters
\W	Any character that is not an alphanumeric character
\b	Backspace character

Table 5-7   Character class escape characters

The following statements demonstrate how to exclude numeric characters from a pattern match using the \D escape character:

```
Regex alphaPattern = new Regex(@"[\D]");
string textString = "A";
Match regExMatch = alphaPattern.Match(textString);
Response.Write("<p>" + regExMatch.Success
   + "</p>"); // prints true
textString = "5";
regExMatch = alphaPattern.Match(textString);
Response.Write("<p>" + regExMatch.Success
   + "</p>"); // prints false
```

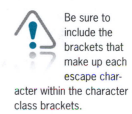

Be sure to include the brackets that make up each escape character within the character class brackets.

As a more complex example, the following statement demonstrates how to compose the e-mail validation regular expression with class expressions:

```
Regex emailPattern = new Regex(
   @"^[_\w\-]+(\.[_\w\-]+)*
   @[\w\-]+(\.[\w\-]+)*(\.[\D]{2,3})$");
```

Matching Multiple Pattern Choices

To allow a string to contain an alternate set of substrings, you separate the strings in a regular expression pattern with the | metacharacter. This is essentially the same as using the Or operator (||) to perform multiple evaluations in a conditional expression. For example, to allow a string to contain either "vegetarian" or "vegan", you include the pattern "vegetarian | vegan".

The following code demonstrates how to check whether a domain identifier at the end of a string contains a required value of either .com, .org, or .net. The first Match() method returns a value of false because the URL contains a domain identifier of .gov, while the second Match() method returns a value of true because the domain identifier contains a valid value of .com.

```
Regex identifierPattern = new Regex(@"\.(com|org|net)$");
string url = "http://www.dongosselin.gov";
Match regExMatch = identifierPattern.Match(url);
Response.Write("<p>" + regExMatch.Success
    + "</p>"); // prints false
url = "http://www.dongosselin.com";
regExMatch = identifierPattern.Match(url);
Response.Write("<p>" + regExMatch.Success
    + "</p>"); // prints true
```

Next, you modify the validateAddress() method so it uses an e-mail regular expression to validate e-mail addresses.

To modify the validateAddress() method so it uses an e-mail regular expression to validate e-mail addresses:

1.   Return to the **Default.aspx.cs** file in the Visual Studio IDE.

2.   Replace the four statements at the beginning of the validateAddress() method with the following Regex and Match object declarations. The Regex object is assigned an e-mail regular expression and the Match object tests the address parameter against the e-mail regular expression.

```
Regex emailPattern = new Regex(
    @"^[_\w\-]+(\.[_\w\-]+)*@[\w\-]
    +(\.[\w\-]+)*(\.[\D]{2,3})$");
Match emailMatch = emailPattern.Match(address);
```

3.   Replace the conditional expressions in the if statement with a single conditional expression that checks the Success property of the emailMatch object, as follows:

```
...
if (emailMatch.Success)
    return true;
...
```

4.   Start the Web site. The Default.aspx file opens in a Web browser.

5.   Enter some invalid e-mail addresses in the sender and recipient e-mail fields and click the **Send** button. You should see the message informing you that one or more of the e-mail addresses are invalid.

6.   Close your Web browser window and then close the project by selecting the **File** menu and then selecting **Close Project**.

Setting Regular Expression Options

You can use the **RegexOptions enumeration** to configure how C# executes regular expressions. An **enumeration** is a special C# construct that contains a set of named constants called an **enumerator list**. One of the most commonly used `RegexOptions` enumerators is the `IgnoreCase` enumerator, which determines whether to ignore letter case when executing a regular expression. By default, regular expression executions take case into account, so you must use the `IgnoreCase` enumerator if you want case to be ignored. To use the `RegexOptions` enumeration, you pass it as a second argument to the `Regex()` constructor and append to it the enumerator you want to use. The following statement demonstrates how to use the `IgnoreCase` enumerator of the `RegexOptions` enumeration to configure a regular expression to ignore case:

```
Regex identifierPattern = new Regex(@"\.(com|org|net)$",
    RegexOptions.IgnoreCase);
```

To use multiple `RegexOptions` enumerators, you separate them with a piping symbol (|). For example, another `RegexOptions` enumerator is `IgnorePatternWhitespace`, which causes the `Regex()` constructor to ignore white space. The following `Regex()` constructor includes both the `IgnoreCase` and `IgnorePatternWhitespace` enumerator:

```
Regex identifierPattern = new Regex(
    @"\.(com|org|net)$",
    RegexOptions.IgnoreCase
    | RegexOptions.IgnorePatternWhitespace);
```

 Refer to the Microsoft Developer Network (MSDN) at *http://msdn.microsoft.com* for information on other enumerators that are available with the `RegexOptions` enumeration.

Using the `RegularExpressionValidator` Control

To programmatically use regular expressions to check multiple data, you must use the `Regex` class techniques explained earlier in this chapter. You can also use the **`RegularExpressionValidator` control** to validate a regular expression that a user enters into a field. Like other validation controls, the field to be validated is identified by the `ControlToValidate` property. You assign the regular expression pattern that you want to validate against to the `ValidationExpression` property.

The following example demonstrates how to use the phone number regular expression pattern with a `RegularExpressionValidator` control to validate a field that should contain a telephone number:

```
Telephone: <asp:TextBox ID="phone" runat="server" />
<asp:RegularExpressionValidator
ID="phoneValidator" runat="server"
ErrorMessage="Invalid phone number"
ValidationExpression=
'"^(1-)?(\(.{3}\) )?(.{3})(\-.{4})$"' />
```

Short Quiz 3

1. What are some of the types of data you would validate with regular expressions?

2. What classes do you use to create a regular expression and to determine whether a particular string matches a regular expression pattern?

3. Describe the metacharacters you can use with regular expressions.

4. What does a period in a regular expression represent?

5. Explain how to define a character class with a regular expression.

Summing Up

- When applied to text strings, the term *parsing* refers to the act of extracting characters or substrings from a larger string.

- All literal strings and string variables in C# are represented by a String class, which contains methods for manipulating text strings.

- Simple Mail Transfer Protocol (SMTP) is a protocol that most e-mail systems use to send messages over the Internet.

- A namespace is an abstract container that manages the identifiers in a C# program.

- You use the MailMessage class to create an e-mail object that contains message information such as the sender, recipient, subject, and body.

- The MailAddress class allows you to identify the e-mail address and display the name of the sender.

- To administer and configure your Web site, you use the ASP.NET Web Site Administration Tool.

- The SmtpClient class allows you to send e-mail messages with SMTP.

- The String class contains a property, the Length property, which returns the number of characters in a string.

- The `IsNullOrEmpty()` method returns either a value of true if a string variable contains an empty string or a value of false if a string variable contains one or more characters.

- To use special characters within text strings, you can use numeric character references, character entities, or escape sequences.

- The `String` class includes various methods that you can use to change the case of letters in a string, trim spaces or characters from a text string, remove characters from the beginning or end of a string, and search for and extract characters and substrings in C#.

- The `String` class includes a `Chars` property that you can use to retrieve a character by its specified index in a text string.

- You use the `Replace()` method of the `String` class to replace all instances of a specified character or text within a string.

- You use the `Split()` method of the `String` class to split a string into an indexed array.

- You use the `Join()` method of the `String` class to combine array elements into a string, separated by specified characters.

- You can compare strings by using comparison operators or with methods of the `String` class.

- The `String` class also includes the `Concat()` method, which creates a new string by combining strings that are passed as arguments.

- If you want to insert text into a string, you use the `Insert()` method of the `String` class to insert the text after a specified index position within the string.

- Regular expressions are patterns that are used for matching and manipulating strings according to specified rules.

- To define a regular expression pattern in C#, you must use the `Regex()` constructor.

- The `Regex` class represents regular expressions in C# and contains methods and properties for working with regular expressions.

- To determine whether a particular string matches a regular expression pattern, you use the `Match` class, which represents the results of a regular expression match.

- Regular expression patterns consist of literal characters and metacharacters, which are special characters that define the pattern matching rules in a regular expression.

- You use a period (`.`) to match any single character in a pattern.

- A pattern that matches the beginning or end of a line is called an anchor. To specify an anchor at the beginning of a line, the pattern must begin with the ^ metacharacter.

- To match any metacharacters as literal values in a regular expression, you must precede the character with a backslash.

- Metacharacters that specify the number of matches are called quantifiers.

- Characters contained in a set of parentheses within a regular expression are referred to as a subexpression or subpattern.

- You use character classes in regular expressions to treat multiple characters as a single item.

- To allow a string to contain an alternate set of substrings, you separate the strings in a regular expression pattern with the | metacharacter.

- You can use the RegexOptions enumeration to configure how C# executes regular expressions.

- An enumeration is a special C# type construct that contains a set of named constants called an enumerator list.

- The RegularExpressionValidator control validates a regular expression that a user enters into a field.

Comprehension Check

1. When applied to text strings, the term _____ refers to the act of extracting characters or substrings from a larger string.

    a. stripping

    b. compiling

    c. rendering

    d. parsing

2. Which of the following properties returns the number of characters in a string?

    a. Size

    b. Length

    c. Chars

    d. Width

3. The `ToUpper()` and `ToLower()` methods do not convert the contents of the string to which they are appended. True or False?

4. Which of the following functions returns a value of -1 if the character or string is not found? (Choose all that apply.)

   a. `IndexOf()`

   b. `LastIndexOf()`

   c. `Contains()`

   d. `Substring()`

5. What is the difference between the `Contains()` and `IndexOf()` methods?

6. Which of the following methods adds characters to the beginning of a string? (Choose all that apply.)

   a. `AddLeft()`

   b. `PadLeft()`

   c. `InsertFirst()`

   d. `Concat()`

7. All search and extraction methods of the `String` class return a value of true or false. True or False?

8. You use the `Chars` property to retrieve a character by appending brackets and a character position to a string, similar to the way you append brackets and an element number to an array. True or False?

9. Which of the following is the correct syntax for using the `Replace()` method to replace commas with semicolons in a variable named `userQuery`?

   a. `userQuery.Replace(",", ";")`

   b. `Replace.userQuery(",", ";")`

   c. `userQuery = Replace(",", ";")`

   d. `userQuery(",").Replace(";")`

10. Which of the following is the correct syntax for splitting a
string variable that contains stock prices separated by semicolons into an array named `stockPriceArray[]`?

a. `stockPrices.Split(";") = new Array(`
   `stockPricesArray);`

b. `Split(stockPrices, stockArray, ";");`

c. `var stockPriceArray.Split(";",stockPrices);`

d. `string[] stockPriceArray`
   `= stockPrices.Split(';');`

11. Which of the following methods compares two strings
according to the numeric values of the characters within
each string?

a. `Equals()`

b. `Compare()`

c. `CompareOrdinal()`

d. `CompareTo()`

12. Which of the following methods can you use to combine text
strings? (Choose all that apply.)

a. `Concat()`

b. `Insert()`

c. concatenation operator (+)

d. compound assignment operator (+=)

13. What are regular expressions and what are they used for?

14. Which of the following namespaces must you import in order
to use regular expressions?

a. `System.Regex`

b. `System.RegularExpressions`

c. `System.Text.RegularExpressions`

d. `System.Strings.RegularExpressions`

15. Which of the following provides correct syntax for creating a regular expression variable named `ftpProtocol` that contains the text ftp://? (Choose all that apply.)

    a. `Regex ftpProtocol = new Regex("ftp://");`

    b. `var ftpProtocol = new Regex(ftp://);`

    c. `var ftpProtocol = "ftp://";`

    d. `var ftpProtocol = /ftp:\/\//;`

16. Which property contains the result returned from the `Match()` method?

    a. `Exp`

    b. `Match`

    c. `Result`

    d. `Success`

17. Which of the following metacharacters used in regular expressions matches characters at the beginning of a string?

    a. `^`

    b. `$`

    c. `()`

    d. `[]`

18. Which of the following quantifiers used in regular expressions specifies that zero or more of the preceding characters can match?

    a. `?`

    b. `+`

    c. `*`

    d. `{n}`

19. Explain why you would use subexpressions.

20. You use _____ in regular expressions to treat multiple characters as a single item.

    a. metacharacters

    b. character classes

    c. subexpressions

    d. curly braces ({ })

Reinforcement Exercises

Exercise 5-1

In this exercise, you will create a document that uses `String` class methods and the `Length` property.

1. Create a new ASP.NET Web site in the Visual Studio IDE and save it in a folder named StringClassExamples in your Exercises folder for Chapter 5. Change the content of the `<title>` element to "String Class Examples".

2. Open the **Default.aspx.cs** file in the Code Editor window and add the following statements to the `Page_Load()` event handler. These statements contain examples of string operators. Use your own first and last name and place of birth instead of the names and locations shown here.

```
string name = "";
string firstName = "Don";
string lastName = "Gosselin";
string placeOfBirth;
name = firstName + " ";
name += lastName;
placeOfBirth = "Hartford";
placeOfBirth += ", Connecticut";
```

3. Add the following statements (which use `String` class methods and the `Length` property) to the end of the `Page_Load()` event handler:

```
string[] nameArray = name.Split(' ');
Response.Write("<p>My first name is: " + nameArray[0]
    + "<br />");
Response.Write("My last name is: " + nameArray[1]
    + "<br />");
Response.Write("There are " + firstName.Length
    + " characters in my first name" + "<br />");
Response.Write("I was born in "
    + placeOfBirth + "<br />");
Response.Write("My initials are: "
    + firstName.Substring(0, 1)
    + lastName.Substring(0, 1)
    + "</p>");
```

4. Start and test the Web site.

5. Close your Web browser window and then close the project by selecting the **File** menu and then selecting **Close Project**.

Exercise 5-2

In this exercise, you will create a program that converts cardinal numbers to ordinal numbers. For example, the program should be able to convert the cardinal number 23 to the ordinal number 23rd.

1. Create a new ASP.NET Web site in the Visual Studio IDE and save it in a folder named OrdinalNumbers in your Exercises folder for Chapter 5. Change the content of the `<title>` element to "Ordinal Numbers".

2. Add the following text and elements to the `<div>` section of the `<form>` element in the Default.aspx file. The `<asp:TextBox>` control is where you will input a cardinal number and the `<asp:Literal>` control will display the associated ordinal number. The `<asp:Button>` control submits the Web form. The statements also include an `<asp:CompareValidator>` control to ensure that users enter integers into the `<asp:TextBox>` control.

```
<h1>
    Ordinal Number</h1>
<hr />
<p>
  Cardinal number:
  <asp:TextBox ID="cardinalNumber" runat="server" />
  <asp:CompareValidator ID="numValidator"
  runat="server" Type="Integer"
  ControlToValidate="cardinalNumber"
  Operator="DataTypeCheck">You must
  enter an integer greater than 0
  </asp:CompareValidator><br />
  Ordinal number: <asp:Label
  ID="ordinalNumber" runat="server" />
</p>
<p>
  <asp:Button ID="convert" runat="server"
  Text="Convert" />
</p>
```

3. Open the **Default.aspx.cs** file in the Code Editor window and add the following statements to the `Page_Load()` event handler to determine whether the current request was caused by a post back event and to determine if the controls on the form are valid:

```
if (Page.IsPostBack)
{
    Page.Validate();
    if (Page.IsValid)
    {
    }
}
```

4. Add the following statements to the `if` statement. These statements convert the cardinal number to an ordinal. The first `if` statement checks whether the number contains more than two digits. If it does, the first statement uses the `Substring()` function and `Length` property to retrieve just the last two

digits in the variable. The nested `if` determines the ordinal form for just the numbers 11 through 13, because numbers that end with these values use "th" in their ordinal form. The `else` clause then determines the ordinal form for all other numbers. The last `else...if` clause determines the ordinal form for the numbers 1 through 9.

```csharp
int lastCharacters = 0;
if (cardinalNumber.Text.Length > 1)
{
    lastCharacters = Convert.ToInt16(
        cardinalNumber.Text.Substring(
        cardinalNumber.Text.Length - 2));
    if (lastCharacters > 10
        && lastCharacters < 14)
        ordinalNumber.Text
        = cardinalNumber.Text + "th";
    else
    {
        lastCharacters = Convert.ToInt16(
        cardinalNumber.Text.Substring(
        cardinalNumber.Text.Length - 1));
        if (lastCharacters == 1)
            ordinalNumber.Text
            = cardinalNumber.Text + "st";
        else if (lastCharacters == 2)
            ordinalNumber.Text
            = cardinalNumber.Text + "nd";
        else if (lastCharacters == 3)
            ordinalNumber.Text
            = cardinalNumber.Text + "rd";
        else
            ordinalNumber.Text
            = cardinalNumber.Text + "th";
    }
}
else if (cardinalNumber.Text.Length == 1)
{
    if (Convert.ToInt16(cardinalNumber.Text) == 1)
        ordinalNumber.Text
        = cardinalNumber.Text + "st";
    else if (Convert.ToInt16(
        cardinalNumber.Text) == 2)
        ordinalNumber.Text
        = cardinalNumber.Text + "nd";
    else if (Convert.ToInt16(
        cardinalNumber.Text) == 3)
        ordinalNumber.Text
        = cardinalNumber.Text + "rd";
    else
        ordinalNumber.Text
        = cardinalNumber.Text + "th";
}
```

5. Start the Web site. Test the form to see if the correct ordinal number prints.

6. Close your Web browser window and then close the project by selecting the **File** menu and then selecting **Close Project**.

Exercise 5-3

In this exercise, you will create a script that uses regular expressions to validate a credit card number. Major credit card numbers must be in the following formats:

- **American Express**—Start with 34 or 37 and consist of 15 digits.

- **Diners Club**—Start with 36, 38, or any number between 300 through 305, and consist of 14 digits.

- **Discover**—Start with 6011 or 65 and consist of 16 digits.

- **JCB**—Start with 2131 or 1800 and consist of 15 digits or start with 35 and consist of 16 digits.

- **Mastercard**—Start with the numbers 51 through 55 and consist of 16 digits.

- **Visa**—Start with a 4; new cards consist of 16 digits and old cards consist 13.

1. Create a new ASP.NET Web site in the Visual Studio IDE and save it in a folder named ValidateCreditCards in your Exercises folder for Chapter 5. Change the content of the `<title>` element to "Validate Credit Cards".

2. Add the following text and elements to the `<div>` section of the `<form>` element in the Default.aspx file. The `<asp:DropDownList>` control contains the names of the credit cards and the `<asp:TextBox>` control receives the credit card numbers. The `<asp:Button>` control submits the Web form. The statements also include an `<asp:RequiredFieldValidator>` control to ensure that users enter integers into the `<asp:TextBox>` control and an `<asp:Literal>` control that displays a message indicating whether the credit card number is valid.

The regular expressions that are used in this exercise are from http://www.regular-expressions.info/regexbuddy.html.

```
<h1>
    Validate Credit Cards</h1>
<p>
    Credit card:
    <asp:DropDownList ID="cardName" runat="server">
        <asp:ListItem>American Express
        </asp:ListItem>
        <asp:ListItem>Diners Club</asp:ListItem>
```

```
          <asp:ListItem>Discover</asp:ListItem>
          <asp:ListItem>JCB</asp:ListItem>
          <asp:ListItem>Mastercard</asp:ListItem>
          <asp:ListItem>Visa</asp:ListItem>
      </asp:DropDownList>
      <br />
      Number:
      <asp:TextBox ID="cardNumber" runat="server" />
      <asp:RequiredFieldValidator
          ID="ccNumValidator" runat="server"
          ErrorMessage="Required field"
          ControlToValidate="cardNumber" />
  </p>
  <p>
      <asp:Button ID="validateCard" runat="server"
      Text="Validate" />
  </p>
  <p>
      <asp:Literal ID="ccResult" runat="server">
      </asp:Literal>
  </p>
```

3. Open the **Default.aspx.cs** file in the Code Editor window
   and add the following `using` statement to the directives list to
   import the `System.Text.RegularExpressions` namespace:

   ```
   using System.Text.RegularExpressions;
   ```

4. Add the following statements to the `Page_Load()` event handler to determine whether the current request was caused by
   a post back event and if the controls on the form are valid:

   ```
   if (Page.IsPostBack)
   {
       Page.Validate();
       if (Page.IsValid)
       {
       }
   }
   ```

5. Add the following statements to the nested `if` statement to
   validate the number for each credit card type:

   ```
   if (cardName.SelectedItem.Value
       == "American Express")
   {
       Regex urlProtocol = new Regex(
         @"^3[47][0-9]{13}$");
       Match regExMatch = urlProtocol.Match(
         Convert.ToString(cardNumber.Text));
       if (regExMatch.Success)
           ccResult.Text = "Valid credit card number";
       else
           ccResult.Text = "Invalid credit card number";
   }
   ```

```csharp
else if (cardName.SelectedItem.Value == "Diners Club")
{
    Regex urlProtocol = new Regex(
      @"^3(?:0[0-5]|[68][0-9])[0-9]{11}$");
    Match regExMatch = urlProtocol.Match(
        Convert.ToString(cardNumber.Text));
    if (regExMatch.Success)
        ccResult.Text = "Valid credit card number";
    else
        ccResult.Text = "Invalid credit card number";
}
else if (cardName.SelectedItem.Value == "Discover")
{
    Regex urlProtocol = new Regex(
      @"^6(?:011|5[0-9]{2})[0-9]{12}$");
    Match regExMatch = urlProtocol.Match(
      Convert.ToString(cardNumber.Text));
    if (regExMatch.Success)
        ccResult.Text = "Valid credit card number";
    else
        ccResult.Text = "Invalid credit card number";
}
else if (cardName.SelectedItem.Value == "JCB")
{
    Regex urlProtocol = new Regex(
      @"^(?:2131|1800|35\d{3})\d{11}$");
    Match regExMatch = urlProtocol.Match(
      Convert.ToString(cardNumber.Text));
    if (regExMatch.Success)
        ccResult.Text = "Valid credit card number";
    else
        ccResult.Text = "Invalid credit card number";
}
else if (cardName.SelectedItem.Value == "Mastercard")
{
    Regex urlProtocol = new Regex(
      @"^5[1-5][0-9]{14}$");
    Match regExMatch = urlProtocol.Match(
      Convert.ToString(cardNumber.Text));
    if (regExMatch.Success)
        ccResult.Text = "Valid credit card number";
    else
        ccResult.Text = "Invalid credit card number";
}
else if (cardName.SelectedItem.Value == "Visa")
{
    Regex urlProtocol = new Regex(
      @"^4[0-9]{12}(?:[0-9]{3})?$");
    Match regExMatch = urlProtocol.Match(
        Convert.ToString(cardNumber.Text));
    if (regExMatch.Success)
        ccResult.Text = "Valid credit card number";
    else
        ccResult.Text = "Invalid credit card number";
}
```

6. Start the Web site. Test the form to see if it correctly validates credit card numbers.

7. Close your Web browser window and then close the project by selecting the **File** menu and then selecting **Close Project**.

Discovery Projects

Save the following projects in the Discovery folder for Chapter 5.

Project 5-1

Create a script that presents a word guessing game. Allow users to guess the word one letter at a time by entering a character in a form. Start by assigning a secret word to a variable. After each guess, print the word using asterisks for each remaining letter, but fill in the letters that the user guessed correctly. For example, if the word you want users to guess is *suspicious* and the user has successfully guessed the letters *s* and *i*, then you would store s*s*i*i**s in the form field. Save the project as **GuessingGame**.

Project 5-2

A palindrome is a word or phrase that is identical forward or backward, such as the word *racecar*. A standard palindrome is similar to a perfect palindrome except that spaces and punctuation are ignored. For example, "Madam, I'm Adam" is a standard palindrome because the characters are identical forward or backward, provided you remove the spaces and punctuation marks. Write a script that checks whether a word or phrase entered by a user is a palindrome. Use a form where the user can enter the word or phrase, and include one button that checks if the word or phrase is a perfect palindrome and another button that checks if the word or phrase is a standard palindrome. For the standard palindrome, use a regular expression to determine whether each character is an alphanumeric character; if not, then you need to remove the nonalphanumeric character (or space) before you can determine if the word or phrase is a standard palindrome. Save the project as **Palindromes**.

Project 5-3

Although the `String` object includes the `ToUpper()` and `ToLower()` methods for converting strings to upper- or lowercase letters, it does not include a method for converting text to title case capitalization (Text That Appears Like This). Create a script that takes text that a user enters into a form field and converts it to title case capitalization. To accomplish this, use the `Split()` method to split the words in the string into an indexed array. Then, create a `for` loop that uses another `Split()` method that splits each word in the elements of the indexed array into another indexed array of characters. Within the `for` loop, use the `ToUpper()` method to convert the first element in the second array (which represents the first character in the word to uppercase) to uppercase, and then use the `Join()` method to rebuild the array of words in the text string. Execute a final `Join()` method to convert the array of words back into a single text string. Save the project as **TitleCase**.

Project 5-4

Create a Web page that contains a text box in which users can enter a date. Also include a button that executes C# code to validate the date against a regular expression. Write a regular expression pattern that allows users to enter a one- or two-digit month, one- or two-digit date, and two- or four-digit year. Also, allow users to separate the month, day, and year by using either dashes or forward slashes. Users should be able to enter any of the following date formats: 11-2-07, 1-25-2007, or 01/25/2007. Save the project as **DateValidation**.

Debugging and Error Handling

In this chapter you will:

◎ Study debugging concepts

◎ Use basic debugging techniques

◎ Trace errors with the Visual Studio Debugger

◎ Handle exceptions and errors

The more programs you write, the more likely you are to write programs that generate error messages. At times, it might seem like your programs never function quite the way you want. Regardless of experience, knowledge, and ability, all programmers incorporate errors in their programs at one time or another. Thus, all programmers must devote part of their programming education to mastering the art of debugging, which is an essential skill for any programmer, regardless of the programming language.

In this chapter, you will learn techniques and tools that you can use to trace and resolve errors. However, you will not create any new programs. Instead, you will learn how to use debugging techniques to locate errors in an existing Web site for a moving company. Figure 6-1 shows an example of the Web site's home page.

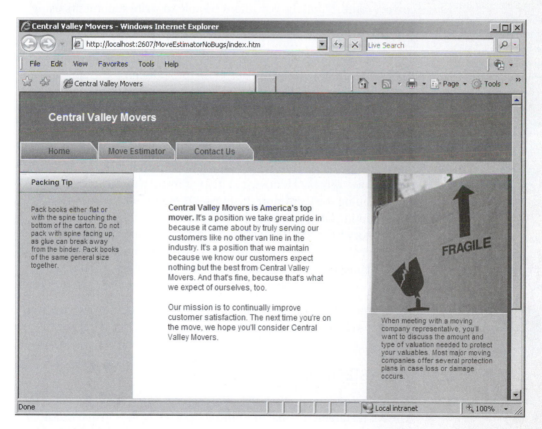

Figure 6-1 Central Valley Movers home page

Note that you will not be working with the MoveEstimatorNoBugs project in this chapter. Rather, you will work with a version of the document that contains bugs, MoveEstimatorWithBugs, which is also contained in your Chapter folder for Chapter 6. You need to use the "buggy" version to learn the debugging techniques presented in this chapter. If you get stuck, however, you can use the no-bugs version as a reference.

Introduction to Debugging

All programming languages, including C#, have their own **syntax**, or rules. To write a program, you must understand the syntax of the programming language you are using. You must also understand computer-programming logic. The term **logic** refers to the order in which various parts of a program run, or execute. The statements in a program must execute in the correct order to produce the desired results. In an analogous situation, although you know how to drive a car well, you might not reach your destination if you do not follow the correct route. Similarly, you might be able to write statements using the correct syntax, but be unable to construct an entire, logically executed program that works the way you want. A typical logical error might be multiplying two values when you meant to divide them. Another might be producing output before obtaining the appropriate input (for example, printing an order confirmation on the screen before asking the user to enter the necessary order information).

Any error in a program that causes it to function incorrectly, whether because of incorrect syntax or flaws in logic, is called a **bug**. The term **debugging** refers to the act of tracing and resolving errors in a program. Grace Murray Hopper, a mathematician who was instrumental in developing the Common Business-Oriented Language (COBOL) programming language, is said to have first coined the term *debugging*. As the story from the 1940s goes, a moth short-circuited a primitive computer that Hopper was using. Removing the moth from the computer "debugged" the system and resolved the problem. Today, a bug refers to any sort of problem in the design and operation of a program.

Three types of errors can occur in a program: syntax errors, run-time errors, and logic errors. First, you will learn about syntax errors.

Understanding Syntax Errors

Syntax errors occur when the interpreter fails to recognize code. In ASP.NET, statements that are not recognized by the Visual Studio IDE generate syntax errors. Syntax errors can be caused by incorrect usage of C# code or references to objects, methods, and variables that do not exist. For example, if a programmer attempts to use a method that does not exist or omits a method's closing parenthesis, Visual Studio generates a compiler error message. Many syntax errors are generated by incorrectly spelled or mistyped words. For example, the

Do not confuse bugs with computer viruses. Bugs are problems within a program that occur because of syntax errors, design flaws, or run-time errors. Viruses are self-contained programs designed to "infect" a computer system and cause mischievous or malicious damage.

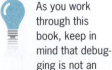

Virus programs themselves can contain bugs if they contain syntax errors or do not perform as their creators envisioned.

As you work through this book, keep in mind that debugging is not an exact science. Every program you write is different and requires different methods of debugging. Although there are some tools available to help you debug your code, your own logical and analytical skills are the best debugging resources you have.

statement `Response.Wrte("Hello World");` causes a syntax error because the `Write()` method is misspelled as *Wrte()*. Similarly, the statement `response.write("Hello World");` causes a syntax error because the `Response` object is incorrectly typed with a lowercase *r*.

Interpreting Error and Warning Messages

Recall from Chapter 1 that the Error List window displays two types of messages: compiler error messages and warning messages. Compiler error messages occur for any syntax errors in a source file and contain a description of the error and the name of the file in which the error occurred; warning messages occur in response to any potential problems in your code that are not serious enough to cause a compiler error message.

Compiler error messages that alert you to a syntax error in a line of code are the most useful. For instance, the statement `mileageCost = miles * 1.25` raises the compiler error message shown in Figure 6-2 because it does not include an ending semicolon.

	Description	File	Line	Column	Project
1	; expected	Default.aspx	11	29	C:\...\WebSite1\

Figure 6-2 Compiler error message for a statement that does not end with a semicolon

Logic errors do not generate compiler errors because computers are not smart enough (yet) to identify a flaw in your logic. For example, if you create an infinite loop with a `for` statement, the interpreter has no way of telling whether you really wanted to continually execute the `for` statement's code. Later in this chapter, you will learn how to trace the flow of your program's execution to locate logic errors.

To jump to the statement that is causing a compiler error, double-click the error message in the Error List window.

Some compiler error messages do not exactly identify the cause of a compiler error. The `Response.Write()` statement in the following code causes a compiler error because C# cannot locate the `result` variable within the scope of the function. The `result` variable is not in scope because it is declared inside the `if` statement. Therefore, it is not visible to the rest of the `calculatePercentage()` function, causing the error. Although the `Response.Write()` statement generates the compiler error because it attempts to access a variable that is not in scope, the real bug in the code is that the `result` variable must be declared outside of the `if` statement.

```
void calculatePercentage() {
    double amount = 500;
    double percentage = .05;
    if (amount < 100) {
            double result;
            result = amount * percentage;
    }
    Response.Write(result);
}
```

Now that you've had a chance to review some examples of compiler errors and compiler error messages, let's turn our attention to warning messages. One common warning message occurs when you declare a variable that you do not actually use in your program. For example, consider again the following function:

```
void calculateProfits()
{
    int payRate = 15;
    int numHours = 40;
    double grossPay;
    double netPay = (payRate * numHours) / .20;
}
```

Because the grossPay variable is never used, the following warning message appears in the Error List window:

```
The variable 'grossPay' is declared but never used
```

The WarningLevel attribute of the @ Page directive specifies the types of warnings to report during compilation. You can assign values 0 through 4 to the WarningLevel attribute. The higher the number, the stricter the compiler is about what it considers to be a warning. The default value is 4, which is the strictest warning level. Assigning a value of 0 to the WarningLevel attribute disables warnings entirely. Changing the warning level severity does not prevent warnings from occurring; it only determines whether ASP.NET will report them during compilation.

Next, you will use error and warning messages to help locate syntax errors in the Move Estimator program.

To locate build errors with error messages:

1. Start Visual Web Developer.

2. Select the **File** menu and then select **Open Web Site**. The Open Web Site dialog box opens. Locate the MoveEstimatorWithBugs folder in your Chapter folder for Chapter 6, highlight the folder name, and then click **Open**. After the project opens, double-click the **page1.aspx** file in the Solution Explorer window to open it in the Code Editor.

3. Build the Web site by selecting the **Build** menu and then selecting **Build Page**. You should see several of the errors shown in Figure 6-3.

		Description	File	Line	Column	Project
✖	1	) expected	page1.aspx.cs	27	64	C:\...\MoveEstimatorWithBugs\
✖	2	; expected	page1.aspx.cs	29	62	C:\...\MoveEstimatorWithBugs\
✖	3	; expected	page1.aspx.cs	30	27	C:\...\MoveEstimatorWithBugs\
✖	4	No overload for 'calculate_Click' matches delegate 'System.EventHandler'	page1.aspx	232		
✖	5	Operator '*' cannot be applied to operands of type 'string' and 'double'	page1.aspx.cs	27	47	C:\...\MoveEstimatorWithBugs\
✖	6	Only assignment, call, increment, decrement, and new object expressions can be used as a statement	page1.aspx.cs	29	62	C:\...\MoveEstimatorWithBugs\
✖	7	The name 'Cost' does not exist in the current context	page1.aspx.cs	30	27	C:\...\MoveEstimatorWithBugs\
✖	8	'double' does not contain a definition for 'Text' and no extension method 'Text' accepting a first argument of type 'double' could be found (are you missing a using directive or an assembly reference?)	page1.aspx.cs	30	62	C:\...\MoveEstimatorWithBugs\
✖	9	The name 'appliancesCost' does not exist in the current context	page1.aspx.cs	35	22	C:\...\MoveEstimatorWithBugs\

Figure 6-3 Build error messages in the Move Estimator program

4. Double-click the first error to go to the statement that is causing the error message, and the page1.aspx.cs file opens with the cursor placed on the statement that uses the Convert. ToDouble() method to assign the value of the miles text box to a variable named mileageCost. The problem with the statement is that the closing parenthesis for the Convert. ToDouble() method is missing. Add the missing parenthesis, and rebuild the page by selecting the **Build** menu and then selecting **Build Page**. You should see seven errors in the error list.

5. The first two errors state that semicolons are missing on Lines 22 and 23. Double-click the first error to jump to the first offending statement, which uses the Convert.ToDouble() method to assign the value of the flights text box to a variable named flightsCost. The problem is that the statement is missing a multiplication operator. Add a multiplication operator to the statement so it appears as follows:

```
double flightsCost = Convert.ToDouble(flights.Text) * 50;
```

6. Examine Line 23 and notice that the problem with this statement is the space between appliances and Cost. Remove the space, and then go to Line 21.

7. Rebuild the page again by selecting the **Build** menu and then selecting **Build Page**. You should see one error stating that no

overload for `'calculate_Click'` matches delegate `'System.EventHandler'`. This means that the compiler is not recognizing the `calculate_Click()` function as an event handler. Why? Because the event handler is missing the required `Object` argument, which represents the raised event, and the `EventArgs` parameter, which is used for passing data with an event. Fix the problem by adding the arguments to the `calculate_Click()` function, as follows:

```
protected void calculate_Click(Object Source, EventArgs E)
{
    double mileageCost = Convert.ToDouble(
    miles.Text) * 1.25;
...
```

8. Rebuild the page once more by selecting the **Build** menu and then selecting **Build Page**. You should receive no more error messages. However, do not try and use the program yet because it still contains plenty of bugs.

Handling Run-Time Errors

The second type of error, a **run-time error** is an error that occurs while a program is executing. Run-time errors differ from syntax errors in that they do not necessarily represent C# language errors. Instead, run-time errors occur when your program encounters code that it cannot execute. Some of the most common run-time errors occur for numeric calculations. For example, run-time errors occur if you attempt to divide by 0. Data types behave differently when dividing by zero. Floating-point data types, such as the `double` data type, are assigned a value of "Infinity," whereas integer data types display an error in the browser window. The following statements assign a value of "Infinity" to the `grossHourlyPay` variable because the `numberOfHours` variable is assigned a value of 0.

```
double grossPay = 1000;
double numberOfHours = 0;
double grossHourlyPay = grossPay / numberOfHours;
```

In comparison, the following version of the preceding code displays the error shown in Figure 6-4 because the divide-by-zero calculation is performed using integer data types.

```
int grossPay = 1000;
int numberOfHours = 0;
int grossHourlyPay = grossPay / numberOfHours;
```

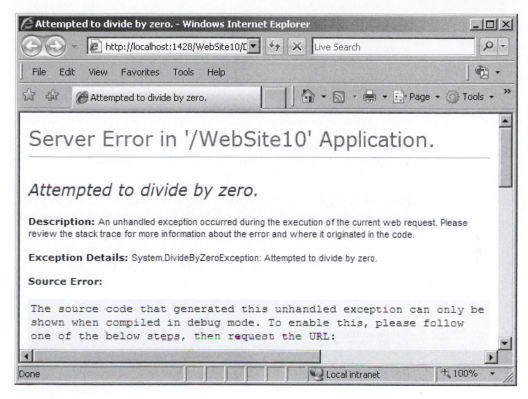

Figure 6-4 Divide-by-zero error

The C# compiler will raise an error for other types of potential run-time errors. For example, a typical run-time error occurs if you attempt to divide by a variable that has not been initialized. The following statements raise an error because the `numberOfHours` variable is not initialized.

```
int grossPay = 1000;
int numberOfHours;
int grossHourlyPay = grossPay / numberOfHours;
```

Identifying Logic Errors

The third type of error, **logic errors**, are flaws in a program's design that prevent the program from running as you anticipate. In this context, the term *logic* refers to the execution of program statements and procedures in the correct order to produce the desired results. You're already accustomed to performing ordinary, nonprogramming tasks according to a certain logic. For example, when you do the laundry, you normally wash, dry, iron, and then fold your clothes. If you decided to iron, fold, dry, and then wash the clothes, you would end up with a pile of wet laundry rather than the clean and pressed garments you desired. The problem, in that case, would be a type of logic error—you performed the steps in the wrong order.

One simple example of a logic error in a computer program is multiplying two values when you mean to divide them, as in the following code:

```
double divisionResult = 10 * 2;
Response.Write("<p>Ten divided by two is equal to "
    + divisionResult + "</p>");
```

Another example of a logic error is the creation of an infinite loop, in which a loop statement never ends because its conditional expression is never updated or is never false. The following code creates a `for` statement that results in the logic error of an infinite loop. The cause of the infinite loop is that the third argument in the `for` statement's parentheses never changes the value of the `count` variable.

```
for (int count = 10; count >= 0; count)
{
    Response.Write("We have liftoff in " + count + "<br />");
}
```

Because the `count` variable is never updated in the preceding example, it continues to have a value of 10 through each iteration of the loop, resulting in the repeated printing of the text "We have liftoff in 10". To correct this logic error, you add a decrement operator to the third argument in the `for` statement's constructor, as follows:

```
for (int count = 10; count >= 0; --count)
{
    Response.Write("We have liftoff in " + count + "<br />");
}
```

Short Quiz 1

1. What is debugging and where does the term come from?

2. What is the difference between syntax errors, run-time errors, and logic errors?

3. How do you specify the types of warnings to report during compilation?

Using Basic Debugging Techniques

Most advanced programming languages or environments, including Visual Studio, provide advanced features for debugging code. Before using these advanced features (which are covered later in this chapter), you need to understand how to use basic debugging techniques. Before studying basic debugging techniques, you should understand that the best weapon against bugs is writing good code.

Writing Good Code

The first and most important step in creating bug-free programs is to write good code. The more disciplined you are in your programming technique, the fewer bugs you will find in your programs. Although error and warning messages will help you catch basic syntax errors, some syntax errors are still difficult to pinpoint. For example, if you have a deeply nested set of control structures and one of the control structures is missing a closing brace, the syntax error might not be able to tell you exactly which control structure is malformed.

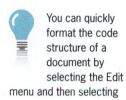
You can quickly format the code structure of a document by selecting the Edit menu and then selecting Format Document.

With this reminder about the importance of good syntax in mind, you are ready to turn your attention to debugging techniques. First, you will learn how to enable debugging.

Enabling Debugging

By default, ASP.NET displays a generic error message, similar to the one shown in Figure 6-4, which includes only a description and exception details about the run-time error that occurred. To print detailed information about errors to the browser window for a particular Web page, you need to include the `Debug` attribute in the @ Page directive and assign it a value of true. The following code, which raises a divide-by-zero error, displays the error information shown in Figure 6-5 because the page includes a `Debug="true"` attribute in the @ Page directive:

You also need to include a `Debug="true"` attribute in the @ Page directive to trace errors with the Visual Studio Debugger, as described later in this chapter.

```
int grossPay = 1000;
int numberOfHours = 0;
int grossHourlyPay = grossPay / numberOfHours;
```

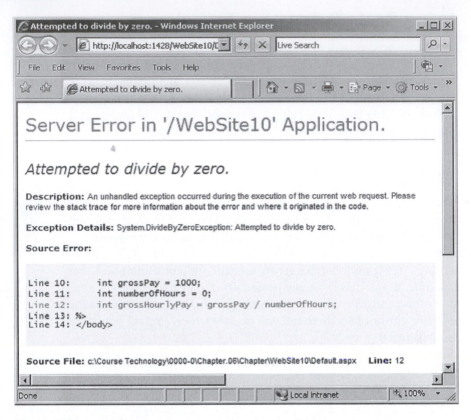

Figure 6-5 Detailed debugging information about a divide-by-zero error

Be sure to disable debugging for Web sites that run in production environments because hackers can use any displayed error messages to identify potential weaknesses in your Web site.

To enable debugging for all of the pages in your project, run the ASP.NET Web Site Server Administration Tool by selecting the Website menu and then selecting ASP.NET Configuration. This displays the Welcome page of the Web Site Administration Tool. Click the Application Configuration link, and then click the Configure debugging and tracing link to display the Configure Debugging and Tracing page. On this page, click the Enable debugging box. Note that an individual page's Debug attribute in the @ Page directive takes precedence over the application-level debugging setting. In other words, even though an application's debugging setting is enabled, debugging for an individual page will be disabled if the page's @ Page directive includes a Debug attribute assigned a value of true.

When you enable debugging for a page or project, you accomplish two things: You allow the Visual Studio Debugger to display detailed error information for any run-time errors it encounters and you allow yourself to manually debug a program. After you enable debugging, you can still use the Start Without Debugging command from the Debug menu, although Visual Studio Debugger will display any run-time error information. Later in this chapter, you will learn how to run the Start Debugging command from the Debug menu to manually debug your programs.

Next, you will locate and correct a run-time error in the Move Estimator program.

To fix a run-time error:

1. Return to the **page1.aspx** file in the Visual Studio IDE.

2. Start the Web site with the **Start Without Debugging** command. The program should build successfully and the Web page opens in the browser.

3. Enter a numeric value, such as 1000, in the Distance in Miles text box, and then click **Calculate**. You see an error page with the message "Input string was not in a correct format." Because you have not enabled debugging, you cannot see any more details of the error. Close your Web browser window.

4. Add a Debug="true" attribute to the @ Page directive, and start the Web site with the **Start Without Debugging** command. Enter a numeric value in the Distance in Miles text box, and click **Calculate**. You see the same error page, but this time with debugging details, as shown in Figure 6-6.

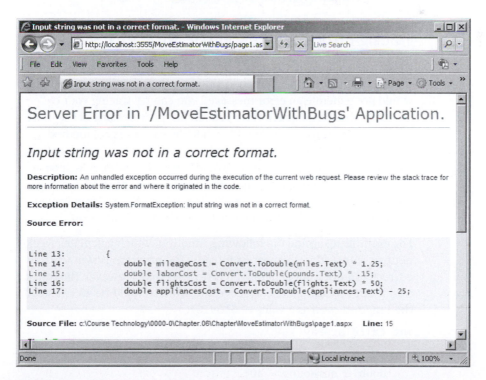

Figure 6-6 Error page with debugging enabled for the Move Estimator Web page

5. Close your Web browser window.

6. Notice in Figure 6-6 that the error occurred in the second statement in the `calculate_Click()` event handler. The first statement, which calculates the mileage cost, executed successfully after you entered a numeric value in the Distance in Miles text box. The problem occurred because the fields in the Move Estimator form do not contain values, causing run-time errors when the statements in the `calculate_Click()` event handler attempt to convert the values using the `Convert.ToDouble()` methods. To fix this problem, add a zero to the five <asp:TextBox> elements in the form. For example, the miles <asp:TextBox> element should appear as follows:

    ```
    <asp:TextBox ID="miles" runat="server" Width="50"
    AutoPostBack="True">0</asp:TextBox>
    ```

7. Start the Web site again with the **Start Without Debugging** command. Enter a numeric value in the Distance in Miles text box, and click **Calculate**. You won't receive the run-time error, but the code still contains several bugs that prevent the calculation from working correctly.

8. Close your Web browser window and remove the `Debug="true"` attribute from the @ `Page` directive.

Tracing Errors with `Response.Write()` Statements

When you are unable to locate a bug in your program by using error messages or examining your code, or if you suspect a logic error (which would not generate an error message), you can try tracing your code manually. The `Response.Write()` statement provides one of the most useful ways to trace code. You place a `Response.Write()` method at different points in your program and use it to display the contents of a variable, an array, or the value returned from a function. A `Response.Write()` statement is especially useful when you want to trace a bug in your program by analyzing a list of values. Using this technique, you can monitor values as they change during program execution.

For example, examine the following function, which calculates weekly net pay, rounded to the nearest integer. The program is syntactically correct and does not generate an error message. However, the function is not returning the correct result, which should be 485. Instead, the function returns a value of 5169107.

```
int calculatePay()
{
    double payRate = 15;
    double numHours = 40;
```

```
        double grossPay = payRate * numHours;
        double federalTaxes = grossPay * .06794;
        double stateTaxes = grossPay * .0476;
        double socialSecurity = grossPay * .062;
        double medicare = grossPay * .0145;
        double netPay = grossPay - federalTaxes;
        netPay *= stateTaxes;
        netPay *= socialSecurity;
        netPay *= medicare;
        return Convert.ToInt32(netPay);
}
```

To trace the problem, you can place a `Response.Write()` statement at the point in the program where you think the error might be located. For example, the first thing you might want to check in the `calculatePay()` function is whether the `grossPay` variable is being calculated correctly. To check whether the program calculates `grossPay` correctly, place a `Response.Write()` statement in the function following the calculation of the `grossPay` variable as follows:

 Place any `Response.Write()` statements used to trace program execution at a different level of indentation than other statements to clearly distinguish them from the actual program.

```
int calculatePay()
{
        double payRate = 15;
        double numHours = 40;
        double grossPay = payRate * numHours;
Response.Write("<p>" + grossPay + "</p>");
        double federalTaxes = grossPay * .06794;
        double stateTaxes = grossPay * .0476;
        double socialSecurity = grossPay * .062;
        double medicare = grossPay * .0145;
        double netPay = grossPay - federalTaxes;
        netPay *= stateTaxes;
        netPay *= socialSecurity;
        netPay *= medicare;
        return Convert.ToInt32(netPay);
}
```

Because the `grossPay` variable contains the correct value (600), you would move the `Response.Write()` statement to check the value of the `netPay` variable. You then continue with this technique until you discover the error. If you did, you would find that the `calculatePay()` function does not perform properly because the lines that add the `stateTaxes`, `socialSecurity`, and `medicare` variables to the `netPay` variable are incorrect; they use the multiplication assignment operator (`*=`) instead of the subtraction assignment operator (`-=`).

An alternative to using a single `Response.Write()` statement is to place multiple `Response.Write()` statements throughout your code to check values as the code executes. For example, you can trace the

calculatePay() function by using multiple Response.Write()
statements, as follows:

```
int calculatePay()
{
    double payRate = 15;
    double numHours = 40;
    double grossPay = payRate * numHours;
Response.Write("<p>" + grossPay + "</p>");
    double federalTaxes = grossPay * .06794;
    double stateTaxes = grossPay * .0476;
    double socialSecurity = grossPay * .062;
    double medicare = grossPay * .0145;
    double netPay = grossPay - federalTaxes;
Response.Write("<p>" + netPay + "</p>");
    netPay *= stateTaxes;
Response.Write("<p>" + netPay + "</p>");
    netPay *= socialSecurity;
Response.Write("<p>" + netPay + "</p>");
    netPay *= medicare;
Response.Write("<p>" + netPay + "</p>");
    return Convert.ToInt32(netPay);
}
```

Don't forget
to remove any
Response.
Write()
statements
that you are using to
debug your program
before you deploy it on
the Web, or you might
unintentionally expose
sensitive information that
a hacker could exploit.

The key to using multiple Response.Write() statements to trace program values is using them selectively at key points throughout a program.
For example, suppose you were debugging a large accounting program
with multiple functions. You could place a Response.Write() statement
at key positions within the program, such as wherever a function returns
a value or a variable is assigned new data. In this way, you can find the
bug's approximate location—for instance in a particular function. You
can then concentrate your debugging efforts on that one function.

Next, you will use Response.Write() statements to locate a bug in
the Move Estimator program.

To locate a bug with Response.Write() statements:

1. Return to the **page1.aspx** file in the Visual Studio IDE.

2. Start the Web site with the **Start Without Debugging** command. The program should build successfully and the Web
   page opens in the browser.

Do not enter
values into any
of the other
text boxes—
the program
still contains
many bugs.

3. Click the **No. of Appliances** text box, type **3**, and click
   Calculate. The value in the Move Estimate text box should
   have changed to $75. Instead, it changes to $-22. This means
   you need to check for bugs.

4. To trace the problem, close your Web browser window, and
   then locate the calculate_Click() event handler in the
   page1.aspx.cs file. Add two Response.Write() statements to
   the calculate_Click() event handler, as follows. The first

Response.Write() function checks to see if the value from the text box is correct. The second Response.Write() function checks to see if the calculation that totals the cost of moving the appliances assigns the correct value to the appliancesCost variable.

```
protected void calculate_Click(Object Source, EventArgs E)
{
    double mileageCost = Convert.ToDouble(
      miles.Text) * 1.25;
    double laborCost = Convert.ToDouble(pounds.Text)
      * .15;
    double flightsCost = Convert.ToDouble(
      flights.Text) * 50;
Response.Write(appliances.Text + "<br />");
    double appliancesCost = Convert.ToDouble(
      appliances.Text) - 25;
Response.Write(appliancesCost + "<br />");
    ...
```

5. Start the Web site with the **Start Without Debugging** command. The program should build successfully and the Web page opens in the browser.

6. Click the **No. of Appliances** text box, type **3**, and click **Calculate**. The first Response.Write() correctly displays 3, which is the number you typed into the text box. The second Response.Write() displays a value of $-22 instead of the correct cost for moving three appliances ($75). This tells you that there is something wrong with the statement preceding the second Response.Write() statement.

7. Close your Web browser window and examine the statement above the second Response.Write() statement. Note that instead of an assignment operator, the statement includes a subtraction operator.

8. Replace the subtraction operator with a multiplication operator as follows:

```
double appliancesCost = Convert.ToDouble(
  appliances.Text) * 25;
```

9. Remove the two Response.Write() statements from the calculate_Click() event handler.

10. Start the Web site with the **Start Without Debugging** command. The program should build successfully and the Web page opens in the browser. Click the **No. of Appliances** text box, type **3**, and click **Calculate**. The value in the Move Estimate text box should correctly change to $75. Leave your Web browser window open.

When using `Response.Write()` statements to trace bugs, it is helpful to use a **driver program**, which is a simplified, temporary program that is used for testing functions and other code. A driver program is simply an ASP.NET page that contains only the code you are testing. Driver programs do not have to be elaborate; they can be as simple as a single function you are testing. This technique allows you to isolate and test an individual function without having to worry about Web page elements, event handlers, global variables, and other code that form your program's functionality as a whole. A testing technique that is essentially the opposite of driver programs is the use of stub functions. **Stub functions** are empty functions that serve as place-holders (or "stubs") for a program's actual functions. Typically, a stub function returns a hard-coded value that represents the result of the actual function. Using stub functions allows you to check for errors in your program from the ground up. You start by swapping stub functions for the actual function definition. Each time you add the actual function definition, you rebuild and test the program. You repeat the process for each function in your program. This technique allows you to isolate and correct bugs within functions, or to correct bugs that occur as a result of how an individual function operates within your program as a whole.

Using Comments to Locate Bugs

 The cause of an error in a particular statement is often the result of an error in a preceding line of code.

Another method of locating bugs in a program is to transform lines that you think might be causing problems into comments. In other words, you can "comment out" problematic lines. This technique helps you isolate the statement that is causing the error. In some cases, you might choose to comment out individual lines that might be causing the error, or you might choose to comment out all lines except the lines that you know work. When you first receive an error message or your program doesn't work as expected, start by commenting out only the statement specified by the line number in the error message, or that you suspect is causing the problem, and rebuild the project. If you receive additional error messages or problems, comment out additional statements. Then, examine the commented out statements for the cause of the bug.

The following statements demonstrate how to use comments to help debug the `calculatePay()` function. This example comments out all of the statements with the exception of the statements that calculate net pay minus federal taxes. After verifying that net pay minus federal taxes calculates correctly, you would remove the comment tags for the state tax calculations, check the result assigned to the `netPay` variable, and keep removing comment tags until you've isolated the problem.

```
int calculatePay()
{
    double payRate = 15;
    double numHours = 40;
    double grossPay = payRate * numHours;
    double federalTaxes = grossPay * .06794;
    // double stateTaxes = grossPay * .0476;
    // double socialSecurity = grossPay * .062;
    // double medicare = grossPay * .0145;
    double netPay = grossPay - federalTaxes;
    // netPay *= stateTaxes;
    // netPay *= socialSecurity;
    // netPay *= medicare;
    return Convert.ToInt32(netPay);
}
```

The problem with the preceding example is that the three statements that assign a value to the netPay variable use the compound multiplication operator (*=) instead of the compound subtraction operator (-=). Although the error might seem somewhat simple, it is typical of the types of errors you will encounter. Often you will see the error right away, making it unnecessary to comment out code or use any other tracing technique. However, when you have been staring at the same code for long periods of time, simple spelling errors are not always easy to spot. Commenting out the lines you know are giving you trouble is a good technique for isolating and correcting even the simplest types of bugs.

Next, you will use comments to locate bugs in the Move Estimator program.

To use comments to locate bugs in the Move Estimator program:

1. Return to the Web browser window that is running the page1. aspx file, enter the following data, and click **Calculate**:

   ```
   Distance in Miles: 400
   Weight in Pounds: 900
   No. of Flights: 2
   ```

2. Note the total value displayed in the Moving Estimate box. Instead of a correct value of 735, you see an incorrect value of 535. To locate the code that is causing this problem, you need to add comments to the calculate_Click() event handler.

3. Close your Web browser and add comments to the four statements that assign values to the moveTotal variable in the calculate_Click() event handler. Your function should appear as follows:

   ```
   protected void calculate_Click(Object Source, EventArgs E)
   {
       double mileageCost = Convert.ToDouble(
         miles.Text) * 1.25;
   ```

```
double laborCost = Convert.ToDouble(pounds.Text)
   * .15;
double flightsCost = Convert.ToDouble(
   flights.Text) * 50;
double appliancesCost = Convert.ToDouble(
   appliances.Text) * 25;
double pianosCost = Convert.ToDouble(
   pianos.Text) * 3.5;
double moveTotal = mileageCost;
// moveTotal += laborCost;
// moveTotal -= flightsCost;
// moveTotal += appliancesCost;
// moveTotal += pianosCost;
total.Text = "$" + moveTotal;
}
```

4. Start the Web site with the **Start Without Debugging** command. Enter **400** as the Distance in Miles value and click **Calculate**. The correct value of 500 is assigned to the Move Estimate box. Therefore, the `mileageCost` variable is not the problem.

5. Close your Web browser and remove the comment from the `moveTotal += laborCost;` statement. Start the Web site with the **Start Without Debugging** command. Enter **400** as the Distance in Miles value, press the **Tab** key, enter **900** as the Weight in Pounds value and click **Calculate**. At 15 cents a pound, the total cost of 900 pounds is $135. Adding 135 to the Distance in Miles amount of 500 results in 635. This tells us that the program is functioning correctly so far.

6. Close your Web browser and remove the comment from the `moveTotal -= flightsCost;` statement and then start the Web site with the **Start Without Debugging** command. Enter **400** as the Distance in Miles value, press the **Tab** key, enter **900** as the Weight in Pounds value, press the **Tab** key, enter **2** as the No. of Flights value and then click **Calculate**. At $50 per flight, a value of 2 should only increase the moving estimate by 100, for a total of 735. However, the Moving Estimate box incorrectly displays 535. As you might have already noticed, the `moveTotal -= flightsCost;` statement uses a decrement assignment operator (-=) instead of an addition assignment operator (+=). Do not think this is a trivial example. As you develop your own applications, you will often find yourself adding and deleting statements that can introduce simple, hard-to-detect bugs in your programs.

7. Close your Web browser and modify the `moveTotal -= flightsCost;` statement so it uses an addition assignment operator (+=), as follows: `moveTotal += flightsCost;`.

Remove the remainder of the comments from the statements in the `calculate_Click()` event handler. Restart the Web site with the **Start Without Debugging** command. Enter the data listed in Step 1. The correct value of 735 should appear in the Moving Estimate box. Do not enter any numbers for the other calculations because the program still contains some errors.

8. Close your Web browser window.

Combining Debugging Techniques

When searching for errors, it's often helpful to combine debugging techniques. For example, the following code uses comments combined with `Response.Write()` statements to trace errors in the `calculatePay()` function. Suppose that the `double grossPay = payRate * numHours;` statement is the last statement in the function that operates correctly. Therefore, all of the lines following that statement are commented out. You would then use a `Response.Write()` statement to check the value of each statement, removing comments from each statement in a sequential order, and checking and correcting syntax as you go.

```
int calculatePay()
{
    double payRate = 15;
    double numHours = 40;
    double grossPay = payRate * numHours;
Response.Write("<p>" + grossPay + "</p>");
    // double federalTaxes = grossPay * .06794;
    // double stateTaxes = grossPay * .0476;
    // double socialSecurity = grossPay * .062;
    // double medicare = grossPay * .0145;
    // double netPay = grossPay - federalTaxes;
    // netPay *= stateTaxes;
    // netPay *= socialSecurity;
    // netPay *= medicare;
    // return Convert.ToInt32(netPay);
}
```

Checking XHTML Elements

There will be occasions when you cannot locate the source of a bug, no matter how long you search. In such cases, the flaw might not lie in your C# code at all, but in your XHTML elements. If you cannot locate a bug using any of the methods described in this chapter, perform a line-by-line analysis of your XHTML code, making sure that all tags have opening and closing brackets. Also, be sure that all necessary opening and closing tags, such as the <body>...</body> tag pair are included. Better yet, be sure to look at the IDE's Error List window for validation errors; this is usually much easier than performing a line-by-line analysis.

The following code contains a flawed XHTML element that prevents an ASP.NET program from running. The project builds successfully, but the statements in the code render block do not execute. Examine the code and look for the error, which can be difficult to spot.

```
<%@ Page Language="C#" AutoEventWireup="true"
CodeFile="Default.aspx.cs" Inherits="_Default" %>
<!DOCTYPE html PUBLIC "-//W3C//DTD XHTML 1.0
Transitional//EN" "http://www.w3.org/TR/xhtml1/DTD/xhtml1-
transitional.dtd">
<html xmlns="http://www.w3.org/1999/xhtml">
<head runat="server">
    <title>Untitled Page</title>
</head>
<body>
<%
double divisionResult = 10 / 2;
Response.Write("<p>Ten divided by two is equal to "
    + divisionResult + "</p>");
%>
</body>
</html>
```

The problem with the preceding code is that the value assigned to the xmlns attribute of the <html> tag is missing a closing quotation mark. Without the closing quotation mark, the compiler will not be able to identify any of the elements in the document, including the code declaration block. It's worth mentioning that although the project will build successfully, the error is listed in the Error List window.

Analyzing Logic

At times, code errors stem from logic problems that are difficult to spot using tracing techniques. When you suspect that your code contains logic errors, you must analyze each statement on a case-by-case basis. For example, the following code contains a logic flaw that prevents it from functioning correctly:

```
if (!emailMatch.Success)
    Response.Write("<p>Invalid e-mail address!</p>");
    throw new Exception("<p>One or more of the
        e-mail addresses you entered does not appear
        to be valid.</p>");
```

If you were to execute the preceding code, the exception will always be thrown, even if the e-mail address is valid. If you examine the `if` statement more closely, you would see that the `if` statement ends after the `Response.Write()` statement because it does not enclose the statements within braces (which is legal). For the code to execute properly, the `if` statement must include braces as follows:

```
if (!emailMatch.Success)
{
    Response.Write("<p>Invalid e-mail address!</p>");
    throw new Exception("<p>One or more of the
        e-mail addresses you entered does not appear
        to be valid.</p>");
}
```

The following `for` statement shows another example of an easily overlooked logic error:

```
int count = 0;
for (count = 1; count < 6; ++count);
    Response.Write(count + "<br />");
```

The preceding code should print the numbers 1 through 5 to the screen. However, the line `for (count = 1; count < 6; ++count);` contains an ending semicolon, which marks the end of the `for` loop. The loop executes five times and changes the value of `count` to 6, but does nothing else, because there are no statements before its ending semicolon. The line `Response.Write(count + "<br />");` is a separate statement that executes only once, printing the number 6 to the screen. The code is syntactically correct, but does not function as you anticipated. As you can see from these examples, it is easy to overlook very minor logic errors in your code.

 Trace output is appended to the bottom of the Web page that ran the program. This means that for long Web pages, you might need to scroll down to see the trace output.

Viewing Diagnostic Trace Information

If you are unable to locate a bug in your program by using error messages, or if you suspect a logic error (which does not generate error messages), you must trace your code. **Tracing** is the examination of individual statements in an executing program. You can view diagnostic trace information for page requests by assigning a value of true to the `Trace` attribute of the `@ Page` processing directive. This prints a page's execution details to the browser window, which you can use to help identify problems in your code. Figure 6-7 displays the diagnostic trace output.

 To configure how diagnostic trace messages are displayed, assign a value of SortByCategory or SortByTime to the TraceMode attributes of the @ Page processing directive. The default TraceMode value is SortByTime.

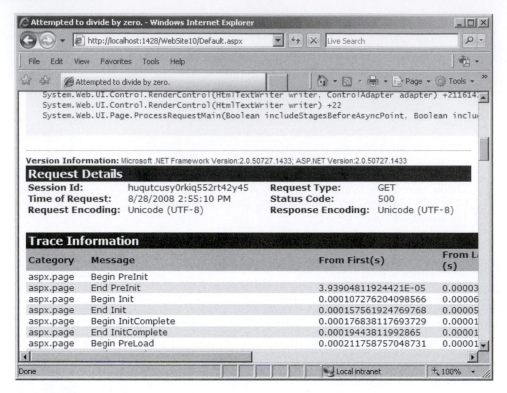

Figure 6-7   Diagnostic trace output

Note that an individual page's Trace attribute in the @ Page directive takes precedence over the application-level trace setting. In other words, even though an application's trace setting is enabled, tracing for an individual page will be disabled if the page's @ Page directive includes a Trace attribute assigned a value of false.

You can store diagnostic trace information for each page request in a log, but you must first enable application-level tracing by selecting the Website menu and then selecting ASP.NET Configuration. This displays the Welcome page of the Web Site Administration Tool. Click the Application Configuration link, click the Configure debugging and tracing link to display the Configure Debugging and Tracing page, and then click the Capture tracing information box.

After enabling application-level tracing, you can view the trace information log using Trace Viewer. To view the trace information log with Trace Viewer, open a file named Trace.axd, which is located in your project's root folder. For example, if your project is stored in a folder named BookStore, you can open Trace Viewer with a URL similar to *http://localhost:1452/BookStore/Trace.axd*. The Trace Viewer page contains links that allow you to view tracing details for each page request and a link that clears the trace log. Figure 6-8 shows the Trace Viewer for the Big River Kayaking site that you created in Chapter 4.

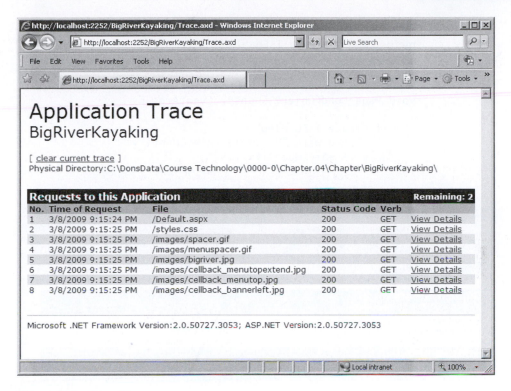

Figure 6-8 Trace Viewer

The default trace diagnostic messages can be very useful for quickly examining critical request information such as events and object collection variables like the Form collection of the Request object. However, they don't list code details, such as the value assigned to a variable. You can add your own custom messages to the trace diagnostic output using the Trace.Write() and Trace.Warn() methods of the TraceContext class. Both of these methods write messages to the Trace Information section of the trace diagnostic output, within the event from which they were called. For example, if the methods were called from the Page_Load() event handler, the messages will print between the Begin Load and End Load events in the Trace Information section. The difference between the Trace.Write() and Trace.Warn() methods is that the Trace.Warn() method prints its messages with red text. The basic syntax for these methods is Trace. Write(*message*).

Any debugging code in your application should only run if tracing is enabled. For this reason, you should use the Trace.IsEnable property to ensure tracing has been enabled for the page before executing the Trace.Write() or Trace.Warn() methods. The following

 As with debugging, be sure to turn off the display of trace information for Web sites that run in production environments because hackers can use any displayed information to identify potential weaknesses in your Web site.

Page_Load() event handler demonstrates how to use the Trace.Warn() method and the Trace.IsEnable property to print the value of a variable named salesQuantity if tracing is enabled. Figure 6-9 shows the output.

```csharp
void Page_Load(Object Source, EventArgs E)
{
    if (Trace.IsEnabled)
        Trace.Warn("Variable salesQuantity: "
            + salesQuantity);
}
```

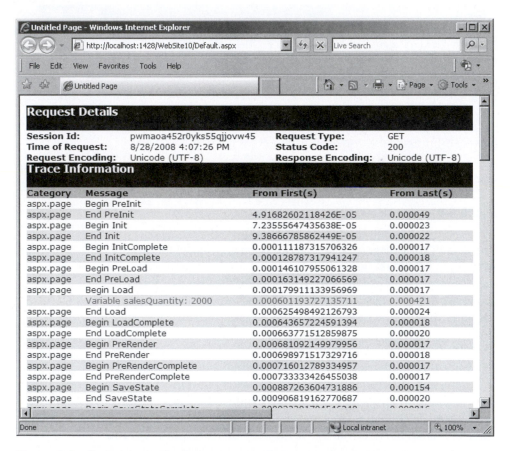

Figure 6-9 Custom trace message

One of the problems with using Response.Write() statements to debug your code is that you can easily forget to remove them before deploying your application, which can pose a serious security risk by potentially making sensitive data visible to hackers. With diagnostic tracing, you don't need to remove any Trace.Write() and Trace.Warn() methods from your code. Instead, you just need to remember to turn off page-level tracing by assigning a value of true to the Trace attribute of the @ Page processing directive or by disabling application-level tracing with the Web Site Administration Tool.

Next, you will enable tracing for the moving Web site.

To enable tracing:

1. Return to the **page1.aspx** file in the Visual Studio IDE.

2. Add Trace="true" to the @ Page processing directive and assign it a value of true.

3. Add the following statements to the end of the Page_Load() event handler in the page1.aspx.cs file. These statements print the values in the Distance in Miles, Weight in Pounds, and No. of Flights fields.

```
if (Trace.IsEnabled)
{
    Trace.Warn("Miles: " + miles.Text);
    Trace.Warn("Pounds: " + miles.Text);
    Trace.Warn("Flights: " + miles.Text);
}
```

4. Enable application-level tracing by selecting the **Website** menu and then selecting **ASP.NET Configuration**. The Welcome page of the Web Site Administration Tool displays. Click the **Application Configuration** link, click the **Configure debugging and tracing** link to display the Configure Debugging and Tracing page, and then click the **Capture tracing information** box. Close the Web Site Administration Tool.

5. Start the Web site with the **Start Without Debugging** command, enter the following data, and click **Calculate**:

```
Distance in Miles: 400
Weight in Pounds: 900
No. of Flights: 2
```

6. After the page reloads, scroll down until you see the trace output. You should see the preceding values printed from the Trace.Warn() methods.

7. Place your cursor in the address box of your Web browser, replace page1.aspx with **Trace.axd**, and press **Enter**. You should see the Trace View page for the MoveEstimatorWithBugs project.

8. Close the Web browser window, and then remove the Trace="true" attribute from the @ Page directive in the page1.aspx file.

9. Disable application-level tracing by selecting the **Website** menu and then selecting **ASP.NET Configuration**. The

Welcome page of the Web Site Administration Tool displays. Click the **Application Configuration** link, click the **Configure debugging and tracing** link to display the Configure Debugging and Tracing page, and then deselect the **Capture tracing information** box. Close the Web Site Administration Tool.

Short Quiz 2

1. How do you enable debugging at both the page and application levels?

2. Explain how to trace errors with `Response.Write()` statements.

3. Explain how to trace errors with comments.

4. Why would you need to check XHTML elements to locate a bug in an ASP.NET program?

5. Explain how to enable tracing and how to add your own custom messages to the trace diagnostic output.

Tracing Errors with the Visual Studio Debugger

Many programming tools such as the Visual Studio IDE have debugging capabilities built directly into their development environments. These built-in debugging capabilities provide sophisticated commands for tracking errors. Up to this point, you have learned how to interpret error messages and correct the statements that cause the errors. As helpful as they are, error messages are useful only in resolving syntax and run-time errors. You have also learned some techniques that assist in locating logic errors. Examining your code manually and using an alert dialog box to track values are usually the first steps in locating a logic error.

These techniques work fine with smaller programs. However, they're not so useful for finding logic errors in larger programs. For instance, you might have a function that contains multiple calls to other functions, which themselves might call other functions. Attempting to trace the logic and flow of such a program using simple tools such as output statements can be difficult. The Visual Studio IDE provides a program called the **debugger**, which is a tool that contains several options that can help you trace each line of code, creating a much more efficient method of finding and resolving logic errors.

Stepping Through Your Code

You start the debugger by selecting the Debug menu and then selecting the Start Debugging, Step Into, or Step Over commands. The **Step Into command** executes an individual line of code and then pauses until you instruct the debugger to continue. This feature gives you an opportunity to evaluate program flow and structure as code is being executed. If you prefer to skip functions that you know are working correctly, you can use the **Step Over command**, which allows you to skip function calls. With this command, the program still executes the function that you step over, but it appears in the debugger as if a single statement executes. These commands allow you to monitor values and trace program execution one command at a time.

Before you can use the Step Into and Step Over commands, you need to insert breakpoints into your code. A **breakpoint** is a statement that switches program execution to break mode. In **break mode**, program execution is temporarily suspended, thereby allowing you to monitor values and trace program execution one command at a time. Once a program is paused at a breakpoint, you can use the commands on the Debug menu to trace program execution. To resume program execution after entering break mode, select Continue from the Debug menu. The **Continue command** executes the rest of the program normally or until another breakpoint is encountered. Multiple breakpoints provide a convenient way to pause program execution at key positions in your code at which you think there might be a bug. You can also end a debugging session without executing the rest of the program by selecting the Debug menu and then selecting the **Stop Debugging command**.

Once your program is in break mode, you can use the **Step Out command** to execute all remaining code in the current function. If the current function was called from another function, all remaining code in the current function executes and the debugger stops at the next statement in the calling function. You can also trace program execution with the Run To Cursor command on the shortcut menu, which appears when you right-click a statement. When you select the **Run To Cursor command**, the program runs normally until it reaches the statement where your cursor is located, at which point the program enters break mode. You can then use the Step Into, Step Over, and Step Out commands to continue tracing program execution. The Run To Cursor command is useful if you are sure that your program is functioning correctly up to a certain point in the code.

Before you can work with your program in break mode, you must first enable application-level debugging with the Web Site Administration Tool.

When you first enter break mode, two new windows, Locals and Watch, appear at the bottom of the Visual Studio IDE. The debugger also includes other windows that will help you debug your programs. You will learn more about these windows later in the chapter.

336

You can also set a breakpoint by clicking next to a statement in the left margin of the Code Editor or by right-clicking a statement, pointing to the Breakpoint submenu on the shortcut menu, and then clicking Insert Breakpoint.

To insert a breakpoint, place your cursor in the statement where you want the program to pause and select Toggle Breakpoint from the Debug menu. A red circle appears in the margin to identify the breakpoint. Once you enter break mode, icons appear in the left margin to indicate various elements. For example, a yellow arrow points to the statement that executes next.

Although you can make changes to code in break mode, they will not take effect while the program is executing. You must end program execution (using the Stop Debugging command), rebuild the project, and then start the program again. You can also select the Debug menu and then select Restart, which stops, rebuilds, and then reexecutes the program in the debugger.

After you are finished debugging your program, you need to clear all the breakpoints or your program will continue to enter break mode each time it encounters one. To clear a breakpoint, place your cursor anywhere in a line that contains the breakpoint, select the Debug menu, and then select Toggle Breakpoint. To remove all breakpoints from a program, select the Debug menu and then select Delete All Breakpoints. Instead of removing a breakpoint, you can enable and disable it by right-clicking the statement containing the breakpoint, pointing to the Breakpoint submenu on the shortcut menu, and then clicking Disable Breakpoint. A disabled breakpoint appears as a hollow circle in the left margin of the Code Editor.

Next, you will use the commands on the Debug menu to trace a bug on the Contact Us form of the mover Web site that is causing an error message.

To use commands on the Debug menu to trace a bug:

1. Return to the Visual Studio IDE and enable application-level debugging by selecting the **Website** menu and then selecting **ASP.NET Configuration**. This displays the Welcome page of the Web Site Administration Tool. Click the **Application Configuration** link, click the **Configure debugging and tracing** link to display the Configure Debugging and Tracing page, and then select the **Enable debugging** box. Close the Web Site Administration Tool. Next, you will run the Web site without debugging so that you can see the bug in action.

2. Open the **page2.aspx** file in the Code Editor, and then start the Web site as usual with the **Start Without Debugging** command. Select a date on the calendar and verify that you see the following error: "Page.IsValid cannot be called before validation has taken place." After reviewing the error message, close your Web browser window.

3. When you click a date on the calendar, the `dateSelected()` event handler is called, so it makes sense to start tracing there. Open the **page2.aspx.cs** file in the Code Editor and move your cursor to the statement within the `dateSelected()` event handler, select the **Debug** menu, and then select **Toggle Breakpoint**. A red circle appears in the margin to identify the breakpoint. Now that you have inserted the breakpoint, you are ready to start debugging.

4. Select the **Debug** menu and then select **Start Debugging** (not Start Without Debugging). Select a date on the calendar. At this point, the IDE window is paused at the statement containing the breakpoint in the `dateSelected()` event handler.

5. Select the **Debug** menu and then select **Step Into** twice. This executes the statement in the `dateSelected()` event handler. Control transfers to the `dateSelected()` event handler's closing brace.

6. Select the **Debug** menu and then select **Step Into**. This transfers control to the `Page_LoadComplete()` event handler.

7. Select **Step Into** from the **Debug** menu twice to skip over the event handler's opening brace and to execute the `lastName. Focus();` statement. Control transfers to the `if` statement that checks if post back has occurred and if it was initiated by the calendar.

8. Select the **Debug** menu and then select **Step Into**. Because the statements within the `if` statement should only execute if the page initiated post back (when a user clicks the Submit button), control skips over the `if` statement to the body of the `if` statement. This alerts you to a problem within the `if` statement's conditional expression. This conditional expression should return a value of true only if post back occurred and if the control that initiated the post back is not the calendar control.

9. Examine the conditional expression closely and notice that the portion of the statement that checks the control uses an equality operator (==) when it should use an inequality operator (!=).

10. Select the **Debug** menu and then select **Stop Debugging**, and modify the `if` statement's conditional expression so that the portion of the statement that checks the control uses an inequality operator instead of an equality operator, as follows:

```
...
if (Page.IsPostBack && Page.Request.Params.Get(
    "__EVENTTARGET") != "Calendar1")
{
...
```

11. Remove the breakpoint from the `dateSelected()` event handler by placing your cursor in the breakpoint statement, selecting the **Debug** menu, and then selecting **Toggle Breakpoint**. Start the Web site again with the **Start Without Debugging** command. Select a date from the calendar. At this point, you should no longer receive an error message. However, if you enter values into the other fields and click **Submit**, you will not see the text about your message being received. Close the Web browser window.

Next, you will use the commands on the Debug menu to trace a logic error on the Contact Us form of the mover Web site.

To use commands on the Debug menu to trace a logic error:

1. Return to the Visual Studio IDE and add a breakpoint to the nested `if` statement in the `Page_LoadComplete()` event handler. Start the program in debugging mode by selecting the **Debug** menu and then selecting **Start Debugging**.

2. Enter values into each of the fields and click **Submit**. Focus switches to the IDE again, paused at the breakpoint in the `Page_LoadComplete()` event handler. Because you entered valid values in each field, the statements within the nested `if` statement should execute. However, when you select **Step Into** from the **Debug** menu, the nested `if` statement is bypassed completely. If you're observant, you probably already noticed that the `if (!Page.IsValid)` statement contains an unnecessary Not operator (!), which prevents the statements with the nested `if` statement from executing, even if the page is valid.

3. Select the **Debug** menu and then select **Stop Debugging**, and then remove the Not operator from the nested `if` statement's conditional expression, as follows:

```
...
if (Page.IsValid)
...
```

4. Remove the breakpoint from the `Page_LoadComplete()` event handler by placing your cursor in the breakpoint statement, selecting the **Debug** menu, and then selecting **Toggle Breakpoint**.

5. Start the Web site again with the **Start Without Debugging** command. Enter values into the fields and click **Submit**. You should see the text about your message being received.

6. Close the Web browser window and disable application-level debugging by selecting the **Website** menu and then selecting **ASP.NET Configuration**. The Welcome page of the Web Site Administration Tool displays. Click the **Application Configuration** link, click the **Configure debugging and tracing** link to display the Configure Debugging and Tracing page, and then deselect the **Enable debugging** box. Close the Web Site Administration Tool.

Working with the Debugger Windows

As you trace program execution using the commands on the Debug menu, you might also need to trace how variables and expressions change during the course of program execution. For example, suppose you have a statement that reads `resultNum = firstNum / secondNum;`. You know this line is causing a divide-by-zero error, but you do not know exactly when `secondNum` is being changed to a zero value. To pinpoint the cause of the logic problem, you need a way to trace program execution and locate the exact location at which `secondNum` is being changed to a zero value. The debugger includes several windows that you can use to monitor variables and expressions in break mode.

When your program enters break mode, four debugging windows become available: Locals, Watch, Immediate, and Call Stack. Depending on how your instance of Visual Web Developer is configured, you might or might not see the windows when you enter break mode. However, you can display all of the windows by selecting the Debug menu and then selecting the Windows submenu.

The **Locals window** displays all local variables within the currently executing function, regardless of whether they have been initialized. The Locals window helps you see how different values in the currently executing function affect program execution. You use the Locals window when you need to be able to see all of a function's variables, regardless of whether they have been assigned a value. You can change the value of a variable in the Locals window by right-clicking the variable and selecting Edit Value from the shortcut menu. Figure 6-10 displays the Locals window in break mode.

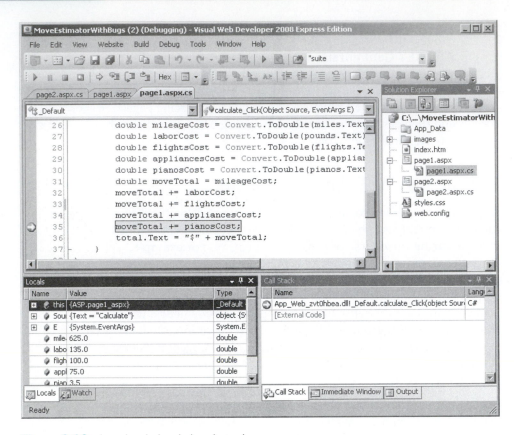

Figure 6-10 Locals window in break mode

To edit or remove a watch expression, right-click the expression in the Watch window and select Edit Value or Delete Watch.

The **Watch window** monitors both variables and expressions in break mode. To display the value of a variable or expression in the Watch window, enter a variable or expression in the first column in the empty row in the Watch window. (You can also right-click a variable or expression in your code and select Add Watch from the shortcut menu.) The variable or expression you enter (or right-click) is then displayed in the Watch window, along with its value. The Watch window in Figure 6-11 shows the value of the `mileageCost` and `moveTotal` variables in the `calculate_Click()` function.

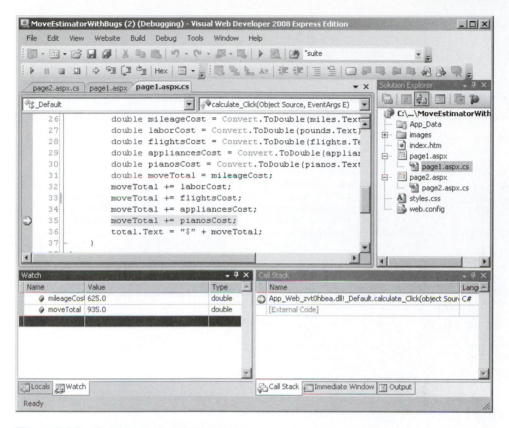

Figure 6-11 Variables in the Watch window

You can use the **Immediate window** to monitor specific variables and expressions in break mode. To open the Immediate window, point to Windows on the Debug menu and then click Immediate. To display the value of a variable or expression in the Immediate window, you enter the variable or expression in the white portion of the window and press Enter. The value is displayed directly beneath the variable or expression in the Immediate window. To change the value of a variable, type the variable name in the Immediate window followed by an equal sign and the new value, and then press Enter. The new value is displayed beneath the statement you entered. Figure 6-12 shows the Immediate window as it monitors the value of the `mileageCost` and `moveTotal` variables in the `calculate_Click()` function.

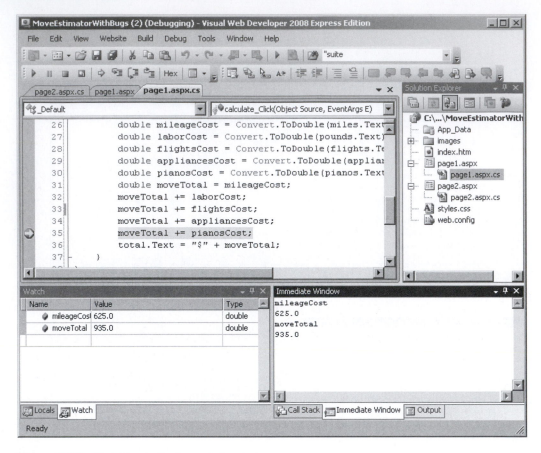

Figure 6-12   Variables in the Immediate window

Next, you will use the Watch window to find a bug on the Move Estimator page.

To use the Watch window to find a bug on the Move Estimator page:

1. Return to the **page1.aspx.cs** file in the Visual Studio IDE and start the Web site, as you normally do, with the **Start Without Debugging** command.

2. Enter the following data for each of the moving cost calculations and click **Calculate**.

    ```
    Distance in Miles: 1000
    Weight in Pounds: 500
    No. of Flights: 2
    No. of Appliances: 3
    No. of Pianos: 2
    ```

3. After you enter the preceding numbers and click Calculate, the Moving Estimate text box displays a value of $1,507,

which isn't right. (The value should be $1,570.) Because you know the Distance in Miles, Weight in Pounds, and No. of Flights calculations are working correctly, you will start by examining the No. of Appliances calculation. You will examine the two values required by the appliances calculation: the appliances control value, which contains the number of appliances on the form, and the appliancesCost variable, which receives the result of the calculation. First, close your Web browser window and insert a breakpoint on the following statement:

```
double appliancesCost = Convert.ToDouble(
    appliances.Text) * 25;
```

4. Start the program in debugging mode by selecting **Start Debugging** from the **Debug** menu. Enter the values from Step 2 into the fields and click **Calculate**. The program enters break mode on the preceding statement. Select the **Step Into** command to execute the statement.

5. Select the name cell in the empty row in the Watch window, type **appliancesCost**, and then press **Enter**. The correct value, 75, appears in the Watch window. Therefore, the problem does not appear to be related to the appliances cost calculation.

6. Select the **Debug** menu and then select **Stop Debugging**.

7. Remove the breakpoint from the appliancesCost statement in the calculate_Click() event handler.

8. Next, you will examine the two values required by the piano calculation: the pianos control and the pianosCost variable. Insert a breakpoint on the following statement:

```
double pianosCost = Convert.ToDouble(pianos.Text) * 3.5;
```

9. Start the program in debugging mode by selecting the **Debug** menu and then selecting **Start Debugging**. Enter the values from Step 2 into the fields and click **Calculate**. The program enters break mode on the preceding statement. Select the **Step Into** command to execute the statement.

10. Select the name cell in the empty row in the Watch window, type **pianosCost**, and then press **Enter**. Because the cost to move a single piano is $35, the pianosCost variable should be updated to 70 after you execute the pianosCost = pianos * 3.5; statement. The correct value of 75 should appear in Watch window or the Command window. Instead, a value of 7 appears. You have probably already noticed that the calculation is multiplying the pianos variable by 3.5 instead of 35.

11. Select the **Debug** menu, select **Stop Debugging**, and then modify the incorrect statement so the value of the pianos control is multiplied by 35 instead of 3.5, as follows:

```
double pianosCost = Convert.ToDouble(pianos.Text) * 35;
```

12. Start the program with the **Start Without Debugging** command and enter the values from Step 2. The program should now function correctly, calculating a moving estimate of $1,570.

13. Close your Web browser window and Visual Studio.

Like the Locals, Watch, and Immediate windows, the Call Stack window also appears automatically in the debugger when you enter break mode. The term **call stack** refers to the order in which procedures, such as functions, methods, or event handlers, execute in a program. Each time a program calls a procedure, the procedure is added to the top of the call stack, and then removed after it finishes executing. For example, if you have an accountsPayable() function that calls an accountsReceivable() function, the computer must remember to return to the accountsPayable() function after the accountsReceivable() function finishes executing. Similarly, if the accountsReceivable() function calls a depositFunds() function after it has been called by the accountsPayable() function, the computer must remember to return to the accountsReceivable() function after the depositFunds() function finishes executing, then return to the accountsPayable() function after the accountsReceivable() function finishes executing.

The ability to view the contents of a call stack is very useful when tracing logic errors in large programs with multiple functions. Suppose you have a variable that is passed as an argument among several functions. Suppose also that the variable is being assigned the wrong value. Viewing the call stack, along with using tracing commands, makes it easier to locate the specific function causing the problem.

Short Quiz 3

1. Explain how to use break mode to trace program execution. What commands can you use to enter break mode?

2. Once your program is in break mode, which command do you use to execute all remaining code in the current function?

3. Explain how to use the Locals, Watch, and Immediate windows.

Handling Exceptions and Errors

Although error messages that are generated by programming languages such as C# are very helpful to programmers, they tend to scare users, who might think that they somehow caused the error. Errors can and will occur, but you should never let your users think that they did something wrong. Your goal should be to write code that anticipates any problems and gracefully deals with them. Writing code that anticipates and handles potential problems is often called **bulletproofing**. One bulletproofing technique you have already used has to do with validating submitted form data with validation controls and regular expressions. Another bulletproofing technique, **exception handling**, allows programs to handle problems as they occur in the execution of a program. The term **exception** indicates that something unexpected occurred while a program is running. An exception is not necessarily an error, although it can be. Typically, exceptions identify situations such as when a user enters the wrong type of data or if a database is not currently available.

Many advanced programming languages, including C#, include exception-handling capabilities. You use exception handling to test any type of input or functionality that is external to a program. For many programming languages, exception handling is most useful when connecting to a database or when evaluating user input. Although you could technically use exception handling for all of the code in your programs, your code should be tested thoroughly enough that it anticipates any potential problems that might occur.

There are three levels at which you can handle exceptions: code level, page level, and application level. You should always strive to handle any exceptions at the code level with `try...catch` blocks (as explained in the next section). However, if you can't handle an error at the code level, you can handle it at the page level. For Web sites with multiple pages that could raise exceptions, you can also handle errors at the application level. First, you will look at how to handle exceptions at the code level.

Throwing Exceptions

You execute code that might contain an exception in a **try statement**. The process by which a `try` statement generates an exception class object is referred to as "throwing an exception." The syntax for a `try` statement is as follows:

```
try {
    statements;
}
```

In C#, exceptions are represented by numerous classes that are based on the Exception class. For example, the ArithmeticException class represents exceptions that are thrown for errors in an arithmetic, casting, or conversion operation, and the MissingMemberException represents exceptions that are thrown when attempting to access a class method or property that does not exist. An exception class object is created if the statements within a try statement fail, depending on the type of exception. The following try block throws a DivideByZeroException object because the statements result in a divide-by-zero error:

```
try {
    int grossPay = 1000;
    int numberOfHours = 0;
    int grossHourlyPay = grossPay / numberOfHours;
}
```

You can also manually throw an exception by using a **throw statement** and an Exception object. The following example demonstrates how to use a regular expression to test whether an argument named emailAddress that is passed to a function named validateEmail() contains a valid e-mail address. If the e-mail address is invalid, the throw statement creates and throws an ArgumentException object. If the e-mail address is valid, a value of true is returned to the calling statement.

```
bool validateEmail(string emailAddress)
{
    Regex emailPattern = new Regex(@"^[_\w\-]
        +(\.[_\w\-]+)*@ [\w\-]+(\.[\w\-]+)*(\.[\D]{2,3})$");
    Match emailMatch = emailPattern.Match(emailAddress);
    if (!emailMatch.Success)
    {
        throw new ArgumentException();
    }
    else
        return true;
}
```

Catching Exceptions

The exception objects that are thrown from a try statement contain several properties and methods that describe what went wrong, including the Message property, which contains a message that describes the current exception, and the ToString() method, which returns a more detailed description of the exception. After you throw an error, you use a **catch statement** to handle, or "catch" the exception object. The syntax for a catch statement is as follows:

```
catch(exception_type identifier) {
    statements;
}
```

The `catch` statement is constructed with a single object parameter of the thrown exception type. You add statements to the `catch` statement that handle the exception or print an error message to the user. The following `catch` statement demonstrates how to catch the exception that is thrown by the `try` statement that causes a divide-by-zero exception. The `Response.Write()` statement uses the `Message` property of the `DivideByZeroException` object to print a description of the exception.

```
try
{
    int grossPay = 1000;
    int numberOfHours = 0;
    int grossHourlyPay = grossPay / numberOfHours;
}
catch (DivideByZeroException emailError)
{
    Response.Write(emailError.Message);
}
```

For exceptions that are generated with the `Exception` class, you can use the `Message` property of the exception object to access the error message that was created in the `try` statement. The following `catch` statement demonstrates how to catch the exception that is thrown by the `try` statement that evaluates the e-mail address.

```
catch (Exception emailError)
{
    Response.Write(emailError.Message);
}
```

It's important to understand that whenever a `try` statement throws an exception, the compiler executes the nearest `catch` statement that matches the exception type. If the thrown exception is within a `try` block, the compiler checks the `try` block for a matching `catch` statement. If the statement that throws the exception is within a `try` block, or if no `catch` statement in the current function or method matches the exception type, the compiler looks for a matching `catch` statement in the next function or method in the call stack. The compiler continues searching up the call stack until it locates a matching `catch` statement. If no matching `catch` statement is found within the call stack, the compiler relies on any page-level exception functionality that exists. If no page-level exception-handling functionality exists, the compiler looks to the application-level exception-handling functionality. Finally, if no application-level exception-handling functionality is found, the compiler displays a default error page, similar to the one shown in Figure 6-4. Your goal as a good ASP.NET programmer is to prevent visitors to your Web site from seeing the default error page, which can be extremely confusing to nonprogrammers. Later in this chapter, you will learn how to add error-handling functionality at the page and application levels.

In the last section, you saw a function named validateEmail() that used a throw statement to throw an ArgumentException error. Because the function did not include any catch statements, the compiler looks to the next function or method in the call stack for a matching catch statement. Let's assume that the validateEmail() function was called from within another function named validateFormData(). The function could contain the following try...catch block. The try statement calls the validateEmail() function. If the ArgumentException error is thrown within the validateEmail() function, the compiler will use the catch statement in the validateFormData() function because the validateEmail() function does not contain a matching catch statement.

```
void validateFormData()
{
    try
    {
        validateEmail("don@dongosselin.com");
    }
    catch (ArgumentException e)
    {
        Response.Write(e.Message);
    }
}
```

A try statement can contain more than one catch block. When an exception is thrown, the compiler looks for the first catch statement that can handle the exception, and ignores the other catch statements. For this reason, your catch statements should start with the most specific and proceed to the most general types of exceptions. For example, you can use the Exception class to catch any exception that is thrown. However, because it can handle all exceptions, if it is listed first in a try statement, any additional catch statements will be ignored. In the following example, the more specific ArgumentException catch block is ignored because the Exception argument catch block is listed first in the try statement.

```
void validateFormData()
{
    try
    {
        validateEmail("don@dongosselin.com");
    }
    catch (Exception e)
    {
        Response.Write(e.Message);
    }
    catch (ArgumentException e)
    {
        Response.Write(e.Message);
    }
}
```

The preceding code should instead be written as follows, with the more specific `ArgumentException` catch block coming first:

```csharp
void validateFormData()
{
    try
    {
        validateEmail("don@dongosselin.com");
    }
    catch (Exception e)
    {
        Response.Write(e.Message);
    }
    catch (ArgumentException e)
    {
        Response.Write(e.Message);
    }
}
```

It's considered bad programming form to use the `Exception` class to catch thrown exceptions. Instead, you should always use the most specific exception classes possible.

349

Executing Final Exception-Handling Tasks

The exception-handling functionality in C# also includes a **finally statement** that executes regardless of whether its associated `try` block throws an exception. You normally use a `finally` statement to perform some type of cleanup or any necessary tasks after code is evaluated with a `try` statement. The syntax for a `finally` statement is as follows:

```csharp
finally {
    statements;
}
```

If a construct contains `try` and `finally` statements, but no `catch` statement, the `finally` statement executes before the compiler begins searching at a higher level for a `catch` statement.

The following example demonstrates how to use a `finally` statement with the `try...catch` block that validates the e-mail address. The `finally` statement uses the `ToLower()` method to convert the e-mail address to lowercase.

```csharp
try
{
    Regex emailPattern = new Regex(@"^[_\w\-]
        +(\.[_\w\-]+)*@[\w\-]+(\.[\w\-]+)*(\.[\D]{2,3})$");
    Match emailMatch = emailPattern.Match(email.Text);
    if (!emailMatch.Success)
    {
        throw new Exception("<p>One or more of the e-mail
            addresses you entered does not appear
            to be valid.</p>");
    }
}
```

```
catch (Exception emailError)
{
    Response.Write(emailError.Message);
}
finally
{
    email.Text = email.Text.ToLower();
}
```

Handling Page-Level Errors

The most basic method of handling errors at the page level is to assign an error page to the `ErrorPage` attribute of the `@ Page` directive. The page you assign to the `ErrorPage` attribute should be a generic Web page that informs the user that an error occurred.

To programmatically control page-level error handling, you must create a page error event handler. Unlike other types of page events, the compiler does not automatically recognize a function named `Page_Error()` as the page error event handler. Instead, you must specify the name of the event-handler function with the `System.EventHandler()` function in the `Page_Load()` event handler using a statement similar to the following. The argument passed to the `System.EventHandler()` function is the name you want to use for the error event handler.

```
Page.Error += new System.EventHandler(Page_Error);
```

To redirect the Web browser to an error page from an error event handler, you must pass the name of the page to the `System.Transfer()` method. Note that after handling an error, you must clear it with the `Server.ClearError()` method. The following page error event handler redirects the browser to a page named ErrorPage.htm and then clears the error:

```
void Page_Error(Object Source, EventArgs E)
{
    Server.Transfer("ErrorPage.htm", true);
    Server.ClearError();
}
```

To pass an error to a page error event handler, you must throw it from the code level. For example, assuming there are no additional `catch` statements further up the call stack, the following `catch` statement throws the e-mail error to the page level:

```
catch (Exception emailError)
{
    throw emailError;
}
```

Handling Application-Level Errors

The statements that you use to handle errors at the application level are the same as the page level. For example, you use the `System.Transfer()` method to redirect users to a generic error page, the `Server.ClearError()` method to clear errors, and the `Server.GetLastError()` method to access the last exception that occurred. You can also use the same procedures for logging errors to a file. Unlike page error event handlers, application errors are handled in the **Global.asax file**, which contains event handlers for handling application events. You add a Global.asax file by selecting the Website menu and then selecting Add New Item. In the Add New Item dialog box, select Global Application Class from the Visual Studio installed templates section of the Templates area. Leave the suggested filename set to Global.asax and the Language box set to Visual C# and click Add. The Global.asax file opens in the Code Editor, and contains various empty application-level event handlers, as shown in Figure 6-13.

```
1   <%@ Application Language="C#" %>
2
3   <script runat="server">
4
5       void Application_Start(object sender, EventArgs e)
6       {
7           // Code that runs on application startup
8
9       }
10
11      void Application_End(object sender, EventArgs e)
12      {
13          //  Code that runs on application shutdown
14
15      }
16
17      void Application_Error(object sender, EventArgs e)
18      {
19          // Code that runs when an unhandled error occurs
20
21      }
22
23      void Session_Start(object sender, EventArgs e)
24      {
```

Figure 6-13 Global.asax file

Unlike with the page error event handler, you do not need to specify the name of the application event handler in the `Page_Load()` event handler.

One of the event handlers that is created by default in the Global.asax file is `Application_Error()`. The following example demonstrates how to use the `System.Transfer()` and `Server.ClearError()` methods in the `Application_Error()` event handler.

```
void Application_Error(object sender, EventArgs e)
{
    Server.Transfer("HTMLPage.htm", true);
    Server.ClearError();
}
```

You cannot include `Response.Write()` or other types of output statements in the Global.asax file. Instead, you must redirect the browser to another page with the `System.Transfer()` method.

Short Quiz 4

1. What does the term "bulletproofing" mean when it comes to writing code?

2. What is an exception?

3. Explain how to create a `try...catch` block.

4. What is the purpose of a `finally` statement?

5. How do you programmatically control page-level error handling?

Summing Up

- All programming languages, including C#, have their own syntax, or rules.

- The term logic refers to the order in which various parts of a program run, or execute.

- Any error in a program that causes it to function incorrectly, whether because of incorrect syntax or flaws in logic, is called a bug. The term debugging refers to the act of tracing and resolving errors in a program.

- Syntax errors occur when the interpreter fails to recognize code.

- Compiler error messages occur for any syntax errors in a source file and contain a description of the error and the name of the file in which the error occurred. Warning messages occur for any potential problems that might exist in your code, but they are not serious enough to cause a compiler error.

352

- Run-time errors happen when a problem occurs while a program is executing.

- Logic errors are flaws in a program's design that prevent the program from running as you anticipate.

- To print detailed information about errors to the browser window, you need to include the `Debug` attribute in the `@ Page` directive and assign it a value of true.

- The `Response.Write()` statement provides one of the most useful ways to trace code. You place a `Response.Write()` method at different points in your program and use it to display the contents of a variable, an array, or the value returned from a function.

- When using `Response.Write()` statements to trace bugs, it is helpful to use a driver program, which is a simplified, temporary program that is used for testing functions and other code.

- Stub functions are empty functions that serve as placeholders (or "stubs") for a program's actual functions.

- Another method of locating bugs in a program is to transform lines that you think might be causing problems into comments.

- If you cannot locate a bug using any of the methods described in this chapter, perform a line-by-line analysis of your XHTML code, making sure that all tags have opening and closing brackets.

- When you suspect that your code contains logic errors, you must analyze each statement on a case-by-case basis.

- Tracing is the examination of individual statements in an executing program.

- You can view diagnostic trace information for page requests by assigning a value of true to the `Trace` attribute of the `@ Page` processing directive.

- After enabling application-level tracing, you can view the trace information log using Trace Viewer.

- The Visual Studio IDE provides a program called the debugger that contains several tools that can help you trace each line of code, creating a much more efficient method of finding and resolving logic errors.

- The term break mode refers to the temporary suspension of program execution so that you can monitor values and trace program execution.

- A breakpoint is a statement in the code at which program execution enters break mode.

354

- The Step Into command executes an individual line of code and then pauses until you instruct the debugger to continue.

- The Step Over command allows you to skip function calls.

- The Step Out command executes all remaining code in the current function.

- The Locals window displays all local variables within the currently executing function, regardless of whether they have been initialized.

- The Watch window monitors both variables and expressions in break mode.

- You can use the Immediate window to monitor specific variables and expressions in break mode.

- The term call stack refers to the order in which procedures, such as functions, methods, or event handlers, execute in a program.

- Writing code that anticipates and handles potential problems is often called bulletproofing.

- Exception handling allows programs to handle errors as they occur in the execution of a program. The term exception refers to some type of error that occurs in a program.

- The most basic method of handling errors at the page level is to assign an error page to the `ErrorPage` attribute of the `@ Page` directive.

- To programmatically control page-level error handling, you must create a page error event handler.

- Application errors are handled in the Global.asax file, which contains event handlers for handling application events.

Comprehension Check

1. _____ errors are problems in the design of a program that prevent it from running as you anticipate.

   a. Syntax

   b. Logic

   c. Run-time

   d. Application

2. If the compiler encounters a problem while a program is executing, that problem is called a(n) _____ error.

   a. run-time

   b. logic

   c. application

   d. syntax

3. Which of the following statements causes a syntax error?

   a. `resForm.Visible() = true;`

   b. `Response.Write("Available points: " + availPoints)`

   c. `return salesTotal;`

   d. `Response.Write("Do you really want to submit the form?");`

4. Which of the following functions causes a run-time error?

   a.
   ```
   void calcProfit() {
         double grossProfit = 50000;
         double netProfit = 40000;
         double margin = grossProfit - netProfit;
         double marginPercent = margin / grossProfit;
   }
   ```

   b.
   ```
   void calcProfit() {
         double grossProfit = 60000;
         double netProfit = 50000;
         double margin = grossProfit - netProfit;
         double marginPercent = margin / grossProfit;
   }
   ```

   c.
   ```
   void calcProfit() {
         double grossProfit = 50000;
         double netProfit = 50000;
         double margin = grossProfit - netProfit;
         double marginPercent = margin / grossProfit;
   }
   ```

   d.
   ```
   void calcProfit() {
         double grossProfit = 20000;
         double netProfit = 30000;
         double margin = grossProfit - netProfit;
         double marginPercent = margin / grossProfit;
   }
   ```

5. Which of the following if statements is logically incorrect?

a. ```
if (urlMatch.Success)
      document.write("Valid URL.");
```

b. ```
if (urlMatch.Success) document.write(
    "Valid URL.");
```

c. ```
if (urlMatch.Success);
      document.write("Valid URL.");
```

d. ```
if (urlMatch.Success) {
      document.write("Valid URL.");
   }
```

6. Error messages identify the exact location in a document where the error occurred. True or False?

7. Explain the various techniques and tools that you can use to manually trace the individual statements in an executing program.

8. Explain how to use a driver program.

9. What is the name of the Trace Viewer file?

a. Trace.htm

b. Trace.asp

c. Trace.aspx

d. Trace.axd

10. In which of the following modes is program execution temporarily suspended, or paused, so that you can monitor values and trace program execution?

a. Step

b. Break

c. Continue

d. Suspend

11. Which of the following debugging commands do you use to execute the rest of the program normally or until another breakpoint is encountered?

a. Continue

b. Run

c. Restart

d. Stop Debugging

12. Which debugging command executes all the statements in the next function?

    a. Step

    b. Step Into

    c. Step Out

    d. Step Over

13. What is the purpose of the call stack? How can you use it to debug your programs?

14. When and why should you use exception handling with your programs?

15. After you throw an error, you use a(n) _____ statement to handle the error.

    a. `exception`

    b. `try`

    c. `catch`

    d. `finally`

16. How do you enable application-level debugging?

17. Which of the following windows displays all local variables within the currently executing function, regardless of whether they have been initialized?

    a. Locals

    b. Watch

    c. Immediate

    d. Output

18. What does the compiler do if a `try` block executes and no `catch` statement in the current function or method matches the exception type?

19. The compiler does not automatically recognize a function named `Page_Error()` as the page error event handler. True or False?

20. Which of the following methods redirect users to another Web page?

    a. `System.Redirect()`

    b. `System.Transfer()`

    c. `System.URL()`

    d. `System.Go()`

Reinforcement Exercises

Exercise 6-1

In this project, you will create and fix a program that prints text strings.

1. Create a new Web site and save it in a folder named StringErrors in your Exercises folder for Chapter 6.

2. Open the **Default.aspx** file in the Code Editor and change the content of the `<title>` element to "String Errors".

3. Add a Literal control to the Web form and change its ID to `outputString`:

```
<asp:Literal ID="outputString" runat="server" />
```

4. Open the Default.aspx.cs file in the Code Editor and add the following statement to the Page_Load() event handler:

```
outputString.Text = "Babe Ruth was also known as
    the "Bambino" and the "Sultan of Swat".");
```

5. Select the **Build** menu and then select **Build Page**. You should receive several error messages. The problem with the code is that the string in the `Response.Write()` statement contains nested double quotations. To fix the problem, you need to escape the double quotations with a backslash character.

6. Return to the document and add escape characters to the string in the `Response.Write()` statement, as follows:

```
Response.Write("<p>Babe Ruth was also known as
    the \"Bambino\" and the \"Sultan of Swat\".</p>");
```

7. Select the **Debug** menu and then select **Start Without Debugging**. The text should display correctly without any error messages.

8. Close your Web browser window.

Exercise 6-2

In this project, you will create and fix a program that displays stock values.

1. Create a new Web site and save it in a folder named StockValues in your Exercises folder for Chapter 6.

2. Open the **Default.aspx.cs** file in the Code Editor and add the following statements to the Page_Load() event handler:

```
string stockShares == 100;
string stockValue == 22.75;
Response.Write = "<p>Current stock value: ";
Response.Write = String.Format("{0:C}",
    StockShares * StockValue) + ".</p>";
```

3. Build and debug the program. A single statement, "Current stock value: $2,275.00." should print to the screen.

Exercise 6-3

In this project, you will create and fix a program that contains the formula for converting Fahrenheit temperatures to Celsius.

1. Create a new Web site and save it in a folder named ConvertToCelsius in your Exercises folder for Chapter 6.

2. Open the **Default.aspx** file in the Code Editor and change the content of the `<title>` element to "Convert to Celsius".

3. Add a Literal control to the Web form and change its ID to convertedTemp:

```
<asp:Literal ID="convertedTemp" runat="server" />
```

4. Open the Default.aspx.cs file in the Code Editor and add to the Page_Load() event handler the following declaration for a variable named fTemp that represents a Fahrenheit temperature. The variable is assigned a value of 68 degrees.

```
double fTemp = 68;
```

5. Add the following two statements to the end of the Page_Load() event handler. The first statement declares a variable named cTemp that will store the converted temperature. The right operand includes the formula for converting from Fahrenheit to Celsius. The last statement prints the value assigned to the cTemp variable.

```
double cTemp = fTemp - 32 * 5 / 9;
convertedTemp.Text = fTemp + " degrees Fahrenheit
    is equal to " + Convert.ToInt16(cTemp)
    + " degrees Celsius.";
```

6. Select the **Debug** menu and then select **Start Without Debugging**. 68 degrees Fahrenheit is equivalent to 20 degrees Celsius. However, the formula incorrectly calculates that 68 degrees Fahrenheit is equivalent to a value of 51 degrees Celsius. You will need to modify the formula so that it uses the correct order of precedence to convert the temperature.

7. Close your Web browser window and modify the order of precedence in the Fahrenheit-to-Celsius formula by adding parentheses as follows:

```
double cTemp = (fTemp - 32) * 5 / 9;
```

8. Select the **Debug** menu and then select **Start Without Debugging**. The temperature should calculate correctly as 20 degrees Celsius.

9. Close your Web browser window.

Exercise 6-4

In this project, you will create and fix a simple form that displays the value of a letter grade.

1. Create a new Web site and save it in a folder named Letter-Grades in your Exercises folder for Chapter 6.

2. Open the **Default.aspx** file in the Code Editor and change the content of the `<title>` element to "Letter Grades".

3. Add the following text and controls to the Web form:

```
Letter grade: <asp:TextBox ID="letterGrade"
runat="server"></asp:TextBox>
<asp:Button ID="checkGrade"
runat="server" Text="Button"
OnClick="checkGrade_Click" />
<asp:Literal ID="gradeValue" runat="server" />
```

4. Open the **Default.aspx.cs** file in the Code Editor and add the following event handler:

```
protected void checkGrade_Click()
{
}
```

5. Add the following switch statement to the `checkGrade_Click()` event handler:

```
switch (letterGrade)
    case "A":
        grade.Text = ("Your grade is excellent.");
        break;
```

```
        case "B":
            grade.Text = ("Your grade is good.");
            break;
        case "C":
            grade.Text = ("Your grade is fair.");
            break;
        case "D":
            grade.Text = ("You are barely passing.");
            break;
        case "F":
            grade.Text = ("You failed.");
            break;
        default:
            grade.Text = ("Invalid letter!");
```

6. Select the **Build** menu and then select **Build Page**. You should receive two error messages. The first error is about a missing brace. The problem is that the statements within the `switch` statement are not contained within braces. Modify the `switch` statement so it includes braces, as follows:

```
switch (letterGrade)
{
        case "A":
            grade.Text = ("Your grade is excellent.");
            break;
        case "B":
            grade.Text = ("Your grade is good.");
            break;
        case "C":
            grade.Text = ("Your grade is fair.");
            break;
        case "D":
            grade.Text = ("You are barely passing.");
            break;
        case "F":
            grade.Text = ("You failed.");
            break;
        default:
            grade.Text = ("Invalid letter!");
}
```

7. Select the **Build** menu and then select **Build Page**. You should receive eight more error messages. The first message states that no overload for 'checkGrade_Click' matches delegate 'System.EventHandler'. You should recognize this message from earlier in the chapter. This means that the compiler does not recognize the `checkGrade_Click()` function as an event handler. This is because the event handler is missing the required `Object` argument, which represents the raised event, and the `EventArgs` parameter, which is

used for passing data with an event. Add the following parameters to the checkGrade_Click() function: **Object Source, EventArgs E**.

8. Select the **Build** menu and then select **Build Page**. You should receive seven more error messages. The first message states that the name 'letter' does not exist in the current context. This error is caused by the fact that the checkGrade_Click() event handler does not define a variable named letter, which is used in the switch statement to evaluate the letter grade. The six additional error messages are not so clear. They state that the name 'grade' does not exist in the current context. The cause of this error is not so readily obvious from the message. The problem is that the control's ID is gradeValue, not grade. First, add the following statement to the beginning of the checkGrade_Click() event handler to define the letter variable from the value is the letterGrade control: string letter = letterGrade.Text;. Then, change the control IDs in the switch statement from grade to gradeValue.

9. Select the **Build** menu and then select **Build Page** again. You should receive one more error message. The message states that a control cannot fall through from one case label ('default:') to another. The reason this error message occurs is because the default label in the switch statement is missing a break statement. Add the missing break statement above the switch statement's closing brace.

10. Select the **Debug** menu and then select **Start Without Debugging**. The program should build without any error messages, and the Web page opens. Test the Web page's functionality, and then close your Web browser.

Exercise 6-5

In this project, you will create and fix a program with an if...else statement.

1. Create a new Web site and save it in a folder named Evaluate-Condition in your Exercises folder for Chapter 6.

2. Open the **Default.aspx.cs** file in the Code Editor and add the following statements to the Page_Load() error handler:

```
bool displayAlert = false;
string conditionState = "";
if (displayAlert = true)
    conditionState = "<p>Condition is true.</p>";
    Response.Write(conditionState);
```

```
else if (displayAlert = false)
    conditionState = "<p>Condition is false.</p>";
    Response.Write(conditionState);
else
    conditionState = "<p>No condition.</p>";
    Response.Write(conditionState);
```

3. Build and debug the program. The code you typed should print "Condition is false." to the screen. However, the code prints "Condition is true." to the screen.

Discovery Projects

Project 6-1

The Projects folder for Chapter 6 on your Data Disk contains copies of some of the programs you created earlier in this text. However, all of the programs contain errors. Use any of the debugging skills you have learned in this section to correct the errors. You may review earlier tutorials to see how the program should function—but do *not* copy or review the correct syntax. Use these exercises as an opportunity to test and improve your debugging skills. The chapter number in which you created each program is appended to the name of the document. After you fix each document, rename the directory by replacing the _Chapter0x portion of the name with "_Fixed". The documents you must correct are as follows:

- OrderFulfillment_Chapter02
- BMI_Chapter02
- CentsToDollars_Chapter03
- LeapYear_Chapter03
- TitleCase_Chapter05
- Palindromes_Chapter05

Project 6-2

Your Projects folder for Chapter 6 contains a Web site folder named MinimumAge. This program contains a text box where a user can enter a birth date and then click a Verify button, which determines whether the user is 21 or older. The program has several problems that prevent it from working successfully. Find and debug the errors.

Project 6-3

One of the most important aspects of creating a good program is the design and analysis phase of the project. Conducting a good design and analysis phase is critical to minimizing bugs in your program. Search the Internet or your local library for information on this topic. Explain the best way to handle the design and analysis phase of a software project.

Project 6-4

Equally important as minimizing bugs during software development is the testing phase. Search the Internet or your local library for information on software testing. Then design a plan for thoroughly testing your ASP.NET programs before deploying them on the Web.

CHAPTER 7

Working with Databases and SQL Server Express

In this chapter you will:

- ◎ Study the basics of databases and SQL Server
- ◎ Work with SQL Server databases
- ◎ Define database tables
- ◎ Work with database records

A common use of Web pages is to gather information that is stored in a database on a Web server. Most server-side scripting languages, including ASP.NET, allow you to create Web pages that can read and write data to and from databases. In this chapter, you will take a break from ASP.NET to learn how to work with SQL Server databases. Your goal is to learn the basics of database manipulation. Then, in Chapter 8, you will apply many of the techniques from this chapter to ASP.NET programs that manipulate SQL Server databases.

Introduction to Databases

Formally defined, a **database** is an ordered collection of information from which a computer program can quickly access information. You can probably think of many databases that you work with in your everyday life. For example, your address book is a database. So is the card file containing recipes in your kitchen. Other examples of databases include a company's employee directory and a file cabinet containing client information. Essentially, any information that can be organized into ordered sets of data, then quickly retrieved, can be considered a database. A collection of hundreds of baseball cards thrown into a shoebox is not a database because an individual card cannot be quickly or easily retrieved (except by luck). However, if the baseball card collection was organized in binders by team, and then further organized according to each player's field position or batting average, it could be considered a database because you could quickly locate a specific card.

The information stored in computer databases is actually stored in tables similar to spreadsheets. Each row in a database table is called a record. A **record** in a database is a single complete set of related information. Each recipe in a recipe database, for instance, is a single database record. Each column in a database table is called a field. **Fields** are the individual categories of information stored in a record. Examples of fields that might exist in a recipe database include ingredients, cooking time, cooking temperature, and so on.

To summarize, you can think of databases as consisting of tables, which consist of records, which consist of fields. Figure 7-1 shows an example of an employee directory for programmers at an application development company. The database consists of five records, one for each employee. Each record consists of six fields: `last_name`, `first_name`, `address`, `city`, `state`, and `zip`.

Fields			Rows		
last_name	first_name	address	city	state	zip
Blair	Dennis	204 Spruce Lane	Brookfield	MA	01506
Hernandez	Louis	68 Boston Post Road	Spencer	MA	01562
Miller	Erica	271 Baker Hill Road	Brookfield	MA	01515
Morinaga	Scott	17 Ashley Road	Brookfield	MA	01515
Picard	Raymond	1113 Oakham Road	Barre	MA	01531

Figure 7-1   Employee directory database

The database in Figure 7-1 is an example of a flat-file database, one of the simplest types of databases. A **flat-file database** stores information in a single table. For simple collections of information, flat-file databases are usually adequate. With large and complex collections of information, flat-file databases can become unwieldy. A better solution for large and complex databases is a relational database. A **relational database** stores information across multiple related tables. Although you will not actually work with a relational database in this chapter, understanding how they work is helpful because relational databases are among the most common in use today.

Understanding Relational Databases

Relational databases consist of one or more related tables. In fact, large relational databases can consist of dozens or hundreds of related tables. Although relational databases can consist of many tables, you create relationships within the database by working with two tables at a time. One table in a relationship is always considered to be the primary table, whereas the other table is considered to be the related table. A **primary table** is the main table in a relationship that is referenced by another table. A **related table** (also called a **child table**) references a primary table in a relational database. Tables in a relationship are connected using primary and foreign keys. A **primary key** is a field that contains a unique identifier for each record in a primary table. A primary key is a type of **index**, which identifies records in a database to make retrievals and sorting faster. An index can consist of just a primary key or it can be a combination of multiple fields. A **foreign key** is a field in a related table that refers to the primary key in a primary table. Primary and foreign keys link records across multiple tables in a relational database.

There are three basic types of relationships within a relational database: one-to-one, one-to-many, and many-to-many. A **one-to-one relationship** exists between two tables when a related table contains exactly one record for each record in the primary table. You create one-to-one relationships when you want to break information into multiple, logical sets. It is important to understand that information in the tables in a one-to-one relationship can usually be placed within a single table. However, you might want to break the information into multiple tables to better organize the information into logical sets. Another reason for using one-to-one relationships is that they allow you to make the information in one of the tables confidential and accessible only by certain individuals. For example, you might want to create a personnel table that contains basic information about an employee, similar to the information in the table in Figure 7-1. Yet, you might also want to create a payroll table that contains confidential information about each employee's salary, benefits, and other types of compensation, and that can be accessed only by the Human Resources and Accounting departments. Figure 7-2 shows two tables, Employees and Payroll, with a one-to-one relationship. The primary table is the employee information table from Figure 7-1. The related table is a payroll table that contains confidential salary and compensation information. Notice that each table contains an identical number of records; one record in the primary table corresponds to one record in the related table. The relationship is achieved by adding a primary key to the Employees table and a foreign key to the Payroll table.

Primary key

Employees table

employee_id	last_name	first_name	address	city	state	zip
101	Blair	Dennis	204 Spruce Lane	Brookfield	MA	01506
102	Hernandez	Louis	68 Boston Post Road	Spencer	MA	01562
103	Miller	Erica	271 Baker Hill Road	Brookfield	MA	01515
104	Morinaga	Scott	17 Ashley Road	Brookfield	MA	01515
105	Picard	Raymond	1113 Oakham Road	Barre	MA	01531

Foreign key

Payroll table

employee_id	start_date	pay_rate	health_coverage	year_vested	401K
101	2002	$21.25	none	na	no
102	1999	$28.00	Family Plan	2001	yes
103	1997	$24.50	Individual	na	yes
104	1994	$36.00	Family Plan	1996	yes
105	1995	$31.00	Individual	1997	yes

Figure 7-2 One-to-one relationship

A **one-to-many relationship** exists in a relational database when one record in a primary table has many related records in a related table. You create a one-to-many relationship to eliminate redundant information in a single table. Primary and foreign keys are the only pieces of information in a relational database table that should be duplicated. Breaking tables into multiple related tables to reduce redundant and duplicate information is called **normalization**. The elimination of redundant information (normalization) reduces the size of a database and makes the data easier to work with. For example, consider the table in Figure 7-3. The table lists every programming language in which the programmer is proficient. Notice that each programmer's name is repeated for each programming language with which she is most familiar. This repetition is an example of redundant information that can occur in a single table.

In some databases, the table containing multiple records for one entity (for example, the programming language table in Figure 7-4) is the primary table. In these cases, the relationship is often referred to as a many-to-one relationship.

369

employee_id	last_name	first_name	language
101	Blair	Dennis	JavaScript
101	Blair	Dennis	ASP.NET
102	Hernandez	Louis	JavaScript
102	Hernandez	Louis	ASP.NET
102	Hernandez	Louis	Java
103	Miller	Erica	JavaScript
103	Miller	Erica	ASP.NET
103	Miller	Erica	Java
103	Miller	Erica	C++
104	Morinaga	Scott	JavaScript
104	Morinaga	Scott	ASP.NET
104	Morinaga	Scott	Java
105	Picard	Raymond	JavaScript
105	Picard	Raymond	ASP.NET

Figure 7-3 Table with redundant information

A one-to-many relationship provides a more efficient and less redundant method of storing this information in a database. Figure 7-4 shows the same information organized into a one-to-many relationship.

Employees table ("one" side)

employee_id	last_name	first_name	address	city	state	zip
101	Blair	Dennis	204 Spruce Lane	Brookfield	MA	01506
102	Hernandez	Louis	68 Boston Post Road	Spencer	MA	01562
103	Miller	Erica	271 Baker Hill Road	Brookfield	MA	01515
104	Morinaga	Scott	17 Ashley Road	Brookfield	MA	01515
105	Picard	Raymond	1113 Oakham Road	Barre	MA	01531

Languages table ("many" side)

employee_id	language
101	JavaScript
101	ASP.NET
102	JavaScript
102	ASP.NET
102	Java
103	JavaScript
103	ASP.NET
103	Java
103	C++
104	JavaScript
104	ASP.NET
104	Java
105	JavaScript
105	ASP.NET

One record in the top table is linked to many records in the bottom table

Figure 7-4 One-to-many relationship

Although Figure 7-4 is an example of a one-to-many relationship, the tables are not normalized because the language field contains duplicate values. Recall that primary and foreign keys are the only pieces of information in a relational database that should be duplicated. To further reduce repetition, you could organize the Languages table in Figure 7-4 into another one-to-many relationship. However, a better choice is to create a many-to-many relationship. A **many-to-many relationship** exists in a relational database when many records in one table are related to many records in another table.

Consider the relationship between programmers and programming languages. Each programmer can work with many programming languages, and each programming language can be used by many programmers. To create a many-to-many relationship, you must use a junction table because most relational database systems cannot work directly with many-to-many relationships. A **junction table** creates a one-to-many relationship for each of the two tables in a many-to-many relationship. A junction table contains foreign keys from the two tables in a many-to-many relationship, along with any other fields that correspond to a many-to-many relationship. Figure 7-5 contains an example of a many-to-many relationship between the Employees table and a Languages table. The Employees table contains a primary key named employee_id, and the Languages table contains a primary key named language_id. A junction table named Experience contains two foreign keys, one corresponding to the employee_id primary key in the Employees table and one corresponding to the language_id primary key in the Languages table. The Experience junction table also contains a field named years. You add records to the Experience junction table to build a list of the years that each programmer has been working with a particular programming language.

Employees table

employee_id	last_name	first_name	address	city	state	zip
101	Blair	Dennis	204 Spruce Lane	Brookfield	MA	01506
102	Hernandez	Louis	68 Boston Post Road	Spencer	MA	01562
103	Miller	Erica	271 Baker Hill Road	Brookfield	MA	01515
104	Morinaga	Scott	17 Ashley Road	Brookfield	MA	01515
105	Picard	Raymond	1113 Oakham Road	Barre	MA	01531

Languages table

language_id	language
10	JavaScript
11	ASP.NET
12	Java
13	C++

Experience junction table

employee_id	language_id	years
101	10	5
101	11	4
102	10	3
102	11	2
102	12	3
103	10	2
103	11	3
103	12	6
103	13	3
104	10	7
104	11	5
104	12	8
105	10	4
105	11	2

Figure 7-5   Many-to-many relationship

Working with Database Management Systems

With a grasp of basic database design, you can now begin to consider how to create and manipulate databases. An application or collection of applications used to access and manage a database is called a **database management system**, or **DBMS**. A DBMS is also used to define a database's **schema**, which is the structure of a database, including its tables, fields, and relationships. Database management systems run on many different platforms, ranging from personal computers, to client/server systems, to mainframes. Different database management systems exist for different types of database formats. A database management system that stores data in a flat-file format is called a **flat-file database management system**. A database management system that stores data in a relational format is called a **relational database**

management system, or **RDBMS**. Other types of database management systems include hierarchical and network database management systems. In addition to SQL Server, some of the more popular commercial relational database management systems you might have heard of include Oracle, Sybase, and Informix for high-end computers such as UNIX or Linux systems, and Microsoft Access, Visual FoxPro, and Paradox for PCs. Two popular open source relational database management systems are MySQL and PostgresSQL.

Database management systems perform many of the same functions as other types of applications you might have encountered, such as word-processing and spreadsheet programs. For example, database management systems create new database files and contain interfaces that allow users to enter and manipulate data. One of the most important functions of a database management system is the structuring and preservation of the database file. In addition, a database management system must ensure that data is stored correctly in a database's tables, regardless of the database format (flat-file, relational, hierarchical, or network). In relational databases, the database management system ensures that the appropriate information is entered according to the relationship structure in the database tables. Many DBMS systems also have security features that can be used to restrict user access to specific types of data.

Another important aspect of a database management system is its querying capability. A **query** is a structured set of instructions and criteria for retrieving, adding, modifying, and deleting database information. Most database management systems use a **data manipulation language**, or **DML**, for creating queries. Different database management systems support different data manipulation languages. However, **Structured Query Language**, or **SQL** (pronounced sequel), has become somewhat of a standard data manipulation language among many database management systems.

Many database management systems also use a data definition language, or DDL, for creating databases, tables, fields, and other components of a database.

Although working with an interface to design queries is helpful, you must still learn the database management system's data manipulation language. For example, when accessing databases with ASP.NET, you must use a data manipulation language. Because SQL is the underlying data manipulation language for many database management systems, including SQL Server, you will learn more about the language as you progress through this chapter.

It is important to understand that even though many database management systems support the same database formats (flat-file, relational, hierarchical, or network), each database management system is an individual application that creates its own proprietary file types. For example, even though Access and Paradox are both relational database management systems, Access creates its database files in a proprietary format with an extension of .mdb, whereas Paradox creates its database files in a proprietary format with an extension of .db. Although both Paradox and Access contain filters that allow you to import each other's file formats, the database files are not completely interchangeable between the two programs. The same is true for most database management systems; they can import each other's file formats, but they cannot directly read each other's files.

Querying Databases with Structured Query Language

Programmers at IBM invented SQL in the 1970s as a way to query databases for specific criteria. Since then, SQL has been adopted by numerous database management systems running on mainframes, minicomputers, and PCs. In 1986, the American National Standards Institute (ANSI) approved an official standard for the SQL language. In 1991, the X/Open and SQL Access Group created a standardized version of SQL known as the Common Applications Environment (CAE) SQL draft specification. Even with two major standards available, however, most database management systems use their own version of the SQL language. SQL Server uses Transact-SQL, which corresponds primarily to the ANSI SQL standard, although it includes a few of its own extensions to the language.

 If you ever work directly with another database management system, keep in mind that the SQL you learn in this chapter might not correspond directly to that database management system's version of SQL.

SQL uses fairly easy-to-understand statements to execute database commands. SQL statements are composed of keywords that perform actions on a database. Table 7-1 lists several SQL keywords that are common to most versions of SQL.

Keyword	Description
DELETE	Deletes a row from a table
FROM	Specifies the tables from which to retrieve or delete records
INSERT	Inserts a new row into a table
INTO	Determines the table into which records should be inserted
ORDER BY	Sorts the records returned from a table
SELECT	Returns information from a table
UPDATE	Saves changes to fields in a record
WHERE	Specifies the conditions that must be met for records to be returned from a query

Table 7-1   Common SQL keywords

The simple SQL statement SELECT * FROM Employees returns all fields (using the asterisk * wildcard) from the Employees table. The following code shows a more complex SQL statement that selects

You will study many of the basic SQL keywords in this chapter. For in-depth information on SQL statements supported in SQL Server, refer to the Transact-SQL Reference at *http://msdn.microsoft.com/en-us/library/ms189826.aspx.*

the last_name and first_name fields from the Employees table if the record's city field is equal to "Spencer." The results are then sorted by the last_name and first_name fields using the ORDER BY keyword. Notice that commas separate multiple field names.

```
SELECT last_name, first_name FROM Employees
WHERE city = "Spencer" ORDER BY last_name, first_name
```

Short Quiz 1

1. What are records and fields and how do they differ?

2. What are one-to-one, one-to-many, and many-to-many relationships?

3. What is a query and how do you create one?

Getting Started with SQL Server

The primary tool that you will use in this chapter, **Microsoft SQL Server Management Studio Express**, is a graphic tool for manipulating SQL Server databases. The main SQL Server Management Studio window is displayed in Figure 7-6.

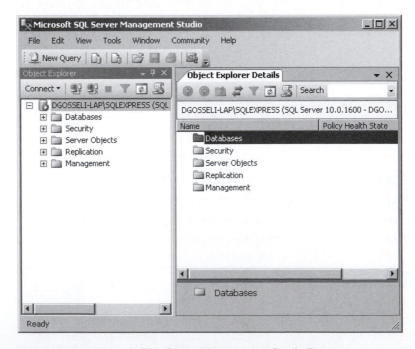

Figure 7-6 Microsoft SQL Server Management Studio Express

The most important tool in the SQL Server Management Studio is the New Query window, which you can use to execute SQL commands. Figure 7-7 displays a query window containing some typical SQL commands that are used for creating a table.

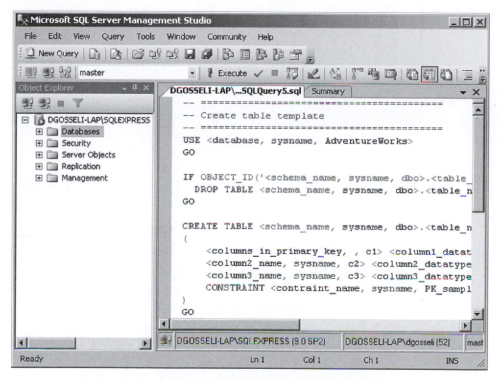

Figure 7-7 Query window in SQL Server Management Studio Express

Many database management systems include tools that make it easier to build queries. Figure 7-8 shows an example of the SQL Server Query Designer, which is a graphic tool for SQL Server that allows you to work with SQL Server queries in a graphical environment. You open SQL Server Query Designer from a query window by selecting Design Query in Editor from the Query menu. You can use the SQL Server Query Designer to create queries by typing SQL commands into the query area at the bottom of the screen or by dragging fields from the table objects in the upper portion of the screen to the criteria grid in the bottom portion of the screen.

Don't worry about trying to understand the SQL commands in Figure 7-7. The purpose of the figure is to simply show how a query window looks in SQL Server Management Studio Express.

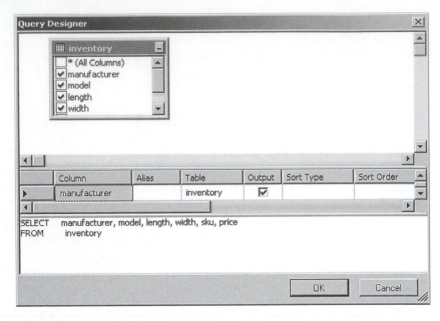

Figure 7-8   Query Designer in SQL Server Management Studio Express

Many of the SQL commands you will study in this chapter can be more easily executed from the Query Designer window. Nevertheless, to successfully execute SQL commands, you must first understand how to write them manually. You also need to know how to write SQL commands manually to access SQL Server databases from ASP. NET programs, as you will do in Chapter 8. For these reasons, you will use the query windows in this chapter to learn how to execute SQL commands. Feel free to experiment with the Query Designer window on your own, but be sure to use query windows to perform the exercises in this chapter.

Next, you install SQL Server Management Studio Express.

Installing SQL Server 2008 Management Studio Express

This section lists the procedures for installing SQL Server 2008 Management Studio Express.

To install SQL Server Management Studio Express:

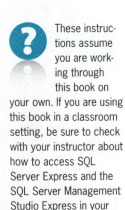

These instructions assume you are working through this book on your own. If you are using this book in a classroom setting, be sure to check with your instructor about how to access SQL Server Express and the SQL Server Management Studio Express in your school's environment.

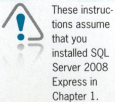

These instructions assume that you installed SQL Server 2008 Express in Chapter 1.

1. Start your Web browser and enter the following URL for the Microsoft Visual Studio Express Editions download page: ***http://www.microsoft.com/express/sql/download***. Click the **SQL Server 2008 Management Studio Express (SSMSE)** link. The Microsoft® SQL Server 2008 Management

Studio Express download page opens. Scroll to the Files in This Download section and click the **Download** button for the SQLManagementStudio_x86_ENU.exe file. When prompted, save the file to a temporary directory on your computer.

2. Open Windows Explorer or My Computer and navigate to the directory where you downloaded the SQLManagement-Studio_x86_ENU.exe file. Double-click the **SQLManage-mentStudio_x86_ENU.exe** file, which opens the SQL Server Installation Center window.

3. Click the **Installation** link on the left side of the SQL Server Installation Center window, and then click the **New SQL Server stand-alone installation or add features to an existing installation** link on the right side of the window. The Setup Support Rules screen of the SQL Server 2008 Setup wizard opens. This screen identifies problems that might occur when you install SQL Server Setup support files. You must correct any failures before continuing setup. Click **OK** if there are no failures. The Setup Support Files screen opens. Click the **Install** button to install the necessary setup support files. Click **Next** after the setup support files have been installed. The Installation Type screen opens.

4. On the Installation Type screen, click **Perform a new installation of SQL Server 2008** and then click **Next**. The Product Key screen of the SQL Server 2008 Setup wizard opens. Because you are installing a free edition, click **Next**. The License Terms screen opens.

5. In the License Terms screen, click the **I accept the license terms** button, and then click **Next**. The Feature Selection screen of the installation wizard opens. In the Feature Selection screen, click **Management Tools - Basic** in the Features area, and then click **Next**. The Disk Space Requirements screen opens.

6. In the Disk Space Requirements screen, verify that your computer contains sufficient disk space to install SQL Server Express, and then click **Next**. The Error and Usage Reporting screen opens.

7. The Error and Usage Reporting screen allows you to select the information that you would automatically like to send to Microsoft to help improve future versions of SQL Server. Leave both boxes on this screen deselected and click **Next**. The Installation Rules screen opens.

8. The Installation Rules screen lists any problems that will block the installation process. You must correct any failures before continuing setup. Click **Next** if there are no failures. The Ready to Install screen opens.

9. Click the **Install** button on the Ready to Install screen. The Installation Progress screen opens. When the setup process is complete, click **Next** to display the Complete screen, and then click **Close**.

10. Close the SQL Server Installation Center window.

Working with the SQL Server Management Studio Express

The query windows in SQL Server Management Studio Express are where most of the action occurs when you create or manipulate databases in SQL Server. If you are familiar with graphical database management systems, such as Microsoft Access, then a query window might take some getting used to because it offers no graphical tools for creating queries. However, keep in mind that most database management systems, including Access, use SQL to manipulate databases. The difference is that a SQL Server Management Studio Express query window includes no graphical "front end," and instead allows you to enter SQL commands directly. Once you get used to working with a SQL Server Management Studio Express query window, you might find that you prefer manipulating databases in this simpler window instead of in a graphical database management system because it provides more exact control over what is happening with your database. It's also worth repeating that you must understand how to write SQL commands manually to access SQL Server databases from ASP.NET programs, as you will do in the next chapter.

When you enter SQL commands in a query window, you must terminate the command with a semicolon. For example, the following SQL statement selects all fields from a table named `inventory` that contains the inventory for a skateboard shop:

```
SELECT * FROM inventory;
```

To execute the SQL commands in a query window, you select Execute from the Query menu. The Results window, which appears below the query window, displays the results of the SQL commands. The preceding statement prints all the records in the `inventory` table to the Results window, as shown in Figure 7-9.

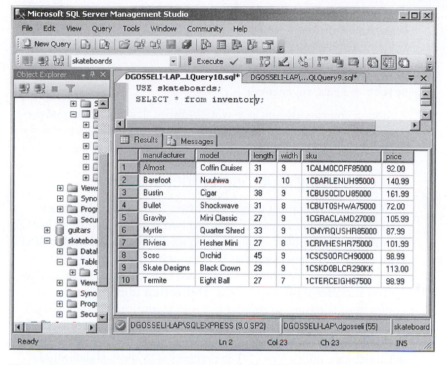

Figure 7-9 Results window showing results of a SQL query

If you omit the concluding semicolon when you enter an SQL statement, the query window assumes that you want to enter a multiple-line command. When entering more complex SQL statements, it's helpful to enter them on multiple lines to make them easier to read. The following example shows a multiple-line SQL command that selects all records from the `inventory` table where the price is less than 100, and sorts the returned records by price. Notice that the terminating semicolon is entered on the third line. Figure 7-10 shows the output in the Results window.

```
SELECT * from inventory
WHERE price < 100
ORDER BY price;
```

	manufacturer	model	length	width	sku	price
1	Bullet	Shockwave	31	8	1CBUTOSHWA75000	72.00
2	Myrtle	Quarter Shred	33	9	1CMYRQUSHR85000	87.99
3	Almost	Coffin Cruiser	31	9	1CALMOCOFF85000	92.00
4	Scsc	Orchid	45	9	1CSCSOORCH90000	98.99
5	Termite	Eight Ball	27	7	1CTERCEIGH67500	98.99

Figure 7-10 Output from a multiline SQL command

The SQL keywords you enter in a query window are not case sensitive, so you can enter any of the following statements to retrieve all fields in the `inventory` table:

```
SELECT * FROM inventory;
select * from inventory;
Select * From inventory;
```

Although you can use any case you like for SQL keywords, most programmers follow the convention of using uppercase letters to clearly distinguish SQL keywords from the names of databases, tables, and fields.

Understanding SQL Server Identifiers

In SQL Server, you must define identifiers (names) for databases, tables, fields, and indexes. You can use two types of identifiers in SQL Server: regular identifiers and delimited identifiers. **Regular identifiers** must begin with a letter, underscore (_), number sign (#), or at sign (@), and subsequent characters are restricted to letters, numbers, underscores, number signs, or at signs. **Delimited identifiers** do not conform to the rules of regular identifiers and can include spaces and other characters that are not allowed in regular identifiers. To use delimited identifiers in SQL statements, you must contain them within double quotations ("") or brackets ([]). Typical delimited identifiers include spaces in the identifier name. For example, suppose you have a table named `Exempt Employees` that contain fields named `First Name` and `Last Name`. To use a SQL SELECT statement to retrieve the `First Name` and `Last Name` records from the `Exempt Employees` table, you must enclose the delimited identifiers within double quotations or brackets, as follows:

```
SELECT * "First Name", "Last Name" FROM "Exempt Employees";
SELECT * [First Name], [Last Name] FROM [Exempt Employees];
```

Next, you will log in to SQL Server Management Studio Express. Before you can log in, you need to understand the Connect to Server dialog box, which is shown in Figure 7-11. Within the Connect to Server dialog box, the Server type list box allows you to select different types of SQL Server engines. To access the basic SQL Server database functionality that this book requires, leave the Server type list box set to Database Engine.

The next item in the Connect to Server dialog box, the Server name list box, identifies the name of the SQL Server instance. The term **instance** refers to a single installation of SQL Server. An SQL Server installation consists of one or more instances. You can use multiple instances of SQL Server for separate test and development environments, or for separate database environments that need to exist on the same server. You can log in with either the default instance or a named instance. The default instance, automatically named

SQLEXPRESS, refers to the instance that is created automatically when you first install SQL Server Express. By default, the Server name box contains a value of *COMPUTER-NAME*\SQLEXPRESS, which refers to the default instance. Instead of specifying the name of your computer, in most cases you can just use .\SQLEXPRESS to refer to your default instance of SQL Server Express. You should use .\SQLEXPRESS in this book, unless your instructor provides you with a named instance.

Next, the Authentication list box identifies the type of authentication for accessing SQL Server. You can choose from Windows Authentication or SQL Server Authentication. The default authentication mode, Windows Authentication, uses your Windows user account and password to log in to SQL Server. SQL Server Authentication requires users to log in with a SQL Server account. This book assumes you are using the default Windows Authentication, although your instructor might provide you with a SQL Server Authentication account.

 You can find your computer name by opening Windows Control Panel, and then by opening the System Properties dialog box. Your computer name is located on the Computer Name tab of the System Properties dialog box.

381

To log in to SQL Server Management Studio Express:

1. To start SQL Server Management Studio Express, click the **Start** button, point to **All Programs**, click **Microsoft SQL Server 2008**, and then click **SQL Server Management Studio**. The Connect to Server dialog box opens, as shown in Figure 7-11.

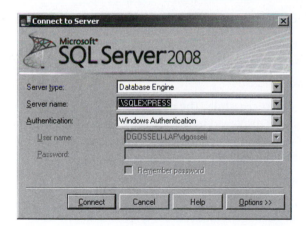

Figure 7-11   Connect to Server dialog box

2. Leave the Server type box set to **Database Engine**.

3. Enter .\SQLEXPRESS in the Server name box, replacing *COMPUTER-NAME* with the name of your computer. If your instructor provided you with a named SQL Server instance, then enter *COMPUTER-NAME\NAMED-INSTANCE* in the Server name box, replacing *COMPUTER-NAME* with the name of your computer and *NAMED-INSTANCE* with the name of your SQL Server instance.

4. To use Windows Authentication, leave the Authentication box set to its default settings and click **Connect**. However, if you chose to use SQL Server Authentication, then enter the username and password that were supplied to you by your instructor and click **Connect**. The SQL Server Management Studio Express window opens, as shown in Figure 7-6.

Short Quiz 2

1. How do you execute a query in a query window?

2. What's the difference between regular and delimited identifiers?

3. What is an SQL Server instance?

Working with SQL Server Databases

This section explains the basics of working with databases in SQL Server.

Creating Databases

You use the CREATE DATABASE statement to create a new database. The following statement creates the skateboards database:

```
CREATE DATABASE skateboards;
```

If the database is created successfully, the message "Command(s) completed successfully." is displayed in the Messages window at the bottom of the query window. If the database already exists, you would see a message similar to the following:

```
Database 'skateboards' already exists. Choose a different
database name.
```

By default, SQL Server Management Studio Express creates new databases in the C:\Program Files\Microsoft SQL Server\MSSQL10. SQLEXPRESS\MSSQL\DATA folder. The databases are created with the name you specified and an extension of .mds. To create a new database in a specific location, you must use the ON keyword, followed by a comma-separated list of items enclosed in parentheses that defines the file information. The ON list requires the NAME and FILENAME keywords. You assign to the NAME keyword a logical name to identify the file. You must use the logical name to refer to the file in SQL Server. You assign to the FILENAME keyword the drive and path where you want to create the database file and a physical filename with an extension of .mds. The following statement demonstrates how to save the `skateboards` database with a logical name of skateboards_inv and a physical name of skateboards_inv.mds in a folder named inventory on the C: drive:

```
CREATE DATABASE skateboards ON (NAME=skateboards_inv,
FILENAME="C:\inventory\skateboards_inv.mds");
```

Keep in mind that the `CREATE DATABASE` statement only creates the specified database. Before you can add records to a new database, you must first define the tables and fields that will store your data. Later in this chapter, you will learn how to define tables and fields in a database.

Next, you will create a database named `forecast`, which will store weather forecasts for various cities.

To create a database named `forecast`:

1. Return to the SQL Server Management Studio Express window.

2. To create a new query window, select the **File** menu, point to **New**, and then select **Query with Current Connection**. A new query window opens.

3. Type the following command to create the database. Change the path to the Chapter file for Chapter 7 in the location where you installed the data files. By default, the path should be C:\Course Technology\0324-2\Chapter.07\Chapter.

   ```
   CREATE DATABASE forecast ON (NAME=forecast_db,
   FILENAME="C:\Course Technology\0324-2\Chapter.07\
   Chapter\forecast_db.mds");
   ```

4. Select the **Query** menu and then select **Execute**. You should see the "Command(s) completed successfully." message in the Messages window, below the query window.

Deleting Databases

To delete a database, you execute the `DROP DATABASE` statement, which removes all tables from the database and deletes the database itself. The syntax for the `DROP DATABASE` statement is as follows:

```
DROP DATABASE database;
```

The following statement deletes the `skateboards` database:

```
DROP DATABASE skateboards;
Query OK, 0 rows affected (0.00 sec)
```

After you drop a database, you should see the "Command(s) completed successfully." message in the Messages window at the bottom of the query window.

You use the logical filename only if you want to refer to the physical file that contains the database; you do not use it to refer to the database itself. For example, you would use the logical file name if you want to move the physical file to a different location.

The specified path must exist before executing a `CREATE DATABASE` statement.

After you create a database, there is no need to save it, like you would with other types of computer files. Instead, the database is saved automatically whenever you run SQL commands that add, remove, and modify the database's tables, records, and fields.

The next two sections explain how to select field data types and create tables, and also how to delete existing tables. Remember that before you can add tables to a database, you must first create the database, as described earlier in this chapter.

Specifying Field Data Types

You can find a complete listing of SQL Server data types in the Data types (Transact-SQL) page of the Transact-SQL Reference at *http://msdn. microsoft.com/en-us/ library/ms187752.aspx.*

By now, you should thoroughly understand that C# variables have different data types, which govern the specific categories of information that a variable can contain. Just like C# variables, the fields in a table also store data according to type. Recall that one of the most important purposes of a variable's data type is that it determines how much memory the computer allocates for the data stored in the variable. Similarly, the data types in database fields determine how much storage space the computer allocates for the data in the database. SQL Server includes numerous data types in categories that include numeric types, string types, monetary types, and date/time types. Table 7-2 lists some of the common SQL Server data types.

Type	Range	Storage
`bigint`	–2^63 (–9,223,372,036,854,775,808) through 2^63-1 (9,223,372,036,854,775,807)	8 bytes
`char(n)`	Fixed length string between 1 to 8000 characters	Number of bytes specified by *n*
`datetime`	January 1, 1753, through December 31, 9999	Two 4-byte integers
`decimal`	–10^38 +1 through 10^38-1	Between 5 and 17 bytes, depending on the number of decimals
float	–1.79E+308 to –2.23E-308, 0 and 2.23E-308 to 1.79E+308	Between 4 and 8 bytes, depending on the number of decimals
`int` or `integer`	–2,147,483,648 through 2,147,483,647	4 bytes
`money`	–922,337,203,685,477.5808 to 922,337,203,685,477.5807	8 bytes
`real`	–3.40E + 38 to –1.18E -38, 0 and 1.18E-38 to 3.40E+38	4 bytes
`smalldatetime`	January 1, 1900 through June 6, 2079	Two 2-byte integers
`smallint`	–32,768 through 32,767	2 bytes
`smallmoney`	–214,748.3648 to 214,748.3647	4 bytes
`tinyint`	0 through 255	1 byte
`varchar(n)`	Variable length string between 0 to 8000 characters	Varies according to the number of bytes specified by *n*

Table 7-2   Common SQL Server data types

To keep your database from growing too large, you should choose the smallest data type possible for each field. For example, the SMALLINT data type stores integer values between −32768 and 32767 and occupies 2 bytes of storage space. In comparison, the BIGINT data type stores integer values between −9,223,372,036,854,775,808 and 9,223,372,036,854,775,807 and occupies 8 bytes of storage space. Regardless of how small the value is that you store in a SMALLINT field, it will occupy 2 bytes of storage space. Similarly, the BIGINT data type occupies 8 bytes of storage space, no matter how small the value. If you know that a value you assign to a field will always be between −32,768 and 32,767, you should use the SMALLINT data type instead of the BIGINT data type, which saves 6 bytes per record. This might not seem like a huge savings, but imagine how much storage space would be saved for a database with millions of records.

To store text in a field, you specify a data type of CHAR(*m*) or VARCHAR(*m*). For both data types, you replace *m* with the maximum number of characters you anticipate the field will store. In general, you should use the VARCHAR(*m*) data type because the amount of storage space it occupies varies according to the number of characters in the field.

Creating Tables

To create a table, you use the CREATE TABLE statement, which specifies the table and column names and the data type for each column. The syntax for the CREATE TABLE statement is as follows:

```
CREATE TABLE table_name (column_name TYPE, ...);
```

To work with a database in a query window, you must first select it by executing the USE *database* statement. For example, the following statement selects the skateboards database:

```
USE skateboards;
```

The following statement selects the skateboards database and then creates the inventory table. The first two columns in the table, manufacturer and model, are VARCHAR data types that can be a maximum of 50 characters. The length and width columns are both DECIMAL data types. The sku column is also a VARCHAR data type, but with a 15-character maximum, and the price field is a SMALLMONEY data type.

```
USE skateboards;
CREATE TABLE inventory (manufacturer VARCHAR(50),
model VARCHAR(50), length DECIMAL, width DECIMAL,
sku VARCHAR(15), price SMALLMONEY);
```

Next, you create in the forecast database a table named outlook, which will contain forecast information for the next week. The table will contain six fields: city, state, day, high, low, and conditions. The city, day, and conditions fields will be VARCHAR data types, the state field will be a char type, and the high and low fields will be float data types.

To create in the forecast database a table named outlook:

1. Return to the query window in SQL Server Management Studio Express.

2. Delete the **CREATE DATABASE** statement.

3. Enter the following command after the USE statement to create the outlook table:

```
USE forecast;
CREATE TABLE outlook (city VARCHAR(25),
state CHAR(2), day VARCHAR(10),
high FLOAT, low FLOAT, conditions VARCHAR(25));
```

4. Select the **Query** menu and then select **Execute**.

Deleting Tables

To delete a table, you execute the DROP TABLE statement, which removes all data and the table definition. The syntax for the DROP TABLE statement is as follows:

```
DROP TABLE table;
```

The following statement deletes the inventory table in the inventory database:

```
DROP TABLE inventory;
```

Short Quiz 3

1. How do you create a new database file in a specific location?

2. How do you decide which data type to use for table fields?

3. How do you create and delete tables?

Working with Records

In this section, you will learn how to add records to a table and how to update and delete existing records.

Adding Records

You add individual records to a table with the INSERT statement. The basic syntax for the INSERT statement is as follows:

```
INSERT INTO table_name VALUES(value1, value2, ...);
```

Text values must be enclosed within single quotations. The values you enter in the VALUES list must be in the same order in which you defined the table fields. For example, the following statement adds a new row to the inventory table in the skateboards database:

```
USE skateboards;
INSERT INTO inventory VALUES('Almost', 'Coffin Cruiser',
31.25, 8.5, '1CALMOCOFF85000', 92.00);
```

You should specify NULL in any fields for which you do not have a value. For example, if you do not know the length or width of the "Coffin Cruiser" skateboard, you can enter NULL values, as follows:

```
USE skateboards;
INSERT INTO inventory VALUES('Almost', 'Coffin Cruiser',
NULL, NULL, '1CALMOCOFF85000', 92.00);
```

Next, you will add two records to the outlook table of the forecast database.

To add two records to the outlook table of the forecast database:

1. Return to the query window in SQL Server Management Studio Express.

2. Delete the **CREATE TABLE** statement, but leave the USE statement.

3. Enter the following command to add a record to the outlook table:

    ```
    INSERT INTO outlook VALUES('Seattle', 'WA',
    'Today', 59, 49, 'Partly cloudy');
    ```

4. Enter the following command to add another record to the outlook table:

    ```
    INSERT INTO outlook VALUES('Boston', 'MA',
    'Today', 74, 53, 'Cloudy');
    ```

5. Select the **Query** menu and then select **Execute**. You should see the message "(1 row(s) affected)" printed twice in the Messages window at the bottom of the query window.

In most cases, you will probably add individual records to a database with the INSERT INTO statement. However, there will be times when you need to add more than one record at the same time. For example, you might need to load multiple records to a new database or append multiple records to an existing database. To add multiple records to a database, you use the BULK INSERT statement with a local text file containing the records you want to add. The syntax for the BULK INSERT statement is as follows:

```
BULK INSERT table_name FROM 'filepath';
```

Place each record in the text file on a separate line and place tabs between each field. Leave any empty fields blank. The values on each line must be in the same order in which you defined the table fields. The following statement loads a file named inventory.txt into the inventory table in the skateboards database:

```
USE skateboards;
BULK INSERT inventory FROM 'inventory.txt';
```

388

Next, you will add new records to the outlook table in the forecast database from a text file named outlook.txt, located in your Chapter directory for Chapter 7.

1. Return to the query window in SQL Server Management Studio Express.

2. Delete the **INSERT INTO** statements, but leave the USE statement.

3. Enter the following BULK INSERT statement that inserts records from the outlook.txt file in your Chapter directory for Chapter 7. Be sure to enter the full path where your data files are stored.

   BULK INSERT outlook FROM '*path*\outlook.txt';

4. Select the **Query** menu and then select **Execute**. You should see the message "(10 row(s) affected)" printed in the Messages window at the bottom of the query window.

5. Replace the BULK INSERT statement with the following SELECT statement, which returns the records that you inserted into the outlook table.

   SELECT * FROM outlook;

6. Select the **Query** menu and then select **Execute**. You should see the records in the Results window, as shown in Figure 7-12.

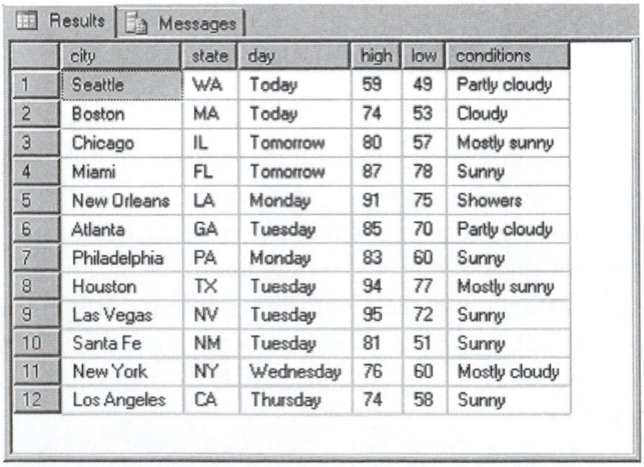

	city	state	day	high	low	conditions
1	Seattle	WA	Today	59	49	Partly cloudy
2	Boston	MA	Today	74	53	Cloudy
3	Chicago	IL	Tomorrow	80	57	Mostly sunny
4	Miami	FL	Tomorrow	87	78	Sunny
5	New Orleans	LA	Monday	91	75	Showers
6	Atlanta	GA	Tuesday	85	70	Partly cloudy
7	Philadelphia	PA	Monday	83	60	Sunny
8	Houston	TX	Tuesday	94	77	Mostly sunny
9	Las Vegas	NV	Tuesday	95	72	Sunny
10	Santa Fe	NM	Tuesday	81	51	Sunny
11	New York	NY	Wednesday	76	60	Mostly cloudy
12	Los Angeles	CA	Thursday	74	58	Sunny

Figure 7-12   Results window after adding records to the outlook table in the forecast database

Retrieving Records

In this chapter, you have seen several examples of how to use a SELECT statement to retrieve records from a table. The basic syntax for a SELECT statement is as follows:

SELECT *criteria* FROM *table_name*;

As you also learned earlier, you use the asterisk * wildcard with the SELECT statement to retrieve all fields from a table. Instead of returning all records by specifying a wildcard, you can specify individual fields to return. To return multiple fields, separate field names with a comma. The following statement returns the manufacturer and make fields from the inventory table in the skateboards database. Figure 7-13 shows the output in the Results window.

SELECT manufacturer, model FROM inventory;

	manufacturer	model
1	Almost	Coffin Cruiser
2	Barefoot	Nuuhiwa
3	Bustin	Cigar
4	Bullet	Shockwave
5	Gravity	Mini Classic
6	Myrtle	Quarter Shred
7	Riviera	Hesher Mini
8	Sesc	Orchid
9	Skate Designs	Black Crown
10	Termite	Eight Ball

Figure 7-13   Individual fields returned with a SELECT statement

Next, you will enter several SELECT statements that return records from the outlook table in the forecast database.

1. Return to the query window in SQL Server Management Studio Express.

2. Modify the SELECT statement so it returns just the city and conditions fields from the outlook table, as follows:

   SELECT city, conditions FROM outlook;

3. Select the **Query** menu and then select **Execute**. You should see the records in the Results window, with the city and conditions fields returned from the outlook table in the forecast database.

4. Modify the SELECT statement so it returns city, day, high, and low fields from the outlook table, as follows:

   SELECT city, day, high, low FROM outlook;

5. Select the **Query** menu and then select **Execute**. You should see the records in the Results window, with the `city`, `day`, `high`, `low` fields returned from the `outlook` table in the `forecast` database.

Sorting Query Results

You use the `ORDER BY` keyword with the `SELECT` statement to perform an alphanumeric sort of the results returned from a query. The following statement returns the `manufacturer`, `model`, and `price` fields from the `inventory` table in the `skateboards` database and sorts the results by the `price` field. Figure 7-14 shows the output in the Results window.

```
USE skateboards;
SELECT manufacturer, model, price FROM inventory
ORDER BY price;
```

	manufacturer	model	price
1	Bullet	Shockwave	72.00
2	Myrtle	Quarter Shred	87.99
3	Almost	Coffin Cruiser	92.00
4	Sosc	Orchid	98.99
5	Termite	Eight Ball	98.99
6	Riviera	Hesher Mini	101.99
7	Gravity	Mini Classic	105.99
8	Skate Designs	Black Crown	113.00
9	Barefoot	Nuuhiwa	140.99
10	Bustin	Cigar	161.99

Figure 7-14 Results returned from `inventory` table of the `skateboards` database sorted by price

To perform a reverse sort, add the `DESC` keyword after the name of the field by which you want to perform the sort. The following statement returns the `manufacturer`, `model`, and `price` fields from the `inventory` table in the `skateboards` database and reverse sorts the results by the `price` field. Figure 7-15 shows the output in the Results window.

```
USE skateboards;
SELECT manufacturer, model, price FROM inventory
ORDER BY price DESC;
```

	manufacturer	model	price
1	Bustin	Cigar	161.99
2	Barefoot	Nuuhiwa	140.99
3	Skate Designs	Black Crown	113.00
4	Gravity	Mini Classic	105.99
5	Riviera	Hesher Mini	101.99
6	Scsc	Orchid	98.99
7	Termite	Eight Ball	98.99
8	Almost	Coffin Cruiser	92.00
9	Myrtle	Quarter Shred	87.99
10	Bullet	Shockwave	72.00

Figure 7-15 Results returned from `inventory` table of the `skateboards` database reverse sorted by price

Next, you will enter several `SELECT` statements that sort records from the `outlook` table in the `forecast` database.

To enter several `SELECT` statements that sort records from the `outlook` table in the `forecast` database:

1. Return to the query window in SQL Server Management Studio Express.
2. Modify the `SELECT` statement so it sorts the returned records by city, as follows:

```
SELECT city, day, high, low FROM outlook ORDER BY city;
```

3. Select the **Query** menu and then select **Execute**. The sorted results should appear in the Results window.
4. Add the `DESC` keyword to the `SELECT` statement so it reverse sorts the returned records by city, as follows:

```
SELECT city, day, high, low FROM outlook
ORDER BY city DESC;
```

5. Select the **Query** menu and then select **Execute**. You should see the records in the Results window, reverse sorted by city.

Filtering Query Results

The *`criteria`* portion of the `SELECT` statement determines which fields to retrieve from a table. You can also specify which records to return by using the `WHERE` keyword. For example, the following statement returns all records from the `inventory` table in the `skateboards` database where the `price` field is less than 100. Figure 7-16 shows the output in the Results window.

```
USE skateboards;
SELECT * FROM inventory WHERE price < 100;
```

	manufacturer	model	length	width	sku	price
1	Almost	Coffin Cruiser	31	9	1CALMOCOFF85000	92.00
2	Bullet	Shockwave	31	8	1CBUTOSHWA75000	72.00
3	Myrtle	Quarter Shred	33	9	1CMYRQUSHR85000	87.99
4	Scsc	Orchid	45	9	1CSCSOORCH90000	98.99
5	Termite	Eight Ball	27	7	1CTERCEIGH67500	98.99

Figure 7-16   Results returned from the inventory table of the skateboards database where price is less than 100

SQL includes the keywords AND and OR that you can use to specify more detailed conditions about the records you want to return. For example, the following statement returns all records from the `inventory` table in the `skateboard` database where the `price` field is greater than 100 AND the `length` field is less than 30. Figure 7-17 shows the output in the Results window.

```
USE skateboards;
SELECT * FROM inventory WHERE price > 100 AND length < 30;
```

	manufacturer	model	length	width	sku	price
1	Gravity	Mini Classic	27	9	1CGRACLAMD27000	105.99
2	Riviera	Hesher Mini	27	8	1CRIVHESHR75000	101.99
3	Skate Designs	Black Crown	29	9	1CSKDOBLCR290KK	113.00

Figure 7-17   Results returned from the inventory table of the skateboards database where price is greater than 100 and length is less than 30

The following statement shows an example of how to use the OR keyword by returning all records from the `inventory` table in the `skateboards` database where the price is greater than 100 OR the length is less than 30. The statement also sorts the returned records by price. Figure 7-18 shows the output in the Results window.

```
USE skateboards;
SELECT * FROM inventory WHERE price > 100
OR length < 30 ORDER BY price;
```

	manufacturer	model	length	width	sku	price
1	Termite	Eight Ball	27	7	1CTERCEIGH67500	98.99
2	Riviera	Hesher Mini	27	8	1CRIVHESHR75000	101.99
3	Gravity	Mini Classic	27	9	1CGRACLAMD27000	105.99
4	Skate Designs	Black Crown	29	9	1CSKDOBLCR290KK	113.00
5	Barefoot	Nuuhiwa	47	10	1CBARLENUH95000	140.99
6	Bustin	Cigar	38	9	1CBUSOCIDU85000	161.99

Figure 7-18   Results returned from the inventory table of the skateboards database where price is greater than 100 or length is less than 30

Next, you will enter several SELECT statements that use the WHERE keyword to filter records from the outlook table in the forecast database.

To enter several SELECT statements that use the WHERE keyword to filter records from the outlook table in the forecast database:

1. Return to the query window in SQL Server Management Studio Express.

2. Modify the SELECT statement so it returns all records for Tuesday, as follows:

    ```
    SELECT * FROM outlook WHERE day='Tuesday';
    ```

3. Select the **Query** menu and then select **Execute**. The Tuesday forecast results should appear in the Results window.

4. Now modify the SELECT statement so it returns all records where the high temperature is greater than 80, as follows:

    ```
    SELECT * FROM outlook WHERE high > 80;
    ```

5. Select the **Execute** command from the **Query** menu. The records with a high temperature greater than 80 should appear in the Results window.

Updating Records

If you need to update records in a table, you use the UPDATE statement. The basic syntax for the UPDATE statement is as follows:

```
UPDATE table_name
SET column_name=value
WHERE condition;
```

The UPDATE keyword specifies the name of the table to update and the SET keyword specifies the value to assign to the fields in the records that match the condition in the WHERE keyword. For example, the following statement modifies the price of the Bullet Shockwave skate-board to $67.00:

```
USE skateboards;
UPDATE inventory SET price=67.00 WHERE manufacturer='Bullet'
AND model='Shockwave';
```

Notice in the preceding statement that to ensure that the correct record is updated, the statement uses the WHERE keyword to specify that the manufacturer field should be equal to 'Bullet' and the model field should be equal to 'Shockwave'. If the statement only specified that the manufacturer field should be equal to 'Bullet', then the price field for all other records in the table that included a manufacturer field with a value of 'Bullet' would also have been updated to 67.00.

Next, you will enter several UPDATE statements to modify records from the outlook table in the forecast database. You modify the day fields with a value of "Today" to "Saturday" and the day fields with a value of "Tomorrow" to "Sunday".

To enter several UPDATE statements to modify records from the outlook table in the forecast database:

1. Return to the query window in SQL Server Management Studio Express.

2. Replace the SELECT statement with the following UPDATE statement that changes day fields with a value of "Today" to "Saturday":

   ```
   UPDATE outlook SET day='Saturday' WHERE day='Today';
   ```

3. Add another update to the end of the query window that changes day fields with a value of "Tomorrow" to "Sunday", as follows:

   ```
   UPDATE outlook SET day='Sunday' WHERE day='Tomorrow';
   ```

4. Select the **Query** menu and then select **Execute**. You should see the message "(2 row(s) affected)" printed twice in the Messages window at the bottom of the query window.

5. Replace the two UPDATE statements with the following SELECT statement that returns all records from the outlook table of the forecast database with the results sorted by the day field:

   ```
   SELECT * FROM outlook ORDER BY day;
   ```

6. Select the **Query** menu and then select **Execute**. The outlook table records should appear in the Results window, sorted by the day field.

Deleting Records

To delete records in a table, you use the DELETE statement. The basic syntax for the DELETE statement is as follows:

```
DELETE FROM table_name
WHERE condition;
```

Be careful when you use the DELETE statement because it will delete all records that match the condition. Therefore, be sure to carefully construct the conditions assigned to the WHERE keyword. For example, the following statement deletes the "Termite Eight Ball" record from the inventory table in the skateboards database:

```
USE skateboards;
DELETE FROM inventory WHERE manufacturer='Termite'
AND model='Eight Ball';
```

To delete all the records in a table, leave off the WHERE keyword. The following statements delete all the records in the inventory table:

```
USE skateboards;
DELETE FROM inventory;
```

Next, you will delete several records from the outlook table in the forecast database.

To delete several records from the outlook table in the forecast database:

Remember that the DELETE statement will delete all records that match the WHERE condition. If you leave off the WHERE keyword, it will delete all of the records in the specified table.

1. Return to the query window in SQL Server Management Studio Express.

2. Replace the SELECT statement with the following DELETE FROM statement that deletes the Chicago record:

   DELETE FROM outlook WHERE city='Chicago';

3. Add the following DELETE FROM statement to the end of the query window to delete the Las Vegas record:

   DELETE FROM outlook WHERE city='Las Vegas';

4. Select the **Query** menu and then select **Execute**. You should see the message "(1 row(s) affected)" printed twice in the Messages window at the bottom of the query window.

5. Replace the two DELETE FROM statements with the following SELECT statement that returns all records from the outlook table of the forecast database with the results sorted by the city field:

   SELECT * FROM outlook ORDER BY city;

6. Select the **Query** menu and then select **Execute**. The outlook table records should appear in the Results window,

sorted by the city field. The table should now only consist of 10 records.

7. Select **Close** from the **File** menu and then select **No** when prompted to save the query. (You can save the more complex queries that you need to run on a regular basis.)

8. To close SQL Server Management Studio Express, select the **File** menu and then select **Exit**.

Short Quiz 4

1. How do you add individual and multiple records to a table?

2. How do you sort and reverse sort the results returned from a query?

3. Explain how to delete records from a table.

Summing Up

- A database is an ordered collection of information from which a computer program can quickly access information.

- A record in a database is a single complete set of related information.

- Fields are the individual categories of information stored in a record.

- A flat-file database stores information in a single table.

- A relational database stores information across multiple related tables.

- A query is a structured set of instructions and criteria for retrieving, adding, modifying, and deleting database information.

- Structured Query Language, or SQL (pronounced sequel), has become somewhat of a standard data manipulation language among many database management systems.

- Microsoft SQL Server Management Studio Express is a graphic tool for manipulating SQL Server databases.

- Regular identifiers must begin with a letter, underscore (_), number sign (#), or at sign (@), and subsequent characters are restricted to letters, numbers, underscores, number signs, or at signs.

Delimited identifiers do not conform to the rules of regular identifiers and can include spaces and other characters that are not allowed in regular identifiers. To use delimited identifiers in SQL statements, they must be contained within double quotations ("") or brackets ([]).

- To work with a database, you must first select it by executing the USE statement.

- You use the CREATE DATABASE statement to create a new database.

- To delete a database, you execute the DROP DATABASE statement, which removes all tables from the database and deletes the database itself.

- The fields in a table also store data according to type. To keep your database from growing too large, you should choose the smallest data type possible for each field.

- To create a table, you use the CREATE TABLE statement, which specifies the table and column names and the data type for each column.

- To delete a table, you execute the DROP TABLE statement, which removes all data and the table definition.

- You add individual records to a table with the INSERT statement.

- To add multiple records to a database, you use the BULK INSERT statement with a local text file containing the records you want to add.

- You use the SELECT statement to retrieve records from a table.

- You use the ORDER BY keyword with the SELECT statement to perform an alphanumeric sort of the results returned from a query. To perform a reverse sort, add the DESC keyword after the name of the field by which you want to perform the sort.

- You can specify which records to return from a database by using the WHERE keyword.

- You use the UPDATE statement to update records in a table.

- You use the DELETE statement to delete records in a table.

Comprehension Check

1. A flat-file database consists of a single table. True or False?

2. Explain how relational databases are organized.

3. What is the correct term for the individual pieces of information that are stored in a database record?

    a. element

    b. field

    c. section

    d. container

4. What is the name of one table's primary key when it is stored in another table?

    a. key symbol

    b. record link

    c. foreign key

    d. unique identifier

5. Breaking tables into multiple related tables to reduce redundant and duplicate information is called _____.

    a. normalization

    b. redundancy design

    c. splitting

    d. simplification

6. Suppose you have a relational database for a dry cleaning company. Each customer of the dry cleaning company can have multiple items in a cleaning order. What type of relationship is this?

    a. one-to-one

    b. one-to-many

    c. many-to-one

    d. many-to-many

7. _____ has become a standard data manipulation language among many database management systems.

    a. Java

    b. SQL

    c. ASP.NET

    d. PERL

8. Files created by different database management systems are completely interchangeable. True or False?

9. What character must terminate SQL commands?

   a. colon (:)

   b. semicolon (;)

   c. ampersand (&)

   d. period (.)

10. Which of the following characters can you include in a regular identifier? (Choose all that apply.)

    a. number sign (#)

    b. dollar sign ($)

    c. at sign (@)

    d. underscore (_)

11. With what characters do you surround delimited identifiers? (Choose all that apply.)

    a. quotation marks (')

    b. double quotation marks (")

    c. backticks (`)

    d. brackets ([])

12. SQL keywords are case sensitive. True or False?

13. Which of the following SQL keywords do you use to delete a database?

    a. DELETE

    b. KILL

    c. DROP

    d. DISCARD

14. Which of the following data types should you use for a column that will store an integer that is smaller than 10,000?

    a. tinyint

    b. smallint

    c. int

    d. bigint

15. Which SQL keyword do you use to select the database you want to work with?

    a. SELECT

    b. OPEN

    c. GET

    d. USE

16. Which of the following statements uses the correct syntax to create a table named students with three VARCHAR columns named firstName, lastName, and studentID?

    a. NEW TABLE students "firstName VARCHAR(25), lastName VARCHAR(25), studentID VARCHAR(10)";

    b. CREATE TABLE students (firstName VARCHAR(25), lastName VARCHAR(25), studentID VARCHAR(10));

    c. INSERT TABLE students firstName VARCHAR(25), lastName VARCHAR(25), studentID VARCHAR(10);

    d. ADD TABLE students [firstName VARCHAR(25) + lastName VARCHAR(25) + studentID VARCHAR(10)];

17. Explain how to add multiple records to a table by using a BULK INSERT statement.

18. Which of the following keywords performs a reverse sort of database records?

    a. DESC

    b. REVERSE

    c. DESCEND

    d. SORTR

19. Which of the following is the correct string for a filter that narrows a recordset to include only records where the State field is equal to California?

    a. "WHERE State = 'California'"

    b. "State = 'California'"

    c. "WHERE State = California"

    d. "State = 'California'"

20. Which of the following SQL keywords do you use in an UPDATE statement to change the value of a matching column?

    a. SET

    b. CHANGE

    c. MODIFY

    d. ALTER

Reinforcement Exercises

Exercise 7-1

In this project, you will create a database with a table containing hitting statistics for major league baseball teams.

1. To start SQL Server Management Studio Express, click the **Start** button, point to **All Programs**, click **Microsoft SQL Server 2008**, and then click **SQL Server Management Studio**. The Connect to Server dialog box opens. Leave the Server type box set to **Database Engine**. Enter .\SQLEXPRESS in the Server name box. If your instructor provided you with a named SQL Server instance, then enter *COMPUTER-NAME\ NAMED-INSTANCE* in the Server name box, replacing *COMPUTER-NAME* with the name of your computer and *NAMED-INSTANCE* with the name of your SQL Server instance. To use Windows Authentication, leave the Authentication box set to its default settings and click **Connect**. However, if you chose to use SQL Server Authentication, then enter the username and password that were supplied to you by your instructor and click **Connect**. The SQL Server Management Studio Express window opens.

2. To create a new query window, select the **File** menu, point to **New**, and then click **Query with Current Connection**. A new query window opens.

3. Type the following command to create the database in your Exercises folder for Chapter 7. Be sure to change the path to where you installed the data files. By default, the path should be C:\Course Technology\0324-2\Chapter.07\Exercises.

```
CREATE DATABASE baseball_stats
ON (NAME=baseball_stats_db,
FILENAME="C:\Course Technology\
0324-2\Chapter.07\Exercises\baseball_stats_db.mds");
```

4. Select the **Query** menu, and then select **Execute**.

5. Replace the CREATE DATABASE command with the following command to select the baseball_stats database:

    USE **baseball_stats**;

6. Leave the query window open in SQL Server Management Studio Express.

Exercise 7-2

In this project, you will create a table named teamstats in the baseball_stats database and add records to the new table from a file named baseball_team_stats.txt in your Exercises folder for Chapter 7.

1. Return to the query window in SQL Server Management Studio Express.

2. Enter the following command to create the flightsessions table, select the **Query** menu, and then select **Execute**. The Team field uses the VARCHAR data type. Thirteen of the columns use INT data types and the last three fields use FLOAT data types. Each of the statistical field names use common baseball acronyms, such as G for games, AB for at bats, R for runs, H for home runs, and so on.

    CREATE TABLE **teamstats** (Team **varchar**(50), G **int**, AB **int**, R **int**, H **int**, [2B] **int**, [3B] **int**, HR **int**, RBI **int**, TB **int**, BB **int**, SO **int**, SB **int**, CS **float**, OBP **float**, SLG **float**, TEAM_AVG **float**);

3. Replace the CREATE TABLE command with a BULK INSERT statement that inserts records from the baseball_team_stats.txt file in your Exercises folder for Chapter 7 into the teamstats table. Replace *path* with the path to your Exercises folder for Chapter 7, and then select **Execute** from the **Query** menu.

    BULK INSERT **teamstats**
    FROM '*path*\baseball_team_stats.txt';

4. Replace the BULK INSERT command with the following command to view all the records in the teamstats table, select the **Query** menu, and then select **Execute**:

    SELECT * FROM **teamstats**;

5. Leave the query window open in SQL Server Management Studio Express.

Exercise 7-3

In this project, you will write SQL statements that return team names, games played, and number of at bats from the teamstats in the baseball_stats database.

1. Return to the query window in SQL Server Management Studio Express.

2. Replace the SELECT statement with the following SELECT statement, which returns the team, G (games played), and AB (at bats) fields from the teamstats table, select the **Query** menu, and then select **Execute**:

   `SELECT team, G, AB FROM teamstats;`

3. Replace the SELECT statement with the following SELECT statement, which returns the team, G (games played), and AB (at bats) fields from the teamstats table, sorted by team name, select the **Query** menu, and then select **Execute**:

   `SELECT team, G, AB FROM teamstats ORDER BY team;`

4. Replace the SELECT statement with the following SELECT statement, which returns the team, G (games played), and AB (at bats) fields from the teamstats table, reverse sorted by team name, select the **Query** menu, and then select **Execute**:

   `SELECT team, G, AB FROM teamstats ORDER BY team DESC;`

5. Leave the query window open in SQL Server Management Studio Express.

Exercise 7-4

SQL includes various functions that you can include in statements, including the SUM() function, which returns the sum of an expression, and the AVG() function, which returns the average of an expression. Both functions can include field names in the expressions assigned to them. In this project, you will write SQL statements that use the SUM() function to return the total number of games played by all teams and the AVG() function to return the common batting average for all teams.

1. Return to the query window in SQL Server Management Studio Express.

2. Replace the SELECT statement with the following SELECT statement, which uses the SUM() function to return the total number of games played by summing the contents of the G fields, select the **Query** menu, and then select **Execute**. You should see a value of 346,316.

   `SELECT SUM(G) FROM teamstats;`

3. Replace the SELECT statement with the following SELECT statement, which uses the AVG() function to return the batting average for all teams by averaging the contents of the AVG

fields, select the **Query** menu, and then select **Execute**. You should see a value of 0.26186666538318.

```sql
SELECT AVG(AVG) FROM teamstats;
```

4. Leave the query window open in SQL Server Management Studio Express.

Discovery Projects

Save the following projects in the Discovery folder for Chapter 7.

Project 7-1
Create a demographics database with a table that contains the following fields: country, primary language, and population. Enter records for at least 10 countries. You can find demographic information for various countries in many places on the Internet, including Wikipedia, a free encyclopedia at *http://www.wikipedia.org/*. Write queries that return the following:

- A list of all records sorted by country name
- The country with the highest population
- The country with the lowest population
- Countries that share a common language, such as French

Project 7-2
Create a database for a used car dealership that includes a table for inventory. Include the following fields in the inventory table: make, model, price, and mpg (miles per gallon). Enter at least 10 records into the table. Write queries that return the following:

- All records
- Make, model, and price, sorted by make and model
- The make and model of the car that gets the best miles per gallon
- The make and model of the car that gets the worst miles per gallon
- The make and model of the highest and lowest priced cars

Project 7-3
Database design techniques include the process of being able to identify and design five normalization levels: first normal form, second normal form, third normal form, fourth normal form, and fifth normal form. Search the Internet or visit your local library for information on these techniques and describe how to identify and design each normalization level.

Manipulating SQL Server Databases with ASP.NET

In this chapter you will:

◎ Connect to SQL Server from ASP.NET

◎ Learn how to handle SQL Server errors

◎ Execute SQL statements with ASP.NET

◎ Use ASP.NET to work with SQL Server databases and tables

One of ASP.NET's greatest strengths is its ability to access and manipulate databases. With its strong ODBC support, you can use ASP.NET to access any database that is ODBC-compliant. ASP.NET also includes functionality that allows you to directly work with different types of databases, without going through ODBC. In this chapter, you will study how to use ASP.NET to directly access SQL Server databases.

As you work through this chapter, keep in mind that almost everything you learned about SQL in Chapter 7 is applicable to this chapter. Although you will need to learn a few new C# techniques to access SQL Server with ASP.NET, you will execute the same SQL statements that you used with SQL Server Management Studio. The great benefit to using ASP.NET or some other server-side scripting language to read from and write to a database server is that it allows you to create a Web-based interface that makes it much easier for visitors to interact with your database.

Connecting to SQL Server with ASP.NET

In today's ever-evolving technology environment, it is often necessary for an application to access multiple databases created in different database management systems. For example, a company might need an ASP.NET program that simultaneously accesses a large legacy database written in dBase and a newer database written in Oracle. In that situation, converting the large dBase database to Oracle would be cost prohibitive. On the other hand, continuing to use the older dBase database would not work because the older database would lack the capabilities the company would require in the future. Somehow, the company must be able to access the data in both the older dBase system and the newer Oracle system.

To allow easy access to data in various database formats, Microsoft established the Open Database Connectivity standard. **Open Database Connectivity**, or **ODBC**, allows ODBC-compliant applications to access any data source for which there is an ODBC driver. ODBC uses SQL commands (known as ODBC SQL) to allow an ODBC-compliant application to access a database. Essentially, an ODBC application connects to a database for which there is an ODBC driver and then executes ODBC SQL commands. Then, the ODBC driver translates the SQL commands into a format that the database can understand. ASP.NET includes strong support for ODBC.

ASP.NET also includes functionality that allows you to directly work with SQL Server and Oracle databases, without going through

ODBC. By eliminating the ODBC layer, your ASP.NET programs will be faster. Further, ASP.NET code that directly accesses a database is also easier to write than code that goes through ODBC. Therefore, your rule of thumb should be to always use direct database access functionality for SQL Server and Oracle databases. Otherwise, use ASP.NET's ODBC functionality to access ODBC-compliant databases.

Accessing SQL Server Databases with ASP.NET

With ASP.NET, you use ActiveX Data Objects to access databases. **ActiveX Data Objects**, or **ADO**, is a Microsoft database connectivity technology that allows ASP and other Web development tools to access ODBC- and OLE DB-compliant databases. **OLE DB** is a data source connectivity standard promoted by Microsoft as a successor to ODBC. One of the primary differences between OLE DB and ODBC is that ODBC supports access only to relational databases, whereas OLE DB provides access to both relational databases and nonrelational data sources, such as spreadsheet programs. The most recent version of ADO is ADO.NET, which allows you to access OLE DB-compliant data sources and XML. You can also use ADO.NET to directly access SQL Server and Oracle databases, without having to go through OLE DB.

ADO and OLE DB are part of the Microsoft Universal Data Access strategy for providing access to data, regardless of its storage format. The components that make up the Universal Data Access technology are called the **Microsoft Data Access Components**, or **MDAC**. MDAC is installed with numerous Microsoft products, including Internet Explorer, Internet Information Services, Microsoft Visual Studio, and the Microsoft .NET Framework SDK. Most of these products, including Internet Explorer, install MDAC automatically. If you are not sure if MDAC is installed on your system, you can check to see if it's installed at *http://support.microsoft.com/kb/301202* or download the latest version at *http://support.microsoft.com/kb/231943/*.

Understanding the `System.Data.SqlClient` Namespace

To access and manipulate SQL Server databases with ASP.NET, you use the classes in the `System.Data.SqlClient` namespace. Table 8-1 lists some of the core classes in the `System.Data.SqlClient` namespace.

Object	Description
DataSet	Represents data retrieved from a data source
SqlCommand	Executes a command, such as a SQL command, against a SQL Server database
SqlConnection	Provides access to a SQL Server database
SqlDataAdapter	Controls the interaction of a DataSet object with a SQL Server database
SqlDataReader	Returns read-only, forward-only data from a SQL Server database
SqlError	Contains error information returned from SQL Server
SqlException	Represents the exception that is thrown when an error or warning is returned from SQL Server

Table 8-1   Core ADO.NET objects

This chapter provides only a brief overview of how to use ASP.NET and ADO.NET to access databases. For more information on ASP.NET database access with ADO.NET, visit the Microsoft Developer Network at *http://msdn. microsoft.com/*.

Next, you will create an ASP.NET program that accesses the forecast database you created in Chapter 7.

To create an ASP.NET program that accesses the forecast database:

1. Create a new ASP.NET Web site in the Visual Studio IDE and save it in a folder named Forecast in your Chapter folder for Chapter 8. Change the content of the <title> element to "Forecast" and add a <link> element above the closing </head> tag that links to the asp_styles.css style sheet file in your data folder. Add the asp_styles.css style sheet to the project by selecting **Add Existing Item** from the **Website** menu.

2. Open the **Default.aspx.cs** file in the Code Editor and add the following directive to the end of the directives section to give the class access to the System.Data.SqlClient namespace:

   ```
   using System.Data.SqlClient;
   ```

Connecting to a SQL Server Database

To connect to a SQL Server database, you instantiate an object of the **SqlConnection class**. The SqlConnection class contains various methods and properties for accessing and manipulating SQL Server databases, as listed in Tables 8-2 and 8-3.

Method	Description
BeginTransaction()	Begins a transaction
ChangeDatabase()	Changes the currently opened database
Close()	Closes a data source connection
CreateCommand()	Creates and returns a Command object associated with the SqlConnection object
GetSchema()	Returns schema information from the data source
Open()	Opens a data source connection
ClearPool()	Empties the SqlConnection object pool for the specified connection
ClearAllPool()	Empties all SqlConnection object pools

Table 8-2   SqlConnection class methods

Property	Description
ConnectionString	The string used to open a SQL Server database
ConnectionTimeout	The time to wait before abandoning a SQL Server database connection attempt
Database	The name of the current SQL Server database to use after a connection has been established
DataSource	The name of the SQL Server instance
ServerVersion	The SQL Server version to which the database is connected
State	A string indicating the current status of the SQL Server database connection

Table 8-3   SqlConnection class properties

The first step in working with a SQL Server database in ASP.NET is to create an object of the SqlConnection class using the following syntax:

```
SqlConnection object = new SqlConnection("connection string");
```

The connection string can contain numerous parameters for connecting to SQL Server. The parameters must be in name=value pair format and be separated with semicolons. The connection string that you pass to the SqlConnection constructor must include the Data Source parameter. You assign to Data Source the name of the SQL Server instance to which you want to connect. To find the name of your SQL Server instance, open SQL Server Management Studio. The name of your SQL Server instance will be located in the Server name box of the Connect to Database Engine dialog box.

The following statement demonstrates how to connect to a SQL Server database instance with a Data Source name of DBSERVER\ SQLEXPRESS:

```
SqlConnection dbConnection = new SqlConnection(
    "Data Source=DBSERVER\\SQLEXPRESS");
```

Instead of specifying the name of your SQL Server instance, in most cases you can just use .\\SQLEXPRESS, as follows:

```
SqlConnection dbConnection = new SqlConnection(
    "Data Source=.\\SQLEXPRESS");
```

Depending on how your SQL Server instance is configured, you might need additional parameters in the connection string. For example, the Integrated Security parameter identifies the type of security that ASP.NET should use when connecting to a SQL Server database. If you are using Windows Authentication as your security mechanism, you must assign the Integrated Security parameter a value of true in the connection string, as follows:

```
SqlConnection dbConnection = new SqlConnection(
    "Data Source=.\\SQLEXPRESS;
    Integrated Security=true");
```

Next, you will add a function to the forecast program that selects the forecast database.

To add a function to the forecast program that selects the forecast database:

1. Return to the **Default.aspx.cs** file in the Visual Studio IDE.

2. Add the following SqlConnection statement to the Page_Load() event handler:

```
SqlConnection dbConnection = new SqlConnection(
    "Data Source=.\\SQLEXPRESS;
    Integrated Security=true");
```

Opening and Closing a Data Source

Once you create an instance of the SqlConnection object, you must use the Open() method to open the specified SQL Server database instance. One SqlConnection object you should use whenever you open a database connection with the Open() method is the Close() method to disconnect the database connection. This is necessary because database connections do not close automatically when an ASP.NET program ends. If you do not close a database connection, it remains open indefinitely (at least until you reboot), and can possibly cause performance problems on the computer where the ASP.NET program is running. The following statement is an example of how

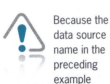

Because the data source name in the preceding example contains a backslash, the connection string contains an escape character (another backslash) to force ASP.NET to treat the backslash as a regular character.

If your connection string contains a backslash, don't forget to escape it with another backslash character.

to connect and disconnect to a database represented by a variable
named dbConnection.

```
SqlConnection dbConnection = new SqlConnection(
    "Data Source=.\\SQLEXPRESS;
    Integrated Security=true");
dbConnection.Open();
additional statements;
dbConnection.Close();
```

Selecting a Database

As you saw in Chapter 7, you must first select a database with the USE
database statement before you can use it. One method of selecting a
database is to include the Database parameter in the connection string
when you first instantiate a SqlConnection object. The following
statement demonstrates how to specify a database named customers
when instantiating a SqlConnection object:

```
SqlConnection dbConnection = new SqlConnection(
    "Data Source=.\\SQLEXPRESS;
    Integrated Security=true;
    Database=customers");
```

You can also select or change a database with the ChangeDatabase()
method of the SqlConnection class. The syntax for the ChangeDatabase()
method is ChangeDatabase("*database*"). For example, instead of
selecting a database by including the Database parameter in the connection string in the SqlConnection instantiation statement, the
following code uses a ChangeDatabase() statement to open the
customers database from the dbConnection database connection:

```
SqlConnection dbConnection = new SqlConnection(
    "Data Source=.\\SQLEXPRESS;
    Integrated Security=true;");
dbConnection.ChangeDatabase("customers");
```

Next, you will add statements to the forecast program that open your
SQL Server instance, select the forecast database, and then close the
database connection.

To add statements to the forecast program that open your SQL
Server instance, select the forecast database, and then close the
database connection:

1. Return to the **Default.aspx.cs** file in the Visual Studio IDE.

2. Add the following statements to the end of the Page_Load()
   event handler to open the database connection, change to the
   forecast database, and then close the database connection:

   ```
   dbConnection.Open();
   dbConnection.ChangeDatabase("forecast");
   dbConnection.Close();
   ```

3. Start the Web site. The Web page will not display anything yet, but if you receive any errors, fix them before continuing.

4. Close your Web browser window.

Short Quiz 1

1. What is ODBC?

2. How do you access databases with ASP.NET?

3. Explain how to select a database after you have instantiated an object of the SqlConnection class.

Handling SQL Server Errors

When accessing SQL Server databases and other types of data sources, you need to understand the errors that can affect the execution of your program. One of the most important errors that you need to consider occurs when you cannot connect to a database server. Reasons that you might not be able to connect to a database server include the following:

- The database server is not running.

- You do not have sufficient privileges to access the data source.

- You entered an invalid username and password.

In addition to database connectivity errors, a number of other types of errors can occur when accessing a database, including errors that occur when you try to open a nonexistent database or when you enter an invalid SQL statement. As you learned in Chapter 6, the standard error messages that ASP.NET generates can be extremely confusing and frustrating for your users. For this reason, you should use bullet-proofing techniques that gracefully handle any errors that might occur. This is especially important when using ASP.NET to manipulate a database. First, you will learn how to check the database connection.

Checking the Database Connection

It is good practice to make sure your program has connected to a database successfully before it attempts to read, write, add, or modify records. The State property of the SqlConnection class contains a string indicating the current status of the database connection. Table 8-4 lists the values that ADO.NET can assign to the State property.

Value	Description
Broken	The connection is broken
Closed	The connection is closed
Connecting	The `Connection` object is connecting to the data source
Executing	The connection is executing a command
Fetching	The connection is retrieving data
Open	The connection is open

Table 8-4 `SqlConnection` class `State` property values

You can use the value assigned to the `State` property to check the database connection, although you must use the `Convert.ToString()` method before you can use it in a conditional expression. The following code adds an `if` statement that checks the `State` property after the statement that creates the new `SqlConnection` object attempts to connect to a database. If the connection was unsuccessful, the ASP.NET `Response.Write()` method returns a message to the client.

```
SqlConnection dbConnection = new SqlConnection(
    "Data Source=.\\SQLEXPRESS;
    Integrated Security=true;
    Database=customers");
dbConnection.Open();
string dbStatus = Convert.ToString(dbConnection.State);
if (dbStatus != "Open")
        Response.Write("The database is not available.");
else
        additional statements;
dbConnection.Close();
```

Next, you will add statements to the forecast program that use the `State` property to check the database connection.

To add statements to the forecast program that use the `State` property to check the database connection:

1. Return to the **Default.aspx.cs** file in the Visual Studio IDE.

2. Add the following `if...else` statement immediately after the `Open()` statement in the `Page_Load()` event handler. If the database connection is successful, the message "Successfully connected to the database instance." displays in the Web browser and the `forecast` database is selected. Otherwise, "The database instance is not available" displays.

```
string dbStatus = Convert.ToString(dbConnection.State);
if (dbStatus == "Open")
{

    Response.Write("Successfully connected to the
        database instance.");
    dbConnection.ChangeDatabase("forecast");
}
```

```
                        else
                            Response.Write("The database instance is
                                not available.");
```

3. Start the Web site. You should see the "Successfully connected to the database instance." message in your Web browser window.

4. Close your Web browser window.

Using Exception Handling to Control SQL Server Errors

Instead of using an `if...else` block and the `State` property to determine whether a database connection was successful, you can also execute the `Open()` method within a `try...catch` block. The `try` block can also contain any database statements that might cause an error, such as the `ChangeDatabase()` method. The following code demonstrates how to use a `try...catch` block to open and select a database. If either the `Open()` or the `ChangeDatabase()` methods return an error, the `catch` block prints "The database is not available."

```
SqlConnection dbConnection = new SqlConnection(
    "Data Source=.\\SQLEXPRESS;
    Integrated Security=true");
try
{
    dbConnection.Open();
    dbConnection.ChangeDatabase("customers");
}
catch
{
        Response.Write("The database is not available.");
}
```

The `System.Data.SqlClient` namespace includes the **SqlException class**, which represents the exception that is thrown when SQL Server returns an error or warning. As an example of how you might use the `SqlException` class, consider an ASP.NET program that allows users to submit a username and password that will be used to log in to SQL Server. For example, a Web page might contain the following simple form that will be submitted to a program named dbAuthenticate.aspx:

```
<form action="dbAuthenticate.aspx" method="POST"
enctype="application/x-www-form-urlencoded">
<p>Username <input type="text" name="userID" /><br />
Password <input type="password" name="password" /></p>
<p><input type="submit" value="Log In" /></p>
</form>
```

If a user enters an invalid username or password with the preceding form, printing a generic message such as "The database server is not available" doesn't help him determine what's wrong. When connecting to a SQL Server database, you should at least use the SqlException class to give the user more information about the error that occurred. For example, the catch statement in the following code uses the Number and Message properties of the SqlException class to print an error code and message if the connection attempt fails. If the user enters an invalid user ID in the form, he will see the error number and description shown in Figure 8-1. As you can see in the figure, the error description informs users that the login failed for the submitted user ID, which means either that the user ID inadvertently included a typo, or that the user does not have authorization to access the database.

```
catch (SqlException exception)
{
    Response.Write("<p>Error code " + exception.Number
        + ": " + exception.Message + "</p>");

}
```

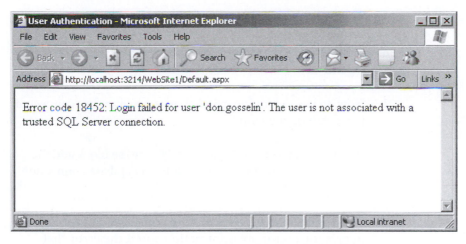

Figure 8-1 Error number and message generated by an invalid user ID

Next, you will modify the forecast program so it uses exception-handling techniques to control SQL Server errors.

To add exception handling to the forecast program:

1. Return to the **Default.aspx.cs** file in the Visual Studio IDE.

2. Delete the dbConnection.Open(); and the Convert. ToString() statement from the Page_Load() event handler.

3. Change the `if...else` statement to a `try` block that contains the `Open()` statement, `ChangeDatabase()` statement, and success message, as follows:

```
try
{
    dbConnection.Open();
    dbConnection.ChangeDatabase("forecast");
    Response.Write("<p>Successfully connected to
        the database instance.</p>");
}
```

4. Add the following `catch` block immediately after the `try` block to handle any SQL exceptions that are thrown:

```
catch (SqlException exception)
{
    Response.Write("<p>Error code " + exception.Number
        + ": " + exception.Message + "</p>");
}
```

5. Start the Web site and you should see the "Successfully connected to the database instance." message in your Web browser window.

6. Close your Web browser window.

Short Quiz 2

1. How do you determine whether your program has connected to a database successfully?

2. What else can you use besides an `if...else` block and the `State` property to determine whether a database connection was successful?

3. What properties of the `SqlException` class can you use to give the user more information about the error that occurred?

Executing SQL Commands Through ASP.NET

The `System.Data.SqlClient` namespace contains various classes that you can use to access and manipulate SQL Server databases. This section discusses the basics of how to work with the `SqlDataReader` and `SqlCommand` classes.

Retrieving Records with the `Sql DataReader` Class

You use the **Sql Command class** to execute commands against Microsoft SQL Server version 7.0 or later. Before you can execute a SQL command, you must create an instance of the `Sql Connection` class using the following syntax:

```
Sql Command object = new Sql Command("command", connection);
```

The *command* parameter you pass to the `Sql Command` object is the SQL command you want to execute. The *connection* parameter represents the `Sql Connection` object that represents the database connection.

The `Sql Command` class contains various methods and properties for executing commands against databases, including the `ExecuteReader()` and `ExecuteNonQuery()` methods. To use the `ExecuteReader()` method, you must first create a **DataReader object**, which retrieves read-only, forward-only data from a data source. **Forward-only** means that the program can only move forward through the record in the returned data, and not backward or to specific records. In other words, your program can sequentially read the records from the first record to the last record, but cannot sequentially read the records from the last record to the first record, or go to a specific record. You use a `DataReader` object when you want to read data from a database, but not add, delete, or modify records. With SQL Server databases, you use the **Sql DataReader class** to retrieve data from Microsoft SQL Server version 7.0 or later.

You use the **ExecuteReader() method** of the `Sql Command` class to create a `Sql DataReader` object, which you must assign to a variable. The following code demonstrates how to create a `Sql DataReader` object named `empRecords` that contains the `last_name` and `first_name` fields from the `Employees` table. The SQL statement uses the `SELECT` keyword to return the data.

```
try
{
    dbConnection.Open();
    dbConnection.ChangeDatabase("employees");
    string SQLString = "SELECT * FROM Employees
            ORDER BY last_name, first_name";
    Sql Command empCommand = new Sql Command(SQLString,
        dbConnection);
    Sql DataReader empRecords = empCommand.ExecuteReader();
}
```

The `Sql DataReader` object contains various properties and methods for reading the returned data. The one method of the `Sql DataReader` object you will study in this chapter is the **Read() method**, which advances the `Sql DataReader` object to the next record. When you work with a `SqlDataReader` object, your position within the record-set is called the **cursor**. When a `SqlDataReader` object is first created, the cursor is initially placed *before* the first row in the recordset. Figure 8-2 shows an example of where the cursor is placed when the `Employees` table is first opened in a `SqlDataReader` object.

Cursor position	101	Blair	Dennis	204 Spruce Lane	Brookfield	MA	01506
	102	Hernandez	Louis	68 Boston Post Road	Spencer	MA	01562
	103	Miller	Erica	271 Baker Hill Road	Brookfield	MA	01515
	104	Morinaga	Scott	17 Ashley Road	Brookfield	MA	01515
	105	Picard	Raymond	1113 Oakham Road	Barre	MA	01531

Figure 8-2   Initial cursor position in a `SqlDataReader` object

You never actually see the record-set in a `SqlDataReader` object as it is shown in Figure 8-2. The illustration in Figure 8-2 is for demonstration purposes only.

The first time you use the `Read()` method, it places the cursor in the first row of the recordset. For example, the following code creates a new `SqlDataReader` object named `empRecords`, and then moves the cursor to the first record in the resulting recordset:

```
string SQLString = "SELECT * FROM Employees
    ORDER BY last_name, first_name";
SqlCommand empCommand = new SqlCommand(SQLString,
    dbConnection);
SqlDataReader empRecords = empCommand.ExecuteReader();
empRecords.Read();
```

When you work with recordsets and the `Read()` method, you can never be certain if there is another record following the current position of the cursor, or even if any records were returned at all from your SQL `SELECT` statement. To determine if a next record is available, you can use the `Read()` method, which returns a value of true if it finds a next row in the recordset or a value of false if it does not find a next row in the recordset. The following code shows how to use an `if` statement to check the value returned by the `Read()` method before moving the cursor. Notice that the `Read()` method is executed as the conditional expression of the `if` statement. Also notice that the conditional expression does not include a comparison operator. The `Read()` method returns a value of true or false automatically as it is executed, eliminating the need for a comparison operator.

```
string SQLString = "SELECT * FROM Employees
    ORDER BY last_name, first_name";
SqlCommand empCommand = new SqlCommand(SQLString,
    dbConnection);
SqlDataReader empRecords = empCommand.ExecuteReader();
if (empRecords.Read()) {
    statements;
}
else
    Response.Write("Your query returned no records.");
```

The field names in a database table are assigned as variables in a SqlDataReader object collection. For example, if you instantiate a SqlDataReader object named empRecords for the Employees database, you can refer to the first_name field by using a statement similar to empRecords["last_name"];. Be aware that whenever you use the Read() method, the content of each variable in a SqlDataReader object changes to reflect the contents of the record at the current location of the cursor. The following code shows a simple program that returns the name of each programmer in the Employees table to the client along with the name of the city where each programmer lives. The program uses a do...while statement to move through the records in the table.

```
string SQLString = "SELECT * FROM Employees
    ORDER BY last_name, first_name";
SqlCommand empCommand = new SqlCommand(SQLString,
    dbConnection);
SqlDataReader empRecords = empCommand.ExecuteReader();
if (empRecords.Read()) {
    do {
        Response.Write(empRecords["first_name"]
        + empRecords["last_name"] + " lives in "
        + empRecords["City"] + ", "
            + empRecords["State"] + ".<br />");
    } while (empRecords.Read());
}
else
    Response.Write("Your query returned no records.");
```

When you are through working with a SqlDataReader object, you must close it with the Close() method, the same way you close a database connection. This allows you to reuse the SqlDataReader object to retrieve other recordsets. Also keep in mind that a SqlDataReader object has exclusive access to the database SqlConnection object. This means you cannot execute any other commands against the database until the SqlDataReader object is closed. To close the empRecords object, use the following statement:

```
empRecords.Close();
```

Next, you will add statements to the try block in the getForecast() function that use the SqlDataReader object to print the results returned from the forecast database in a table.

To print the records from the forecast database in a table:

1. Return to the **Default.aspx.cs** file in the Visual Studio IDE.

2. Delete from the try block the Response.Write() statement that prints the connection success message.

3. Add the following statements to the end of the try block. The first statement creates a string variable named retString that contains SQL statements that return all of the records from the outlook table, sorted by city. The second statement creates a new SqlCommand object using the dbConnection and retString variables. The third statement uses the SqlCommand object to run the ExecuteReader() method.

```
string retString = "SELECT * FROM outlook
    ORDER BY city";
SqlCommand outlookCommand =
    new SqlCommand(retString, dbConnection);
SqlDataReader outlookRecords
    = outlookCommand.ExecuteReader();
```

4. Add the following if statement to the end of the try block. The conditional expression uses the Read() method to determine whether the recordset contains any rows. If so, the first two Response.Write() statements set up a table to contain the records. The do...while statement then uses the Read() method to iterate through and print the contents of the recordset.

```
if (outlookRecords.Read()) {
    Response.Write("<table width='100%' border='1'>");
    Response.Write("<tr><th>City</th><th>State</th>
        <th>Day</th><th>High</th><th>Low</th>
        <th>Conditions</th></tr>");
    do
    {
        Response.Write("<tr>");
        Response.Write("<td>" + outlookRecords["city"]
            + "</td>");
        Response.Write("<td>" + outlookRecords["state"]
            + "</td>");
        Response.Write("<td>" + outlookRecords["day"]
            + "</td>");
        Response.Write("<td>" + outlookRecords["high"]
            + "</td>");
        Response.Write("<td>" + outlookRecords["low"]
            + "</td>");
        Response.Write("<td>"
            + outlookRecords["conditions"] + "</td>");
        Response.Write("</tr>");
    } while (outlookRecords.Read());
    Response.Write("</table>");
}
```

5. Add the following statements to the end of the try block. The else statement prints "Your query returned no results." if no records were returned and the Close() statement closes the outlookRecords object.

```
else
    Response.Write("<p>Your query returned
        no results.</p>");
outlookRecords.Close();
```

6. Start the Web site and you should see the table and database records shown in Figure 8-3.

7. Close your Web browser window.

Figure 8-3 Database records returned with the `SqlDataReader` object

Executing SQL Commands with the SqlCommand Object

Another method of the `SqlCommand` class is the **ExecuteNonQuery()**
method, which executes commands against a database. The
`ExecuteNonQuery()` method is most useful for quickly inserting,
updating, or deleting rows in a SQL Server database. The following
code uses the SQL INSERT statement to add a new employee record to

the Employees database table. If the connection is successful, the try block executes necessary statements to perform the desired actions against the database before disconnecting. The SQL code is assigned to the SQLString variable, and then passed to a SqlCommand object named empCommand, along with the name of the database connection (dbConnection).

```
SqlConnection dbConnection = new SqlConnection(
    "Data Source=.\\SQLEXPRESS;
    Integrated Security=true");
try
{
    dbConnection.Open();
    dbConnection.ChangeDatabase("employees");
    string SQLString = "INSERT INTO Employees VALUES('106',
        'Mbuti', 'Pierre', '106 Flagg Road', 'Spencer',
        'MA', '01562')";
    SqlCommand empCommand = new SqlCommand(SQLString,
        dbConnection);
    empCommand.ExecuteNonQuery();
}
catch (SqlException exception)
{
    Response.Write("<p>Error code " + exception.Number
        + ": " + exception.Message + "</p>");
}
dbConnection.Close();
```

The following code shows another example of the ExecuteNonQuery() method in a try block. This example deletes a row from the Employees table.

```
try
{
    dbConnection.Open();
    dbConnection.ChangeDatabase("employees");
    string SQLString = "DELETE FROM Employees
        WHERE last_name = 'Miller'";
    SqlCommand empCommand = new SqlCommand(SQLString,
        dbConnection);
    empCommand.ExecuteNonQuery();
}
```

The SQL string in the preceding code uses the WHERE clause to look for rows in the table where the last_name field is equal to Miller. Note that the preceding statement would actually delete all rows in the table where the last_name field is equal to Miller. The statement is safe with this example, assuming that there is only one record that contains Miller in the last_name field. However, it's important to understand exactly what records will be deleted before executing the DELETE statement. Also, be sure to include a WHERE clause when using the DELETE statement or all of the rows in the specified table will be deleted.

Next, you will add code to the forecast program that uses the ExecuteNonQuery() method to add two new records to the outlook table in the forecast database.

To add new records to the outlook table in the forecast database:

1. Return to the **Default.aspx.cs** file in the Visual Studio IDE.

2. Add the following new declaration for a new function named addForecast() to the beginning of the code declaration block. Notice that the function definition includes a string parameter named newRecord. You will pass the SQL statements that will create the new record to the newRecord parameter.

```
protected void addForecast(string newRecord)
{
}
```

3. Add the following SqlConnection statement to the addForecast() function. Again, be sure to replace the value assigned to the Data Source property with the name of the SQL Server instance to which you want to connect.

```
SqlConnection dbConnection = new SqlConnection(
    "Data Source=SQL Server instance;
    Integrated Security=true");
```

4. Add the following try block to the end of the addForecast() function. The first two statements open the database connection and change to the forecast database. The third statement uses the newRecord parameter to construct a SqlCommand object and the fourth statement uses the ExecuteNonQuery() method to execute the SQL command. The last statement prints a message if the record was added successfully.

```
try
{
    dbConnection.Open();
    dbConnection.ChangeDatabase("forecast");
    SqlCommand outlookCommand = new SqlCommand(
        newRecord, dbConnection);
    outlookCommand.ExecuteNonQuery();
    Response.Write("<p>Successfully added
        record.</p>");
}
```

5. Now add to the end of the addForecast() function the following catch block, which catches any SQL exceptions, and Close() statement, which closes the database connection.

```
catch (SqlException exception)
{
    Response.Write("<p>Error code "
      + exception.Number + ": "
      + exception.Message + "</p>");
}

dbConnection.Close();
```

424

6. Finally, add the following statements to the end of the Page_Load() event handler, after the statement that closes the database connection. The first statement passes SQL code to the addForecast() function to create a record for Tucson, Arizona, and the second statement passes SQL code that creates a record for Williamsburg, Virginia.

```
addForecast("INSERT INTO outlook VALUES('Tucson',
     'AZ', 'Tuesday', 102, 72, 'Partly cloudy')");
addForecast("INSERT INTO outlook
   VALUES('Williamsburg', 'VA',
   'Wednesday', 90, 71, 'Mostly clear')");
```

7. Start the Web site and you should see two "Successfully added record." messages along with the table containing the new records.

8. Close your Web browser window and then close the project by selecting the **File** menu and then selecting **Close Project**.

Although you will learn in this section how to create databases and tables with ASP.NET, in most cases you should ensure that the database and any necessary tables exist before you put your Web site into production. In other words, you would not normally use ASP.NET to create databases and tables programmatically. The techniques presented in this section are primarily intended to help you better understand how you can use ASP.NET to work with SQL Server databases.

Short Quiz 3

1. How do you use the ExecuteReader() method?

2. When working with a SqlDataReader object, what is a cursor and how do you use it?

3. What do you use the ExecuteNonQuery() method for?

Working with Databases and Tables

In this section, you will learn how to use ASP.NET to work with SQL Server databases, tables, and records. Again, keep in mind that the SQL statements in this section are identical to the SQL statements you saw in Chapter 7. The only difference is that they are executed with ASP.NET instead of with SQL Server Management Studio.

Creating and Deleting Databases

You use the CREATE DATABASE statement with the ExecuteNonQuery() method to create a new database. The following statements create a database named real_estate:

```
SqlConnection dbConnection = new SqlConnection(
    "Data Source=.\\SQLEXPRESS;
    Integrated Security=true");
try
{
    dbConnection.Open();
    SqlCommand sqlCommand = new SqlCommand(
        "CREATE DATABASE real_estate", dbConnection);
    sqlCommand.ExecuteNonQuery();
    Response.Write("<p>Successfully executed
        the query.</p>");
}
catch (SqlException exception)
{
    Response.Write("<p>Error code " + exception.Number
        + ": " + exception.Message + "</p>");
}
dbConnection.Close();
```

If the try block successfully creates the database, you see the "Successfully executed the query." message shown in the preceding example. If the database already exists, you see the error code and message shown in Figure 8-4.

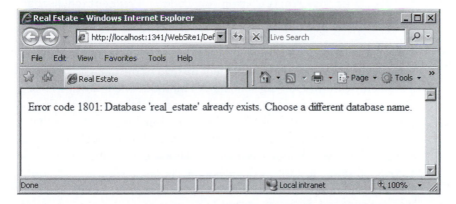

Figure 8-4 Error code and message that prints when you attempt to create a database that already exists

One way to avoid the error message shown in Figure 8-4 is to attempt to access the database with the ChangeDatabase() method. If the database exists, the try block functions successfully. However, if the database does not exist, a SqlException is thrown and the catch block executes. Within the catch block, you can add code that checks the error number to determine whether the exception was thrown when the ChangeDatabase() method attempted to access a nonexistent database. The error number that is returned when you attempt to access a nonexistent database is 911. In the following try block, the ChangeDatabase() method attempts to select the real_estate database. If the database exists, the message "Successfully selected the database." prints to the Web browser. If the database does not yet exist, a SqlException is thrown and the if statement in the catch block executes and checks the error number to see if it is equal to 911. If so, the database is created and "Successfully created the database." prints to the Web browser.

```
try
{
    dbConnection.Open();
    dbConnection.ChangeDatabase("real_estate");
    Response.Write("<p>Successfully selected
        the database.</p>");
}
catch (SqlException exception)
{
    if (exception.Number == 911)
    {
        SqlCommand sqlCommand = new SqlCommand(
            "CREATE DATABASE real_estate", dbConnection);
        sqlCommand.ExecuteNonQuery();
        Response.Write("<p>Successfully created
            the database.</p>");
    }
    else
        Response.Write("<p>Error code " + exception.Number
            + ": " + exception.Message + "</p>");
}
```

Deleting a database is almost identical to creating one, except that you use the DROP DATABASE statement instead of the CREATE DATABASE statement with the ExecuteNonQuery() method. The following code demonstrates how to delete the real_estate database. Notice that the code uses the same error-handling functionality as the code that created the database. In this version, the catch block checks for error number 3702, which indicates that the database does not exist.

```
SqlConnection dbConnection = new SqlConnection(
    "Data Source=.\\SQLEXPRESS;
    Integrated Security=true");
try
{
    dbConnection.Open();
    SqlCommand sqlCommand = new SqlCommand(
        "DROP DATABASE real_estate", dbConnection);
    sqlCommand.ExecuteNonQuery();
    Response.Write("<p>Successfully deleted
        the database.</p>");
}
```

```
catch (SqlException exception)
{
    if (exception.Number == 3701)
    {
        Response.Write("<p>The database does
            not exist.</p>");
    }
    else
        Response.Write("<p>Error code " + exception.Number
            + ": " + exception.Message + "</p>");
}
dbConnection.Close();
```

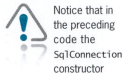

Notice that in the preceding code the SqlConnection constructor does not specify a database to open, nor does the code include a ChangeDatabase() statement to select the database. If you attempt to delete a currently selected database, you will receive an error.

In the rest of this chapter, you will work on a Web site for registering students in energy efficiency classes for a company named Central Valley Utilities. The Web site is already created for you in your Chapter folder for Chapter 8. Figure 8-5 shows how the main page appears in a Web browser.

Figure 8-5   Central Valley Utilities energy efficiency school main Web page

Student information and class registrations will be stored in a SQL Server database named `ConservationSchool` that consists of two tables: `students` and `registration`. The `students` table contains each student's ID, along with other personal information. The `registration` table contains a record for each class in which a student enrolls. The `students` table is the primary table, and the `studentID` field acts as the primary key. The `studentID` field also acts as the foreign key in the `registration` table. Because each student can enroll in more than one class, the relationship between the `students` table and the `registration` table is one-to-many; the `students` table is the one side of the relationship, and the `registration` table is the many side of the relationship.

First, you will start adding code to the New Students page that registers students with the energy efficient school. The New Students page contains a form that students use to enter their name, telephone number, and e-mail address. The form contains validation controls to ensure that students enter values into each field along with RegularExpression-Validator controls that validate the formats of the telephone number and e-mail address. Figure 8-6 shows the New Student page.

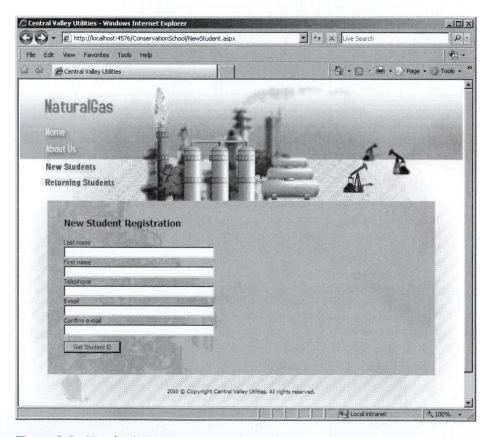

Figure 8-6 New Student page

To start adding code that registers students:

1. Return to the Visual Studio IDE, select the **File** menu and then select **Open Web Site**. The Open Web Site dialog box opens. Locate and select the ConservationSchool folder, located in your Chapter folder for Chapter 8, and then click **Open**. The ConservationSchool Web site opens in the Visual Studio IDE.

2. Open the **NewStudent.aspx.cs** file in the Code Editor and add the following directive to the end of the directives section to give the class access to the `System.Data.SqlClient` namespace:

```
using System.Data.SqlClient;
```

3. Add the following statements to the `Page_Load()` event handler to determine whether the current request was caused by a post back event and if the controls on the form are valid. With the New Student page, post back will occur after students fill out the form and click the Get Student ID button.

```
if (Page.IsPostBack)
{
    Page.Validate();
    if (Page.IsValid)
    {
    }
}
```

4. Add the following statements to the nested `if` statement you created in Step 3. The first two statements hide the Web form and unhide a Literal control that displays results to the student, respectively. The remaining statements assign the values of the form controls to string variables.

```
registrationForm.Visible = false;
regMessage.Visible = true;
string first = firstName.Text;
string last = lastName.Text;
string phone = telephone.Text;
string emailAddress = Request.Form["email"];
```

5. Next, add the following statements to the end of the `if` statement. The first statement establishes a connection to your database. The `try` block attempts to open the database connection and change to the `ConservationSchool` database. If the database does not exist, the `catch` block creates it and then changes to it. The `finally` block prints a message

indicating that the database was selected successfully and the last statement closes the database connection.

```
SqlConnection dbConnection = new SqlConnection(
    "Data Source=.\\SQLEXPRESS;
    Integrated Security=true");
try
{
    dbConnection.Open();
    dbConnection.ChangeDatabase("ConservationSchool");
}
catch (SqlException exception)
{
    if (exception.Number == 911)
    {
        SqlCommand sqlCommand
            = new SqlCommand(
            "CREATE DATABASE ConservationSchool",
            dbConnection);
        sqlCommand.ExecuteNonQuery();
        regMessage.Text = "<p>Successfully created
            the database.</p>";
        dbConnection.ChangeDatabase(
            "ConservationSchool");
    }
    else
        regMessage.Text += "<p>Error code "
          + exception.Number
            + ": " + exception.Message + "</p>";
}
finally
{
    regMessage.Text += "<p>Successfully selected
        the database.</p>";
}
dbConnection.Close();
```

6. Start the Web site and click the **New Students** button. Enter values into each of the form fields and click the **Get Student ID** button. You should see the "Successfully created the database." and "Successfully selected the database." messages, as shown in Figure 8-7.

7. Close your Web browser window.

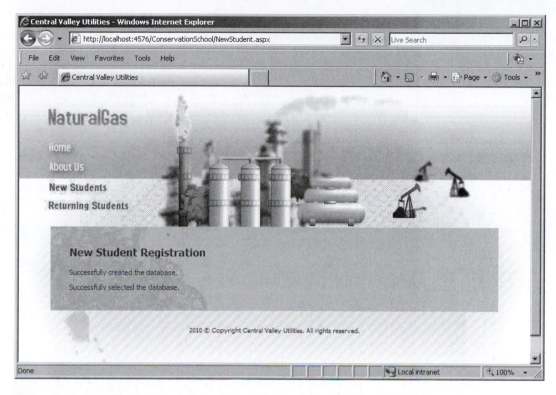

Figure 8-7 New Student page after adding code to create and select the database

Creating and Deleting Tables

To create a table, you use the CREATE TABLE statement with the
ExecuteNonQuery() method. Be sure you have selected the cor-
rected database with the SqlConnection constructor or with the
ChangeDatabase() method before executing the CREATE TABLE statement or you might create your new table in the wrong database. The
following code creates a table named commercial in the real_estate
database.

```
SqlConnection dbConnection = new SqlConnection(
    "Data Source=.\\SQLEXPRESS;
    Integrated Security=true");
try
{
    dbConnection.Open();
    dbConnection.ChangeDatabase("real_estate");
    SqlCommand sqlCommand = new SqlCommand(
        "CREATE TABLE commercial (city VARCHAR(25),
            state VARCHAR(25), sale_or_lease VARCHAR(25),
            type_of_use VARCHAR(40), price INT, size INT)",
            dbConnection);
```

```
        sqlCommand.ExecuteNonQuery();
        Response.Write("<p>Successfully created the
            table.</p>");
    }
    catch (SqlException exception)
    {
        Response.Write("<p>Error code " + exception.Number
            + ": " + exception.Message + "</p>");
    }
    dbConnection.Close();
```

With the preceding code, if the table already exists in the selected database, you will see the error code and message shown in Figure 8-8.

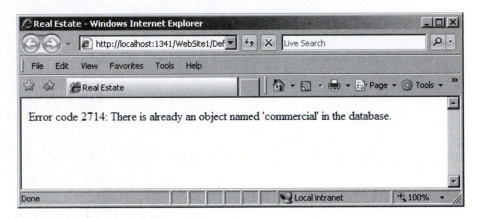

Figure 8-8   Error code and message that prints when you attempt to create a table that already exists

To avoid the error message shown in Figure 8-8, you can use the `ExecuteReader()` or `ExecuteNonQuery()` methods to determine whether the error number thrown is equal to 208, which indicates the object does not exist. In the following `try...catch` block, the `ExecuteReader()` method attempts to select records from the `commercial` table. If the table exists, the `ExecuteReader()` method executes successfully. If the table does not exist, a `SqlException` is thrown and the `if` statement in the `catch` block executes, checking the error number to see if it is equal to 208. If so, the table is created and "Successfully created the table." prints to the Web browser.

```
try
{
    dbConnection.Open();
    dbConnection.ChangeDatabase("real_estate");
    string SQLString = "SELECT * FROM commercial";
    SqlCommand empCommand = new SqlCommand(SQLString,
        dbConnection);
    SqlDataReader empRecords = empCommand.ExecuteReader();
```

```
    empRecords.Close();
    Response.Write("<p>The table already exists.</p>");
    }
catch (SqlException exception)
{
    if (exception.Number == 208)
    {
        SqlCommand sqlCommand = new SqlCommand(
            "CREATE TABLE commercial (city VARCHAR(25),
            state VARCHAR(25), sale_or_lease VARCHAR(25),
            type_of_use VARCHAR(40), price INT, size INT)",
            dbConnection);
        sqlCommand.ExecuteNonQuery();
        Response.Write("<p>Successfully created
            the table.</p>");
    }
    else
        Response.Write("<p>Error code " + exception.Number
            + ": " + exception.Message + "</p>");
}
```

Next, you will add code to the NewStudentID.aspx.cs program that creates the students table the first time the program is called. The students table will use the studentID field as the primary key. To identify a field as a primary key, you include the PRIMARY KEY keywords when you first define a field with the CREATE TABLE statement. The **IDENTITY keyword** is used with a primary key to generate a unique ID for each new row in a table. By default, the value of the first row in a field that is created with the IDENTITY keyword is assigned a value of 1 and the value for each subsequently added row is incremented by 1 from the preceding row. However, you can specify the starting number and the amount each subsequent row is incremented with the syntax IDENTITY(start, increment). For example, IDENTITY(1000,5) assigns a value of 1000 for the first row and increments subsequent rows by 5. As an example, the following SQL statement defines a primary key named id for the inventory table using the SMALLINT data type. The id field definition also includes the IDENTITY keyword.

```
CREATE TABLE inventory (id SMALLINT IDENTITY PRIMARY
KEY, manufacturer VARCHAR(50), model VARCHAR(50),
length DECIMAL, width DECIMAL, sku VARCHAR(15), price
SMALLMONEY);
```

When you add records to a table that includes an IDENTITY field, you do not include a field value for the IDENTITY field. The following SQL statement inserts a new record into the inventory table of the skateboards database. If this is the first record added to the table, its primary key will be a value of 1.

```
INSERT INTO inventory VALUES('Almost', 'Coffin Cruiser',
31.25, 8.5, '1CALMOCOFF85000', 92.00);
```

To add code to the NewStudentID.aspx.cs program that creates the students table the first time the program is called:

1. Return to the **NewStudent.aspx.cs** file in the Visual Studio IDE.

2. Add the following try block above the statement that closes the database connection. The ExecuteReader() method attempts to select records from the students table. If the table exists, the ExecuteReader() method executes successfully. If the table does not exist, a SqlException with error number 208 is thrown.

```
try
{
    string SQLString = "SELECT * FROM students";
    SqlCommand checkIDTable = new SqlCommand(
      SQLString, dbConnection);
    SqlDataReader idRecords
      = checkIDTable.ExecuteReader();
    idRecords.Close();
}
```

3. Add the following catch block immediately above the statement that closes the database connection. The if statement in the catch block creates the students table and executes only if an exception is thrown with error number 208, indicating that the table does not exist. Notice that the CREATE TABLE statement creates the studentID field as an autoincrementing primary key that starts with a value of 100 and increments each subsequent row by one. The else statement executes if any other error number was thrown.

```
catch (SqlException exception)
{
    if (exception.Number == 208)
    {
        SqlCommand sqlCommand = new SqlCommand(
          "CREATE TABLE students (studentID SMALLINT
          IDENTITY(100,1) PRIMARY KEY, first VARCHAR(25),
          last VARCHAR(50), phone VARCHAR(15),
          email VARCHAR(50))", dbConnection);
        sqlCommand.ExecuteNonQuery();
        regMessage.Text += "<p>Successfully created
            the table.</p>";
    }
    else
        Response.Write("<p>Error code "
          + exception.Number + ": "
          + exception.Message + "</p>");
}
```

4. Start the Web site and click the **New Students** button. Enter values into each of the form fields and click the **Get Student ID** button. You should see the "Successfully selected the database." and "Successfully created the table." messages.

5. Close your Web browser window.

To delete a table, you use the DROP TABLE statement with the ExecuteNonQuery() function. The following code demonstrates how to delete the commercial table using similar error-handling functionality as the code that created the table. In this version, the if statement in the try block checks for an exception number of 3701, which indicates that the table does not exist or that you do not have permission to drop it.

```
try
{
    dbConnection.Open();
    dbConnection.ChangeDatabase("real_estate");
    SqlCommand sqlCommand = new SqlCommand(
        "DROP TABLE commercial", dbConnection);
    sqlCommand.ExecuteNonQuery();
    Response.Write("<p>Successfully deleted
        the table.</p>");
    }
catch (SqlException exception)
{
    if (exception.Number == 3701)
    {
        Response.Write("<p>The table does not exist.</p>");
    }
    else
        Response.Write("<p>Error code "
            + exception.Number + ": "
            + exception.Message + "</p>");
}
```

Adding, Deleting, and Updating Records

To add records to a table, you use the INSERT and VALUES keywords with the ExecuteNonQuery() method. Remember that the values you enter in the VALUES list must be in the same order in which you defined the table fields. For example, the following statements add a new row to the inventory table in the skateboards database:

```
SqlConnection dbConnection = new SqlConnection(
    "Data Source=.\\SQLEXPRESS;
    Integrated Security=true");
```

```
dbConnection.Open();
dbConnection.ChangeDatabase("skateboards");
SqlCommand sqlCommand = new SqlCommand(
    "INSERT INTO inventory VALUES('Almost',
    'Coffin Cruiser', 31.25, 8.5,
    '1CALMOCOFF85000', 92.00)", dbConnection);
sqlCommand.ExecuteNonQuery();
Response.Write("<p>Successfully added the record.</p>");
dbConnection.Close();
```

Also remember that you must specify NULL in any fields for which you do not have a value. For example, if you do not know the length, width, or sku for the Almost Coffin Cruiser skateboard, you can enter NULL for each item in the VALUES list, as follows:

```
SqlCommand sqlCommand = new SqlCommand(
    "INSERT INTO inventory VALUES('Almost',
    'Coffin Cruiser', NULL, NULL,
    NULL, 92.00)", dbConnection);
sqlCommand.ExecuteNonQuery();
Response.Write("<p>Successfully added the record.</p>");
```

To add multiple records to a database, you use the BULK INSERT statement and the ExecuteNonQuery() function with a local text file containing the records you want to add. The following statements load a file named inventory.txt into the inventory table in the skateboards database:

```
SqlCommand sqlCommand = new SqlCommand(
    "BULK INSERT inventory from 'inventory.txt'",
    dbConnection);
sqlCommand.ExecuteNonQuery();
Response.Write("<p>Successfully added the records.</p>");
```

To update records in a table, you use the UPDATE, SET, and WHERE keywords with the ExecuteNonQuery() function. The UPDATE keyword specifies the name of the table to update and the SET keyword specifies the value to assign to the fields in the records that match the condition in the WHERE keyword. For example, the following statements modify the price of the Almost Coffin Cruiser skateboard to $97.50.

```
SqlCommand sqlCommand = new SqlCommand("UPDATE inventory
    SET price=97.50 WHERE manufacturer='Almost'
    AND model='Coffin Cruiser'",
    dbConnection);
sqlCommand.ExecuteNonQuery();
Response.Write("<p>Successfully modified the record.</p>");
```

To delete records in a table, you use the DELETE and WHERE keywords with the ExecuteNonQuery() function. Remember that the

WHERE keyword determines which records to delete in the table. For example, the following statements delete the "Almost Coffin Cruiser" record from the `inventory` table in the `skateboards` database:

```
SqlCommand sqlCommand = new SqlCommand("DELETE
    FROM inventory WHERE manufacturer='Almost'
    AND model='Coffin Cruiser'",
    dbConnection);
sqlCommand.ExecuteNonQuery();
Response.Write("<p>Successfully deleted the record.</p>");
```

To delete all the records in a table, omit the WHERE keyword. The following statement deletes all the records in the `inventory` table:

```
SqlCommand sqlCommand = new SqlCommand(
    "DELETE FROM inventory", dbConnection);
sqlCommand.ExecuteNonQuery();
Response.Write("<p>Successfully deleted all records.</p>");
```

In this exercise, you will add code to the NewStudentID.aspx.cs program that adds a new student record to the `students` table in the `ConservationSchool` database. You will add the records using the `ExecuteNonQuery()` function, and then you will retrieve the ID created with IDENTITY in the last INSERT operation by using the Transact-SQL **IDENT_CURRENT() function**, which returns the last identity value that was created for a specified table. Because the IDENT_CURRENT() function is part of Transact-SQL, you assign it to the SQL string that is executed with the `ExecuteReader()` function. More specifically, you use the IDENT_CURRENT() function with the SELECT keyword, and the AS keyword to assign a column name for the returned value. In the following example, the SQL statement assigned to the `SQLString` variable uses the SELECT keyword with the IDENT_CURRENT() function to retrieve the last identity value that was created for the `inventory` table in the `skateboards` database. The returned value is assigned to a column named `inventoryID`, which is then printed to the Web page.

```
string SQLString = "SELECT IDENT_CURRENT('inventory')
    AS inventoryID";
SqlCommand invCommand = new SqlCommand(SQLString,
    dbConnection);
SqlDataReader invRecords = empCommand.ExecuteReader();
invRecords.Read();
Response.Write(invRecords["inventoryID"]);
```

To add code to the NewStudentID.aspx.cs program that adds a new student record to the `students` table in the `ConservationSchool` database:

1. Return to the **NewStudent.aspx.cs** file in the Visual Studio IDE.

2. Add the following statement to the end of the last `finally` block to build a query string that will insert the values into the `students` table:

```
string studentInfo = "INSERT INTO students VALUES('"
    + first + "', '"
    + last + "', '"
    + phone + "', '"
    + emailAddress + "')";
```

3. Add the following statement to the end of the `finally` block to create the `SqlCommand` object and run the `ExecuteNonQuery()` method:

```
SqlCommand sqlCommand = new SqlCommand(studentInfo,
    dbConnection);
sqlCommand.ExecuteNonQuery();
```

4. Add the following statements after the `finally` block but above the statement that closes the database connection. These statements retrieve and print the new student ID. The last statement creates a link to a registration page. Notice that the student ID is appended to the URL as a query string.

```
string idString = "SELECT IDENT_CURRENT('students')
    AS studentID";
SqlCommand newID = new SqlCommand(idString,
dbConnection);
SqlDataReader studentRecord = newID.ExecuteReader();
studentRecord.Read();
string studentID = Convert.ToString(
    studentRecord["studentID"]);
studentRecord.Close();
regMessage.Text += "<p>Thanks " + first
    + "! Your new student ID is <strong>" + studentID
    + "</strong>.</p>";
regMessage.Text += "<p><a href
    ='ReturningStudent.aspx?" + studentID
    + "'>Register for Classes</a></p>";
```

5. Start the Web site and click the **New Students** button. Enter values into each of the form fields and click the

Get Student ID button. You should be assigned a new student ID of 100 and you should see the Web page shown in Figure 8-9.

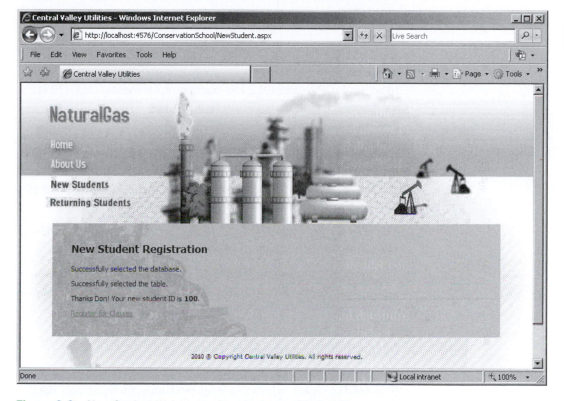

Figure 8-9   New Student Web page after obtaining a student ID

6. Close your Web browser window.

Short Quiz 4

1. How do you create and delete SQL Server databases programmatically with ASP.NET?

2. How do you create and delete tables in SQL Server databases programmatically with ASP.NET?

3. How do you add, update, and delete records in a database?

Summing Up

- Open Database Connectivity, or ODBC, allows ODBC-compliant applications to access any data source for which there is an ODBC driver.

- ActiveX Data Objects, or ADO, is a Microsoft database connectivity technology that allows ASP and other Web development tools to access ODBC- and OLE DB-compliant databases. OLE DB is a data source connectivity standard promoted by Microsoft as a successor to ODBC.

- To access and manipulate SQL Server databases with ASP.NET, you use the classes in the `System.Data.SqlClient` namespace.

- To connect to a SQL Server database, you instantiate an object of the `SqlConnection` class.

- The `State` property of the `SqlConnection` class contains a string indicating the current status of the database connection.

- The `System.Data.SqlClient` namespace includes the `SqlException` class, which represents the exception that is thrown when SQL Server returns an error or warning.

- You use the `SqlCommand` class to execute commands against Microsoft SQL Server version 7.0 or later.

- To use the `ExecuteReader()` method, you must first create a `DataReader` object, which retrieves read-only, forward-only data from a data source. Forward-only means that the program can only move forward through the record in the returned data, and not backward or to specific records.

- With SQL Server databases, you use the `SqlDataReader` class to retrieve data from Microsoft SQL Server version 7.0 or later.

- You use the `ExecuteReader()` method of the `SqlCommand` class to create a `SqlDataReader` object.

- When you work with a `SqlDataReader` object, your position within the recordset is called the cursor.

- The `ExecuteNonQuery()` method of the `SqlCommand` class executes commands against a database.

- To create a new database, you use the `CREATE DATABASE` statement with the `ExecuteNonQuery()` method.

- To create a table, you use the CREATE TABLE statement with the ExecuteNonQuery() function.

- The IDENTITY keyword is used with a primary key to generate a unique ID for each new row in a table.

- To delete a table, you use the DROP TABLE statement with the ExecuteNonQuery() function.

- To add records to a table, you use the INSERT and VALUES keywords with the ExecuteNonQuery() method.

- To add multiple records to a database, you use the BULK INSERT statement and the ExecuteNonQuery() function with a local text file containing the records you want to add.

- To update records in a table, you use the UPDATE, SET, and WHERE keywords with the ExecuteNonQuery() function.

- To delete records in a table, you use the DELETE and WHERE keywords with the ExecuteNonQuery() function.

Comprehension Check

1. ODBC-compliant applications can only access SQL Server databases. True or False?

2. Explain the difference between ODBC and OLE DB.

3. Which of the following namespaces contains classes for directly manipulating SQL Server databases with ASP.NET?

    a. `System.Data.Odbc`

    b. `System.Data.OleDb`

    c. `System.Data.SqlClient`

    d. `System.Data.SqlServer`

4. To connect to a SQL Server database, you instantiate an object of the _____ class.

    a. `SqlServer`

    b. `SqlExpress`

    c. `SqlDatabase`

    d. `SqlConnection`

5. Which of the following parameters is required in the connection string that is used for connecting to SQL Server?

a. Connection String

b. Database

c. Data Source

d. Server Version

6. If you are using Windows Authentication as your security mechanism, to which connection string parameter do you need to assign a value of true?

a. Integrated Security

b. Windows Authentication

c. SQL Server Authentication

d. Native Authentication

7. Explain why you should always use the Close() method to close a database connection.

8. How do you select a database with a SQL Server connection? (Choose all that apply.)

a. by including the Database parameter in the connection string

b. by calling the selectDB() method

c. by assigning the database name to the useDatabase parameter

d. by calling the ChangeDatabase() method

9. What value is assigned to the State property if a connection to a database has been successfully established?

a. True

b. Open

c. Connected

d. Ready

10. Before you can use the value assigned to the State property in a conditional expression to check the database connection, you must first use the Convert.ToString() method. True or False?

11. What is the name of the exception class that is thrown when SQL Server returns an error or warning?

    a. `SqlFailure`

    b. `SqlServerError`

    c. `SqlException`

    d. `SqlConnectionError`

12. What is the second parameter that you must pass to a `SqlCommand` object?

    a. the SQL command you want to execute

    b. the value assigned to the `Connection` object's `State` property

    c. the name of the data provider

    d. the name of the object that represents the database connection

13. The `SqlDataReader` class can move forward, backward, or to a specific record. True or False?

14. Where is the cursor placed when you first create a `SqlDataReader` object?

    a. before the first record

    b. on the first record

    c. on the last record

    d. after the last record

15. What value does the `Read()` method return if it finds a next row in the recordset?

    a. −1

    b. true

    c. false

    d. the record number

16. The `ExecuteNonQuery()` method returns records from a database. True or False?

17. If you attempt to delete a currently selected database, you will receive an error. True or False?

18. Which of the following SQL keywords creates an autoincrementing field?

    a. AUTO

    b. INCREMENT

    c. IDENTITY

    d. COUNT

19. What value must you pass to an autoincrementing field when adding new records to a table?

    a. NULL

    b. VOID

    c. AUTO

    d. You do not include a value for an autoincrementing field.

20. Which Transact-SQL function returns the last autoincremented value that was created for a specified table?

    a. CURRENT()

    b. IDENT()

    c. LAST_IDENT()

    d. IDENT_CURRENT()

Reinforcement Exercises

Exercise 8-1

In this exercise, you will add controls to the Default.aspx file that returning students can use to log in. You will also add code to the Page_Load() event handler that determines whether the student entered a valid ID.

To add login functionality to the Default.aspx file:

1. Return to the Visual Studio IDE and open the **Default.aspx** file in the Code Editor.

2. Locate the Web form and add the following controls. Students will enter their student ID into the TextBox control and click the Returning Students button. Code in the Page_Load() event handler will validate the ID against the database and print a message to the Literal control if it's not valid.

```
<asp:TextBox ID="studentID" runat="server" />
 <asp:Button ID="Button1" runat="server"
Text="Returning Students" /> <asp:Literal
ID="validateMessage" runat="server" />  
<asp:RequiredFieldValidator ID="idValidator"
runat="server" ErrorMessage="**You must enter
your student ID**" ControlToValidate="studentID" />
```

3. Open the **Default.aspx.cs** file in the Code Editor and add the
   following directive to the end of the directives section to give
   the class access to the System.Data.SqlClient namespace:

   ```
   using System.Data.SqlClient;
   ```

4. Add the following statements to the Page_Load() event handler to determine whether the current request was caused by a
   post back event and if the controls on the form are valid. With
   the Default.aspx page, post back will occur after students enter
   a student ID and click the Returning Students button.

   ```
   if (Page.IsPostBack)
   {
       Page.Validate();
       if (Page.IsValid)
       {
       }
   }
   ```

5. Add the following statements to the if statement. The first
   statement instantiates a SqlConnection object. The try statement changes to the ConservationSchool database and uses
   the ExecuteReader() method to query the database to determine whether the ID the student entered is valid. If the Read()
   method returns a value of true, the ID exists and the page is
   redirected to the ReturningStudent.aspx page. Notice that the
   student ID is appended to the URL as a query string. If the ID
   does not exist, an error message is printed to the Literal control.

   ```
   SqlConnection dbConnection = new SqlConnection("Data
   Source=..\\SQLEXPRESS;Integrated Security=true");
   try
   {
       dbConnection.Open();
       dbConnection.ChangeDatabase("ConservationSchool");
       string SQLString = "SELECT * FROM students WHERE
           studentID=" + studentID.Text;
       SqlCommand checkIDTable
         = new SqlCommand(
         SQLString, dbConnection);
       SqlDataReader idRecords
         = checkIDTable.ExecuteReader();
       if (idRecords.Read())
       {
   ```

```
                    Response.Redirect(
                        "ReturningStudent.aspx?studentID="
                        + studentID.Text);
                    idRecords.Close();
                }
                else
                {
                    validateMessage.Text
                        = "<p>**Invalid student ID**</p>";
                    idRecords.Close();
                }
            }
            catch (SqlException exception)
            {
                Response.Write("<p>Error code "
                    + exception.Number + ": "
                    + exception.Message + "</p>");
            }
```

6. Start the Web site, enter an invalid student ID in the text box, and then click the **Returning Students** button. You should see the "**Invalid student ID**" message. Now enter a valid student ID in the text box and then click the **Returning Students** button. You should be successfully redirected to the ReturningStudent.aspx page, which doesn't have any controls yet. You will add controls to the ReturningStudent.aspx page next.

7. Close your Web browser window.

Exercise 8-2

Although you used ASP.NET to create the ConservationSchool database and students table, to ensure that they exist you should manually create the database and any necessary tables with SQL Server Management Studio before you put your Web site into production. In this exercise, you will use SQL Server Management Studio instead of ASP.NET code to create the registration table.

To create the registration table:

1. Start SQL Server Management Studio by clicking the **Start** button, clicking the **Start** button, pointing to **All Programs**, clicking **Microsoft SQL Server 2008**, and then clicking **SQL Server Management Studio**.

2. If necessary, enter your connection information into the Server name, Server type, and Authentication boxes, and then click **Connect**.

3. Create a new query window by selecting the **File** menu, pointing to **New**, and clicking **Query with Current Connection**. A new query window opens.

4. Enter the following command to select the `ConservationSchool` database:

   ```
   USE ConservationSchool;
   ```

5. Enter the following command to create the `registration` table:

   ```
   CREATE TABLE registration (studentID SMALLINT, class VARCHAR(40), days VARCHAR(40), time VARCHAR(40));
   ```

6. Select the **Query** menu and then select the **Execute** command. You should see the "Command(s) completed successfully." message in the Messages window at the bottom of the query window.

7. Select the **File** menu, select **Close**, and then select **No** when prompted to save the query.

8. Close Microsoft SQL Server Management Studio by selecting the **File** menu and then selecting **Exit**.

Exercise 8-3

In this exercise, you will complete the ReturningStudent.aspx program, which adds student registration information to the `registration` table.

1. Return to the Visual Studio IDE and open the **ReturningStudent.aspx** file in the Code Editor.

2. Locate the Web form and add the following controls, which students will use to register for classes. The first Literal control will display the current student ID.

   ```
   <asp:Literal ID="curID" runat="server" />
   <strong>Select the class you would like to take:
   </strong><br />
   <p>
       <asp:RadioButtonList ID="className"
         runat="server">
         <asp:ListItem Value="Solar Power Basics"
             Selected="True">Solar Power Basics
             </asp:ListItem>
         <asp:ListItem Value="Green Construction
             Techniques"> Green Construction
             Techniques</asp:ListItem>
         <asp:ListItem Value="Commercial Energy
             Management">Commercial Energy
             Management</asp:ListItem>
         <asp:ListItem Value="Creating a
             Green Office">Creating a Green
             Office</asp:ListItem>
         <asp:ListItem Value="Residential Energy
             Management">Residential Energy
             Management</asp:ListItem>
       </asp:RadioButtonList>
   </p>
   ```

```
<p>
    <strong>Available Days and Times:</strong><br />
    <asp:ListBox ID="days" runat="server" Rows="1">
        <asp:ListItem Selected="True">Mondays and
            Wednesdays</asp:ListItem>
        <asp:ListItem>Tuesdays and Thursdays
            </asp:ListItem>
        <asp:ListItem>Wednesdays and Fridays
            </asp:ListItem>
    </asp:ListBox>
    <asp:ListBox ID="time" runat="server" Rows="1">
        <asp:ListItem Selected="True">
            9 a.m. - 11 a.m.</asp:ListItem>
        <asp:ListItem>1 p.m. - 3 p.m.</asp:ListItem>
        <asp:ListItem>6 p.m. - 8 p.m.</asp:ListItem>
    </asp:ListBox>
    <p>
        <asp:Button ID="register" runat="server"
            Text="Register" /></p>
```

3. Open the **ReturningStudent.aspx.cs** file in the Code Editor and add the following directive to the end of the directives section to give the class access to the System.Data.SqlClient namespace:

```
using System.Data.SqlClient;
```

4. Add the following statements to the Page_Load() event handler. The if statement determines whether the query string contains a student ID. If it doesn't, the user is redirected to the Default.aspx file. If it does, the user ID is assigned to the curID Literal control. Notice that a link is also added to the Literal control that will be used to display the student's current schedule.

```
if (Request.QueryString["studentID"] == "")
    Response.Redirect("Default.aspx");
else
    curID.Text = "<p>Student ID: "
        + Request.QueryString["studentID"]
        + " <a href='ReviewSchedule.
          aspx?studentID="
        + Request.QueryString["studentID"]
        + "'>Review Current Schedule</a></p>";
```

5. Add the following statements to the end of the Page_Load() event handler to determine whether the current request was caused by a post back event and if the controls on the form are valid. With the Default.aspx page, post back will occur after students enter a student ID and click the Returning Students button.

```
if (Page.IsPostBack)
{
    Page.Validate();
    if (Page.IsValid)
    {
    }
}
```

6. Add the following statements to the if statement. The code uses for loops to determine which class, days, and time are selected. Then, the ExecuteNonQuery() method adds a new record to the registration table.

```
registrationForm.Visible = false;
regMessage.Visible = true;
string studentID = Request.QueryString["studentID"];
string selectedClass = "";
string selectedDays = "";
string selectedTime = "";
for (int i = 0; i < className.Items.Count; ++i)
{
    if (className.Items[i].Selected)
        selectedClass = className.Items[i].Value;
}
for (int i = 0; i < days.Items.Count; ++i)
{
    if (days.Items[i].Selected)
        selectedDays = days.Items[i].Value;
}
for (int i = 0; i < time.Items.Count; ++i)
{
    if (time.Items[i].Selected)
        selectedTime = time.Items[i].Value;
}
SqlConnection dbConnection = new SqlConnection(
    "Data Source=.\\SQLEXPRESS;
    Integrated Security=true");
try
{
    dbConnection.Open();
    dbConnection.ChangeDatabase(
      "ConservationSchool");
    string classInfo = "INSERT INTO
      registration VALUES('"
        + studentID + "', '" + selectedClass
        + "', '" + selectedDays + "', '"
        + selectedTime + "')";
    SqlCommand sqlCommand = new SqlCommand(
        classInfo, dbConnection);
    sqlCommand.ExecuteNonQuery();
    regMessage.Text = "<p>You are registered for "
        + selectedClass + " on " + selectedDays
        + ", " + selectedTime;
    regMessage.Text += "<p>Click your browser's Back
        button to register for more classes.</p>";
}
```

```
catch (SqlException exception)
{
    Response.Write("<p>Error code "
        + exception.Number + ": "
        + exception.Message + "</p>");
}
dbConnection.Close();
```

7. Start the Web site, enter an existing student ID, and then click the **Class Registration** button. The ReturningStudent.aspx page should appear similar to Figure 8-10.

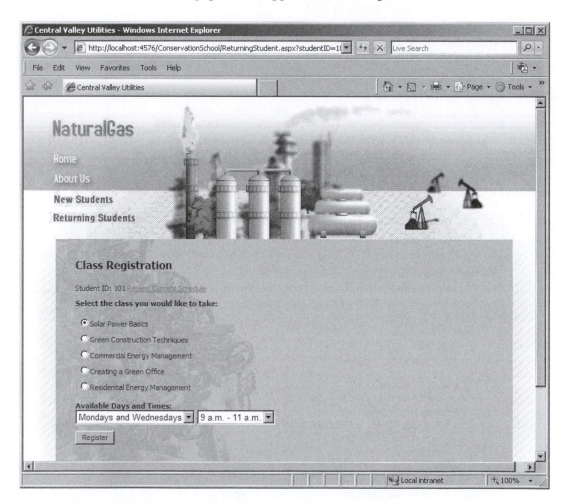

Figure 8-10 ReturningStudent.aspx

8. Select a class, as well as the days and times you want to take it, and then click the Register button. You should see the registration confirmation, as shown in Figure 8-11.

9. Close your Web browser window.

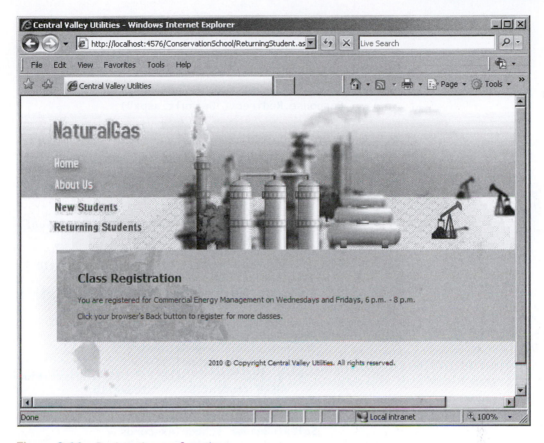

Figure 8-11 Registration confirmation

Exercise 8-4

In this exercise, you will complete the ReviewSchedule.aspx program, which allows students to review the classes in which they are registered.

To create the ReviewSchedule.aspx program:

1. Return to the Visual Studio IDE and open the **ReviewSchedule.aspx** file in the Code Editor.

2. Locate the Web form and add the following Literal control, which will display the student's current schedule:

    ```
    <asp:Literal ID="schedule" runat="server" />
    ```

3. Open the **ReviewSchedule.aspx.cs** file in the Code Editor and add the following directive to the end of the directives section to give the class access to the System.Data.SqlClient namespace:

    ```
    using System.Data.SqlClient;
    ```

4. Add the following statements to the Page_Load() event handler. The if statement determines whether the query string contains a student ID. If it doesn't, the user is redirected to the Default.aspx file.

```
if (Request.QueryString["studentID"] == "")
    Response.Redirect("Default.aspx");
```

5. Add the following statements to the end of the Page_Load() event handler. The code uses an ExecuteReader() method to return the matching records from the registration table.

```
else
{
    SqlConnection dbConnection = new SqlConnection(
        "Data Source=.\\SQLEXPRESS;
        Integrated Security=true");
    string studentID = Request.QueryString["studentID"];
    schedule.Text = "<p>Student ID: "
        + Request.QueryString["studentID"] + "</p>";
    try
    {
        dbConnection.Open();
        dbConnection.ChangeDatabase(
          "ConservationSchool");
        string classInfo = "SELECT * FROM registration
            WHERE studentID=" + studentID;
        SqlCommand studentSchedule = new SqlCommand(
            classInfo, dbConnection);
        SqlDataReader scheduleRecords =
            studentSchedule.ExecuteReader();
        if (scheduleRecords.Read())
        {
            schedule.Text
              += "<table width='100%' border='1'>";
            schedule.Text
              += "<tr><th>Class</th><th>Days</th>
              <th>Time</th></tr>";
            do
            {
                schedule.Text += "<tr>";
                schedule.Text += "<td>"
                    + scheduleRecords["class"]
                    + "</td>";
                schedule.Text += "<td>"
                    + scheduleRecords["days"]
                    + "</td>";
                schedule.Text += "<td>"
                    + scheduleRecords["time"]
                    + "</td>";
                schedule.Text += "</tr>";
            } while (scheduleRecords.Read());
            schedule.Text += "</table>";
        }
}
```

```
        else
            schedule.Text += "<p>You have not
            registered for any classes! Click
            your browser's Back button to
            return to the previous page.</p>";
        scheduleRecords.Close();
    }
    catch (SqlException exception)
    {
        Response.Write("<p>Error code "
            + exception.Number + ": "
            + exception.Message + "</p>");
    }
    dbConnection.Close();
}
```

6. Start the Web site, enter an existing student ID, and then click the **Returning Students** button. Register for several classes, and then click the **Review Current Schedule** button. Figure 8-12 shows the Review Schedule Web page for a student who is signed up for three classes.

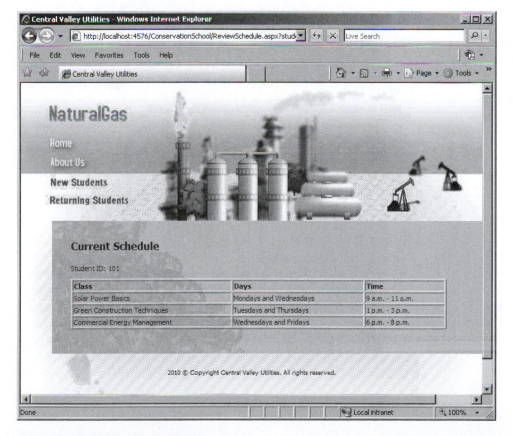

Figure 8-12   Review Schedule Web page

7. Close your Web browser window, close the project, and then close Visual Web Developer.

Discovery Projects

Save the following projects in your Discovery folder for Chapter 8.

Project 8-1
Create a project with a form that registers users for a professional conference. Save the project in a folder named Conference in your Projects folder for Chapter 8.

Project 8-2
Create a telephone directory application that saves entries to a single text file. Save the project in a folder named Directory in your Projects folder for Chapter 8. You should include standard telephone directory fields in the database, such as first name, last name, address, city, state, zip, telephone number, and so on. Create a document to be used as a main "directory," where you can select and retrieve records. Also, create one document that you can use to add new entries to the database and another document that you can use to edit entries.

Project 8-3
Create a Web site to be used for storing software development bug reports in a database. Save the project in a folder named BugReport in your Projects folder for Chapter 8. Include fields such as product name and version, type of hardware, operating system, frequency of occurrence, and proposed solutions. Include links on the main page that allow you to create a new bug report and update an existing bug report.

Project 8-4
Create a Web site for tracking, documenting, and managing the process of interviewing candidates for professional positions. Save the project in a folder named Interviews in your Projects folder for Chapter 8. On the main page, include a form with fields for the interviewer's name, position, and date of interview. Also include fields for entering the candidate's name, communication abilities, intellect computer skills, business knowledge, and interviewer's comments. Clicking the Save Interview button should save the data in a database. Include a link for opening a document that displays each candidate's interview information.

Project 8-5

Create a Web page that stores airline surveys in a database. Save the project in a folder named AirlineSurveys in your Projects folder for Chapter 8. Include fields for the date and time of the flight, flight number, and so on. Also, include groups of radio buttons that allow the user to rate the airline on the following criteria:

- Friendliness of customer staff

- Space for luggage storage

- Comfort of seating

- Cleanliness of aircraft

- Noise level of aircraft

The radio buttons for each question should consist of the following options: No Opinion, Poor, Fair, Good, or Excellent. Separate text files should store the results of a single survey.

CHAPTER 9

Maintaining State Information

In this chapter you will:

◎ Save state information with query strings, hidden form fields, and post back

◎ Save state information with cookies

◎ Save state information with the Session state, Application state, and Profiles

The Web was not originally designed to store information about a user's visit to a Web site. However, the ability to store user information, including preferences, passwords, and other data, is very important because it makes it easier for people to interact with your Web sites. In this chapter, you will study some basic methods for storing user information (known as maintaining state), including the use of query strings, hidden form fields, and post back/view state. You will also learn how to work with cookies and user profiles and how to maintain session and application state.

Understanding State Information

Hypertext Transfer Protocol (HTTP) manages the hypertext links used to navigate the Web and ensures that Web browsers correctly process and display the various types of information contained in Web pages. Information about individual visits to a Web site is called **state information**. HTTP was originally designed to be **stateless**, which means that Web browsers stored no persistent data about a visit to a Web site. The original stateless design of the Web allowed early Web servers to quickly process requests for Web pages because they did not need to remember any unique requirements for different clients. Similarly, Web browsers did not need to know any special information to load a particular Web page from a server. Although this stateless design was efficient, it was also limiting; because a Web server could not remember individual user information, the Web browser was forced to treat every visit to a Web page as an entirely new session. This was true regardless of whether the browser had just opened a different Web page on the same server. This design hampered interactivity and limited the amount of personal attention a Web site could provide. Today, there are many reasons for maintaining state information. Among other things, maintaining state information allows a server to do the following:

- Customize individual Web pages based on user preferences.

- Temporarily store information for a user as a browser navigates within a multipart form.

- Allow a user to create bookmarks for returning to specific locations within a Web site.

- Provide shopping carts that store order information.

- Store user IDs and passwords.

- Use counters to keep track of how many times a user has visited a site.

To learn how to use the various state maintenance tools, in this chapter you will work on the frequent flyer login functionality for the Skyward Aviation Web site. Your Chapter folder for Chapter 9 contains a folder named SkywardAviation where you can find the files that you will need for this project. Figure 9-1 illustrates how visitors navigate through the frequent flyer pages on the Skyward Aviation Web site and Figure 9-2 shows the home page.

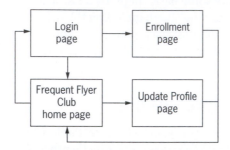

Figure 9-1   Skyward Aviation Web site flow

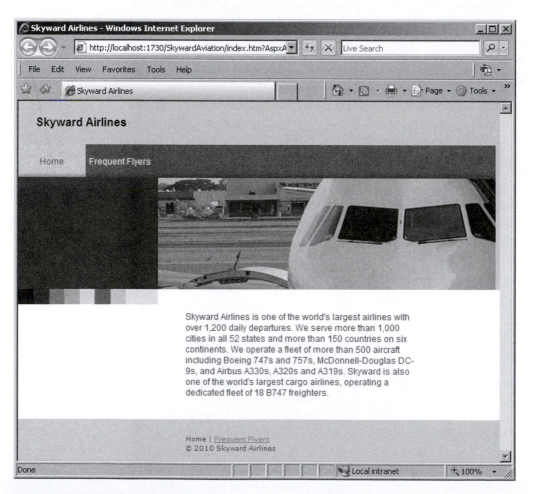

Figure 9-2   Skyward Aviation home page

Visitors who click on the Frequent Flyers tab will be directed to a page that prompts them to log in with their existing username and password or register for a new username and password. After a user logs in, the Web site must keep track of information about the user the entire time the user (that is, the client) navigates through the various pages on the Web site. In other words, the Web site must maintain state information about the client session. In this chapter, you will learn how ASP.NET can maintain state by using post back, cookies, session state, application state, and profiles.

As you work with the Skyward Aviation Web site, keep in mind that the goal of this chapter is to teach you how to maintain state information with C#. The Web site is as simple as possible, to allow you to focus on using state techniques. Most important, remember that, even though the Web site requires user IDs and passwords, *it is not secure*. For information on how to secure your Web sites, visit the Securing ASP.NET Web Sites section on MSDN at *http://msdn. microsoft.com/en-us/library/91f66yxt.aspx*.

First, you will create a database named SkywardAviation along with a table named FrequentFlyers. You will use this database to store profile information for each client.

To create the SkywardAviation database:

1. Click the **Start** button, point to **All Programs**, and then click **Microsoft Visual Web Developer 2008 Express Edition**. The Visual Studio Integrated Development Environment (IDE) opens.

2. Select the **File** menu and then select **Open Web Site**. The Open Web Site dialog box opens. Select the SkywardAviation folder, which is located in your Chapter folder for Chapter 9, and then click **Open**. The Skyward Aviation Web site opens in the Visual Studio IDE.

3. Select the **Website** menu and then select **Add New Item**. The Add New Item dialog box opens. In the Visual Studio installed templates section of the Templates area, select **SQL Server Database**. Change the suggested filename in the Name box to **SkywardAviation.mdf**. If necessary, change the value in the Language box to **Visual C#**.

4. Click the **Add** button to add the SQL Server database to the project, and then click **Yes** when prompted to save the database in the App_Data folder. The SkywardAviation database opens in Database Explorer.

5. Select the **Data** menu, point to **Add New**, and then select **Table**. A new table opens in the Table Definition panel. Add the fields shown in Figure 9-3.

Column Name	Data Type	Allow Nulls
flyerID	smallint	☐
last	varchar(50)	☑
first	varchar(50)	☑
phone	varchar(15)	☑
email	varchar(50)	☑
password	varchar(12)	☑
cardType	varbinary(20)	☑
expireMonth	varchar(2)	☑
expireYear	varchar(4)	☑
cardNumber	varchar(50)	☑
cardholder	varchar(50)	☑
address	varchar(50)	☑
city	varchar(50)	☑
state	varchar(25)	☑
zip	varchar(10)	☑
travelerType	varchar(20)	☑
homeAirport	varchar(50)	☑
class	varchar(50)	☑
seat	varchar(10)	☑
meal	varchar(15)	☑
		☐

Figure 9-3   FrequentFlyers table fields

6. Right-click the **flyerID** field and select **Set Primary Key** from the shortcut menu.

7. Verify that the flyerID field is still selected, and then scroll down in the Column Properties section of the table editor to the section labeled Identity Specification.

8. Expand the Identity Specification section, and then change the **(Is Identity)** property to **Yes** and the **Identity Seed** property to **100**. This causes SQL to automatically assign a unique ID to each flyer starting with a value of 100 for each new flyer.

9. Select the **File** menu and then select **Save Table1**. The Choose Name dialog box opens. Enter **FrequentFlyers** as the name of the table and click **OK**.

10. Select the **File** menu and then select **Close**.

Three of the most basic tools for maintaining state are query strings, hidden form fields, and the post back and view state functionality that is available to Web server controls. First, you will look at query strings.

Query Strings

There will be times when you might want to pass a single piece of data, such as a user ID, between Web pages. To quickly pass data from one Web page to another using a query string, add a question mark (?) immediately after a URL, followed by the query string (in name=value pairs) for the information you want to preserve. In this way, you can pass information to another Web page, similar to the way you pass arguments to a function or method.

You separate individual name=value pairs within the query string using ampersands (&). The following code provides an example of an <a> element that contains a query string consisting of three name=value pairs:

```
<a href="JobListings.aspx?firstName=Don&lastName=Gosselin
    &occupation=writer">Job Listings</a>
```

To access the query string from the JobListings.aspx page, you use the QueryString collection of the Request object, as follows:

```
Response.Write("<p>" + Request.QueryString["firstName"]
    + " " + Request.QueryString["lastName"] +
    ", " + Request.QueryString["occupation"] + "</p>");
```

Hidden Form Fields

As you should know from your study of HTML, a hidden form field, which is not displayed by the Web browser, is useful when you want to hide information from users. You create hidden form fields with the <input> element. Hidden form fields temporarily store data that needs to be sent to a server along with the rest of a form, but that a user does not need to see. Examples of data stored in hidden fields include the result of a calculation or some other type of information that a program on the Web server might need. You create hidden form fields using the same syntax used for other fields created with the <input> element: <input type="hidden">. The only attributes that you can include with a hidden form field are the name and value attributes. In fact, you have already used this technique in Chapter 4 when you used a hidden form field to store a Boolean value that indicated whether a form was being opened for the first time or if it had already been submitted to itself. Further, post back maintains view state by assigning the form values to a hidden form field named __VIEWSTATE.

Saving State with Post Back

In the old days, before advanced development environments such as ASP.NET, Web developers were required to use query strings and hidden form fields to preserve state information for a Web site. Thankfully, ASP.NET includes newer techniques that make state

Because users can see query strings appended to the URL in their browsers' address boxes, be sure not to use query strings to store sensitive data such as passwords.

This same functionality occurs when you submit a Web form with a method of "get". For example, if you submit a form that contains fields with ID values of firstName and lastName, both field IDs and values are submitted to the requested Web page as a query string.

Because the user can see the values assigned to hidden form fields by opening a Web page's source code, you should not use hidden form fields to save sensitive data such as passwords.

preservation easier and more robust, including the post back and view state functionality of Web server controls.

In the previous sections, you were required to create two separate Web pages to maintain state information with query strings and hidden form fields across a multipage form. A better technique is to use the MultiView and View controls or the Wizard Web server control to simulate multipage forms. First, you will study the MultiView and View controls.

Simulating Multipage Forms with the MultiView and View Web Server Controls

The **MultiView control** is used to hide and display areas of a page that are defined by a **View control**, which acts as a container for text, markup, and other controls. The MultiView control is based on the `MultiView` class and the View control is based on the `View` class. One of the primary uses of the MultiView control is to simulate multipage forms. Only one View control displays at a time within a MultiView control. The mechanism for hiding and displaying View controls, which also causes post back to occur, simulates the experience of navigating between multiple, related forms on separate Web pages. Because the View controls are all defined on the same page, any data within the form fields contained within a View control is preserved during post back operations, assuming that the `EnableViewState` attribute is assigned a value of true.

To move between views within a MultiView control, you must add a button control to each View control. Within each button control, you include `CommandName` attributes to control the view to display. You assign to the `CommandName` attribute one of the following values:

- NextView—Displays the next View control
- PrevView—Displays the previous View control
- SwitchViewByID—Displays the View control with the ID value assigned to the `CommandArgument` attribute
- SwitchViewByIndex—Displays a View control according to its index number

The following View control demonstrates how to use the NextView and PrevView values with the `CommandName` attribute. Assuming there are additional View controls before and after the following controls, then the Previous and Next buttons would change the currently displayed View control to the previous or next views. The View control also contains a button with a `CommandName` attribute that is assigned a value of submitView, which jumps directly to the final page (that is assigned an ID of "submitView") in the MultiView control.

```
<asp:View ID="contactInfo" runat="server">
    <p>
        <strong>Contact Information</strong></p>
    <p>
        Telephone:
        <asp:TextBox ID="telephone" runat="server" /><br />
        E-mail:
        <asp:TextBox ID="email" runat="server" />
    </p>
    <p>
        <asp:Button ID="previous" runat="server" Text="Previous"
            CommandName="PrevView" />
        <asp:Button ID="next" runat="server" Text="Next"
            CommandName="NextView" />
        <asp:Button ID="goToLast" runat="server"
            Text="Submit Page" CommandName="submitView" /></p>
</asp:View>
```

The following form contains a more complex example of a MultiView control. This example contains four different views that make up a fitness survey form for a health club. The views include CommandName attributes assigned values of PrevView and NextView to allow users to navigate to the different pages in the form. Figure 9-4 shows the pages of the form.

```
<form id="fitnessSurveyForm" runat="server">
<div>
    <h2>
        Fitness Survey</h2>
    <asp:MultiView ID="FitnessForm" ActiveViewIndex="0"
        runat="server">
        <asp:View ID="gym" runat="server">
            <table cellpadding="4" cellspacing="4">
                <tr>
                    <td><strong>Do you belong to a gym?
                    </strong></td>
                </tr>
                <tr>
                    <td>
                        <asp:RadioButton ID="gymYes"
                            GroupName="gym" runat="server"
                            Checked="True" />Yes
                            <asp:RadioButton ID="gymNo"
                            GroupName="gym" runat="server" />
                        No</td>
                </tr>
                <tr>
                    <td>
                        <asp:Button ID="Button1"
                            runat="server" Text="Next"
                            CommandName="NextView" />
                    </td>
                </tr>
            </table>
```

```
        </asp:View>
        <asp:View ID="regimen" runat="server">
            <table cellpadding="4" cellspacing="4">
                <tr>
                    <td><strong>How do you stay in
                        shape?</strong></td>
                </tr>
                <tr>
                    <td>
                        <asp:CheckBox ID="jogging"
                            runat="server" />
                            Jogging<br />
                        <asp:CheckBox ID="Yoga"
                            runat="server" />Yoga<br />
                        <asp:CheckBox ID="swimming"
                            runat="server" />
                            Swimming<br />
                        <asp:CheckBox ID="teamsports"
                            runat="server" />
                            Team sports<br />
                        <asp:CheckBox ID="classes"
                            runat="server" />
                            Fitness classes<br />
                        <asp:CheckBox ID="weights"
                            runat="server" />
                            Weights</td>
                </tr>
                <tr>
                    <td>
                        <asp:Button ID="Button3"
                            runat="server" Text="Previous"
                            CommandName="PrevView" />
                        <asp:Button ID="Button2"
                            runat="server" Text="Next"
                            CommandName="NextView" />
                    </td>
                </tr>
            </table>
        </asp:View>
        <asp:View ID="frequency" runat="server">
            <table cellpadding="4" cellspacing="4">
                <tr>
                    <td><strong>How often do you
                        exercise?</strong> </td>
                </tr>
                <tr>
                    <td>
                        <asp:RadioButton ID="frequency1"
                            GroupName="frequency" runat="server"
                            Checked="True" />Once
                            per week<br />
                        <asp:RadioButton ID="frequency2"
                            GroupName="frequency" runat="server" />
                            2-3 times per week<br />
```

```
                    <asp:RadioButton ID="frequency3"
                        GroupName="frequency" runat="server" />
                        4-6 times per week<br />
                    <asp:RadioButton ID="frequency4"
                        GroupName="frequency" runat="server" />
                        Every day<br />
                </td>
            </tr>
            <tr>
                <td>
                    <asp:Button ID="Button4" runat="server"
                        Text="Previous" CommandName="PrevView" />
                    <asp:Button ID="Button5" runat="server"
                        Text="Next" CommandName="NextView" />
                </td>
            </tr>
        </table>
    </asp:View>
    <asp:View ID="summary" runat="server">
        <table cellpadding="4" cellspacing="4">
            <tr>
                <td><strong>Summary</strong> </td>
            </tr>
            <tr>
                <td>Do you belong to a gym?
                    <asp:Literal ID="gymResult"
                        runat="server"></asp:Literal>
                </td>
            </tr>
            <tr>
                <td>How do you stay in shape?
                    <asp:Literal ID="regimenResult"
                        runat="server"></asp:Literal></td>
            </tr>
            <tr>
                <td>How often do you exercise?
                    <asp:Literal ID="frequencyResult"
                        runat="server"></asp:Literal></td>
            </tr>
            <tr>
                <td>
                    <asp:Button ID="Button7" runat="server"
                        Text="Previous" CommandName="PrevView" />
                    <asp:Button ID="Button6" runat="server"
                        Text="Submit Survey" />
                </td>
            </tr>
        </table>
    </asp:View>
    </asp:MultiView>
</div>
</form>
```

466

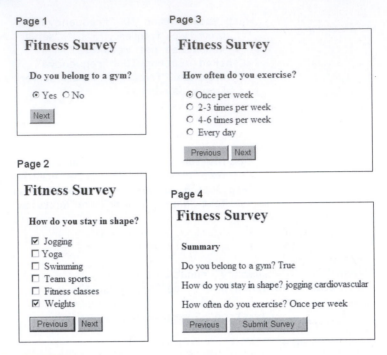

Figure 9-4 Pages of a multipage form

Page 4 of the fitness survey relies on the following `Page_LoadComplete()` event handler to display the information that was gathered on the preceding pages. Notice the `else...if` statement at the end of the event handler. The conditional expression checks the value assigned to the `ActiveViewIndex` property of the `MultiView` class to determine whether it contains a value of -1, which indicates that no view is currently set. This means that the user has clicked the Submit Survey button, so the survey data is stored in a database and confirmation text prints to the screen.

```
protected void Page_LoadComplete(object sender, EventArgs e)
{
    Boolean gymMembership = false;
    string regimen = "";
    string workoutDays = "";
    if (gymYes.Checked)
    {
        gymMembership = true;
    }
    if (jogging.Checked)
        regimen = "jogging ";
    if (swimming.Checked)
        regimen = "swimming ";
    if (yoga.Checked)
        regimen += "yoga ";
```

```
if (teamsports.Checked)
    regimen += "team sports ";
if (classes.Checked)
    regimen += "classes ";
if (weights.Checked)
    regimen += "cardiovascular";
if (frequency1.Checked)
    workoutDays = "Once per week";
if (frequency2.Checked)
    workoutDays = "2-3 times week";
if (frequency3.Checked)
    workoutDays = "4-6 times week";
if (frequency4.Checked)
    workoutDays = "Every day";
    if (Page.IsPostBack && summary.Visible)
    {
        gymResult.Text = gymMembership.ToString();
        regimenResult.Text = regimen;
        frequencyResult.Text = workoutDays;
    }
    else if (Page.IsPostBack
        && FitnessForm.ActiveViewIndex == -1)
    {
        fitnessSurveyForm.Visible = false;
        SqlConnection dbConnection
            = new SqlConnection(
            "Data Source=.\\SQLEXPRESS;
            Integrated Security=true");
        dbConnection.Open();
        dbConnection.ChangeDatabase("fitnessSurvey");
        SqlCommand sqlCommand = new SqlCommand(
            "INSERT INTO surveyResults VALUES("
            + gymMembership + "," + regimen + ","
            + workoutDays + ")", dbConnection);
        sqlCommand.ExecuteNonQuery();
        Response.Write("<p>We have received your survey.
            Thank you for your input.</p>");
    }
}
```

For more information on the methods and properties that are available to the MultiView class, refer to *http://msdn. microsoft.com/en-us/ library/system.web. ui.webcontrols.multiview. aspx*. For more information on the View class, refer to *http://msdn. microsoft.com/en-us/ library/system.web. ui.webcontrols.view.aspx*.

Next, you will create the Enrollment page for the Skyward Aviation Web site. The page will use a MultiView control to gather the following types of information: base profile information, billing information, and travel preferences.

To add a MultiView control to the Enrollment page:

1. Return to the Visual Studio IDE and open the **Registration. aspx** file in the Code Editor.

2. Locate the Web form in the document body and add the following MultiView control to the <div> element:

```
<asp:MultiView ID="enrollmentForm"
    ActiveViewIndex="0" runat="server">
</asp:MultiView>
```

3. Add to the <asp:MultiView> control the following <asp:View> element, which gathers the user's name, telephone, e-mail address, and password to use for the account. Notice that there is a hidden field named hiddenPassword. Because passwords are not preserved during round-trips to the server, the Page_Load() event handler will store the password in this hidden field.

```
<asp:View ID="baseProfile" runat="server">
    <h3>
        Account Details</h3>
    <p>Last name<br />
        <asp:TextBox ID="lastName" runat="server"
            Width="265" /><br />
            First name<br />
        <asp:TextBox ID="firstName" runat="server"
            Width="265" /><br />
            Telephone<br />
        <asp:TextBox ID="telephone" runat="server"
            Width="265" /><br />
            E-mail<br />
        <asp:TextBox ID="email" runat="server"
            Width="265" /><br />
            Confirm e-mail<br />
        <asp:TextBox ID="confirmEmail" runat="server"
            Width="265" /><br />
            Password<br />
        <asp:TextBox ID="password" runat="server"
            Width="265" TextMode="Password" /><br />
            Confirm password<br />
        <asp:TextBox ID="confirmPassword"
            runat="server" Width="265"
            TextMode="Password" />
        <asp:HiddenField ID="hiddenPassword"
            runat="server" /></p>
    <p><asp:Button ID="Button1" runat="server"
        Text="Next" CommandName="NextView" /></p>
</asp:View>
```

4. Add to the end of the <asp:MultiView> control the following <asp:View> element, which gathers the user's billing information:

```
<asp:View ID="billing" runat="server">
    <h3>
        Billing Information</h3>
    <table Width="100%" border="0" cellspacing="0"
    cellpadding="0">
        <tr><td><p>Card type<br />
            <asp:DropDownList ID="creditcard"
            runat="server">
                <asp:ListItem></asp:ListItem>
                <asp:ListItem>Visa</asp:ListItem>
```

```
        <asp:ListItem>Mastercard
            </asp:ListItem>
        <asp:ListItem>Diners Club
            </asp:ListItem>
        <asp:ListItem>American Express
            </asp:ListItem>
    </asp:DropDownList></p></td>
<td><p>Expiration date<br />
        <asp:DropDownList ID="expireMonth"
            runat="server">
            <asp:ListItem></asp:ListItem>
            <asp:ListItem Value="01">01
                </asp:ListItem>
            <asp:ListItem Value="02">02
                </asp:ListItem>
            <asp:ListItem Value="03">03
                </asp:ListItem>
            <asp:ListItem Value="04">04
                </asp:ListItem>
            <asp:ListItem Value="05">05
                </asp:ListItem>
            <asp:ListItem Value="06">06
                </asp:ListItem>
            <asp:ListItem Value="07">07
                </asp:ListItem>
            <asp:ListItem Value="08">08
                </asp:ListItem>
            <asp:ListItem Value="09">09
                </asp:ListItem>
            <asp:ListItem Value="10">10
                </asp:ListItem>
            <asp:ListItem Value="11">11
                </asp:ListItem>
            <asp:ListItem Value="12">12
                </asp:ListItem>
        </asp:DropDownList>
        <asp:DropDownList ID="expireYear"
            runat="server">
            <asp:ListItem></asp:ListItem>
            <asp:ListItem Value="2008">
                2008</asp:ListItem>
            <asp:ListItem Value="2009">
                2009</asp:ListItem>
            <asp:ListItem Value="2010">
                2010</asp:ListItem>
            <asp:ListItem Value="2011">
                2011</asp:ListItem>
            <asp:ListItem Value="2012">
                2012</asp:ListItem>
            <asp:ListItem Value="2013">
                2013</asp:ListItem>
            <asp:ListItem Value="2014">
                2014</asp:ListItem>
            <asp:ListItem Value="2015">
                2015</asp:ListItem>
```

```
                        <asp:ListItem Value="2016">
                            2016</asp:ListItem>
                        <asp:ListItem Value="2017">
                            2017</asp:ListItem>
                    </asp:DropDownList></p>
                </td>
            </tr></table>
        <p>
            Card number<br />
            <asp:TextBox ID="cardnumber" runat="server"
                Width="265" TextMode="SingleLine" /><br />
            Cardholder name<br />
            <asp:TextBox ID="cardholder" runat="server"
                Width="265" TextMode="SingleLine" /><br />
            Address<br />
            <asp:TextBox ID="address" runat="server"
                Width="265" TextMode="SingleLine" /><br />
            City<br />
            <asp:TextBox ID="city" runat="server"
                Width="265" TextMode="SingleLine" /><br />
            State<br />
            <asp:TextBox ID="state" runat="server"
                Width="265" TextMode="SingleLine" /><br />
            Zip<br />
            <asp:TextBox ID="zip" runat="server"
                Width="265" TextMode="SingleLine" /><br />
        </p>
        <p>
            <asp:Button ID="Button3" runat="server"
                Text="Previous" CommandName="PrevView" />
            <asp:Button ID="Button2" runat="server"
                Text="Next" CommandName="NextView" /></p>
    </asp:View>
```

5. Add to the end of the <asp:MultiView> control the following <asp:View> element, which gathers the user's travel preferences:

```
<asp:View ID="preferences" runat="server">
    <h3>
        Travel Preferences</h3>
    <p>
        Traveler type<br />
        <asp:DropDownList ID="travelerType"
            runat="server">
            <asp:ListItem></asp:ListItem>
            <asp:ListItem Value="Adult">Adult
                </asp:ListItem>
            <asp:ListItem Value="Child (2-11)">
                Child (2-11)</asp:ListItem>
            <asp:ListItem Value="Infant (under 2)">
                Infant (under 2)</asp:ListItem>
            <asp:ListItem Value="Senior (65+)">
                Senior (65+)</asp:ListItem>
```

```
</asp:DropDownList><br />
Home airport<br />
<asp:TextBox ID="homeAirport" runat="server"
    Width="265" TextMode="SingleLine" /><br />
Service class<br />
<asp:DropDownList ID="serviceClass"
    runat="server">
    <asp:ListItem></asp:ListItem>
    <asp:ListItem Value="Economy
        (lowest available)"> Economy (lowest)
        </asp:ListItem>
    <asp:ListItem Value="Economy
        (lowest refundable)"> Economy
        (refundable)</asp:ListItem>
    <asp:ListItem Value="Business
        (lowest available)"> Business
        (lowest)</asp:ListItem>
    <asp:ListItem Value="Business
        (lowest refundable)"> Business
        (refundable)</asp:ListItem>
    <asp:ListItem Value="First
        (lowest available)"> First
        (lowest)</asp:ListItem>
    <asp:ListItem Value="First
        (lowest refundable)"> First
        (refundable)</asp:ListItem>
</asp:DropDownList><br />
Seat preference<br />
<asp:DropDownList ID="seatPreference"
    runat="server">
    <asp:ListItem></asp:ListItem>
    <asp:ListItem Value="aisle">aisle
        </asp:ListItem>
    <asp:ListItem Value="window">window
        </asp:ListItem>
</asp:DropDownList><br />
Meal request<br />
<asp:DropDownList ID="mealRequest"
        runat="server">
    <asp:ListItem></asp:ListItem>
    <asp:ListItem Value="standard">
        standard</asp:ListItem>
    <asp:ListItem Value="diabetic">
        diabetic</asp:ListItem>
    <asp:ListItem Value="fruit ">
        fruit </asp:ListItem>
    <asp:ListItem Value="kosher">
        kosher</asp:ListItem>
    <asp:ListItem Value="low sodium">
        low sodium</asp:ListItem>
    <asp:ListItem Value="vegetarian">
        vegetarian</asp:ListItem>
</asp:DropDownList></p>
```

```
<p><asp:Button ID="Button4" runat="server"
    Text="Previous" CommandName="PrevView" />
<asp:Button ID="Button5" runat="server"
    Text="Enroll" CommandName="NextView" /></p>
</asp:View>
```

6. Add to the end of the `<asp:MultiView>` control the following `<asp:View>` element. The `Page_Load()` event handler will set the value assigned to the `<asp:Literal>` control so it contains either a failure message or a success message and the new frequent flyer number.

```
<asp:View ID="success" runat="server">
    <p>
      <asp:Literal ID="successString"
        runat="server"></asp:Literal></p>
    <p><a href="ffClubPage.aspx">Frequent
      Flyer Club home page</a></p>
</asp:View>
```

7. Open the **Registration.aspx.cs** file in the Code Editor and add the following directive to the end of the directives section:

```
using System.Data.SqlClient;
```

8. Modify the `Page_Load()` event handler so it stores the password value in the hidden field, as follows:

```
protected void Page_Load(object sender, EventArgs e)
{
    if (Page.IsPostBack
        && enrollmentForm.ActiveViewIndex == 0)
        hiddenPassword.Value = password.Text;
}
```

9. Add after the `Page_Load()` event handler the following `Page_LoadComplete()` event handler, which determines whether a post back event has occurred and, if the currently active view index is equal to 3, indicates that this is the last page in the form. The `if` statement also contains a statement that instantiates a new `SQLConnection` object. Be sure to change the path location where you created the `SkywardAviation` database.

```
protected void Page_LoadComplete(
    object sender, EventArgs e)
{
    if (Page.IsPostBack
        && enrollmentForm.ActiveViewIndex == 3)
    {
        SqlConnection dbConnection
            = new SqlConnection(
            "Data Source=.\\SQLEXPRESS;
            AttachDbFilename=C:\\Course Technology\\
            0324-2\\Chapter.09\\Chapter\\ SkywardAviation\\
```

```
        App_Data\\SkywardAviation.mdf;
        Integrated Security=True;
        User Instance=True");
    }
}
```

10. Add to the end of the if statement the following try...catch
    block, which uses a ExecuteNonQuery() method to write the
    data to the FrequentFlyers table of the SkywardAviation
    database. The final statements in the try block also retrieve
    and print the frequent flyer number.

```
try
{
    dbConnection.Open();
    SqlCommand sqlCommand = new SqlCommand(
        "INSERT INTO FrequentFlyers (last, first,
        phone, email, password, cardType,
        expireMonth, expireYear, cardNumber,
        cardholder, address, city, state, zip,
        travelerType, homeAirport, class, seat,
        meal) VALUES("
        + "'" + lastName.Text + "',"
        + "'" + firstName.Text + "',"
        + "'" + telephone.Text + "',"
        + "'" + email.Text + "',"
        + "'" + hiddenPassword.Value + "',"
        + "'" + creditcard.Text + "',"
        + "'" + expireMonth.Text + "',"
        + "'" + expireYear.Text + "',"
        + "'" + cardnumber.Text + "',"
        + "'" + cardholder.Text + "',"
        + "'" + address.Text + "',"
        + "'" + city.Text + "',"
        + "'" + state.Text + "',"
        + "'" + zip.Text + "',"
        + "'" + travelerType.Text + "',"
        + "'" + homeAirport.Text + "',"
        + "'" + serviceClass.Text + "',"
        + "'" + seatPreference.Text + "',"
        + "'" + mealRequest.Text + "')",
        dbConnection);
    sqlCommand.ExecuteNonQuery();
    sqlCommand = new SqlCommand(
        "SELECT IDENT_CURRENT('FrequentFlyers')",
        dbConnection);
    SqlDataReader lastID =
        sqlCommand.ExecuteReader();
    if (lastID.Read())
        successString.Text +=
            "<h3>Enrollment Successful</h3>
            <p>Your frequent flyer number is "
            + lastID.GetValue(0) + ".</p>";
}
```

```
catch (SqlException exception)
{
    successString.Text += "<p>Error code "
        + exception.Number
        + ": " + exception.Message + "</p>";
}
```

11. Finally, add the following statement to the end of the if statement to close the database connection:

```
dbConnection.Close();
```

12. Start the Web site. Select the Frequent Flyers tab, and then click the Enroll in Skyward Airlines Frequent Flyer program link. Test the form to ensure that the data is saved properly to the Skyward Aviation Web site. After completing the form, you should see the final page in the enrollment form, as shown in Figure 9-5.

13. Close your Web browser window.

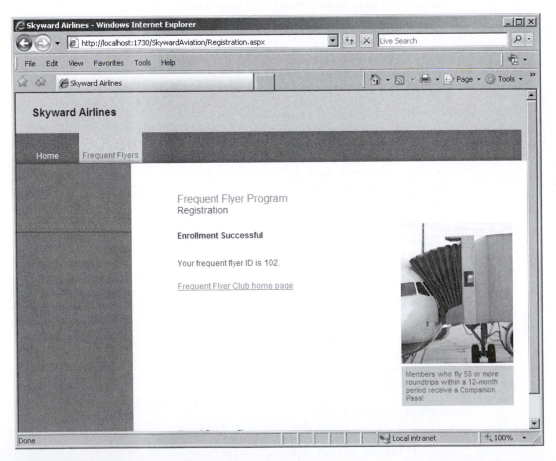

Figure 9-5   Final page of the frequent flyer enrollment form

Next, you will add functionality that allows users to log in with an existing ID and password.

To add functionality that allows users to log in with an existing ID and password:

1. Return to the Visual Studio IDE and open the **ffClubPage.aspx** file in the Code Editor and add the following text and elements to the <div> selection in the <form> element:

    ```
    <p>
        <strong>Customer Name:</strong>
        <asp:Literal ID="firstName" runat="server" />
        <asp:Literal ID="lastName" runat="server" /><br />
        <strong>Frequent Flyer #:</strong>
        <asp:Literal ID="flyerIDValue" runat="server" /><br />
    </p>
    <p>
        <a href="ContactInfo.aspx">Update Contact
            Info</a><br />
        <asp:LinkButton ID="logout" runat="server">
            Logout</asp:LinkButton></p>
    ```

2. Open the **ffClubPage.aspx.cs** file in the Code Editor and add the following directive to the end of the directives section:

    ```
    using System.Data.SqlClient;
    ```

3. Add to the Page_Load() event handler the following if statement, which contains a single statement that redirects users to the Login.aspx page if the URL does not include a query string that contains the flyerID variable. You will pass the flyerID variable to the ffClubPage.aspx page from the Login. aspx page.

    ```
    if (Request.QueryString["flyerID"] == null)
        Response.Redirect("Login.aspx");
    ```

4. Add the following else statement to the end of the Page_Load() event handler. If the URL includes a query string that contains the flyerID variable, the statements in the else statement populate the text boxes in the ffClubPage.aspx file's Web form with the user's frequent flyer number and name.

    ```
    else
    {
        SqlConnection dbConnection = new SqlConnection(
            "Data Source=.\\SQLEXPRESS;AttachDbFilename=
            C:\\Course Technology\\0324-2\\Chapter.09\\
            Chapter\\SkywardAviation\\App_Data\\
            SkywardAviation.mdf;Integrated Security=True;
            User Instance=True");
        dbConnection.Open();
        try
        {
    ```

```csharp
SqlCommand sqlCommand = new SqlCommand(
    "SELECT flyerID, first, last FROM
    FrequentFlyers WHERE flyerID = "
    + Request.QueryString["flyerID"],
    dbConnection);
SqlDataReader userInfo
    = sqlCommand.ExecuteReader();
if (userInfo.Read())
{
    flyerIDValue.Text
        = userInfo["flyerID"].ToString();
    firstName.Text
        = userInfo["first"].ToString();
    lastName.Text
        = userInfo["last"].ToString();
}
userInfo.Close();
}
catch (SqlException exception)
{
    Response.Write("<p>Error code "
        + exception.Number + ": "
        + exception.Message + "</p>");
}
dbConnection.Close();
}
```

5. Open the Login.aspx file and add the following lines of code to the `<div>` section in the `<form>` element:

```
<p>
    Frequent flyer ID<br />
    <asp:TextBox ID="account" runat="server"
        Width="200px"></asp:TextBox></p>
<p>
    Password<br />
    <asp:TextBox ID="password" runat="server"
        Width="200px" TextMode="Password">
        </asp:TextBox></p>
    <asp:Literal ID="badLogin" runat="server">
        </asp:Literal><p>
    <asp:Button ID="Login" runat="server"
        Text="Login" />
</p>
```

6. Open the **Login.aspx.cs** file in the Code Editor and add the following directive to the end of the directives section:

```csharp
using System.Data.SqlClient;
```

7. Add the following code to the `Page_Load()` event handler. The Login.aspx page contains a Web form with two fields, Frequent flyer number and Password. When the user submits the Web form, the following statements use these two values

to determine whether a corresponding record exists in the SkywardAviation database. If so, the user is redirected to ffClubPage.aspx. Be sure to change the path location where you created the SkywardAviation database.

```
if (Page.IsPostBack)
{
    SqlConnection dbConnection = new SqlConnection(
        "Data Source=.\\SQLEXPRESS;AttachDbFilename=
        C:\\Course Technology\\0324-2\\Chapter.09\\
        Chapter\\SkywardAviation\\App_Data\\
        SkywardAviation.mdf;Integrated Security=True;
        User Instance=True");
    try
    {
        dbConnection.Open();
        SqlCommand sqlCommand = new SqlCommand(
            "SELECT flyerID, first, last, password
            FROM FrequentFlyers WHERE flyerID = "
            + Convert.ToInt16(account.Text)
            + " AND password = '" + password.Text
            + "'", dbConnection);
        SqlDataReader curUser
            = sqlCommand.ExecuteReader();
        if (curUser.Read())
            Response.Redirect(
                "ffClubPage.aspx?flyerID="
                + curUser["flyerID"]);
        else
            badLogin.Text = "<p style='color:red'>
                <strong>Incorrect ID or password.
                <strong></p>";
    }
    catch (SqlException exception)
    {
        Response.Write("<p>Error code "
            + exception.Number + ": "
            + exception.Message + "</p>");
    }
}
```

8. Finally, add the following statement to the end of the if statement to close the database connection:

   dbConnection.Close();

9. Start the Web site. Select the Frequent Flyers tab, enter a valid frequent flyer number and password, and then click Login. The Account Profile page opens and appears similar to Figure 9-6.

10. Close your Web browser window.

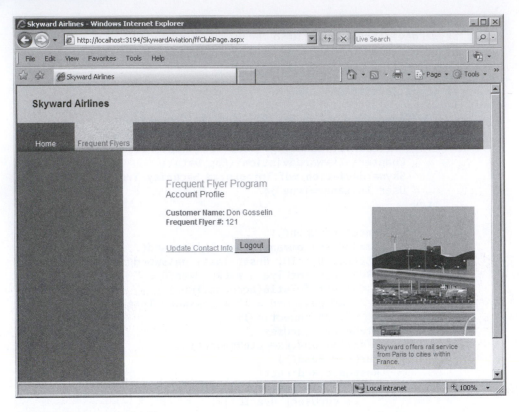

Figure 9-6   Account Profile page

Simulating Multipage Forms with the Wizard Web Server Control

As with MultiView controls, **Wizard Web server controls** allow you to create a multistep interface for gathering user input. Wizard Web server controls function very similar to MultiView controls in that they are used to hide and display areas of a page to simulate multipage forms. However, Wizard controls are more powerful because they automate navigation and other functionality and they contain a wide variety of options for formatting the display of the control. The basic syntax for a Wizard control is as follows:

```
<asp:Wizard ID="Wizard2" runat="server">
    <WizardSteps>
        <asp:WizardStep ID="WizardStep5" runat="server"
            Title="Step 1">
        </asp:WizardStep>
        <asp:WizardStep ID="WizardStep6" runat="server"
            Title="Step 2">
        </asp:WizardStep>
    </WizardSteps>
</asp:Wizard>
```

The `<asp:Wizard>` control contains a nested `<WizardSteps>` element that further contains `<asp:WizardStep>` controls that represent each step in the wizard. The preceding example contains two steps. Notice that each step includes a `Title` attribute. The Wizard control uses this text to generate navigation links that control navigation within the wizard. You nest within each `<asp:WizardStep>` control the text, markup, and other controls that apply to the step.

Table 9-1 lists some of the critical Wizard control behavior attributes and Table 9-2 lists the attributes of the WizardStep control. The Wizard control includes dozens of appearance, behavior, and layout attributes. There are too many attributes to list here, so refer to the Wizard Members page on MSDN at *http://msdn.microsoft.com/en-us/library/system.web.ui.webcontrols.wizard_members.aspx.*

Attribute	Description
CancelDestinationPageURL	Identifies a Web page to which the user is redirected after clicking the Cancel button
DisplayCancelButton	Determines whether the wizard includes a Cancel button
DisplaySideBar	Determines whether the wizard displays a sidebar containing links to each step
FinalDestinationPageURL	Identifies a Web page where the user is redirected after clicking the Finish button on the final page; by default the Complete step opens
HeaderText	Specifies the text that will appear at the top of each step in the wizard

Table 9-1   Common Wizard control behavior attributes

Attribute	Description
Title	Specifies a step title that is displayed in the sidebar.
AllowReturn	Determines whether a user can return to a previous step in the wizard.
EnableTheming	Determines whether the step can use themes, which are collections of property settings that you can use to define a consistent look and feel for Web pages.
EnableViewState	Determines whether view state is enabled for the step.
StepType	Identifies the step as one of the following types: Start, Step, Finish, Complete, or Auto. The Start value identifies the first page in the wizard, whereas the Step value identifies an intermediate step in the wizard. Start pages contain Next links, whereas Step buttons contain Previous and Next links. The Finish value creates a final page that contains Previous and Finish links. The Complete value creates a final page in the wizard that does not contain any navigation links. You can think of a Complete page as being equivalent to the Summary View page you created with the MultiView control in the preceding section.

Table 9-2   WizardStep control attributes

Navigation in a wizard can be linear or non-linear. In linear navigation, you can navigate backward and forward through the wizard steps. In nonlinear navigation, you can navigate by clicking a specific step. To specify whether a user can return to a previous step in the wizard, assign a value of true or false to the `<asp:WizardStep>` control's `AllowReturn` attribute.

480

Although you can manually build a Wizard control in the Code Editor, you can also use some automated tools, called Wizard Tasks, which are available in Design view. Position the mouse pointer over a Wizard control in Design view to display the tools shown in Figure 9-7.

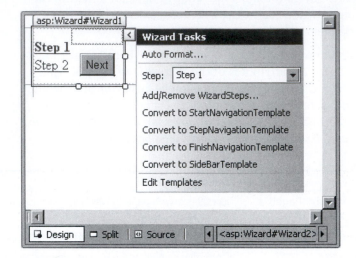

Figure 9-7   Wizard Tasks menu

The Styles section of a Wizard's Properties page contains several objects for which you can assign formatting to control the appearance of various parts of a wizard. For example, the `StepStyle` object contains style options for formatting an interim wizard step. If you assign a value to a style of one of the objects in the Styles section, the IDE adds a Web server control to the end of the `<asp:Wizard>` control. For example, changing the background color to blue and the border color to black for the `StepStyle` object adds the following markup to the end of the `<asp:Wizard>` control:

```
<StepStyle BackColor="Blue" BorderColor="Black" />
```

The Auto Format command on the Wizard Tasks menu displays a dialog box from which you can select a predefined formatting scheme. When you select a predefined formatting scheme from the Auto Format command on the Wizard Tasks menu, the IDE automatically adds the necessary Style objects to the end of the `<asp:Wizard>` control. Selecting the Simple predefined formatting scheme adds the following markup to the end of the `<asp:Wizard>` control:

```
<SideBarButtonStyle ForeColor="White" />
<NavigationButtonStyle BackColor="White"
    BorderColor="#C5BBAF"
    BorderStyle="Solid" BorderWidth="1px"
    Font-Names="Verdana" Font-Size="0.8em"
    ForeColor="#1C5E55" />
```

```
<SideBarStyle BackColor="#1C5E55" Font-Size="0.9em"
    VerticalAlign="Top" />
<HeaderStyle HorizontalAlign="Center"
    BackColor="#666666" BorderColor="#E6E2D8"
    BorderStyle="Solid" BorderWidth="2px"
    Font-Bold="True" Font-Size="0.9em"
    ForeColor="White"></HeaderStyle>
```

The Step box on the Wizard Tasks menu allows you to change the currently displayed wizard step in Design view. The Add/Remove WizardSteps command displays the WizardStep Collection Editor, shown in Figure 9-8, which assists you in adding steps to and removing steps from the wizard.

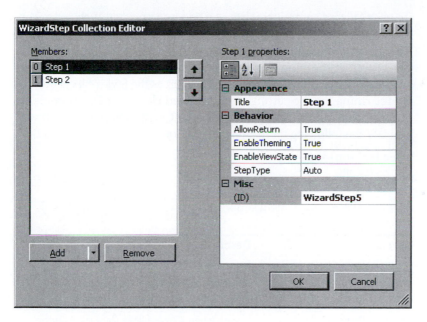

Figure 9-8 WizardStep Collection Editor

The remaining commands in the Wizard Tasks menu deal with the templates that are available to the Wizard control. A template allows you to control the appearance of specific portions of a Web server control. Table 9-3 lists the templates that are available to the Wizard control.

Template	Description
HeaderTemplate	Controls the appearance of a Wizard control's header area
SidebarTemplate	Controls the appearance of a Wizard control's sidebar area
StartNavigationTemplate	Controls the appearance of the navigation area of a Wizard control's starting step
StepNavigationTemplate	Controls the appearance of the navigation area of a Wizard control's intermediate steps
FinishNavigationTemplate	Controls the appearance of the navigation area of a Wizard control's finish step

Table 9-3　Wizard control templates

Instead of using templates and Style objects, you can also format the appearance and basic aspects of a wizard by using the appearance and layout attributes of the `<asp:Wizard>` control. However, using templates and Style objects gives you much greater control over the design and layout of a wizard.

To use a Wizard control template, you add its associated Web server control to the end of the `<asp:Wizard>` section, the same as for Style objects. The primary difference between Wizard control templates and Style objects is that the templates primarily determine the text and elements to place in a specific area of the wizard, whereas the Style objects primarily determine the formatting of the text and elements. For example, to automatically print "Fitness Survey" at the top of each step in a wizard, you add the following template to the end of the `<asp:Wizard>` section:

```
<HeaderTemplate>
    <strong>Fitness Survey</strong>
</HeaderTemplate>
```

The `<asp:Wizard>` control supports the events listed in Table 9-4.

Event	Description
ActiveStepChanged	Raised when a different wizard step becomes active
CancelButtonClick	Raised when a user clicks the Cancel button
FinishButtonClick	Raised when a user clicks the Finish button
NextButtonClick	Raised when a user clicks the Next button
PreviousButtonClick	Raised when a user clicks the Previous button
SideBarButtonClick	Raised when a user clicks a sidebar button

Table 9-4　Wizard control events

The `<asp:WizardStep>` control supports the Activate event, which is raised when a wizard step becomes active, and the Deactivate event, which is raised when the current wizard step is deactivated.

The following code shows a wizard version of the Fitness Survey form. The wizard is formatted with the Professional predefined formatting scheme. Figure 9-9 shows the wizard steps.

```
<form ID="form1" runat="server"><div>
    <asp:Wizard ID="FitnessSurvey" runat="server"
        BackColor="#F7F6F3" BorderColor="#CCCCCC"
        BorderStyle="Solid" BorderWidth="1px"
        Font-Names="Verdana" Font-Size="0.8em">
```

```
<StepStyle BorderWidth="0px" ForeColor="#5D7B9D" />
<WizardSteps>
    <asp:WizardStep ID="WizardStep5" runat="server"
        Title="Question 1">
        <table cellpadding="4" cellspacing="4">
            <tr><td><strong>Do you belong to
            a gym?</strong></td></tr>
            <tr><td><asp:RadioButton ID="gymYes"
            GroupName="gym" runat="server"
            Checked="True" />Yes
            <asp:RadioButton ID="gymNo" GroupName="gym"
            runat="server" />No</td></tr></table>
    </asp:WizardStep>
    <asp:WizardStep ID="WizardStep6" runat="server"
        Title="Question 2">
        <table cellpadding="4" cellspacing="4">
            <tr><td><strong>How do you stay in
                shape?</strong></td></tr>
            <tr><td>
                <asp:CheckBox ID="jogging"
                runat="server" />Jogging<br />
                <asp:CheckBox ID="yoga"
                    runat="server" />Yoga<br />
                <asp:CheckBox ID="swimming"
                    runat="server" />Swimming<br />
                <asp:CheckBox ID="teamsports"
                    runat="server" />Team sports<br />
                <asp:CheckBox ID="classes"
                    runat="server" />
                    Fitness classes<br />
                <asp:CheckBox ID="weights"
                    runat="server" />
                    Weights</td></tr>
        </table>
    </asp:WizardStep>
    <asp:WizardStep ID="WizardStep1"
    runat="server" Title="Question 3">
        <table cellpadding="4" cellspacing="4">
            <tr><td><strong>How often do you
                exercise?</strong></td></tr>
            <tr><td>
                <asp:RadioButton ID="frequency1"
                    GroupName="frequency"
                    runat="server"
                    Checked="True" />
                    Once per week<br />
                <asp:RadioButton ID="frequency2"
                    GroupName="frequency"
                    runat="server" />
                    2-3 times per week<br />
                <asp:RadioButton ID="frequency3"
                    GroupName="frequency"
                    runat="server" />
                    4-6 times per week<br />
```

```
                              <asp:RadioButton ID="frequency4"
                                  GroupName="frequency"
                                  runat="server" />
                                  Every day<br /></td>
                          </tr></table>
            </asp:WizardStep>
            <asp:WizardStep ID="Summary" runat="server"
            Title="Summary"
                StepType="Finish">
                <table cellpadding="4" cellspacing="4">
                    <tr><td><strong>Summary</strong>
                    </td></tr>
                    <tr><td>Do you belong to a gym?
                        <asp:Literal ID="gymResult"
                            runat="server"></asp:Literal>
                        </td></tr>
                    <tr><td>How do you stay in shape?
                        <asp:Literal ID="regimenResult"
                            runat="server"></asp:Literal>
                        </td></tr>
                    <tr><td>How often do you exercise?
                        <asp:Literal ID="frequencyResult"
                            runat="server"></asp:Literal>
                        </td></tr>
            </table></asp:WizardStep>
            <asp:WizardStep ID="Complete" runat="server"
                Title="Complete" StepType="Complete">
                <asp:Label ID="finishMessage"
                    runat="server" />
            </asp:WizardStep>
        </WizardSteps>
        <SideBarButtonStyle BorderWidth="0px"
            Font-Names="Verdana"
            ForeColor="White" />
        <NavigationButtonStyle BackColor="#FFFBFF"
            BorderColor="#CCCCCC" BorderStyle="Solid"
            BorderWidth="1px" Font-Names="Verdana"
            Font-Size="0.8em"
            ForeColor="#284775" />
        <SideBarStyle BackColor="#7C6F57"
            BorderWidth="0px"
            Font-Size="0.9em" VerticalAlign="Top" />
        <HeaderStyle BackColor="#5D7B9D"
            BorderStyle="Solid"
            Font-Bold="True" Font-Size="0.9em"
            ForeColor="White" HorizontalAlign="Left" />
        <HeaderTemplate>
            <strong>Fitness Survey</strong>
        </HeaderTemplate>
    </asp:Wizard>
</div></form>
```

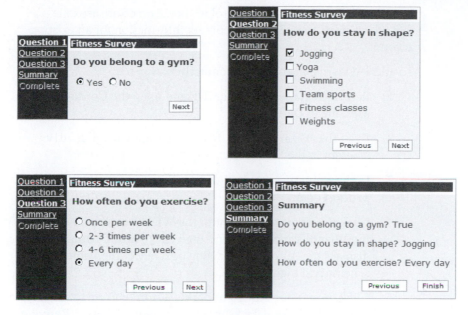

Figure 9-9   Steps in the Fitness Survey wizard

The Summary page of the Fitness Survey wizard relies on the same `Page_LoadComplete()` event handler to display the information that was gathered on the preceding pages. However, the `if` and `else...if` statements at the end of the event handler instead check the ID of the `ActiveStep` property of the wizard object to determine which form is displayed, as follows:

The Complete step of the Fitness Survey wizard simply prints the text "We have received your survey. Thank you for your input." to the browser window.

```
...
        if (FitnessSurvey.ActiveStep.ID == "Summary")
        {
            gymResult.Text = gymMembership.ToString();
            regimenResult.Text = regimen;
            frequencyResult.Text = workoutDays;
        }
        else if (FitnessSurvey.ActiveStep.ID == "Complete") {
            SqlConnection dbConnection = new SqlConnection(
                "Data Source=.\\SQLEXPRESS;
                Integrated Security=true");
            dbConnection.Open();
            dbConnection.ChangeDatabase("fitnessSurvey");
            SqlCommand sqlCommand = new SqlCommand(
                "INSERT INTO surveyResults VALUES("
                + gymMembership + "," + regimen + ","
                + workoutDays + ")", dbConnection);
            sqlCommand.ExecuteNonQuery();
            finishMessage.Text = "<p>We have received your
                survey. Thank you for your input.</p>";
        }
    }
```

Next, you will add a Wizard control to the ContactInfo.aspx file that allows users to update their contact information for an existing account.

To add a Wizard control to the ContactInfo.aspx file:

1. Return to the Visual Studio IDE and open the **ContactInfo. aspx** file in Design view.

2. Drag the Wizard control from the Toolbox to the `<div>` element in the Web form.

3. In the Properties window, change the Wizard control's ID to **profileForm**.

4. Click the arrow to the right of the Wizard control to display the Wizard Tasks menu, and then click **Auto Format**, which displays the Auto Format dialog box. Select the **Professional** scheme and then click **OK**.

5. Click the arrow to the right of the Wizard control again to display the Wizard Tasks menu, and then click **Add/Remove WizardSteps**, which displays the WizardStep Collection Editor dialog box.

6. In the WizardStep Collection Editor dialog box, select **Step 1** and change its `Title` attribute to **Account Details** and its `StepType` attribute to **Start**. Select **Step 2** and change its `Title` attribute to **Billing Information** and its `StepType` attribute to **Step**.

7. In the WizardStep Collection Editor dialog box, use the Add button to add third and fourth wizard steps. For the third wizard step, change its `Title` attribute to **Travel Preferences** and its `StepType` attribute to **Finish**. For the fourth wizard step, change its `Title` attribute to **Profile Updated** and its `StepType` attribute to **Complete**. Click **OK** to close the WizardStep Collection Editor dialog box.

8. Return to the Registration.aspx file in the Code Editor and copy the text and elements within the `<asp:View>` element with the `ID` attribute of "baseProfile", except for the Next button. Open the ContactInfo.aspx in the Code Editor and paste the text and elements into the `<asp:WizardStep>` element with the `title` attribute of "Account Details".

9. Return to the Registration.aspx file in the Code Editor and copy the text and elements within the `<asp:View>` element with the `ID` attribute of "billing", except for the Next

and Previous buttons. Return to the ContactInfo.aspx in the Code Editor and paste the text and elements into the `<asp:WizardStep>` element with the `title` attribute of "Billing Information".

10. Return to the Registration.aspx file in the Code Editor and copy the text and elements within the `<asp:View>` element with the `ID` attribute of "preferences", except for the Previous and Enroll buttons. Return to the ContactInfo.aspx in the Code Editor and paste the text and elements into the `<asp:WizardStep>` element with the `title` attribute of "Travel Preferences".

11. Add the following Literal control to the `<asp:WizardStep>` element with the `title` attribute of "Profile Updated".

```
<asp:Literal ID="updateOK" runat="server" />
```

12. Finally, add the following Literal control immediately after the closing `</asp:Wizard>` tag. This control will display any errors that occur when attempting to update user information.

```
<asp:Literal ID="updateErrors" runat="server" />
```

Next, you will add functionality that allows users to update their contact information for an existing account.

To add functionality that allows users to update their contact information for an existing account:

1. Return to the Visual Studio IDE and open the **ffClubPage. aspx** file in the Code Editor.

2. Locate the link to the ContactInfo.aspx file and modify it as follows so it appends the frequent flyer number to the URL as a query string:

```
<a href=<% Response.Write("ContactInfo.aspx?flyerID="
+ Request.QueryString["flyerID"]); %>>
Update Contact Info</a>
```

3. Open the **ContactInfo.aspx.cs** file in the Code Editor.

4. Add the following directive to the end of the directives section:

```
using System.Data.SqlClient;
```

5. Add to the `Page_Load()` event handler the following statements. The first `if` statement redirects the browser to the Login.aspx page if the URL does not include a `flyerID` query

string value. The second if statement stores the password in a hidden form field when the wizard's start page opens:

```
if (Request.QueryString["flyerID"] == null)
    Response.Redirect("Login.aspx");
 if (profileForm.ActiveStep.StepType
    == WizardStepType.Start)
    hiddenPassword.Value = password.Text;
```

6. Add the following statements to the end of the Page_Load() event handler to populate the fields in the wizard:

```
SqlConnection dbConnection = new SqlConnection(
    "Data Source=.\\SQLEXPRESS;AttachDbFilename=
    C:\\Course Technology\\0324-2\\Chapter.09\\Chapter\\
    SkywardAviation\\App_Data\\SkywardAviation.mdf;
    Integrated Security=True;User Instance=True");
dbConnection.Open();
try
{
SqlCommand sqlCommand = new SqlCommand(
    "SELECT * FROM FrequentFlyers WHERE flyerID = "
    + Request.QueryString["flyerID"], dbConnection);
SqlDataReader userInfo = sqlCommand.ExecuteReader();
if (userInfo.Read())
{
    firstName.Text = userInfo["first"].ToString();
    lastName.Text = userInfo["last"].ToString();
    telephone.Text = userInfo["phone"].ToString();
    email.Text = userInfo["email"].ToString();
    confirmEmail.Text = userInfo["email"].ToString();
    creditcard.Text = userInfo["cardType"].ToString();
    expireMonth.Text = userInfo["expireMonth"]
        .ToString();
    expireYear.Text = userInfo["expireYear"]
        .ToString();
    cardnumber.Text = userInfo["cardNumber"]
        .ToString();
    cardholder.Text = userInfo["cardholder"]
        .ToString();
    address.Text = userInfo["address"].ToString();
    city.Text = userInfo["city"].ToString();
    state.Text = userInfo["state"].ToString();
    zip.Text = userInfo["zip"].ToString();
    travelerType.Text = userInfo["travelerType"]
        .ToString();
    homeAirport.Text = userInfo["homeAirport"]
        .ToString();
    serviceClass.Text = userInfo["class"]
        .ToString();
    seatPreference.Text = userInfo["seat"]
        .ToString();
    mealRequest.Text = userInfo["meal"].ToString();
```

```
updateOK.Text = "<p>Account successfully
    updated.</p><p><a href='ffClubPage.aspx?
    flyerID=" + Request.QueryString["flyerID"]
    + "'>Account Profile page</a></p>";
}
else
{
    profileForm.Visible = false;
    updateErrors.Text = "<p>Invalid frequent
        flyer number!</p>";
}
userInfo.Close();
}
catch (SqlException exception)
{
    Response.Write("<p>Error code "
        + exception.Number
        + ": " + exception.Message + "</p>");
}
dbConnection.Close();
```

7. Immediately after the Page_Load() event handler, add a Page_LoadComplete() event handler containing an if statement that opens a database connection when the complete step of the wizard opens. Be sure to change the path location where you created the SkywardAviation database.

```
protected void Page_LoadComplete(
    object sender, EventArgs e)
{
    if (profileForm.ActiveStep.StepType
        == WizardStepType.Complete)
    {
        SqlConnection dbConnection = new SqlConnection(
            "Data Source=.\\SQLEXPRESS;AttachDbFilename=
            C:\\Course Technology\\0324-2\\Chapter.09\\
            Chapter\\SkywardAviation\\App_Data\\
            SkywardAviation.mdf;Integrated Security=True;
            User Instance=True");
    }
}
```

8. Add to the end of the if statement the following try...catch block, which uses a SQL UPDATE command to update the database record:

```
try
{
    dbConnection.Open();
    SqlCommand sqlCommand = new SqlCommand(
        "UPDATE FrequentFlyers SET "
        + "last= '" + lastName.Text + "',"
        + "first ='" + firstName.Text + "',"
```

```
            + "phone ='" + telephone.Text + "',"
            + "email='" + email.Text + "',"
            + "password='" + hiddenPassword.Value + "',"
            + "cardtype='" + creditcard.Text + "',"
            + "expireMonth ='" + expireMonth.Text + "',"
            + "expireYear ='" + expireYear.Text + "',"
            + "cardnumber ='" + cardnumber.Text + "',"
            + "cardholder ='" + cardholder.Text + "',"
            + "address ='" + address.Text + "',"
            + "city ='" + city.Text + "',"
            + "state ='" + state.Text + "',"
            + "zip ='" + zip.Text + "',"
            + "travelerType = '" + travelerType.Text + "',"
            + "homeAirport ='" + homeAirport.Text + "',"
            + "class ='" + serviceClass.Text + "',"
            + "seat ='" + seatPreference.Text + "',"
            + "meal ='" + mealRequest.Text
            + "' WHERE flyerID = "
            + Request.QueryString["flyerID"], dbConnection);
        sqlCommand.ExecuteNonQuery();
    }
    catch (SqlException exception)
    {
        updateOK.Text = "<p>Error code " + exception.Number
            + ": " + exception.Message + "</p>";
    }
```

9. Finally, add the following statement to the end of the if statement to close the database connection:

```
dbConnection.Close();
```

10. Start the Web site. Select the Frequent Flyers tab, enter a valid
    frequent flyer number and password, and then click **Login**.
    The Account Profile page opens. Select the **Update Contact
    Info** link. The Contact Information page opens, as shown in
    Figure 9-10.

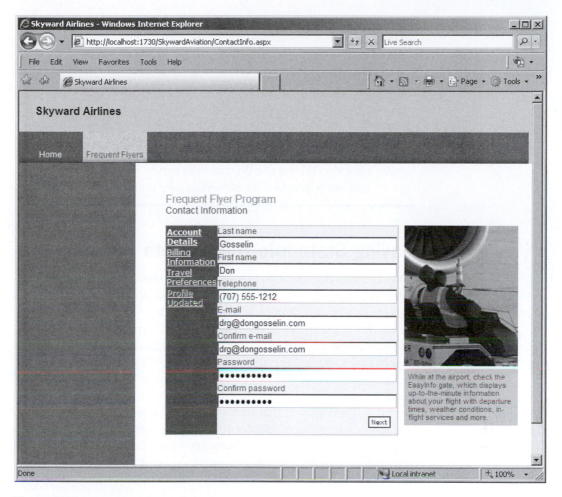

Figure 9-10   Contact Information page

11.   Use the wizard to change some of the information in the record, and then close your Web browser window.

12.   In the Visual Studio IDE, select the **View** menu and then select **Database Explorer**. In the Database Explorer window, expand the **SkywardAviation** database and then expand **Tables**. Right-click the **FrequentFlyers** table and select **Show Table Data**. Verify that the information you changed was updated in the table.

Short Quiz 1

1. Explain how to use query strings and hidden form fields to maintain state information.

2. How do you simulate multipage forms with the MultiView and View Web server controls?

3. How do you use the Wizard Web server control to create a multistep interface for gathering user input?

Saving State Information with Cookies

Query strings do not permanently maintain state information. The information contained in a query string is available only during the current session of a Web page. Once a Web page that reads a query string closes, the query string is lost. Hidden form fields and Web server controls maintain state information between Web pages, but the data they contain are also lost once the Web page that reads the hidden fields closes. You can save the contents of a query string or hidden form fields by submitting the form data using a server-side scripting language, but that method requires a separate server-based application. To make it possible to store state information beyond the current Web page session, Netscape created cookies. **Cookies** are small pieces of information about a user that are stored by a Web server in text files on the user's computer.

Each time the Web client visits a Web server, the client sends saved cookies for the requested Web site to the server. The server then uses the cookies to customize the Web page for the client. Cookies were originally created for use with CGI scripts, but are now commonly used by JavaScript and server-side scripting tools such as ASP.NET.

 Web browsers enforce a number of limitations on the use of cookies. Each individual server or domain can store only a maximum of 20 cookies on a user's computer with a maximum size of 4 kilobytes. In addition, the total cookies per browser cannot exceed 300. If these limits are exceeded, a Web browser might start discarding older cookies.

You have probably seen cookies in action if you have ever visited a Web site where you entered a username in a prompt dialog box or in a text field, and then found that you were greeted by that username the next time you visited the Web site. This could occur with each subsequent visit to the same Web site, whether during the same browser session or during a different browser session days or weeks later. The Web page remembers this information by storing it locally on your computer in a cookie. Another example of a cookie is a counter that counts the number of times an individual user has visited a Web site.

Cookies can be temporary or persistent. **Temporary cookies** remain available only for the current browser session. **Persistent cookies** remain available beyond the current browser session and are stored in a text file on a client computer. In this section, you will create both persistent and temporary cookies.

Creating Cookies

ASP.NET includes a number of ways to store cookies. The easiest way to store a cookie is to use the following syntax to define a variable in the `Cookies[]` collection of the Response object:

```
Response.Cookies["cookieName"].Value = "cookie value";
```

The following statement creates a cookie named `firstName` that is assigned the value "Don":

```
Response.Cookies["firstName"].Value = "Don";
```

The preceding statement stores the cookie as a name=value pair (firstName=Don) in the browser.

You can also create a cookie by declaring an object of the `HttpCookie` class, as follows:

```
HttpCookie firstName = new HttpCookie("firstName");
```

The `HttpCookie` class contains other properties that you can use to create the cookie, including a `Value` property to which you assign the cookie value. After you finish creating the cookie, you store it in the browser with the `Response.Cookies.Add()` method statement. You pass to the `Response.Cookies.Add()` method the name of the object you created with the `HttpCookie` class. The following code demonstrates how to create a cookie named `firstName` with the `HttpCookie` class, assign it a value of "Don", and then store the cookie in a browser with the `Response.Cookies.Add()` method statement.

```
HttpCookie firstName = new HttpCookie("firstName");
firstName.Value = "Don";
Response.Cookies.Add(firstName);
```

Should you use the `Cookies[]` collection or the `HttpCookie` class? Both techniques work in essentially the same way. However, the `HttpCookie` class allows you to treat cookies as objects and gives you greater flexibility and control over your cookies. For example, instead of relying on the response mechanism provided by the `Cookies[]` collection, you can take advantage of the `HttpCookie` class, which gives you greater control over when the cookie is added to the browser. You need to understand how to use both techniques, but in most cases, you should use the `HttpCookie` class.

ASP.NET also supports storing multiple name=value pairs in a single cookie. Multiple name=value pairs that are stored in a single cookie are called **subkeys**. Using subkeys is helpful because each individual server or domain can store only a maximum of 20 cookies on a user's

493

computer, and subkeys allow you to remain below your limit of 20 cookies. This technique is especially useful for large Web sites with numerous pages that store cookies. Further, each individual cookie requires approximately 50 bytes, plus the storage required for the assigned cookie value. If you can use one cookie with subkeys instead of 10 individual cookies, you can save approximately 450 bytes, which is more than 10% of the 4 kilobytes maximum amount of cookie storage space that most browsers enforce for individual servers and domains.

The syntax for using `Response.Cookies()` statements to create cookies with multiple subkeys is as follows:

```
Response.Cookies["cookieName"]["subkeyName"] = "value";
```

> Be sure not to include the Value property at the end of the left operands in the preceding statements.

The following statements create a cookie named `userInfo` with three subkeys: firstName, lastName, and occupation:

```
Response.Cookies["userInfo"]["firstName"] = "Don";
Response.Cookies["userInfo"]["lastName"] = "Gosselin";
Response.Cookies["userInfo"]["occupation"] = "writer";
```

To create subkeys with the `HttpCookie` class, you must use the `Values()` property to create individual subkeys. The syntax for creating a cookie subkey using the `HttpCookie` class and the `Values()` property is as follows:

```
cookieObject.Values["subkeyName"] = "subkeyValue";
```

The following code demonstrates how to use the `HttpCookie` class to create the `userInfo` cookie:

```
HttpCookie userInfoObject = new HttpCookie("userInfo");
userInfoObject.Values["firstName"] = "Don";
userInfoObject.Values["lastName"] = "Gosselin";
Response.Cookies.Add(userInfoObject);
```

A Web browser automatically separates cookie subkeys with an ampersand (&). Therefore, the value assigned to the `userInfo` cookie contains the following value:

```
firstName=Don&lastName=Gosselin&occupation=writer
```

Setting Cookie Expiration Dates

For a cookie to persist beyond the current browser session, you must use the `Expires` property of the cookie object. The **Expires property** determines how long a cookie can remain on a client system before it is deleted. Cookies created without an `Expires` property are available for only the current browser session. You must assign to the `Expires` property the `DateTime` structure, which represents an instance in time. The `DateTime` structure includes various methods and properties that you can use to retrieve and modify date and time information. The most common way to use the DateTime structure with a cookie's Expires property is to use the Now property and one of the Add() methods of the DateTime structure. The Now property returns the current date and time. The DateTime structure's various Add() methods, such as AddDays() and AddMonths(), adds the specified amount of time to the date in the Now property. The following statements demonstrate how to configure the userInfo cookie with the Response.Cookies[] collection so it expires in seven days:

```
Response.Cookies["userInfo"]["firstName"] = "Don";
Response.Cookies["userInfo"]["lastName"] = "Gosselin";
Response.Cookies["userInfo"]["occupation"] = "writer";
Response.Cookies["userInfo"].Expires
    = DateTime.Now.AddDays(7);
```

The following statements demonstrate how to configure the userInfo cookie with HttpCookie object so it expires in seven days. Notice that the expiration statement is placed before the Add() statement.

```
HttpCookie userInfoObject = new HttpCookie("userInfo");
userInfoObject.Values["firstName"] = "Don";
userInfoObject.Values["lastName"] = "Gosselin";
userInfoObject.Expires = DateTime.Now.AddDays(7);
Response.Cookies.Add(userInfoObject);
```

When developing a program, you might accidentally create persistent cookies that your program does not need. Unused persistent cookies can sometimes interfere with the execution of a program. For this reason, it's a good idea to delete your browser cookies periodically, especially while developing a program that uses cookies. To delete cookies in Internet Explorer, select the Tools menu and then select Internet Options. Click the General tab of the Internet Options dialog box, and then click the Delete button. In the Delete Browsing History dialog box, select Delete cookies and select Yes when prompted. To delete cookies in Firefox, select Options from the Tools menu, select the Privacy tab in the Options dialog box, and then click the Clear Now button. Select the Cookies check box and click Clear Private Data Now.

Configuring Cookie Availability to Other Web Pages on the Server

The **Path property** determines the availability of a cookie to other Web pages on a server. You append the path attribute to the cookie object and assign it a path. By default, a cookie is available to all Web pages in the same directory. However, if you specify a path, then a cookie is available to all Web pages in the specified path as well as to all Web pages in all subdirectories in the specified path. For example, the following Response.Cookies[] collection example makes the cookie named `userInfo` available to all Web pages located in the/marketing directory or any of its subdirectories:

```
Response.Cookies["userInfo"]["firstName"] = "Don";
Response.Cookies["userInfo"]["lastName"] = "Gosselin";
Response.Cookies["userInfo"]["occupation"] = "writer";
Response.Cookies["userInfo"].Expires = DateTime.Now.AddDays(7);
Response.Cookies["userInfo"].Path = "/marketing";
```

The following example demonstrates how to set the path using the `HttpCookie` object:

```
HttpCookie userInfoObject = new HttpCookie("userInfo");
userInfoObject.Values["firstName"] = "Don";
userInfoObject.Values["lastName"] = "Gosselin";
userInfoObject.Expires = DateTime.Now.AddDays(7);
userInfoObject.Path = "/marketing";
Response.Cookies.Add(userInfoObject);
```

To make a cookie available to all directories on a server, use a slash to indicate the root directory, as in the following examples:

```
// Response.Cookies[] collection
Response.Cookies["userInfo"].Path = "/";
// HttpCookie object
userInfoObject.Path = "/";
```

When you are developing programs that create cookies, your programs might not function correctly if the directory containing your Web page contains other programs that create cookies. Cookies from other programs that are stored in the same directory along with unused cookies you created during development can cause your cookie program to run erratically. Therefore, it is a good idea always to place cookie programs in their own directory and use the `Path` property to specify any subdirectories your program requires.

Sharing Cookies Across a Domain

Using the `Path` property allows you to share cookies across a server. Some Web sites, however, are very large and use a number of servers. The **Path property** determines the availability of a cookie to other Web sites on a server. (Note that you cannot share cookies outside of a domain.) You append the `path` attribute to the `cookie` object and assign it a domain. For example, if the Web server `programming.gosselin.com` needs to share cookies with the Web server `writing.gosselin.com`, the `Domain` property for cookies set by `programming.gosselin.com` should be set to `.gosselin.com`. That way, cookies created by `programming.gosselin.com` are available to `writing.gosselin.com` and to all other servers in the domain `gosselin.com`.

The following code shows examples with the `Response.Cookies[]` collection and `HttpCookie` object methods on how to make a cookie at `programming.gosselin.com` available to all servers in the `gosselin.com` domain:

```
// Response.Cookies[] collection
Response.Cookies["userInfo"].Domain = "gosselin.com";
// HttpCookie object
userInfoObject.Path = "gosselin.com";
```

Securing Cookie Transmissions

Internet connections are not always considered safe for transmitting sensitive information. It is possible for unscrupulous people to steal personal information, such as credit card numbers, passwords, Social Security numbers, and other types of private information online. To protect private data transferred across the Internet, Netscape developed **Secure Sockets Layer**, or **SSL**, to encrypt data and transfer it across a secure connection. The URLs for Web sites that support SSL usually start with the HTTPS protocol instead of HTTP. The **Secure property** indicates that a cookie can only be transmitted across a secure Internet connection using HTTPS or another security protocol.

To enable SSL for cookies, append the `Secure` property to the `Response.Cookies[]` collection or the `HttpCookie` object, and assign it a value of true, as follows:

```
// Response.Cookies[] collection
Response.Cookies["userInfo"].Secure = true;
// HttpCookie object
userInfoObject.Secure = true;
```

The Skyward Aviation Web site currently maintains state by passing the frequent flyer number to each page. Next, you will modify the Login page so a user's frequent flyer number is stored in a cookie.

To modify the Login page so a user's frequent flyer number is stored in a cookie:

1. Return to the **Login.aspx.cs** file in the Visual Studio IDE.

2. The `if` statement within the `try` block appends the frequent flyer number to the ffClubPage.aspx URL as a query string. Modify the `if` statement as follows so the ID is instead stored with a cookie. The cookie is configured to expire in 30 days.

```
if (curUser.Read())
{
    HttpCookie flyerIDObject = new HttpCookie("flyerID");
    flyerIDObject.Value = curUser["flyerID"].ToString();
    flyerIDObject.Expires = DateTime.Now.AddDays(30);
    Response.Cookies.Add(flyerIDObject);
    Response.Redirect("ffClubPage.aspx");
}
```

Reading Cookies

When a browser requests a Web page, it sends any existing cookies for the Web site along with the request. The cookies are then available in the Request.Cookies[] collection, the same as form values are available in the Request.Forms[] and Request.QueryString[] collections. To retrieve the value of a specific cookie, you refer to it as a variable of the Request.Cookies[] collection and append the Value property, as in the following statement that prints the value of the firstName cookie:

```
Response.Write(Request.Cookies["firstName"].Value);
```

Use the following format to refer to a cookie value with an HttpCookie object:

```
HttpCookie userFirstName
    = Request.Cookies["firstName"];
Response.Write(userFirstName.Value);
```

When attempting to read a cookie, your program should always check first to see if the cookie exists with a conditional expression that determines whether the cookie is not equal to null. Otherwise, you will receive the NullReferenceException exception. The following code demonstrates how to determine if the firstName cookie exists using both the Request.Cookies[] collection and an HttpCookie object:

```
// Response.Cookies[] collection
if (Request.Cookies["firstName"] != null)
    Response.Write(Request.Cookies["firstName"].Value);
// HttpCookie object
if (Request.Cookies["firstName"] != null)
{
    HttpCookie userFirstName
        = Request.Cookies["firstName"];
    Response.Write(userFirstName.Value);
}
```

To refer to a cookie's subkeys, append the subkey name to the Request.Cookies[] collection, surrounded by brackets and quotations. The following code demonstrates how to print each of the subkeys in the userInfo cookie:

```
if (Request.Cookies["userInfo"] != null)
{
    Response.Write(Request.Cookies["userInfo"]["firstName"]
        + " ");
    Response.Write(Request.Cookies["userInfo"]["lastName"]
        + " is a ");
    Response.Write(Request.Cookies["userInfo"]["occupation"]);
}
```

Here's the same code using the `HttpCookie` object:

```
if (Request.Cookies["userInfo"] != null)
{
    HttpCookie userInfoObject
        = Request.Cookies["userInfo"];
    Response.Write(userInfoObject.Values["firstName"] + " ");
    Response.Write(userInfoObject.Values["lastName"]
        + " is a ");
    Response.Write(userInfoObject.Values["occupation"]);
}
```

Next, you will modify the pages in the Skyward Aviation Web site so they maintain state with a cookie instead of a query string.

To modify the pages in the Skyward Aviation Web site so they maintain state with a cookie instead of a query string:

1. Return to the Visual Studio IDE.

2. Return to the **ffClubPage.aspx** file and locate the link to the ContactInfo.aspx file and modify it so the `href` attribute is simply assigned the ContactInfo.aspx URL:

   ```
   <a href="ContactInfo.aspx">Update Contact Info</a>
   ```

3. Return to the **ContactInfo.aspx.cs** file and locate the statement at the end of the `try` block that assigns a value to the `Text` property of the `updateOK` control. Modify the assign values as follows so it does not append the frequent flyer number to the URL:

   ```
   updateOK.Text = "<p>Account successfully updated.
       </p><p><a href='ffClubPage.aspx'>Account
       Profile page</a></p>";
   ```

4. Select the **Edit** menu, point to **Find and Replace**, and then select **Quick Replace**. The Find and Replace dialog box opens.

5. In the Find and Replace dialog box, enter **Request. QueryString["flyerID"]** in the Find what box and enter **Request.Cookies["flyerID"]** in the Replace with box. Click the **Look in** box and select **Current Project**, and then click **Replace All**. The replace operation replaces six occurrences.

6. Close the Find and Replace dialog box.

7. Return to the **ContactInfo.aspx.cs** file and locate the `SqlCommand` statement in the `Page_Load()` event handler and add **.Value** to Request.Cookies["flyerID"], as follows:

   ```
   SqlCommand sqlCommand = new SqlCommand(
       "SELECT * FROM FrequentFlyers WHERE flyerID = "
       + Request.Cookies["flyerID"].Value, dbConnection);
   ```

8. Locate the `SqlCommand` statement in the `Page_LoadComplete()` event handler and add **`.Value`** to Request.Cookies["flyerID"], as follows:

```
...
+ Request.Cookies["flyerID"].Value, dbConnection);
```

9. Return to the **ffClubPage.aspx.cs** file and locate the `SqlCommand` statement in the `try` block in the `Page_Load()` event handler and add **`.Value`** to Request.Cookies["flyerID"], as follows:

```
SqlCommand sqlCommand = new SqlCommand("SELECT flyerID,
    first, last FROM FrequentFlyers WHERE flyerID = "
    + Request.Cookies["flyerID"].Value, dbConnection);
```

10. Start the Web site. Select the **Frequent Flyers** tab, enter a valid frequent flyer number and password, and then click **Login**. The Account Profile page opens. Select the **Home Page** tab and then select the **Frequent Flyers** tab. You should still be logged in to the application.

11. Close your Web browser window.

Modifying and Deleting Cookies

You cannot directly modify the value assigned to a cookie or subkey. Instead, you must overwrite the old cookie with a new cookie. For example, suppose you want to store the date of the user's last visit. In the following code, the first `if` statement checks if the `lastVisit` cookie is available. If it is, it prints the date of the user's last visit. If not, it prints a message telling the user that this is his or her first visit in six months. The last two statements then re-create the `lastVisit` cookie and assign to it the current month, date, and year, using properties of the `DateTime` structure.

```
if (Request.Cookies["lastVisit"] != null)
    Response.Write("<p>Your last visit was on "
        + Request.Cookies["lastVisit"].Value + ".</p>");
else
    Response.Write("<p>This is your first visit in six
        months.</p>");
Response.Cookies["lastVisit"].Value = DateTime.Now
    .ToShortDateString();
Response.Cookies["lastVisit"].Expires = DateTime.Now
    .AddMonths(6);
```

Here's the same code using the `HttpCookie` class:

```
if (Request.Cookies["lastVisit"] != null)
    Response.Write("<p>Your last visit was on "
        + Request.Cookies["lastVisit"].Value + ".</p>");
```

```
else
    Response.Write("<p>This is your first visit in six
        months.</p>");
HttpCookie lastVisitObject = new HttpCookie("lastVisit");
lastVisitObject.Value = DateTime.Now.ToShortDateString();
Response.Cookies.Add(lastVisitObject);
```

You can delete cookies, although the way in which you delete them is not intuitive. To delete a cookie, you must set its expiration to a date in the past. The following code demonstrates how to delete the userInfo cookie by using the AddDays() method to assign a value of yesterday to the cookie's Expires property. Notice that you assign a value of yesterday to the cookie by passing an argument of -1 to the AddDays() method.

```
// Response.Cookies[] collection
if (Request.Cookies["userInfo"] != null)
    Response.Cookies["userInfo"].Expires
        = DateTime.Now.AddDays(-1);
// HttpCookie object
if (Request.Cookies["userInfo"] != null)
{
    HttpCookie userInfoObject
        = Request.Cookies["userInfo"];
    userInfoObject.Expires = DateTime.Now.AddDays(-1);
    Response.Cookies.Add(userInfoObject);
}
```

To delete a subkey, you must call the Remove() method of the Values collection, as follows:

```
// Response.Cookies[] collection
Response.Cookies["userInfo"].Values.Remove("occupation");
// HttpCookie object
userInfo.Values.Remove("occupation");
```

Next, you will add an event handler for the Logout link button on the Account Profile page that deletes the flyerID cookie.

To add an event handler for the Logout link button on the Account Profile page that deletes the flyerID cookie:

1. Return to the **ffClubPage.aspx** file in the Visual Studio IDE and open it in Design view.

2. Double-click the **Logout** link button and an event handler named logout_Click() is created in the ffClubPage.aspx.cs file.

3. Add the following statements to the event handler. The first statement deletes the cookie by changing its Expires property to one day in the past and the second statement redirects the user to the Login.aspx page.

    ```
    Response.Cookies["flyerID"].Expires
        = DateTime.Now.AddDays(-1);
    Response.Redirect("Login.aspx");
    ```

4. Start the Web site. Try logging in and out several times to see if the new functionality works.

5. Close your Web browser window.

Short Quiz 2

1. Explain the difference between temporary and persistent cookies. How do you configure a cookie to be persistent?

2. How do you configure cookies to be available to other Web pages on the server?

3. How do you secure cookie transmissions?

4. How do you determine if a cookie exists?

5. How do you modify and delete cookies?

Working with Session State, Application State, and Profiles

In this section, you will learn how to save state information with session state, application state, and profile properties. First, you will examine session state.

Storing Session Information with Session State

A new `Request` object is instantiated each time a client requests an ASP.NET URL, and then destroyed once the URL is delivered to the client. However, an ASP.NET application might be composed of multiple documents. Because the `Request` object is destroyed once the URL is delivered to the client, you cannot use the same `Request` object with different pages in an application. If you want to preserve client information across multiple pages in an ASP.NET application, you must use **session state**, which stores specific client information and makes that information available to all the pages for the current ASP.NET session. Session data is stored in a `SessionStateItemCollection` object that you can access through the `Session[]` collection. A `SessionStateItemCollection` object is instantiated the first time a client accesses a URL in a given application. For example, you might store the values from the `Request` object `Form` collection in the `Session` collection to make the form information available across all the pages in an ASP.NET application.

The following code shows an example of an ASP.NET application that assigns the values of form fields submitted with the `get` method to variables of the `Session` collection:

```
Session["name"] = Request.QueryString["name"];
Session["address"] = Request.QueryString["address"];
Session["city"] = Request.QueryString["city"];
Session["state"] = Request.QueryString["state"];
Session["zip"] = Request.QueryString["zip"];
Session["email"] = Request.QueryString["email"];
```

You configure session state with a `<sessionState>` element in the Web.config file. Table 9-5 lists some of the common attributes that you can use in the `<sessionState>` element.

Attribute	Description
cookieless	Specifies how a session uses cookies; a value of true. You can assign one of the following values to this attribute: **AutoDetect**—Determines whether the requesting browser accepts cookies; if the browser accepts cookies, the session ID is stored in a cookie; if the browser does not accept cookies, the session ID is added to the page's URL **UseCookies** (default)—Specifies that the session stores user data in cookies, regardless of whether the browser supports them **UseDeviceProfile**—Uses the `HttpBrowserCapabilities` setting to determine whether a browser accepts cookies; if the browser accepts cookies, the session ID is stored in a cookie; if the browser does not accept cookies, the session ID is added to the page's URL **UseURI**—Specifies that the session ID is always stored in the URI
cookieName	Specifies the name of the cookie that stores the session ID; the default value is ASP.NET_SessionId
mode	Specifies where to store session state values. You can assign one of the following values to this attribute: **Custom**—Session state is stored in a custom data store **InProc** (default)—Session state is stored within the ASP.NET process **Off**—Session state is disabled **SQLServer**—Session state is stored in a SQL Server database **StateServer**—Session state is stored in the Windows operating system process
Timeout	Specifies the life span of the session

Table 9-5　Common attributes of the `<sessionState>` element

It's important to keep in mind that the ASP.NET session has a default life span of 20 minutes. A default life span is necessary because the Web does not contain any links between a client and a server as a real network does; it relies instead on HTTP to send requests and responses back and forth over the Internet. Therefore, ASP.NET has no way of knowing whether a client has left the Web site. For example, when users access a Web site, they are only requesting a document. Once an ASP. NET server returns the requested document, it has no way of knowing whether the client will request other Web pages. From the server's point of view, the only possible indication that a client hasn't left the Web site occurs when the client requests another document. If the client fails to make another request within 10 minutes, the ASP.NET session that was created for the client's initial request is deleted. If you want to allocate more time before a session expires, you use the `Timeout` attribute, which determines the life span of a session. The following XML example demonstrates how to use the `<sessionState>` element in the Web.config file to decrease the session timeout to 15 minutes:

See *http://msdn. microsoft.com/ en-us/library/ h6bb9cz9.aspx* for a complete list of available attributes for the `<sessionState>` element.

```
<system.web>
<sessionState
    timeout="15" />
</system.web>
```

Next, you will modify the pages in the Skyward Aviation Web site so they maintain state with the `Session[]` collection instead of a cookie.

To modify the pages in the Skyward Aviation Web site so they maintain state with the `Session[]` collection instead of a cookie:

1. Return to the **Login.aspx.cs** file in the Visual Studio IDE.

2. Replace the first four statements in the `if` statement within the `try` block with a single statement that creates a `flyerID` session variable, as follows:

```
if (curUser.Read())
{
    Session["flyerID"] = curUser["flyerID"].ToString();
    Response.Redirect("ffClubPage.aspx");
}
```

3. Select the **Edit** menu, point to **Find and Replace**, and then select **Quick Replace**. The Find and Replace dialog box opens.

4. In the Find and Replace dialog box, enter **Request. Cookies["flyerID"]** in the Find what box and enter **Session["flyerID"]** in the Replace with box. Click the **Look in** box and select **Current Project**, and then click **Replace All**. The replace operation replaces six occurrences.

5. Close the Find and Replace dialog box.

6. Return to the **ffClubPage.aspx.cs** file. Remove ".Value" from `Session["flyerID"]` in the statement that creates the `sqlCommand` object:

```
SqlCommand sqlCommand = new SqlCommand(
    "SELECT flyerID, first, last FROM
    FrequentFlyers WHERE flyerID = "
    + Session["flyerID"], dbConnection);
```

7. Return to the **ContactInfo.aspx.cs** file and remove ".Value" from Session["flyerID"] in the statement that creates the sqlCommand object in the Page_Load() event handler:

```
SqlCommand sqlCommand = new SqlCommand("SELECT * FROM
    FrequentFlyers WHERE flyerID = "
    + Session["flyerID"], dbConnection);
```

8. Remove ".Value" from Session["flyerID"] in the statement that creates the sqlCommand object in the Page_LoadComplete() event handler:

```
...
+ Session["flyerID"], dbConnection);
```

9. Start the Web site. The functionality should work the same as it did before you replaced the cookie with a session variable.

10. Close your Web browser window.

Using Cookieless Sessions

By default, ASP.NET keeps track of an individual session by storing a session ID in a cookie on the user's browser. However, if a browser does not accept cookies, then ASP.NET cannot use a cookie to store the session ID. To get around this problem, ASP.NET supports **cookieless sessions**, which store the session ID in a Web page's URL instead of in a cookie. To configure a Web site to use cookieless sessions, you must add the cookieless attribute to the <sessionState> element. In most cases, you should assign a value of "AutoDetect" if you want your application to support sessions for browsers that do not accept cookies. When "AutoDetect" is assigned to the cookieless attribute, then if the browser accepts cookies, the session ID is stored in a cookie. However, if the browser does not accept cookies, the session ID is added to the page's URL.

The following XML example demonstrates how to use the <sessionState> element in the Web.config file to assign a value of "AutoDetect" to the cookieless attribute:

```
</system.web>
<sessionState
    cookieless="AutoDetect"
    timeout="20" />
</system.web>
```

Next, you will modify the Skyward Aviation Web site so it supports cookieless sessions:

506

To modify the Skyward Aviation Web site so it supports `cookieless` sessions:

1. Return to the Visual Studio IDE and open the **Web.config** file in the Code Editor.

2. Add the following element above the closing `</system.web>` tag:

```
<sessionState
    cookieless="AutoDetect"/>
```

3. Open your Web browser and disable cookies. To disable cookies in Internet Explorer, select the **Tools** menu and then select **Internet Options**. Click the **Privacy** tab and then click the **Advanced** button. The Advanced Privacy Settings dialog box opens. Select the **Override automatic cookie handling** box, and then select **Block** for both **First-party Cookies** and **Third-Party Cookies**. Select the **Always allow session cookies** box and click **OK** to close the Advanced Privacy Settings dialog box and **OK** again to close the Internet Options dialog box. To disable cookies in Firefox, select the **Tools** menu and then select **Options**. Select the **Privacy** tab, and then clear the Advanced Privacy Settings dialog box by clicking the **Clear Now** button. Click **OK** to close the Options dialog box.

4. Start the Web site. The functionality should work the same as it did before you configured the Web site to use cookieless sessions.

5. Turn cookies back on in your Web browser.

6. Close your Web browser window.

Storing Global Information with Application State

An ASP.NET application is restarted whenever you modify the Web.config file, global.asax file, or other types of configuration files.

You use **application state** to preserve information that can be shared by all clients accessing an application. Application data is stored in an `HttpApplicationState` object that you can access through the `Application[]` collection. Each application has its own `HttpApplicationState` object that runs in memory on the server. ASP.NET application state automatically starts the first time a client requests one of the application pages, and runs until the server shuts down or is restarted or until the application is restarted.

You create your own application state variables in the `Application[]` collection. One common application state variable is some type of unique number used to identify clients. You can create a variable in the `Application[]` collection that keeps track of the last assigned number, and then update the number and assign it to a client. For example, suppose you have a Web application that takes online orders. Each time a client accesses the application, you want to assign a unique invoice number. The following code assigns to the curInvoiceNum variable the value of the lastInvoiceNum variable of the Application[] collection. The curInvoiceNum variable is then incremented by one. Then, a new invoiceNum variable is created in the Session[] collection and assigned the value of the curInvoiceNum variable. The example also contains code that determines whether the Application["lastInvoiceNum"] variable exists. If so, the last invoice number is incremented by one. If not, the variable is assigned an initial value of 1000. You place this code in the first page of the online order application to assign an invoice number to a client that accesses the page.

```
if (Application["lastInvoiceNum"] != null)
{
    int curInvoiceNum = Convert.ToInt16(
        Application["lastInvoiceNum"]);
    ++curInvoiceNum;
    Application["lastInvoiceNum"] = curInvoiceNum;
    Session["invoiceNum"] = curInvoiceNum.ToString();
    Response.Write(Session["invoiceNum"]);

}
else
{
    Application["lastInvoiceNum"] = 1000;
    Session["invoiceNum"] = Application["lastInvoiceNum"];
    Response.Write(Session["invoiceNum"]);
}
```

You can remove application state variables by using the Remove() and RemoveAll() methods of the HttpApplicationState.Contents property. You access the Contents property through the Application[] collection. For example, to remove all variables stored in application state, you execute the statement Application.Contents.RemoveAll();. See *http://msdn.microsoft.com/en-us/library/system.web.httpapplicationstate. aspx* for additional methods and properties that you can use with the HttpApplicationState.Contents property.

Application state variables are available to all clients that access the application, and it is possible that one client might try to access a property before another client is through with it. To prevent one client from accessing an application state variable until another client is through with it, you use the Lock() and UnLock() methods of the HttpApplicationState class. The **Lock() method** prevents other clients from accessing properties of the HttpApplicationState object, and the Unlock() method cancels the Lock() method. You place an Application.Lock(); statement before any code that accesses

Application object properties. Following the last statement that accesses Application object properties, you place an Application.UnLock(); statement. For example, to prevent data integrity problems with the lastInvoiceNum code example, you use the Lock() and UnLock() methods as follows:

```
if (Application["lastInvoiceNum"] != null)
{
    Application.Lock();
    int curInvoiceNum = Convert.ToInt16(
        Application["lastInvoiceNum"]);
    ++curInvoiceNum;
    Application["lastInvoiceNum"] = curInvoiceNum;
    Session["invoiceNum"] = curInvoiceNum.ToString();
    Response.Write(Session["invoiceNum"]);
    Application.UnLock();
}
else
{
    Application.Lock();
    Application["lastInvoiceNum"] = 1000;
    Session["invoiceNum"] = Application["lastInvoiceNum"];
    Response.Write(Session["invoiceNum"]);
    Application.UnLock();
}
```

Storing User Information in Profiles

As you learned in the preceding section, ASP.NET application state automatically starts the first time a client requests one of the application pages, and runs until the server shuts down or is restarted, or if the application is restarted. The problem with application state is that, because data is stored in memory on the server, all data is lost if the application shuts down or restarts. Although you could write code that saves the data to a database, a better solution is to use **profiles**, which automatically store and retrieve strongly typed state information to and from a SQL Server database. The beauty of profiles is that you do not need to write a single line of code to access the database; ASP.NET automatically takes care of accessing the information in the database for you.

It is important to note that profiles are much more powerful than the other ASP.NET state preservation techniques. However, this chapter just skims the surface on how to use them. Refer to the ASP.NET Profile Properties Overview on MSDN at *http://msdn.microsoft.com/ en-us/library/2y3fs9xs.aspx* for advanced profile techniques, including how to create new profile classes, group profile properties, and serialize profile properties.

Before you can use profiles, you must perform the following steps:

1. Run the aspnet_regsql.exe tool to configure the aspnetdb SQL Server database, which is the database that ASP.NET uses by default to store profile information.

2. Configure the connection information to the SQL Server database.

3. Define the profile properties by using the `<profile>` element in the Web.config file.

The aspnet_regsql.exe tool is located in the following folder:

```
C:\WINDOWS\Microsoft.NET\Framework\v#.#.#####
```

When you execute this tool without specifying any parameters, a wizard opens that walks you through the process of configuring the aspnetdb database. In the Select a Setup Option page, select Configure SQL Server for application services, and in the Select the Server and Database page, be sure to enter .\SQLEXPRESS or the correct server name for your instance of SQL Server.

To set the connection information to the SQL Server database, you need to edit the machine.config file, which by default, is located in the C:\Windows\Microsoft.NET\Framework\v2.0.xxxx\Config. The file contains a `<connectionStrings>` element, similar to the following, which you need to modify by adding the connection string information for your SQL Server database. Notice that the connection string assigns a value of "aspnetdb" to the Initial Catalog property.

```
<connectionStrings>
    <add name="LocalSqlServer" connectionString="Integrated
        Security=SSPI;Data Source=.\\SQLEXPRESS;Initial
        Catalog=aspnetdb;"
        providerName="System.Data.SqlClient"/>
</connectionStrings>
```

If you further examine the machine.config file, you will see an element similar to the following:

```
<profile>
    <providers>
        <add name="AspNetSqlProfileProvider"
            connectionStringName="LocalSqlServer"
            applicationName="/"
            type="System.Web.Profile.SqlProfileProvider />
    </providers>
</profile>
```

The preceding element specifies that ASP.NET will use SQL Server to store the profile information. It does this by assigning a value of AspNetSqlProfileProvider to the name attribute. The

The # symbols in the preceding path represent the version of the .NET Framework installed on your computer.

510

`AspNetSqlProfileProvider` value represents an object of the `SqlProfileProvider` class, which manages the storage of profile information for an ASP.NET application in a SQL Server database. You do not need to make any changes to this element if you want to use the default aspnetdb SQL Server database. However, you must modify this element if you want to use a different SQL Server database or a different relational database management system to store profile information.

To define profile properties, you add to the `<system.web>` element in the Web.config file a `<profile>` element containing nested `<properties>` elements for each profile property. The syntax for the `<profile>` element is as follows:

```
<profile>
    <properties>
        <add name="property_name"
            type="type" />
    </properties>
    ... additional properties
</profile>
```

Notice that the preceding property definition includes a `type` attribute. One of the more powerful aspects of profiles is that, unlike other state preservation techniques, you can optionally specify a type for each property definition. The type you assign to a property can be any .NET class, although in most cases you would use basic types such as integers and doubles. Note that .NET class types are slightly different than C# types. For example, the equivalent C# `int` data type in .NET is the `int32` data type. Further, to refer to basic data types, you must append them to the `System` object, as in `System.int32`.

For more information on the differences between C# and .NET types, see the .NET Framework Class Library Overview page on MSDN at *http://msdn.microsoft.com/en-us/library/hfa3fa08.aspx*.

The following example demonstrates how to define string and double profile properties:

```
<profile>
    <properties>
        <add name="city"
            type="System.String" />
        <add name="population"
            type="System.Double" />
    </properties>
</profile>
```

To set or retrieve the value of a profile property in your code, you simply append the property name to the `Profile` object. For example, the following statements assign values to the `city` and `population` profile properties:

```
Profile.city = "Sacramento";
Profile.population = 475743;
```

Short Quiz 3

1. Why would you use session state?

2. Why and how would you use application state?

3. What are the benefits to using sessions?

Summing Up

- Information about individual visits to a Web site is called state information.

- HTTP was originally designed to be stateless, which means that Web browsers stored no persistent data about a visit to a Web site.

- To pass data from one Web page to another using a query string, add a question mark (?) immediately after a URL, followed by the query string (in name=value pairs) for the information you want to preserve.

- Hidden form fields temporarily store data that needs to be sent to a server along with the rest of a form, but that a user does not need to see.

- The MultiView Web server control hides and displays areas of a page that are defined by a View control, which acts as a container for text, markup, and other controls.

- Wizard Web server controls allow you to create a multistep interface for gathering user input.

- Cookies are small pieces of information about a user that are stored by a Web server in text files on the user's computer.

- Temporary cookies remain available only for the current browser session. Persistent cookies remain available beyond the current browser session and are stored in a text file on a client computer.

- Session state stores specific client information and makes that information available to all the pages in an ASP.NET application.

- Cookieless sessions store the session ID in a Web page's URL instead of in a cookie.

- You use application state to preserve information that can be shared by all clients accessing an application.

- Profiles automatically store and retrieve strongly typed state information to and from a SQL Server database.

Comprehension Check

1. HTTP was originally designed to store data about individual visits to a Web site. True or False?

2. Stored information about a previous visit to a Web site is called _____ information.

   a. HTTP

   b. client-side

   c. state

   d. prior

3. Describe the different types of information about a user that a Web server might need to store.

4. What is the name of the hidden form field that post back uses to maintain view state?

   a. _VIEWSTATE

   b. __VIEWSTATE

   c. __viewstate

   d. ViewState

5. In what format are items in a query string appended to a target URL?

   a. in comma-delimited format

   b. as name&value pairs

   c. as name=value pairs

   d. in name, value, length format

6. Which of the following values can you assign to a MultiView control's CommandName attribute to move to the next View control? (Choose all that apply.)

   a. Next

   b. NextView

   c. SwitchViewByID

   d. SwitchViewByIndex

7. Which value assigned to the `ActiveViewIndex` property of the `MultiView` class indicates that no view is currently set?

    a. −1

    b. 0

    c. false

    d. null

8. Which of the following Wizard control step types creates a final page that contains Previous and Finish links?

    a. summary

    b. auto

    c. finish

    d. complete

9. Explain how to determine a wizard's currently selected step type.

10. Which of the following statements correctly creates a cookie using the `HttpCookie` class?

    a. `Response.Cookies.Value(firstName);`

    b. `Response.Cookies.Add(firstName);`

    c. `Response.Cookies.Value["firstName"];`

    d. `Response.Cookies.Add["firstName"];`

11. By default, cookies created without the `Expires` property are available for 24 hours. True or False?

12. Cookies created without the `Expires` property are called _____ .

    a. transient

    b. temporary

    c. permanent

    d. persistent

13. The availability of a cookie to other Web pages on a server is determined by the _____ property.

    a. Path

    b. Directory

    c. System

    d. Server

14. How do you delete cookies before the time assigned to the Expires property elapses?

    a. Assign a NULL value to the Expires property.

    b. Set its expiration to a date in the past.

    c. Execute the DeleteCookie() function.

    d. You cannot delete a cookie before the time assigned to the Expires property elapses.

15. Which of the following objects has the shortest life span?

    a. Request

    b. Cookies

    c. Session

    d. Application

16. Which attribute of the <sessionState> element in the Web.config file determines the life span of a Session object?

    a. timeout

    b. expires

    c. lifespan

    d. duration

17. Explain how to configure cookieless sessions.

18. Which method prevents other clients from accessing properties of the Application object?

    a. lock()

    b. Lock()

    c. Closed()

    d. InUse()

19. Describe the steps you must follow before you can use profiles.

20. You can specify C# data types for profile properties. True or False?

Reinforcement Exercises

Exercise 9-1

You can use the MultiView control to create a page with tabs, although you need to use some additional CSS. You also need to use the Menu control, which allows you to create menus for your ASP.NET Web pages.

To create a page with tabs:

1. Create a new ASP.NET Web site in the Visual Studio IDE and save it in a folder named MultiViewTabs in your Exercises folder for Chapter 9. Change the content of the `<title>` element to **"MultiViewTabs"**.

2. Add the following inline style sheet above the closing `</head>` tag:

```css
<style type="text/css">
    html
    {
        background-color:aqua;
    }
    p {
        font-family:Arial;
        font-size:small;
    }
    .backgroundTab
    {
        border:solid 1px black;
        background-color:purple;
        padding:2px 10px;
        font-family:Arial;
        font-size:small;
        color:White;
    }
    .visibleTab
    {
        background-color:white;
        border-bottom:solid 1px white;
        font-family:Arial;
        font-size:small;
        color:Black;
    }
    .tabBody
    {
```

```
            border:solid 1px black;
            padding:10px;
            background-color:white;
        }
        .tabPositioning
        {
            position:relative;
            top:1px;
            left:10px;
        }
    </style>
```

3. Add the following Menu control to the Web form. This control defines three menu items (Products, Services, and Support), which will represent the tabs.

```
<asp:Menu
    ID="siteMenu"
    Orientation="Horizontal"
    StaticMenuItemStyle-CssClass="backgroundTab"
    StaticSelectedStyle-CssClass="visibleTab"
    CssClass="tabPositioning"
    Runat="server"
    OnMenuItemClick="tabMenu_MenuItemClick">
    <Items>
        <asp:MenuItem Text="Products" Value="0"
        Selected="true" />
        <asp:MenuItem Text="Services" Value="1" />
        <asp:MenuItem Text="Support" Value="2" />
    </Items>
</asp:Menu>
```

4. Immediately after the closing </asp:Menu> tag, add the following MultiView control, which handles the display of the tabs:

```
<div class="tabBody">
    <asp:MultiView ID="tabContents"
     ActiveViewIndex="0" runat="server">
        <asp:View ID="View1" runat="server">
            <p>
                Use this page to display product
                information.</p>
        </asp:View>
        <asp:View ID="View2" runat="server">
            <p>
                Use this page to offer service
                options.</p>
        </asp:View>
        <asp:View ID="View3" runat="server">
            <p>
                Use this page to list support
                services.</p>
        </asp:View>
    </asp:MultiView>
</div>
```

5. Finally, open the **Default.aspx.cs** file and add the following event handler for the Menu control:

```
protected void tabMenu_MenuItemClick(
    object sender, MenuEventArgs e)
{
    int curTab = Int32.Parse(e.Item.Value);
    tabContents.ActiveViewIndex = curTab;
}
```

6. Start the Web site. You see the Web page displayed in Figure 9-11.

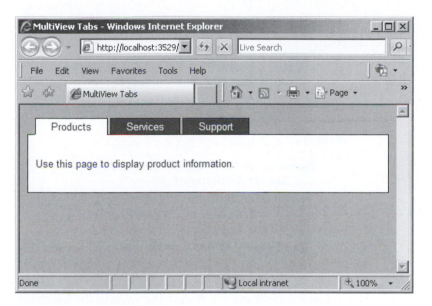

Figure 9-11   MultiView Tabs page

7. Close your Web browser window and the MultiViewTabs project

Exercise 9-2

As you know, users can disable cookies in their Web browsers. However, no error or exception will be raised if you attempt to create a cookie in a browser in which cookies have been disabled. If your Web site absolutely requires cookies, your program should first check whether the browser accepts cookies; otherwise, your program might not run correctly. One way to determine if a browser accepts cookies is to write and then attempt to read a cookie. If you cannot read the cookie, the browser has cookies disabled. The following exercise demonstrates how to check if a browser accepts cookies.

To check if a browser accepts cookies:

1. Create a new ASP.NET Web site in the Visual Studio IDE and save it in a folder named CookieChecker in your Exercises folder for Chapter 9. Change the content of the `<title>` element to **"Cookie Checker"**.

2. Open the **Default.aspx.cs** file and add the following code to the Page_Load() event handler. This page writes out a cookie named CookieCheck, and then redirects the browser to second page, named CookiesTest.

```
if (!Page.IsPostBack)
{
    if (Request.QueryString["AcceptsCookies"] == null)
    {
        Response.Cookies["CookieCheck"].Value = "ok";
        Response.Cookies["CookieCheck"].Expires =
            DateTime.Now.AddMinutes(1);
        Response.Redirect("CookiesTest.aspx?redirect=" +
            Server.UrlEncode(Request.Url.ToString()));
    }
    else
    {
        Response.Write("Accept cookies = " +
            Server.UrlEncode(
            Request.QueryString["AcceptsCookies"]));
    }
}
```

3. Select the **Website** menu and then select **Add New Item**. The Add New Item dialog box opens. Select **Web form** from the Templates area. Change the suggested filename in the Name box to **CookiesTest.aspx**, but leave the value in the Language box set to **Visual C#**. Click the **Add** button. The new page opens in the IDE.

4. Open the **CookiesTest.aspx** file in the Code Editor.

5. Add the following code to the Page_Load() event handler. This code determines whether the browser accepts cookies, and then redirects users back to the Default.aspx page.

```
string redirect = Request.QueryString["redirect"];
string acceptsCookies;
if (Request.Cookies["CookieCheck"] == null)
    acceptsCookies = "no";
else
{
    acceptsCookies = "yes";
    Response.Cookies["TestCookie"].Expires =
        DateTime.Now.AddDays(-1);
}
```

```
Response.Redirect(redirect + "?AcceptsCookies="
    + acceptsCookies, true);
}
```

6. Start the Web site. Test the Web pages by disabling cookies in your Web browsers, but be sure to reenable cookies when you are through.

7. Close your Web browser window and the CookieChecker project.

Exercise 9-3

In this exercise, you will create a Web form that saves user preferences with session state.

1. Create a new ASP.NET Web site in the Visual Studio IDE and save it in a folder named PreferencesSession in your Exercises folder for Chapter 9. Change the content of the `<title>` element to **"Preferences Session"**.

2. Add the following text and elements to the Web form in the Default.aspx file. The table contains selection lists that display values for the color, font-size, font-family, background-color, border-style, border-color, and border-width CSS styles. Users will select from these lists to customize the display of the Web form.

```
<table>
    <tr>
        <td>Text Color</td>
        <td>
            <select id="textColor" runat="server">
                <option>red</option>
                <option>yellow</option>
                <option>blue</option>
                <option>green</option>
                <option>white</option>
                <option>black</option>
            </select>
        </td>
    </tr>
    <tr>
        <td>Font Size</td>
        <td>
            <select id="fontSize" runat="server">
                <option>8pt</option>
                <option>10pt</option>
                <option>12pt</option>
                <option>14pt</option>
            </select>
        </td>
```

```
            </tr>
            <tr>
                <td>Font Name</td>
                <td>
                    <select id="fontName" runat="server">
                        <option>verdana</option>
                        <option>tahoma</option>
                        <option>arial</option>
                        <option>times</option>
                    </select>
                </td>
            </tr>
            <tr>
                <td>Background Color</td>
                <td>
                    <select id="backColor" runat="server">
                        <option>red</option>
                        <option>yellow</option>
                        <option>blue</option>
                        <option>green</option>
                        <option>white</option>
                        <option>black</option>
                    </select>
                </td>
            </tr>
            <tr>
                <td>Border Style</td>
                <td>
                    <select id="borderStyle" runat="server">
                        <option>none</option>
                        <option>hidden</option>
                        <option>dotted</option>
                        <option>dashed</option>
                        <option>solid</option>
                        <option>double</option>
                        <option>groove</option>
                        <option>ridge</option>
                        <option>inset</option>
                        <option>outset</option>
                    </select>
                </td>
            </tr>
            <tr>
                <td>Border Color</td>
                <td>
                    <select id="borderColor" runat="server">
                        <option>red</option>
                        <option>yellow</option>
                        <option>blue</option>
                        <option>green</option>
                        <option>white</option>
                        <option>black</option>
                    </select>
                </td>
```

```
        </tr>
        <tr>
            <td>Border Width</td>
            <td>
                <select id="borderWidth" runat="server">
                    <option>thin</option>
                    <option>medium</option>
                    <option>thick</option>
                </select>
            </td>
        </tr>
    </table>
    <p>
    <asp:Button ID="setPrefs" runat="server"
        Text="Set Preferences" /></p>
    <p>
        <a href="TestSessionVariables.htm">
            Test Session Variables</a></p>
```

3. Open the **Default.aspx.cs** file in the Code Editor and add the following Page_LoadComplete() event handler. The if statement only executes if the textColor session variable exists, which means that the session variables have already been initialized when the user clicked the Set Preferences button. The statements within the if statement initialize the session variables that will store the user preferences. These statements assign the CSS preferences stored in the session variables to the Web form.

```
protected void Page_LoadComplete(
    object sender, EventArgs e)
{
    if (Session["textColor"] != null)
        {
            prefsForm.Attributes.CssStyle
                .Add("color",
                Session["textColor"].ToString());
            prefsForm.Attributes.CssStyle
                .Add("font-size",
                Session["fontSize"].ToString());
            prefsForm.Attributes.CssStyle
                .Add("font-family",
                Session["fontName"].ToString());
            prefsForm.Attributes.CssStyle
                .Add("background-color",
                Session["backColor"].ToString());
            prefsForm.Attributes.CssStyle
                .Add("border-style",
                Session["borderStyle"].ToString());
            prefsForm.Attributes.CssStyle
                .Add("border-color",
                Session["borderColor"].ToString());
```

```
                    prefsForm.Attributes.CssStyle
                        .Add("border-width",
                        Session["borderWidth"].ToString());
            }
        }
```

4. Switch to **Design View** and double-click the **Set Preferences** button, which creates a new event handler named `setPrefs_Click()`. Add the following statements to the `setPrefs_Click()` event handler. These statements update the values stored in the session variables when the user clicks the Set Preferences button.

```
Session["textColor"] = textColor.Value;
Session["fontSize"] = fontSize.Value;
Session["fontName"] = fontName.Value;
Session["backColor"] = backColor.Value;
Session["borderStyle"] = borderStyle.Value;
Session["borderColor"] = borderColor.Value;
Session["borderWidth"] = borderWidth.Value;
```

5. Select the **Website** menu and then select **Add New Item**. In the Add New Item dialog box, click **HTML Page** and change the name to **TestSessionVariables.htm**. Click the **Add** button. The new Web page opens in Code Editor.

6. Add the following paragraph and link to the document body. This link simply takes you back to the Default.aspx page to test the session variables.

```
<p><a href="Default.aspx">Main Page</a></p>
```

7. Start the Web site, select some values in the list boxes, and then click **Set Preferences**. The page should update with the preferences you select. Then, click the **Test Session Variables** link, which takes you to the TestSessionVariables.htm file. In the TestSessionVariables.htm file, click the **Main Page** link, which takes you back to the Default.aspx file. The preferences you selected should still be set.

8. Close your Web browser window.

Exercise 9-4

In this exercise, you will add code to the PreferencesSession project that sets default values for the user preferences and also allows the user to reset their preferences to the default values.

1. Return to the **Default.aspx.cs** file in the Visual Studio IDE.

2. Add the following `else` clause to the end of the
    `Page_LoadComplete()` event handler:

    ```
    else
    {
        prefsForm.Attributes.CssStyle
            .Add("color", "black");
        prefsForm.Attributes.CssStyle
            .Add("font-size", "8");
        prefsForm.Attributes.CssStyle
            .Add("font-family", "tahoma");
        prefsForm.Attributes.CssStyle
            .Add("background-color", "green");
        prefsForm.Attributes.CssStyle
            .Add("border-style", "double");
        prefsForm.Attributes.CssStyle
            .Add("border-color", "black");
        prefsForm.Attributes.CssStyle
            .Add("border-width", "2");
    }
    ```

3. Open the **Default.aspx** file in Design view and add a new
    Button control beneath the Set Preferences button. Change
    its ID attribute to **"resetPrefs"** and its Text attribute to
    "Reset Preferences". Double-click the **Reset Prefer-
    ences** button, which creates a new event handler named
    `resetPrefs_Click()`. Add the following statements to
    the `resetPrefs_Click()` event handler, which delete the
    session variables:

    ```
    Session["textColor"] = null;
    Session["fontSize"] = null;
    Session["fontName"] = null;
    Session["backColor"] = null;
    Session["borderStyle"] = null;
    Session["borderColor"] = null;
    Session["borderWidth"] = null;
    ```

4. Start the Web site, select some values in the list boxes, and
    then click **Set Preferences**. The page should update with
    the preferences you selected. Now click the **Reset Prefer-
    ences** button. The page should update with the default
    values.

5. Close your Web browser window and the PreferencesSession
    project.

Discovery Projects

Project 9-1

Copy the SkywardAviation folder from your Chapter folder to a folder named SkywardAviationValidation in your Projects folder for Chapter 9. Add validation controls for the e-mail and password fields in the registration form. For the e-mail fields, be sure to use a regular expression to determine whether the e-mail is valid. For the password fields, use a regular expression that verifies the password is between 6 and 10 characters in length and that it contains at least one uppercase letter, one lowercase letter, and a number.

Project 9-2

Copy the SkywardAviationValidation folder from your Projects folder to a folder named SkywardAviationProfiles in your Projects folder for Chapter 9. Redesign the chapter project so it uses profiles. Be sure to replace the existing database connection code and session functionality with references to the profile variables.

Project 9-3

Create a Web site with a "nag" counter that reminds users to register. Save the counter in a cookie that expires in 30 days and display a message reminding users to register every fifth time they visit your site. Create a Web form in the body of the document that includes text boxes for a user's name and e-mail address along with a Registration button. After a user fills in the text boxes and clicks the Registration button, delete the nag counter cookie and replace it with cookies containing the user's name and e-mail address. After registering, print the name and e-mail address cookies whenever the user revisits the site. Save the project as **NagCounter**.

CHAPTER 10

Developing Object-Oriented C# Programs

In this chapter you will:

- ◎ Study object-oriented programming concepts
- ◎ Define custom classes
- ◎ Declare class fields
- ◎ Work with class methods

The C# programs you have written so far have mostly been self-contained. That is, most of the code—including variables, statements, and functions—exists within a script section. For example, you might create a Web page for an online retailer that uses C# to calculate the total for a sales order that includes state sales tax and shipping. However, suppose the retailer sells different types of products on different Web pages, with one page selling baseball uniforms, another page selling jelly beans, and so on. If you want to reuse the C# sales total code on multiple Web pages, you must copy all of the statements or re-create them from scratch for each Web page. Object-oriented programming takes a different approach. Essentially, object-oriented programming allows you to use and create self-contained sections of code—known as objects—that can be reused in your programs. In other words, object-oriented programming allows you to reuse code without having to copy or re-create it.

Introduction to Object-Oriented Programming

As you learned in Chapter 2, object-oriented programming (OOP) refers to the creation of reusable software objects that can be easily incorporated into another program. An object is programming code and data that can be treated as an individual unit or component. Objects are often also called **components**. In object-oriented programming, the code that makes up an object is organized into classes. Objects can range from simple controls, such as a button, to entire programs, such as a database application. In fact, some programs consist entirely of other objects. You'll often encounter objects that have been designed to perform a specific task. For example, in a retail sales program, you could refer to all of the code that calculates the sales total as a single object. You could then reuse that object over and over again in the same program just by typing the object name.

Popular object-oriented programming languages include C++, Java, and Visual Basic. Using any of these or other object-oriented languages, programmers can create objects themselves or use objects created by other programmers or supplied by the manufacturer. For example, if you are creating an accounting program in Visual Basic, you can use an object named `Payroll` that was created in C++. The `Payroll` object might contain one method that calculates the amount of federal and state tax to deduct, another function that calculates the FICA amount to deduct, and so on. Properties of the `Payroll` object might include an employee's number of tax withholding allowances, federal and state tax percentages, and the cost of insurance premiums. You do not need to know how the `Payroll` object was created in C++, nor do you need to re-create it in Visual Basic. You only need to know how to access the methods and properties of the `Payroll` object from the Visual Basic program.

Understanding Encapsulation

Objects are **encapsulated**, which means that all code and required data are contained within the object itself. In most cases, an encapsulated object consists of a single computer file that contains all code and required data. Encapsulation places code inside what programmers like to call a "black box." When an object is encapsulated, you cannot see "inside" it—all internal workings are hidden. The code (methods and statements) and data (variables and constants) contained in an encapsulated object are accessed through an interface. The term **interface** refers to the methods and properties that are required for a source program to communicate with an object. For example, interface elements required to access a `Payroll` object might be a method named `calcNetPay()`, which calculates an employee's net pay, and properties containing the employee's name and pay rate.

When you include encapsulated objects in your programs, users can see only the methods and properties of the object that you allow them to see. By removing the ability to see inside the black box, encapsulation reduces the complexity of the code, allowing programmers who use the code to concentrate on the task of integrating the code into their programs. Encapsulation also prevents other programmers from accidentally introducing a bug into a program, or from possibly even stealing the code and claiming it as their own.

You can compare a programming object and its interface to a handheld calculator. The calculator represents an object, and you represent a program that wants to use the object. You establish an interface with the calculator object by entering numbers (the data required by the object) and then pressing calculation keys (which represent the methods of the object). You do not need to know, nor can you see, the inner workings of the calculator object. As a programmer, you are concerned only with an object's methods and properties. To continue the analogy, you are only concerned with the result you expect the calculator object to return. Figure 10-1 illustrates the idea of the calculator interface.

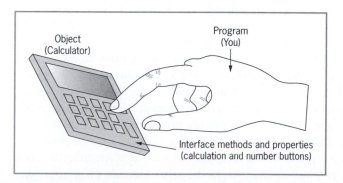

Figure 10-1   Calculator interface

Another example of an object and its interface is Microsoft Word. Word itself is actually an object made up of numerous other objects. The program window (or user interface) is one object. The items you see in the interface, such as the menu and toolbars, are used to execute methods. For example, the Bold button on the toolbar executes a bold method. The text of your document is the data you provide to the program. Word is a helpful tool that you can use without knowing how the various methods work. You only need to know what each method does. To get full satisfaction out of Word, you only need to provide the data (text) and execute the appropriate methods (such as the bold method), when necessary. In the same way, when using objects in your code, you only need to provide the necessary data (such as an employee's gross pay) and execute the appropriate method (such as the `calcNetPay()` method).

Using Objects in C# Programs

Up to this point, all of the C# programs you have written have contained procedural statements that did not rely on objects. This does not mean that the skills you have learned so far are useless in constructing object-oriented programs. However, object-oriented techniques will help you build more extensible code that is easier to reuse, modify, and enhance.

In object-oriented programming, the code, methods, attributes, and other information that make up an object are organized into classes. Essentially, a class is a template, or blueprint, that serves as the basis for new objects. When you use an object in your program, you actually create an instance of the class of the object. In other words, an instance is an object that has been created from a class. When you create an object from a class, you are said to be **instantiating** the object.

Later in this chapter, you will learn how to create, or instantiate, an object from custom classes that you write yourself. However, as a conceptual example, consider an object named `BankAccount` that contains methods and properties that you might use to record transactions associated with a checking or savings account. The `BankAccount` object is created from a `BankAccount` class. To use the `BankAccount` class, you create an instance of the class. A particular instance of an object **inherits** its methods and properties from a class—that is, it takes on the characteristics of the class on which it is based. The `BankAccount` object, for instance, would inherit all of the methods and properties of the `BankAccount` class. To give another example, when you create a new word-processing document, which is a type of object, it usually inherits the properties of a template on which it is based. The template is a type of class. The document inherits characteristics of the template, which might include font size, line spacing, and boilerplate text. In the same manner, programs that include instances of objects inherit the object's functionality.

You use the following constructor syntax to instantiate an object from a class:

```
ClassName objectName = new ClassName();
```

The identifiers you use for an object name must follow the same rules as identifiers for variables: They must begin with an upper-case or lowercase ASCII letter, can include numbers (but not as the first character), cannot include spaces, cannot be keywords, and are case sensitive. The following statement instantiates an object named checking from the BankAccount class:

```
BankAccount checking = new BankAccount();
```

Class constructors are primarily used to initialize properties when an object is first instantiated. For this reason, you can pass arguments to many constructor methods. For example, the BankAccount class might require you to pass three arguments: the checking account number, a check number, and a check amount, as follows:

```
BankAccount checking = new BankAccount(01234587, 1021, 97.58);
```

After you instantiate an object, you use a period to access the methods and properties contained in the object. With methods, you must also include a set of parentheses at the end of the method name, just as you would with functions. Like functions, methods can also accept arguments. The following statements demonstrate how to call two methods, getBalance() and getCheckAmount(), from the checking object. The getBalance() method does not require any arguments, whereas the getCheckAmount() method requires an argument containing the check number.

```
double balance = checking.getBalance();
checkNumber = 1022;
double amount = checking.getCheckAmount(checkNumber);
```

To access property values in an object, you do not include parentheses at the end of the property name, as you do with functions and methods. The following statements update and display the value in a property named balance in the checking object:

```
checkAmount = 124.75;
checking.balance = checking.balance + checkAmount;
Response.Write("<p>Your updated checking account balance is "
    + String.Format("{0:C}", checking.balance) + "</p>");
```

In this chapter, you will work on a Web site for an online bakery named Central Valley Bakery. The store includes four shopping categories: cakes, cookies, pies, and breads. The purpose of the Web site is to demonstrate code reuse with classes. As you progress through this chapter, you will develop a class named ShoppingCart that handles the functionality of building and updating a shopping cart as a user selects items to purchase. Shopping cart classes are very popular with Web developers because of the many Web sites that offer online shopping.

Rather than re-creating shopping cart functionality for each online Web site you develop, you can much more easily develop the Web site by reusing an existing shopping cart class. As you create the ShoppingCart class, notice that its functionality has nothing to do with the products sold by Central Valley Bakery. Instead the code is generic enough that it can be used with any Web site that sells products, provided the pages in the site and the associated database conform to the requirements of the class. Your Chapter folder for Chapter 10 contains a folder named Bakery where you can find the files that you will need for this project. The Web site and a database named Bakery have already been created; you only need to focus on the class development techniques. Figure 10-2 shows the Central Valley Bakery home page.

Figure 10-2   Central Valley Bakery home page

First, you will add to each of the product pages a Literal control that displays messages from the ShoppingCart class and a GridView control that displays product information. The ShoppingCart class requires that product information is stored in tables containing four fields: productID, name, description, and price. The productID field is the primary key and consists of a unique text field. For example, the primary key for the first cake product is CAKE001. To keep things simple, the ShoppingCart class does not store customer or payment information.

You'll start by adding the Literal control to the cakes.aspx page.

To add controls to the cakes.aspx page:

1. Start Visual Web Developer, select the **File** menu and then select **Open Web Site**. The Open Web Site dialog box opens. Locate and select the **Bakery** folder, located in your Chapter folder for Chapter 10, and then click **Open**. The Bakery Web site opens in the Visual Studio IDE.

2. Open the **cakes.aspx** file in Design view.

3. Replace [**Add code here**] with a Literal control and change its ID to **ProductPage**.

4. Expand the **App_Data** folder in Solution Explorer and then double-click the **Bakery.mdf** file to open the database in Database Explorer.

5. Add a GridView control with an ID of **ProductGrid** immediately after the Literal control. After you add the control, select **Choose Data Source** from the GridView Tasks menu, and then select **<New data source ...>**. The Choose a Data Source Type page of the Data Source Configuration Wizard opens.

6. On the Choose a Data Source Type page, select **Database**, and enter an ID of **BakeryDataSource**. Click **OK**. The Choose Your Data Connection page opens.

7. On the Choose Your Data Connection page, click the data connection box and then select **Bakery.mdf**. Click **Next**. The Save the Connection String to the Application Configuration File opens.

8. On the Save the Connection String to the Application Configuration File page, change the name of the connection string to **BakeryConnectionString**, and then click **Next**. The Configure the Select Statement page opens.

9. On the Configure the Select Statement page, select Cakes from the Name box and * from the Columns list, and then click **Next**. The Test Query page opens.

10. On the Test Query page, click the **Test Query** button. You should see a list of cake and their product IDs, descriptions, and prices. Click **Finish** to close the Data Source Configuration Wizard.

Next, you will format the GridView control on the cakes.aspx page.

To format the GridView control on the cakes.aspx page:

1. With the GridView control selected in Design view, expand the **Font** property in the Properties window and select **Smaller** in the Size box.

2. If necessary, change the value assigned to the DataKeyNames property to **productID**.

3. Select the **GridView** control in Design view and then click the arrow to the right of the control to display the **GridView Tasks** menu.

4. Select the **Auto Format** command from the GridView Tasks menu. The AutoFormat dialog box displays. Select the **Brown Sugar** scheme and then click **OK**.

5. From the GridView Tasks menu, select **Enable Selection** and then select **Edit Columns**. The Fields dialog box opens.

6. In the Fields dialog box, click the **Select** field in the Selected fields list, and then click the down arrow until the Select field is the last control in the list.

7. In the CommandField properties section, change the Button-Type property to **Button** and the SelectImageUrl property to **~/images/ordernow.gif**. The ordernow.gif file is located in the images folder within the project folder.

8. Click the **productID** field in the Selected fields list and click the **X** button to remove it from the list.

9. Click the **name** field in the Selected fields list and change its HeaderText property to **Name**.

10. Click the **description** field in the Selected fields list and change its HeaderText property to **Description**.

11. Click the **price** field in the Selected fields list and change its HeaderText property to **Price**. Also, change its DataFormatString property to **{0:c}**, which displays price fields as currency.

12. Click **OK** to close the Fields dialog box.

Next, you will copy the controls from the cakes.aspx file to the breads.aspx, cookies.aspx, and pies.aspx files.

To copy the GridView control from the cakes.aspx file to the breads.aspx, cookies.aspx, and pies.aspx files:

1. Click the **Source** button at the bottom of the IDE window to view the cakes.aspx page in the Code Editor window.

2. Locate and copy the `<asp:Literal>`, `<asp:GridView>`, and `<asp:SqlDataSource>` controls.

3. Open the **breads.aspx** file in the Code Editor window.

4. Locate the text [**Add code here**] and replace it with the controls you copied from the cakes.aspx file. Then, locate the

ConnectionString property in the **<asp:SqlDataSource>** control and replace [Cakes] with **[Breads]**.

5. Open the **cookies.aspx** file in the Code Editor window.

6. Locate the text **[Add code here]** and replace it with the controls you copied from the cakes.aspx file. Then, locate the ConnectionString property in the **<asp:SqlDataSource>** control and replace [Cakes] with **[Cookies]**.

7. Open the **pies.aspx** file in the Code Editor window.

8. Locate the text **[Add code here]** and replace it with the controls you copied from the cakes.aspx file. Then, locate the ConnectionString property in the **<asp:SqlDataSource>** control and replace [Cakes] with **[Pies]**.

9. Start the Web site and test the product pages. Figure 10-3 shows the Cakes product page. Be sure not to click any of the Order Now buttons because you still need to add code to give them their functionality.

10. Close your Web browser window.

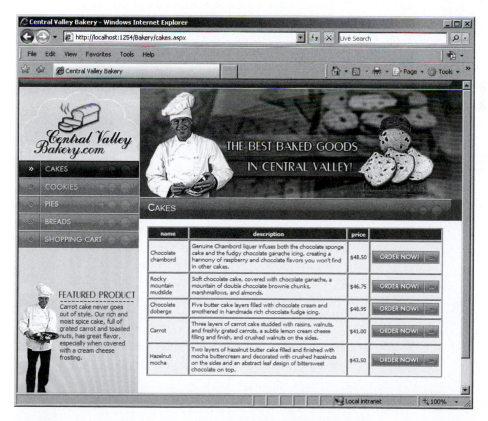

Figure 10-3   Cakes product page after adding Web server controls

Short Quiz 1

1. Why do programmers refer to encapsulation as a black box?

2. What is instantiation as it relates to classes, objects, and object-oriented programming?

3. Explain how to instantiate an object from a class.

4. What are class constructor statements primarily used for?

5. How do you access an object's methods and properties?

Defining Custom C# Classes

Classes were defined earlier in this chapter as the code, methods, attributes, and other information that make up an object. In C#, classes more specifically refer to data structures that contain fields along with methods for manipulating the fields. The term **data structure** refers to a system for organizing data, whereas the term **field** refers to variables that are defined within a class. Some of the data structures you have already used include arrays and lists. The methods and fields defined in a class are called **class members** or simply **members**. Class variables are referred to as **data members** or **member variables**, whereas methods are referred to as **function members** or **member functions**. To use the fields and methods in a class, you instantiate an object from that class. After you instantiate a class object, class data members (or fields) are referred to as properties of the object and class function members (or methods) are referred to as methods of the object.

Classes themselves are also referred to as *user-defined data types* or *programmer-defined data types*. These terms can be somewhat misleading, however, because they do not accurately reflect the fact that classes can contain function members. In addition, classes usually contain multiple fields of different data types, so calling a class a data type becomes even more confusing. One reason classes are referred to as user-defined data types or programmer-defined data types is that you can work with a class as a single unit, or object, in the same way you work with a variable. In fact, the terms variable and object are often used interchangeably in object-oriented programming. The term object-oriented programming comes from the fact that you can bundle variables and functions together and use the result as a single unit (a variable or object).

What this means will become clearer to you as you progress through this chapter. For now, think of the handheld calculator example. A calculator could be considered an object of a `Calculation` class. You access all of the `Calculation` methods (such as addition and subtraction) and its fields (operands that represent the numbers you are calculating) through your calculator object. You never actually work with the `Calculation` class yourself, only with an object of the class (your calculator).

But why do you need to work with a collection of related fields and methods as a single object? Why not simply call each individual field and method as necessary, without bothering with all this class business? The truth is: You are not required to work with classes; you can create much of the same functionality without classes as you can by using classes. In fact, many of the scripts that you create—and that you find in use today—do not require object-oriented techniques to be effective. Classes help make complex programs easier to manage, however, by logically grouping related methods and fields and by allowing you to refer to that grouping as a single object. Another reason for using classes is to hide information that users of a class do not need to access or know about. Information hiding, which is explained in more detail later in this chapter, helps minimize the amount of information that needs to pass in and out of an object, which helps increase program speed and efficiency. Classes also make it much easier to reuse code or distribute your code to others for use in their programs. Without a way to package fields and methods in classes and include those classes in a new program, you would need to copy and paste each segment of code you wanted to reuse (methods, fields, and so on) into any new program.

You will learn how to create your own classes and include them in your scripts shortly.

An additional reason to use classes is that instances of objects inherit their characteristics, such as class members, from the class upon which they are based. This inheritance allows you to build new classes based on existing classes without having to rewrite the code contained in the existing classes.

Working with Access Modifiers

The first thing you need to understand about classes is **access modifiers**, which control a client's access to classes, individual fields, and methods and their members. Table 10-1 lists the access modifiers you can use with C# classes:

Access modifier	Descriptions
public	Allows anyone to access a class or class member.
private	Prevents clients from accessing a class or class member and is one of the key elements in information hiding. Private access does not restrict a class's internal access to its own members; a class method can modify any private class member.
protected	Allows only the class or a derived class to access the class or class member.
internal	Allows a class or class member to be accessed from anywhere in the application, but not from external applications.
protected internal	Allows only code in the same structure, or from a derived class, to access the class or class member.

Table 10-1   C# access modifiers

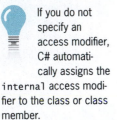

If you do not specify an access modifier, C# automatically assigns the internal access modifier to the class or class member.

Derived classes are used with a more advanced object-oriented programming technique called inheritance.

Next, you will learn how to use access modifiers with classes you define.

Creating a Class Definition

A **class definition** contains the class members that make up the class. To create a class definition in C#, you use the **class** keyword and precede it with an access modifier, as follows:

```
accessModifier class ClassName
{
    // Class member definitions
}
```

The *ClassName* portion of the class definition is the name of the new class. You can use any name you want for a structure, as long as you follow the same naming conventions that you use when declaring other identifiers, such as variables and functions. Also, keep in mind that class names usually begin with an uppercase letter to distinguish them from other identifiers. Within the class's curly braces, you declare the fields and methods that make up the class.

You have already seen examples of class definitions with the event handlers that you have worked with since Chapter 4. For example, the following code shows the default code-behind page for an ASP.NET Web site. As you can see, the **_Default** class uses a public access modifier, whereas the **Page_Load()** event handler method uses a protected access modifier.

```
public partial class _Default : System.Web.UI.Page
{
    protected void Page_Load(object sender, EventArgs e)
    {
        // Class member definitions
    }
}
```

The `partial` keyword in the preceding definition indicates that the class can be split across multiple files, which allows multiple programmers to work on the same code simultaneously. The colon and `System.Web.UI.Page` at the end of the class definition header indicates that the `_Default` class derives from the `System.Web.UI.Page` class, which means that the `_Default` class inherits the members of the `System.Web.UI.Page` class.

The following code demonstrates how to declare a public class named `BankAccount` that inherits the members of the `System.Web.UI.Page` class. The statements following the class definition instantiate an object of the class named `checking` and print the object's type (`BankAccount`):

```
public class BankAccount : System.Web.UI.Page
{
    // Class member definitions
}
BankAccount checking = new BankAccount();
Response.Write(checking.GetType());
```

Next, you will start creating the `ShoppingCart` class.

To start creating the `ShoppingCart` class:

1. Select the **Website** menu and then select **Add New Item**. The Add New Item dialog box opens.

2. In the Add New Item dialog box, select **Class** from the Templates list and then change the name of the class file to **ShoppingCart.cs**. Click **Add** and then click **Yes** when prompted to save the file in the App_Code folder. The `ShoppingCart` class file opens in the Code Editor window and contains the following statements:

    ```
    using System;
    using System.Collections.Generic;
    using System.Linq;
    using System.Web;
    /// <summary>
    /// Summary description for ShoppingCart
    /// </summary>
    public class ShoppingCart
    {
        public ShoppingCart()
        {
            //
            // TODO: Add constructor logic here
            //
        }
    }
    ```

3. Replace the "Summary description for ShoppingCart" comment with **Generic shopping cart class**.

Class names in a class definition are not followed by parentheses, as are function names in a function definition.

4. Open the **shopping_cart.aspx** file in the Code Editor window. Locate the text [**Add code here**] and replace it with a Literal control. Change the ID of the Literal control to **CartBody**.

5. Open the **shopping_cart.aspx.cs** file in the Code Editor window. Add the following statements to the Page_Load() event handler to instantiate a ShoppingCart object. The statements write success or failure messages to a Literal control with an ID of CartBody in the shopping_cart.aspx file.

```
try
{
    ShoppingCart cart = new ShoppingCart();
    CartBody.Text = "<p>Successfully instantiated an
        object of the ShoppingCart class.</p>";
}
catch
{
    CartBody.Text = "<p>The ShoppingCart class
        is not available!</p>";
}
```

6. Start the Web site and open the Shopping Cart page. You should see the message shown in Figure 10-4.

7. Close your Web browser window.

Figure 10-4   Shopping Cart page after instantiating a ShoppingCart object

Collecting Garbage

If you have worked with other object-oriented programming languages, you might be familiar with the term **garbage collection**, which refers to cleaning up, or reclaiming, memory that is reserved by a program. When you declare a variable or instantiate a new object, you are actually reserving computer memory for the variable or object. With some programming languages, you must write code that deletes a variable or object after you are through with it to free the memory for use by other parts of your program, or by other programs running on your computer. With C#, you do not need to worry about reclaiming memory that is reserved for your variables or objects because C# knows when your program no longer needs a variable or object and automatically cleans up the memory for you. The one exception has to do with open database connections. As you learned in Chapter 8, because database connections can take up a lot of memory, you should explicitly close a database connection when you are through with it by calling the `Close()` method. This ensures that the connection doesn't keep taking up space in your computer's memory while the script finishes processing.

Short Quiz 2

1. What is a data structure and what are some of the types of data structures you have worked with in this book?

2. Why are classes referred to as user-defined data types or programmer-defined data types, and why are these terms somewhat misleading?

3. What are some of the benefits to working with classes and objects?

4. Explain the level of protection provided by each of the C# access modifiers.

5. How do you specify in a class definition a class from which another class should inherit its class members?

Declaring Class Fields

In this section, you will learn how to declare fields within a class. Declaring and initializing fields is a little more involved than declaring and instantiating standard C# variables. Before you can declare fields, you must first understand the principle of information hiding, which you will study first.

What Is Information Hiding?

One of the fundamental principles in object-oriented programming is the concept of information hiding. Information hiding gives an encapsulated object its black box capabilities so that users of a class can see only the members of the class that you allow them to see. Essentially, the principle of **information hiding** states that any class members that other programs, sometimes called clients, do not need to access or know about, should be hidden. Information hiding helps minimize the amount of information that needs to pass in and out of an object; this in turn helps increase program speed and efficiency. Information hiding also reduces the complexity of the code that clients see, allowing them to concentrate on the task of integrating an object into their programs. For example, if a client wants to add to her accounting program a `Payroll` object, she does not need to know the underlying details of the `Payroll` object's methods, nor does she need to modify any local fields that are used by those methods. The client only needs to know which of the object's methods to call and what data (if any) needs to be passed to those methods.

Now consider information hiding on a larger scale. Professionally developed software packages are distributed in an encapsulated format, which means that the casual user—or even an advanced programmer—cannot see the underlying details of how the software is developed. Imagine what would happen if Microsoft distributed Excel without hiding the underlying programming details. Most users of the program would be bewildered if they accidentally opened the source files. There is no need for Microsoft to allow users to see the underlying details of Excel because users do not need to understand how the underlying code performs the various types of spreadsheet calculations. Microsoft also has a critical interest in protecting proprietary information, as do you. The design and sale of software components is big business. You certainly do not want to spend a significant amount of time designing an outstanding software component, only to have an unscrupulous programmer steal the code and claim it as his own.

This same principle of information hiding needs to be applied in object-oriented programming. There are few reasons why clients of your classes need to know the underlying details of your code. Of course, you cannot hide all of the underlying code, or other programmers will never be able to integrate your class with their applications. But you need to hide most of it.

Information hiding on any scale also prevents other programmers from accidentally introducing a bug into a program by modifying a class's internal workings. Programmers are curious creatures and will often attempt to "improve" your code, no matter how well it is written.

Before you distribute your classes to other programmers, your classes should be thoroughly tested and bug-free. With tested and bug-free classes, other programmers can focus on the more important task of integrating your code into their programs using the fields and methods you designate.

The opposite of software that adheres to the principles of information hiding is open source software, for which the source code can be freely used and modified. Instead of intentionally hiding the internal workings of a software application for proprietary purposes, open source software encourages programmers to use, change, and improve the software. Open source software can be freely distributed or sold, provided it adheres to the software's copyright license.

To enable information hiding in your classes, you must designate access modifiers for each of your class members, similar to the way you must designate an access modifier for a class definition.

Using Access Modifiers with Fields

You declare a field in the same way that you declare a standard variable, except that you must include an access modifier at the beginning of a field declaration statement. For example, the following statement declares a public field named `balance` in the BankAccount class and initializes it with a value of 0:

It is common practice to list public class members first to clearly identify the parts of the class that can be accessed by clients.

```
public class BankAccount : System.Web.UI.Page
{
    public double balance = 0;
}
```

As with standard C# variables, it is considered good programming practice to assign an initial value to a field when you first declare it. The best way to initialize a field is with a constructor method (discussed later in this chapter), although you can also assign values to fields when you first declare them.

Recall that to access a field as an object property, you append the property name to the object with a period. The following statements assign a new value to the `balance` field and then print its value:

```
BankAccount checking = new BankAccount();
checking.balance = 743.26;
Response.Write("<p>Your updated checking account balance is "
    + String.Format("{0:C}", checking.balance) + "</p>");
```

Next, you will declare four data members, `dbConnection`, `sqlString`, `tableName`, and `orders[]`, in the ShoppingCart class. The `dbConnection`, `sqlString`, and `tableName` fields store the database connection details. The `orders[]` array is an array list that keeps track of the

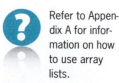

Refer to Appendix A for information on how to use array lists.

products in a customer's shopping cart. The array will consist of three elements, each of which contains another array list. The first dimension stores product IDs, the second dimension stores the quantity of each product purchased, and the third dimension stores the table in the Bakery database that contains the product information. To adhere to the principles of information hiding, you must declare all of the data members as private. Later in this chapter, you will write member functions that access and manipulate the values in each array.

To declare four data members in the ShoppingCart class:

1. Return to the **ShoppingCart.cs** file in the Code Editor window.

2. Add the following using directives to the end of the using directives list.

```
using System.Collections;
using System.Data.SqlClient;
```

3. Add the following declaration statements to the class. Be sure to replace the value assigned to the Data Source property with the name of the SQL Server instance to which you want to connect. Note that you must include the entire path to the Bakery.mdf file.

```
public class ShoppingCart
{
    private SqlConnection dbConnection
        = new SqlConnection("Data Source=
        .\\SQLEXPRESS;AttachDbFilename
        ='path\\Bakery.mdf'; Integrated Security=True;
         User Instance=True");
    private ArrayList productID = new ArrayList();
    private ArrayList productQuantity = new ArrayList();
    private ArrayList productTable = new ArrayList();
    public ShoppingCart()
    {
        //
        // TODO: Add constructor logic here
        //
    }
}
```

Serializing Objects

In Chapter 9, you learned about C#'s various state preservation techniques, including how to use sessions. In addition to keeping track of current Web site visitors, session variables can store information that can be shared among multiple scripts that are called as part of the same session. But how do you share objects within the same session or across multiple sessions and applications? You could assign the value of an object's fields to session variables, but you would need to instantiate a new object and reassign the session variable values to the fields each time you execute a program. However, this approach would be difficult if you have an object with dozens of fields. A better choice is to serialize the object.

Serialization refers to the process of converting an object's fields into a string that you can store for reuse. The .NET Framework supports two types of serialization technologies: binary serialization and XML serialization. **Binary serialization** converts object properties to a binary format, whereas **XML serialization** converts object properties to XML. Binary serialization is more efficient in terms of speed and memory usage, and it converts all of an object's fields to binary format while maintaining their data types. XML serialization converts only an object's public fields and properties to XML and does not maintain their data types. Because only the .NET Framework can read binary serialized objects created with C#, you would use XML serialization if you need to share the serialized data with another application. This chapter discusses binary serialization.

Before you can serialize a class object, you must mark the class as serializable by adding the `Serializable` attribute immediately above the class definition, surrounded by brackets (`[]`), as follows:

```
[Serializable]
public class BankAccount : System.Web.UI.Page
{
    // Class member definitions
}
```

Binary serialized objects are most commonly stored in binary files on a local computer. For this reason, you need to understand how to create a **file stream**, which is used for accessing a resource, such as a file, that you can read from and write to. An **input stream** reads data from a resource (such as a file), whereas an **output stream** writes data to a resource (again, such as a file). You have already used an output stream frequently with `Response.Write()` statements, which send data to an output stream (the Web browser window). Using a file stream involves the following steps:

1. Create an object of the `FileStream` class, passing to the class constructor the name and path of the file and a parameter that specifies what to do with the file. To create a file, you pass `FileMode.Create` as the second parameter of the class constructor. To open a file, you pass `FileMode.Open` as the second parameter of the class constructor.

2. Write data to or read data from the file stream.

3. Close the file stream with the `Close()` method.

You must include the `System.IO` namespace before you can use the `FileStream` class.

This section only covers the most basic methods for working with the `FileStream` class. For more information, refer to the "FileStream Class" page on MSDN at *http://msdn.microsoft.com/en-us/library/system.io.filestream.aspx*.

You must include the `System.Runtime.Serialization.Formatters.Binary` namespace before you can use the `BinaryFormatter` class.

544

The following statements demonstrate how to create, work with, and then close a `FileStream` object named `accountFile`. The class constructor creates a new file named accountInfo.dat in a folder named accountData on the C drive.

```csharp
FileStream accountFile =
    new FileStream(
    @"C:\\accountData\\accountInfo.dat",
    FileMode.Create);
// Statements that write data to or read data from
    the file stream
accountFile.Close();
```

To serialize an object, you must first create an object of the `BinaryFormatter` class, which serializes and deserializes objects in binary format. The following statements demonstrate how to create the `checking` object and a `BinaryFormatter` object named `savedAccount`:

```csharp
BankAccount checking = new BankAccount();
BinaryFormatter savedAccount = new BinaryFormatter();
```

Once you have created an object of the class you want to serialize along with a `FileStream` object and a `BinaryFormatter` object, you call the `Serialize()` method of the `BinaryFormatter` object, passing to it the `FileStream` object and then the class object you want to serialize. The following statements show a complete example of how to serialize a `BankAccount` object and save its data to a file named accountInfo.dat:

```csharp
BankAccount checking = new BankAccount();
// Statements that modify the fields in the BankAccount object
BinaryFormatter savedAccount = new BinaryFormatter();
FileStream accountFile =
    new FileStream(
    @"C:\\accountData\\accountInfo.dat",
    FileMode.Create);
savedAccount.Serialize(accountFile, checking);
accountFile.Close();
```

To convert serialized data back into an object, you must first open a file stream, passing to it a value of `FileMode.Open` as the second parameter of the `FileStream` class constructor. The remainder of the steps are the same as the preceding serialization steps, except that you call the `Deserialize()` method instead of the `Serialize()` method of the `BinaryFormatter` object. The following statements demonstrate how to serialize a binary file and deserialize its data back into a `BankAccount` object. Notice that the deserialization statement instantiates an object of the `BankAccount` class and then casts the result returned from the `Deserialize()` method into a `BankAccount` class object.

```
BinaryFormatter savedAccount = new BinaryFormatter();
FileStream accountFile =
    new FileStream(@"C:\\accountData\\accountInfo.dat",
    FileMode.Open);
BankAccount checking =
    (BankAccount)savedAccount.Deserialize(accountFile);
accountFile.Close();
```

Recall that binary serialization converts all of an object's fields to binary format. However, you don't necessarily have to serialize each and every field in a class, particularly for large objects that contain numerous fields. For fields that you do not need to serialize, add the NonSerialized attribute before the declaration statement, surrounded by brackets ([]). The following statement demonstrates how to prevent a field named interestRate from being serialized:

```
[NonSerialized]
public double interestRate;
```

When working with a shopping cart, you do not normally need to serialize and store order information in a file. Instead, you just use session state to maintain the shopping cart for the duration of the current session. The following statement demonstrates how to assign the checking object to a session variable named myAccount:

```
Session["myAccount"] = checking;
```

To restore a serialized object from a session variable, you must cast the session variable to the BankAccount class, and then assign the session variable to a BankAccount object, as follows:

```
curAccount = (BankAccount)Session["myAccount"];
```

Event handlers that are called when a user clicks a product's Order Now button will handle the creation and storage of ShoppingCart objects. When a user clicks an Order Now button, the button's event handler will check if a ShoppingCart object exists in a session variable named savedCart. If the object does exist, the event handler calls a method that adds the selected product to the ShoppingCart object. If the object does not exist, the event handler creates it before attempting to add the selected product. The Shopping Cart page will use the Page_Load() event handler to check if the savedCart session variable exists. If so, the selected products are printed to a table. If not, a message prints to a Literal control named CartBody that informs the user that the shopping cart is empty.

Next, you will add code to the Shopping Cart page's Page_Load() event handler that checks if the savedCart session variable exists.

To add code to the Shopping Cart page's Page_Load() event handler that checks if the savedCart session variable exists:

1. Return to the **shopping_cart.aspx.cs** file in the Code Editor window.

2. Add the following statement to the beginning of the Page_Load() event handler to instantiate a ShoppingCart object:

```
ShoppingCart curCart;
```

3. Replace the try...catch block with the following if statement that checks if the savedCart session variable exists. Later in the chapter, you will learn how to create methods that access the fields stored in the ShoppingCart object.

```
if (Session["savedCart"] != null)
{
    curCart =
        (ShoppingCart)Session["savedCart"];
}
```

4. Add the following else statement to the end of the Page_Load() event handler.

```
else
{
    CartBody.Text = "<p>Your shopping cart is empty.</p>";
}
```

5. Start the Web site and open the Shopping Cart page. You should see the message indicating that the shopping cart is empty.

6. Close your Web browser window.

Short Quiz 3

1. Why should you hide any class members that other programmers do not need to access or know about?

2. How do the principles of information hiding compare with open source software?

3. What are the two ways in which you can assign an initial value to a field?

4. What are the differences between binary and XML serialization? When would you use each type of serialization method?

5. What class do you use to serialize and deserialize objects in binary format, and what class do you use to create a file stream object? How do these two classes work together in the serialization/deserialization processes?

Working with Class Methods

Because methods perform most of the work in a class, you now learn about the various techniques associated with them. Methods are usually declared as public or private, but they can also be declared with any of the other types of access modifiers. Public methods can be called by anyone, whereas private methods can be called only by other methods in the same class.

You might wonder about the usefulness of a private method, which cannot be accessed by a client of the program. Suppose your program needs some sort of utility method that clients have no need to access. For example, the BankAccount class might need to calculate interest by calling a method named calcInterest(). Because the calcInterest() method can be called automatically from within the BankAccount class, the client does not need to access the calcInterest() method directly. By making the calcInterest() method private, you protect your program and add another level of information hiding. A general rule of thumb is to create as public any methods that clients need to access and to create as private any methods that clients do not need to access. The protected and protected internal access modifiers are more flexible than the private access modifier because they also allow derived classes to access a method. The internal access modifier allows a method to be accessed from anywhere in the application, but not from external applications.

You declare a method within the body of a class definition and include an access modifier before the method's return type. Other than including an access modifier, there is little difference between standard functions and methods. You are not required to define a method with an access modifier. If you do exclude the access modifier, the method's default access is internal. However, it's good programming practice to include an access modifier with any method definition to clearly identify the scope of the method. The following statement demonstrates how to declare a method named withdrawal() in the BankAccount class:

```
public class BankAccount : System.Web.UI.Page
{
    public double balance = 958.20;
    public void withdrawal(double amount) {
        balance -= amount;
    }
}
BankAccount checking = new BankAccount();
checking.withdrawal(200);
Response.Write("<p>Your updated checking account balance is "
    + String.Format("{0:C}", checking.balance) + "</p>");
```

548

Initializing with Constructor Methods

When you first instantiate an object from a class, you will often want to assign initial values to fields or perform other types of initialization tasks, such as calling a method that might calculate and assign values to fields. Although you can assign simple values to fields when you declare them, a better choice is to use a constructor method. A **constructor method** is a special method that is called automatically when an object from a class is instantiated. You define and declare constructor methods the same way you define other methods, although you do not include a return type because constructor methods do not return values. Each class definition can contain one or more constructor methods whose names are the same as the class. You must specify the public access modifier with a constructor method. The following code demonstrates how to use the BankAccount() constructor method to initialize the fields in the BankAccount class:

```
public class BankAccount : System.Web.UI.Page
{
        private string accountNumber;
        private string customerName;
        private double balance;
        public BankAccount() {
                accountNumber = "012345678";
                balance = 0;
                customerName = "";
        }
}
```

Constructor methods are commonly used to handle database connection tasks. Next, you will add to the ShoppingCart class's constructor method that contains statements that instantiate a new database object.

To add to the ShoppingCart class's constructor method statements that instantiate a new database object:

1. Return to the **ShoppingCart.cs** file in the Code Editor window.

2. Replace the comments in the constructor method with the following statement, which opens the database connection:

   dbConnection.Open();

Cleaning Up with Destructor Methods

Just as a default constructor method is called when a class object is first instantiated, a destructor method is called when the object is destroyed. A **destructor method** cleans up any resources allocated to an object after the object is destroyed. You cannot explicitly call a destructor method. Instead, it is called automatically by the C#

garbage collection. You generally do not need to use a destructor method, although many programmers use one to close file database connections. To add a destructor method to a C# class, create a method with the same name as the class, but preceded by a tilde symbol (~). Note that you do not specify an access modifier or data type for a destructor method. The following code contains a destructor method that closes an open database connection:

```csharp
public class BankAccount : System.Web.UI.Page
{
    private SqlConnection dbConnection;
    public BankAccount()
    {
        dbConnection = new SqlConnection(
            "Data Source=DBSERVER\\SQLEXPRESS;
            Integrated Security=true");
        dbConnection.Open();
        dbConnection.ChangeDatabase("accountDB");
    }
    ~BankAccount()
    {
        dbConnection.Close();
    }
}
```

Next, you will add to the ShoppingCart class a destructor method that closes the database object that you instantiated with the constructor method.

To add a destructor method:

1. Return to the **ShoppingCart.cs** file in the Code Editor window.

2. Add the following destructor method definition to the end of the class:

   ```csharp
   ~ShoppingCart()
   {
   }
   ```

3. Add to the destructor method the following statement that closes the database object:

   ```csharp
   dbConnection.Close();
   ```

Writing Accessors

Even if you make all fields in a class private, you can still allow your program's clients to retrieve or modify the value of fields via accessor methods. **Accessor methods** are public methods that a client can call to retrieve or modify the value of a field. Because accessor methods often begin with the words "set" or "get," they are also referred to as set or get methods. Set methods modify field values; get methods retrieve field values. To allow a client to pass a value to your program that will be assigned to a private field, you include parameters in a set method's definition. You can then write code in the body of the set method that validates the data passed from the client, prior to assigning values to private fields. For example, if you write a class named `Payroll` that includes a private field containing the current state income-tax rate, you could write a public accessor method named `getStateTaxRate()` that allows clients to retrieve the variable's value. Similarly, you could write a `setStateTaxRate()` method that performs various types of validation on the data passed from the client (such as making sure the value is not null, is not greater than 100%, and so on) prior to assigning a value to the private state tax rate field.

The following code demonstrates how to use set and get methods with the `balance` field in the `BankAccount` class. The `setBalance()` method is declared with an access modifier of `public` and accepts a single parameter containing the value to assign to the `balance` field. The `getBalance()` method is also declared as `public` and contains a single statement that returns the value assigned to the `balance` field. Statements at the end of the example call the methods to set and get the `balance` field.

```csharp
public class BankAccount : System.Web.UI.Page
{
    private double balance = 0;
    public void setBalance(double newBalance)
    {
        balance = newBalance;
    }
    public double getBalance()
    {
        return balance;
    }
}
BankAccount checking = new BankAccount();
checking.setBalance(457.63);
Response.Write("<p>Your updated checking account balance is "
    + String.Format("{0:C}", checking.getBalance()) + "</p>");
```

Next, you will add two accessor methods to the `Bakery` class: `addItem()` and `showCart()`. When the user clicks one of the Order Now buttons from a product page, the `addItem()` method will add new elements to the `productID`, `productQuantity`, and `productTable` fields for the selected item. The `showCart()` method displays the shopping cart when the user selects a new item or opens the Shopping Cart page.

To add `addItem()` and `showCart()` accessor methods to the `Bakery` class:

1. Return to the **ShoppingCart.cs** file in the Code Editor window.

2. Add the following `addItem()` method definition above the class constructor method. This method returns a Boolean value of true if the item was added successfully or false if it already exists in the shopping cart.

```
public bool addItem(string prodID, string table)
{
}
```

3. Add to the `addItem()` method the following `foreach` statement, which loops through the elements in the `productID[]` array list. If the product ID is found, the method returns a value of false and ends because the item already exists in the shopping cart.

```
foreach (string item in productID)
{
    if (item == prodID)
        return false;
}
```

4. Add to the end of the `addItem()` method the following statements, which assign values to the `productID`, `productQuantity`, and `productTable` fields for the selected item. The last statement returns a value of false, indicating that the item was successfully added to the shopping cart.

```
productID.Add(prodID);
productQuantity.Add(1);
productTable.Add(table);
return true;
```

5. Add the following `showCart()` method definition above the class constructor method. This method works by building a table containing the products in the shopping cart. The table is then returned to the calling function.

```
public string showCart()
{
}
```

6. Add the following statements to the `showCart()` method to begin building the table string. The `total` variable will store a running total of the items in the shopping cart.

```
string retValue = "<table width='100%'
    cellspacing='2' cellpadding='3' rules='all'
    border='1' id='ProductGrid'
    style='background-color:#DEBA84;
    border-color:#DEBA84;border-width:1px;
    border-style:None;font-size:Smaller;'>";
```

```
retValue += "<tr style='color:White;
    background-color:#A55129;
    font-weight:bold;'><th align='center'>
    Product</th><th align='center'>
    Quantity</th><th align='center'>
    Price Each</th></tr>";
double total = 0;
```

7. Add the following for loop to the end of the showCart()
   method. These statements run an ExecuteReader() method to
   open a recordset for each item in the shopping cart. The code
   reads the price for each item and builds the body of the table.

```
for (int i = 0; i < productID.Count; ++i)
{
    string sqlString = "SELECT * FROM "
        + productTable[i] + " WHERE productID='"
        + productID[i] + "'";
    SqlCommand prodCommand = new
        SqlCommand(sqlString, dbConnection);
    SqlDataReader prodRecords =
        prodCommand.ExecuteReader();
    if (prodRecords.Read())
    {
        retValue += "<tr style='color:#8C4510;
            background-color:#FFF7E7;'>"
            + "<td>" + prodRecords["name"] + "</td>"
            + "<td align='center'>"
            + productQuantity[i] + "</td>"
            + "<td align='center'>"
            + String.Format("{0:C}",
            prodRecords["price"])
            + "</td></tr>";
        double price = Convert.ToDouble(
            prodRecords["price"]);
        int quantity = Convert.ToInt16(
            productQuantity[i]);
        total += price * quantity;
    }
    prodRecords.Close();
}
```

8. Add to the end of the showCart() method the following
   statements, which complete the table and return the string
   to the calling function:

```
retValue += "<td align='center' colspan='2'>
    <strong>Your shopping cart contains "
    + productQuantity.Count
    + " product(s).</strong></td>";
retValue += "<td align='center'><strong>Total: "
    + String.Format("{0:C}", total)
    + "</strong></td></tr>";
retValue += "<asp:Button runat='server'
    Text='Button' /></table>";
return retValue;
```

9. Return to the shopping_cart.aspx.cs file in the Code Editor window.

10. Add the following statements to the end of the if statement. These statements call the showCart() function and assign the returned results to the CartBody literal.

```
string retString = curCart.showCart();
CartBody.Text = retString;
```

Next, you will add code to the product pages and Shopping Cart page that calls the new ShoppingCart class methods.

To add code to the product pages and Shopping Cart page that calls the new ShoppingCart class methods:

1. Open **breads.aspx.cs** in the Code Editor window and add the following definition for an event handler named ProductGrid_SelectedIndexChanged().

```
protected void ProductGrid_SelectedIndexChanged(
    object sender, EventArgs e)
{
}
```

2. Add to the ProductGrid_SelectedIndexChanged() event handler the following statements. These statements create a new ShoppingCart object or open the existing ShoppingCart object from the session variable, then execute the addItem() method. Depending on the result returned from the addItem() method, the remaining statements either print "You already selected that item" in the Literal control or redirect the browser to the Shopping Cart page.

```
ShoppingCart curCart;
if (Session["savedCart"] == null)
    curCart = new ShoppingCart();
else
{
    curCart = (ShoppingCart)Session["savedCart"];
}
bool addResult = curCart.addItem(
ProductGrid.SelectedValue.ToString(), "Breads");
if (addResult == false)
    ProductPage.Text = "<p>You already selected
    that item!</p>";
else
{
    Session["savedCart"] = curCart;
    Response.Redirect("shopping_cart.aspx");
}
```

3. Return to **breads.aspx** in the Code Editor window and add the following event handler just before the closing bracket (>) for the <asp:GridView> control:

```
onselectedindexchanged="ProductGrid_
SelectedIndexChanged"
```

4. Repeat Steps 1 and 3 for the cakes.aspx, cookies.aspx, and the pies.aspx files. Replace the second argument that is passed to the addItem() function with the appropriate product type. For example, you should change the argument in the cakes.aspx file from "Breads" to "Cakes".

5. Return to the **shopping_cart.aspx.cs** file in the Code Editor window.

6. Start the Web site and test the product pages and Shopping Cart page. Figure 10-5 shows the Shopping Cart page after adding several items.

7. Close your Web browser window.

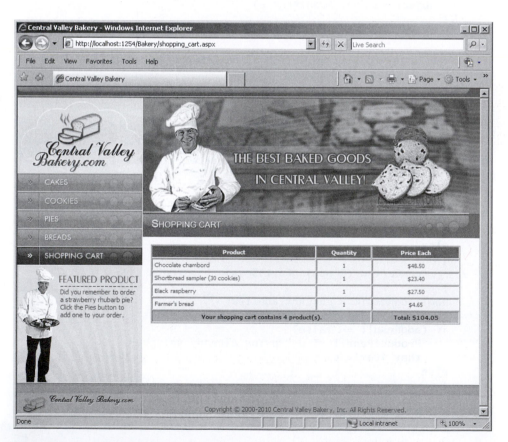

Figure 10-5   Shopping Cart page after adding several items

The preceding techniques are the traditional ways of creating accessors in object-oriented programming languages. C# allows you to create accessors using **properties**, which are special methods that you can use as public data members to set and get field values. To create a property, you create a constructor that is similar to a method definition and includes an accessor level and data type, but does not include parentheses at the end of the method name. To create a property's set and get methods, you include the set and get keywords within the property definition. Following the set and get keywords, you place the necessary statements for each method within a set of braces. For the get method, you can perform any type of computation and then return the value using a return statement. The set method includes an implicit parameter named value that represents the value being assigned to the field. The following example demonstrates how to set and get the balance in the BankAccount program as a property:

```
public class BankAccount : System.Web.UI.Page
{
    private double balance = 0;
    public double Balance {
        get { return balance; }
        set { balance = value; }
    }
}
BankAccount checking = new BankAccount();
checking.Balance = 457.63;
Response.Write("<p>Your updated checking account balance is "
    + String.Format("{0:C}", checking.Balance) + "</p>");
```

Short Quiz 4

1. Why would you use a private class method?

2. If you exclude an access modifier when declaring a class method, what access level does C# use by default?

3. What is the required syntax for declaring constructor and destructor methods?

4. Why would you use accessor methods? Why do they often begin with the words "set" or "get"?

5. How are accessor methods related to C# properties? How do you create C# properties and access them through an instantiated class object?

Summing Up

- An object is programming code and data that can be treated as an individual unit or component.

- Objects are encapsulated, which means that all code and required data are contained within the object itself. Encapsulation places code inside what programmers like to call a "black box." When an object is encapsulated, you cannot see "inside" it—all internal workings are hidden.

- The term *interface* refers to the methods and properties that are required for a source program to communicate with an object.

- In object-oriented programming, the code, methods, attributes, and other information that make up an object are organized into classes, which is essentially a template, or blueprint, that serves as the basis for new objects.

- When you create an object from an existing class, you are said to be instantiating the object. A particular instance of an object inherits its methods and properties from a class—that is, it takes on the characteristics of the class on which it is based.

- In C#, the term *class* more specifically refers to data structures that contain fields along with methods for manipulating the fields. The term *data structure* refers to a system for organizing data, whereas the term *field* refers to variables that are defined within a class.

- The methods and fields defined in a class are called class members or simply members. Class variables are referred to as data members or member variables, whereas class methods are referred to as function members or member functions.

- Classes help make complex programs easier to manage by logically grouping related methods and fields and by allowing you to refer to that grouping as a single object.

- Access modifiers control a client's access to classes, individual data members, and function members.

- To create a class in C#, you use the `class` keyword and an access modifier to write a class definition, which contains the class members that make up the class.

- The term *garbage collection* refers to cleaning up, or reclaiming, memory that is reserved by a program. With C#, you do not need to worry about reclaiming memory that is reserved for your variables or objects because C# knows when your program no longer needs a variable or object and automatically cleans up the memory for you. The one exception has to do with open database connections, which you do need to close manually.

- The principle of information hiding states that any class members that other programmers, sometimes called clients, do not need to access or know about should be hidden.

- You declare a field in the same way that you declare a standard variable, except that you must include an access modifier at the beginning of a field declaration statement.

- Serialization is the process of converting an object's fields into a string that you can store for reuse. Binary serialization converts object properties to a binary format, whereas XML serialization converts object properties to XML.

- A file stream is used for accessing a resource, such as a file, that you can read from and write to. An input stream reads data from a resource (such as a file), whereas an output stream writes data to a resource (again, such as a file).

- Methods are usually declared as public or private, but they can also be declared with any of the other types of access modifiers. Public methods can be called by anyone, whereas private methods can be called only by other methods in the same class.

- A general rule of thumb is to create as public any methods that clients need to access and to create as private any methods that clients do not need to access.

- A constructor method is a special method that is called automatically when an object from a class is instantiated.

- A destructor method cleans up any resources allocated to an object after the object is destroyed.

- Accessor methods are public methods that a client can call to retrieve or modify the value of a field. Because accessor methods often begin with the words "set" or "get," they are also referred to as set or get methods.

- C# allows you to create accessors using properties, which are special methods that you can use as public data members to set and get field values.

Comprehension Check

1. Reusable software objects are often referred to as _____.

   a. methods

   b. components

   c. widgets

   d. functions

2. Explain the benefits of object-oriented programming.

3. The term *black box* refers to _____.

   a. a property

   b. debugging

   c. encapsulation

   d. an interface

4. Users can see all of the methods and properties within an encapsulated object. True or False?

5. A(n) _____ is an object that has been created from an existing class.

   a. pattern

   b. structure

   c. replica

   d. instance

6. What is inheritance? How is it used with classes?

7. The functions associated with an object are called _____. (Choose all that apply.)

   a. properties

   b. function members

   c. methods

   d. attributes

8. The terms *variable* and *object* are often used interchangeably in object-oriented programming. True or False?

9. Class names usually begin with a(n) _____ to distinguish them from other identifiers.

    a. number

    b. exclamation mark (!)

    c. ampersand (&)

    d. uppercase letter

10. Which of the following access specifiers prevents clients from calling methods or accessing fields? (Choose all that apply.)

    a. `public`

    b. `private`

    c. `protected`

    d. `internal`

11. Which access modifier does C# use by default if you do not include one in a class or class member definition?

    a. `public`

    b. `private`

    c. `protected`

    d. `internal`

12. Explain how to create a class definition.

13. Class names in a class definition are followed by parentheses, the same as with a function definition. True or False?

14. For which of the following programmatic constructs do you need to perform garbage collection?

    a. `variables`

    b. `objects`

    c. `database connections`

    d. `file streams`

15. Explain the principle of information hiding.

16. What types of serialization does the .NET Framework support? (Choose all that apply.)

    a. binary

    b. unary

    c. XML

    d. database

17. Explain how to serialize a class object to a file.

18. When is a destructor called?

    a. when the object is destroyed

    b. when the constructor method ends

    c. when you delete a class object with the `unset()` method

    d. when you call the `serialize()` method

19. Explain the use of accessor functions. How are they often named?

20. What is a property in the context of a C# class? How do you create a property?

Reinforcement Exercises

Exercise 10-1

In this exercise, you will add two member functions, `removeItem()` and `emptyCart()`, to the `ShoppingCart` class. These functions allow you to remove individual items or empty all items from the shopping cart.

To add the `removeItem()` and `emptyCart()` member functions to the `ShoppingCart` class:

1. Return to the **ShoppingCart.cs** file in the Code Editor window.

2. Add the following `removeItem()` method definition above the class constructor:

```
public void removeItem(string prodID)
{
}
```

3. Add to the removeItem() method the following statements, which loop through the productID[] array list until the element that matches the prodID parameter is found. Then, the if statement deletes the associated elements in the productID[], productQuantity[], and productTable[] methods.

```
for (int i = 0; i < productID.Count; ++i)
{
    if (productID[i].ToString() == prodID)
    {
        productID.RemoveAt(i);
        productQuantity.RemoveAt(i);
        productTable.RemoveAt(i);
        break;
    }
}
```

4. Add the following emptyCart() method definition above the class constructor:

```
public void emptyCart(string prodID)
{
}
```

5. Add the following statements to the emptyCart() method definition. The statements empty the cart by calling the Clear() method for the productID[], productQuantity[], and productTable[] methods.

```
productID.Clear();
productQuantity.Clear();
productTable.Clear();
```

6. Next, you need to modify the showCart() method so it displays links that call the removeItem() and emptyCart() functions. First, modify the second statement that creates the table header (<th>) elements so it includes another column for the remove item links, as follows:

```
retValue += "<tr style='color:White;
    background-color:#A55129;
    font-weight:bold;'><th align='center'>
    Remove</th><th align='center'>
    Product</th><th align='center'>
    Quantity</th><th align='center'>
    Price Each</th></tr>";
```

7. Modify the value assigned to the retValue variable in the if statement in the showCart() function as follows. These statements create new table cells containing Remove Item links. Notice that a query string named operation is appended to

the shopping_cart.aspx URL. This query string notifies the class which method to call. In this case, the removeItem() method is being called.

```
retValue += "<tr style='color:#8C4510;
   background-color:#FFF7E7;'>"
+ "<td align='center'>
<a href='shopping_cart.aspx?operation
=removeItem&productID=" + productID[i]
+ "'>Remove</a></td>" + "<td>"
+ prodRecords["name"] + "</td>"
+ "<td align='center'>" + productQuantity[i]
+ "</td>" + "<td align='center'>"
+ String.Format("{0:C}", prodRecords["price"])
+ "</td></tr>";
```

8. Add the following statement after the for loop's closing brace. This statement adds an Empty Cart link to the end of the shopping cart table.

```
retValue += "<td align='center'>
<a href='shopping_cart.aspx?operation=emptyCart'>
Empty Cart</a></td>";
```

9. Return to the **shopping_cart.aspx.cs** script in the Code Editor window and modify the if statement that checks if the savedCart session variable exists so it includes nested if statements that call the removeItem() and emptyCart() methods, as follows. Also, enclose within an else construct the statements that call the showCart() method and assign the return value to the Literal control. Your statements should appear as follows:

```
if (Session["savedCart"] != null)
{
    curCart = (ShoppingCart)
      Session["savedCart"];
    if (Request.QueryString["operation"]
      == "removeItem")
    {
        curCart.removeItem(
          Request.QueryString["productID"]);
        Response.Redirect("shopping_cart.aspx");
    }
    else if (Request.QueryString["operation"]
      == "emptyCart")
    {
        curCart.emptyCart(Request.QueryString
          ["productID"]);
        Response.Redirect("shopping_cart.aspx");
```

```
    }
    else
    {
        string retString = curCart.showCart();
        CartBody.Text = retString;
    }
}
else
{
    CartBody.Text = "<p>Your shopping cart
      is empty.</p>";
}
```

10. Start the Web site and test the Remove and Empty Cart links on the Shopping Cart page. Figure 10-6 shows the Shopping Cart page after adding the remove item and empty cart functionality.

11. Close your Web browser window.

Figure 10-6 Shopping Cart Web page after adding the remove item and empty cart functionality

Exercise 10-2

In this project, you will add two member functions, addOne() and removeOne(), to the ShoppingCart class. These functions allow you to change the quantities of products in the shopping cart.

To add the addOne() and removeOne() member functions to the ShoppingCart class:

1. Return to the **ShoppingCart.cs** file in the Code Editor window.

2. Add the following addOne() method definition above the class constructor:

    ```
    public void addOne(string prodID)
    {
    }
    ```

3. Add to the addOne() method the following statements, which increment a product's quantity:

    ```
    for (int i = 0; i < productID.Count; ++i)
    {
        if (productID[i].ToString() == prodID)
        {
            productQuantity[i] = Convert.ToInt16(
                productQuantity[i]) + 1;
            break;
        }
    }
    ```

4. Add the following removeOne() method definition above the class constructor:

    ```
    public void removeOne(string prodID)
    {
    }
    ```

5. Add to the removeOne() method the following statements, which decrement a product's quantity:

    ```
    for (int i = 0; i < productID.Count; ++i)
    {
        if (productID[i].ToString() == prodID)
        {
        productQuantity[i] = Convert.ToInt16(
            productQuantity[i]) - 1;
        if (Convert.ToInt16(productQuantity[i]) == 0)
        {
    ```

```
            productID.RemoveAt(i);
            productQuantity.RemoveAt(i);
            productTable.RemoveAt(i);
        }
        break;
        }
    }
```

6. Modify the value assigned to the retValue variable in the if statement in the showCart() function, as follows. These statements create Add and Remove links within the cell containing the product quantity.

```
retValue += "<tr style='color:#8C4510;
    background-color:#FFF7E7;'>"
    + "<td align='center'>
    <a href='shopping_cart.aspx?operation
    =removeItem&productID=" + productID[i]
    + "'>Remove</a></td>" + "<td>"
    + prodRecords["name"] + "</td>"
    + "<td align='center'>" + productQuantity[i]
    + "<br /><a href='shopping_cart.aspx?
    operation=addOne&productID="
    + productID[i] + "'>Add</a> 
    <a href='shopping_cart.aspx?
    operation=removeOne&productID="
    + productID[i] + "'>Remove</a>"
    + "<td align='center'>" + String.Format("{0:C}",
    prodRecords["price"]) + "</td></tr>";
```

7. Return to the **shopping_cart.aspx.cs** script in the Code Editor window and modify the Page_Load() event handler so it includes nested if statements that call the addOne() and removeOne() methods, as follows:

```
if (Request.QueryString["operation"] == "removeItem")
{
    curCart.removeItem(
    Request.QueryString["productID"]);
    Response.Redirect("shopping_cart.aspx");
}
else if (Request.QueryString["operation"] == "emptyCart")
{
    curCart.emptyCart(Request.QueryString["productID"]);
    Response.Redirect("shopping_cart.aspx");
}
else if (Request.QueryString["operation"] == "addOne")
{
    curCart.addOne(Request.QueryString["productID"]);
    Response.Redirect("shopping_cart.aspx");
}
```

```csharp
else if (Request.QueryString["operation"] == "removeOne")
{
    curCart.removeOne(Request.QueryString["productID"]);
    Response.Redirect("shopping_cart.aspx");
}
else
{
    string retString = curCart.showCart();
    CartBody.Text = retString;
}
```

8. Start the Web site and test the Add and Remove links on the Shopping Cart page. Figure 10-7 shows the Shopping Cart page after adding functionality to change the product quantity.

9. Close your Web browser window.

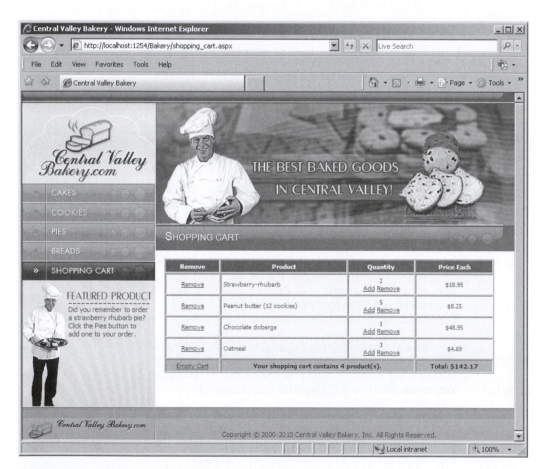

Figure 10-7 Shopping Cart Web page after adding functionality to change the product quantity

Discovery Projects

Save the Web sites you create for the following projects in your Projects folder for Chapter 10.

Project 10-1

Create a `HitCounter` class that counts the number of hits to a Web page and stores the results in a database. Use a private data member to store the number of hits and include public set and get member functions to access the private counter member variable. Save the project in a folder named **HitCounter** in your Projects folder for Chapter 10.

Project 10-2

Create a `GuestBook` class that stores Web site visitor names in a database. Use a private data member to store visitor names and include public set and get member functions to access the private visitor name member variable. Save the project in a folder named **GuestBook** in your Projects folder for Chapter 10.

Project 10-3

Create a `Movies` class that determines the cost of a ticket to a cinema, based on the moviegoer's age. Assume that the cost of a full-price ticket is $10. Assign the age to a private data member. Use a public member function to determine the ticket price, based on the following schedule:

Age	Price
Under 5	Free
5 to 17	Half price
18 to 55	Full price
Over 55	$2 off

Save the project in a folder named **Movies** in your Projects folder for Chapter 10.

Project 10-4

Create a program that calculates how long it takes to travel a specified number of miles, based on speed, number of stops, and weather conditions for a passenger train that averages a speed of 50 mph. Each stop of the train adds an additional five minutes to the train's schedule. In addition, during bad weather the train can only average a speed of 40 mph. Write a class-based version of this script with a class named Train. Save each piece of information you gather from the user in a private data member, and write the appropriate get and set functions for setting and retrieving each data member. Save the project in a folder named **Train** in your Projects folder for Chapter 10.

Project 10-5

In Chapter 5, you wrote a script that calculates the correct amount of change to return when performing a cash transaction. Write a class-based version of this script with a class named Change. Allow the user (a cashier) to enter the cost of a transaction and the exact amount of money that the customer hands over to pay for the transaction. Use set and get functions to store and retrieve both amounts to and from private data members. Then use member functions to determine the largest amount of each denomination to return to the customer. Assume that the largest denomination a customer will use is a $100 bill. Therefore, you will need to calculate the correct amount of change to return for $50, $20, $10, $5, and $1 bills, along with quarters, dimes, nickels, and pennies. For example, if the price of a transaction is $5.65 and the customer hands the cashier $10, the cashier should return $4.35 to the customer. Include code that requires the user to enter a numeric value for the cash transaction. Save the project in a folder named **Change** in your Projects folder for Chapter 10.

Project 10-6

Create a BankAccount class that allows users to calculate the balance in a bank account. The user should be able to enter a starting balance, and then calculate how that balance changes when she makes a deposit, withdraws money, or enters any accumulated interest. Add the appropriate data members and member functions to the BankAccount class that will enable this functionality. Also, add code to the class that ensures that the user does not overdraw her account. Be sure that the program adheres to the information-hiding techniques presented in this chapter. Save the project in a folder named **BankAccount** in your Projects folder for Chapter 10.

Working with Array Lists

Introduction to Array Lists

The arrays you have seen so far have been traditional arrays created with the following syntax:

```
type arrayName = new type[elements];
```

Although these types of arrays are fine for basic purposes, they are somewhat limited in that they have a fixed size. In other words, you cannot dynamically add and remove elements. A better solution is to use the **ArrayList class** to create an array that can be dynamically resized. The basic syntax for creating an array list is as follows:

```
ArrayList arrayName = new ArrayList();
```

 In order to use an ArrayList, you must include the `System.Collections` namespace.

To add elements to an array list, you use the **Add() method** of the ArrayList class. You pass to the Add() method the value of the element that you want to add to the array list. An added benefit of the ArrayList class is that, unlike traditional arrays, it does not restrict you to including only elements of a single data type. The following code creates an array and stores values with different data types in the array list elements:

 You do not need to specify the number of elements when you define an array list because its elements are resized dynamically.

```
ArrayList hotelReservation  = new ArrayList();
hotelReservation.Add("Don Gosselin"); // guest name (string)
hotelReservation.Add(2); // # of nights (integer)
hotelReservation.Add(89.95); // price per night
  (floating point)
hotelReservation.Add(true); // nonsmoking room (Boolean)
```

You access the elements of an array list the same as a traditional array, by specifying the element number within brackets appended to the array name. The following statements demonstrate how to print the values assigned to the `hotelReservation[]` array list:

```
Response.Write(hotelReservation[0] + "<br />");
Response.Write(hotelReservation[1] + "<br />");
Response.Write(hotelReservation[2] + "<br />");
Response.Write(hotelReservation[3] + "<br />");
```

This section discusses basic `ArrayList` class techniques. For more advanced `ArrayList` class techniques, refer to the Microsoft Developer Network (MSDN) at *http://msdn.microsoft.com*.

To manipulate array lists in your scripts, you use the methods and properties of the `ArrayList` class. Unlike with arrays that you create with the `Array` class, you do not use the `Length` property to return the number of elements in an array list. Instead, you must use the **Count property** of the `ArrayList` class to return the number of elements in an array list. The following statement demonstrates how to use the `Count` property of the `ArrayList` class to return the number of elements in the `hotelReservation[]` array list.

```
Response.Write("<p>The hotelReservation[] array
   list contains " + hotelReservation.Count
   + " elements.</p>");
```

Finding and Extracting Elements and Values

This section discusses methods for finding and extracting elements and values in an array. One of the most basic methods for finding a value in an array or array list is to use a looping statement to iterate through the array list until you find a particular value. For example, the `for` statement in the following code loops through the `travelItinerary[]` array list to determine if it contains "Ireland". If it does, a message prints and the `break` statement ends the `for` loop.

```
ArrayList travelItinerary = new ArrayList();
travelItinerary.Add("Ireland");
travelItinerary.Add("France");
travelItinerary.Add("Germany");
travelItinerary.Add("England");
travelItinerary.Add("Italy");
for (int i=0; i<travelItinerary.Count; ++i) {
    if (travelItinerary[i] == "Ireland") {
        Response.Write("<p>The tour will stop in Ireland.</p>");
        break;
    }
}
```

You can also find elements and values in an array list by using the methods of the `ArrayList` class that are listed in Table A-1.

Method	Description
Contains(*item*)	Performs a case-sensitive search and returns true if the *item* argument is found within the array list or false if the item is not found
IndexOf(*item*[, *index*])	Performs a case-sensitive search and returns the element number in an array list of the first instance of the first character in the *item* argument; if the *index* argument is included, the IndexOf() method starts searching at that position within the array list; returns –1 if the *item* argument is not found
LastIndexOf(*item*[, *index*])	Performs a case-sensitive search and returns the element number in an array list of the last instance of the first character in the *item* argument; if the *index* argument is included, the LastIndexOf() method starts searching at that position within the array list; returns –1 if the *item* argument is not found

Table A-1 Search methods of the ArrayList class

The search methods of the ArrayList class listed in Table A-1 are virtually identical to the String class methods of the same name. For example, the Contains() method of the ArrayList class returns a value of true or false to indicate whether the specified item is located within an array list, similar to the way the Contains() method of the String class returns a value of true or false to indicate whether the specified text is located within a string. The following statements demonstrate how to use the Contains() method of the ArrayList class to determine whether the travelItinerary[] array list contains "Ireland":

```
if (travelItinerary.Contains("Ireland"))
    Response.Write("<p>The tour will stop in Ireland.</p>");
```

The IndexOf() and LastIndexOf() methods of the ArrayList class return the element number of the specified item within an array list. If the item is not found, the methods return a value of -1. The following code uses the IndexOf() method to determine whether the travelItinerary[] array list contains "Ireland".

```
if (travelItinerary.IndexOf("Ireland")>0)
    Response.Write("<p>The tour will stop in Ireland.</p>");
```

To extract elements and values from an array list, you use the GetRange() method of the ArrayList class to return (copy) a portion of an array list and assign it to another array list. The syntax for the GetRange() method is *arrayName*.GetRange(*start*, *end*);. The *arrayName* argument indicates the name of the array list from which you want to extract elements. The *start* argument indicates the start position within the array list to begin extracting elements. The *end* argument is an integer value that indicates the number of elements to return from the array list, starting with the element indicated by the *start* argument.

The following example demonstrates how to use the `GetRange()` method to return the first two elements in the `travelItinerary[]` array list. The elements are assigned to a new array list named `travelStops[]`. Figure A-1 shows the output.

```
ArrayList travelStops = travelItinerary.GetRange(0, 2);
Response.Write("<p>The first two stops in the
   European tour are " + travelStops[0] + " and "
   + travelStops[1] + ".</p>");
```

Figure A-1 Output of example of how to use the `GetRange()` method to return the first two elements in the `travelItinerary[]` array list

Manipulating Elements

As you use array lists in your scripts, you will undoubtedly need to add and remove elements. For example, suppose you have a shopping cart program that uses an array list to store the names of products that a customer plans to purchase. As the customer selects additional products to purchase, or changes her mind about an item, you will need to manipulate the elements in the array of products.

An important difference between arrays and array lists in C# is that array sizes are immutable (cannot change), whereas array lists can be sized dynamically. In other words, you cannot add or remove the number of elements in an array after you define it. In comparison, the `ArrayList` class contains various methods for adding and removing elements from an array list. First, you will learn how to add elements to an array list.

Adding Elements from the End of an Array List

As you already learned, you use the Add() method of the ArrayList class to add individual elements to the end of an array list. You can also use the **AddRange() method** of the ArrayList class to add multiple elements to the end of an array list. To use the AddRange() method, you must pass to it the name of an array or another array list. The following code demonstrates how to use the AddRange() method to add multiple elements to an array. Figure A-2 shows the output in a Web browser.

```
ArrayList travelItinerary = new ArrayList();
travelItinerary.Add("Ireland");
travelItinerary.Add("France");
travelItinerary.Add("Germany");
travelItinerary.Add("England");
travelItinerary.Add("Italy");
string[] newCountries = new string[2];
newCountries[0] = "Romania";
newCountries[1] = "Russia";
travelItinerary.AddRange(newCountries);
for (int i = 0; i < travelItinerary.Count; ++i)
{
    Response.Write(travelItinerary[i] + "<br />");
}
```

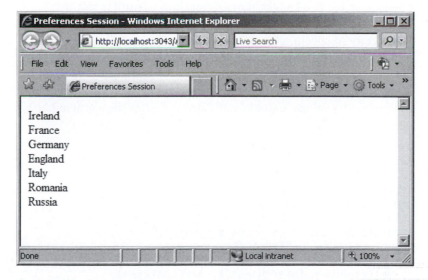

Figure A-2 Output of the travelItinerary[] array list after adding new elements with the AddRange() method

Adding Elements Within an Array List

So far, you have learned to add elements to the end of an array list. To add elements anywhere else in an array list, you need to use the Insert() and InsertRange() methods of the ArrayList class. The **Insert() method** adds a single element to a specified position within an array list, whereas the **InsertRange() method** adds a range of elements to a specified position within an array list. The syntax for the Insert() method is *arrayName*.Insert(*index*, *value*);. The *arrayName* argument indicates the name of the array list you want to modify. The *index* argument indicates the element within the array at which point to add the new element. The *value* arguments represent the value of the new element you want to add the array list. The Insert() method in the following code adds an element containing the value "Denmark" to the beginning of the travelItinerary[] array:

```
ArrayList travelItinerary = new ArrayList();
travelItinerary.Add("England");
travelItinerary.Add("France");
travelItinerary.Add("Germany");
travelItinerary.Add("Ireland");
travelItinerary.Add("Italy");
travelItinerary.Insert(0, "Denmark");
```

The syntax for the InsertRange() method is similar to the AddRange() method, except that you must pass two arguments: The first argument specifies the position within the array list where you want to insert the new elements and the second argument identifies the array or array list containing the elements you want to insert. The InsertRange() method in the following code inserts two elements containing the values "Estonia" and "Finland" after the element containing "Ireland":

```
ArrayList travelItinerary = new ArrayList();
travelItinerary.Add("Ireland");
travelItinerary.Add("France");
travelItinerary.Add("Germany");
travelItinerary.Add("England");
travelItinerary.Add("Italy");
string[] newCountries = new string[2];
newCountries[0] = "Estonia";
newCountries[1] = "Finland";
travelItinerary.InsertRange(1, newCountries);
```

Removing Elements from an Array List

To remove elements from an array list, you must use one of the methods of the ArrayList class listed in Table A-2.

Method	Description
Clear()	Deletes all elements from an array list
Remove(*item*)	Deletes the first element that matches the specified *item*
RemoveAt(*index*)	Deletes the element at the specified *index*
RemoveRange(*index*, *length*)	Deletes a range of elements started at the specified *index* up to the number of elements specified by the *length* argument

Table A-2   Remove methods of the ArrayList class

The following statement demonstrates how to use the Remove() method to delete the "France" element from the travelItinerary[] array list:

```
travelItinerary.Remove("France");
```

Here is an other example of how to remove the "France" element from the travelItinerary[] array list, this time by specifying its index with the RemoveAt() method:

```
travelItinerary.RemoveAt(1);
```

Finally, the following statement demonstrates how to use the RemoveRange() method to delete multiple elements from the travelItinerary[] array list. In this example, the elements for France, Germany, and England are removed.

```
travelItinerary.RemoveRange(1, 3);
```

Manipulating Array Lists

In the preceding section, you studied techniques for working with the individual elements in an array list. In this section, you will study techniques for manipulating an entire array list. More specifically, this section discusses how to sort array lists and how to convert them to arrays. First, you will learn how to sort arrays.

Sorting Array Lists

To sort elements of an array list alphabetically, you use the **Sort() method** of the ArrayList class. You append the Sort() method to the name of the array list you want to sort using the following syntax: *arrayList*.Sort();. The following code shows how to use the Sort() method to sort the elements of the travelItinerary[] array list. Figure A-3 shows the order of the elements after executing the Sort() method.

```
ArrayList travelItinerary = new ArrayList();
travelItinerary.Add("Ireland");
travelItinerary.Add("France");
travelItinerary.Add("Germany");
travelItinerary.Add("England");
travelItinerary.Add("Italy");
travelItinerary.Sort();
for (int i = 0; i < travelItinerary.Count; ++i)
{
    Response.Write(travelItinerary[i] + "<br />");
}
```

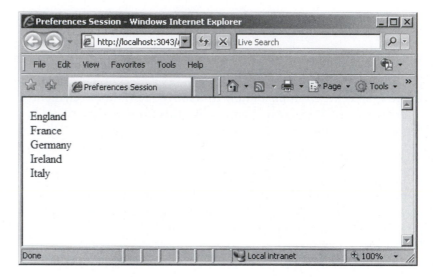

Figure A-3   Output of a sorted array list

To reverse the order of elements in an array list, you use the
Reverse() method of the ArrayList class. The Reverse() method
simply transposes, or reverses, the order of the elements in an array
list; it does not perform a reverse sort (Z to A instead of A to Z). If
you want to perform a reverse sort on an array list, you first need to
execute the Sort() method to sort the array list alphabetically, and
then call the Reverse() method to transpose the array list elements.
The following code shows how to perform a reverse sort on the
travelItinerary[] array. Figure A-4 shows the output of the code
in a Web browser.

```
ArrayList travelItinerary = new ArrayList();
travelItinerary.Add("Ireland");
travelItinerary.Add("France");
travelItinerary.Add("Germany");
travelItinerary.Add("England");
travelItinerary.Add("Italy");
travelItinerary.Sort();
travelItinerary.Reverse();
```

```
for (int i = 0; i < travelItinerary.Count; ++i)
{
    Response.Write(travelItinerary[i] + "<br />");
}
```

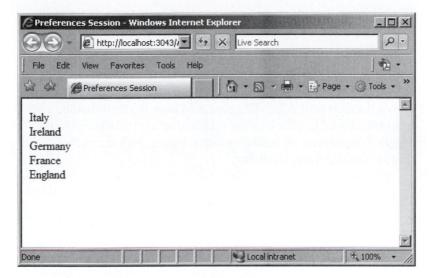

Figure A-4   Output of a reverse-sorted array list

Converting Array Lists to Arrays

You already know that you can convert an array to an array list by passing the name of the array to the AddRange() or InsertRange() methods of the ArrayList class. To convert an array list to an array requires the CopyTo() and ToArray() methods of the ArrayList class. The **CopyTo() method** copies an entire array list to an array with the syntax *arrayListName*.CopyTo(*arrayName*);. Here's how to convert the travelItinerary[] array list to an array named travelArray[]. Notice that the first statement uses the Count() method of the array list to determine the size of the new array.

```
string[] travelArray = new string[travelItinerary.Count];
travelItinerary.CopyTo(travelArray);
for (int i = 0; i < travelArray.Length; ++i)
{
    Response.Write(travelArray[i] + "<br />");
}
```

The array to which you want to copy an array list must be defined before calling the CopyTo() method. The **ToArray() method** also copies an entire array list to an array, but it also allows you to define the new array. In other words, you do not need a separate statement to define the new array, as you do with the CopyTo() method. The following syntax for the `ToArray()` method is a little more complicated than the `CopyTo()` method:

```
type[] arrayName = (type[])arrayListName
    .ToArray(typeof(type));
```

The following statement shows how to use the `ToArray()` method to convert the `travelItinerary[]` array list to an array named `travelArray[]`:

```
string[] travelArray = (string[])travelItinerary
    .ToArray(typeof(string));
```

As you develop your ASP.NET programs, keep in mind that in many cases you should continue to use standard arrays. However, if your program requires more flexibility when dealing with arrays, you should consider using array lists.

Using AJAX with ASP.NET

Introduction to AJAX

This appendix explains how to use AJAX with ASP.NET. But first, you need to understand a little history of JavaScript.

The most recent version of the JavaScript language is ECMAScript Edition 3, which was first released in December of 1999. The next major edition of the JavaScript language will be ECMAScript Edition 4, although at the time of this writing, the developers of the language have not made a great deal of progress on the new version and it is not known when it will be complete. Although there have been numerous browser enhancements since Edition 3 was released in 1999, the core JavaScript language has remained essentially unchanged for eight years. This is unusual with software development technologies because the Web developers who use these technologies are constantly looking for new and better tools for writing their programs. Unwilling simply to await the arrival of Edition 4, JavaScript programmers have managed to accommodate their own demand for increased JavaScript functionality by combining JavaScript with other technologies.

One such technology is DHTML, which makes Web pages dynamic by combining JavaScript, XHTML, CSS, and the Document Object Model. DHTML does a great job of making Web pages more dynamic and will continue to be a vital Web page development technique. The fact that DHTML runs entirely within a user's Web browser used to be considered an advantage because it made external resources, such as server data, unnecessary. However, as the Internet matured and broadband access became commonplace, Web developers began demanding a way to make their Web pages interact more dynamically with a Web server. To understand why, consider a Web browser's request for a Web page. In response, the Web server returns the requested page. If the user wants to refresh the Web page, the Web server returns the entire page again—not just the changed portions of the page. For Web page data that must always be up to date, such as stock prices, continuously reloading the entire page is too slow, even at broadband speeds.

The solution was **Asynchronous JavaScript and XML (AJAX)**, which refers to a combination of technologies that allow Web pages displayed on a client computer to quickly interact and exchange data with a Web server without reloading the entire Web page. Although its name implies a combination of JavaScript and XML, AJAX primarily relies on JavaScript and HTTP requests to exchange data between a client computer and a Web server. AJAX gets its name from the fact that XML is often the format used for exchanging data between a client computer and a Web server (although it can also exchange data using standard text strings). The other technologies that make up AJAX include XHTML, CSS, and the Document Object Model (DOM). However, these technologies primarily handle the display and presentation of data within the Web browser (the same as with DHTML), whereas HTTP and XML are responsible for data exchange. JavaScript ties everything together.

The term AJAX was first used in an article written in 2005 by Jesse James Garrett titled "Ajax: A New Approach to Web Applications" (*http://adaptivepath.com/publications/essays/archives/000385.php*). The article discussed how Garrett's company, Adaptive Path, was using a combination of technologies, which they referred to collectively as AJAX, to add richness and responsiveness to Web pages. Since then, AJAX has become hugely popular among JavaScript developers.

Understanding the `XMLHttpRequest` Object

It's important to note that Garrett and Adaptive Path did not invent anything new. Rather, they improved Web page interactivity by combining JavaScript, XML, XHTML, CSS, and the DOM with the key component of AJAX, the `XMLHttpRequest` object, which is available in modern Web browsers. The **`XMLHttpRequest` object** uses HTTP to exchange data between a client computer and a Web server. Unlike standard HTTP requests, which usually replace the entire page in a Web browser, the `XMLHttpRequest` object can be used to request and receive data without reloading a Web page. By combining the `XMLHttpRequest` object with DHTML techniques, you can update and modify individual portions of your Web page with data received from a Web server. The process of using the `XMLHttpRequest` object to update parts of a Web page with server data without reloading the entire page is called **partial-page rendering**. The `XMLHttpRequest` object has been available in most modern Web browsers since around 2001. However, Garrett's article was the first to clearly document the techniques for combining the XMLHttpRequest object with other techniques to exchange data between a client computer and a Web server.

Another factor contributing to AJAX's popularity was the release in 2005 of the Google Suggest Web site (*http://www.google.com/webhp? complete=1*), which was one of the first commercial Web sites to implement an AJAX application. Google Suggest was similar to the standard Google Web page, except that, as you type, Google Suggest listed additional search suggestions based on the text you type. The Google Suggest AJAX functionality has since been incorporated into the main Google search page. For example, if you type "san francisco hotels" in the Google text box, the search suggestions shown in Figure B-1 appear. The important thing to understand about Google is that, as you type each letter, JavaScript code uses the XMLHttpRequest object to send the string in the text box to the Google server, which attempts to match the typed characters with matching suggestions. The Google server then returns the suggestions to the client computer (without reloading the Web page), and JavaScript code populates the suggestion list with the response text.

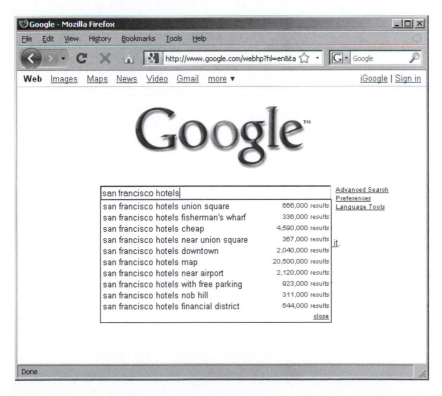

Figure B-1   Google Web site search functionality

Figures B-2 and B-3 conceptually illustrate the difference between a standard HTTP request and an HTTP request with the XMLHttpRequest object. In Figure B-2, the client makes a standard HTTP request for the *http://www.google.com* Web page, which is returned from the server and displayed in the client's Web browser. Figure B-3 illustrates the request process with the Google Suggest page when a user types the text "las vegas hotels discount" into the text box. Instead of requesting an entire Web page, the XMLHttpRequest object only requests recommended search terms for the "las vegas hotels discount" string. The server returns recommended search terms to the client, which in turn uses JavaScript to display the terms in the suggestion list.

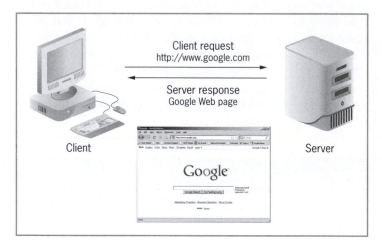

Figure B-2   Standard HTTP request

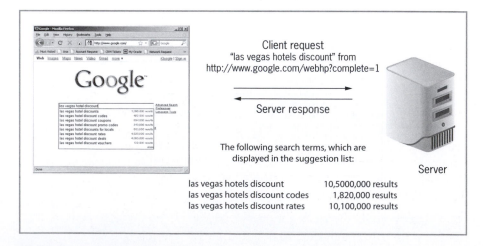

Figure B-3   HTTP request with the XMLHttpRequest object

Why Should You Use AJAX with ASP.NET?

As you know, updating any portion of a page in an ASP.NET application requires a round-trip to the server, regardless of how small the data is that needs updating. This means that your Web page will need to perform a round-trip to the server for every control event, which can seriously degrade the performance of your Web page. This can be enormously inefficient, especially if you need to update a small piece of data, such as a stock quote, on a regular basis. As mentioned in Chapter 1, an important question in the design of any client/server system is deciding how much processing to place on the client or server. In the context of Web site development, you must decide whether to use client-side JavaScript or a server-side script. This is an important consideration because the choice you make can greatly affect the performance of your program. In some cases, the decision is simple. For example, if you want to control the Web browser, you must use JavaScript. If you want to access a database on a Web server, you must use a server-side script. However, there are tasks that both languages can accomplish, such as validating forms and manipulating cookies. Further, both languages can perform the same types of calculations and data processing. A general rule of thumb is to allow the client to handle the user interface processing and light processing, such as data validation, but have the Web server perform intensive calculations and data storage. This division of labor is especially important when dealing with clients and servers over the Web. Unlike with clients on a private network, it's not possible to know in advance the computing capabilities of each client on the Web. You cannot assume that each client (browser) that accesses your client/server application (Web site) has the necessary power to perform the processing required by the application. For this reason, intensive processing should be placed on the server.

To allow ASP.NET applications to dynamically update portions of a Web page without performing a round-trip to the server, you can use AJAX server controls. This technique can significantly increase the speed of your dynamic applications because it allows them to perform a partial-page update instead of a full-page post back whenever data needs updating. Behind the scenes in an ASP.NET program, these controls use the same JavaScript, XML, XHTML, CSS, HTTP, and DOM technologies that client-side scripts use. In other words, the updates to your ASP.NET application are handled by the client instead of by the server. However, ASP.NET handles writing all of the code. You only need to understand how to add the AJAX controls to your Web forms and how to configure them to access and update the necessary data for your application.

It's important to understand that, although you can use AJAX to update portions of a Web page without performing a round-trip to the server, the partial-page rendering mechanism still executes each of the post back page events (PreInit through Unload) every time it is called. This means that if you have complex code in your Page_Load() or other event handler, it executes every time you perform a partial-page update. For example, if your Page_Load() event handler contains code that opens and queries a database and performs other complex tasks, using AJAX techniques might not do much to improve the performance of your Web site. Therefore, if you plan to incorporate AJAX techniques into your Web pages, be judicious with the code that you need to run during post back.

Using the AJAX Server Controls

This section discusses the basic AJAX server controls, starting with the ScriptManager control.

ScriptManager Control

The **ScriptManager control** manages the JavaScript for any AJAX controls on an ASP.NET Web page. You must place the ScriptManager control on any page that will contain AJAX controls. The Script-Manager control enables partial-page rendering and provides access to the **Microsoft AJAX Library**, which contains the namespaces, classes, and types for developing AJAX applications. You must place the ScriptManager control before any AJAX controls on a Web page.

```
<%@ Page Language="C#" AutoEventWireup="true"
CodeFile="Default3.aspx.cs" Inherits="Default3" %>
<!DOCTYPE html PUBLIC "-//W3C//DTD XHTML 1.0
Transitional//EN"
"http://www.w3.org/TR/xhtml1/DTD/xhtml1-transitional.dtd">
<html xmlns="http://www.w3.org/1999/xhtml">
<head runat="server">
    <title></title>
</head>
<body>
    <form id="form1" runat="server">
    <div>
        <asp:ScriptManager ID="ScriptManager1"
            runat="server" />
    </div>
    </form>
</body>
</html>
```

To use the basic AJAX controls discussed in this appendix, you don't need to know anything more about the ScriptManager control. To use more advanced AJAX controls, you need to familiarize yourself with the ScriptManager control, which includes various properties that you can find listed on MSDN at *http://msdn.microsoft.com/en-us/library/system.web.ui.scriptmanager_properties.aspx.*

UpdatePanel Control

The **UpdatePanel control** specifies regions on a Web page that will be updated with partial-page rendering. You can include multiple UpdatePanel controls on a Web page, provided you place them after the ScriptManager control. Within each UpdatePanel control, you place server controls that will perform the partial-page update. When a server control event within an UpdatePanel control is raised, post back is initiated. However, only the controls within the UpdatePanel control are updated. Remember that, even though the UpdatePanel controls are the only Web page content updated, the partial-page rendering mechanism still executes each of the post back page events (`PreInit` through `Unload`) every time it is called.

You must place the content of an UpdatePanel control inside of a `<ContentTemplate>` element, as follows:

```
<form id="form1" runat="server">
<div>
    <asp:ScriptManager ID="ScriptManager1"
        runat="server" />
    <asp:UpdatePanel ID="UpdatePanel1"
        runat="server">
        <ContentTemplate>
            UpdatePanel content
        </ContentTemplate>
    </asp:UpdatePanel>
</div>
</form>
```

As an example of an AJAX control, consider Figure B-4, which shows a Web page for a hotel. Notice the navigation arrows on either side of the image. Clicking either image scrolls through a series of five photos. Keep in mind that AJAX was used with this Web page to prevent a complete page reload. Instead of reloading the entire page, only the next photo in the series is loaded.

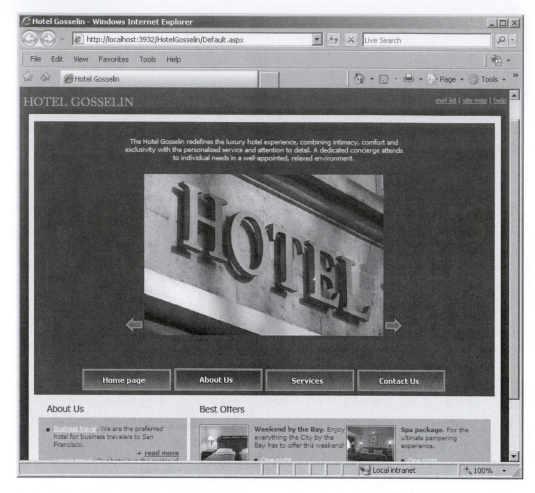

Figure B-4   Web page with an AJAX control

The following code gives the Web page in Figure B-4 its functionality. The image in the figure is rendered with an `<asp:Image>` control that is contained within an UpdatePanel control. Left and right `<asp:ImageButton>` controls are contained within the UpdatePanel control to initiate the partial-page render.

```
<form id="form1" runat="server">
<div>
    <asp:ScriptManager ID="ScriptManager1"
        runat="server">
    </asp:ScriptManager>
    <asp:UpdatePanel ID="UpdatePanel1"
        runat="server">
        <ContentTemplate>
            <table style="width: 60%">
                <tr>
                    <td>
```

```
            <p>
                The Hotel Gosselin redefines
                the luxury hotel experience,
                combining intimacy, comfort
                and exclusivity with the
                personalized service and
                attention to detail. A dedicated
                concierge attends to individual
                needs in a well-appointed,
                relaxed environment.</p>
            <asp:ImageButton ID="leftButton"
                runat="server"
                ImageUrl="images/left.gif"
                OnClick="leftButton_Click" />
            <asp:Image ID="roomImage"
                runat="server"
                ImageUrl="images/suite1.jpg" />
            <asp:ImageButton ID="rightButton"
                runat="server"
                ImageUrl="images/right.gif"
                OnClick="rightButton_Click" />
        </td>
    </tr>
</table>
        </ContentTemplate>
    </asp:UpdatePanel>
</div>
</form>
```

Notice the OnClick event handlers for the left and right button controls in the preceding code, which call the following functions. The Contains() method of the String class determines which photo is currently displayed and whether to display the next or previous photo in the series.

```
protected void leftButton_Click(object sender,
    EventArgs e)
{
    string curImage = roomImage.ImageUrl;
    if (curImage.Contains("5"))
        roomImage.ImageUrl = "images/suite4.jpg";
    else if (curImage.Contains("4"))
        roomImage.ImageUrl = "images/suite3.jpg";
    else if (curImage.Contains("3"))
        roomImage.ImageUrl = "images/suite2.jpg";
    else if (curImage.Contains("2"))
        roomImage.ImageUrl = "images/suite1.jpg";
    else
        roomImage.ImageUrl = "images/suite5.jpg";

}
protected void rightButton_Click(object sender,
    EventArgs e)
```

You can find a working example of the Hotel Gosselin Web site in the HotelGosselin folder in your Appendix.B folder.

```
{
    string curImage = roomImage.ImageUrl;
    if (curImage.Contains("1"))
        roomImage.ImageUrl = "images/suite2.jpg";
    else if (curImage.Contains("2"))
        roomImage.ImageUrl = "images/suite3.jpg";
    else if (curImage.Contains("3"))
        roomImage.ImageUrl = "images/suite4.jpg";
    else if (curImage.Contains("4"))
        roomImage.ImageUrl = "images/suite5.jpg";
    else
        roomImage.ImageUrl = "images/suite1.jpg";
}
```

In the previous example, the UpdatePanel for the Hotel Gosselin Web site contains the `<asp:ImageButton>` controls that perform the partial-page render. By default, any Web server control that is contained within an UpdatePanel will cause a partial-page render for that UpdatePanel. However, you can also configure controls that are not contained with an UpdatePanel to perform the partial-page render for that UpdatePanel. To authorize controls that are outside of an UpdatePanel control to perform a partial-page render, you add a `<Triggers>` element to an UpdatePanel control. Within the `<Triggers>` element, you nest `<asp:AsyncPostBackTrigger>` controls for each control that should be able to perform a partial-page render. The `<asp:AsyncPostBackTrigger>` control contains a single property, `ControlID`, to which you assign the ID of the control that you want to authorize as a trigger.

The following code contains a modified version of AJAX controls for the Hotel Gosselin Web page. In this version, the `<asp:ImageButton>` controls are placed outside of the UpdatePanel control, but are identified as triggers in the `<Triggers>` element. The arrow controls render below the image, as shown in Figure B-5.

```
<form id="form1" runat="server">
<div>
    <asp:ScriptManager ID="ScriptManager1"
        runat="server">
    </asp:ScriptManager>
    <asp:UpdatePanel ID="UpdatePanel1"
        runat="server">
```

You can find a working example of the triggers version of the Hotel Gosselin Web site in the HotelGosselin_ triggers folder in your Appendix.B folder.

```
    <Triggers>
        <asp:AsyncPostBackTrigger
            ControlID="leftButton" />
        <asp:AsyncPostBackTrigger
            ControlID="rightButton" />
    </Triggers>
<ContentTemplate>
    <table style="width: 60%">
        <tr>
            <td>
                <p>
                    The Hotel Gosselin redefines
                    the luxury hotel experience,
                    combining intimacy, comfort
                    and exclusivity with the
                    personalized service and
                    attention to detail. A dedicated
                    concierge attends to individual
                    needs in a well-appointed,
                    relaxed environment.</p>
                <asp:Image ID="roomImage"
                    runat="server"
                    ImageUrl="images/suite1.jpg" />
            </td>
        </tr>
    </table>
</ContentTemplate>
</asp:UpdatePanel>
<asp:ImageButton ID="leftButton" runat="server"
    ImageUrl="images/left.gif"
    OnClick="leftButton_Click" /> 
<asp:ImageButton ID="rightButton" runat="server"
    ImageUrl="images/right.gif"
    OnClick="rightButton_Click" />
</div>
</form>
```

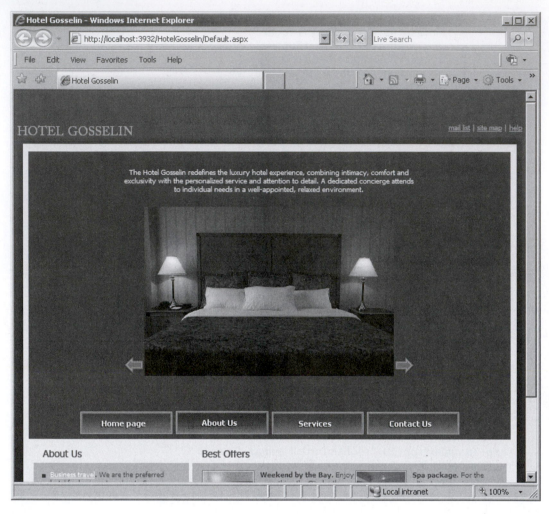

Figure B-5 Hotel Gosselin Web page after adding trigger code

Timer Control

As you develop Web pages, you might need to have some code execute repeatedly without user intervention. Alternatively, you might want to create animations or allow for some kind of repetitive task that executes automatically. For example, you might want to include an advertising image that changes automatically every few seconds. You use the **Timer control** to perform post backs at defined intervals. As with other AJAX controls, a Web page that uses the Timer control must also include a ScriptManager control.

The easiest way to use the Timer control is to add it to a Content-Template control. The Timer control includes three behavior properties: `Enabled`, `EnableViewState`, and `Interval`. The `Enabled` property determines whether the Timer control is enabled and the `EnableViewState` property determines whether view state is enabled for the UpdatePanel control. You assign to the `Interval` property a value in milliseconds to specify how long to wait before repeating the post back. By default, the `Interval` property repeats post back every 60,000 milliseconds (one minute).

A millisecond is one thousandth of a second; there are 1000 milliseconds in a second. For example, five seconds is equal to 5000 milliseconds.

Instead of making the user click the right and left buttons on the Hotel Gosselin Web page, you can use the Timer control to cycle through the photos automatically. The following modified version of the Web form for the Hotel Gosselin Web page includes a Timer control that is set to repeat post back every five seconds:

```
<form id="form1" runat="server">
<div>
    <asp:ScriptManager ID="ScriptManager1"
        runat="server">
    </asp:ScriptManager>
    <asp:UpdatePanel ID="UpdatePanel1"
        runat="server">
        <ContentTemplate>
        <asp:Timer id="photoChanger" runat="server"
            Interval="5000" />
        <table style="width: 60%">
                <tr>
                    <td>
                        <p>
                            The Hotel Gosselin redefines
                            the luxury hotel experience,
                            combining intimacy, comfort
                            and exclusivity with the
                            personalized service and
                            attention to detail. A dedicated
                            concierge attends to individual
                            needs in a well-appointed,
                            relaxed environment.</p>
                        <asp:Image ID="roomImage"
                            runat="server"
                            ImageUrl="images/suite1.jpg" />
                    </td>
                </tr>
            </table>
        </ContentTemplate>
    </asp:UpdatePanel>
</div>
</form>
```

Remember that while the partial-page rendering mechanism only updates the controls within an UpdatePanel control, it still executes each of the post back page events every time it is called. When you place the Timer control in the ContentTemplate control as shown in

You can find a working example of the page load event version of the Hotel Gosselin Web site in the HotelGosselin_Page_Load folder in your Appendix.B folder.

the preceding example, the updates to the UpdatePanel control must be handled with the page load event or other page events. For the photos on the Hotel Gosselin page to change during each post back, you must add code similar to the following to the `Page_Load()` event handler:

```
protected void Page_Load(object sender, EventArgs e)
{
    string curImage = roomImage.ImageUrl;
    if (curImage.Contains("1"))
        roomImage.ImageUrl = "images/suite2.jpg";
    else if (curImage.Contains("2"))
        roomImage.ImageUrl = "images/suite3.jpg";
    else if (curImage.Contains("3"))
        roomImage.ImageUrl = "images/suite4.jpg";
    else if (curImage.Contains("4"))
        roomImage.ImageUrl = "images/suite5.jpg";
    else
        roomImage.ImageUrl = "images/suite1.jpg";
}
```

Instead of relying on the `Page_Load()` event handler, you can write your own event handler that is called by the Timer control's `OnTick` event, which executes each time that the Timer control performs a post back. To create an `OnTick` event handler, open a form in Design view and double-click the Timer control. Here's how the Timer control appears for the Hotel Gosselin Web page after adding an `OnTick` event handler:

```
<asp:Timer id="photoChanger" runat="server"
Interval="5000" OnTick="photoChanger_Tick" />
```

You can find a working example of the timer event version of the Hotel Gosselin Web site in the HotelGosselin_timer_event folder in your Appendix.B folder.

The `photoChanger_Tick()` event handler would contain the same code that you saw in the `Page_Load()` event handler before you added the `OnTick` event, as follows:

```
protected void photoChanger_Tick(object sender,
    EventArgs e)
{
    string curImage = roomImage.ImageUrl;
    if (curImage.Contains("1"))
        roomImage.ImageUrl = "images/suite2.jpg";
    else if (curImage.Contains("2"))
        roomImage.ImageUrl = "images/suite3.jpg";
    else if (curImage.Contains("3"))
        roomImage.ImageUrl = "images/suite4.jpg";
    else if (curImage.Contains("4"))
        roomImage.ImageUrl = "images/suite5.jpg";
    else
        roomImage.ImageUrl = "images/suite1.jpg";
}
```

You can place the Timer control outside of the UpdatePanel, although the Timer control must be identified as a trigger with the `<Triggers>` element, as follows:

```
<form id="form1" runat="server">
<div>
    <asp:Timer ID="photoChanger" runat="server"
        Interval="5000" OnTick="photoChanger_Tick" />
    <asp:ScriptManager ID="ScriptManager1"
        runat="server" />
    <asp:UpdatePanel ID="UpdatePanel1" runat="server">
        <Triggers>
            <asp:AsyncPostBackTrigger
                ControlID="photoChanger" />
        </Triggers>
        <ContentTemplate>
        ...
```

AJAX is a much larger subject than is covered in this appendix. However, it is fast becoming one of the most important technologies in Web development. If you intend to pursue a career in Web development, be sure that you have a thorough understanding of AJAX development techniques.

 Although the Timer control is most frequently used for partial-page rendering, it can also be used to automatically repost the entire page at a specified interval. To use a Timer control to repost an entire page, place the control outside of an UpdatePanel control and do not identify the Timer control as a trigger with the `<Triggers>` element.

Solutions to Short Quizzes

Chapter 1

Short Quiz 1

1. When and who developed the Internet and what was its original purpose?

   The Internet is a vast network that connects computers all over the world. The original plans for the Internet grew out of a series of memos written by J. C. R. Licklider of the Massachusetts Institute of Technology (MIT), in August 1962, discussing his concept of a "Galactic Network." Licklider envisioned a global computer network through which users could access data and programs from any site on the network. The Internet was actually developed in the 1960s by the Advanced Research Projects Agency (or ARPA) of the U.S. Department of Defense, which later changed its name to Defense Advanced Research Projects Agency (or DARPA). The goal of the early Internet was to connect the main computer systems of various universities and research institutions that were funded by this agency. This first implementation of the Internet was referred to as the ARPANET. More computers were connected to the ARPANET in the years following its initial development in the 1960s, although access to the ARPANET was still restricted by the U.S. government primarily to academic researchers, scientists, and the military.

2. What is the Web in relation to the Internet and how do they differ?

   A common misconception is that the words *Web* and *Internet* are synonymous. The Web is only one *part* of the Internet, and is a means of communicating on the Internet. The Internet is also composed of other communication methods such as e-mail systems that send and receive messages. However, because of its enormous influence on computing, communications, and the economy, the World Wide Web is arguably the most important part of the Internet today and is the primary focus of this book.

3. What were the browser wars, and how did they begin and end?

The so-called browser wars began when Microsoft and Netscape fought for control of the browser market. Earlier versions of Internet Explorer and Navigator included DHTML elements that were incompatible. Furthermore, Microsoft and Netscape each wanted its version of DHTML to become the industry standard. To settle the argument, the World Wide Web Consortium set out to create a platform-independent and browser-neutral version of DHTML. The **World Wide Web Consortium**, or W3C, was established in 1994 at MIT to oversee the development of Web technology standards. While the W3C was drafting a recommendation for DHTML, versions 4 of both Internet Explorer and Navigator added a number of proprietary DHTML elements that were completely incompatible with the other browser. As a result, when working with advanced DHTML techniques such as animation, a programmer had to write a different set of HTML code for each browser type. Unfortunately for Netscape, the W3C adopted as the formal standard the version of DHTML found in version 4 of Internet Explorer, which prompted many loyal Netscape followers to defect to Microsoft.

4. What is the process called that a Web browser uses to assemble and format an HTML document?

When you open an HTML document in a Web browser, the document is assembled and formatted according to the instructions contained in its elements. The process by which a Web browser assembles and formats an HTML document is called **parsing** or **rendering**.

5. What are the basic parts of a URL and what is each part's purpose?

A Web page is identified by a unique address called the URL. A Web page's URL is similar to a telephone number. Each URL consists of two basic parts: a protocol (usually HTTP) and either the domain name for a Web server or a Web server's Internet Protocol address. **Hypertext Transfer Protocol (HTTP)** manages the hypertext links that are used to navigate the Web. HTTP ensures that Web browsers correctly process and display the various types of information contained in Web pages (text, graphics, audio, and so on). The protocol portion of a URL is followed by a colon, two forward slashes, and a host. The term **host** refers to a computer system that is being accessed by a remote computer. In the case of a URL, the host portion of a URL is usually *www* for "World Wide Web." A **domain name** is a unique address used for identifying a computer, often a Web server, on the Internet. The domain name consists of two parts separated by a period. The first part of a domain name is usually text that easily identifies a person or an organization, such as DonGosselin or Course. The last part of a domain name, known as the **domain identifier**, identifies the type of institution or organization. Common domain identifiers include .biz, .com, .edu, .info, .net, .org, .gov, .mil, or .int. Each domain identifier briefly describes the type of business or organization it represents. For instance, com (for *commercial*) represents private companies, gov (for *government*) represents government agencies, and edu (for *educational*) represents educational institutions. Therefore, the domain name consists of descriptive text for the Web site combined with the domain identifier. For example, course.com is the domain name for Course Technology. An example of an entire URL is *http://www.DonGosselin.com* or *http://www.course.com*.

Short Quiz 2

1. What are the differences in Web page design, Web page authoring, and Web development?

   Web page design, or **Web design**, refers to the visual design and creation of the documents that appear on the World Wide Web. Most businesses today—both prominent and small—have Web sites. To attract and retain visitors, and to stand out from the crowd, Web sites must be exciting and visually stimulating. Quality Web design plays an important role in attracting first-time and repeat visitors. However, the visual aspect of a Web site is only one part of the story. Equally important is the content of the Web site and how that content is structured. **Web page authoring** (or **Web authoring**) refers to the creation and assembly of the tags, attributes, and data that make up a Web page. There is a subtle, but important distinction between Web design and Web page authoring: Web design refers to the visual and graphical design aspects of creating Web pages, whereas a book on Web page authoring refers to the physical task of assembling the Web page tags and attributes. **Web development**, or **Web programming**, refers to the design of software applications for a Web site. Generally, a Web developer works "behind the scenes" to develop software applications that access databases and file systems, communicate with other applications, and perform other advanced tasks. The programs created by a Web developer will not necessarily be seen by a visitor to a Web site, although the visitor will certainly use a Web developer's programs, particularly if the Web site writes and reads data to and from a database. Although JavaScript lives more in the realm of Web page authoring, there is certainly some overlap between Web authoring and Web development, especially when it comes to sending and receiving data to and from a Web server.

2. What are the primary roles of the client and the server in a two-tier system architecture?

One of the primary roles of the **client**, or **front end**, in a two-tier system is the presentation of an interface to the user. The user interface gathers information from the user, submits it to a server, or **back end**, then receives, formats, and presents the results returned from the server. The main responsibility of a server is usually data storage and management. On client/server systems, heavy processing, such as calculations, usually takes place on the server. As desktop computers become increasingly powerful, however, many client/server systems have begun placing at least some of the processing responsibilities on the client. In a typical client/server system, a client computer might contain a front end that is used for requesting information from a database on a server. The server locates records that meet the client request, performs some sort of processing, such as calculations on the data, and then returns the information to the client. The client computer can also perform some processing, such as building the queries that are sent to the server or formatting and presenting the returned data.

3. What is the purpose of the processing tier in a three-tier system architecture?

The processing tier performs any necessary processing or calculations based on the request from the client tier, and then reads information from or writes information to the data storage tier. The processing tier also handles the return of any information to the client tier. Note that the processing tier is not the only place where processing can occur. The Web browser (client tier) still renders Web page documents (which requires processing), and the database or application in the data storage tier might also perform some processing.

4. Why are scripts written with the JavaScript programming language restricted to executing only within a Web browser?

For security reasons, the JavaScript programming language cannot be used outside of the Web browser. For example, to prevent mischievous scripts from stealing information, such as your e-mail address or credit card information you use for an online transaction, or from causing damage by changing or deleting files, JavaScript does not allow any file manipulation whatsoever. Similarly, JavaScript does not include any sort of mechanism for creating a network connection or accessing a database. This limitation prevents JavaScript programs from infiltrating a private network or intranet from which information might be stolen or damaged. Another helpful limitation is the fact that JavaScript cannot run system commands or execute programs on a client. The ability to read and write cookies is the only type of access to a client that JavaScript has. Web browsers, however, strictly govern cookies and do not allow access to cookies from outside the domain that created them. This security also means that you cannot use JavaScript to interact directly with Web servers that operate at the processing tier. Although the programmer can employ a few tricks (such as forms and query strings) to allow JavaScript to interact indirectly with a Web server, if you want true control over what's happening on the server, you need to use a server-side scripting language.

5. How does the execution and use of client-side scripting differ from server-side scripting?

Server-side scripting is a technology that processes a request for a Web page by executing a script on a server. One of the primary reasons for using server-side scripting is to develop interactive Web sites that communicate with a database. Server-side scripts work in the processing tier and have the ability to handle communication between the client tier and the data storage tier. At the processing tier, a server-side script usually prepares and processes the data in some way before submitting it to the data storage tier.

Short Quiz 3

1. What files does Visual Studio use to store a Web site's project settings and where are these files stored?

   A Web site's project settings are stored in two files: a **Visual Studio Solution** file with an extension of .sln and a Solution User Options file with an extension of .suo. These files are referred to as solution files. The Visual Studio Solution file stores all of the settings that are required by a Web site project, whereas the Solution User Options file stores customization options for the project. These files are assigned the name of the folder where you chose to store your Web site. The solution files are always stored in the folder that is designated as your Visual Studio projects location, although your Web site files can be stored in a separate directory. In other words, the files that make up your Web site do not need to be stored in the same folder as the project's solution files. For example, suppose you create a new project in C:\WebSites\StoreFront. This folder will contain all of your project's files, with the exception of the solution files, which will be stored in a folder named StoreFront in the designated Visual Studio projects location. The default Visual Studio projects location is usually set to C:\Documents and Settings*user name*\My Documents\Visual Studio 2008\WebSites. Because you will be saving your Web sites in the location where you installed the data files, separate folders containing solution files for each of your projects will also be created in your default Visual Studio projects location.

2. What is the primary difference between a Visual Web Developer project and solution?

   Within the IDE, the program you are writing is referred to as a **project** or a **solution**. The difference between projects and solutions is that a solution can contain multiple projects. In Visual Web Developer, a project is the Web site you are creating.

3. What window in the IDE do you use to change the various properties, attributes, and other settings that are associated with a project?

   An ASP.NET project contains various settings, or properties, that determine how a project and its files appear and behave. You use the **Properties window** to change the various properties, attributes, and other settings that are associated with a project. The properties listed in the Properties window change according to the programmatic element that is selected in an editor.

4. What must happen before you can execute source code?

Source code is the original programming code in which an application was written. Before you can use source code, it must be **compiled**, or processed and assembled into an executable format. In Visual Web Developer, the tools for compiling the source code that makes up a Web site are located on the Build menu. You have two options for compiling: You can compile the files containing your source code (such as ASP.NET with an extension of .aspx) individually using the Build Page command or you can compile all the source files in the Web site simultaneously using the Build Web Site command. Both commands check code syntax and compile the source files.

5. What is the difference between compiler error messages and warning messages?

Compiler error messages occur for any syntax errors in a source file and contain a description of the error, the name of the file in which the error occurred, the line and column number in the document, and the project that contains the file. **Warning messages** occur for any potential problems that might exist in your code, but that are not serious enough to cause a compiler error message.

Short Quiz 4

1. Why has XHTML replaced HTML?

HTML has been replaced because it is useful only for rendering documents in traditional Web browsers like Firefox or Internet Explorer. That worked well as long as browsers running on computers were the main source of requests for files over the Web. These days, however, many types of devices besides computers use the Web. For example, mobile phones and PDAs are commonly used to browse the Web. An application that is capable of retrieving and processing HTML and XHTML documents is called a **user agent**. A user agent can be a traditional Web browser or a device such as a mobile phone or PDA, or even an application such as a crawler for a search engine that simply collects and processes data instead of displaying it. Although user agents other than browsers can process HTML, they are not ideally suited to the task, primarily because HTML is more concerned with how data appears than with the data itself. As Web browsers have evolved over the years, they have added extensions (elements and attributes) to HTML to provide functionality for displaying and formatting Web pages. For instance, one extension to the original HTML language is the <font> element, which allows you to specify the font for data in an HTML document. The <font> element has nothing to do with the type of data in an HTML document. Instead, its sole purpose is to display data in a specific typeface within a Web browser. There is nothing wrong with continuing to author your Web pages using HTML and design elements such as the <font> element—provided your Web pages will be opened only in a Web browser. However, many user agents (such as mobile phones and PDAs) display only black-and-white or grayscale text and are incapable of processing HTML elements that handle the display and formatting of data. User agents such as these require a language that truly defines data (such as a paragraph or heading) independently of the way it is displayed.

2. Which HTML elements have been deprecated in XHTML?

<applet>	Executes Java applets
<basefont>	Specifies the base font size
<center>	Centers text
<dir>	Defines a directory list
<font>	Specifies a font name, size, and color
<isindex>	Creates automatic document indexing forms
<menu>	Defines a menu list
<s> or <strike>	Formats strikethrough text
<u>	Formats underlined text

3. What are some of the important components of a well-formed document?

- All XHTML documents must use <html> as the root element. The xmlns attribute is required in the <html> element and must be assigned the *http://www.w3.org/ 1999/xhtml* URI.

- XHTML is case sensitive.

- All XHTML elements must have a closing tag.

- Attribute values must appear within quotation marks.

- Empty elements must be closed.
- XHTML elements must be properly nested.

4. What is the difference between formatting elements and phrase elements?

Formatting elements provide specific instructions about how their contents should be displayed. Two of the most commonly used formatting elements are the <b> element (for boldface) and the <i> element (for italic). **Phrase elements**, on the other hand, primarily identify or describe their contents. For instance, the <em> element is an emphasized piece of data, similar to a quotation. How the <em> element is rendered is up to each user agent, although most current Web browsers display the contents of the <em> element using italic. However, a user agent for the vision impaired might use the <em> element to pronounce the text or phrase it contains with more emphasis, to get the meaning across to the vision-impaired visitor to the Web site. Although text-formatting elements are commonly used and work perfectly well for displaying text with a specific style of formatting, it's better to format the text on your Web pages using a phrase element that describes its content. Using phrase elements helps ensure that your Web pages are compatible with user agents that might not be capable of handling formatting elements.

5. How will most Web browsers respond when opening an XHTML document that is not well formed?

When you open an XHTML document that is not well formed in a Web browser, the browser simply ignores the errors, as it would with an HTML document with errors, and renders the Web page as best it can. The Web browser cannot tell whether the XHTML document is well formed. To ensure that your XHTML document is well formed and that its elements are valid, you need to use a validating parser.

Chapter 2

Short Quiz 1

1. What is a processing directive and how are they used in ASP.NET?

An **ASP processing directive** provides a Web server with information on how to process the code in an ASP.NET document.

2. What are the different types of code render blocks?

Code render blocks are the most basic way of adding ASP.NET to a Web page. **Code render blocks** define inline code or inline expressions that execute when a Web page renders. **Inline code** refers to one or more individual code lines, or **statements**, contained within a code render block. You use the delimiters <% and %> to designate inline code. A **delimiter** is a character or sequence of characters used to mark the beginning and end of a code segment. You include within the script delimiters any commands that are valid for the scripting language you are using.

3. Should you use code render blocks in a production environment?

In practice, code render blocks are of limited use and can be difficult to maintain and debug. Further, it is considered poor programming practice to use code render blocks to create complex programs.

4. Explain the relationship between classes and objects.

An **object** is programming code and data that can be treated as an individual unit or component. In object-oriented programming, the code that makes up an object is organized into **classes**. Essentially, a class is a template, or blueprint, that serves as the basis for new objects. When you use an object in your program, you actually create an instance of the class of the object. An **instance** is an object that has been created from an existing class. When you create an object from an existing class, you are said to be **instantiating** the object. For example, you might create a ShoppingCart class for a Web site that calculates the total cost of a sales transaction. The ShoppingCart class might store information about the purchased items, shipping costs, and so on. To use the ShoppingCart class, you must instantiate a ShoppingCart object.

5. Which processing directives are used to create server-side comments?

Server-side comments allow you to leave comments anywhere within an ASP.NET file, with the exception of code render and code declaration blocks. Server-side comments are not processed on the server and do not display in the rendered page. You create server-side comments with the <%-- and --%> delimiters.

Short Quiz 2

1. What rules and conventions must you observe when naming a variable in C#?

   - Identifiers must begin with an uppercase or lowercase ASCII letter or underscore (_).

   - You can use numbers in an identifier, but not as the first character.

   - You cannot include spaces in an identifier.

   - You cannot use keywords for identifiers.

2. How can you use keywords as identifiers in C# and is this a good programming practice?

   You can actually use keywords as identifiers in your C# programs if you precede them with the @ character. However, this is considered a very poor programming technique because it makes code confusing and difficult to read, so you should avoid using it in your C# programs.

3. Why should you initialize a variable when you first declare it?

   Although you can assign a value when a variable is declared, you are not required to do so because your program might assign the value later. However, if for some reason the program fails to assign a value to the variable and then attempts to use it, you will receive an error message when your program executes. Therefore, it is good programming practice always to initialize your variables when you declare them.

4. What convention should you follow when naming a constant?

   You use the same rules for naming constants as you do for naming variables—that is, constant names must begin with an uppercase or lowercase ASCII letter or underscore. You can use numbers in a constant name, but not as the first character, and you cannot use spaces in a constant name or use keywords for constant names. Note that it is common practice to use all uppercase letters for constant names, such as STATE_SALES_TAX.

5. Can you modify the value assigned to a constant after you first initialize it?

   No. An existing constant cannot change after it is initialized.

Short Quiz 3

1. What is the difference between loosely typed and strongly typed programming languages?

    Many programming languages require that you declare the type of data that a variable contains. Programming languages that require you to declare the data types of variables are called **strongly typed programming languages**. Strong typing is also known as **static typing** because data types do not change after they have been declared. Programming languages that do not require you to declare the data types of variables are called **loosely typed programming languages**. Loose typing is also known as **dynamic typing** because data types can change after they have been declared. C# is a strongly typed programming language. When you declare a variable in C#, you *must* designate a data type. As with integer variables, you designate data types for other types of variables by placing the data type name and a space in front of the variable name.

2. How do you decide which numeric data type to use for a variable?

    Deciding which numeric data type to use is often confusing to beginning programmers. Whenever you declare a variable, C# reserves for the variable the amount of memory that the specified data type requires. How much space is reserved for the two integer data types? C# reserves 32 bits of memory for int variables and 64 bits of memory for long variables. The basic rule of thumb is to use the smallest data type possible to conserve memory. Therefore, if you need to use an integer variable in your program and you know that the values it stores will always be between -2,147,483,648 and 2,147,483,647, you should use the int data type because it requires less memory than the long data type.

3. What is the hexadecimal numeral system and how is it used with C# char variables?

    Hexadecimal is a numeral system based on a value of 16 that uses combinations of 16 characters, the numbers 0 through 9 and the letters A through F, to represent values. For example, the hexadecimal Unicode number for the copyright symbol is 00A9. To assign a hexadecimal Unicode character to a char variable, it must be preceded by the \u escape sequence and enclosed in single quotations.

4. What are the two techniques you can use to cast data types?

The C# syntax for casting types is *newVariable =
(newType)oldVariable;*. The *newType* portion of the
syntax is the keyword representing the type to which you
want to cast the variable. In addition to type casting, you can
manually convert variables to other types by using one of the
methods of the Convert class methods. For example, the
Convert.ToString() method converts a variable to a string
data type and the Convert.ToDouble() method converts a
variable to a double data type.

5. How do you declare and initialize an array?

When you declare an array, you must declare the array's data
type and the number of elements it will contain. The syntax
for declaring an array is as follows:

```
type[] arrayName = new type[elements];
```

Notice that when declaring an array, you must declare its
data type, just as you would with regular variables. Some languages, such as JavaScript and PHP, allow you to use different
data types within the same array. With C#, all elements must
be of the same data type.

You assign values to individual array elements in the same
fashion as you assign values to a standard variable, except that
you include the index for an individual element of the array.

Short Quiz 4

1. What is the difference between operands and operators?

Operands are variables and literals contained in an expression. A **literal** is a value such as a literal string or a number.
Operators, such as the addition operator (+) and multiplication operator (*), are symbols used in expressions to manipulate operands.

2. Explain the difference between binary and unary operators.

C# operators are binary or unary. A **binary operator** requires
an operand before and after the operator. The equal sign in
the statement int orderNumber = 300; is an example of a
binary operator. A **unary operator** requires a single operand
either before or after the operator. For example, the increment
operator (++), an arithmetic operator, is used for increasing
an operand by a value of one. The statement orderNumber++;
changes the value of the orderNumber variable to "301".

3. How do you use prefix and postfix operators?

The increment (++) and decrement (--) unary operators can be used as prefix or postfix operators. A **prefix operator** is placed before a variable. A **postfix operator** is placed after a variable. The statements ++myVariable; and myVariable++; both increase myVariable by one. However, the two statements return different values. When you use the increment operator as a prefix operator, the value of the operand is returned *after* it is increased by a value of one. When you use the increment operator as a postfix operator, the value of the operand is returned *before* it is increased by a value of one. Similarly, when you use the decrement operator as a prefix operator, the value of the operand is returned *after* it is decreased by a value of one, and when you use the decrement operator as a postfix operator, the value of the operand is returned *before* it is decreased by a value of one. If you intend to assign the incremented or decremented value to another variable, it makes a difference whether you use the prefix or postfix operator.

4. Explain how the C# interpreter compares nonnumeric values.

When two nonnumeric values are used as operands, the C# interpreter compares them according to their hexadecimal Unicode number, not alphabetically. For example, the Unicode number for the uppercase letter *A* is 0041, whereas the Unicode number for the lowercase letter *a* is 0061. The statement returnValue = 'A' > 'a'; returns false because the lowercase letter *a* has a higher hexadecimal Unicode number than the uppercase letter *A*.

5. How do you use the conditional operator?

The **conditional operator** returns one of two results, based on the results of a conditional expression. The syntax for the conditional operator is *conditional_expression* ? *result1* : *result2*;. If the conditional expression evaluates to true, *result1* is assigned as the result of the operation. If the conditional expression evaluates to false, *result2* is assigned as the result of the operation.

Short Quiz 5

1. What is associativity and how does it affect operator precedence?

When performing operations with operators in the same precedence group, the order of precedence is determined by the operator's **associativity**—that is, the order in which operators of equal precedence execute. Associativity is evaluated from left to right or from right to left depending on the operators involved.

2. Which operators have the highest order of precedence?

.	Objects
()	Function calls/evaluations
[]	Array elements
++	Increment (postfix)
--	Decrement (postfix)
new	New object
typeof	Data type

3. Which operators have the lowest order or precedence?

=	Assignment
+=	Compound addition assignment
-=	Compound subtraction assignment
*=	Compound multiplication assignment
/=	Compound division assignment
%=	Compound modulus assignment

Chapter 3

Short Quiz 1

1. How do you use code declaration blocks and what types of code can they contain?

   Code declaration blocks use `<script>` elements to contain ASP.NET functions and global variables. With ASP.NET, you use two attributes in a code declaration block: `runat="server"` and `language`. The `runat="server"` attribute is required to identify the script section as an ASP.NET program. The `language` attribute identifies the scripting language used within the code declaration block. Recall that with ASP.NET, you can use Visual Basic or C# as the scripting language within a code render block.

2. What is the difference between arguments and parameters?

   The variables or values that you place in the parentheses of a function call statement are called **arguments** or **actual parameters**.

A **parameter** is a variable that is used within a function. Placing a parameter name within the parentheses of a function definition is the equivalent of declaring a new variable. As with regular variables, you must declare a parameter's data type.

3. How do you execute a function?

To execute a function, you must invoke, or **call**, it from elsewhere in your program. The code that calls a function is referred to as a **function call** and consists of the function name followed by parentheses that contain any variables or values to be assigned to the function parameters.

4. Why would you want to return a value from a function?

In many instances, you might want your program to receive the results from a called function and then use those results in other code. For instance, consider a function that calculates the average of a series of numbers that are passed to it as arguments. Such a function would be useless if your program could not print or use the result elsewhere. You can return a value from a function to a calling statement by assigning the calling statement to a variable.

5. What is variable scope?

When you use a variable in a C# program, particularly a complex ASP.NET program, you need to be aware of the **variable's scope**—that is, you need to think about where in your program a declared variable can be used. A variable's scope can be either global or local. A **global variable** is one that is declared within a code declaration block, but outside a function, and is available to all parts of your page. A **local variable** is declared inside a function or code render block and is only available within the function or code render block in which it is declared. Local variables cease to exist when the function or code render block ends. If you attempt to use a local variable outside the function in which it is declared, you will receive an error message.

Short Quiz 2

1. What are collections and how do you access them?

Collections are data structures similar to arrays that store object properties. You can access an object collection with the syntax *object.collection("property");*.

2. How do you access form data submitted with the "post" and "get" methods?

The Request object collection that you will use most is the Form collection, which contains variables representing form elements from a requesting Web page that is submitted with a method of "post." ASP.NET takes all of the named elements in a form on the user's browser and adds them as variables to the Form collection of the Request object. When a user clicks a form's Submit button, each field on the form is submitted to the server as a name=value pair. The name portion of the name=value pair becomes a variable name in the Form collection, and the value portion is assigned as the value of the variable. When you submit a form with a method of "get," name=value pairs are attached to the URL as a query string, and are assigned as variables to the Request object QueryString collection. This means that you need to refer to the form values using the QueryString collection instead of the Form collection.

3. How do you return the number of variables in a collection?

ASP.NET collections support a count property, which returns the number of variables in a collection. You append the count property to the collection name with a period.

Short Quiz 3

1. When will an if statement execute?

The if statement is one of the more common ways to control program flow. The **if statement** is used to execute specific programming code if the evaluation of a conditional expression returns a value of true. If the condition being evaluated returns a value of true, the statement immediately following the conditional expression executes. After the if statement executes, any subsequent code executes normally.

2. Why would you use a command block with a decision-making statement?

You can use a command block to construct a decision-making structure containing multiple statements. A **command block** is a set of statements contained within a set of braces, similar to the way function statements are contained within a set of braces. Each command block must have an opening brace ({) and a closing brace (}). If a command block is missing either the opening or closing brace, an error occurs.

3. Why would you nest decision-making statements?

You can use a control structure such as an `if` or `if...else` statement to allow a program to make decisions about what statements to execute. In some cases, however, you might want the statements executed by the control structure to make other decisions. For instance, you might have a program that uses an `if` statement to ask users if they like sports. If users answer yes, you might want to run another `if` statement that asks users whether they like team sports or individual sports. You can include any code you want within the code block for an `if` statement or an `if...else` statement, and that includes other `if` or `if...else` statements.

4. What type of label represents a specific value and contains one or more statements that execute if its value matches the value of the `switch` statement's expression?

A **case label** in a switch statement represents a specific value and contains one or more statements that execute if the value of the `case` label matches the value of the switch statement's expression. The result returned from the expression must be an integer data type, which includes the `int` and `long` types.

5. Describe how the statements in a `switch` statement execute. When does a `switch` statement end?

When a `switch` statement executes, the value returned by the expression is compared with each `case` label in the order in which it is encountered. When a matching label is found, its statements execute. Unlike with the `if...else` statement, execution of a `switch` statement does not automatically stop after particular `case` label statements execute. Instead, the `switch` statement continues evaluating the rest of the `case` labels in the list. When a matching `case` label is found, evaluation of additional `case` labels is unnecessary. If you are working with a large `switch` statement with many `case` labels, evaluation of additional `case` labels can potentially slow down your program. To avoid slow performance, then, you need to give some thought to how and when to end a `switch` statement. A `switch` statement ends automatically after the interpreter encounters its closing brace (}). You can, however, use a special kind of statement, called a **break statement**, to end a `switch` statement after it has performed its required task. To end a `switch` statement after it performs its required task, include a `break` statement within each `case` label.

Short Quiz 4

1. Why is a counter critical to repetition statements?

   To ensure that a repetition statement ends after the desired tasks have been performed, you must include code that tracks the progress of the loop and changes the value produced by the conditional expression. You track the progress of a loop with a counter, which is a variable that increments or decrements with each iteration of a loop statement.

2. How do you break out of an infinite loop?

   If you do not include code that changes the value used by the conditional expression, your program will be caught in an infinite loop. In an **infinite loop**, a loop statement never ends because its conditional expression is never false. If a C# program is caught in an infinite loop, the server will eventually run out of memory and halt the program. To manually halt an infinite loop, you need to restart the Visual Studio IDE.

3. Which type of repetition statement always executes its statements once, even if the conditional expression returns a value of false?

   The **do...while statement** executes a statement or statements once, and then repeats the execution as long as a given conditional expression evaluates to true.

4. What are the primary differences between the `while` statement and the `for` statement?

   One of the primary differences between the `while` statement and the `for` statement is that, in addition to a conditional expression, the `for` statement can also include code that initializes a counter and changes its value with each iteration. This is useful because it provides a specific place for you to declare and initialize a counter, and to update its value, which helps prevent infinite loops.

5. How do you restart a repetition statement?

   You use the **continue statement** when you want to stop the loop for the current iteration, but want the loop to continue with a new iteration.

Chapter 4

Short Quiz 1

1. Why should you use ASP.NET instead of JavaScript to validate submitted data?

   JavaScript is often used with forms to validate or process form data before the data is submitted to a server-side program. For example, customers might use an online order form to order merchandise from your Web site. When a customer clicks the form's Submit button, you can use JavaScript to ensure that the customer has entered important information, such as his name, shipping address, and so on. The problem with using JavaScript to validate form data is that you cannot always ensure that the data submitted to your ASP.NET program was submitted from the Web page containing the JavaScript validation code. Every self-respecting hacker knows how to bypass JavaScript validation code in an HTML form by appending a query string directly to the URL of the ASP.NET program that processes the form. If a user does bypass the form and type the URL and a query string in the Address box of a Web browser, any JavaScript validation code in the Web page containing the form fails to execute. Because JavaScript validation code can be bypassed in this way, you should always include C# code to validate any submitted data. If your program lacks such code, you cannot be sure that all of the necessary data was submitted (such as a shipping address for an online order) nor can you tell if an unscrupulous hacker is attempting to submit malicious data that might cause problems in your script or on your Web site.

2. Explain how to use the `TryParse()` method to convert a string variable to a particular data type.

   Each of the primitive numeric data types in C# includes a **TryParse() method** that you can use to convert a string variable to that particular data type. The basic syntax for the `TryParse()` methods is `type.TryParse(string, out variable)`. The `TryParse()` methods perform two tasks: They return a Boolean value indicating whether the conversion was successful and they also assign the converted value to the variable in the second argument. However, this assignment only occurs when the string value is in the proper format. If it is not in the proper format, the original value in the variable remains unaltered. Note that the `TryParse()` methods require the use of the `out` keyword as the second argument.

3. How do you use a single Web form to gather and process submitted data?

Web forms can submit data to a server, but how the server receives the data differs significantly from standard HTML forms. The most critical thing you need to understand is that a Web form only submits data to itself, in the same way that the Web page you saw in the last section submitted data to itself. In fact, you cannot submit a Web form to another URL; if you include the `action` attribute that identifies a URL to which a form should be submitted, it will be ignored. Instead, if you submit a Web form by clicking a submit button, by default its data will be posted back to the Web page itself. The process by which form data is posted back to the same page with a Web form is called **post back**. After a Web form is submitted, the post back mechanism automatically restores the form's value. Whether or not data is posted back to a Web page is determined by its **view state**. With post back and view state, you do not need to retrieve the form values that were submitted with the `Response.QueryString()` or `Response.Form()` collections.

4. What is a code-behind page?

The preferred method for working with C# code is to place it in a **code-behind page**, which is a separate class file that contains properties for an associated page. Every ASP.NET page has an associated code-behind page with an extension of .cs.

5. When is a post back event initiated?

With ASP.NET server controls, post back occurs every time a server control event executes. In other words, the form is submitted each time a control event occurs. After post back occurs, the event handler for the control that raised the event executes on the server and a response is returned to the client, thus causing page events to execute.

Short Quiz 2

1. Explain how to use a Literal control and why you would use one.

The **Literal control** adds literal text that is not rendered in any HTML elements, but that can be created and manipulated programmatically on the server. The difference between the Label control and the Literal control is that whereas a Label control is rendered with a `<span>` element using properties associated with the control itself, a Literal control is only rendered with the text and markup that you specify. This allows you to dynamically generate text and HTML markup with ASP.NET. You assign the text and markup that you want rendered to the Literal control's `Text` property or place it between the `<asp:Literal>` element's tag pairs. To programmatically modify the contents of a Label control, you assign a value to the `Text` property of the element ID.

2. Why would you use an Image control instead of an `<img>` element?

    The only reason to use the Image control instead of the HTML `<img>` element is if you want to programmatically manipulate the image with ASP.NET.

3. What are the values you can assign to the `HotSpotMode` property and how do you use them?

    You can select one of four values for the `HotSpotMode` property: Inactive, Navigate, NotSet, and Postback. The Inactive value disables the hot spot. The Navigate value causes the page to navigate to the specified URL. If the NotSet value is selected for an individual control, the control performs the behavior that is assigned to the HyperLink control's `HotSpotMode` property. However, if the HyperLink control's `HotSpotMode` property is assigned the value of NotSet, each hot spot that does not have a value assigned to its own `HotSpotMode` property navigates to its specified target URL. The Postback value causes the Web form to post back to itself.

4. Explain the difference between the Button, ImageButton, and LinkButton controls.

    With the Button control, you can create two types of buttons: a submit button that causes a Web form to post back to itself and a push button that is similar to the OK and Cancel buttons you see in dialog boxes. The primary purpose of push buttons is to execute code that performs some type of function, such as a calculation. The Button control's default functionality is as a submit button. However, if you have multiple Button controls in a form, you must specify which button to use as the submit button by setting the control's

UseSubmitBehavior property to true, which is the default value. The ImageButton control creates an image submit button that displays a graphical image and performs exactly the same function as a submit button in that it transmits a form's data to a Web server. The LinkButton control creates a hyperlink that posts the form to the server instead of navigating to another URL. A link button performs the same tasks as a submit button. Although a link button is rendered with the anchor element (<a>), ASP.NET adds JavaScript code on the Web page that causes post back to occur.

5. Explain how to use the RadioButtonList and CheckBoxList controls.

Radio buttons, or option buttons, refer to groups of controls from which the user can select only one value. The CheckBoxList control makes it easier to organize multiple check boxes, except that you can select multiple check boxes within a check box list.

Short Quiz 3

1. Explain how to use a RequiredFieldValidator control to ensure that a user enters a value into a specified field.

You assign the message that you want to appear to the RequiredFieldValidator control's Text property or place it between the <asp:RequiredFieldValidator> control element's tag pairs. The field that is to be validated is identified by the ControlToValidate property.

2. Which validation control property identifies the control to validate?

The ControlToValidate property.

3. How do you force the browser to display a validation control only when it's needed?

When you add a validation control to a Web page, the browser automatically reserves space for it when the page renders, even if there are no validation errors. To force the browser to display a validation control only when it's needed, assign a value of "dynamic" to its Display property.

4. Explain how to use a CompareValidator control to verify that a user has entered a value of a specified data type into a field.

To identify another control against which to compare the control identified with the `ControlToValidate` property, you use the `ControlToCompare` property. The CompareValidator control also includes the `Type`, `Operator`, and `ValueToCompare` properties. You assign to the `Type` property the data type that you want users to enter into the field: `string`, `integer`, `double`, `date`, or `currency`. The `Operator` property accepts one of several comparison types, which determine how to compare the field value.

5. How do you configure a CompareValidator control to check a field's data type?

You assign to the Type property of the CompareValidator control the data type that you want users to enter into the field: `string`, `integer`, `double`, `date`, or `currency`.

Chapter 5

Short Quiz 1

1. Why do you need to manipulate data in strings? List some examples in which you would use string manipulation techniques.

One of the most important reasons for needing to manipulate data in strings is for processing form data with C#. You will often find it necessary to count characters and words in strings, particularly with strings from form submissions. For example, you might need to count the number of characters in a password to ensure that a user selects a password with a minimum number of characters. Or, you might have a Web page that allows users to submit classified ads that cannot exceed a maximum number of characters.

2. Explain how to use the classes of the `System.Net.Mail` namespace to send e-mail to an SMTP server.

The `System.Net.Mail` namespace contains classes for sending e-mail to an SMTP server. You import the namespace in a Web form with the `@ import` processing directive or into a class file with the `using` directive. You use the `MailMessage` class to create an e-mail object that contains message information such as the sender, recipient, subject, and body. After initializing an object, you use properties of the `MailMessage` object to construct the message. The six basic properties of the `MailMessage` object are From, To, CC, Bcc, Subject, and Body. The values you assign to the From, To, CC, and

Bcc properties can either be e-mail addresses in the format *name@domain.identifier* or an object of the MailAddress class, which allows you to identify the e-mail address and display name of the sender.

3. What Visual Studio IDE tool would you use to administer a Web site?

   To administer a Web site, you use the ASP.NET Web Site Administration Tool, which you can run by selecting the Website menu and then by selecting ASP.NET Configuration.

4. Why would you need to count the number of characters in a text string?

   You might need to count the number of characters in a password to ensure that a user selects a password with a minimum number of characters. Or, you might have a Web page that allows users to submit classified ads that cannot exceed a maximum number of characters.

5. Explain the three ways in which you can include special characters within a text string.

   When you want to include basic types of special characters, such as quotation marks, within a literal string, you must use an escape sequence. The escape sequence for double quotation marks is \" and the escape sequence for single quotation marks is \'. For other types of special characters, you need to use Unicode. In most cases, you can use XHTML numeric character references or character entities to represent Unicode characters in text strings. For example, the copyright symbol (©) can be represented in HTML by the numeric character reference © and the character entity is ©. Instead of using numeric character references or character entities to specify special characters within text strings, you can use an escape sequence in the form \xhhhh. The hhhh characters represent the four digits of a hexadecimal Unicode symbol.

Short Quiz 2

1. Explain why you might need to find and extract characters and substrings from a string.

   In some situations, you will need to find and extract characters and substrings from a string. For example, if your program receives an e-mail address, you might need to extract the name portion of the e-mail address or domain name.

2. What types of values are returned from the various search and extraction methods of the String class?

Some of the search and extraction methods of the String class return true if the *string* argument is found within the string or false if the string is not found. Other methods return the position of a specified character or string or -1 if the character or string is not found.

3. Explain how to convert between strings and arrays.

You use the Split() method of the String class to split a string into an indexed array. The Split() method splits each character in a string into an array element, using the syntax *array* = *string*.Split(*separator*[, *limit*]);. The opposite of the Split() method is the String class's Join() method, which combines array elements into a string, separated by specified characters. The syntax for the Join() method is stringVariable = String.Join(["separator", arrayName]);.

4. What operators and String class methods can you use to compare strings?

You can use the comparison operator (==) and various methods of the String class, including the Equals() method, to perform the same function as the comparison operator in that it determines whether two strings contain the same value. It returns either a value of true if the two strings are equal or false if they are not. The syntax for the Equals() method is *string*.Equals(*string*);. The String class also includes several compare methods that compare strings according to the particular sort order of a language or country. For example, the Compare() method compares two strings that are passed as arguments. The syntax for the Compare() method is string.Compare(*string1*, *string2*). If *string1* is equivalent to *string2*, the method returns a value of 0; if *string2* sorts before *string1*, the method returns a value greater than 0, usually 1; if *string2* sorts after *string1*, the method returns a value less than 0, usually -1. If you want to perform a case-insensitive comparison of two strings, you need to pass a value of true as a third argument to the Compare() method.

5. What operators and String class methods can you use to combine strings?

To combine strings, you can use the concatenation operator (+) and the compound assignment operator (+=) to combine text strings. The String class also includes the Concat()

method, which creates a new string by combining strings that are passed as arguments. The syntax for the `Concat()` method is `string.concat(string1, string2, ...)`. If you want to insert text into a string, you use the `Insert()` method of the `String` class to insert the text after a specified index position within the string. The syntax for the `Insert()` method is `string.concat(index, text)`.

Short Quiz 3

1. What are some of the types of data you would validate with regular expressions?

   You can use a regular expression to ensure that a user enters a date in a specific format, such as *mm*/*dd*/*yyyy*, or a telephone number in the format (###) ###-####. Other types of data you would commonly validate with regular expressions include credit card numbers and e-mail addresses.

2. What classes do you use to create a regular expression and to determine whether a particular string matches a regular expression pattern?

   To define a regular expression pattern in C#, you must use the `Regex()` constructor. The `Regex()` constructor is part of the `Regex` class, which represents regular expressions in C# and contains methods and properties for working with regular expressions. To determine whether a particular string matches a regular expression pattern, you must use the `Match` class, which represents the results of a regular expression match. You instantiate an object of the `Match` class and assign to it the results from the `Match()` method of the `Regex` class. The `Match()` method returns a value of true or false, depending on whether the string matches the regular expression. The `Match()` class contains various methods and properties, the most important of which is the `Success` property, which returns a value of true or false, depending on the result of the `Match()` method.

3. Describe the metacharacters you can use with regular expressions.

   You use a period (.) to match any single character in a pattern. A period in a regular expression pattern really specifies that the pattern must contain a value where the period is located. A pattern that matches the beginning or end of a line is called an anchor. To specify an anchor at the beginning of a line, the pattern must begin with the ^ metacharacter. To specify an anchor at the end of a line, the pattern must end with the $ metacharacter. To match any metacharacters as literal values in a regular expression, you must precede the character with a backslash. Metacharacters that specify the number of matches are called quantifiers. The question mark quantifier specifies that the preceding character in the pattern is optional. The addition quantifier (+) specifies that one or more of the preceding characters match, whereas the asterisk quantifier (*) specifies that zero or more of the preceding characters match. The { } quantifier allows you to specify more precisely the number of times that a character must repeat.

4. What does a period in a regular expression represent?

   A period (.) in a regular expression matches any single character in a pattern. If you want to ensure that a string contains an actual period and not any character, you need to escape it with a backslash.

5. Explain how to define a character class with a regular expression.

   You create a character class by enclosing the characters that make up the class with bracket [] metacharacters. Any characters included in a character class represent alternate characters that are allowed in a pattern match. You use a hyphen metacharacter (-) to specify a range of values in a character class. You can include alphabetical or numerical ranges. You specify all lowercase letters as "[a-z]" and all uppercase letters as "[A-Z]". To specify optional characters to exclude in a pattern match, include the ^ metacharacter immediately before the characters in a character class.

Chapter 6

Short Quiz 1

1. What is debugging and where does the term come from?

   The term **debugging** refers to the act of tracing and resolving errors in a program. Grace Murray Hopper, a mathematician who was instrumental in developing the Common Business-Oriented Language (COBOL) programming language, is said to have first coined the term *debugging*. As the story from the 1940s goes, a moth short-circuited a primitive computer that Hopper was using. Removing the moth from the computer "debugged" the system and resolved the problem. Today, a bug refers to any sort of problem in the design and operation of a program.

2. What is the difference between syntax errors, run-time errors, and logic errors?

    Syntax errors occur when the interpreter fails to recognize code. In ASP.NET, statements that are not recognized by the Visual Studio IDE generate syntax errors. Syntax errors can be caused by incorrect usage of C# code or references to objects, methods, and variables that do not exist. The second type of error, a **run-time error**, occurs while a program is executing. Run-time errors differ from syntax errors in that they do not necessarily represent C# language errors. Instead, run-time errors occur when your program encounters code that it cannot execute. The third type of error, **logic errors**, are flaws in a program's design that prevent the program from running as you anticipate. In this context, the term *logic* refers to the execution of program statements and procedures in the correct order to produce the desired results.

3. How do you specify the types of warnings to report during compilation?

    The `WarningLevel` attribute of the `@ Page` directive specifies the types of warnings to report during compilation. You can assign values 0 through 4 to the `WarningLevel` attribute; the higher the number, the stricter the compiler is about what it considers to be a warning. The default value is 4, which is the strictest warning level. Assigning a value of 0 to the `WarningLevel` attribute disables warnings entirely. Changing the warning level severity does not prevent warnings from occurring; it only determines whether ASP.NET will report them during compilation.

Short Quiz 2

1. How do you enable debugging at both the page and application levels?

    To print detailed information about errors to the browser window for a particular Web page, you need to include the `Debug` attribute in the `@ Page` directive and assign it a value of true. To enable debugging for all of the pages in your project, run the ASP.NET Web Site Administration Tool by selecting the Website menu and then by selecting ASP.NET Configuration.

This displays the Welcome page of the Web Site Administration Tool. Click the Application Configuration link, and then click the Configure debugging and tracing link to display the Configure Debugging and Tracing page. On this page, click the Enable debugging box. Note that an individual page's `Debug` attribute in the `@ Page` directive takes precedence over the application-level debugging setting. In other words, even though an application's debugging setting is enabled, debugging for an individual page will be disabled if the page's `@ Page` directive includes a `Debug` attribute assigned a value of true.

2. Explain how to trace errors with `Response.Write()` statements.

When you are unable to locate a bug in your program by using error messages or examining your code, or if you suspect a logic error (which would not generate an error message), you can try tracing your code manually. The `Response.Write()` statement provides one of the most useful ways to trace PHP code. You place a `Response.Write()` method at different points in your program and use it to display the contents of a variable, an array, or the value returned from a function. A `Response.Write()` statement is especially useful when you want to trace a bug in your program by analyzing a list of values. Using this technique, you can monitor values as they change during program execution.

3. Explain how to trace errors with comments.

Another method of locating bugs in a program is to transform lines that you think might be causing problems into comments. In other words, you can "comment out" problematic lines. This technique helps you isolate the statement that is causing the error. In some cases, you might choose to comment out individual lines that might be causing the error, or you might choose to comment out all lines except the lines that you know work. When you first receive an error message or your program doesn't work as expected, start by commenting out only the statement specified by the line number in the error message, or that you suspect is causing the problem, and rebuild the project. If you receive additional error messages or problems, comment out additional statements. Then, examine the commented out statements for the cause of the bug.

4. Why would you need to check XHTML elements to locate a bug in an ASP.NET program?

There will be occasions when you cannot locate the source of a bug, no matter how long you search. In such cases, the flaw might not lie in your C# code at all, but in your XHTML elements. If you cannot locate a bug using any of the methods described in this chapter, perform a line-by-line analysis of your XHTML code, making sure that all tags have opening and closing brackets. Also, be sure that all necessary opening and closing tags, such as the <body>...</body> tag pair are included. Better yet, be sure to look at the IDE's Error List window for validation errors; this is usually much easier than performing a line-by-line analysis.

5. Explain how to enable tracing and how to add your own custom messages to the trace diagnostic output.

You can view diagnostic trace information for page requests by assigning a value of true to the Trace attribute of the @ Page processing directive. You can enable application-level tracing by selecting the Website menu and then by selecting ASP.NET Configuration. This displays the Welcome page of the Web Site Administration Tool. Click the Application Configuration link, click the Configure debugging and tracing link to display the Configure Debugging and Tracing page, and then click the Capture tracing information box.

Short Quiz 3

1. Explain how to use break mode to trace program execution. What commands can you use to enter break mode?

In **break mode**, program execution is temporarily suspended, thereby allowing you to monitor values and trace program execution one command at a time. Once a program is paused at a breakpoint, you can use the commands on the Debug menu to trace program execution, including the Step Into, Step Over, Step Out, Continue, and Stop commands.

2. Once your program is in break mode, which command do you use to execute all remaining code in the current function?

Once your program is in break mode, you can use the **Step Out command** to execute all remaining code in the current function. If the current function was called from another function, all remaining code in the current function executes and the debugger stops at the next statement in the calling function.

3. Explain how to use the Locals, Watch, and Immediate windows.

    The **Locals window** displays all local variables within the currently executing function, regardless of whether they have been initialized. The Locals window helps you see how different values in the currently executing function affect program execution. You use the Locals window when you need to be able to see all of a function's variables, regardless of whether they have been assigned a value. You can change the value of a variable in the Locals window by right-clicking the variable and selecting Edit Value from the shortcut menu. The **Watch window** monitors both variables and expressions in break mode. To display the value of a variable or expression in the Watch window, enter a variable or expression in the first column in the empty row in the Watch window. (You can also right-click a variable or expression in your code and select Add Watch from the shortcut menu.) The variable or expression you enter (or right-click) is then displayed in the Watch window, along with its value. You can use the **Immediate window** to monitor specific variables and expressions in break mode. To open the Immediate window, point to Windows on the Debug menu and then click Immediate. To display the value of a variable or expression in the Immediate window, you enter the variable or expression in the white portion of the window and press Enter. The value is displayed directly beneath the variable or expression in the Immediate window. To change the value of a variable, type the variable name in the Immediate window followed by an equal sign and the new value, and then press Enter. The new value is displayed beneath the statement you entered.

Short Quiz 4

1. What does the term bulletproofing mean when it comes to writing code?

    Writing code that anticipates and handles potential problems is often called **bulletproofing**. One bulletproofing technique you have already used has to do with validating submitted form data with validation controls and regular expressions. Another bulletproofing technique, **exception handling**, allows programs to handle problems as they occur in the execution of a program.

2. What is an exception?

    The term **exception** indicates that something unexpected occurred while a program is running. An exception is not

626

necessarily an error, although it can be. Typically, exceptions identify situations such as when a user enters the wrong type of data or if a database is not currently available.

3. What are `try...catch` blocks?

You execute code that might contain an exception in a **try statement**. The process by which a `try` statement generates an exception class object is referred to as "throwing an exception." The exception objects that are thrown from a `try` statement contain several properties and methods that describe what went wrong, including the `Message` property, which contains a message that describes the current exception, and the `ToString()` method, which returns a more detailed description of the exception. After you throw an error, you use a **catch statement** to handle, or "catch" the exception object.

4. What is the purpose of a `finally` statement?

A **finally statement** executes regardless of whether its associated `try` block throws an exception. You normally use a `finally` statement to perform some type of cleanup or any necessary tasks after code is evaluated with a `try` statement.

5. How do you programmatically control page-level error handling?

To programmatically control page-level error handling, you must create a page error event handler. Unlike other types of page events, the compiler does not automatically recognize a function named `Page_Error()` as the page error event handler. Instead, you must specify the name of the event handler function with the `System.EventHandler()` function in the `Page_Load()` event handler. The argument passed to the `System.EventHandler()` function is the name you want to use for the error event handler.

Chapter 7

Short Quiz 1

1. What are records and fields and how do they differ?

A **record** in a database is a single complete set of related information. Each recipe in a recipe database, for instance, is a single database record. Each column in a database table is called a field. **Fields** are the individual categories of information stored in a record. Examples of fields that might exist in a recipe database include ingredients, cooking time, cooking temperature, and so on.

2.   What are one-to-one, one-to-many, and many-to-many relationships?

A **one-to-one relationship** exists between two tables when a related table contains exactly one record for each record in the primary table. A **one-to-many relationship** exists in a relational database when one record in a primary table has many related records in a related table. You create a one-to-many relationship to eliminate redundant information in a single table. A **many-to-many relationship** exists in a relational database when many records in one table are related to many records in another table.

3.   What is a query and how do you create one?

A **query** is a structured set of instructions and criteria for retrieving, adding, modifying, and deleting database information. Most database management systems use a **data manipulation language**, or **DML**, for creating queries. Different database management systems support different data manipulation languages. However, **structured query language**, or **SQL** (pronounced sequel), has become somewhat of a standard data manipulation language among many database management systems.

Short Quiz 2

1.   How do you execute a query in a query window?

When you enter SQL commands in a query window, you must terminate the command with a semicolon. To execute the SQL commands in a query window, you select Execute from the Query menu. The Results window, which appears below the query window, displays the results of the SQL commands.

2.   What is the difference between regular and delimited identifiers?

Regular identifiers must begin with a letter, underscore (_), number sign (#), or at sign (@), and subsequent characters are restricted to letters, numbers, underscores, number signs, or at signs. **Delimited identifiers** do not conform to the rules of regular identifiers and can include spaces and other characters that are not allowed in regular identifiers. To use delimited identifiers in SQL statements, you must contain them within double quotations ("") or brackets ([]).

3. What is a SQL Server instance?

A SQL Server installation consists of one or more **instances**, which refer to a single installation of SQL Server. You can use multiple instances of SQL Server for separate test and development environments, or for separate database environments that need to exist on the same server. You can log in with either the default instance or a named instance. The default instance, automatically named SQLEXPRESS, refers to the instance that is created automatically when you first install SQL Server Express.

Short Quiz 3

1. How do you create a new database file in a specific location?

To create a new database in a specific location, you must use the ON keyword, followed by a comma-separated list of items enclosed in parentheses that defines the file information. The ON list requires the NAME and FILENAME keywords. You assign to the NAME keyword a logical name to identify the file. You must use the logical name to refer to the file in SQL Server. You assign to the FILENAME keyword the drive and path where you want to create the database file, and a physical filename with an extension of .mds.

2. How do you decide which data type to use for table fields?

To keep your database from growing too large, you should choose the smallest data type possible for each field. For example, the SMALLINT data type stores integer values between -32768 and 32767 and occupies 2 bytes of storage space. In comparison, the BIGINT data type stores integer values between -9223372036854775808 and 9223372036854775807 and occupies 8 bytes of storage space. Regardless of how small the value is that you store in a SMALLINT field, it will occupy 2 bytes of storage space. Similarly, the BIGINT data type occupies 8 bytes of storage space, no matter how small the value. If you know that a value you assign to a field will always be between -32768 and 32767, you should use the SMALLINT data type instead of the BIGINT data type, which saves 6 bytes per record. This might not seem like a huge savings, but imagine how much storage space would be saved for a database with millions of records.

3. How do you create and delete tables?

To create a table, you use the CREATE TABLE statement, which specifies the table and column names and the data type for each column. To delete a table, you execute the DROP TABLE statement, which removes all data and the table definition.

Short Quiz 4

1. How do you add individual and multiple records to a table?

You add individual records to a table with the INSERT statement. Text values must be enclosed within single quotations. The values you enter in the VALUES list must be in the same order in which you defined the table fields. You should specify NULL in any fields for which you do not have a value. To add multiple records to a database, you use the BULK INSERT statement with a local text file containing the records you want to add. Place each record in the text file on a separate line and place tabs between each field. Leave any empty fields blank. The values on each line must be in the same order in which you defined the table fields.

2. How do you sort and reverse sort the results returned from a query?

You use the ORDER BY keyword with the SELECT statement to perform an alphanumeric sort of the results returned from a query. To perform a reverse sort, add the DESC keyword after the name of the field by which you want to perform the sort.

3. Explain how to delete records from a table.

To delete records in a table, you use the DELETE statement. Be careful when you use the DELETE statement because it will delete all records that match the condition. Therefore, be sure to carefully construct the conditions assigned to the WHERE keyword. To delete all the records in a table, leave off the WHERE keyword.

Chapter 8

Short Quiz 1

1. What is ODBC?

Open database connectivity, or **ODBC**, allows ODBC-compliant applications to access any data source for which there is an ODBC driver. ODBC uses SQL commands (known as ODBC SQL) to allow an ODBC-compliant application to access a database. Essentially, an ODBC application connects to a database for which there is an ODBC driver and then executes ODBC SQL commands. Then, the ODBC driver translates the SQL commands into a format that the database can understand. ASP.NET includes strong support for ODBC.

2. How do you access databases with ASP.NET?

With ASP.NET, you use ActiveX Data Objects to access databases. **ActiveX Data Objects**, or **ADO**, is a Microsoft database connectivity technology that allows ASP and other Web development tools to access ODBC- and OLE DB-compliant databases. **OLE DB** is a data source connectivity standard promoted by Microsoft as a successor to ODBC. One of the primary differences between OLE DB and ODBC is that ODBC supports access only to relational databases, whereas OLE DB provides access to both relational databases and non-relational data sources, such as spreadsheet programs. The most recent version of ADO is ADO.NET, which allows you to access OLE DB-compliant data sources and XML. You can also use ADO.NET to directly access SQL Server and Oracle databases, without having to go through OLE DB.

3. Explain how to select a database after you have instantiated an object of the `SqlConnection` class.

You can also select or change a database with the `ChangeDatabase()` method of the `SqlConnection` class. The syntax for the `ChangeDatabase()` method is `ChangeDatabase("database")`.

Short Quiz 2

1. How do you determine whether your program has connected to a database successfully?

The `State` property of the `SqlConnection` class contains a string indicating the current status of the database connection. The `State` property contains one of the following values that indicate the status of the database connection: Broken, Closed, Connecting, Executing, Fetching, or Open. You can use the value assigned to the `State` property to check the database connection, although you must use the `Convert.ToString()` method before you can use it in a conditional expression.

2. What else can you use besides an `if...else` block and the `State` property to determine whether a database connection was successful?

   You can also execute the `Open()` method within a `try...catch` block. The `try` block can also contain any database statements that might cause an error, such as the `ChangeDatabase()` method. The `System.Data.SqlClient` namespace includes the **SqlException class**, which represents the exception that is thrown when SQL Server returns an error or warning.

3. What properties of the `SqlException` class can you use to give the user more information about the error that occurred?

   You can use the `Number` and `Message` properties of the `SqlException` class to print an error code and message if the connection attempt fails.

Short Quiz 3

1. How do you use the `ExecuteReader()` method?

   You use the **ExecuteReader() method** of the `SqlCommand` class to create a `SqlDataReader` object, which you must assign to a variable. To use the `ExecuteReader()` method, you must first create a **DataReader object**, which retrieves read-only, forward-only data from a data source. **Forward-only** means that the program can only move forward through the record in the returned data, and not backward or to specific records. In other words, your program can sequentially read the records from the first record to the last record, but cannot sequentially read the records from the last record to the first record, or go to a specific record. You use a `DataReader` object when you want to read data from a database, but not add, delete, or modify records.

2. When working with a `SqlDataReader` object, what is a cursor and how do you use it?

   When you work with a `SqlDataReader` object, your position within the recordset is called the **cursor**. When a `SqlDataReader` object is first created, the cursor is initially placed *before* the first row in the recordset. The first time you use the `Read()` method, it places the cursor in the first row of the recordset. When you work with recordsets and the `Read()` method, you can never be certain if there is another record following the current position of the cursor, or even if any records were returned at all from your SQL SELECT statement. To determine if a next record is available, you can use the Read() method, which returns a value of true if it finds a next row in the recordset or a value of false if it does not find a next row in the recordset.

3. What do you use the ExecuteNonQuery() method for?

The ExecuteNonQuery() method executes commands against a database and is most useful for quickly inserting, updating, or deleting rows in a SQL Server database.

Short Quiz 4

1. How do you create and delete SQL Server databases programmatically with ASP.NET?

You use the CREATE DATABASE statement with the ExecuteNonQuery() method to create a new database. To ensure that the database does not already exist, you should first attempt to access the database with the ChangeDatabase() method in a try...catch block. If the database exists, the try block functions successfully. However, if the database does not exist, a SqlException is thrown and the catch block executes. Within the catch block, you can add code that checks the error number to determine whether the exception was thrown when the ChangeDatabase() method attempted to access a nonexistent database. The error number that is returned when you attempt to access a nonexistent database is 911. You can trap this error number and create the database from within the catch block.

Deleting a database is almost identical to creating one, except that you use the DROP DATABASE statement instead of the CREATE DATABASE statement with the ExecuteNonQuery() method.

2. How do you create and delete tables in SQL Server databases programmatically with ASP.NET?

To create a table, you use the CREATE TABLE statement with the ExecuteNonQuery() function. Be sure you have selected the correct database with the SqlConnection constructor or with the ChangeDatabase() method before executing the CREATE TABLE statement or you might create your new table in the wrong database. To delete a table, you use the DROP TABLE statement with the ExecuteNonQuery() function.

3. How do you add, update, and delete records in a database?

To add records to a table, you use the INSERT and VALUES keywords with the ExecuteNonQuery() method. To add multiple records to a database, you use the BULK INSERT statement and the ExecuteNonQuery() function with a local text file containing the records you want to add. To update records in a table, you use the UPDATE, SET, and WHERE keywords with the ExecuteNonQuery() function. The UPDATE keyword specifies the name of the table to update and the SET keyword specifies the value to assign to the fields in the records that match the condition in the WHERE keyword. To delete records in a table, you use the DELETE and WHERE keywords with the ExecuteNonQuery() function.

Chapter 9

Short Quiz 1

1. Explain how to use query strings and hidden form fields to maintain state information.

To quickly pass data from one Web page to another using a query string, add a question mark (?) immediately after a URL, followed by the query string (in name=value pairs) for the information you want to preserve. In this manner, you are passing information to another Web page, similar to the way you can pass arguments to a function or method. You separate individual name=value pairs within the query string using ampersands (&).

Hidden form fields temporarily store data that needs to be sent to a server along with the rest of a form, but that a user does not need to see. Examples of data stored in hidden fields include the result of a calculation or some other type of information that a program on the Web server might need. You create hidden form fields using the same syntax used for other fields created with the <input> element: <input type="hidden">. The only attributes that you can include with a hidden form field are the name and value attributes. In fact, you have already used this technique in Chapter 4 when you used a hidden form field to store a Boolean value that indicated whether a form was being opened for the first time or if it had already been submitted to itself. Further, post back maintains view state by assigning the form values to a hidden form field named __VIEWSTATE.

2. How do you simulate multipage forms with the MultiView and View Web Server controls?

   The MultiView control is used to hide and display areas of a page that are defined by a View control, which acts as a container for text, markup, and other controls. The MultiView control is based on the `MultiView` class and the View control is based on the `View` class. One of the primary uses of the MultiView control is to simulate multipage forms. Only one View control displays at a time within a MultiView control. The mechanism for hiding and displaying View controls, which also causes post back to occur, simulates the experience of navigating between multiple, related forms on separate Web pages. Because the View controls are all defined on the same page, any data within the form fields contained within a View control is preserved during post back operations, assuming that the `EnableViewState` attribute is assigned a value of true.

3. How do you use the Wizard Web server control to create a multistep interface for gathering user input?

   Wizard Web server controls function very similar to Multi-View controls in that they are used to hide and display areas of a page to simulate multipage forms. However, Wizard controls are more powerful because they automate navigation and other functionality, and they contain a wide variety of options for formatting the display of the control. The `<asp:Wizard>` control contains a nested `<WizardSteps>` element that further contains `<asp:WizardStep>` controls that represent each step in the wizard. You nest within each `<asp:WizardStep>` control the text, markup, and other controls that apply to the step.

Short Quiz 2

1. Explain the difference between transient and persistent cookies. How do you configure a cookie to be persistent?

   Cookies can be temporary or persistent. **Temporary cookies** remain available only for the current browser session. **Persistent cookies** remain available beyond the current browser session and are stored in a text file on a client computer. For a cookie to persist beyond the current browser session, you must use the `Expires` property of the cookie object. The **Expires property** determines how long a cookie can remain on a client system before it is deleted. Cookies created without an `Expires` property are available for only the current browser session. You must assign to the `Expires` property the `DateTime` structure, which represents an instance in time. The `DateTime` structure includes various methods and properties that you can use to retrieve and modify date and time information. The most common way to use the `DateTime` structure with a cookie's `Expires` property is to use the `Now` property and one of the `Add()` methods of the `DateTime` structure. The `Now` property returns the current date and time. The `DateTime` structure's various `Add()` methods, such as `AddDays()` and `AddMonths()`, adds the specified amount of time to the date in the `Now` property.

2.   How do you configure cookies to be available to other Web pages on the server?

The **Path property** determines the availability of a cookie to other Web pages on a server. You append the `path` attribute to the `cookie` object and assign it a path. By default, a cookie is available to all Web pages in the same directory. However, if you specify a path, then a cookie is available to all Web pages in the specified path as well as to all Web pages in all subdirectories in the specified path.

3.   How do you secure cookie transmissions?

Internet connections are not always considered safe for transmitting sensitive information. It is possible for unscrupulous people to steal personal information, such as credit card numbers, passwords, Social Security numbers, and other types of private information online. To protect private data transferred across the Internet, Netscape developed **Secure Sockets Layer**, or **SSL**, to encrypt data and transfer it across a secure connection. The URLs for Web sites that support SSL usually start with the HTTPS protocol instead of HTTP. The **Secure property** indicates that a cookie can only be transmitted across a secure Internet connection using HTTPS or another security protocol.

4.   How do you determine if a cookie exists?

When attempting to read a cookie, your program should always check first to see if the cookie exists with a conditional expression that determines whether the cookie is not equal to null. Otherwise, you will receive a `NullReferenceException` exception.

5. How do you modify and delete cookies?

You cannot directly modify the value assigned to a cookie or subkey. Instead, you must overwrite the old cookie with a new cookie. To delete a cookie, you must set its expiration to a date in the past.

Short Quiz 3

1. Why would you use session state?

A new `Request` object is instantiated each time a client requests an ASP.NET URL and is then destroyed once the URL is delivered to the client. However, an ASP.NET application can be composed of multiple documents. Because the `Request` object is destroyed once the URL is delivered to the client, you cannot use the same `Request` object with different pages in an application. If you want to preserve client information across multiple pages in an ASP.NET application, you must use **session state**, which stores specific client information and makes that information available to all the pages for the current ASP.NET session. Session data is stored in a `SessionStateItemCollection` object that you can access through the `Session[]` collection. A `SessionStateItemCollection` object is instantiated the first time a client accesses a URL in a given application.

2. Why and how would you use application state?

You use **application state**, which refers to preserved information that can be shared by all clients accessing an application. Application data is stored in an `HttpApplicationState` object that you can access through the `Application[]` collection. Each application has its own `HttpApplicationState` object that runs in memory on the server. ASP.NET application state automatically starts the first time a client requests one of the application pages, and runs until the server shuts down or is restarted, or if the application is restarted. You create your own application state variables in the `Application[]` collection. One common application state variable is some type of unique number used to identify clients. You can create a variable in the `Application[]` collection that keeps track of the last assigned number, and then update the number and assign it to a client.

3. What are the benefits to using profiles?

ASP.NET application state automatically starts the first time a client requests one of the application pages, and runs until the server shuts down or is restarted, or if the application is restarted. The problem with application state is that, because data is stored in memory on the server, all data will be lost if the application shuts down or restarts. Although you could write code that saves the data to a database, a better solution is to use **profiles**, which automatically store and retrieve strongly typed state information to and from a SQL Server database. The beauty of profiles is that you do not need to write a single line of code to access the database; ASP.NET automatically takes care of accessing the information in the database for you.

Chapter 10

Short Quiz 1

1. Why do programmers refer to encapsulation as a black box?

    Objects are **encapsulated**, which means that all code and required data are contained within the object itself. In most cases, an encapsulated object consists of a single computer file that contains all code and required data. Encapsulation places code inside what programmers like to call a "black box." When an object is encapsulated, you cannot see "inside" it—all internal workings are hidden. The code (methods and statements) and data (variables and constants) contained in an encapsulated object are accessed through an interface.

2. What is instantiation as it relates to classes, objects, and object-oriented programming?

    In object-oriented programming, the code, methods, attributes, and other information that make up an object are organized into classes. Essentially, a class is a template, or blueprint, that serves as the basis for new objects. When you use an object in your program, you actually create an instance of the class of the object. In other words, an instance is an object that has been created from a class. When you create an object from a class, you are said to be **instantiating** the object.

3. Explain how to instantiate an object from a class.

    You use the following constructor syntax to instantiate an object from a class:

    ```
    ClassName objectName = new ClassName();
    ```

4. What are class constructor statements primarily used for?

When you first instantiate an object from a class, you will often want to assign initial values to fields or perform other types of initialization tasks, such as calling a method that might calculate and assign values to fields. Although you can assign simple values to fields when you declare them, a better choice is to use a constructor method. A **constructor method** is a special method that is called automatically when an object from a class is instantiated. You define and declare constructor methods the same way you define other methods, although you do not include a return type because constructor methods do not return values. Each class definition can contain one or more constructor methods whose names are the same as the class. You must specify the public access modifier with a constructor method.

5. How do you access an object's methods and properties?

After you instantiate an object, you use a period to access the methods and properties contained in the object. With methods, you must also include a set of parentheses at the end of the method name, just as you would with functions. Like functions, methods can also accept arguments.

Short Quiz 2

1. What is a data structure and what are some of the types of data structures you have worked with in this book?

The term **data structure** refers to a system for organizing data, whereas the term **field** refers to variables that are defined within a class. Some of the data structures you have already used include arrays and lists.

2. Why are classes referred to as user-defined data types or programmer-defined data types and why are these terms somewhat misleading?

Classes themselves are also referred to as *user-defined data types* or *programmer-defined data types*. These terms can be somewhat misleading, however, because they do not accurately reflect the fact that classes can contain function members. In addition, classes usually contain multiple fields of different data types, so calling a class a data type becomes even more confusing. One reason classes are referred to as user-defined data types or programmer-defined data types is that you can work with a class as a single unit, or object, in the same way you work with a variable. In fact, the terms variable and object are often used interchangeably in object-oriented programming. The term object-oriented programming comes from the fact that you can bundle variables and functions together and use the result as a single unit (a variable or object).

3. What are some of the benefits to working with classes and objects?

Classes help make complex programs easier to manage, however, by logically grouping related methods and fields and by allowing you to refer to that grouping as a single object. Another reason for using classes is to hide information that users of a class do not need to access or know about. Information hiding, which is explained in more detail later in this chapter, helps minimize the amount of information that needs to pass in and out of an object, which helps increase program speed and efficiency. Classes also make it much easier to reuse code or distribute your code to others for use in their programs. Without a way to package fields and methods in classes and include those classes in a new program, you would need to copy and paste each segment of code you wanted to reuse (methods, fields, and so on) into any new program.

4. Explain the level of protection provided by each of the C# access modifiers.

`public`	Allows anyone to access a class or class member.
`private`	Prevents clients from accessing a class or class member and is one of the key elements in information hiding. Private access does not restrict a class's internal access to its own members; a class method can modify any private class member.
`protected`	Allows only the class or a derived class to access the class or class member.
`internal`	Allows a class or class member to be accessed from anywhere in the application, but not from external applications.
`protected internal`	Allows only code in the same structure, or from a derived class, to access the class or class member.

5. How do you specify in a class definition a class from which another class should inherit its class members?

You append a colon and the class name to the end of the class definition header.

Short Quiz 3

1. Why should you hide any class members that other program-
    mers do not need to access or know about?

    One of the fundamental principles in object-oriented pro-
    gramming is the concept of information hiding. Information
    hiding gives an encapsulated object its black box capabili-
    ties so that users of a class can see only the members of the
    class that you allow them to see. Essentially, the principle
    of **information hiding** states that any class members that
    other programs, sometimes called clients, do not need to
    access or know about, should be hidden. Information hiding
    helps minimize the amount of information that needs to pass
    in and out of an object; this in turn helps increase program
    speed and efficiency. Information hiding also reduces the
    complexity of the code that clients see, allowing them to con-
    centrate on the task of integrating an object into their pro-
    grams. For example, if a client wants to add to her accounting
    program a `Payroll` object, she does not need to know the
    underlying details of the `Payroll` object's methods, nor does
    she need to modify any local fields that are used by those
    methods. The client only needs to know which of the object's
    methods to call and what data (if any) needs to be passed to
    those methods.

2. How do the principles of information hiding compare to open
    source software?

    The opposite of software that adheres to the principles of
    information hiding is open source software, for which the
    source code can be freely used and modified. Instead of inten-
    tionally hiding the internal workings of a software application
    for proprietary purposes, open source software encourages
    programmers to use, change, and improve the software. Open
    source software can be freely distributed or sold, provided it
    adheres to the software's copyright license.

3. What are the two ways in which you can assign an initial value
    to a field?

    The best way to initialize a field is with a constructor method,
    although you can also assign values to fields when you first
    declare them.

4. What are the differences between binary and XML serializa-
    tion? When would you use each type of serialization method?

Binary serialization converts object properties to a binary format, whereas **XML serialization** converts object properties to XML. Binary serialization is more efficient in terms of speed and memory usage, and it converts all of an object's fields to binary format while maintaining their data types. XML serialization converts only an object's public fields and properties to XML and does not maintain their data types. Because only the .NET Framework can read binary serialized objects created with C#, you would use XML serialization if you need to share the serialized data with another application.

5. What class do you use to serialize and deserialize objects in binary format, and what class do you use to create a file stream object? How do these two classes work together in the serialization/deserialization processes?

To serialize an object, you must first create an object of the `BinaryFormatter` class, which serializes and deserializes objects in binary format. Once you have created an object of the class you want to serialize along with a `FileStream` object and a `BinaryFormatter` object, you call the `Serialize()` method of the `BinaryFormatter` object, passing to it the `FileStream` object and then the class object you want to serialize. To convert serialized data back into an object, you must first open a file stream, passing to it a value of `FileMode.Open` as the second parameter of the `FileStream` class constructor. The remainder of the steps are the same as the preceding serialization steps, except that you call the `Deserialize()` method instead of the `Serialize()` method of the `BinaryFormatter` object.

Short Quiz 4

1. Why would you use a private class method?

Suppose your program needs some sort of utility method that clients have no need to access. For example, the `BankAccount` class might need to calculate interest by calling a method named `calcInterest()`. Because the `calcInterest()` method can be called automatically from within the `BankAccount` class, the client does not need to access the `calcInterest()` method directly. By making the `calcInterest()` method private, you protect your program and add another level of information hiding. A general rule of thumb is to create as public any methods that clients need to access and to create as private any methods that clients do not need to access.

2. If you exclude an access modifier when declaring a class method, what access level does C# use by default?

If you do exclude the access modifier, the method's default access is internal. However, it's good programming practice to include an access modifier with any method definition to clearly identify the scope of the function.

3. What is the required syntax for declaring constructor and destructor methods?

You define and declare constructor methods the same way you define other methods, although you do not include a return type because constructor methods do not return values. Each class definition can contain one or more constructor methods whose names are the same as the class. You must specify the public access modifier with a constructor method. To add a destructor method to a C# class, create a method with the same name as the class, but preceded by a tilde symbol (~). Note that you do not specify an access modifier or data type for a destructor method.

4. Why would you use accessor methods? Why do they often begin with the words "set" or "get"?

Accessor methods are public methods that a client can call to retrieve or modify the value of a field. Because accessor methods often begin with the words "set" or "get," they are also referred to as set or get methods. Set methods modify field values; get methods retrieve field values. To allow a client to pass a value to your program that will be assigned to a private field, you include parameters in a set method's definition. You can then write code in the body of the set method that validates the data passed from the client, prior to assigning values to private fields. For example, if you write a class named `Payroll` that includes a private field containing the current state income tax rate, you could write a public accessor method named `getStateTaxRate()` that allows clients to retrieve the variable's value. Similarly, you could write a `setStateTaxRate()` method that performs various types of validation on the data passed from the client (such as making sure the value is not null, is not greater than 100%, and so on) prior to assigning a value to the private state tax rate field.

5. How are accessor methods related to C# properties? How do you create C# properties and access them through an instantiated class object?

C# allows you to create accessors using **properties**, which are special methods that you can use as public data members to set and get field values. To create a property, you create a constructor that is similar to a method definition and includes an accessor level and data type, but does not include parentheses at the end of the method name. To create a property's set and get methods, you include the set and get keywords within the property definition. Following the set and get keywords, you place the necessary statements for each method within a set of braces. For the get method, you can perform any type of computation and then return the value using a return statement. The set method includes an implicit parameter named `value` that represents the value being assigned to the field.

Index

Note: Page numbers in **boldface** type indicate pages where key terms are defined.